"This lively, capacious history of Christianity emphasizes the extent to which the religion still underpins Western liberal values."
—*New Yorker*

"A galloping tour of Christianity's influence across the last 2,000 years, with vivid vignettes scattered across the centuries, and a concluding argument the Christian faith, 'the most influential framework for making sense of human existence that has ever existed,' still shapes the way that even the most secular modern people think about the world."
—Ross Douthat, *New York Times*

"If great books encourage you to look at the world in an entirely new way, then *Dominion* is a very great book indeed."
—*Sunday Times* (UK), History Book of the Year

"A sweeping narrative.... [Holland] is an exceptionally good story-teller with a marvelous eye for detail.... Excellent fun."
—*Economist*

"An absorbing survey of Christianity's subversive origins and enduring influence is filled with vivid portraits, gruesome deaths, and moral debates.... Holland has all the talents of an accomplished novelist: a gift for narrative, a lively sense of drama, and a fine ear for the rhythm of a sentence."
—*Guardian* (UK)

"Christianity may not be on the march, but its principles continue to dominate in much of the world; this thoughtful, astute account describes how and why.... Holland delivers penetrating, often jolting discussions on great controversies of Western civilization in which war, politics, and culture have formed a background to changes in values.... An insightful argument that Christian ethics, even when ignored, are the norm worldwide."
—*Kirkus* (starred review)

"Sustained with all the breadth, originality, and erudition that we have come to associate with Holland's writing." —*Spectator*

"An exhaustive, demanding, and hugely impressive interpretation of our past, bursting with fresh ideas and perspectives on every page." —*Sunday Times* (UK)

"An ambitious account of the history and enduring influence of Christianity. Holland argues that the modern world has been shaped by the consequences of the life and death of Jesus." —*Daily Mail*, The Year's Most Essential Books

"What in other hands could have been a dry pedantic account of Christianity's birth and evolution becomes in Holland's an all-absorbing story.... It takes a master storyteller to translate the development of a philosophical notion into a captivating story, and Holland proves to be one.... Holland offers a remarkably nuanced and balanced account of two millennia of Christian history—intellectual, cultural, artistic, social, and political. The book's scope is breathtaking." —*Literary Review*

"A masterpiece of scholarship and storytelling, *Dominion* surpasses Holland's earlier books in its sweeping ambition and gripping presentation.... *Dominion* presents a rich and compelling history of Christendom." —*New Statesman*

"It is hard to overstate the importance of Holland's book.... [He] punctures common myths about Christianity and secularism in every chapter. In no way does he let the church off the hook for its innumerable failures. Nor will he let secular people live with the illusion that their values are just self-evident, the result of reason and scientific investigation. If both sides would allow themselves to be chastened by Holland, future conversations will be much more fruitful, and more tethered to reality." —Tim Keller, *Gospel Coalition*

"Tom Holland has done a great service to current discussions on the relationship between Christianity and Western civilization."

—*Providence Magazine*

"The history of Christian influence could not be better served than with Tom Holland's *Dominion*.... Holland's exploration of Christianity's notion of inherent worth in all humans is deftly handled, and at times it rises to something akin to greatness.... This latest work elevates him to the front of the top ranks of our scholarly, yet popular, historians."

—*LA Daily Journal*

"Terrific: bold, ambitious, and passionate."

—Peter Frankopan, author of *The Silk Roads: A New History of the World*

"Tom Holland is fun to read, monstrously erudite, wickedly joyful, and ahead of the established consensus, on average, by four years, three months, and two days."

—Nassim Nicholas Taleb, author of *The Black Swan*

"This extraordinary book is vintage Tom Holland: history boldly and elegantly retold, with fascinating interconnections traced to create a narrative that cannot fail to stimulate, for it leads to a never-ending question."

—Diarmaid MacCulloch, author of *The Reformation: A History* and *Christianity: The First 3000 Years*

"At a moment when popular debates over 'faith' and 'reason' have become fashionable, Tom Holland brilliantly reminds us that the most essential values claimed by all sides arise from a long and complex cultural history of Christian moral imagination—one we would do well to remember."

—David Bentley Hart, author of *The Experience of God*

DOMINION

HOW THE CHRISTIAN REVOLUTION
REMADE THE WORLD

❖

TOM HOLLAND

BASIC BOOKS

New York

Basic Books
Hachette Book Group
1290 Avenue of the Americas, New York, NY 10104
www.basicbooks.com

Printed in the United States of America
Originally published in 2019 by Little, Brown in the United Kingdom
First US Edition: October 2019
First Trade Paperback Edition: March 2021

Published by Basic Books, an imprint of Perseus Books, LLC, a subsidiary of Hachette Book Group, Inc. The Basic Books name and logo is a trademark of the Hachette Book Group.

The Hachette Speakers Bureau provides a wide range of authors for speaking events. To find out more, go to www.hachettespeakersbureau.com or call (866) 376-6591.

The publisher is not responsible for websites (or their content) that are not owned by the publisher.

Library of Congress Control Number: 2019948347

ISBNs: 978-0-465-09350-2 (hardcover), 978-0-465-09352-6 (ebook), 978-1-5416-7559-9 (paperback)

LSC-C

Printing 1, 2021

In memory of Deborah Gillingham.
Much loved, much missed.

'Love, and do as you will.'

—*Saint Augustine*

'That you feel something to be right may have its cause in your never having thought much about yourself and having blindly accepted what has been labelled right since your childhood.'

—*Friedrich Nietzsche*

'All you need is love.'

—*John Lennon and Paul McCartney*

CONTENTS

CONTENTS

Part III:
MODERNITAS

Illustration section appears between pages 360 and 361

PREFACE

Some three or four decades before the birth of Christ, Rome's first heated swimming pool was built on the Esquiline Hill. The location, just outside the city's ancient walls, was a prime one. In time, it would become a showcase for some of the wealthiest people in the world: an immense expanse of luxury villas and parks. But there was a reason why the land beyond the Esquiline Gate had been left undeveloped for so long. For many centuries, from the very earliest days of Rome, it had been a place of the dead. When labourers first began work on the swimming pool, a corpse-stench still hung in the air. A ditch, once part of the city's venerable defensive system, was littered with the carcasses of those too poor to be laid to rest in tombs. Here was where dead slaves, 'once they had been slung out from their narrow cells',[1] were dumped. Vultures, flocking in such numbers that they were known as 'the birds of the Esquiline',[2] picked the bodies clean. Nowhere else in Rome was the process of gentrification quite so dramatic. The marble fittings, the tinkling fountains, the perfumed flower beds: all were raised on the backs of the dead.

The process of reclamation, though, took a long time. Decades on from the first development of the region beyond the Esquiline Gate, vultures were still to be seen there, wheeling over a site named the Sessorium. This remained what it had always been: 'the place set aside for the execution of slaves'.[3] It was not—unlike the arenas in which criminals were put to death for the delectation of

1

cheering crowds—a place of glamour. Exposed to public view like slabs of meat hung from a market stall, troublesome slaves were nailed to crosses. Even as seedlings imported from exotic lands began to be planted across the emerging parkland of the Esquiline, these bare trees remained as a token of its sinister past. No death was more excruciating, more contemptible, than crucifixion. To be hung naked, 'long in agony, swelling with ugly weals on shoulders and chest',[4] helpless to beat away the clamorous birds: such a fate, Roman intellectuals agreed, was the worst imaginable. This in turn was what rendered it so suitable a punishment for slaves. Lacking such a sanction, the entire order of the city might fall apart. Luxury and splendour such as Rome could boast were dependent, in the final reckoning, on keeping those who sustained it in their place. 'After all, we have slaves drawn from every corner of the world in our households, practicing strange customs, and foreign cults, or none—and it is only by means of terror that we can hope to coerce such scum.'[5]

Nevertheless, while the salutary effect of crucifixion on those who might otherwise threaten the order of the state was taken for granted, Roman attitudes to the punishment were shot through with ambivalence. Naturally, if it were to serve as a deterrent it needed to be public. Nothing spoke more eloquently of a failed revolt than the sight of hundreds upon hundreds of corpse-hung crosses, whether lining a highway or else massed before a rebellious city, the hills all around it stripped bare of their trees. Even in peacetime, executioners would make a spectacle of their victims by suspending them in a variety of inventive ways: 'one, perhaps, upside down, with his head towards the ground, another with a stake driven through his genitals, another attached by his arms to a yoke'.[6] Yet in the exposure of the crucified to the public gaze there lurked a paradox. So foul was the carrion-reek of their disgrace that many felt tainted even by viewing a crucifixion. The Romans, for all that they had adopted the punishment as the 'supreme penalty',[7] refused to countenance the possibility that it might have originated with them. Only a people famed for their barbarousness and cruelty could ever have devised such a torture: the Persians, perhaps, or the Assyrians, or the Gauls. Everything about the practice of nailing a man to a cross—a *'crux'*— was repellent. 'Why, the very word is harsh on our ears.'[8] It was this disgust that crucifixion uniquely inspired which explained why, when slaves were condemned to death, they were executed in the meanest, wretchedest stretch of land beyond the city walls; and why, when Rome burst its ancient limits, only the planting of the world's most exotic and aromatic plants could serve to mask the taint. It was also why, despite the ubiquity of crucifixion across the Roman world, few cared to think much about it. Order, the order loved by the gods and upheld by magistrates vested with the full authority of the greatest power on earth, was what counted—not the elimination of such vermin as presumed to challenge it. Criminals broken on implements of torture: who were such filth to concern men of breed-ing and civility? Some deaths were so vile, so squalid, that it was best to draw a veil across them entirely.

The surprise, then, is less that we should have so few detailed descriptions in ancient literature of what a crucifixion might actually involve, than that we should have any at all.* The corpses of the cru-cified, once they had first provided pickings for hungry birds, tended to be flung into a common grave. In Italy, undertakers dressed in red, ringing bells as they went, would drag them there on hooks. Oblivion, like the loose earth scattered over their tortured bodies, would then entomb them. This was a part of their fate. Neverthe-less, amid the general silence, there is one major exception which proves the rule. Four detailed accounts of the process by which a man might be sentenced to the cross, and then suffer his punish-ment, have survived from antiquity. Remarkably, they all describe

---

* Indeed, so sparse are descriptions of the punishment in ancient sources that Gunnar Samuelsson, in a recent monograph, has (controversially) argued that 'there was no defined punishment called crucifixion before the execution of Jesus' (p. 205).

the same execution: a crucifixion that took place some sixty or seventy years after the building of the first heated swimming pool in Rome. The location, though, was not the Esquiline, but another hill, outside the walls of Jerusalem: Golgotha, 'which means the place of a skull'.[9] The victim, a Jew by the name of Jesus, a wandering preacher from an obscure town named Nazareth, in a region north of Jerusalem named Galilee, had been convicted of a capital offence against Roman order. The four earliest accounts of his execution, written some decades after his death, specify what this meant in practice. The condemned man, after his sentencing, was handed over to soldiers to be flogged. Next, because he had claimed to be 'the king of the Jews', his guards mocked him, and spat on him, and set a crown of thorns on his head. Only then, bruised and bloodied, was he led out on his final journey. Hauling his cross as he went, he stumbled his way through Jerusalem, a spectacle and an admonition to all who saw him, and onwards, along the road to Golgotha.* There, nails were driven into his hands and feet, and he was crucified. After his death, a spear was jabbed into his side. There is no reason to doubt the essentials of this narrative. Even the most sceptical historians have tended to accept them. 'The death of Jesus of Nazareth on the cross is an established fact, arguably the only established fact about him.'[10] Certainly, his sufferings were nothing exceptional. Pain and humiliation, and the protracted horror of 'the most wretched of deaths':[11] these, over the course of Roman history, were the common lot of multitudes.

Decidedly not the common lot of multitudes, however, was the fate of Jesus' corpse. Lowered from the cross, it was spared a common grave. Claimed by a wealthy admirer, it was prepared reverently for burial, laid in a tomb and left behind a heavy boulder.

---

* Although Jesus is described in the Gospels as carrying a *stauros*, the Greek word for a cross, the likelihood is that he carried what in Latin was termed a *patibulum*: a horizontal cross bar. 'Let him carry his *patibulum* through the city, and then be nailed to his cross.' So wrote the Roman playwright Plautus, a couple of centuries before the crucifixion of Jesus.

Such, at any rate, is the report of all four of the earliest narratives of Jesus' death—narratives that in Greek were called *euangelia*, 'good news', and would come to be known in English as gospels.* The accounts are not implausible. Certainly, we know from archaeological evidence that the corpse of a crucified man might indeed, on occasion, be granted dignified burial in the ossuaries beyond the walls of Jerusalem. Altogether more startling, though—not to say unprecedented—were the stories of what happened next. That women, going to the tomb, had found the entrance stone rolled away. That Jesus, over the course of the next forty days, had appeared to his followers, not as a ghost or a reanimated corpse, but resurrected into a new and glorious form. That he had ascended into heaven and was destined to come again. Time would see him hailed, not just as a man, but as a god. By enduring the most agonising fate imaginable, he had conquered death itself. 'Therefore God has highly exalted him and bestowed on him the name which is above every name, that at the name of Jesus every knee should bow, in heaven and on earth and under the earth...'[12]

The utter strangeness of all this, for the vast majority of people in the Roman world, did not lie in the notion that a mortal might become divine. The border between the heavenly and the earthly was widely held to be permeable. In Egypt, the oldest of monarchies, kings had been objects of worship for unfathomable aeons. In Greece, stories were told of a 'hero god'[13] by the name of Heracles, a muscle-bound monster-slayer who, after a lifetime of spectacular feats, had been swept up from the flames of his own pyre to join the immortals. Among the Romans, a similar tale was told of Romulus, the founder of their city. In the decades before the crucifixion of Jesus, the pace of such promotions into the ranks of the gods had begun to quicken. So vast had the scope of Roman power become that any man who succeeded in making himself its master

---

* The earliest Christian texts, Paul's letters, also report that Jesus was 'buried' (1 Corinthians 15.4).

was liable to seem less human than divine. The ascent into heaven of one of those, a warlord by the name of Julius Caesar, had been heralded by the blaze across the skies of a fiery-tailed star; that of a second, Caesar's adopted son, who had won for himself the name of Augustus, by a spirit seen rising—just as Heracles had done—from a funeral pyre. Even sceptics who scorned the possibility that a fellow mortal might truly become a god were happy to concede its civic value. 'For the human spirit that believes itself to be of divine origin will thereby be emboldened in the undertaking of mighty deeds, more energetic in accomplishing them, and by its freedom from care rendered more successful in carrying them out.'[14]

Divinity, then, was for the very greatest of the great: for victors, and heroes, and kings. Its measure was the power to torture one's enemies, not to suffer it oneself: to nail them to the rocks of a mountain, or to turn them into spiders, or to blind and crucify them after conquering the world. That a man who had himself been crucified might be hailed as a god could not help but be seen by people everywhere across the Roman world as scandalous, obscene, grotesque. The ultimate offensiveness, though, was to one particular people: Jesus' own. The Jews, unlike their rulers, did not believe that a man might become a god; they believed that there was only the one almighty, eternal deity. Creator of the heavens and the earth, he was worshipped by them as the Most High God, the Lord of Hosts, the Master of all the Earth. Empires were his to order; mountains to melt like wax. That such a god, of all gods, might have had a son, and that this son, suffering the fate of a slave, might have been tortured to death on a cross, were claims as stupefying as they were, to most Jews, repellent. No more shocking a reversal of their most devoutly held assumptions could possibly have been imagined. Not merely blasphemy, it was madness.

Even those who did come to acknowledge Jesus as '*Christos*', the Anointed One of the Lord God, might flinch at staring the manner of his death full in the face. 'Christians', as they were called, were as wise to the connotations of crucifixion as anyone. 'The mystery of the cross, which summons us to God, is something despised and dishonourable.'[15] So wrote Justin, the foremost Christian apologist of his generation, a century and a half after the birth of Jesus. The torture of the Son of the Most High God was a horror simply too shocking to be portrayed in visual form. Scribes copying the gospels might on occasion draw above the Greek word for 'cross' delicate pictograms that hinted at the crucified Christ, but otherwise it was left to sorcerers or satirists to illustrate his execution. Yet this, to many across the Roman world, was not as deep a paradox as perhaps it might have seemed. So profound were some mysteries that mortals had no choice but to keep them veiled. The naked radiance of the gods was far too dazzling for the human eye. No one, by contrast, had been blinded by the spectacle of the Son of the Most High God being tortured to death; but Christians, although accustomed to make the sign of the cross as a gesture of piety, and to contemplate with wide-eyed reverence the gospel accounts of their Saviour's sufferings, seem to have shrunk from seeing them represented in physical form.

Only centuries after the death of Jesus—by which time, astonishingly, even the Caesars had been brought to acknowledge him as Christ—did his execution at last start to emerge as an acceptable theme for artists. By AD 400 the cross was ceasing to be viewed as something shameful. Banned as a punishment decades earlier by Constantine, the first Christian emperor, crucifixion had come to serve the Roman people as an emblem of triumph over sin and death. An artist, carving the scene out of ivory, might represent Jesus in the skimpy loincloth of an athlete, no less muscled than any of the ancient gods. Even as the western half of the empire began to slip away from the rule of the Caesars and fall to barbarian invaders, so in the eastern half, where Roman power endured, the Cross provided assurance to an embattled people that victory would ultimately be theirs. In Christ's agonies had been the index of his defeat of evil. This was why, triumphant even on the implement of his torture, he was never shown as suffering pain. His expression was one of serenity. It proclaimed him Lord of the Universe.

So it was, in an empire that—although today we call it Byzantine—never ceased to insist that it was Roman, a corpse came to serve as an icon of majesty. Byzantium, though, was not the only Christian realm. In the Latin-speaking West, a millennium and more after the birth of Christ, a fresh revolution was brewing. Increasingly, there were Christians who, rather than keeping the brute horror of crucifixion from their gaze, yearned instead to fix their eyes fully upon it. 'Why, O my soul, did you fail to be there, to be stabbed by a sword of bitter grief, that you could not endure the piercing of your Saviour's side by a spear? Why could you not bear to see the nails violate the hands and feet of your Creator?'[16] This prayer, written some time around AD 1070, was not just to the God who reigned in glory on high, but to the condemned criminal he had been when he suffered his humiliating death. Its author, a brilliant scholar from northern Italy by the name of Anselm, was a man of noble birth: a correspondent of countesses, an associate of kings. Such it was to be a prince of the Church: the *ecclesia* or 'assembly' of the Christian people. Anselm was a man who combined birth, ability and a famous name. Nevertheless, even as he laboured to sway the destiny of Christendom, he could not help but find in his own eminence a cause of dread. So upset was he when appointed to lead the English Church that he promptly suffered a spectacular nosebleed. 'The very name of private property was to him a thing of horror.'[17] Seeing a cornered hare, he burst into tears, and bade the terrified animal be set free. No matter how high in the affairs of the world he rose, he never forgot that it was in lowliness, and nakedness, and persecution that his Saviour had redeemed him. In his prayer to the crucified Christ, copied as it was and read across the whole of the Latin West, Anselm articulated a new and momentous understanding of the Christian God: one in which the emphasis was laid not upon his triumph, but upon his suffering humanity.

'With this lament, suddenly, shockingly, we are in the presence of rupture...'[18] The Jesus portrayed by medieval artists, twisted, bloody, dying, was a victim of crucifixion such as his original executioners would have recognised: no longer serene and victorious, but racked by agony, just as any tortured slave would have been. The response to the spectacle, however, was far removed from the mingled revulsion and disdain that had typified that of the ancients to crucifixion. Men and women, when they looked upon an image of their Lord fixed to the cross, upon the nails smashed through the tendons and bone of his feet, upon the arms stretched so tightly as to appear torn from their sockets, upon the slump of his thorn-crowned head onto his chest, did not feel contempt, but rather compassion, and pity, and fear. There was certainly no lack of Christians, in medieval Europe, to identify with the sufferings of their God. Rich still trampled down poor. Gibbets stood on hills. The Church itself, thanks in large part to the exertions of men like Anselm, was able to lay claim to the ancient primacy of Rome—and uphold it, what was more. And yet, for all that, something fundamental had indeed changed. 'Patience in tribulation, offering the other cheek, praying for one's enemies, loving those who hate us':[19] such were the Christian virtues as defined by Anselm. All derived from the recorded sayings of Jesus himself. No Christians, then, not even the most callous or unheeding, could ignore them without some measure of reproof from their consciences. That the Son of God, born of a woman, and sentenced to the death of a slave, had perished unrecognised by his judges, was a reflection fit to give pause to even the haughtiest monarch. This awareness, enshrined as it was in the very heart of medieval Christianity, could not help but lodge in its consciousness a visceral and momentous suspicion: that God was closer to the weak than to the mighty, to the poor than to the rich. Any beggar, any criminal, might be Christ. 'So the last will be first, and the first last.'[20]

To the Roman aristocrats who, in the decades before the birth of Jesus, first began to colonise the Esquiline Hill with their marble fittings and their flowers beds, such a sentiment would have seemed grotesque. And yet it had come to pass. Nowhere bore more spectacular witness to this than Rome itself. In 1601, in a church that had originally been built to exorcise the ghost of Nero, a particularly flamboyant and malignant Caesar, a painting was installed that paid homage to the outcast origins of the city's Christian order. The artist, a young man from Milan by the name of Caravaggio, had been commissioned to paint a crucifixion: not of Christ himself, but of his leading disciple. Peter, a fisherman who, according to the gospels, had abandoned his boat and nets to follow Jesus, was said to have become the 'overseer'—the *episcopos* or 'bishop'—of the first Christians of Rome, before being put to death by Nero. Since Peter's execution, more than two hundred men had held the bishopric, an office that brought with it a claim to primacy over the entire Church, and the honorary title of *Pappas* or 'Father'—'Pope'. Over the course of the fifteen centuries and more that had followed Peter's death, the authority of the popes had waxed and waned; but it remained, in the lifetime of Caravaggio, a formidable thing. The artist, however, knew better than to celebrate its pomp, its splendour, its wealth. The earthly greatness of the papacy was turned literally on its head. Peter, the story went, had demanded to be crucified upside down, so as not to share in the fate of his Lord; and Caravaggio, choosing as his theme the very moment when the heavy cross was levered upwards, portrayed the first pope as he had authentically been—as a peasant. No ancient artist would have thought to honour a Caesar by representing him as Caravaggio represented Peter: tortured, humiliated, stripped almost bare. And yet, in the city of the Caesars, it was a man broken to such a fate who was honoured as the keeper of 'the keys of the kingdom of heaven'.[21] The last had indeed become first.

The relationship of Christianity to the world that gave birth to it is, then, paradoxical. The faith is at once the most enduring legacy of classical antiquity, and the index of its utter transformation. Formed of a great confluence of traditions—Persian and Jewish, Greek and Roman—it has long survived the collapse of the empire from which it first emerged, to become, in the words of one Jewish scholar, 'the most powerful of hegemonic cultural systems in the history of the world'.²² In the Middle Ages, no civilisation in Eurasia was as congruent with a single dominant set of beliefs as was the Latin West with its own distinctive form of Christianity. Elsewhere, whether in the lands of Islam, or in India, or in China, there were various understandings of the divine, and numerous institutions that served to define them; but in Europe, in the lands that acknowledged the primacy of the pope, there was only the occasional community of Jews to disrupt the otherwise total monopoly of the Roman Church. Such exclusivity was sternly guarded. Those who disturbed it, and refused to repent, might expect to be silenced, expelled or put to death. A Church that worshipped a God executed by heedless authorities presided over what has aptly been termed 'a persecuting society'.* Here, in the conviction that beliefs served to define a man or woman, was yet a further index of the transformative impact of the Christian revolution. That Christians had been willing to die as witnesses for their beliefs, as martyrs, was precisely what had marked them out to the Roman authorities as sinister and aberrant. All that, though, had changed. Time had seen the subversive prevail. In medieval Christendom, the bones of martyrs were treasured, and it was the Church that patrolled belief. To be human was to be Christian; to be Christian was to believe.

Well might the Roman Church have termed itself 'catholic': 'universal'. There was barely a rhythm of life that it did not define. From dawn to dusk, from midsummer to the depths of winter, from the hour of their birth to the very last drawing of their breath, the men and women of medieval Europe absorbed its assumptions into their bones. Even when, in the century before Caravaggio, Catholic Christendom began to fragment, and new forms of Christianity to emerge, the conviction of Europeans that their faith was universal remained deep-rooted. It inspired them in their exploration of continents undreamed of by their forefathers; in their conquest of those that they were able to seize, and reconsecrate as a Promised Land;

---

* The phrase is from the title of R. I. Moore's *The Formation of a Persecuting Society.*

in their attempt to convert the inhabitants of those that they were not. Whether in Korea or in Tierra del Fuego, in Alaska or in New Zealand, the cross on which Jesus had been tortured to death came to serve as the most globally recognised symbol of a god that there has ever been. 'Thou hast rebuked the nations, thou hast destroyed the wicked; thou hast blotted out their name for ever and ever.'[23] The man who greeted the news of the Japanese surrender in 1945 by quoting scripture and offering up praise to Christ was not Truman, nor Churchill, nor de Gaulle, but the Chinese leader, Chiang Kai-shek. Even in the twenty-first century, as the tide of Western dominance palpably retreats, assumptions bred of Europe's ancestral faith continue to structure the way that the world organises itself. Whether in North Korea or in the command structures of jihadi terrorist cells, there are few so ideologically opposed to the West that they are not sometimes obliged to employ the international dating system. Whenever they do so, they are subliminally reminded of the claims made by Christianity about the birth of Jesus. Time itself has been Christianised.

How was it that a cult inspired by the execution of an obscure criminal in a long-vanished empire came to exercise such a transformative and enduring influence on the world? To attempt an answer to this question, as I do in this book, is not to write a history of Christianity. Rather than provide a panoramic survey of its evolution, I have sought instead to trace the currents of Christian influence that have spread most widely, and been most enduring into the present day. That is why—although I have written extensively about the Eastern and Orthodox Churches elsewhere, and find them themes of immense wonder and fascination—I have chosen not to trace their development beyond antiquity. My ambition is hubristic enough as it is: to explore how we in the West came to be what we are, and to think the way that we do. The moral and imaginative upheaval that saw Jesus enshrined as a god by the same imperial order that had tortured him to death did not bring to an end the capacity of Christianity for inspiring profound transformations in societies. Quite the opposite. Already, by the time that Anselm died in 1109, Latin Christendom had been set upon a course so distinctive that what today we term 'the West' is less its heir than its continuation. Certainly, to dream of a world transformed by a reformation, or an enlightenment, or a revolution is nothing exclusively modern. Rather, it is to dream as medieval visionaries dreamed: to dream in the manner of a Christian.

Today, at a time of seismic geopolitical realignment, when our values are proving to be not nearly as universal as some of us had assumed them to be, the need to recognise just how culturally contingent they are is more pressing than ever. To live in a Western country is to live in a society still utterly saturated by Christian concepts and assumptions. This is no less true for Jews or Muslims than it is for Catholics or Protestants. Two thousand years on from the birth of Christ, it does not require a belief that he rose from the dead to be stamped by the formidable—indeed the inescapable—influence of Christianity. Whether it be the conviction that the workings of conscience are the surest determinants of good law, or that Church and state exist as distinct entities, or that polygamy is unacceptable, its trace elements are to be found everywhere in the West. Even to write about it in a Western language is to use words shot through with Christian connotations. 'Religion', 'secular', 'atheist': none of these are neutral. All, though they derive from the classical past, come freighted with the legacy of Christendom. Fail to appreciate this, and the risk is always of anachronism. The West, increasingly empty though the pews may be, remains firmly moored to its Christian past.

There are those who will rejoice at this proposition; and there are those who will be appalled by it. Christianity may be the most enduring and influential legacy of the ancient world, and its emergence the single most transformative development in Western history, but it is also the most challenging for a historian to write about.

In the West, and particularly in the United States, it remains easily the dominant faith. Worldwide, over two billion people—almost a third of the planet's population—subscribe to it. Unlike Osiris, or Zeus, or Odin, the Christian God still goes strong. The tradition of interpreting the past as the tracing of patterns upon time by his forefinger—a tradition that reaches back to the very beginnings of the faith—is far from dead. The crucifixion of Jesus, to all those many millions who worship him as the Son of the Lord God, the Creator of heaven and earth, was not merely an event in history, but the very pivot around which the cosmos turns. Historians, however, no matter how alert they may be to the potency of this understanding, and to the way in which it has swayed the course of the world's affairs, are not in the business of debating whether it is actually true. Instead, they study Christianity for what it can reveal, not about God, but about the affairs of humanity. No less than any other aspect of culture and society, beliefs are presumed to be of mortal origin and shaped by the passage of time. To look to the supernatural for explanations of what happened in the past is to engage in apologetics: a perfectly reputable pursuit, but not history as today, in the modern West, it has come to be understood.

Yet if historians of Christianity must negotiate faith, so also must they negotiate doubt. It is not only believers whose interpretation of Christian history is liable to be something deeply personal to them. The same can be equally true of sceptics. In 1860, in one of the first public discussions of Charles Darwin's recently published *On the Origin of Species*, the Bishop of Oxford notoriously mocked the theory that human beings might be the product of evolution. Now, though, the boot is on the other foot. 'It is the case that since we are all 21st century people, we all subscribe to a pretty widespread consensus of what's right and what's wrong.'[24] So Richard Dawkins, the world's most evangelical atheist, has declared. To argue that, in the West, the 'pretty widespread consensus of what's right and what's wrong' derives principally from Christian teachings and presumptions can risk seeming, in societies of many faiths and none, almost offensive. Even in America, where Christianity remains far more vibrant a force than it does in Europe, growing numbers have come to view the West's ancestral faith as something outmoded: a relic of earlier, more superstitious times. Just as the Bishop of Oxford refused to consider that he might be descended from an ape, so now are many in the West reluctant to contemplate that their values, and even their very lack of belief, might be traceable back to Christian origins.

I assert this with a measure of confidence because, until quite recently, I shared in this reluctance. Although as a boy I was taken every Sunday to church by my mother, and would solemnly say my prayers at night, I found myself at an early age experiencing what I can now recognise as having been an almost Victorian crisis of faith. I still remember the shock I felt when, at Sunday school one day, I opened a children's Bible and found an illustration on its first page of Adam and Eve with a brachiosaur. Respectful of Bible stories I may have been, but of one thing—to my regret—I was rock-solid certain: no human being had ever seen a sauropod. That the teacher seemed not to care about this error only compounded my sense of outrage and perplexity. Had there been dinosaurs in the Garden of Eden? My teacher seemed neither to know nor to care. A faint shadow of doubt had been brought to darken my confidence in the truth of what I was being taught about the Christian faith.

With time, it darkened further still. My obsession with dinosaurs—glamorous, ferocious, extinct—evolved seamlessly into an obsession with ancient empires. When I read the Bible, the focus of my fascination was less the children of Israel or Jesus and his disciples than their adversaries: the Egyptians, the Assyrians, the Romans. In a similar manner, although I vaguely continued to believe in God, I found him infinitely less charismatic than the gods of the Greeks: Apollo, Athena, Dionysus. I liked the way that they did not lay down laws, or condemn other deities as demons; I liked their rock-star glamour. As a result, by the time I came to read Edward Gibbon and his great history of the decline and fall of the Roman Empire, I was more than ready to accept his interpretation of the triumph of Christianity: that it had ushered in an 'age of superstition and credulity'.[25] My childhood instinct to see the biblical God as the po-faced enemy of liberty and fun was rationalised. The defeat of paganism had ushered in the reign of Nobodaddy, and of all the various crusaders, inquisitors and black-hatted Puritans who had served as his acolytes. Colour and excitement had been drained from the world. 'Thou hast conquered, O pale Galilean,' wrote the Victorian poet Algernon Charles Swinburne, echoing the apocryphal lament of Julian the Apostate, the last pagan emperor of Rome. 'The world has grown grey from thy breath.'[26] Instinctively, I agreed.

Yet over the course of the past two decades, my perspective has changed. When I came to write my first works of history, I chose as my themes the two periods that had always most stirred and moved me as a child: the Persian invasions of Greece and the last decades of the Roman Republic. The years that I spent writing these twin studies of the classical world, living intimately in the company of Leonidas and of Julius Caesar, of the hoplites who had died at Thermopylae and of the legionaries who had crossed the Rubicon, only confirmed me in my fascination: for Sparta and Rome, even when subjected to the minutest historical enquiry, retained their glamour as apex predators. They continued to stalk my imaginings as they had always done: like a great white shark, like a tiger, like a tyrannosaur. Yet giant carnivores, however wondrous, are by their nature terrifying. The more years I spent immersed in the study of classical antiquity, so the more alien I increasingly found it. The values of Leonidas, whose people had practised a peculiarly murderous form of eugenics and trained their young to kill uppity *Untermenschen* by night, were nothing that I recognised as my own; nor were those of Caesar, who was reported to have killed a million Gauls, and enslaved a million more. It was not just the extremes of callousness that unsettled me, but the complete lack of any sense that the poor or the weak might have the slightest intrinsic value. Why did I find this disturbing? Because, in my morals and ethics, I was not a Spartan or a Roman at all. That my belief in God had faded over the course of my teenage years did not mean that I had ceased to be Christian. For a millennium and more, the civilisation into which I had been born was Christendom. Assumptions that I had grown up with—about how a society should properly be organised, and the principles that it should uphold—were not bred of classical antiquity, still less of 'human nature', but very distinctively of that civilisation's Christian past. So profound has been the impact of Christianity on the development of Western civilisation that it has come to be hidden from view. It is the incomplete revolutions which are remembered; the fate of those which triumph is to be taken for granted.

The ambition of *Dominion* is to trace the course of what one Christian, writing in the third century AD, termed 'the flood-tide of Christ':[27] how the belief that the Son of the one God of the Jews had been tortured to death on a cross came to be so enduringly and widely held that today most of us in the West are dulled to just how scandalous it originally was. This book explores what it was that made Christianity so subversive and disruptive; how completely it came to saturate the mindset of Latin Christendom; and why, in a West that is often doubtful of religion's claims, so many of its instincts remain—for good and ill—thoroughly Christian.

It is—to coin a phrase—the greatest story ever told.

Part I

❖

ANTIQUITY

1

ATHENS

479 BC: The Hellespont

At one of the narrowest points on the Hellespont, the thin channel of water that snakes from the Aegean up towards the Black Sea, and separates Europe from Asia, a promontory known as the Dog's Tail extended from the European shore. Here, 480 years before the birth of Christ, a feat so astonishing as to seem the work of a god had been completed. Twin pontoon bridges, stretching from the Asian shore to the tip of the Dog's Tail, had yoked the two continents together. That none but a monarch of infinite resources could possibly have tamed the currents of the sea in so imperious a manner went without saying. Xerxes, the King of Persia, ruled the largest empire that the world had ever seen. From the Aegean to the Hindu Kush, all the teeming hordes of Asia marched at his command. Going to war, he could summon forces that were said to drink entire rivers dry. Few had doubted, watching Xerxes cross the Hellespont, that the whole continent beyond would soon be his.

One year on, the bridges were gone. So too were Xerxes' hopes of conquering Europe. Invading Greece, he had captured Athens; but the torching of the city was to prove the high point of his campaign. Defeat by sea and land had forced a Persian retreat. Xerxes himself had returned to Asia. On the Hellespont, where command of the strait had been entrusted to a governor named Artaÿctes, there was particular alarm. He knew himself, in the wake of the debacle in Greece, ominously exposed. Sure enough, late in the summer of 479, a squadron of Athenian ships came gliding up the Hellespont. When they moored beside the Dog's Tail, Artaÿctes first barricaded himself inside the nearest stronghold; and then, after a lengthy siege, made a break for safety, accompanied by his son. Despite a successful escape in the dead of night, they did not get far. Hunted down, father and son were soon being hauled back in chains to the Dog's Tail. There, on the furthermost tip of the promontory, Artaÿctes was fixed by his Athenian captors to a wooden board, and hung from it. 'Then, before his very eyes, they stoned his son to death.'[1] Artaÿctes himself was left to a much more lingering end.

How had his executioners succeeded in keeping him attached to the upright plank? In Athens, criminals convicted of particularly heinous crimes might be fastened to an instrument of torture called the *apotumpanismos*, a board furnished with shackles for securing the neck, wrists and ankles. There is no suggestion, however, that this particular device was employed by the killers of Artaÿctes. Instead, in the one account of his death we have, we are told that he was fastened to the board with *passaloi*: 'pins'.* The executioners, forcing their victim onto his back, had evidently driven spikes through his living flesh, hammering them deep into the wood. Bone would have rubbed and scraped against iron as the board was then levered erect. Artaÿctes, watching as his son was left a pulped and broken mess, would also have been able to look up to the skies, and see the birds there wheeling, impatient to settle on him, to feast on his eyes. Death, when it finally claimed him, would have come as a release.

His captors, in making such a protracted spectacle of Artaÿctes' suffering, were also making a statement. To execute him on the very spot where Xerxes had first stepped onto European soil broadcast an

---

* Specifically, the word used by Herodotus is *prospassaleusantes*: 'fastened with pins'.

unmistakable message. To humiliate the Great King's servant was to humiliate the Great King himself. The Greeks, who had long lived in the shadow of Persia, had good reason to regard it as the home of ingenious tortures. It was the Persians, they believed, who had first initiated the practice of exposing criminals on stakes or crosses, so that humiliation compounded the agonies of death. Certainly, the punishments inflicted on those who defied the royal dignity were as excruciating as they were minatory. Some forty years before Xerxes' invasion of Greece, his father, Darius, had dealt with those who disputed his right to the throne by torturing them in the most public manner possible. Entire forests of stakes had been erected, on which his rivals, writhing and screaming as they felt the wood start to penetrate their innards, had been impaled. 'I cut off both his nose and his ears, and put out one of his eyes, and kept him bound at my palace entrance, where all could see him.' So Darius had boasted, detailing his treatment of one particularly noxious rebel. 'Then I had him impaled.'[2]

Not every victim of the Great King's anger, though, was necessarily suspended and exposed as he died. The Greeks reported in hushed tones of disgust one particularly revolting torture: the *scaphe*, or 'trough'. The executioner, after placing his victim inside a boat or hollowed-out tree trunk, would then attach a second one over the top of it, so that only the wretched man's head, hands and feet were left sticking out. Fed continuously with rich food, the criminal would have no choice but to lie in his own excrement; smeared all over with honey, he would find himself powerless to brush away the buzzing flies. 'Worms and swarms of maggots were bred of the rottenness and the putrefaction of the excrement; and these, eating away at his body, bored into his intestines.'[3] The victim would finally expire only once his flesh and organs had been almost entirely consumed. One man, so it was reliably reported, had endured the *scaphe* for seventeen days before finally breathing his last.

Yet cruel though such a torture might be, it was not wantonly so. The Greeks, when they charged the Great King with heedless displays of despotism, mistook for barbarous savagery the sense of responsibility that characterised his concern for justice. In truth, from the perspective of the Persian court, it was the Greeks who were the barbarians. Although the Great King was content to allow his subject peoples to uphold their own laws—provided, of course, that they were dutifully submissive—he never doubted the cosmic character of his own prerogatives and responsibilities. 'By the favour of Ahura Mazda am I king,' declared Darius. 'Ahura Mazda bestowed kingship upon me.'⁴ Greatest of the gods, the Wise Lord, who had created both the heavens and the earth, and clad himself in the crystalline beauty of the skies above the snows and sands of Iran, he was the only patron whom Darius acknowledged. The justice the Great King gave to his subjects was not of mortal origin but derived directly from the Lord of Light. 'The man who is loyal, I reward; the man who is faithless, I punish. It is by the favour of Ahura Mazda that people respect the order I uphold.'⁵

This conviction, that the rule of a king might be as beneficent as a god's, was not original to Darius. It reached back to the very beginning of things. To the west of Iran, watered by two mighty rivers, stretched the mudflats of the region known to the Greeks as Mesopotamia: 'the land between the rivers'. Here, in cities older by far than the Persians, monarchs had long been in the habit of thanking the gods for their assistance in administering justice. A thousand years and more before Darius, a king named Hammurabi had declared himself charged with a divine mandate: 'to bring about the rule of righteousness in the land, and to destroy the wicked and the evil-doers, so that the strong should not harm the weak'.⁶ The influence of this claim, that a king best served his people by providing them with equity, was to prove an enduring one. Babylon, the city ruled by Hammurabi, regarded itself as the capital of the world. This was not mere wishful thinking. As wealthy as it was sophisticated, the metropolis had long attracted superlatives. Although its greatness had ebbed and flowed over the course of the centuries, the grandeur and antiquity of its traditions were grudgingly acknowledged across Mesopotamia. Even in Assyria, a land to the north of

Babylon, and which, until the collapse of its ferociously militarist regime in 612 BC, had repeatedly launched punitive expeditions against the great city, its kings echoed the pretensions of Hammurabi. They too claimed a dazzling and intimidating status for their rulings. 'The word of the King,' so one of them ringingly declared, 'is as perfect as that of the gods.'[7]

In 539 BC, when Babylon was conquered by the Persians, just as Assyria seven decades previously had been conquered by the Babylonians, the gods of the vanquished metropolis had not hesitated to hail its new master as their favourite. Cyrus, the founder of his people's greatness, and whose capture of the world's largest city had set the seal on a lifetime of astonishing victories, had graciously accepted their patronage. The Persian king boasted of having entered Babylon at their explicit invitation; of having restored their temples; of having cared daily for their worship. Cyrus, as deft a propagandist as he was effective a military commander, knew full well what he was doing. Starting his reign as the king of an obscure and upstart people, he ended it as lord of the largest agglomeration of territories that the world had ever seen—and on a scale, certainly, that far exceeded the wildest fantasies of any Assyrian or Babylonian monarch. Yet Cyrus, when he looked to promote himself as a global ruler, had little option but to look to the heritage of Mesopotamia. Nowhere else in his dominions had offered him a model of kingship so rooted in antiquity, so burnished by self-satisfaction. 'King of the universe, mighty king, king of Babylon':[8] here were titles that the Persian conqueror had been eager to make his own.

Nevertheless, Mesopotamian tradition had in the long run proven inadequate to the needs of his heirs. The Babylonians, despite all Cyrus' flattering of their pretensions, had only reluctantly accepted their loss of independence. Among the rebels who rose against Darius when, seventeen years after the fall of Babylon, he seized the Persian throne, there was one who claimed to be the son of the city's last native king. Defeated in battle, the wretched man and his lieutenants—as was only to be expected, of course—were all briskly impaled. Darius also made sure, though, to skewer his defeated rival's reputation. Inscriptions broadcast to the world the full scale of the pretender's deceptions. Far from having been a prince of the blood, it was announced, he had not even been a Babylonian, but an Armenian by the name of Arakha. 'He was a liar.'[9] This, of all the many accusations that a Persian might level against an adversary, was easily the most damning. The falsehood of which Arakha had been convicted was an offence, not just against Darius, but against the very stability of the universe. All good and all wise though the Lord Mazda was, his creation, so the Persians believed, was menaced by a darkness to which they gave the name of *Drauga*: 'the Lie'. In fighting Arakha and his fellow rebels, Darius had not merely been defending his own interests. Infinitely more had been at stake. The spreading filth of the Lie, had it had not been purged by Darius, would have ended up splashing the radiance of all that was good with the poison of its sewage. Rebels against his authority as king were also rebels against that of the Wise Lord. 'Ignorant of the worship of Ahura Mazda,'[10] they had assailed a cosmic order that was synonymous with Truth itself. Not for nothing did the Persians use the same word, *Arta*, for them both. Darius, in committing himself to the defence of Truth, was setting an example for all who would follow him onto the throne. 'You, who shall be king hereafter, be firmly on your guard against the Lie. The man who shall be a follower of the Lie—punish him well.'

And his heirs had done so. Like Darius, they knew themselves engaged in a conflict as old as time, and as wide as the universe. Between the light and the darkness, all had to choose their side. There was nothing so tiny, no creeping or coiling thing so insignificant, that it might not rank as a minion of the Lie. The worms and maggots that fed on a man sentenced to the *scaphe*, bred of his filth, confirmed by consuming his flesh that both were agents of falsehood and darkness. In a similar manner, those barbarians who lurked beyond the limits of Persian order, where the writ of the Great King did not run, were the servants not of gods, but of demons. Naturally, this did not mean blaming foreigners merely because, unlucky not to have been born Persian, they were ignorant of Ahura Mazda. Such a policy would have been grotesque: an offence against all accepted custom. Cyrus, by lavishing patronage on the temples of Babylon, had blazed a path that his heirs made sure to follow. Who was any mortal, even the Great King, to mock the gods of other peoples? Nevertheless, as the man charged by Ahura Mazda with the defence of the world against the Lie, it was his responsibility to purge strife-torn lands of demons no less than of rebels. Just as Arakha had seduced Babylon into revolt by taking on the appearance of their dead king's son, so did demons similarly practise deception by aping the appearance of gods. Faced with such a danger, what recourse did a Great King have save to take punitive action?

So it was that Darius, looking to the lands beyond his northern frontiers, and alerted to the fractious character of a people named the Scythians, had recognised in their savagery something ominous: a susceptibility to the seductions of demons. 'They were vulnerable, these Scythians, to the Lie'[11]—and so Darius, ever the dutiful servant of Ahura Mazda, had made sure to pacify them. In similar manner, after capturing Athens, Xerxes had ordered the temples on the Acropolis be scoured clean with fire; and only then, once he could be certain that they were purged of demons, had he permitted the gods of the city to be offered sacrifice once again. Power such as the Great King wielded was something unprecedented. More than any other ruler before him, he was able, by virtue of the sheer immensity of his territorial possessions, to believe himself charged with a universal mission. The word he gave to his empire, *bumi*, was synonymous with the world. The Athenians, when they thought to defy Xerxes' claim to Europe by crucifying one of his servants beside the Hellespont, only confirmed themselves as adherents of the Lie.

Beyond the physical apparatus of the Great King's vast empire, then, beyond the palaces, and the barrack rooms, and the way-posts on dusty roads, there shimmered a sublime and momentous conceit. The dominion forged by Cyrus and secured by Darius served as a mirror to the heavens. To resist it or to subvert it was to defy Truth itself. Never before had a monarchy with ambitions to rule the world endowed its sway with quite so potent an ethical character. The reach of the Great King's power, which extended to the limits of east and west, even cast its light into the grave. 'These are the words of Darius, the King: that whosoever worships Ahura Mazda will be blessed with divine favour, both living and dead.'[12] Perhaps, as he endured his death-agonies, Artaÿctes was able to find comfort in such a reflection.

Certainly, the news of his execution would only have confirmed the Great King in his disdain for the Athenians as terrorists. Truth or falsehood; light or darkness; order or chaos: these were the choices that humans everywhere had to make.

It was a way of comprehending the world that was destined to have an enduring afterlife.

Tell Me Lies

In Athens, of course, they saw things rather differently. In 425 BC, a dramatist by the name of Aristophanes made comic play of just how differently. Fifty-four years had passed since Xerxes put the Acropolis to the torch, and the summit of the rock, cleaned of rubble and adorned with 'marks and monuments of empire',[13] bore dazzling witness to the scale of the city's revival. Below the Parthenon, largest and most beautiful of the temples that now adorned the Athenian skyline, citizens would gather every winter within the natural curve of the hillside, there to take their seats in a theatre for an annual display of drama.* In a year marked by the rhythm of festivals, the Lenaia was a particular celebration of comedy—and Aristophanes, although only at the start of his career, had already proven himself a master of the medium. In 425, he made his debut in the Lenaia with

---

* The plays staged in honour of the Lenaia were moved there two or three decades before Aristophanes' debut.

a play, *The Acharnians*, that ridiculed everything it touched—and among its targets were the vaunts of the Persian king.

'He has many eyes.'[14] To the Greeks, the claim of their traditional enemy to a universal rule could hardly help but seem sinister in the extreme. Within the limits of his empire, spies were believed to enforce a perpetual surveillance. 'Everyone feels himself under watch by a king who is omnipresent.'[15] Such a target, for Aristophanes, was too tempting to resist. When the actor given the part of a Persian ambassador in *The Acharnians* walked onto the stage, he did so wearing an enormous eye on his head. Invited to deliver the Great King's message, he solemnly declaimed a line of gibberish. Even his name, Pseudartabas, was a pointed joke: for just as *arta* in Persian meant 'truth', so did *pseudes* in Greek mean 'lying'.[16] Aristophanes could recognise a deserving target when he saw it. Insolently, indomitably, he exposed the profoundest convictions of Darius and his heirs to the laughter of the Athenian crowd.

That truth might deceive was a paradox with which the Greeks were well acquainted. In the mountains north-west of Athens, at Delphi, there stood an oracle; and so teasing were its revelations, so ambiguous and riddling its pronouncements, that Apollo, the god who inspired them, was hailed as *Loxias*—'the Oblique One'. A deity less like Ahura Mazda it would have been hard to imagine. Greek travellers marvelled at peoples in distant lands who obeyed oracles to the letter: for those delivered by Apollo were invariably equivocal. In Delphi, ambivalence was the prerogative of the divine. Apollo, most golden of the gods, who in time would come to be identified with the charioteer of the sun, dazzled those he raped. Famed though he was for his powers of healing, and for the magical potency of his musicianship, he was dreaded too as the lord of the silver bow, whose arrows were tipped with plague. Light, which the Persians saw as the animating principle of the universe, wholly good and wholly true, was also the supreme quality of Apollo; but there was a darkness to the Greek god as well. He and his twin sister Artemis, a virgin huntress no less deadly with the bow, were famed for their sensitivity to insult. When a king's daughter named Niobe boasted of how many more children she had than Leto, the mother of Apollo and Artemis, who had only ever had the two, the twin gods exacted a terrible vengeance. A firestorm of golden arrows felled her sons and daughters. For nine days their corpses lay unburied in their mother's hall, caked with blood. The princess herself, worn to the bone with weeping, took to the hills. 'There, stuck into stone, Niobe still broods on the spate of griefs the gods poured out to her.'[17]

How were mortals to avoid offending these capricious and ever status-conscious deities? It was not enough merely to refrain from insulting an immortal's mother. There were dues of sacrifice to be paid, as well as of respect. The bones of animals slaughtered before white-chalked altars, glistening with fat and burned in fires perfumed with incense, were the portion owed the gods. While offerings certainly never guaranteed their favour, failure to make sacrifice was bound to provoke the gods' rage. The risk was one shared by all. No wonder, then, that it should have been the rituals of sacrifice which tended to bring a community most closely together. Men and women, boys and girls, free and slaves: all had their part to play. Festivals, hallowed by time, were hallowed as well by mystery. There were some altars built entirely out of blood; others where no flies ever swarmed around the shambles. The whim of a god was a variable thing, and differed from place to place. In her shrine at Patrae, in southern Greece, Artemis demanded a holocaust of living creatures, birds, and boars, and bears; at Brauron, east of Athens, the robes of women who had died in childbirth; at Sparta, the blood of young men lashed to ribbons. Naturally, with so many different ways of paying the gods what was owed them, and with so many different gods to honour, there was always a nagging anxiety that some might be overlooked. A citizen set the task of collating and inscribing the traditions of Athens discovered, to his horror, a long list of sacrifices that everyone had forgotten. The expense of restoring them, so he calculated, would bankrupt the city.

The grim truth was that the immortals, with the passage of time, had withdrawn from the company of men, and a golden age became an age of iron. Once, back in the distant past, even Zeus, the king of the gods, who ruled from the heights of Mount Olympus, had delighted in joining the banquets of mortals. Increasingly, though, he had chosen to disguise himself, and to descend from his palace not to share in a feast, but to rape. Whether as a shower of gold, or as a white bull, or as a swan with beating wings, he had forced himself on a whole succession of women; and thereby bred a race of heroes. Warriors of incomparable prowess, these men had cleansed mountains and swamps of monsters, ventured to the limits of the world, and fathered entire peoples, 'the noblest and most righteous of generations'.[18] The doom of the heroes, when it finally arrived, had proven fully worthy of their peerless stature; for they had been culled in the most renowned and terrible of wars. Ten years it had lasted; and at the end of it, when Troy, the greatest city in Asia, had been left a pile of smoking ruins, few were the victors who had not themselves then succumbed to shipwreck, or to murder, or to a battalion of sorrows. Justly could it be said of Zeus, 'No one is more destructive than you.'[19]

The fate of Troy never ceased to haunt the Greeks. Even Xerxes, arriving at the Hellespont, had demanded to be shown its site. The *Iliad*, the poem that enshrined the memory of those who had fought amid the dust of the Trojan plain, also provided the Greeks with their most popular window onto the workings of the gods, and of their relationship to mortals. Its author, a man whose dates and place of birth were endlessly debated, was himself a figure touched by a certain quality of the divine. Some went so far as to claim that Homer's father had been a river and his mother a sea-nymph; but even those who accepted that his origins had been more mundanely human stood in awe of his achievements. 'Best and most godlike of all poets':[20] so he was hailed. Never had there been a poem as vivid with a sense of brightness as the *Iliad*. The play of light was everywhere in its verses. No woman in it was so insignificant that she could not be described as 'white-armed'; no man so fleetingly mentioned that he might not be cast as 'bronze-armoured'. The queen who dressed herself did so by putting on robes that dazzled the eye. The warrior preparing for battle sheathed himself in refulgence, 'brighter than gleaming fire'.[21] Beauty was everywhere—and invariably it hinted at violence.

To blaze like a golden flame, and to attain a godlike pitch of strength and valour: this it was, in the *Iliad*, to be most fully a man. Physical perfection and moral superiority were indissoluble: this was the assumption. On the battlefield at Troy, only the base were ugly. Such men might on occasion merit being mocked and beaten, but they were hardly fitting opponents of a hero. The surest measure of greatness was in a contest worthy of the name: an *agon*. This was why, in the fighting between Greek and Trojan, the gods themselves would sometimes descend onto the battlefield; not merely to watch the serried lines of men, their shields and armour glinting, as they moved in for the kill, but to fight in the cause of their favourites— and whenever they alighted, they would quiver with anticipation 'like nervous doves'.[22] It was why, as well, sitting in their golden halls, the gods might not hesitate to sacrifice whole cities and peoples to their enmities. When Hera, the queen of the gods, demanded of her husband that he surrender Troy, which he loved above all other cities, to her quenchless hatred, and Zeus demurred, she refused to cede the field.

> The three cities that I love best of all
> are Argos and Sparta, Mycenae with streets as broad as Troy's.
> Raze them—whenever they stir the hatred in your heart.[23]

What mattered was victory, not the cost.

This spirit, this ferocious commitment to being the best, was one in which all aspired to share. In Homer's poetry, the word for 'pray', *euchomai*, was also a word for 'boast'. The gods invariably looked with favour upon an *agon*. Rare was the sanctuary that did not serve as the venue for some competition, be it for dancers, poets or weavers. From athletics to beauty contests, all had their divine sponsors. When Aristophanes wrote *The Acharnians* he did so as a contender in an *agon*. The Lenaia was held in honour of Dionysus, a god whose fondness for drunken revelry and female company rendered him a more than appropriate patron for Aristophanes' brand of comedy. Kings and princes, of the kind who on the plain of Troy had dared to fight even with gods, no longer reigned in Athens. Less than a century before the time of Aristophanes, revolution had come to the city and a radically new form of government, one in which power was entrusted to the people, had been enshrined there. In a democracy, the right to contend with one's peers was no longer the prerogative of aristocrats alone. Indeed, the ethos of gods and heroes might come to seem, when viewed through the prism of a more egalitarian age, more than a little comic. Aristophanes, who was nothing if not competitive himself, did not hesitate to portray them as oafs, or cowards, or liars. In one of his comedies, he even dared to show Dionysus, disguised as a slave, shitting himself as he was threatened with torture, and then being scourged with a whip. The play, like *The Acharnians*, was awarded first prize.

The tension, though, between ancient song and the values of those who were not heroes, was never simply a matter for laughter. 'Are there no guidelines set by heaven for mortal men, no path to follow that will please the gods?'[24] This question, which the sick, the bereaved or the oppressed could hardly help but ask, had no ready answer. The gods, inscrutable and whimsical as they were, rarely deigned to explain themselves. They certainly never thought to regulate morals. The oracle at Delphi might offer advice, but not ethical instruction. 'The god does not rule by issuing commands.'[25] Such guidelines as mortal men had set for them derived from tradition, not revelation. Law was so dependent on custom as to be indistinguishable from it. With the coming of democracy, though, that assumption was challenged. The right of the people to determine legislation emerged as something fundamental to their authority. 'For everyone would agree that it is the city's laws which are chiefly responsible for its prosperity, its democracy and its freedom.'[26] Only in the assemblies, where citizens met as equals to deliberate and vote, was there to be found a source of legitimacy appropriate to the rule of Athens by the people. What value liberty otherwise?

Nevertheless, the Athenians could not help but be nagged by a certain anxiety. To submit themselves to laws of human origin was to run the risk of tyranny: for what was to stop an over-ambitious citizen from framing legislation designed to subvert the democracy? Unsurprisingly, then, the laws most reassuring to the Athenians were those that seemed to sprout from the very soil of their homeland, like the olive trees in the fields beyond Athens, their roots clinging fast to stone. This was why, in an attempt to give legislation a comforting patina of age, it became the habit to attribute its authorship to sages from the city's distant past. There were many, though, who believed in something infinitely more venerable: indeed, a law so transcendent that it had no origin at all. Some four or five years before the first performance of *The Acharnians*, another play staged in the theatre of Dionysus gave potent voice to this conviction.* Sophocles, its author, was not, like Aristophanes, a writer of comedies. There were no jokes in *Oedipus the King*. Tragedy, the genre of which Sophocles was a prize-winning master, took the ancient stories told of gods and heroes, and made play with them to often disorienting effect; but not for laughs. The downfall of Oedipus had been dramatised many times before, but never to such bleak effect as in the version presented by Sophocles. King of Thebes, a city to the north-west of Athens much detested by the Athenians, Oedipus had killed his father and married his mother. That he had committed these crimes unwittingly, having been exposed as a baby and brought up by foster parents, did not serve to extenuate his offence. His crime was against laws that were timeless, eternal, sacred. 'Begotten in the clear

---

* Assuming, that is, that the plague which ravages Thebes in the play is an echo of the plague that had devastated Athens in 430 BC. No source specifically gives us the play's date.

aether of heaven, fathered by Olympus alone, nothing touched by the mortal is their parent, nor shall oblivion ever lull them to sleep.'[27]

These laws, unlike those of mortal origin, were not written down: it was precisely their lack of an author which distinguished them as divine. 'Neither today or yesterday were they born; they are eternal, and no one knows when they first appeared.'[28] Quite how, if lacking a written form, they were to be recognised, still more to be distinguished from human legislation, was an issue that did not much concern the average citizen; most Greeks—whose capacity to hold two dissonant points of view at the same time was considerable—were not greatly perturbed by the resulting tensions. But some were; and among them was Sophocles. *Oedipus the King* was not the only play he wrote about the curse brought down on Thebes by the crimes of his hero. In an earlier tragedy, *Antigone*, he had portrayed the ultimate doom of Oedipus' house. The play opened amid the aftermath of civil war. Oedipus' two sons, fighting over the kingdom, both lay dead before the walls of Thebes. Only one, though, Eteocles, was to be afforded proper burial: for their uncle, Creon, succeeding to the throne, had decreed the second brother, Polynices, to blame for the war, and that as punishment his corpse be left as food for dogs and birds. Even to mourn the traitor, so the new king had pronounced, would mean death. Yet this edict, for all that it had the force of law, did not satisfy everyone that it was legal. Antigone, Oedipus' daughter, dared to defy her uncle, and give Polynices a symbolic burial by scattering dust on his corpse. Brought before Creon, she scorned his edict. 'I do not believe your laws, you being only a man, sufficient to overrule divine ordinances—unwritten and unfailing as they are.'[29] Sentenced to be walled up alive in a tomb, Antigone hanged herself. Creon's son, who had been betrothed to her, likewise committed suicide; so too his queen. The ruin was total. The chorus, witness to the tragedy, drew the seeming lesson. 'The chiefest part of happiness is wisdom—that, and not to insult the gods.'[30]

Such a resolution, in light of the ruin visited upon the house of Oedipus, seemed barely adequate to the terrifying nature of the divine order that had sanctioned it. Yet it seems unlikely, as the stage was cleared and the spectators rose to leave the theatre, that many were brought to question the glaring contradictions that lay at the heart of how they conceived the gods. That the immortals were held to be simultaneously whimsical and purposeful, amoral and sternly moral, arbitrary and wholly just, did not perturb most Athenians. Leaving the theatre of Dionysus, they would have been able to look up at the brilliant array of monuments on the rock above them, where Athena, the divine virgin whose name their city bore, had her greatest temple. No god better exemplified the paradoxes that characterised how most Greeks comprehended the divine. To enter the Parthenon and to look upon its colossal statue of Athena, fashioned out of gold and ivory, magnificent, imperious and sublime, was to behold a deity who offered up a mirror to the Athenian people themselves. Like them, she was famed both for her wisdom and for her quicksilver moods; like her city, she was mistress both of handicrafts and of 'the clamorous cry of war'.[31] Although, in the theatre below her temple, the Athenians were content every year to watch new drafts of the stories told of the gods, and be brought by the spectacle either to laugh or to weep, it did not prompt most of them to smooth out the inconsistencies in their attitudes to the divine. Most preferred not to worry. Most barely paused to reflect that their beliefs might perhaps be a bit inconsistent.

Most—but not all.

Lovers of Wisdom

A century and more after Aristophanes had mocked the pretensions of the Persian king in *The Acharnians*, a great array of bronze statues began to appear across Athens. By 307 BC, the city had come to be dotted with over three hundred of them, some equestrian, some complete with chariot, but all portraying the same man. Demetrius of Phaleron was a native of the old port of Athens, and from a resolutely working-class background—indeed, according to his enemies, he had once been a slave.* Nevertheless, while still only in his early thirties he had secured a more absolute authority over the city than anyone had wielded since the founding of the democracy. Blessed as a youth with the kind of long-lashed beauty that was liable to make Athenian statesmen go weak at the knees, Demetrius had not hesitated to capitalise on the head start this advantage gave him. Even as he continued to dye his hair blond and make liberal use of mascara, he had also proven himself, over the course of the decade that he had ruled as the master of Athens, an effective legislator. Not merely a statesman, he was also bred of the city's intellectual marrow: a *philosophos.*

'Lover of wisdom,' the word literally meant. Although it had become a recognisable job only a few decades previously, the origins of philosophy were venerable.† For two centuries and more, while most Greeks had been perfectly content to rely upon Homer for their understanding of the gods, and upon local tradition, and upon what custom defined as the dues of sacrifice, there had been some who were not. To these thinkers, the contradictions between the timeless laws that were presumed to prescribe correct behaviour, and the readiness of the immortals in the *Iliad* to ignore them, were a scandal. Homer and his fellow poets, so the philosopher Xenophanes complained, 'have attributed to the gods all kinds of things that among humans are shameful and matters of reproach: theft, adultery, deceit'.[32] Were cattle only capable of drawing, he scoffed, they would portray their deities as bulls and cows. Yet this bracing scepticism—although in time it would tempt some thinkers to atheism—did not in the main result in a godless materialism. Quite the opposite. If philosophers disdained to believe in the quarrelsome and intemperate immortals of song, then it was generally so that they might better contemplate what was truly divine about both the

---

* This, it has justly been observed, was almost certainly 'a piece of vindictive gossip.' (Fortenbaugh and Schütrumpf, p. 315).

† The first use of the word is traditionally ascribed to Pythagoras, but in fact it seems to have originated with Plato.

universe and themselves. To fathom what underlay matter was also to fathom how humans should properly behave. 'For all the various laws of men are nourished by the single law—which is divine.'[33]

Beyond the buzzing of flies above a sticky altar, beyond the statues of gods smiling or frowning in shadow-cooled temples, beyond all the manifold variety and flux of human custom, there existed a pattern to things. Eternal and perfect, it needed only to be identified. It was not in the lies of poets but in the workings of the cosmos that it was to be located. Nowhere was this conviction more fruitfully explored than in Athens. By the time that Demetrius of Phaleron was born, some time around 350 BC, it had come to be accepted by the city's most celebrated philosophers that the seemingly irregular motions of the stars in truth obeyed unchanging geometric laws. The universe itself stood revealed as rational—and hence divine. Xenophanes, a century and a half before, had proclaimed the existence of a single ungenerated and morally perfect deity, who guided everything through the sheer power of his consciousness—his *nous*. Demetrius, studying as a young man, could trace in the movements of the stars the evidence for a subtler, and yet no less chilly conception of the divine. 'There is something which moves without being moved—something eternal.'[34] So wrote Aristotle, a philosopher from the north of Greece who, settling in Athens, had established a school so influential that it continued to flourish even after his death in 322. In the heavens, so Aristotle had taught, beyond the sublunar world to which mortals were confined, bodies were eternal and obedient to unchanging circular orbits; and yet these movements, perfect though they were, depended in turn upon a mover which itself never moved. 'This, then, is the god—the principle on which heaven and nature depend.'[35] Such a deity—off-puttingly metaphysical though it might appear to those without a schooling in philosophy—was properly the object of every mortal's love. Whether that love was reciprocated, however, appeared exceedingly improbable. Aristotle certainly disdained to say that it might be.

The sublunar world, lacking as it did the inerrant order of the stars, and far distant from them, could hardly be expected to concern the unmoving mover.

Nevertheless, the earth as well as the heavens bore witness to its controlling *nous*. Aristotle, to a degree unprecedented among philosophers, sought to fathom its workings by anatomising whatever he could. Sometimes, whether dissecting a cuttlefish or examining the stomach of an elephant, he would do so literally: for even amid the slipperiness of a dead creature's intestines there was proof to be found of the eternal structure of the cosmos. To love wisdom, so Aristotle taught, was to train the mind in the skills required to trace its laws. This was why, not content with studying as many different organisms as he could, he also investigated the numerous ways that humanity sought to organise itself: 'for man alone of animals is capable of deliberation'.[36] The goal, as ever with Aristotle, was not merely to compile a catalogue, but to distinguish the lineaments of a cosmic order. The need to achieve this was evident. Only the law that pervaded the universe, and was equivalent to the divine *nous*, could truly provide a city with proper governance, 'for to be ruled by men, whose appetites will be something feral, and whose passions— no matter how upstanding they may be—are bound to warp them, is to be ruled by wild beasts'.[37]

Yet there lurked in this conviction, for any philosopher anxious to act upon it, a familiar puzzle. How, when the affairs of the world so signally failed to mimic the smooth and regular movement of the heavens, was a city best to be ordered? Naturally, there were certain fundamentals upon which everyone could agree. It hardly required an anatomist of Aristotle's genius to observe the most obvious ways in which society should obey the laws of nature. 'He used to say, it is reported, that he thanked Fortune for three things: "first, that I am a human and not a beast; second, that I am a man and not a woman; third, that I am a Greek and not a barbarian".'[38] This anecdote, so widely repeated that it was told of several philosophers, was certainly nothing with which Aristotle disagreed. Satisfied as he was that humans were superior to all the other 494 species he had identified over the course of his researches, that man was the master of woman, and that barbarians were fitted by nature to be the slaves of Greeks, he drew the logical—indeed, the only possible—conclusion. 'That one should command and another obey is not just necessary but expedient.'[39]

And now, less than a decade after the death of Aristotle, a philosopher ruled over Athens. Demetrius, following the prescriptions of his master, had little patience with the masses. Aristotle, anxious that the reins of state be held only by those with the time and money to be educated in the true nature of things, had wrinkled his nose at the thought of sailors—men more habituated to the rowing bench than to the philosopher's salon—wielding influence over public affairs. 'Such a mob should never rank as citizens.'[40] Demetrius, despite his own upbringing in a port, had enthusiastically followed this prescription. Under his rule, the poor were disenfranchised. Property was defined as the qualification for having a vote. Assemblies were abolished, laws revised, spending cuts imposed. The machinery of government, no longer subject to the chaotic whims of the people, was set on a new and regular course. His labour of reform completed, Demetrius then settled back and devoted his attention to prostitutes and young boys. What else was there for him to do? Athens' new constitution had not been crafted by a philosopher for nothing. Like the stars in their orbits, revolving with smooth precision around the earth, it was designed to be obedient to the eternal and unchanging laws that governed the cosmos.

A reflection certainly fit to delight philosophers—but not, perhaps, the vast mass of those who had little time for abstract speculation. To them, the deity enshrined by Aristotle at the heart of the universe, heedless as it was of humanity's cares, remained as impersonal and colourless as it had ever been. A people with the rhythms of the *Iliad* in their minds still wanted glamour when they looked to the heavens. Sure enough, far beyond the walls of Athens, deeds were being achieved of what seemed to many a god-like order. In 334 BC, Alexander, the king of Macedon, on the northern periphery of Greece, and himself a one-time student of Aristotle, had crossed the Hellespont at the head of an army. By the time he died eleven years later, he had humbled the pride of the Persian monarchy and conquered an empire that stretched all the way to the Indus. The proud claims of Darius a century and a half earlier stood revealed as vain. The greatness of his dynasty's dominion was not, after all, eternal. Carved up in the wake of Alexander's death by predatory Macedonian generals, its provinces now funded the ambitions of men who cared nothing for Ahura Mazda. 'The strong do what they have the power to do, and the weak must suck it up.'[41] This grim parody of the law discerned by philosophers in the workings of the universe—formulated by an Athenian a century previously—was one which Demetrius too, in his heart of hearts, had little choice but to acknowledge. His regime was ultimately dependent, not on the approbation of his fellow citizens but on foreign spears. The true master of Athens was not Demetrius at all, but his sponsor, a Macedonian nobleman named Cassander who, in the wake of Alexander's death, had seized control of Macedon—and with it the rule of Greece. Philosophers too, no less than women or slaves, might be dependents. Any weakening of Cassander's position was liable to leave Demetrius as collateral damage.

And so it turned out. In the spring of 307, a large fleet appeared in the waters off Athens. A second Macedonian warlord was making a pitch for Greece. Demetrius, rather than stand and fight, promptly fled to Thebes. The Athenian people, in an ecstasy of delight, celebrated by felling his statues, melting them down, and converting them into chamberpots. Even so, they had hardly been liberated. One man named Demetrius had merely been exchanged for another. Unlike the Athenians' previous ruler, though, the second Demetrius was at least an authentic hero. Young, dashing and handsome, he had palpable shades of Alexander. Far too restless to linger in Athens, he had no sooner captured the city than he was off again, fighting a series of epic engagements and winning for himself a splendid honorific: 'the Besieger'. Time would see him outlive Cassander, murder his rival's son, and make himself king of Macedon. Returning to Athens in 295, the Besieger assembled the people in the theatre of Dionysus and then appeared to them on the stage, as though he were the hero of a drama—or a god. Five years later, when Demetrius made a further visit to the city, his claim to divinity could hardly have been rendered any more flamboyant. Stars embroidered on his cloak identified him with the sun. Dancers adorned with giant phalluses greeted him as though he were Dionysus. Choirs sang a hymn that proclaimed him a god and saviour. 'For the other gods are far distant, or have no ears, or do not exist, or ignore us—but you we can see before us. You are not made of stone or wood. No, you are real.'[42]

Disappointment followed soon after. An unseasonal frost blasted the Athenian harvest; an altar raised to Demetrius was overgrown by hemlock; the Besieger himself, having been chased off the Macedonian throne, died in 283 the prisoner of a rival warlord. Nevertheless, the yearning of the Greeks for what they termed a *parousia*, the physical presence of a deity, did not fade away. The gods who had manifested themselves on the battlefield at Troy had been absent too long for kings of the order of Demetrius not to impress many as enticing substitutes. The Athenians were far from alone in feeling their smallness before the immensity of the world revealed by Alexander's conquests. The descendants of his generals ruled from capitals so vast and multicultural that Athens, by comparison, could only seem diminished. The largest of them all, a city founded by Alexander on the coast of Egypt and named by him—with his customary modesty—Alexandria, was consciously promoted as the new heartbeat of Greek civilisation. When Demetrius of Phaleron, licking his wounds, looked around for alternative employment, it was to Alexandria that he duly headed. There, sponsored by a Macedonian general who had made himself pharaoh, he helped to establish what would endure for centuries as the greatest repository of learning in the world. For all the scope and scale of its research facilities, though, Alexandria was not solely a monument to the philosophy of Aristotle. Beyond its incomparable library, and the cloisters and gardens where scholars enjoyed a richly subsidised opportunity to catalogue the wisdom of the ages, the city served as a microcosm, not of the chilly perfection of the stars, but of the teeming diversity of the sublunar world. Planted where previously there had been nothing but sand and wheeling sea birds, Alexandria rested on shallow foundations. Its gods as well as its citizens were immigrants. Statues of Apollo and Athena stood in the streets alongside those of strange deities with the heads of crocodiles or rams. It did not take long, though, for new gods, distinctively Alexandrian, to emerge. One in particular, who combined the luxuriant facial hair of Zeus with echoes of Osiris, the Egyptian judge of the dead, had soon become the face of the megalopolis. Serapis—whose vast temple, the Serapeum, would come to rank as the greatest in Alexandria—provided its ruling dynasty with a patron that they avidly promoted as their own. Philosophers, alert to the source of their funding, proved happy to do their bit as well. When Demetrius of Phaleron, miraculously cured after going blind, wrote a hymn of thanks to Serapis, no mention was made of the motionless mover at the heart of the cosmos. Even a disciple of Aristotle might sometimes prefer a god with the personal touch.

Not only that, but he might doubt the very value of his role as a philosopher. 'It is not intelligence which guides the affairs of mortals, but Fortune.'[43] This claim, when made by Demetrius' teacher back in Athens, had generated much outrage among his peers; but Demetrius himself, over the course of his turbulent life, had been brought to acknowledge its force. Fortune—*Tyche*, as the Greeks knew her—had revealed herself the most terrible and powerful of deities. 'Her influence on our lives,' wrote Demetrius, 'is as beyond computation as the manifestations of her power are unpredictable.'[44] Small wonder, in an age that had seen great empires dismembered and kings rise from nothing to rank as gods, that she should have come to be worshipped as the truest mistress of things. Even as philosophers continued their search for the patterns that governed the cosmos, the dread of what might be wrought by Tyche could not help but shadow their efforts. The affairs of the world did not stand still. Demetrius, wondering at the downfall of Persian greatness, had foretold that the Macedonians would in their turn be brought low—and so it came to pass. A new people emerged to claim the rule of the world. In 167 BC, the king of Macedon—a descendant of Demetrius the Besieger, no less—was dragged in chains through the streets of a barbarous capital. Famous cities were put to the torch. Multitudes were sold on the auctioneer's block. The fate of the Trojans was visited on countless Greeks. Nevertheless, the gods who on the battlefield of Troy had given such free rein to their murderous whims appeared inadequate to explain the sheer jaw-dropping scale of change. 'For the affairs of Italy and Africa, interwoven with those of Asia and Greece, now tended towards a single end.'[45] Surely only a deity as great as Tyche could explain the rise to world empire of the Roman republic?

Yet even Tyche, perhaps, could be tamed. In 67 BC, the most celebrated Roman general of his day arrived on Rhodes. Pompey the Great was, as his soubriquet implied, a man whose conceit had never found it much of a challenge to keep pace with his own achievements. Accustomed since a young man to being idolised, he was always delighted to burnish his reputation with a well-devised publicity stunt. So it was, prior to embarking on a campaign to clear the Mediterranean of pirates, that he dropped in on the world's most famous philosopher. Posidonius, like his guest, had an international reputation. He was a noted athlete; he had dined with barbarian headhunters; he had calculated the size of the moon. Among the Roman elite, however, he was famed for one particular accomplishment: the equation of their city's conquests with the order of the cosmos. Five hundred years after Darius had promoted a very similar vision of empire, Posidonius was able to reassure his Roman patrons that their triumph was born of more than chance. Tyche, who had repeatedly granted victory to their legions, and rewarded them with slaves harvested from across the Mediterranean, and brought them riches beyond the avarice of kings, had not bestowed her blessings merely on a whim. Rather, she had done so because of what one of Posidonius' students, the great Roman orator Cicero, described as 'the highest reason, ingrafted in nature'.[46] Rome had become a superpower in obedience of 'natural law'.

This phrase had not originated with Posidonius. Like so many other eminent philosophers, he had been educated in Athens, and his thought bore the stamp of the school that he had attended there. Zeno, its founder, had himself arrived in Athens from Cyprus back in 312, when Demetrius of Phaleron was still in power. He and his followers had come to be known—from Zeno's habit of teaching students in a painted *stoa*, or colonnade—as 'Stoics'. Just as Aristotle had done, they wrestled with the tension between the perfection of a heavenly order governed by mathematical laws and a sublunar realm governed by chance. Their solution was as radical as it was neat: to deny that any such tension existed. Nature, the Stoics argued, was itself divine. Animating the entire universe, God was active reason: the *Logos*. 'He is mixed with matter, pervading all of it and so shaping it, structuring it, and making it into the world.'[47] To live in accordance with nature, therefore, was to live in accordance with God. Male or female, Greek or barbarian, free or slave, all were equally endowed with the ability to distinguish right from wrong. *Syneidesis*, the Stoics termed this spark of the divine within every mortal: 'conscience'. 'Alone of all creatures alive and treading the earth, it is we who bear a likeness to a god.'[48]

It was not merely in the conscience common to humanity, however, that natural law was manifest. If the entire fabric of the cosmos was divine, then it followed that everything was bound to be for the best. To those who lacked this understanding, it might indeed seem that Tyche was a motiveless thing of caprice; but to Stoics, who could recognise in the universe a living thing, in which the explanations for everything that ever happens are bound together like the mesh of an infinite net, cast out deep into the future, none of her works were motiveless. 'If there only existed a mortal with the capacity to discern the links that join causes together, nothing would ever deceive him. For the man who grasps the causes of future events necessarily grasps what lies in the future.'[49] So wrote Cicero—whose admiration for Posidonius was such that at one point he even vainly begged the philosopher to write a treatise on his feats as a statesman. The appeal of Stoic teaching to Roman statesmen was hardly difficult to fathom. Their conquests and their rule of the world; the wealth that they had won, and the teeming populations of slaves, uprooted and transported to Italy; the rank that was theirs, and the dignity, and the renown: all had been fated to happen.

It was unsurprising, perhaps, that Rome's leaders should have come to see their city's empire as an order destined as universal. Not for the first time, sway of a global scope served to foster a matching conceit. Pompey did not, however, cast himself as an agent of truth and light. The notion of the world as a battleground between good and evil was foreign to him. Iron courage, unbending discipline, mastery of body and soul: these were the qualities that had won the Roman people their rule of the world. The role of Greek philosophers was merely to gild this self-image. 'Always fight bravely, and be superior to others.'[50] Such was the admonition with which Posidonius sent Pompey on his way. The tag, though, was not his own. It came from the *Iliad*. As on the battlefield of Troy, so in the new world order forged by Rome—it was only by putting others in the shade that a man most fully became a man. Setting sail at the head of his war fleet, Pompey could reflect with satisfaction upon the perfect elision of his own ambitions and a beneficent providence. All was for the best. The whole world was there to be set in order. The future belonged to the strong.

2

JERUSALEM

63 BC: Jerusalem

A violent shuddering of masonry, the collapse of an entire tower, and a great rent was left in the line of fortifications. As the dust cleared, legionaries were already piling into the gap. Officers, eager to secure the glory of the feat for themselves, led their men over the mounds of rubble, scrambling up through the breach. Eagles—the battle-standards of the Roman army—bobbed over the fray. The defenders, whose obduracy and courage had been powerless in the final reckoning to stop the advance of Pompey's battering rams, knew themselves doomed. Many chose to torch their own homes, rather than leave them to be looted by their conquerors; others to hurl themselves from the battlements. Some twelve thousand in all, when the work of killing was finally done, lay littered as corpses across the city. 'Roman casualties, though, were very light.'[1] Pompey was an efficient general. Four years had passed since his meeting with Posidonius, and in that time he had swept the Mediterranean clear of pirates, humbled a succession of Near Eastern potentates, and brought their kingdoms directly under the sway of Rome. Now, after a three-month siege, he had added another victory to his stunning roster of battle-honours. Jerusalem was his.

The city, distant as it was from the sea and isolated from major trade routes, was in many ways a backwater. Judaea, the kingdom of which it was the capital, ranked as very much a second-rate power. To Pompey, a man who had swaggered his way around much of the Mediterranean, it could hardly help but seem a bit lacking in glamour. Nevertheless, Jerusalem was not entirely without interest. Its conqueror, who had a connoisseur's fascination with monumental architecture, and viewed the oddities of defeated peoples as so much grist to his own fame, took considerable delight in the exotic. The Jews, for all that they looked and dressed much like other people, were renowned for their peculiarities. They refused to eat pork. They circumcised their sons. They rested every seventh day, to mark what they termed the Sabbath. Most perversely of all, they refused to pay respects to any god save for the single one they acknowledged as their own. Even the dues of worship demanded by this jealous and exacting deity were liable to seem to Greeks or Romans bizarrely exclusive. In all the world, there stood only a single shrine regarded by the vast majority of his devotees as legitimate. The Jewish Temple, raised on a plateau of rock named Mount Moria on the eastern flank of Jerusalem, had for centuries dominated the skyline of the city. Naturally enough—now that the siege had been concluded— Pompey was keen to pay it a visit.

In truth, his attention had been fixed on the Temple complex ever since he first appeared with his legions before the walls that surrounded it. Long after the rest of Jerusalem had surrendered, defenders there had persisted in defying him; and now the great rock on which it stood was piled with bodies and sticky with blood. That Jews might be dogmatic in their eccentric beliefs was something of which Pompey was well aware; for the refusal of his opponents to fight on the Sabbath had greatly eased the task of his engineers in constructing their siege works. Now, though, the Temple was secured; and Pompey, as he approached its gateways, did so in a spirit of respect as well as of curiosity. That the Jews gave their god a barbarous name and ascribed perplexing commandments to him did not mean that he was any less worthy of reverence for that. To scholars learned in the study of the heavens, it appeared plain that 'the Jews worshipped the supreme god—who was to be identified with the king of all the gods'.[2] Jupiter, the Romans called him—just as the Greeks knew him as Zeus. This practice, of identifying the gods worshipped in one land with those honoured in another, was a venerable one. For a millennium and more, diplomats had depended upon it to render practicable the very concept of international law. How, after all, were two powers to agree to a treaty without invoking gods that both parties could acknowledge as valid witnesses to their covenant? Different rites might be practised in different cities; but Pompey, like other conquerors before him, never doubted that more united the various peoples of the world in their worship of the gods than divided them. Why, then, should he not inspect the Temple?

'It was as a victor that he claimed the right to enter it.'[3] That the Jews, jealous of the sanctity of their shrine, banned outsiders was hardly a consideration fit to perturb the conqueror of Jerusalem. His men, in capturing the Temple, had already stormed its outer court-yard. The priests, surprised as they were pouring libations and burning incense, had not so much as paused in their rites. Throughout the entire siege, twice a day, once in the morning and once at twilight, trumpets had sounded: the signal for the burning of a lamb on a great square altar. Now, though, piled up in the outer court-yard, priests lay slaughtered; and it was their blood, borne on the water that gushed from the base of the altar, that was being sluiced away. Pompey could not help but admire their fortitude in the face of death; but nothing about their ministrations would have struck him as particularly deserving notice. Sacrifices were practised across the Mediterranean, after all. The mystery for which the Temple was notorious awaited Pompey deep within the complex: a chamber treasured by the Jews as the single holiest place in the world. With such reverence did they regard this room that no one was permitted to enter it except for their high priest—and even then only once a year. To Greek scholars, the question of what might be found within this 'Holy of Holies' was a tantalising one. Posidonius, never knowingly without a theory, claimed that it contained a golden ass's head. Others believed that it held 'the stone image of a man with a long beard sitting on a donkey'.[4] Others yet reported that it served as the prison of a Greek captive, who, after a year of being fattened up, would then, amidst awful solemnity, be sacrificed and devoured. Pompey, pausing before the curtain that screened the room from a treasure-filled antechamber, could have no certain idea what lay beyond.

In the event, he found only emptiness. There was no statue in the chamber, no image of any kind, and certainly no fattened prisoner— just a bare block of stone. Yet Pompey, although bemused, left not unimpressed by what he had seen. He refrained from stripping the Temple of its treasures. He ordered its custodians to scrub the complex clean of the marks of battle and permitted them to perform the daily sacrifices. He appointed a new high priest. Then, freighted with prisoners, he departed Jerusalem, bound for a hero's welcome back in Rome. Pompey could reflect with double satisfaction on his achievements in Judaea. The Jews had been roundly defeated, the boundaries of their kingdom redrawn in accord with Roman interests, and a substantial tribute imposed. Simultaneously, due respect had been paid to their god. Pompey could bask in the assurance that he had fulfilled his duty, not just to Rome, but to the cosmos. Taking ship for home, he stopped off in Rhodes, where for a second time he called on Posidonius, presenting to the philosopher a living reassurance that the forging of a universal dominion, one that reflected the timeless order of the heavens, was proceeding apace. Posidonius, refusing to let an attack of arthritis deny him the chance to grandstand, signified approval of his visitor by delivering an oration from his sickbed. His theme, explored amid numerous flamboyant groans: 'only what is honourable is good'.[5]

Meanwhile, back in Jerusalem, the perspective on Pompey's conquests was—unsurprisingly—rather different. When Jews sought to make sense of their city's fall, they did not look to philosophy. Instead, in pain and bewilderment, they turned to their god.

When the sinner became proud he struck down the fortified walls
with a battering ram,
and You did not restrain him.
Foreign nations went up to Your altar,
in pride they trampled it with their sandals...⁶

This howl of anguish, addressed to the god who had permitted his
house to be stormed and his innermost sanctuary intruded upon,
was not one that Pompey could ever realistically have hoped to calm.
The respect that he believed himself to have shown the Jewish deity
cut little ice with most Jews. The very idea of equating the Temple
with the shrines of foreign gods was unspeakably offensive to them.
Perhaps, had the man installed by Pompey as high priest met with his
patron as an equal, he might have sought to explain why. That there
was only the one God; and that the Temple stood as a replica of the
universe that he alone had brought into being. In the robes worn by
the high priest were to be seen mirrors held up to the cosmos; in the
rituals he performed an echo of the divine labour of creation at the
beginning of time; on the golden plate he wore on his forehead an
awesome inscription, that of the name of God himself, which sacred
custom ordained should only ever be uttered by the high priest—and
even then only once a year, when he went into the Holy of Holies. To
desecrate the Temple was to desecrate the universe itself. The Jews,
no less than Posidonius, recognised in the expansion of Roman
power an event that reverberated to the heavens.

'To the victor is granted the right to lay down laws.'⁷ Such was
the maxim that Pompey, as he deposed kings and redrew boundaries, took for granted. The Jews, though, in defiance of earthly
power, claimed a status for themselves that no empire, not even one
as mighty as Rome, could ever hope to emulate. Once, many generations back, when Troy was yet to be founded and Babylon was still
young, a man named Abram had lived in Mesopotamia. There, it
was taught by Jewish scholars, he had come by a profound insight:

that idols were mere painted stone or wood, and that there existed, unique, intangible and omnipotent, just the single deity. Rather than stay in a city polluted by idolatry, Abram had chosen instead to leave his home, travelling with his wife and household to the land that would one day be called Judaea, but was then known as Canaan. All was part of the divine plan. God, appearing to Abram, had told him that, despite the great age of his childless wife, she would bear him a son, and that his descendants would one day inherit Canaan: a 'Promised Land'. As token of this, Abram was given a new name, 'Abraham'; and it was commanded by God that he and his male heirs, all of them, down countless generations, be circumcised. Abraham, obedient to every divine instruction, did as he was told; and when, sure enough, he was rewarded with a child, and God told him to take this child, Isaac, to a high place, and there to sacrifice the boy, 'your son, your only son, whom you love',[8] he showed himself willing to do it. Yet at the very last moment, even as Abraham was reaching for the cleaver, an angel spoke from the heavens, telling him to hold his hand; and Abraham, looking to where a ram had been caught in the thickets, had taken the animal and slain it on the altar. And God, because Abraham had been willing to offer in sacrifice the most precious thing that he had, confirmed the promise that his offspring would be as numerous as the stars in the sky. 'And through your offspring all nations on earth will be blessed, because you have obeyed me.'[9]

Where had this fateful episode taken place? Many generations later, when Abraham's descendants had come to settle the Promised Land and to name it Israel, an angel had materialised for a second time over the site where Isaac had almost perished—and this site, so it was recorded by Jewish scholars, had been none other than Mount Moria. Past and future, earth and heaven, mortal endeavour and divine presence: all had stood revealed as conjoined. Jerusalem itself, at the time of the angel's appearance, had only recently come under Israelite control. The man who had captured the city, a one-time shepherd boy and harpist by the name of David, from a small town called Bethlehem, had risen to become king over the whole of Israel; and now, at the very moment when he had established it as his capital, an angel had been sent to its heights, there to 'show him the spot where the Temple was to be built'.[10] David himself had been forbidden by God from embarking on the project; but under his son Solomon—a king of such wealth and wisdom that his name would ever after serve the Jews as a byword for splendour—Mount Moria had become 'the mountain of the house of the LORD'.[11] It was Solomon, after the completion of the Temple, who had placed in the Holy of Holies the greatest treasure that the Israelites possessed: a gilded chest, or ark, made to precise specifications laid down by God himself, and in which his presence was manifest on earth. This, then, was the glory of Israel: that its Temple was truly the house of the Lord God.

But such a glory was not merely given; it had to be earned. The charge laid upon his people by God, to worship him as was his due, came hedged about with warnings. 'See, I am setting before you today a blessing and a curse—the blessing if you obey the commands of the LORD your God that I am giving you today; the curse, if you disobey the commands of the LORD your God.'[12] Over the centuries that followed Solomon's building of the Temple, the people had repeatedly strayed—and sure enough, after four hundred years of disobedience, they had reaped a bitter harvest. First, the Assyrians conquered the north of the Promised Land: ten of the twelve tribes who traced their lineage back to Israel had been taken into captivity, and vanished into the maw of Mesopotamia. Not even the fall of Assyria to Babylon in 612 BC had seen them return. Then, in 587 BC, it had been the turn of Judah, the kingdom that took its name from the fourth son of Israel, and of its capital, Jerusalem. The King of Babylon had taken the city by storm. 'And he burnt the house of the LORD and the house of the king and all the houses of Jerusalem, and every great house he burnt in fire.'[13] Nothing of the Temple built by Solomon, not its fittings of cypress wood, nor its gilded gates, nor its bronze pillars ornamented with pomegranates, had been spared.

Only ruins and weeds remained. And when in her turn Babylon had fallen, and the Persians had wrested from her the mantle of empire, and Cyrus had given permission for the Temple to be rebuilt, the complex that arose on Mount Moria was merely a shadow of what had stood before. 'Who of you is left who saw this house in its former glory? How does it look to you now? Does it not seem to you like nothing?'[14] Starkest of all the reminders of vanished glories was the Holy of Holies. The Ark, upon which the glory of God Himself, in a cloud of impenetrable darkness, had been accustomed to descend, was gone. No one could say for certain what its fate had been. Only the block of stone seen by Pompey when he stepped into the chamber, bare and unadorned, served to mark the spot where it had once stood.

And now foreign invaders had desecrated Mount Moria again. Even as the high priest and his acolytes sought to cleanse it of the traces of the Roman siege, and to restore to the Temple its accustomed rites, so were there Jews who scorned their efforts. Why, after all, would God have permitted an alien conqueror to trespass within the Holy of Holies unless it were to express his anger with its guardians? To critics of the Temple priests, the explanation for the catastrophe appeared manifest: 'it was because the sons of Jerusalem had defiled the Lord's sanctuary, they profaned the offerings to God with lawlessness'.[15] Just as centuries previously, amid the calamities of the Assyrian and Babylonian conquests, men known as *nevi'im*, or 'prophets', had appeared, to urge their countrymen to reform their ways or else risk obliteration, so now, in the wake of Pompey's conquests, were there Jews who in a similar manner despaired of the Temple establishment. 'Because you have plundered many nations, the peoples who are left will plunder you.'[16] Moralists convinced of God's anger did not hesitate to apply this warning, delivered many centuries earlier, to the priests in Jerusalem. That Pompey had spared the treasures of the Temple did not mean that the troops of some future Roman warlord might not seize them. 'Their horses are swifter than leopards, fiercer than wolves at dusk. Their cavalry gallops headlong, their horsemen come from afar. They fly like a vulture swooping to devour.'[17] Only if the priests repented of their greed, and of their avarice for gold harvested from across the world, would they be spared. Otherwise, the judgement of God would be swift and certain: 'their riches and loot will be given into the hands of the army of the Romans'.[18]

Most Jews, it was true, did not despair of the Temple and its guardians. The very scale of the wealth banked on Mount Moria served as the witness of that. As critics of its priests pointed out, the offerings made to the Temple derived not just from Judaea, but from across the civilised world. Many more Jews lived beyond the limits of the Promised Land than within them. For the vast majority of these, the Temple remained what it had ever been: the central institution of Jewish life. Yet it was not the only one. Had it been, then it would have been hard for Jews settled beyond the Promised Land to remain as Jews for long. Distance from the Temple, from its rituals, and sacrifices, and prayers, would gradually have seen their sense of Jewish identity blur and fade. But as it was, they did not need to travel to Jerusalem on one of the three pilgrim festivals held every year to feel themselves in the presence of God. Rather, they had only to go to one of the numerous houses of prayer and instruction that were to be found wherever Jews were congregated: a 'house of assembly', or 'synagogue'. Here, boys would be taught to read, and adults schooled throughout their lives in the interpretation of some very specific texts. These, lovingly transcribed onto parchment scrolls, were kept, when they were not being studied, in a box that deliberately echoed the long-vanished Ark: an awesome marker of their holiness. Other peoples too could claim possession of texts from gods—but none were so charged with a sense of holiness, none so attentively heeded, none so central to the self-understanding of an entire people as the collection of writings cherished by Jews as their holiest scripture.

Torah, they called it: 'teachings'. Five scrolls portrayed the original working of God's purposes: from the creation of the world to the arrival on Canaan's borders, after many hardships and wanderings, of Abraham's descendants, ready at last to claim their inheritance. The story did not end there, though. There were many other writings held sacred by the Jews. There were histories and chronicles, detailing everything from the conquest of Canaan to the destruction and rebuilding of the Temple. There were records of prophecy, in which men who had felt the word of God like a burning fire within their bones gave it utterance. There were collections of proverbs, tales of inspirational men and women, and an anthology of poems named psalms. All these various writings, by many different hands over the course of many years, served to provide Jews beyond the Promised Land with a much-craved reassurance: that living in foreign cities did not make them any the less Jewish. Nor, three centuries on from Alexander's conquest of the world, did the fact that the vast majority of them spoke not the language of their ancestors but Greek. A bare seventy years after Alexander's death there had begun to emerge in Alexandria large numbers of Jews who struggled to understand the Hebrew in which most of their scriptures had been written. The commission to translate them, so the story went, had come from none other than Demetrius of Phalerum. Keen to add to the stock of the city's great library, he had sent to Jerusalem for seventy-two scholars. Arriving in Alexandria, these had set diligently to work translating the holiest text of all, the five scrolls, or *pentateuch*, as they were called in Greek.* Other texts had soon followed. Demetrius, so it was improbably claimed, had defined them as 'philosophical, flawless—and divine'.[19] Not merely books, they were hailed by Greek-speaking Jews as *ta biblia ta hagia*—'the holy books'.†

---

* It is possible that the categorisation of the various Jewish holy books—what Jews today call the Tanakh and Christians the Old Testament—derived originally from the way that they were catalogued in the Library of Alexandria.

† At this stage, the Jewish collection of sacred writings was yet to correspond fully to what Jews today would recognise as the Tanakh. The phrase *ta biblia ta hagia* first appears in 1 Maccabees 12.9.

Here was the manifestation of a subtle yet momentous irony. A body of writings originally collated and adapted by scholars who took for granted the centrality of Jerusalem to the worship of their god was slipping its editors' purposes: the *biblia* came to possess, for the Jews of Alexandria, a sanctity that rivalled that of the Temple itself. Wherever there existed a scribe to scratch their verses onto parchment, or a student to commit them to memory, or a teacher to explicate their mysteries, their sanctity was affirmed. Their eternal and indestructible nature as well. Such a monument, after all, was not easily stormed. It was not constructed out of wood and stone, to be levelled by a conquering army. Wherever Jews might choose to live, there the body of their scriptures would be present as well. Those in Alexandria or Rome, far distant from the Temple though they were, knew that they possessed in their holy books—and the Torah especially—a surer path to the divine than any idol could provide. 'What other nation is so great as to have their gods near them the way the LORD our God is near us whenever we pray to Him?'[20]

The Romans might have the rule of the world; the Greeks might have their philosophy; the Persians might claim to have fathomed the dimensions of truth and order; but all were deluded. Darkness covered the earth, and thick darkness was over the nations. Only once the Lord God of Israel had risen upon them, and his glory appeared over them, would they come into the light, and kings to the brightness of dawn.

For there was no other god but him.

Like Humans You Shall Die

Half a millennium and more before Pompey's capture of Jerusalem, when the Babylonians stormed the original Temple and burnt it to the ground, they transported the elite of the conquered kingdom to Babylon. There, in a city vast beyond their wildest imaginings, the exiles found themselves amid temples so steepling that they seemed to brush the sky. The greatest of them all, the Esagila, was hailed by the Babylonians as the oldest building in the world, and the very axis of the cosmos. No earthly hand had raised it. Instead, it was the gods who had erected its stupefying bulk, to serve as the palace of Marduk, the king of the heavens. Within it stood sculptures fashioned by Marduk himself, and a mighty bow: 'marks never to be forgotten'[21] of a victory won by the god at the beginning of time. Then it was, so the Babylonians claimed, that Marduk had fought with a dragon of terrifying size, a monster of the heaving ocean, and split her in two with his arrows, and fashioned the heavens and the earth from the twin halves of her corpse. Next, rather than condemn the gods to perpetual toil, Marduk had commissioned a further act of creation. 'I will make man,' he had declared, 'who shall inhabit the earth, that the service of the gods may be established, and their shrines built.'[22] Humanity, moulded out of dust and blood, had been bred to labour.

It would have been easy for the exiles from Jerusalem, numbed by defeat and a sense of their own puniness before the immensity of Babylon, to have accepted this bleak understanding of man's purpose. But they did not. Rather than fall to the worship of Marduk, they clung instead to the conviction that it was their own god who had brought humanity into being. Man and woman, in the various stories told by the exiles, had been endowed with a uniquely privileged status. They alone had been shaped in God's image; they alone had been granted mastery over every living creature; they alone, after six days of divine labour, which had seen heaven itself, and earth, and everything within them brought into being, had been fashioned as the summit of creation. Humans shared in the dignity of the one God, who had not, like Marduk, fought with a monster of the seas before embarking on His labour of creation, but had crafted the entire cosmos unaided and alone. To priests transported from the ruins of Jerusalem, the story provided a desperately needed reassurance: that the object of their worship still reigned supreme. Generation after generation, versions of it were retold. Written down, spliced together, fashioned into a single, definitive account, the story came to serve as the opening of the Torah itself. Long after the greatness of Marduk had been humbled into the dust, and the Esagila become the haunt of jackals, the book known to its Greek translators as Genesis continued to be copied, studied and revered. 'And God saw all that he had done, and it was very good.'[23]

Yet this assertion—for Jews struggling to make sense of the ruin that had periodically overwhelmed them, and of the humiliations visited on them by a succession of conquerors—raised a problem. Why, if the world created by God was good, did he permit such things to happen? Jewish scholars, by the time that Pompey came to storm the Temple, had arrived at a sombre explanation. The entire history of humanity was one of disobedience to God. Making man and woman, he had given them a garden named Eden to tend, filled with every kind of exotic plant; and all its fruit was theirs to eat, save only that of a single tree, 'the tree of the knowledge of good and evil'.[24] But the first woman, Eve, had been tempted by the serpent to taste the fruit of the tree; and the first man, Adam, had taken it from her and tasted it as well. God, to punish them, had expelled the couple from Eden, and cursed them, decreeing that from that time on women were to suffer the agonies of childbirth, and men to labour for their food, and die. A grim sentence—and yet not, perhaps, the full limit of humanity's fall. Banished from Eden, Eve had borne Adam children; and Cain, their eldest, had slain Abel, their second-born. From that moment on, it was as though the taint of violence were endemic to mankind. Blood had never ceased to splash the earth. Jewish scholars, tracking the wearying incidence of crimes down the generations, could not help but wonder from what—or who—such a capacity for evil derived. A century before Pompey's capture of Jerusalem, a Jewish sage named Jesus Ben Sirah had arrived at the logical, the baneful, conclusion. 'From a woman sin had its beginning, and because of her we all die.'[25]

For Jews, this inclination to disobedience, this natural proclivity for offending against God, represented a particular challenge. After all, it was they alone, of the many peoples of the world, who had been graced with his especial favour. They had not, as others had done, forgotten the Creator of the universe. The same God who had walked with Adam and Eve in Eden had appeared to their ancestors, and given them Canaan to be their own, and wrought a multitude of miracles on their behalf. All this was known to every Jew. Recorded in the scrolls that constituted the very essence of Jewish identity, it could be read in any synagogue. Yet these scriptures were a chronicle of mutiny as well as of submission; of whoring after idols as well as of faithfulness to God. The narratives of the conquest of Canaan portrayed a land filled with altars that demanded to be smashed, and sanctuaries that required to be despoiled—but which, even as they were destroyed, exerted an awful fascination. Not even the gift of the Promised Land had been able to keep Israel from idolatry. 'They chose new gods.'[26] In book after book the same cycle was repeated: apostasy, punishment, repentance. Jews, reading of how their forebears had been seduced by the gods of neighbouring peoples—the Canaanites, the Syrians, the Phoenicians—knew as well what the ultimate, the crowning, chastisements had been: Israel enslaved; Jerusalem sacked; the Temple destroyed. These were the traumas that haunted every Jew. Why had God permitted them to happen? Such was the question, in the wake of the Babylonian exile, that had done more than anything to inspire the compilation of the Jewish scriptures. Jews who read the scrolls that told of their people's history could be in no doubt as to the retribution that might again be visited on them were they ever to abandon the worship of God; but there was hope in their scriptures as well as warning. Even if ruin were to be visited on Jerusalem again, and the Jews dispersed to the ends of the earth, and salt and brimstone rained down upon their fields, God's love would endure. Repentance, as it ever did, would see them forgiven. 'And the LORD your God will restore your fortunes and have compassion on you and gather you again from all the nations where he scattered you.'[27]

Here, in this demanding, emotional and volatile deity, was a divine patron like no other. Apollo might have favoured the Trojans, and Hera the Greeks, but no god had ever cared for a people with the jealous obsessiveness of the God of Israel. Wise, he was also wilful; all-powerful, he was also readily hurt; consistent, he was also alarmingly unpredictable. Jews who pondered the evidence of their scriptures never doubted that he was a deity with whom it was possible to have a profoundly personal relationship; but the key to his identity, vivid though it was, lay in its manifold contradictions. A warrior, who in his wrath might panic armies, annihilate cities and command the slaughter of entire peoples, he also raised the poor from the dust and the needy from dungheaps. Lord of the heavens and the earth, 'the Rider of Clouds',[28] he served too as a comfort to those who called upon him amid dark nights of misery and dread. A creator and a destroyer; a husband and a wife; a king, a shepherd, a gardener, a potter, a judge: the God of Israel was hailed in the Jewish holy books as all these things, and more. 'I am the first and I am the last; apart from me there is no God.'[29] A historic vaunt. Recorded in the wake of Babylon's fall to Cyrus in 539 BC, it asserted a proposition that had never before in history been made quite so baldly. Just as Marduk had claimed the credit for the Persian victory, so too—in almost identical terms—had the God of Israel; but Marduk, despite the insistence of his priests that it was he who had chosen Cyrus to rule the world, had ranked as only one of an immense multitude of gods. Male gods and female gods; warrior gods and craftsmen gods; storm gods and fertility gods: 'you are less than nothing.'[30] Long after the death of Cyrus, with the temples of Babylon in ruins, and their idols lost to mud, Jews could read in their synagogues assurances given centuries previously to the Persian king—and know them to be true. 'I will strengthen you,' the One God of Israel had announced to Cyrus, 'though you have not acknowledged me, so that from the rising of the sun to the place of its setting men may know there is none besides me. I am the LORD, and there is no other.'[31]

Yet if their scriptures, in the age of the spread of Roman power, were understood by Jews to demonstrate the truth of this vaunting statement, so also, scattered throughout them, were vestiges of assumptions older by far. The immense tapestry woven by priests and scribes in the wake of the Babylonian destruction of the Temple had been fashioned from numerous ancient threads. Nothing better illustrated the variety of sources from which these had been spun than the sheer range of names given throughout the Jewish *biblia* to God: Yahweh, Shaddai, El. That these had always referred to the same deity was, naturally enough, the guiding assumption of every Jewish scholar; and yet there lingered hints enough to suggest a rather different possibility. 'Who among the gods is like you, O LORD?'[32] Such a question was an echo from a distant, barely imaginable world—one in which Yahweh, the deity to whom it was put, had ranked as only one among various gods of Israel. How, then, had he evolved to become the universal Lord of the heavens and earth, without peer or rival? The priests and scribes who compiled the writings that told their story would have been appalled even to contemplate such a question. Nevertheless, despite all the care and attentiveness of their editing, not every trace of the deity that Yahweh had originally been was erased from Jewish scripture. It was still possible to detect, preserved like insects in amber, hints of a cult very different from that practised in the Temple: that of a storm god worshipped in the form of a bull, sprung 'from the land of Edom'[33] in the land to the south of Canaan, and who had come to rule as supreme in the council of the gods.* 'For who in the skies above can compare with the LORD? Who is like the LORD among the sons of the gods?'[34]

That there existed a strict hierarchy in the heavens was taken for granted by peoples everywhere. How otherwise would Marduk have been able to press his fellow gods to labour for him? Zeus too, enthroned on the summit of Olympus, presided over a court. Nevertheless, the radiance of his glory had its limits. The other gods

---

* The worship of Yahweh in the form of a bull is attested by 1 Kings 12.28 and Hosea 8.6. The description of Yahweh coming from Edom appears in the Song of Deborah—a hymn that most scholars identify as one of the oldest passages in the Bible.

on Olympus were not consumed by it. Zeus did not absorb various of their attributes into his own being, and then dismiss their phantasms as demons. How different was the God of Israel! From what did all the manifold complexities and contradictions of his character ultimately derive? Perhaps from a process that had been the precise opposite of that celebrated by the Jewish holy books: a process by which Yahweh, to a degree unparalleled by any other deity, had come to contain multitudes within himself. When, in the very first sentence of Genesis, he was described as creating the heavens and the earth, the Hebrew word for God—*Elohim*—was tellingly ambiguous. Used throughout Jewish scripture as a singular, the noun's ending was plural. 'God' had once been 'gods'.

That the Israelites, far from announcing their arrival in Canaan by toppling idols and smashing temples, might originally have shared in the customs of their neighbours, and indeed been virtually indistinguishable from them, was a possibility that Jewish scripture emphatically, and even violently, rejected.* But did it, perhaps, protest too much? Indeed, had there even been a conquest of Canaan at all? The account preserved by the Jews, which told of a succession of spectacular victories by the general Joshua, narrated the downfall of cities that had either been long abandoned by the time the Israelite invasion was supposed to have occurred, or else were yet to be founded.† The conviction of those who composed the Book of Joshua, that God had bestowed lands upon his Chosen People in return for their obedience, reflected the perils of their own age: for it was most likely written in the spreading shadow of Assyrian

---

* It is telling, perhaps, that the author of Chronicles, a history of Israel written in the fourth century BC, does not describe an Israelite conquest of Canaan. 'Israel's presence in and right to the land is presented as an unproblematic and established fact.' (Satlow, p. 93).

† Jericho, the walls of which supposedly came tumbling down before the trumpets of Joshua's army, had in reality been lying abandoned for centuries before the supposed date of the Israelite army. Gibeon, which in the Book of Joshua supplies the Israelites with 'hewers of wood and drawers of water' (9.21), was founded well after the Bronze Age.

greatness. Nevertheless, it also reflected something more. The insistence in the Book of Joshua that the Israelites had come as conquerors to Canaan hinted at a nagging and persistent anxiety: that the worship of their god might originally have owed more to Canaanite practice than Jewish scholars cared to acknowledge. Customs they condemned as monstrous innovations—the worship of other gods, the feeding of the dead, the sacrifice of children—were perhaps the very opposite: venerable traditions, compared to which their own evolving cult constituted the novelty.

The revolutionary quality of this—the way in which, from the cocoon of Canaanite, and Syrian, and Edomite beliefs, a new and portentous conception of the divine had come to unfold its wings—was veiled by Jewish scripture. Not entirely, though. In the Book of Psalms, one poem in particular served to dramatise the confused and lengthy process by which *elohim*—'the gods'—had become the one supreme Lord: *Elohim*.

God presides in the great assembly;
he gives judgement among the gods.[35]

Injustice; favouring the wicked; scorning the poor, the lowly and the wretched: such were the crimes of which the assembled gods stood guilty. Their offences had cast the world into darkness and made it totter. Their punishment: to be dethroned from the heavens for evermore. Elohim himself pronounced their sentence.

I said, 'You are gods;
you are all sons of the Most High.
But you will die like mere men;
you will fall like every other ruler.[36]

In the council of the heavens, there would henceforward rule only the single God.

The Jews may have been an insignificant people, peripheral to the concerns of great powers; and yet the deity of their scriptures, who had toppled gods much as conquerors like Alexander or Pompey toppled kings, was one whose dominion spanned the whole of creation, and brooked no rival. 'My name will be great among the nations, from the rising to the setting of the sun.'[37] This, very consciously, was to echo the Persian king. The magnanimity shown by Cyrus towards the exiles from Jerusalem had not been forgotten. Unlike the rulers of Egypt, or Assyria, or Babylon, he had shown respect for the God of Israel. More than any other foreign monarch in the annals of the exiles' history, Cyrus had provided them with a model of kingship. The heavens, in the wake of their return from Babylon, had taken on something of the appearance of the Persian court. 'From where do you come?' So asked God, in the Book of Job, of an official in his retinue titled the Adversary—the *Satan*. Back came the reply: 'From roaming through the earth and going to and fro in it.'[38] In Athens, dread of the Great King's secret agents had inspired Aristophanes to portray one of them as a giant eye; but in Jewish scripture there was no laughing at the royal spies. They were far too potent, far too menacing, for that. When God points to Job as 'blameless and upright, a man who fears God and shuns evil',[39] the Satan responds mockingly that it is easy for the prosperous to be good. 'But stretch out your hand and strike everything he has, and he will surely curse you to your face.'[40] So God, accepting the wager, delivers Job into the Satan's hands. Innocent of fault though he is, all his worldly goods are destroyed; his children slain; his skin covered with boils. 'Then Job took a piece of broken pottery and scraped himself with it as he sat among the ashes.'[41]

A criminal sentenced to the *scaphe* had no free hands with which to scrape himself, of course; and yet the power to make flesh rot on the bones was, in the age of Persian greatness, a peculiarly terrifying marker of royal power. What, though, of the claim made by Darius and his heirs, that when they put their victims to torture they did so in the cause of truth, and justice, and light? Job, as he lay hunched among the ashes, was approached by three companions, and after sitting with him in silence for seven days and seven nights, they sought to make sense of the torments inflicted on him.

'Would God pervert justice,
would Shaddai pervert what is right?
   If your children offended Him,
      He dispatched them because of their crime.[42]

Such was the assurance offered elsewhere in Jewish scripture: that God only ever punished wrongdoers, just as he only ever favoured the righteous. Job, however, dismisses this comforting notion. 'Why do the wicked live, grow rich and gather wealth?' Most startlingly of all, the story ends with God himself speaking to Job from a whirlwind and flatly rejecting the proposition put forward by his companions. 'You have not spoken rightly of Me,' he informs them, 'as did My servant Job.'[43] Yet to the question of why—despite his innocence—Job had been punished so cruelly, no answer is given. God restores to him everything that he had lost, and doubles it, and blesses Job with new sons and daughters. But those children he had lost are not redeemed from the dust to which they had been returned. The bereaved father does not get them back.

When Apollo slew the children of Niobe, no one thought to complain that his vengeance had been excessive. Lord of the silver bow, he dealt with those who offended him as he pleased. It was not by answering the complaints of mortals that Apollo made manifest his divinity, but by performing deeds infinitely beyond their scope. Like Marduk, he had even felled a dragon. In Canaan, too, stories were told of how gods had fought with dragons and sea serpents—and thereby demonstrated their worthiness to rule the heavens. Such a conceit was, to the writers of Genesis, a nonsense and a blasphemy; and so it was, in their account of the Creation, that they made sure to specify that Elohim had fashioned, not fought with, the creatures of the deep. 'And God created the sea monsters.'[44] Yet the surface calm of the Jewish holy books was deceptive. Every so often, stirring from the depths of memories and traditions that not even the most careful editing could entirely erase, the sinuous bulk of a monster that had indeed fought with God would hove into view. Named variously Rahab, Tanin and Leviathan, it was the same seven-headed serpent that had twisted and coiled in poetry composed almost a millennium before the Book of Job. 'Could you draw Leviathan with a hook, and with a cord press down his tongue?'[45] The question, demanded of Job from the whirlwind, was, of course, rhetorical. Only God could tame Leviathan. If he was portrayed in the Book of Job as ruling in the manner of a Persian king, the Lord of agents who post over land and ocean, then so also, when he spoke to a man who had arraigned him of injustice, did he draw on vastly more ancient wellsprings to articulate his power. No wonder that Job ended up brow-beaten. 'I know You can do anything.'[46]

Yet Job had never doubted God's power—only his justice. On that score, God had nothing to say. The Book of Job—written when, for the first time, the existence of a deity both omnipotent and all-just was coming to be contemplated—dared to explore the implications with an unflinching profundity. That Jewish scholars should have included it in their great compilation of scripture spoke loudly of their struggle to confront a novel and pressing problem: the origin of evil. For other peoples, with their multitudes of deities, the issue had barely raised its head. After all, the more gods there were in the cosmos, the more explanations there were for human suffering. How, though, to explain it in a cosmos with just a single god? Only the devotees of Ahura Mazda—who, like the Jews, believed in a universe created by an all-wise, all-good deity—had ever had to wrestle with a question of this order. Perhaps, then, in the presence before God's throne of the Satan, who inflicts such sufferings on Job and then vanishes mysteriously from the story, there was a hint of the solution proposed by the Persians to explain the potency of evil: that it existed as a rival and equal principle to good. Yet if so, it was not one that Jewish scholars were willing to countenance. Deeply though they might revere the memory of Cyrus, they had no place in their scriptures for anything resembling the cosmic battle between *Arta* and *Drauga*. There could be only the one God. Less blasphemous to attribute to him the creation of evil than to imply that it might ever be a threat to his power. Yahweh, speaking to Cyrus, was portrayed as scorning the notion of a universe contested by the Truth and the Lie. 'I form the light and create darkness, I bring prosperity and create disaster. I, the LORD, do all these things.'[47]

Nowhere else in Jewish scripture was there anything resembling this bald assertion. If God was omnipotent, then so too was he all-just. These were twin convictions that the Jews, no matter the patent tension between them, had come to enshrine as the very essence of their understanding of the divine. That God might have sponsored the Roman storming of the Temple, not as a punishment for the faults of his chosen people but because he was as much the author of chaos as of order, was a possibility so grotesque as to be inconceivable. All his works served the cause of order. That his purposes might sometimes be veiled in mystery did not prevent him from fathoming human despair, from caring for the wretched, and from providing comfort where there was grief.

> 'The poor and needy search for water,
> but there is none;
> their tongues are parched with thirst,
> But I the LORD will answer them,
> I, the God of Israel, will not forsake them.'[48]

Never before had such incongruities been so momentously combined within a single deity: power and intimacy, menace and compassion, omniscience and solicitude.

And this god—all-powerful, all-good, who ruled the entire world, and upheld the harmony of the cosmos—was the god who had chosen for his especial favour the Jews. Helpless before the might of Rome's legions though they might be, unable to prevent a conqueror from intruding upon even their holiest shrine, a people with no prospect of ever winning global rule, they had this consolation: the certitude that their God was indeed the one, the only Lord.

Covenant

Hard proof was not long in coming. Divine punishment caught up with Pompey. In 49 BC, the Roman world collapsed into civil war, and the following year, in Greece, the man who had dominated Rome for two decades was routed in battle by a rival warlord: Julius Caesar. Barely seven weeks later, Pompey the Great was dead. The speed and scale of his downfall stunned the world—and was greeted in Judaea with exultant delight. Just as God had triumphed over Leviathan, so now had he crushed 'the pride of the Dragon'.[49] A poet, writing in emulation of the Psalms, chronicled the details: how Pompey had sought refuge in Egypt; how he had been run through with a spear; how his corpse, bobbing on the waves, had been left without a grave. 'He had failed to recognise that God alone is great.'[50]

The scene of Pompey's death was a particularly potent one in Jewish imaginings. Nowhere had more spectacularly, or more momentously, borne witness to the power of their God than Egypt. Once, before they came into their inheritance and took possession of Canaan, the Children of Israel had been slaves there. Pharaoh, fearful of their growing numbers, had 'worked them ruthlessly.[51] He and all his gods, though, had been humbled into the dust. Ten plagues had devastated his kingdom. The Nile had turned to blood; vermin had variously slithered or swarmed across every corner of the land; the entire country had been cast into darkness. For a long while, though, Pharaoh had remained obdurate. Only after a climactic horror, when the firstborn of every Egyptian was struck down in a single night, 'and the firstborn of all the livestock as well',[52] had he finally let the Israelites go. Even then, he had soon recanted. Pursuing the fugitive slaves, he and his squadron of chariots had cornered them on the shores of the Red Sea. Still the miracles had not ceased.

A mighty east wind had blown up, and the waters split apart; and the children of Israel, crossing the seabed, made it to the far shore. Onwards in pursuit of them Pharaoh and his warriors had sped. 'The water flowed back and covered the chariots and horsemen— the entire army of Pharaoh that had followed the Israelites into the sea. Not one of them survived.'[53]

Here, then, in a world where the gods tended to bestow their favours upon kings and conquerors, was yet another mark of the distinctive character of the God of Israel: that he had chosen as his favourites slaves. The memory of how he had set their ancestors free would always be tended and treasured by the Jews. As cloud by day, and fire by night, he had been more visibly present than at any time before or since: first as a column guiding them through the desert, and then imminent within a tent fashioned to serve as his throne-room. Upon one man in particular he had bestowed an exceptional grace: 'for,' as the Lord God told him, 'you have found favour in My eyes and I have known you by name'.[54] No other prophet in Israel's history would have a bond with God such as Moses had enjoyed. He it was who had spoken for the Lord before Pharaoh, who had summoned the plagues that harrowed Egypt, who had raised his staff to split the waters of the Red Sea. Most awesome of all, and most intimate, was the meeting of God with Moses upon a mountain named Sinai.* As the Israelites gathered on the plain below, heavy cloud concealed its heights, and there had been thunder and lightning, and the great blaring of a ram's horn. 'Watch yourselves not to go up on the mountain or to touch its edge. Whosoever touches the mountain is doomed to die.' But as the ram's horn sounded ever louder, and the mountain began to shake, and the Lord God himself descended upon it amid smoke and fire, Moses was summoned to climb its slopes. Heaven met with Earth; the celestial with the human. What followed was to prove the axle on which the course of history itself would turn.

---

* In Deuteronomy, Sinai is referred to as Horeb.

The Jews did not hold to this conviction lightly. They could be confident of what had happened when Moses climbed Sinai, for the fruits of it were still in their charge. Inscribed in the Torah were commandments that had originally been written by the finger of God himself on tablets of stone. 'You shall have no other gods before me.'[55] Nine similarly lapidary instructions followed: orders to obey the Sabbath and to honour one's parents; to refrain from carving likenesses and taking the name of God in vain; never to murder or commit adultery, nor to steal, bear false witness or covet. All ten commandments, though, were dependent for their potency on the first. There were other gods, after all, who did not put the same value on moral principles as did the God of Israel. Some placed a premium on beauty; some on knowledge; some on power. The Ten Commandments were not merely instructions, but an expression of the very identity of the God of Israel. His Chosen People were being called to live, not as his slaves, but as men and women brought closer to him, to share in his nature. This was why, even as he gave the Ten Commandments to Moses, he warned that he was 'a jealous god'.[56] His love was of an order that might, if betrayed or rejected, turn murderously coercive. When Moses, descending Sinai after an absence of forty days and forty nights, discovered that the Israelites had set up a golden calf, and fallen to worshipping it, so angry was he that he smashed the tablets of stone, and ordered the slaughter of three thousand men. Yet God's anger was even more terrible. His initial intention was to wipe out the Israelites altogether. Only after Moses had climbed Mount Sinai again and implored him for mercy did God finally relent.

Yet that love was what their divine patron felt for them the Jews never doubted. 'For you are a holy people to the LORD your God. You the LORD has chosen to become for Him a treasured people among all the peoples that are on the face of the earth.' As token of this he had given to Moses, after the Ten Commandments, an altogether fuller body of ordinances. Among these were instructions on how altars were to be constructed, and priests to purify themselves, and sacrifices to be conducted; but priests were not alone in being subjected to his instructions. So too were all the Children of Israel. The laws given by God to Moses specified what foods they could and could not eat; with whom they could and could not have sex; how they were to keep the Sabbath; how they were to treat their slaves; that they were to leave gleanings for the poor in orchards; that they were not to sport pudding-bowl haircuts. To contravene these dictates was to call down upon Israel the most terrifying punishment; and yet, like the Ten Commandments, they served as an expression not of tyranny, but of devotion. The Lord God, the creator of the heavens and the earth, had granted to the Children of Israel a momentous and unprecedented honour: a covenant. No other people had so much as contemplated that such a thing might be possible. Gods served to witness treaties, after all—not to enter into one themselves. Who were mortals, to imagine that they might contract an alliance with a deity? Only the Jews had dared entertain such a novel, such a blasphemous conceit. That they had entered into an accord with the Lord God provided the foundation-stone of their entire understanding of the divine. It was the Covenant, written on the tablets borne by Moses, that the Ark had been built to contain; it was the Covenant, reverently placed in the Holy of Holies, that lay at the heart of the Temple raised by Solomon. Nor, even after the ruin visited on Jerusalem by the Babylonians, had the treaty between the Lord God and His Chosen People been rendered void. The terms of it endured. The Jewish scriptures, edited and re-edited in the centuries that followed the disappearance of the Ark, had been compiled in large part to enshrine them. Every Jew who studied it renewed the Covenant in his heart.

Moses, so it was recorded at the end of the Torah, had died on the eve of Joshua's conquest of Canaan. Despite having freed the Israelites from their bondage in Egypt, and then led them for forty years in the wilderness, he never set foot in the Promised Land. 'And no man has known his burial place to this day.'[57] The mystery that veiled the location of his tomb helped to veil as well how his story came to be told in the way that it did. No mention of Moses was to be found in

Egypt; no mention of the plagues; no mention of the miraculous part-
ing of the Red Sea. It was as though, outside Jewish scripture, he had
never existed. Yet the quality of myth that attached itself to Moses,
the degree to which he was—in the words of one scholar—'a figure of
memory but not of history',[58] was precisely what endowed his encounter on the summit of Sinai with its transcendent and incomparable
power. The authors of the Torah, when they formulated the covenant
that bound them to the Lord God, naturally drew on the conventions
of the age. 'I am the LORD your God, who brought you out of Egypt,
out of the land of slavery.'[59] Such was the custom in the Near East:
for a king to begin a proclamation with a ringing vaunt. When the
Lord God threatened that disobedience would see the heavens over
Israel's head turn to bronze, and the earth beneath her feet turn to
iron, he echoed the menacing terms of an Assyrian conqueror. When
he promised that he would scourge 'all the peoples whom you fear',[60]
he offered protection much as a pharaoh committing himself to an
alliance might have done. Yet the record of his covenant, couched
though it may have been in terms familiar to the diplomats of the
Near East, gave to the Jews something utterly without parallel: legislation directly authored by a god.

It needed no mortals to supplement this. Such was the clear lesson of the Jewish holy books. Even the oil with which David and
Solomon were anointed, as the mark of their election, did not endow
them with what Hammurabi and his heirs in Babylon had always
taken for granted: the right of a king to issue laws. Monarchy in
Israel, compared to that of Mesopotamia, was a pallid and a gelded
thing. Only by abandoning the Covenant altogether could it hope to
assert itself—and this, so Jewish scripture recorded, was precisely
what had happened. Kings had grown uppity. They had burned
incense to gods other than the Lord God and issued laws of their
own. Then, a few decades before Jerusalem fell to the Babylonians,
a king named Josiah reported the discovery in the Temple of something astonishing: a long-lost 'Book of the Law'.[61] Summoning the
priests, 'and all the people from the least to the greatest',[62] he read

them what it decreed. The mysterious book proved to be the record of the Covenant itself. Josiah, calling his people to the proper worship of the LORD, did not do so in his own name. He, no less than the meanest of his subjects, was subject to the dictates of God's law. Legislation was the prerogative of the divine. Repeatedly in Jewish scripture, doubts were expressed as to whether Israel, as God's people, needed kings at all. 'The LORD will rule over you.'[63]

And so it proved. Monarchy in Jerusalem was extirpated in 587 BC by the triumphant King of Babylon; but Torah endured. Great powers rose and fell, and conquerors came and went; but still, amid all the ebb and surge of the passing centuries, the Jews held fast to the Covenant. Without it, they, like so many other peoples, would surely have been dissolved in the relentless churning of empires: Babylon, Persia, Macedon, Rome. Even as it was, though, many Jews could not escape a nagging dread. What if they forgot the precise details of the Covenant? As justification for this anxiety, moralists would point to the people who inhabited what had, until its destruction by the Assyrians, been the kingdom of Israel, and who presumed, like the Jews, to lay claim to a Pentateuch. The similarities between the two peoples, though, only emphasised their differences. The Samaritans dismissed the holiness of Jerusalem; scorned the authority of the scriptures written since the time of Moses; insisted that they alone had preserved the untarnished law of God. No wonder, then, that they should have appeared to the Jews a race as mongrel as they were perverse—and as such a standing warning. To abandon God's law was to cease to be 'a wise and understanding people'.[64] It was the Covenant, and the Covenant alone, that enabled the Jews to make sense of the world's affairs. That infractions would be punished as swiftly as they had ever been was evident from the legions' capture of Jerusalem; that the Lord God held to his own side of the bargain was evident from Pompey's miserable end.

Yet it was not merely the flux of past events that Jewish scholars, when they contemplated the implications of the Covenant, believed themselves able to explain. There was the future as well. Vivid in the books of the prophets were visions of what, at the end of days, was to come: of ruin visited on the earth, of new wine drying up and the vine withering; of the leopard lying down with the goat, and a little child leading 'the calf and the lion and the yearling'.[65] A universal kingdom of righteousness was destined to emerge, with Jerusalem as its capital, and a prince of the line of David as its king. 'With justice he will give decisions for the poor of the earth. He will strike the earth with the rod of his mouth; with the breath of his lips he will slay the wicked.'[66] It was as God's Anointed that this prince was destined to rule: as his 'Messiah', or—translated into Greek—his *Christos*. Already, in the visions of a prophet named Isaiah, the title had been applied to Cyrus; but now, in the wake of Pompey's desecration of the Temple, it had come to possess a far more urgent significance. Anticipation of a messiah sprung from David's line, who would impose the covenant with a new vigour, winnowing the wheat from the chaff and restoring the lost tribes to Jerusalem, crackled in the air. All foreign practices were to be purged from Israel. The messiah would smash the arrogance of unrighteous rulers like a potter's vessel. 'And he shall have the peoples of the nations to serve him under his yoke, and he shall glorify the LORD in the sight of all the earth, and he shall purify Jerusalem in holiness as it was at the beginning.'[67]

And briefly, in the wake of Pompey's murder, it seemed as though the end of days might indeed be drawing near. The rivalries of Roman warlords continued to convulse the Mediterranean. Legion clashed with legion, battle-fleet with battle-fleet. Nor were the Jews alone in looking to the heavens and dreaming of better times to come.

Now virginal Justice and the golden age return,
Now its first-born is sent down from high heaven.
With the birth of this boy, the generation of iron will pass,
And a generation of gold will inherit all the world.[68]

These lines, written by a Roman poet named Virgil, spoke loudly of the hopes for a golden age that were as common in Italy as in Judaea; and when, a few years later, they came to be answered, it was not a Jewish messiah who sat enthroned as the master of the world, but a man who claimed descent from a god.

Augustus was the adopted son of Julius Caesar, the vanquisher of Pompey and a man whose feats had seen him, in the wake of his death, installed by official proclamation in the halls of heaven. Nor was that all: for there were those who claimed, just for good measure, that Augustus had been fathered by Apollo in the form of a snake. Certainly, it was not hard to believe that he might indeed rank doubly as *Divi Filius*: 'Son of God'. The dominion of the Roman people, which had seemed as though it might be on the verge of disintegration, was set by him on a new and formidable footing. Peace, to a man like Augustus, was no passive virtue, and the order he brought to the world was imposed at the point of a sword. Roman governors, charged with maintaining order in the Empire's various provinces, wielded a monopoly of violence. Fearsome sanctions were theirs to command: the right to condemn anyone who offended against Rome to be burnt alive, or thrown to wild beasts, or nailed to a cross. In AD 6, when direct rule was imposed on Judaea, the prefect sent to administer the province was 'entrusted by Augustus with full powers—including the infliction of capital punishment'.[69] The Jews' noses were rubbed humiliatingly in the brute fact of their subordination. Rather than dull their expectation that some great change in the world's affairs was approaching, however, and that the end days might well be drawing near, the Roman occupation served only to heighten it. The Jews responded in various ways. Some, taking to the wilderness east of Jerusalem, withdrew from the world; others, cleaving to the Temple, clung for their hopes of salvation to the rites and services ordained of the priesthood. Others yet—scholars known as 'Pharisees'—dreamed of an Israel in which obedience to the laws given by God to Moses would be so absolute, so universal, that every Jew would come to serve as a priest. 'For he left no excuse for ignorance.'[70]

Distinctiveness, in the age of an empire that proclaimed itself universal, might well rank as defiance. The more that different peoples found themselves joined together under the rule of Rome, so the more did Jews, hugging the Covenant close to their hearts, assert their status as a people apart. To the Roman elite, schooled in the range of human custom as only the masters of the world could be, they appeared paradigms of perversity. 'Everything that we hold sacred they scorn; everything that we regard as taboo they permit.'[71] Yet these idiosyncrasies, while they certainly provoked suspicion, were capable of inspiring admiration as well. Among Greek intellectuals, the Jews had long been viewed as a nation of philosophers. Their presence in Alexandria, in the bustling streets that lay beyond the city's library, rendered the story of how the Israelites had escaped Egypt—the *Exodos*, as it was called in Greek—a topic of particular fascination. Some philosophers claimed that Moses had been a renegade priest, and his followers a band of lepers; others cast him as a visionary, who had sought to fathom the mysteries of the cosmos. He was praised both for having forbidden the portrayal of gods in human form, and for having taught that there existed only a single deity. To scholars in the age of Augustus, he appeared a thinker fit for a rapidly globalising world. 'For that which encompasses us all, including earth and sea—that which we call the heavens, the world and the essence of things—this one thing only is God.'[72]

That such an interpretation of Moses' teachings owed more to the Stoics than to Torah did not alter a momentous truth: that the Jewish conception of the divine was indeed well suited to an age that had seen distances shrink and frontiers melt as never before. The God of Israel was a 'great King over all the earth'.[73] Author of the Covenant that bound him uniquely to the Jews, he was at the same time capable of promising love to 'foreigners who bind themselves to the LORD'.[74] Of these, in the great melting pot of the Roman

Mediterranean, there were increasing numbers. Most, it was true, opted to lurk on the sidelines of the synagogue, and rest content there with a status not as Jews, but as *theosebeis*: 'God-fearers'. Men in particular shrank from taking the ultimate step. Admiration for Moses did not necessarily translate into a willingness to go under the knife. Many of the aspects of Jewish life that appeared most ridiculous to outsiders—circumcision, the ban on eating pork—were dismissed by admirers of Moses' teaching as much later accretions, the work of 'superstitious tyrants and priests'.[75] Jews themselves naturally disagreed; and yet there was, in the widespread enthusiasm for their prophets and their scriptures, a hint of just how rapidly the worship of their god might come to spread, were the prescriptions of the Torah only to be rendered less demanding.

Even as it was, there were converts. In an age where more Jews spoke Greek than Hebrew, it was perfectly possible for a Greek— or indeed anyone else—to become a Jew. Nowhere was this more evident than in Alexandria, the original cosmopolis; but increasingly, wherever there were synagogues, there converts were to be found as well. In Rome, where the elite's suspicion of foreign cults had long been the measure of their appeal among the masses, suspicions of this trend were particularly strong. Conservatives did not need to consult the Torah to recognise the fundamental incompatibility of the Jewish god with those of their own city. 'The first lesson absorbed by converts is to despise the gods, to renounce their country, and to view their parents, their children and their brothers as expendable.'[76] Jews were hardly alone in dreading where a multicultural world might lead.

A tension that had always existed within Jewish scripture was being brought to a head. How was the deity whose words and deeds it recorded best understood: as the God of the Covenant or as the Creator of all humanity? The question had long been brewing; but the rise to greatness of a dominion as globe-spanning as Rome's could not help but give it an added urgency. Mutual suspicion between Jews and Gentiles—all the various other peoples of the world—co-existed with an equally mutual fascination. The wilderness east of Jerusalem, where men gathered among lonely hills to live in accordance with Torah, and to tend a hatred of the unrighteous, had its counterpoint in Alexandria, where Greek-speaking scholars of Moses might have no hesitation in expressing admiration for Roman order, or hailing Augustus as 'an instructor in piety'.[77] Just as the Pharisees dreamed of an Israel become a nation of priests, so were there scholars who imagined peoples everywhere brought to obey the laws of Moses: 'barbarians, and Greeks, the inhabitants of continents and islands, the eastern nations and the western, Europe and Asia; in short, the whole habitable world from one extremity to the other'.[78]

Perhaps, far from speaking of God's anger, the absorption of the Jews into the universal empire ruled by Augustus signalled something very different: the imminent fulfilment of his plan for all humankind.

3

MISSION

AD 19: Galatia

Five years after the death of Augustus, the dignitaries of the *Koinon Galaton*—the 'Galatian League'—met in solemn convocation. Loyal to the memory of the Caesar who now, alongside his divine father, reigned in heaven, they looked to honour him as their Saviour and Lord. As elsewhere in the empire, so in Galatia: there was peace and order where before there had always been war. The Galatians, for most of their existence, had been a people largely defined by their aptitude for violence. Three centuries before the death of Augustus, twenty thousand of them, migrants from distant Gaul, had swarmed across the straits from Europe into Asia Minor, a land celebrated for the wealth of its cities, the softness of its citizens, and the talents of its celebrity chefs. Here, in the central highlands of what is now Turkey, the Galatians had quickly carved out a new home for themselves. What the mountains lacked in resources they had more than made up for in location. Barren though Galatia was, it was ideally placed for launching raids on neighbouring kingdoms. Tall, red-haired and prone to fighting in the nude, the Galatians had made their living out of 'their talent for inspiring terror'.[1] Not for nothing was one of the three tribes that together constituted their kingdom named the Tectosages: the 'Searchers after Loot'.

But then the legions had appeared on the scene. Rome briskly put an end to the Galatians' roistering tradition of banditry. In due course, after a century and more of clientage, they were deprived by Augustus of even the figleaf of independence. The borders of the new province were extended far beyond those of the original kingdom; colonies filled with retired soldiers planted across its southern reaches; roads scored through the mountains and desert plains. Engineers, taming the savagery of the landscape, had set the seal on a great feat of pacification. The *Via Sebaste*, a mighty gash of stone and compacted gravel that snaked for four hundred miles across the length of southern Galatia, served the province as both guarantor and symbol of Roman might. The road was worthily named: for *Sebastos*, in Greek, meant 'Augustus'. Merely to travel it was to pay homage to the *Divi Filius*: the Son of a God who, by his exertions and his wisdom, had ushered humanity into a golden age.

And even now, despite his death, he had not abandoned the world. In this conviction, the cities of Galatia could find a shared sense of identity and purpose. The need for this was great. The order that Augustus had brought to the region served to dizzy as well as to settle. Once, back in the swaggering days of their independence, chieftains had gathered in oak glades and feasted beneath the stars, and offered up garlanded prisoners in sacrifice to their gods; but no longer. Now the Galatians lived in marble cities of the kind that their ancestors had delighted in raiding, in a province dotted with Roman colonies, where the common language was Greek. No longer could the *Koinon Galaton* define itself exclusively in terms of its past. Instead, the three Galatian tribes had come by a new marker of identity. The title of *Sebastenos*—'favoured by Augustus'—had been bestowed on them by Caesar himself. To pay honour to their divine patron was, then, for the Galatian elite, no matter of mere expediency, but a deeply felt obligation. This was why, five years after his ascension into heaven, it was decreed that Augustus' own account of his career, which in the year of his death had been inscribed on bronze tablets and attached to his mausoleum in Rome, should be reproduced across Galatia.² One transcript was carved into the wall of a newly consecrated temple to Rome; another etched in red down the piers of a triple-arched gateway; another adorned with statues of the *Divi Filius* and assorted members of his family on horseback. To visit the cities of Galatia was constantly to be reminded of the sheer scale of Augustus' achievements. His birth had set the order of things on a new course. War was over. The world stood as one. Here, so inscriptions proclaimed to a grateful people, was *Euangelion*— 'Good News'.*

Certainly the renown of a god had never before spread so fast, so far. 'Across islands and entire continents, all humanity pays him reverence with temples and sacrifices.'³ In Galatia, as the decades passed, so the cult of Augustus, and of the Caesars who succeeded him on the throne of the world, put down ever stronger roots. It served as the vital sap that sustained civic life. Cities, amid the bleak steppes and jagged mountains, were hardly natural grafts. Out in the wilds of Galatia, where the *pagani*—the country people—lived, the squares and fountains of the cities founded by Augustus might well seem a world away. Long before the coming of the Galatians, the region had been notorious for the savagery of its inhabitants, the potency of its witches, and the vengefulness of its gods. One was dreaded for rendering liars blind, or else rotting their genitals; another for punching women who offended him in the breasts. Fearsome deities such as these were perfectly at home amid the wilds. Bands of itinerant priests, dancing as they travelled and playing flutes and kettledrums, were a common sight on Galatian roads. Some were famed for working themselves up into a lather of prophecy by indulging in spectacular orgiastic rites; but there could be no copulation for the most celebrated of them all. The *Galli*, men dressed as women, were

---

* 'He brings war to an end; he orders peace; by manifesting himself, he surpasses the hopes of all who were looking for good news.' These words, inscribed on stone in 9 BC, came from a decree issued by a consortium of cities similar to the Galatian League, but centred on the Aegean coast of Asia Minor. It uses the plural form of *euangelion—euangelia*.

servants of Cybele, the Mother Goddess who sat enthroned amid the highest peaks of Galatia; and the mark of their submission to this most powerful and venerable of all the region's gods was the severing with a knife or a sharp stone of their testicles. The same feat of pacification that had fostered the cult of Caesar across the Mediterranean had also encouraged the *Galli* to broaden their horizons, and take to the freshly laid roads. Increasingly, they were even to be seen in Rome itself—to the natural dismay of conservatives in the capital. 'If a god desires worship of this kind,' so one of them sternly opined, 'then she does not deserve to be worshipped in the first place.'[4]

Yet the *Galli*, though certainly offensive to Roman values, presented no conceivable threat to the cult of Augustus. Cybele herself had already been worshipped in Rome for over two centuries; and Virgil, describing the world's new 'age of gold',[5] had imagined her gazing on it with a fond and benignant eye. Only the Jews, with their stiff-necked insistence that there existed just a single god, refused as a matter of principle to join in acknowledging the divinity of Augustus; and so perhaps it was no surprise, in the decades that followed the building to him of temples across Galatia, that the visitor there most subversive of his cult should have been a Jew. 'Formerly, when you did not know God, you were slaves to those who by nature are not gods.'[6] So wrote Paul, a traveller to Galatia who, some four decades after the death of Augustus, fell ill in the province—where, precisely, we do not know—and was offered shelter by attentive well-wishers. The visitor, a man as indomitable as he was charismatic, was not the kind to stay silent, even on his sickbed. That his carers, far from merely tolerating his contemptuous dismissal of the Caesars, should have listened to him as though he were 'an angel of God',[7] suggests that he had found refuge with *theosebeis*. Paul, as fluent in Greek as he was well-versed in Torah, was a man ideally qualified to school his hosts in the glory of the Jewish deity. 'You would have torn out your eyes,' he so fondly recalled later, 'and given them to me.'[8] Clearly, even in Galatia, a province where the achievements of Augustus had been publicly transcribed in city after city, and where the honours due to Caesar hallowed the rhythms of the months, the seasons and the years, there were those keen to learn what they might from a Jew.

Jews, though, came in many forms, and what Paul had to say was no less subversive of Torah than it was of Caesar. A decade, perhaps, before his arrival in Galatia, his life had been upended. As a young man he had been a Pharisee, ferociously committed to his studies; it was as a scholar 'zealous in the extreme for the traditions of my fathers'⁹ that he had sought to patrol the boundaries of what a Jew might acceptably believe. Inevitably, then, the followers of an itinerant teacher named Jesus, who insisted, despite the wretched man's crucifixion, that he had risen from the dead and ascended into heaven, there to reign as the Son of God, could not help but arouse in Paul profound emotions of shock and revulsion. Such a claim was not to be endured. It was a repellent folly. It had to be silenced. Paul had duly set himself to the destruction of the cult. But then, unexpectedly, traumatically, rapturously, the tipping point of his entire existence. Some decades later, a version of what had happened would be reported by one of Paul's followers, a historian to whom tradition would give the name of Luke: how it had occurred on the road from Jerusalem to Damascus, words uttered from a blinding light. 'Have I not seen Jesus our Lord?'¹⁰ So Paul himself, when challenged, might demand of his critics. The vision that had been granted him, of a new understanding of God, and of divine love, and of how time itself, like the tucking-in of a bird's wings, or the furling of a ship's sails, had folded in on itself, and of how everything was changed, had overwhelmed him. Paul, in his correspondence with those who shared his new conviction—that Jesus was indeed the Christ, the Anointed One of God—could never leave the wonder of it alone. That he had been called in person to spread the Good News, to serve as an apostle of Christ, was at once the proudest and the most humbling confession of his life. 'For I am the least of the apostles and do not even deserve to be called an apostle, because I persecuted the church of God.'[11]

If the strangeness of it all was something that Paul himself found overwhelming, then so too was it bound to raise eyebrows in Galatia. His scorn for the pretensions of the *Divi Filius* was total. The Son of God proclaimed by Paul did not share his sovereignty with other deities. There were no other deities. 'For us there is but one God, the Father, from whom all things came and for whom we live; and there is but one Lord, Jesus Christ, through whom all things came and through whom we live.'[12] This conviction, that a crucified criminal might somehow be a part of the identity of the one God of Israel—a conviction that Paul, in all his correspondence, took absolutely for granted—was shocking to Galatians as well as to Jews. Command and swagger were the very essence of the cult of the Caesars. To rule as an emperor—an *imperator*—was to rule as a victorious general. In every town in Galatia, in every square, statues of Caesar served as a reminder to his subjects that to rank as the son of a god was, by definition, to embody earthly greatness. No wonder, then, that Paul, proclaiming to the Galatians that there was only the one Son of God, and that he had suffered the death of a slave, not struggling against it but submitting willingly to the lash, should have described the cross as a 'scandal'.[13] The offensiveness of it was not something that Paul ever sought to palliate. That it was 'a stumbling block to Jews, and foolishness to everyone else'[14] did not inhibit him in the slightest. Quite the opposite. Paul embraced the mockery that his gospel brought him—and the dangers. Recuperating from his illness, he would not have concealed from his hosts the trellis-work of scars across his back: the marks of the beatings that he had suffered for the sake of Christ. 'I bear on my body the marks of Jesus.'[15]

Why should this have persuaded anyone in Galatia to accept the truth of Paul's message? To abandon the cult of the Caesars was not merely to court danger, but to risk the very stitching that held together the patchwork society of the province's cities. Yet some, for all this, did find in the new identity proclaimed by Paul not a menace, but a liberation. The love felt by the Jewish god for his chosen people—so unlike anything displayed by the heedless gods of Galatia—had long aroused in Gentiles emotions of envy as well as suspicion. Now, by touring cities across the entire span of the Roman world, Paul set himself to bringing them the news of a convulsive upheaval in the affairs of heaven and earth. Once, like a child under the protection of a tutor, the Jews had been graced with the guardianship of a divinely authored law; but now, with the coming of Christ, the need for such guardianship was past. No longer were the Jews alone 'the children of God'.[16] The exclusive character of their covenant was abrogated. The venerable distinctions between them and everyone else—of which male circumcision had always been the pre-eminent symbol—were transcended. Jews and Greeks, Galatians and Scythians: all alike, so long as they opened themselves to belief in Jesus Christ, were henceforward God's holy people. This, so Paul informed his hosts, was the epochal message that Christ had charged him to proclaim to the limits of the world. 'The only thing that counts is faith expressing itself through love.'[17]

The appeal of such a sentiment to those already sympathetic to the teachings of Jewish scripture was evident. Once, in a town called Gordium, before the coming there of the Galatians, who had adorned it with the severed heads and twisted corpses of their foes, Alexander the Great had been confronted by a celebrated wonder: the drawbar of a cart that for generations had been knotted to its yoke. 'Whoever succeeds in untying it,' so a prophecy ran, 'is destined to conquer the world.'[18] Alexander, rather than waste time trying to pick at the knot with his fingers, had severed it with his sword. Now, with his preaching that Jesus was the fulfilment of God's plans for the world, long foretold by the prophets, Paul had achieved a similar feat. A single deft stroke, and the tension that had always been manifest within Jewish scripture, between the claims of the Jews upon the Lord of all the Earth and those of everyone else, between a God who favoured one people and a God who cared for all humanity, between Israel and the world, appeared resolved. To an age which—in the shadow first of Alexander's empire, and then of Rome's—had become habituated to yearnings of a universal order, Paul was preaching a deity who recognised no borders, no divisions. Paul had not ceased to reckon himself a Jew; but he had come to view the marks of his distinctiveness as a Jew, circumcision, avoidance of pork and all, as so much 'rubbish'.[19] It was trust in God, not a line of descent, that was to distinguish the children of Abraham. The Galatians had no less right to the title than the Jews. The malign powers that previously had kept them enslaved had been routed by Christ's victory on the cross. The fabric of things was rent, a new order of time had come into existence, and all that previously had served to separate people was now, as a consequence, dissolved. 'There is neither Jew nor Greek, slave nor free, male nor female, for you are all one in Christ Jesus.'[20]

Only the world turned upside down could ever have sanctioned such an unprecedented, such a revolutionary, announcement. If Paul did not stint, in a province adorned with monuments to Caesar, in hammering home the full horror and humiliation of Jesus' death, then it was because, without the crucifixion, he would have had no gospel to proclaim. Christ, by making himself nothing, by taking on the very nature of a slave, had plumbed the depths to which only the lowest, the poorest, the most persecuted and abused of mortals were confined. If Paul could not leave the sheer wonder of this alone, if he risked everything to proclaim it to strangers likely to find it disgusting, or lunatic, or both, then that was because he had been brought by his vision of the risen Jesus to gaze directly into what it meant for him and for all the world. That Christ—whose participation in the divine sovereignty over space and time he seems never to have doubted—had become human, and suffered death on the ultimate instrument of torture, was precisely the measure of Paul's understanding of God: that He was love. The world stood transformed as a result. Such was the gospel. Paul, in proclaiming it, offered himself as the surest measure of its truth. He was nothing, worse than nothing, a man who had persecuted Christ's followers, foolish and despised; and yet he had been forgiven and saved. 'I live by faith in the Son of God, who loved me and gave himself for me.'[21]

And if Paul, then why not everybody else?

The Spirit of the Law

Naturally, he could not stay to instruct the Galatians in the gospel forever. The whole world had to hear it. Paul's ambition was one bred of the age. Never before had a single power controlled all the shipping lanes of the Mediterranean; never before had there been such a network of roads along its shores. Paul, born in the port city of Tarsus, on the coast to the south of Galatia, had always known that horizons were there to be crossed. Now, shaking off the dust of Galatia from his sandals, he headed westwards, towards the gleaming cities that circled the Aegean: Ephesus, Thessalonica, Philippi. Admittedly, it was not always easy. 'We have become the scum of the earth, the refuse of the world.'[22] Paul spoke as a man forever on the road, one who had suffered beatings and imprisonments, shipwrecks and the extortions of bandits. Nevertheless, despite the manifold dangers of travel, he had no intention of gathering moss. How could he complain of hardship, when for his sake his Saviour had been tortured to death? So on he went.

By the end of Paul's life, it has been estimated, he had travelled some ten thousand miles.[23] Always there were new churches to be established, fresh peoples to be won for Christ. But Paul was not merely a visionary. He also understood the value of strategy. Like any good general, he knew better than to neglect his rear. Daily, along the roads built with such effort and proficiency by Caesar's engineers, missives were borne in the service of the Roman state. Paul too, in the service of his own Lord, dispatched a steady stream of letters. Sufficiently tutored in the art of rhetoric to deny that he had ever learnt it, he was a brilliant, expressive, highly emotional correspondent. One letter might be marked by his tears; another with expostulations of rage; another with heartfelt declarations of love for its recipients; many with all three. At times of particular stress, Paul might even seize the pen from the scribe and start scratching with it himself, his writing large and bold. To read his correspondence was not just to track the pattern of his thoughts, but almost to hear his voice.

When brought disturbing news from Galatia, his immediate response was to write a frantic and impassioned letter. 'You foolish Galatians, who has put a spell on you?'[24] Paul knew full well the sinister aura of sorcery that clung to their homeland; but it was not the local witches who had provoked him to outrage. Instead, by a bitter irony, it was men claiming, like him, to be preaching the gospel of Christ who now threatened his mission with ruin. To accept Jesus as Lord, they had been instructing the churches of Galatia, was to accept the Law of Moses—and in full. This, as a flat contradiction of everything that Paul had been telling them, struck at the very heart of his understanding of Christ's death on the cross. Unsurprisingly, then, in his determination to combat the 'false brothers'[25] and their teachings, he did not pull his punches. 'I wish they would go the whole way, and castrate themselves!'[26] Scabrous and bitter, the joke dramatised for the Galatians the twin perils that Paul dreaded now threatened them. Circumcision was little better than castration. To submit to the Law of Moses would be as sure a betrayal of Christ as to take to the roads in praise of Cybele. This was not because Paul himself ever doubted that Torah had come from God, but because—in the wake of the great rupture in the affairs of heaven and earth that he believed himself commanded to proclaim—'neither circumcision nor the lack of it has any value'.[27] To demand of the Galatians that they submit to the knife would be to assume that Christ had been inadequate to save them. It would be to reinstate precisely the division between the Jews and the other peoples of the world that Paul believed to have been ended by his Lord's crucifixion. It would be to geld any sense of his mission as universal. No wonder, then, in his letter to the Galatians, that Paul should alternately have cajoled and implored them to stay true to his teaching. 'You, my brothers, were called to be free.'[28]

Such a slogan, though, might cut both ways. Perhaps it was not surprising, in the wake of Paul's departure from Galatia, that some of those he had won for Christ should have come to feel a lack of moorings. To repudiate a city's gods was to repudiate as well the rhythms of its civic life. It was to imperil relations with family and friends. It was to show disrespect to Caesar himself. The crisis in Galatia had taught Paul a sobering lesson: that so extreme might be the sense of dislocation experienced by his converts that some of them, groping after a way to reorient themselves, could seriously contemplate circumcision. The Jews, after all, were an ancient people, and their laws famously strict. The appeal of an identity that was simultaneously venerable and exclusive was stronger, perhaps, than Paul had appreciated. Yet he refused to compromise. Instead, he doubled down. By urging his converts to consider themselves neither Galatian nor Jewish, but solely as the people of Christ, as citizens of heaven, he was urging them to adapt an identity that was as globalist as it was innovative. This, in an age that took for granted local loyalties and tended to look upon novelty with suspicion, was a bold strategy—but one for which Paul refused to apologise. If he was willing to grant the Law of Moses any authority at all, then it was only to insist that what God most truly wanted was a universal amity. 'The entire law is summed up in a single command: "Love your neighbour as yourself."'[29] All you need is love.

That Paul, in the same letter, had openly fantasised about his opponents castrating themselves, did not for a moment give him pause. After all, the truth of his message had been vouchsafed for him by Christ himself: not only on the road to Damascus, but on a subsequent occasion as well, in a vision of heaven, where he had heard 'inexpressible things, things that man is not permitted to tell'.[30] Then, in Galatia, further wonders. The Spirit of God, which, in the beginning, before the creation of things, had hovered over the face of the primordial waters, had descended upon Paul's converts.

Miracles had been performed: the infallible sign of a new covenant between heaven and earth. It was here, in Paul's utter conviction that the breath of God had descended upon the Galatian church, that the explanation for his inner certitude was to be found, and his scorn for his opponents. 'The letter kills, but the Spirit gives life.'[31] What need, then, for Gentiles touched by the divine to obey the Law of Moses? 'For the Lord is the Spirit—and where the Spirit of the Lord is, there is freedom.'[32]

So Paul wrote to a second church, preaching the redemption from old identities that lay at the heart of his message. Corinth, unlike Galatia, enjoyed an international reputation for glamour. Dominating the narrow isthmus linking southern Greece to the north, and with a history that reached back to before the Trojan War, it was wealthy as only a city with two crowded harbours, the headquarters of the provincial governor, and a wide array of banks could be. Even in Rome, the excellence of its bronzes and the proficiency of its prostitutes were spoken of with awe. 'Not everyone has the good fortune to visit Corinth.'[33] Yet the city, despite the antiquity of its name, was in truth barely much older than those planted by Augustus in Galatia. Like them, it was a colony, founded on the site of the original settlement, which a Roman army, in a brutal display of strength, had wiped out some two centuries before. As much as anywhere in Greece, then, Corinth was a melting pot. The descendants of Roman freedmen settled there by Julius Caesar mingled with Greek plutocrats; shipping magnates with cobblers; itinerant philosophers with Jewish scholars. Identity, in such a city, might easily lack deep roots. Unlike in Athens, where even Paul's greatest admirers found it hard to pretend that he had enjoyed much of an audience, in Corinth he had won a hearing. His stay in the city, where he had supported himself by working on awnings and tents, and sleeping among the tools of his trade, had garnered various converts. The church that he had founded there—peopled by Jews and non-Jews, rich and poor, some with Roman names and some with Greek—served as a monument to his vision of a new people: citizens of heaven.

To many in Corinth, it was true, there would not have appeared anything particularly startling about such a sect. The city had a long tradition of hosting eccentrics. Back in the time of Alexander, the philosopher Diogenes had notoriously proclaimed his contempt for the norms of society by living in a large jar and masturbating in public. Paul, though, demanded of the Corinthians a far more total recalibration of their most basic assumptions. To commit to Christ was to be plunged into water: to be baptised. Old identities were washed away. Converts were born anew. In a city famed for its wealth, Paul proclaimed that it was the 'low and despised in the world, mere nothings',[34] who ranked first. Among a people who had always celebrated the *agon*, the contest to be the best, he announced that God had chosen the foolish to shame the wise, and the weak to shame the strong. In a world that took for granted the hierarchy of human chattels and their owners, he insisted that the distinctions between slave and free, now that Christ himself had suffered the death of a slave, were of no more account than those between Greek and Jew. 'For he who was a slave when he was called by the Lord is the Lord's freedman; similarly, he who was a free man when he was called is Christ's slave.'[35] Even Corinth itself, seen through Paul's eyes, appeared transfigured. Its theatres and stadia served as monuments, not to the honouring of the city's ancient festivals, but to the radical novelty of his message. To preach the gospel of Christ was to stand like an actor before the gaze of an entire people; it was to train for the great games staged on the Isthmus, as a runner, as a boxer. Once, back in the darkest year of the city's history, it had been a Roman general who led the Corinthians in long lines as the mark of his triumph; but now it was God. There was no shame in joining such a procession. Just the opposite. To walk incense-perfumed in the divine train was not to be a captive, but truly to be free.

Freedom, though, as Paul was discovering, might easily bring its own stresses. If in Galatia it had left some of his converts so dizzied that the Law of Moses had come to seem to them a welcome crutch, then in Corinth it inspired a giddy sense that anything might be permitted. Some years after Paul had left the city, news was brought to him of a shocking development: one of his converts had gone to bed with his father's wife. Paul, unsurprisingly, was horrified. Yet when he wrote to the church in Corinth, warning it against incest and prostitution, against greed, and drunkenness, and back-biting, he could not ignore the charge that he himself might have sanctioned them. What was freedom, after all, if not a license to do as one pleased? Paul, never one to duck a challenge, met the question head on. 'Everything is permissible,' he wrote to the Corinthians, 'but not everything is beneficial. 'Everything is permissible—but not everything is constructive.'[36] Here, plucked from the seeming implosion of the church in Corinth, was a momentous argument: that law was most properly 'the law of Christ'[37] when it served the good of those who obeyed it. Commandments were just, not because God had decreed that they were, not because he had uttered them to a prophet, not because he had issued them amid fire and thunder from some distant mountain in a desert, but because they worked for the common good.

But how were Paul's followers to judge what ranked as mutually beneficial? As with the Galatians, so with the Corinthians: the apostle sought to answer this question by preaching the primacy of love. Without it, so he stirringly proclaimed, a knowledge of right and wrong was as nothing. 'If I speak in the tongues of men and of angels, but have not love, I am only a resounding gong or a clanging cymbal. If I have the gift of prophecy and can fathom all mysteries and all knowledge, and if I have a faith that can move mountains, but have not love, I am nothing.'[38] Consistent though Paul was in preaching this message, he nevertheless remained haunted by a dilemma that he struggled to resolve. He had travelled widely enough to know how various were the customs of different peoples. Like the great salesman that he was, he always made sure to pitch his message to his audience. 'I have become all things to all men, so that by all possible means I might save some.'[39] Despite this claim, and despite the convulsive transformation in his understanding of what it meant to be a Jew, in his instincts and prejudices he remained the product of his schooling. Confronted by Greek traditions about what love might mean, the disgust he felt was recognisably that of a Pharisee. Paul, brought up to regard monogamous marriage as the only acceptable form of sexual relationship, and sex between two men as utterly beyond the pale, did not hesitate to identify these teachings as the will of God. That he could no longer draw on the Law of Moses to back up these convictions did not inhibit him in the slightest. Indeed, if anything, it seems only to have rendered him the more assertive. Paul, in the final reckoning, did not trust his converts to recognise for themselves what was beneficial and constructive.

The result, lurking at the very heart of his teachings, was a paradox with seismic implications. Between the rupture in the fabric of things preached by Paul and the interminable challenges of daily life, between the volcano-blast of revolution and the shelter from it provided by tradition, a tension existed that he could never entirely resolve. Why, for instance, if male and female were indeed 'all one in Christ Jesus',[40] should women not take on the full prerogatives of men? Paul, wrestling with this question, found himself torn. Revelation and upbringing pulled him in opposite directions. His faith in the transformative impact of Christ's gospel was everywhere manifest among his converts: for whenever the Spirit was believed to have descended upon a woman, her standing among them would be no less than that of a man. Paul himself took for granted that this should be so. Women risked their lives for him; helped to fund his missions; served as leaders in his churches. Yet the notion of equivalence between the two sexes—liable to be as startling to a Jew as it was to a Greek—could not help but give Paul pause. That men might become indistinguishable from women was, after all, the very curse that he had pronounced upon his opponents in Galatia. Understandably, then, the possibility that the church in Corinth might be serving to incubate the mirror image of the *Galli*, women who looked like men, was one that he refused to countenance. Short hair on a woman, so Paul sternly informed the Corinthians, was as repellent as long hair on a man; a woman praying without a veil was unacceptable, because—among other horrors—it would offend any visiting angels. So might a man who had just scuttled a ship clutch on the swelling of a wave after its wreckage. 'The head of every man is Christ, and the head of the woman is man.'[41]

Paul himself, even as he delivered these rulings, never for a moment forgot his own limitations. He was not such a hypocrite as to set himself up as a second Moses. If asked for counsel, he would give it; but this was not to be mistaken for commandments from God. His correspondence was no second Torah. Rather than lay down the law of Christ, his role as an apostle was altogether more modest: to help his converts recognise it within themselves. 'You show that you are a letter from Christ, the result of our ministry, written not with ink but with the Spirit of the living God, not on tablets of stone but on tablets of human hearts.'[42] Paul, in struggling to articulate what he meant by this, naturally looked to the scriptures: for there, in the writings of the prophets, assurances were indeed to be found of a time when God, making a new covenant with his chosen people, would put his law 'upon their hearts'.[43] These haunting promises, though, did not provide Paul with the only precedent for what he was trying to express—and he knew it. Writing from Corinth to the churches of Rome, he freely acknowledged that Jews were not alone in having a sense of right and wrong. Other peoples too, however dimly, possessed one. How had they come by it? Since God had never given them a Law, it could only have derived 'from nature'.[44] This, for a Jew, was an astonishing acknowledgement to make. The concept of natural law had no place in Torah. Yet Paul—as he struggled to define the law that he believed, in the wake of the crucifixion and the resurrection, to be written on the heart of all who acknowledged Christ as Lord—did not hesitate to adapt the teachings of the Greeks. The word he used for it—*syneidesis*—clearly signalled which philosophers in particular he had in mind. Paul, at the heart of his gospel, was enshrining the Stoic concept of conscience.

Here, in the great struggle to define what the coming of Christ had meant for the world, was a decisive moment. The opponents so forthrightly dismissed by Paul in his letter to the Galatians, the missionaries who preached that to be baptised meant submitting to circumcision as well, were not yet defeated; but they were in retreat. In the churches that Paul had laboured so hard to establish across the span of the Mediterranean, his was the understanding of God's purpose that was destined to prevail. Never before had Jewish morality and Greek philosophy been fused to such momentous effect. That the law of the God of Israel might be read inscribed on the human heart, written there by his Spirit, was a notion that drew alike on the teachings of Pharisees and Stoics—and yet equally was foreign to them both. Its impact was destined to render Paul's letters—the correspondence of a bum, without position or reputation in the affairs of the world—the most influential, the most transformative, the most revolutionary ever written. Across the millennia, and in societies and continents unimagined by Paul himself, their impact would reverberate. His was a conception of law that would come to suffuse an entire civilisation.

He was indeed—just as he proclaimed himself to be—the herald of a new beginning.

Light My Fire

'The night is nearly over; the day is almost here.'[45] So Paul wrote to the *Hagioi*, or saints, who constituted the churches of Rome. The urgency with which he kept travelling the Mediterranean—now planning a trip to Judaea, now an expedition to Spain—reflected his enduring anxiety that the world was running out of time. The whole of creation was in labour. The revolution in the affairs of heaven and earth preached by Paul was of a literally cosmic order. With a mighty blasting of trumpets, with the acclamation of angels, Christ would soon be coming again. Paul, even as he ached for his Lord's return, shivered at the prospect. 'May your whole spirit, soul and body,' he urged his converts, 'be kept blameless at the coming of our Lord Jesus Christ.'[46] The word that he used to describe this impending arrival, *parousia*, was one full of resonance for any Greek. The yearning to behold a god walk the earth, which had seen meretricious warlords like Demetrius the Besieger fêted as divine, was fused by Paul with the natural awe felt by Jews for the one God of Israel. Here, in the prospect of Christ's return, was a message ripe with multicultural appeal.

Rome, though, was already the stage-set for a spectacular *parousia*. As Paul travelled from city to city, warning that time was short, so in the capital a young Caesar had come to power who took flamboyant pleasure in blurring the boundaries between human and divine. The great-great grandson of Augustus, Nero also ranked— courtesy of an adoptive father who, following his death, had been briskly promoted to the heavens—as the son of a god. Divine favour had touched him from the very moment of his nativity, when the first rays of a December dawn had bathed him in gold. Flatterers compared him to Apollo, praising him for putting the scattered stars to flight, for bringing a new age of joy, and for 'giving to silenced laws new breath'.[47] More literally than Augustus had ever done, he pushed such propaganda to ferocious limits. When Nero brought his *euangelion* to Greece, he did so in the flashiest manner possible: by remitting the province's taxes, starting a canal across the Isthmus of Corinth, and starring in the Olympic Games. The resources of the entire world were at his service. Coins, statues, banners: all promoted Nero as a being haloed with divine fire. In the streets of the capital he would pose as the charioteer of the sun. When he made his public debut on the lyre, an instrument to which he had devoted much practice, he pointedly chose to sing of the punishment of Niobe. Apollo, radiant in his cruelty and splendour, seemed to Nero's dazzled admirers manifest on earth.

To Paul, of course, it was all worse than folly—and not only to Paul. Nero, by appearing in public as a charioteer or a musician, was riding roughshod over a venerable Roman prejudice: that to entertain the public was to become the lowest of the low. Yet the offence, far from giving him pause, only served his purpose. On one thing, at least, the emperor and the apostle were agreed: in a world newly touched by the divine, nothing could quite be as it had been before. Nero, as the son of a god and the ruler of the world, was not bound by the drab and wearisome conventions that governed the affairs of mortals. Instead, like some figure sprung from tragedy, he killed his mother; he kicked his pregnant wife to death; he was married, dressed as a woman, to a man. Such it was to live as a hero of myth. What, in a city ruled by a superhuman figure, were mere proprieties? Rome itself was rendered complicit in their repeated and spectacular subversion. In the summer of AD 64, a great street party was thrown to celebrate the new order of things. In the very heart of the city, a lake was filled with sea-monsters. Along its edge, brothels were staffed with whores ranging from the cheapest streetwalkers to the most blue-blooded of aristocrats. For a single night, to the delight of the men who visited them and knew that the women were forbidden to refuse anyone, there was no slave or free. 'Now a minion would take his mistress in the presence of his master; now a gladiator would take a girl of noble family before the gaze of her father.'[48]

Yet out in the vast sprawl of the capital, in the apartment blocks and workshops of the largest city in the world, there were scattered communities of people who, in their rejection of conventions and norms, put even Nero in the shade. Paul was not the founder of the churches in Rome. Believers in Christ had appeared well before his own arrival there. Nevertheless, the letter that he had sent these *Hagioi* from Corinth, a lengthy statement of his beliefs that was designed as well to serve as an introduction to 'all in Rome who are loved by God',[49] was like nothing they had ever heard before. The most detailed of Paul's career, it promised to its recipients a dignity more revolutionary than even any of Nero's stunts. When the masses were invited by the emperor to his street parties, the summons was to enjoy a fleeting taste of the pleasures of a Caesar; but

Paul, in his letter to the Romans, had something altogether more startling to offer. 'The Spirit himself testifies with our spirit that we are God's children.'[50] Here, baldly stated, was a status that Nero would never have thought to share. It was not given to householders filthy and stinking with the sweat of their own labours, the inhabitants at best of a mean apartment or workshop on the outskirts of the city, to lay claim to the title of a Caesar. And yet that, so Paul proclaimed, was indeed their prerogative. They had been adopted by a god.

And not only the householders. In the great parties thrown by Nero for the Roman people, the subversion of tradition sponsored by the emperor had manifest limits. The nobleman's daughter obliged to work as a prostitute, and serve whoever might demand to use her, was the emblem of a brute truth that most in the capital took for granted: the potency of a Roman penis. Sex was nothing if not an exercise of power. As captured cities were to the swords of the legions, so the bodies of those used sexually were to the Roman man. To be penetrated, male or female, was to be branded as inferior: to be marked as womanish, barbarian, servile. While the body of a free-born Roman was sacrosanct, those of others were fair game. 'It is accepted that every master is entitled to use his slave as he desires.'[51] Nero, by depriving the aristocratic women who worked at his parties of the inviolability that was theirs by right of law, was certainly—even if only for one night—making scandalous play with the Roman class system; but not with a far more fundamental proposition. In Rome, men no more hesitated to use slaves and prostitutes to relieve themselves of their sexual needs than they did to use the side of a road as a toilet. In Latin, the same word, *meio*, meant both ejaculate and urinate. To the presumptions that underlay this, however, Paul brought a radically different perspective. 'Do you not know that your bodies are members of Christ himself?'[52] So he had demanded of the Corinthians. How could any man, knowing his limbs consecrated to the Lord, think to entwine them with those of a whore, mingle his sweat with hers, become one flesh with her? But

Paul, by proclaiming the body 'a temple of the Holy Spirit',[53] was not merely casting as sacrilege attitudes towards sex that most men in Corinth or Rome took for granted. He was also giving to those who serviced them, the bar girls and the painted boys in brothels, the slaves used without compunction by their masters, a glimpse of salvation. To suffer as Christ had done, to be beaten, and degraded, and abused, was to share in his glory. Adoption by God, so Paul assured his Roman listeners, promised the redemption of their bodies. 'And if the Spirit of him who raised Jesus from the dead is living in you, he who raised Christ from the dead will also give life to your mortal bodies through his Spirit, who lives in you.'[54]

The revolutionary implications of this message, to those who heard it, could not help but raise pressing questions. In the cramped workshops that provided the *Hagioi* of Rome with their places of assembly, where they would meet to commemorate the arrest and suffering of Christ with a communal meal, men rubbed shoulders with women, citizens with slaves. If all were equally redeemed by Christ, if all were equally beloved of God, then what of the hierarchies on which the functioning of even the humblest Roman household depended? Paul, in giving his answer, betrayed a certain ambivalence. Certainly, he refuted any notion that the divine justice promised to those baptised in the name of Christ might be determined by their rank. 'God,' he declared firmly, 'does not show favouritism.'[55] All were equally redeemed from the servitude of sin and death. The master of a household was no more or less a son of God than his slaves. Everyone, then, should be joined together by a common love. Yet even as Paul urged this, he did not push the radicalism of his message to its logical conclusion. A slave might be loved by his master as a brother, and renowned for his holiness, and blessed with the gift of prophecy—but still remain a slave. 'We have different gifts,' so Paul explained, 'according to the grace given us. If a man's gift is prophesying, let him use it in proportion to his faith. If it is serving, let him serve.' And if he combined the gifts, then, of course, let him do both.

Paul, in urging this manifesto, could at least argue that he practised what he preached. Willingly, he had abandoned the privileges
of his upbringing. Not just a scribe and a scholar, he had inherited
from his father—if Luke's history is to be trusted—the rights of a
Roman citizen.* He rarely stood upon them, though. Fearless in proclaiming what he believed, he perfectly accepted that those placed in
authority were entitled to punish him for what he said. Repeatedly,
rather than abandon his right to speak in synagogues, he submitted
to their codes of discipline. 'Five times have I received at the hands of
the Jews the thirty-nine lashes.'[56] In a similar spirit, and despite his
scorn for the pretensions of the Caesars, Paul warned the churches
of Rome not to offer open resistance to Nero. 'Everyone must submit
himself to the governing authorities, for there is no authority except
that which God has established.'[57] Paul's conviction that the only true
citizenship was that of heaven was matched by his determination to
exploit the manifestations of earthly authority as effectively as he
possibly could. If synagogues offered him a chance to win his fellow
Jews for Christ, then he would seize it. If householders in Corinth
or Rome provided him with financial backing, and with spaces in
which his various converts could meet, and with funds to help relieve
a famine back in Judaea, then he would take full advantage of their
generosity. If Roman power upheld the peace that enabled him to
travel the world, then he would not jeopardise his mission by urging
his converts to rebel against it. Too much was at stake. There was no
time to weave the entire fabric of society anew. What mattered, in
the brief window of opportunity that Paul had been granted, was to
establish as many churches as possible—and thereby to prepare the
world for the *parousia*. 'For the day of the Lord will come like a thief
in the night.'[58]

And increasingly, it seemed that the world's foundations were
indeed starting to shake. In the summer of 64, a few weeks after

---

* Even if Luke is not to be trusted—and scholarly opinion is divided on the question
of whether Paul was truly a Roman citizen—the fact that the claim could be made
implies much about his background.

Nero's notorious street party, a deadly fire broke out in Rome. For days it raged. When at last it was extinguished, perhaps a third of the city was left as smoking rubble. Nero, looking around for culprits, fixed on the *Hagioi*. The charges against them—arson, and 'hatred of humankind'⁵⁹—betrayed no detailed interrogation of their beliefs. They were scapegoats, nothing more. Nero, ever fond of a spectacle, displayed a vengefulness worthy of Artemis and Apollo. Some of the condemned, dressed in animal skins, were torn to pieces by dogs. Others, lashed to crosses, were smeared in pitch and used as torches to illumine the night. Nero, riding in his chariot, mingled with the gawping crowds. Among those put to death, so later tradition would record, were two famous names. One was Peter. The other—beheaded, as befitted a Roman citizen—was Paul. Whether, in truth, he perished in the wake of the great fire, or some time before, is unclear; but that he was indeed executed seems certain enough. Within thirty years of his death, he was being hailed in Rome as the very archetype of a witness to the glory of God: as a *martus*, a 'martyr'. 'For after he had been bound in chains seven times, driven into exile and stoned; after he had preached in both the East and the West; after he had taught what it was to be righteous to the whole world, even to the furthest limits of the West; then he won the noble glory that was the reward for his faith.'⁶⁰

Paul died disappointed in his hope that he would live to see the return in glory of Christ. Yet the most revolutionary of all his teachings—that the Lord of Hosts, rather than preparing amid fire and thunder to rescue Israel from foreign oppression, had opted instead to send His Son to perish on a Roman cross, and thereby to usher in a new age—was soon to receive what, to his followers, could only seem awful confirmation. In AD 66, the smouldering resentments of the Jews in Judaea burst into open revolt. Roman vengeance, when it came, was terrible. Four years after the launch of the rebellion, Jerusalem was stormed by the legions. The wealth of the Temple was carted off to Rome, and the building itself burnt to the ground. 'Neither its antiquity, nor the extent of its treasures, nor the global range of those who regarded it as theirs, nor the incomparable glory of its rites, proved sufficient to prevent its destruction.'[61] God, whose support the rebels had been banking upon, had failed to save his people. Many Jews, cast into an abyss of misery and despair, abandoned their faith in him altogether. Others, rather than blame God, chose instead to blame themselves, arraigning themselves on a charge of disobedience, and turning with a renewed intensity to the study of their scriptures and their laws. Others yet—those who believed that Jesus was Christ, and whom the Roman authorities had increasingly begun to categorise as *Christiani**—found in the ruin visited on God's Chosen People the echo of an even more dreadful spectacle: that of God's Son upon the gallows. Paul, although he had not lived to see the destruction of the Temple, had been expecting it. The conviction that God was a warrior bound by a timeless covenant to the defence of a particular people was one that he had abandoned after his first vision of Christ. It was a new covenant that he had preached. The Son of God, by becoming mortal, had redeemed all humanity. Not as a leader of armies, not as the conqueror of Caesars, but as a victim the Messiah had come. The message was as novel as it was shocking—and was to prove well suited to an age of trauma. 'Jews demand miraculous signs and Greeks look for wisdom—but we preach Christ crucified.'[62]

It was hardly surprising, then, in the wake of Jerusalem's destruction, and with Jesus starting to pass out of living memory, that Christians should have set to transcribing reports of his life and sayings. Paul, in his letters, had often made allusion to the passion of

---

* According to Acts, 'the disciples were called Christians first at Antioch' (11.26). The distinctive form of the Greek word *Christianos* strongly suggests that 'it was first coined in Latin, in the sphere of Roman administration' (Horrell, p. 364). Indeed, Tacitus explicitly states that those condemned by Nero were abusively referred to by the name of *Chrestiani*. Unsurprisingly, then, neither in Paul's letters nor in the Gospels does the word appear; but already, by AD 100 at the latest, Christians themselves seem to have begun to appropriate it.

Christ—to the night of his arrest, to his flogging, to his crucifixion—
but, confident that his correspondents already knew the details, had
neglected to make it the focus of his communications. The gospels
written in the tense and terrible years that immediately preceded and
followed the annihilation of Jerusalem were different.* The four earliest and most influential all had as their climax the death and resurrection of Christ. But these were not their only theme. 'You have
one teacher.'[63] So Jesus, in one of the gospels, declared. His manner
of teaching, though, was nothing like that of a philosopher. Those
who paraded their virtue, and condemned the faults of others, he
dismissed as painted tombs heaving with maggots and corruption. The standards of virtue he preached—to love one's enemy, to
abandon all one's worldly goods—were so demanding as to seem
impossible to meet. He was peculiarly tender with sinners. He dined
with Jews who violated the law and talked beside wells with adul-
terers. He had a genius for simile. The kingdom of God was like
a mustard seed; it was like the world as seen through the eyes of a
child; it was like yeast in dough. Again and again, in the stories that
Jesus loved to tell, in his parables, the plot was as likely to be drawn
from the world of the humble as it was from that of the wealthy or
the wise: from the world of swineherds, servants, sowers. And yet,
for all that, they had an eerie quality. Repeatedly, the familiar was
rendered strange. Seed falling among thorns; a lost sheep; brides-
maids waiting for a wedding to start: all, in Jesus' teaching, shed a
haunting light on the purposes of God. Yet nothing was remotely
as uncanny as the character of Jesus himself. No one quite like him
had ever before been portrayed in literature. The measure of this
was that Christians, when they read the gospels, were able to believe
that the man whose life they depicted, a man whom they described
as weeping, sweating and bleeding, a man whose death they vividly

---

* The four canonical gospels continue to defy precise dating. Estimates range from
the 50s to the 90s. The evidence for a later date is no longer as solid as it was once
thought to be.

and unsparingly related, had indeed been what Paul claimed him to be: 'the Son of God'.[64]

SIX AND A HALF CENTURIES before the Roman sack of Jerusalem, when the Babylonians had visited a similar fate on the city, those hauled away into captivity had kept faith with their god by imagining that all would ultimately be for the best. Israel would be restored, and princes bow down before her. The darkness would ultimately be lifted. So the Lord God himself had declared.

'I will give you as a light to the nations,
 that my salvation may reach to the ends of the earth.'[65]

Now, in the wake of a second Temple's destruction, the darkness seemed only to have thickened. What prospect, then, of light? To this question, the writers of the gospels provided a startling answer: it had already appeared. 'The light shines in the darkness, but the darkness has not understood it.'[66] So began a gospel which Christians in due course would attribute to John, youngest of the twelve original disciples of Jesus, and the one whom he had particularly loved. The *Logos*, which was with God, and was God, and through whom the world was made, had come into the world, and the world had failed to recognise him. No less than Paul's letters, it was—in its fusion of Jewish scripture with Greek philosophy—a recognisable monument to the age. Certainly, the notion that light and truth were synonymous was not original to John. It reached back at least to Darius. Yet what followed had no parallel in the utterances of Persian kings, nor of Greek philosophers, nor of Jewish prophets. The *Logos*—the Word—had become flesh. His disciples had been fishermen and tax collectors. They had trodden dusty roads together, and slept on hard floors. Then, when the night came of Jesus' arrest, they had abandoned him. Even Peter, standing by a fire in a courtyard outside where Jesus had been taken, had three times denied him before cockcrow. The betrayal had seemed beyond forgiveness. But then, at the end of the gospel, it had come. John described how the risen Christ had appeared to the disciples as they were out on a lake fishing, and had lit a fire, and had invited them to cook their fish on it. Then, when they had finished eating, he had turned to Peter, and three times asked him, 'Do you love me?' Three times Peter had answered that he did. And three times Jesus had commanded him, 'Feed my sheep.'[67]

So ended a gospel that had begun with the Word that was with God, and was God, at the moment of creation: beside a barbecue on the shores of a lake. Hope from despair; reconciliation from betrayal; healing from trauma.

It was a message, amid the convulsions of the age, to which many would find themselves drawn—and for which some, as time would prove, were more than willing to die.

4

BELIEF

AD 177: Lyon

The churches of the Rhône valley were on the rack. News of their agonies could not help but shadow Irenaeus as he set out on his journey. Some years previously, travelling from his native Asia Minor, he had settled in Vienne, a city twenty miles south of Lyon. The Gauls—like their distant cousins the Galatians—had long since submitted to Roman arms. Vienne had originally been founded by Julius Caesar, while Lyon had been serving as the effective capital of Gaul since the time of Augustus. Irenaeus, arriving in the Rhône valley from the Aegean, had found a home away from home. Lyon in particular was proudly cosmopolitan. It possessed a temple complex dedicated to Augustus quite as impressive as anything to be seen in Asia Minor; it teemed with officers, administrators and merchants drawn from across the Roman world; it even had an altar to Cybele. Most significantly, from Irenaeus' point of view, there were Christians. Their companionship had always provided him with the bedrock of his life. As a young man, he had sat at the feet of the local bishop, 'a steadfast witness of truth'[1] by the name of Polycarp—and who, so Irenaeus reported, had in his turn known the gospel-writer John. 'And I remember how he spoke of his conversations with John and with others who had seen the Lord, how he would recite their words from memory, and recall what he had heard from them concerning the Lord, his mighty works, and his teaching.'[2] Arriving in the Rhône valley, Irenaeus had brought with him something incalculably precious to the infant churches there: reminiscences, derived from a celebrated witness, of the generation of the apostles. The church in Vienne had welcomed him with open arms. His learning and his palpable commitment to Christ set the seal on his reputation. This was why, anxious to settle various disagreements that had arisen among the churches of the Rhône valley, and eager to consult with those of Rome, the elders of Lyon and Vienne had chosen Irenaeus as their ambassador to the capital. And so off he had set.

Arriving in Rome, Irenaeus found himself moved by the witness that Christians there had for so long borne to Christ. Twelve men in succession, so he reported, had presided over 'the venerable and universally renowned church founded by those two most glorious apostles, Peter and Paul'.[3] The state-sponsored persecution unleashed by Nero had long since petered out. Christians in the city had, by and large, been left to their own devices—and had become, in their own turn, just that little bit more Roman. The heady days when Paul had preached the imminent return of Christ were by now a century and more in the past. Christians might still hourly expect the *parousia*, but the original, unsettling radicalism of Paul's own message had been diluted. Letters written in his name and that of Peter now sternly instructed women to submit to their husbands, and slaves to obey their 'earthly masters in everything'.[4] The Christians of Rome were advised not to court death at the hands of Caesar, but rather to 'honour' him.[5] Irenaeus himself, that seasoned traveller, knew full well on what the order of the world depended, and did not hesitate to acknowledge it. 'It is thanks to them,' he wrote of the imperial authorities, 'that the world is at peace. It is thanks to them that we are able to walk along well-kept roads without fear, and take ship wherever we wish.'[6]

Efficiently organised transport infrastructure might, however, come at a price. Irenaeus knew, even as he carried out his mission, that the churches he had left behind stood in mortal peril. The lack of any systematic persecution did not mean that Christians could ever afford to relax. Despite a legal obligation on governors not to disturb the order of their provinces by rooting them out, mobs were perfectly happy to take on the task themselves. Christians, who prided themselves on the distinctiveness of their worship, were—unsurprisingly—the objects of much prurient gossip. They committed incest; they worshipped the genitals of their elders and bishops; they staged 'monstrous rituals involving a tethered dog'.[7] No matter how indignantly Christians themselves might refute these calumnies, the conviction that there was no smoke without fire proved difficult to rebut. Nor did it help, in Lyon and Vienne, that the churches were largely peopled by immigrants. Hostility towards foreigners who refused to engage in the cities' rituals of sacrifice, who scorned so much as to swear by 'the fortune of Caesar',[8] who hailed a crucified criminal as Lord, was easily stoked. All Christians, no matter where they were, had to live with the knowledge that they might be lynched. In the Rhône valley, the threat was particularly severe. In 177, when the storm finally broke, so capriciously did the violence spread, and so savagely did it manifest itself, that it seemed to its victims to have erupted from a realm of darkness beyond the merely human. Thugs roamed the streets, hunting out Christians wherever they could find them. Men and women of all ages and of all classes were dragged through a rain of fists and stones to the central square of Lyon, then flung into cells. There they were kept, to await the pleasure of the governor.

It was from gaol that the elders of the two Gallic churches had given Irenaeus his commission; and it was from gaol, once the bravest of the arrested Christians had refused the governor's offer to spurn Christ, and thereby secure their freedom, that they were led to an amphitheatre. Cities the size of Lyon possessed one as a matter of course: for it was in the arena, where cheering crowds would gather to watch criminals thrown to wild animals, or fight one another to death, or endure cruelly inventive forms of torture, that the Roman genius for making a show out of death attained its quintessence. Yet that genius met its match in the Christians of Lyon. 'We have been made a spectacle to the whole universe.'⁹ So Paul, comparing himself to a man condemned to death in the arena, had once written. Opposed to the brutally coercive power of the Roman state, Christians brought a conviction as potent as it was subversive: that they were actors in a cosmic drama. They did not shrink from the blast of the crowd's breath, nor cower before the revolting humiliations visited on them. On the contrary: they fashioned out of their ordeals a public display of their devotion to Christ. Whether gored by bulls, or savaged by dogs, or roasted on red-hot chairs of iron, they cried out only 'the words they had repeated all along— the declarations of their faith'. So, at any rate, it was reported to the churches of Asia Minor, in an account written quite possibly by Irenaeus himself.* With this letter, a momentous discovery was being put into effect: that to be a victim might be a source of strength. Turn on their heads the guiding assumptions of the Roman authorities, and submission might be redefined as triumph, degradation as glory, death as life. In Lyon, over the course of that terrible summer, the paradox of a crucified king held the most public stage in Gaul.

Not that the Christian concept of martyrdom—original though it certainly was—would have seemed altogether unfamiliar to spectators in the amphitheatre. Greeks and Romans were no strangers to tales of self-sacrifice. Their more edifying histories were rife with them. A philosopher might gnaw off his own tongue and spit it in a tyrant's face; a warrior, captured by an enemy, might demonstrate his resolve by plunging his hand into a blazing fire. Exemplars such as these had always been a feature of the Roman schoolroom. The values that they instilled in the young were precisely what had

---

* The letter is quoted by Eusebius, a historian of the church writing a century and a half after the events it describes (*History of the Church*, 5.1). It is perfectly possible— indeed likely—that he added his own touches to it; and yet, for all that, allusions in the narrative to doctrinal controversies contemporaneous with Irenaeus make it clear that the bulk of the letter must be authentic. It may even be by Irenaeus himself.

enabled Rome to conquer the world. They served to illustrate the qualities of steel that had made the Roman people great. All the more grotesque, then, that criminals condemned to the arena, obliged to submit to the ministrations of torturers, penetrated by spears or swords, should have presumed to lay claim to them as well. Indeed, to the Roman authorities, the pretensions of martyrs were liable to seem so ludicrous, so utterly offensive, as to verge on the incomprehensible. Had the governor who sentenced to death the Christians of Lyon and Vienne read the account of his actions sent to the churches of Asia, he would only have been the more disgusted. 'Those things reckoned by men low, and invisible, and contemptible,' so the letter proclaimed, 'are precisely what God ranks as deserving of great glory.'[10] In illustration of this subversive message, it dwelt particularly on a slavegirl named Blandina. Every torture inflicted on her, every torment, she had fearlessly endured. The radiance of her heroism had put even her fellow martyrs in the shade. Blandina's mistress, although sentenced to the arena as well, did not merit being named. Other Christians, those who had lost their nerve and renounced Christ, were dismissed as 'flabby athletes who had failed to train'.[11] It was Blandina who had won every bout, every contest— and thereby secured the crown.

That a slave, 'a slight, frail, despised woman',[12] might be set among the elite of heaven, seated directly within the splendour of God's radiant palace, ahead of those who in the fallen world had been her immeasurable superiors, was a potent illustration of the mystery that lay at the heart of the Christian faith. In the arena, so it was reported to the churches of Asia, Blandina's broken body had seemed transfigured. Her fellow martyrs, in the midst of their own agonies, 'had looked upon their sister, and seen in her person the One who was crucified for them'.[13] Irenaeus had no doubt that a woman such as Blandina, when the lash bit her, felt pain just as Christ had done. This was the assurance that steeled a martyr for death. The willingness of Christians to embrace excruciating tortures—which to those who sentenced them could only appear as lunacy—was founded on an awesome conviction: that their Saviour was by their side. More than the temples and the fields for which the antique heroes of Rome had been willing to sacrifice themselves, Christ's presence was something real. He was there in the arena, as once he had been nailed to the cross. To emulate his sufferings was to impose a meaning on the blankness and inscrutability of death.

But what if he had not suffered? Here was a question, as Irenaeus knew all too well, infinitely more unsettling than any that a Roman governor might think to demand. For some Christians, the teaching within Paul's letters, and within the four earliest gospels—that Jesus, a man tortured to death on a cross, was also, in some mysterious way, a part of the identity of the One God of Israel—was simply too radical to tolerate. Who, then, might he actually have been? Rather than commingling the earthly with the heavenly, some Christians argued, was it not likelier that his humanity had been mere illusion? How could the Lord of the Universe possibly have been born of a mortal woman, still less have experienced pain and death? Various Christian teachers attempted solutions to these puzzles. In Rome, Irenaeus had come across a range of schools, each with their own opinions: their own *haereses*. Some taught that Christ was pure spirit; others that the mortal Jesus 'was merely a receptacle of Christ';[14] others still that Christ and Jesus, although distinct from one another, were both of them supernatural entities, part of a bewilderingly complex cast of divine beings who, far beyond the bounds of the material earth, inhabited what was termed the *pleroma*, or 'fullness'. One thing, though, these various 'heresies' did tend to have in common: revulsion at the idea that Christ might literally have suffered death. 'The man who believes that is still a slave.'[15] Such was the opinion of Basilides, a Christian living in Alexandria, who taught that Jesus, when the time came for him to be crucified, had swapped his form with that of an unfortunate passer-by. 'And Jesus had stood laughing, as the man, through ignorance and error, was crucified in his place.'[16] To Irenaeus, in his determination to define for the Christian people the true path of belief, the *orthodoxia*, doctrines such as Basilides' constituted a treacherous diversion. They made a mockery of any notion that Christ might be imitated. Those who taught that he had been nothing but spirit, so Irenaeus reported, 'go so far as to mock the martyrs'.[17] The implications were devastating. Blandina, far from sharing in Christ's glory, had been pathetically deluded. Her agonies had been in vain. She had died a slave.

That different Christians might have different views on the nature of their Saviour was, perhaps, inevitable. Irenaeus knew perfectly well that he was competing for customers in an open market. Hence his enthusiasm for the momentous new concept of orthodoxy. Beliefs, after all, did not patrol themselves. They had to be promoted, and upheld against their rivals. This was no less the case in Gaul than it was in Rome. There were Christians in Lyon, even after the devastating persecution of 177, who mocked the ideal of martyrdom and denied the authority of the local bishop. Irenaeus, who had been elected to the post following the death of his predecessor in a prison cell, was predictably dismissive of them in turn. Their teachings he despised as high-flown gibberish; their rituals as an excuse to foist aphrodisiacs on gullible women. 'The cunning of necromancers is joined to buffoonery.'[18]

Yet Irenaeus, despite his occasional expostulations of contempt, never doubted that he was engaged in an authentic battle of ideas. To condemn wild and unfounded *haereses* was to approve *orthodoxia*. Truth shone the brighter for being framed by lies. Such was the conviction that Irenaeus brought to his systematic cataloguing of those teachings by self-proclaimed Christians that he condemned as false. If he was unfair in deriving them all from a single source— a Samaritan necromancer named Simon, supposedly converted by Peter—then he was not entirely so. Teachers like Basilides had made sure to trace the origin of their doctrines back to the time of the apostles. This, though, was a battlefield on which Irenaeus found it easy to train overwhelming force. When Basilides claimed that he had received his gospel from a single follower of Peter, by means of a secret channel of communication, it inevitably highlighted how plentiful and public were the sources for the authority claimed by bishops such as Irenaeus himself. 'Although dispersed throughout the whole world, even to the ends of the earth, the church has received from the apostles, and from the disciples of the apostles, one single faith.'[19] To Irenaeus, who in his native Asia had sat at the feet of Polycarp, and in Rome had traced whole generations of bishops back to the time of Peter, the continuity of his beliefs with the primordial beginnings of the Church appeared self-evident. He did not claim any privileged source of wisdom. Just the opposite. Irenaeus, in his attempt to define orthodoxy, was defiantly contemptuous of radical speculations. The Church that he defended rested on foundations that spanned the entire Roman world. Decades earlier, while travelling through Asia Minor on his way to Rome, Ignatius, a bishop from Syria, had proudly defined it as *katholikos*: 'universal'[20]. This—the catholic Church—was the one with which Irenaeus identified.

Even so, despite his claim to be defending primal Christian tradition, he was not above appropriating the innovations of his rivals when it suited his purpose. Although most of them, as he dismissively pointed out, alleged that 'truth was to be derived elsewhere than from written documents',[21] the most formidable had not. Marcion was a Christian from the Black Sea coast, a wealthy shipping magnate whose arrival in Rome some four decades before Irenaeus travelled there had generated a sensation. Outraged that the churches in the capital refused to accommodate his teachings, he had indignantly turned his back on them and founded his own. Marcion, like numerous other Christian intellectuals, was revolted by any notion that Christ might have had a human body, with human limitations and human functions—but that was hardly the most eye-opening of his teachings. Altogether more so was his take on the God of Israel, who, so Marcion had insisted, was not the supreme deity at all. Instead, he was the lesser of two gods. The supreme God, the God who was the true father of Christ, had not created the world, nor ever had anything to do with it, until, in his infinite mercy, he had sent his son to redeem it. A novel and startling doctrine—but manifest, so Marcion had claimed, in the contradictions between Jewish scripture and the letters of Paul. Rather than struggle to square these differences, he had instead proposed, as a means of calibrating God's true purpose, a precise and infallible measuring device, like the chalked string used by carpenters to mark a straight line: in Greek, a *canon*. Christians, so Marcion had taught, should regard as definitive only a closed selection of writings: ten of Paul's letters, and a carefully edited version of the gospel written by his follower Luke. Here, in place of Jewish scripture, was a witness to the divine purpose that Christians could authentically regard as their own: a new testament.[22] It was a momentous innovation. Never before—so far as we know—had a Christian proposed a canon. The concept was one that Irenaeus found too suggestive to ignore.

Naturally, not sharing Marcion's contemptuous attitude towards Jewish scripture, Irenaeus made sure to reinstate it at the head of his own canon. It was, so he declared, essential reading for all Christians: 'a field in which hidden treasure is revealed and explained by the cross of Christ'.[23] Yet Irenaeus, even as he sought to repudiate Marcion's influence, could not help but betray it. In what role, after all, was he casting Jewish scripture, if not as an 'old testament'? What hope of finding treasure in it, except by the light of a new? This was why, just as Marcion had done fifty years previously, Irenaeus promoted a corpus of writings from the age of the apostles. Alongside Luke's gospel, he included John's, and the two others most widely accepted as authoritative: one attributed to Matthew, a tax-collector summoned by Jesus to follow him, and the second to Mark, the reputed founder of the church in Alexandria. Compared to these, so Irenaeus declared, all other accounts of Christ's life and teachings were but 'ropes woven out of sand'.[24] As the generations passed, and the memories of those who had known the apostles with them, so could the faithful find in the gospels of Irenaeus' canon a sure and certain mooring to the bedrock of the past: a new testament indeed.

'I AM A CHRISTIAN.'[25] So a prisoner from Vienne arrested in 177 had replied to every question put to him by his interrogators. Rather than tell them his name, or where he had been born, or whether he were slave or free, he had instead repeatedly insisted that he had no status save that of a follower of Christ. Such obduracy, to his judges, was baffling as well as infuriating. The refusal of Christians to identify themselves as belonging to one of the familiar peoples of the earth— the Romans, or the Greeks, or the Jews—branded them as rootless, just as bandits and runaways were. Their delight in posing as aliens, as transients, made a boast out of what should properly have been a cause of shame. 'To them, a homeland is a foreign country, and a foreign country a homeland.'[26] And yet, for all that, Christians did believe they belonged to a common *ethnos*: a people. The bonds of their shared identity spanned the world, and reached back across the generations. When the martyrs of Lyon and Vienne embraced death for the sake of their Lord, they knew themselves bound in fellowship with others who had suffered a similar fate: in Jerusalem, in Asia Minor, in Rome. They knew themselves as well to stand in a line of descent from those martyrs who had gone before them: Polycarp, and Ignatius, and Paul. They knew their citizenship to be that of heaven.

The feat of Irenaeus, labouring in the wake of their deaths, was to give substance and solidity to these convictions. Already, within his own lifetime, his achievements and those of Christians who thought like him were becoming apparent even to hostile observers. They led an organisation that, in its scale and scope, was not merely one among a crowd of churches, but something altogether more impos- ing: the 'Great Church'.[27] Never before had there been anything quite like it: a citizenship that was owed not to birth, nor to descent, nor to legal prescriptions, but to belief alone.

Living Stones

The Roman elite, of course, had their own views on how a universal order should properly be constituted. The surest way to shape one out of all the manifold peoples of the world—as Posidonius had long before pointed out to Pompey—was for Rome to rule the lot. In 212, an edict was issued that would have warmed the old Stoic's heart. By its terms, all free men across the vast expanse of the empire were granted Roman citizenship. Its author, a thuggish Caesar by the name of Marcus Aurelius Severus Antoninus, was a living embodiment of the increasingly cosmopolitan character of the Roman world. The son of an African nobleman, he had been proclaimed emperor in Britain and was nicknamed *Caracalla*— 'Hoodie'—after his fondness for Gallic fashions. He understood, as only a man who had toured the world could, how various were the customs of humanity—and it perturbed him. Caracalla, who had seized power over the corpse of his murdered brother, knew what he owed the gods for their backing, and did not care to think that sacrifices made on his behalf might be failing to please them. This was why, despite the sneers of his critics that he was only interested in broadening the tax-base, he had granted a common citizenship to all the peoples of the empire. The more Roman they became, the more pleasing to the heavens their cults were bound to be. 'So it is that I think my act worthy of the majesty of the gods.'[28] Caracalla's divine patrons, who had bestowed on him and on Rome the rule of the world, were at last to receive their proper due: their *religio*.

The word came incense-trailed in the imaginings of pious Romans by a sense of deep antiquity. It conjured up for them visions of primordial rites: of the honours paid to the gods back in the very earliest days of their city, and which had first served to win divine favour for Rome. As in Greek cities, the abiding dread was of what might happen should rituals be neglected. Any obligation owed the gods in exchange for their protection, any tradition or custom, constituted a *religio*. 'Sacrificial offerings, the chastity of virgins, the whole range of priesthoods garlanded with dignity and titles':[29] all were *religiones*. But even Rome was merely one among a vast number of cities. Caracalla knew that as well as anyone. Hence the need for *religiones* that could join all the peoples of the world. The emperor, in his decree, boasted that he would lead them in a single procession 'to the sanctuaries of the gods'. That he had one sanctuary particularly in mind was made clear when, in the autumn of 215, he arrived in Egypt. His night-time entry into Alexandria, complete with 'torch-lit processions and garlands',[30] shared in the splendour of the city's most celebrated festival, when the dark streets would be lit up in honour of Serapis. The god held a particular place in Caracalla's affections. Even before travelling to Egypt, he had commissioned a Serapeum in Rome. Inscriptions in Alexandria proclaimed him *Philoserapis*: 'Devoted to Serapis.' The appeal of the city's most multi-cultural god was evident. Nevertheless, the cult the emperor wished to promote was not primarily that of Serapis. On coins, the god was shown passing the sceptre of the cosmos to another figure: the emperor himself. Just as Serapis, the divine father, ruled in the heavens, so did Caracalla, haloed and radiant, exercise a rule no less universal on earth. In the wake of his grant of citizenship to all the peoples of the empire, it was Caesar alone who could worthily mediate between them and their various gods. The great web of dues and obligations that had always bound the Roman people to the dimension of the supernatural now spanned the world. To poke a hole in it was not merely sacrilege but treason.

The full implications of this were soon to drench the streets of Alexandria in blood. Caracalla, who was rumoured to put to death anyone who so much as urinated in the presence of his portrait busts, was not a man to disrespect. The Alexandrians, who found his affectations risible, and made sure to let him know it, discovered this too late. Caracalla, summoning them to a public meeting, had the crowd surrounded by his troops and cut to pieces. The lesson could not have been more brutally rubbed home. Sacrilege was intolerable. To be a Roman citizen brought responsibility as well as honour. Any insult to Caesar was an insult to the gods. All that winter, Caracalla's indignation continued to smoulder. His soldiers, roaming the streets, killed and plundered at will. Most Alexandrians had no option save to cower, and wait for the emperor's departure. Not all, though. Some—those able to find refuge abroad—opted to slip away. Among them was a man particularly renowned for his meditations on the nature of the divine, and on the proper relationship of mortals to the heavens: the most brilliant scholar in a city renowned for its scholarship.

Yet Origen enjoyed no cushy billet, as intellectuals in Alexandria had traditionally done. Well before the arrival of Caracalla, he had learned to dread the Roman state's capacity for violence. In 202, when he was only seventeen, his father had been arrested and beheaded; Origen himself, in the years that followed, frequently had to evade angry lynch mobs, 'moving from house to house, driven from pillar to post'.[31] The son of Christian parents, his precocious commitment to the defence of his faith was steeled by adversity. Like Irenaeus—whose writings had reached Alexandria within only a few years of their composition—he dreaded that the Great Church was under constant siege. Only by delineating its frontiers so that none could ever mistake them, and lining them with fortifications, could it hope to be defended. The need was as pressing in Alexandria as anywhere in the Christian world. The city teemed with adversaries. It was where Basilides had founded his school. It was where, for many centuries, Jewish society had shown its most cosmopolitan face. Above all, it was where the great conqueror who had founded the city boasted his ultimate monument, a vision of Greece stamped on Egyptian soil, so that there was nowhere, not in Athens, not in Rome, where the study of Homer and Aristotle was more fruitfully nourished. To live in Alexandria—even for the most devout follower of Christ—was to experience the full dazzling potency of Greek culture.

Origen, though, was nothing daunted. Christians might have no monuments to compare with those that had drawn Caracalla to the city, no rivals to the massive bulk of the Serapeum; but they did not need them. 'All of us who believe in Christ Jesus are said to be living stones.'[32] Here, constructed out of the world's Christians, and with Christ himself as 'the chief cornerstone',[33] was the great temple that Origen aimed to buttress against its adversaries. Unlike the homelands of other peoples, that of the Christian people existed beyond the dimensions of altars, and hearth-fires, and fields. Indeed, without their belief in Christ as Lord, it would not have existed at all. It was Ignatius, a century before Origen, who had first given it the name that would endure forever after.[34] *Christianismos*, he had called it: 'Christianity'.

'Every time we understand,' wrote Origen, 'we owe it to our faith that we understand.'[35] So novel was what Christians meant by *Christianismos* that it could not help but colour the way that they saw the rest of the world. The various *haereses* taught by Basilides and his ilk did not, in the opinion of Origen, constitute simply a range of different opinions and philosophies, but rather a hydra-headed parody of the one True Church. *Ioudaismos*, a word that in the centuries before Christ had sometimes signified a Jewish way of life, and sometimes its propagation and defence, had come to possess for Christians a much more precise meaning, one that cast Jews as the citizens of a presumed counterpoint to 'Christianity': 'Judaism'. Most baneful of all, though, were the cults of those whom Paul had termed 'outsiders':[36] those who, from the rising to the setting of the sun, set up idols. Christians, precisely because they defined themselves in terms of their faith, could not help but assume the same of those who worshipped other gods. That a *Philoserapis* like Caracalla was concerned pre-eminently not with whether Serapis existed or not, but rather with honouring him in the mandated way, with respecting the taboos that hedged about his worship, and with paying him the correct dues of sacrifice, tended to pass them by. Even Origen, who knew perfectly well that many of those who made offerings to idols 'do not take them for gods, but only as offerings dedicated to the gods',[37] shuddered before the horror that such rituals seemed to imply. To spatter an altar with gore betrayed much about the beings that could demand such an offering. That they battened onto carcasses. That they were vampiric in their appetites. 'That they delighted in blood.'[38] To propitiate them was to feed the very forces that threatened humanity with darkness.

Yet there was a paradox. Origen, for all his hostility towards the seductions and the assumptions of the great city in which he lived, remained a native of it through and through. More completely, perhaps, than anyone before him, he blended Alexandria's various traditions within himself. Diverse though the city was, it had never been a true melting pot. The interest that many Greeks took in Jewish teachings, and that many Jews took in philosophy, had always been circumscribed by the prescriptions of the Mosaic covenant. Christianity, though, provided a matrix in which the Jewish and the Greek were able to mingle as well as meet. No one demonstrated this to more fruitful effect than Origen. A devotion to Christianity's inheritance from the Jews was manifest in all he wrote. Not only did he go to the effort of learning Hebrew from a Jewish teacher, but the Jewish people themselves he hailed as family: as the Church's 'little sister', or else 'the brother of the bride'.[39] Marcion's sneer that orthodox Christians were Jew-lovers was not one that Origen would necessarily have disputed. Certainly, he did more to embed the great body of Jewish scripture within the Christian canon, and to enshrine it as an 'Old Testament', than anyone before or since. A critic as honest as he was subtle, he did not deny the challenge that this represented. That the sacred books of the Jews, their *biblia*, were rife 'with riddles, parables, dark sayings, and various other forms of obscurity'[40] he readily acknowledged. Yet all of them derived from God. Contradictions only hinted at hidden truths. The challenge for the reader was to access them. Scripture was like a mansion with an immense number of locked rooms, and an equal number of keys, all of which lay scattered about the house. This haunting image, so Origen declared, had been suggested to him by his Hebrew teacher; and yet, in his own efforts to track down the keys, to open the locked doors, he relied on methods that derived from a very different source. In the great library of Alexandria, scholars had long been honing methods for making sense of ancient texts: treating their subject matter as allegory, and their language as an object of the most methodical study. Origen, in his own commentaries, adopted both techniques. Jewish the great mansion of the Old Testament may have been; but the surest method for exploring it was Greek.

'Whatever men have rightly said, no matter who or where, is the property of us Christians.'[41] That God had spoken to the Greeks as well as to the Jews was not a theory that originated with Origen. Just as Paul, in his correspondence, had approvingly cited the Stoic concept of conscience, so had many Christians since found in philosophy authentic glimmerings of the divine. No one in the Church, though, had ever before rivalled Origen for his sheer mastery of the discipline. Schooled in the classics of Greek literature since childhood, and familiar with the most cutting-edge work of his philosophical contemporaries, he identified in it the same quest to which he had devoted his own life: the search for God. Christianity, in Origen's opinion, was not merely compatible with philosophy, but the ultimate expression of it. 'No one can truly do duty to God,' he declared, 'who does not think like a philosopher.'[42] Sure enough, even when Origen left Alexandria he never forgot his roots in the capital of Greek learning. First in 215, in temporary flight from Caracalla, and then again in 234 on a permanent basis, he settled in Caesarea, a port on the coast of what he termed the 'Holy Land'—and established there a school that embodied the very best of his native city. 'No subject was forbidden us,' one of his students would later recall, 'nothing hidden or put away. Every doctrine—Greek or not—we were encouraged to study. All the good things of the mind were ours to enjoy.'[43]

Naturally, Origen did not propose that philosophy be studied as an end in itself. That, he warned his students, would be to wander forever lost in a swamp, or a labyrinth, or a forest. Shot through with errors though the speculations of philosophers might be, they nevertheless could still help to illumine Christian truth. Just as traditions of textual inquiry honed in Alexandria had helped Origen to elucidate the complexities of Jewish scripture, so did he use philosophy to shed light on an even more profound puzzle: the nature of God himself. The need was urgent. The gospel proclaimed by Paul, the conviction that had animated him and all the first generation of Christians, the revelation that a crucified criminal had in some unspecified but manifest way been an aspect of the very Creator of the heavens and the earth, constituted the molten heart of Christianity. Yet it raised an obvious question. How, when Christians accorded Jesus a status that was somehow divine, could they possibly claim to worship only the single god? Greek philosophers no less than Jewish scholars, when they deigned to take note of the upstart faith, would relentlessly home in on this point. The challenge could not be ducked. The struggle, then, was to find an adequate way of expressing a mystery that seemed to defy expression. It was not just Jesus who had to be integrated into the oneness of God, but his Spirit as well. The solution, by the time Origen came to this puzzle, was already clear in its outline. The unity of God came, not in spite of his Son and Spirit, but through them. One was Three; Three were One. God was a Trinity.

It was Origen, though, more comprehensively and more brilliantly than anyone before him, who drew on the resources of philosophy to fashion for the Church an entire *theologia*: a science of God. The language he used to explore the paradoxes of the divine was deployed in the full knowledge of the uses to which it had long previously been put by a Xenocrates or a Zeno. His school in Caesarea, for all its insistence on the Christian canon as the ultimate summit of wisdom, was recognisably in a line of descent that reached back to

Aristotle, and beyond. No one, after Origen's labours in the service of his faith, would be able to charge that Christians appealed only to 'the ignorant, the stupid, the unschooled'.[44] The potency of this achievement, in a society that took for granted the value of education as an indicator of status, was immense. Contempt for those who lacked a grounding in philosophy ran deep. Knowledge—*gnosis*—was widely viewed as a definitive marker of class. Even Christians were not immune to this prejudice. When Irenaeus described teachers such as Basilides as 'Gnostics', he was identifying as their defining characteristic their claim to be better informed than everyone else. 'Tradition they scorn, insisting that they know things that neither the elders of the Church knew, nor even the apostles—for they alone have identified the unadulterated truth.'[45] This was the temptation against which Origen, in labouring to shape a theology that could satisfy the learned, had to guard. Much was at stake. Cults, after all, were rarely categorised as philosophies; nor philosophies cults. The claim of Christianity to a universal message could not rest merely on the presence of churches from Mesopotamia to Spain. It had to appeal to people of every class, and of every level of education. In a society that ranked philosophy alongside vintage statuary and exotic spices as one of the perks of the rich, Origen was a living, breathing paradox: a philosopher who defied elitism.

That an identity might be defined by belief was in itself a momentous innovation; but that the learned and the illiterate alike might be joined by it, 'becoming—despite their multitude—one single body',[46] was no less startling a notion. The genius of Origen was to create out of the inheritance of Greek philosophy an entire new universe of the mind—one in which even the least educated could share. When he hailed God as 'pure intelligence',[47] he was arguing nothing that Aristotle had not long previously said. Philosophy, though, was only the beginning of what Origen had to teach. The divine *nous*, far from lingering in the motionlessness of a chilly perfection, had descended to earth. The mystery of it was at once beyond the comprehension of even the greatest of scholars, and a cause of wonder that labourers and kitchen maids could admire. If Origen, drawing on the great treasury of Greek and Jewish literature, would sometimes describe Christ as divine reason, and sometimes as 'the stainless mirror of the activity of God',[48] then there were times as well when he confessed himself quite as stupefied as the littlest child. When contemplating how the Wisdom of God had entered the womb of a woman, and been born a baby, and cried for milk, the paradox of it all was too much even for him. 'For since we see in Christ some things so human that they appear to share in every aspect in the common frailty of humanity, and some things so divine that they are manifestly the expression of the primal and ineffable nature of the Divine, the narrowness of human understanding is inadequate to cope. Overcome with amazement and admiration, it knows not where to turn.'[49]

Here, in this fusion of deeply read sophistication and wide-eyed awe, was something recognisably of the seedbed of Alexandria—and yet also disconcertingly new. By scorning to see the contemplation of heaven's mysteries as philosophers had traditionally done, as the exclusive preserve of the educated and the wealthy, Origen had created a matrix for the propagation of philosophical concepts that would prove to have momentous reach. Far from damaging his reputation, his refusal to behave in the manner of a conventional philosopher ended up only enhancing his fame. Turning sixty, Origen could reflect with pride on a career so influential that even the mother of an emperor, intrigued by his celebrity, had once summoned him to instruct her in the nature of God. Such fame, though, was as likely to stoke hostility as admiration. The age was a treacherous one. The violence brought by Caracalla to the streets of Alexandria had been an ominous portent of even darker times ahead. In the decades that followed, sorrows had come not as single spies, but in battalions. Caracalla himself, murdered while relieving himself on campaign, had been just one of a succession of emperors slain in a blizzard of assassinations and civil wars. Meanwhile, taking full advantage of the escalating chaos, barbarian warbands had begun to seep across the frontiers. On the empire's eastern doorstep, a new Persian dynasty—the most formidable to have emerged since the time of Darius—visited a succession of humiliations on Roman power. The gods, it seemed, were angry. The correct *religiones* were manifestly being neglected. The fault, in the wake of Caracalla's mass grant of citizenship, lay not just in Rome, but in the empire as a whole. Accordingly, early in 250, a formal decree was issued that everyone—with the sole exception of the Jews—offer up sacrifice to the gods. Disobedience was equated with treason; and the punishment for treason was death. For the first time, Christians found themselves confronted by legislation that directly obliged them to choose between their lives and their faith. Many chose to save their skins—but many did not. Among those arrested was Origen. Although put in chains and racked, he refused to recant. Spared execution, he was released after days of brutal treatment a broken man. He never recovered. A year or so later, the aged scholar was dead of the sufferings inflicted on him by his torturers.

The magistrate presiding over his case, respectful of his reputation, had taken no pleasure in the torments inflicted on such a brilliant man. As they had ever done, the Roman authorities found the refusal of Christians to make sacrifice to the gods as pig-headed as it was subversive. Why citizens who insisted on their loyalty to the empire should refuse to demonstrate it and simply make a pledge of allegiance bewildered them. That a ritual sanctified by both tradition and patriotism might cause anyone offence was an idea that they struggled to comprehend. Origen had been put to torture as much in sorrow as in anger.

How different it would have been, of course, had the empire itself been Christian! A remote, a fantastical possibility—and yet, just a couple of years before his arrest, Origen himself had thought to float it. 'Should the Romans embrace the Christian faith,' he had declared, 'then their prayers would see them overcome their enemies; or rather, having come under the protection of God, they would have no enemies at all.'[50]

But to believe that a Caesar might be won for Christ was indeed to believe in miracles.

Keeping the Faith

In the summer of 313, Carthage was a city on edge. An ancient rival of Rome for the rule of the western Mediterranean, destroyed by the legions and then—just as Corinth had been—refounded as a Roman colony, its commanding position on the coastline across from Sicily had won for it an undisputed status as the capital of Africa. Like Rome and Alexandria, it had grown to become one of the great centres of Christianity: a status much seeded, in the words of one Carthaginian Christian, by 'the blood of the martyrs'.[51] In Africa, the Church had long treasured the scars of persecution. The judicial execution in 258 of Carthage's most celebrated bishop, a noted scholar by the name of Cyprian, had confirmed them in a peculiarly militant understanding of their faith. Purity was all. There could be no compromising with the evils of the world. Belief was nothing if it was not worth dying for. This was why, in 303, when an imperial edict was issued commanding Christians to hand over their books of scripture or face death, Africa had been at the forefront of resistance to the decree. The provincial authorities, determined to break the Church, had expanded on the edict by commanding that everyone make sacrifice to the gods. Recalcitrant Christians were rounded up and brought in chains to Carthage. Batches of them had been executed. By the time, two years later, that the persecution finally petered out, the conviction of Christians across Africa that God demanded a purity of belief, absolute and untainted, had been fertilised with yet more martyrs' blood. Ten years on from the most savage persecution endured by the church of Carthage, the mood in the city was anxious, fractious, fraught. The death of its bishop, Majorinus, served as a lightning rod for various tensions. One question predominated. How, in the wake of a concentrated effort to wipe the Church from the face of Africa, were Christians best to defend the sanctity of their faith?

Three centuries on from the birth of Christ, this was an issue with ramifications far beyond the Church itself. Bishops in the great cities were well on their way to becoming public figures. If the state was prone to targeting them with persecution, then so also, on occasion, might an emperor opt to grant them favours. Back in 260, only a decade after the arrest and torture of Origen, a change of regime had seen churches granted a particularly significant privilege: the right to own property. Bishops, already armed with considerable powers of patronage, had thereby accrued an even greater heft. That they were elected only served to enhance the potency and scope of their leadership. Authority such as theirs, exercised over growing flocks, was something that any Roman official might grudgingly respect. The devastating persecution launched in 303 had done nothing to diminish this. Indeed, if anything, the failure of the provincial authorities to uproot the Church served only to enhance the prestige of those leaders who had defied it. When, in the summer of 313, a new bishop was elected in succession to Majorinus, he might not have seemed, by the traditional standards of the Roman ruling classes, an impressive figure. Donatus came from Casae Nigrae, an obscure town far to the south of Carthage, perched on the fringes of the desert, 'where the burnt land bears nothing but venomous snakes'.[52] Yet this stern and rugged provincial—precisely because he rejected all markers of status—could lay claim to an influence in Carthage that owed nothing to either wealth or breeding. Power rendered him dangerous—and being dangerous made him feared.

The bishop's bitterest enemies, however, were not the provincial authorities. They were his fellow Christians. Donatus was not the only man to have claimed the leadership of the Carthaginian church. He had a rival. Caecilian had won the bishopric two years previously—but his election had been furiously contested. Able though he was, a forceful and experienced administrator, he was notorious for scorning the pre-eminence of martyrs as God's favourites. This reputation, even at the best of times, would have rendered him unacceptable to many Christians in Carthage; but the times were not the best. The Church in Africa was riven from top to bottom. While many of its leaders had upheld the conviction of one bishop that it was better for him 'to be burned in the fire than the holy scriptures', others had not. There were Christians who, in the heat of persecution, had handed them over. This, to Donatus and his followers, was a betrayal that could not be forgiven. Those who had surrendered the scriptures in their keep—the *traditores*, as they were contemptuously termed—were no longer seen as Christian. They had saved their skins at the cost of their souls. Their very voices were cancerous with infection. Only re-immersion in the waters of baptism could hope to cleanse them of their sin. Yet the *traditores*, far from acknowledging their fault, had installed as their bishop Caecilian, a man darkly rumoured not merely to have been a *traditor* himself, but to have colluded in the persecution of those who had refused to hand over the scriptures. Between two such opposed points of view, between those who insisted on defiance of the world and those who preferred to compromise with it, between Donatists and Caecilianists, what reconciliation could there possibly be? A grim and unsettling truth stood revealed: that shared beliefs might serve to divide as well as bring together the Christian people.

Donatus, in his ambition to heal the schism, naturally turned to the heavens. His followers believed with a devout literalism the claim of their bishop to have a direct line of communication with God. Nevertheless, in the absence of a divine response sufficient to persuade the Caecilianists, Donatus found himself with a pressing need for an alternative source of authority. Fortunately, only a year before his election as bishop, a miracle had occurred. Or so, at any rate, the events of 312 appeared to startled Christians. In that year, a renewed bout of civil war had shaken Italy. A claimant to the rule of Rome named Constantine had marched on the city. There, on the banks of the river Tiber, beside the Milvian Bridge, he had won a decisive victory. His rival had drowned in the river. Constantine, entering the ancient capital, had done so with the head of his defeated enemy held aloft on a spear. Provincial officials from Africa, summoned to meet their new master, had dutifully admired the trophy. Shortly afterwards, as a token of Constantine's greatness, it had been dispatched to Carthage. But so too had something much more unexpected. A package of letters arrived in the city, which betrayed clear Christian sympathies. The governor was instructed to restore to the church any possessions confiscated from it; Caecilian—who, shrewd operator that he was, had already made sure to write to Constantine, offering his most profuse congratulations—was personally assured of the emperor's sympathies for 'the most holy Catholic Church'.[53] Shortly afterwards, another letter from the emperor arrived in Carthage. In it, the governor was instructed to spare Caecilian and his fellow priests the burden of civic dues. Donatus, scandalised by the favouritism shown his rival, was nevertheless alert to its broader implications. Constantine was not merely gracing the Church with toleration: it was almost as though he had written as a Christian.

And so it proved. Over time, remarkable stories would be told of how Constantine had been won for Christ: of how, on the eve of his great victory at the Milvian Bridge, he had seen a cross in the sky, and then, in his dreams, been visited by the Saviour himself. For the rest of his life, the emperor would never doubt to whom he owed the rule of the world. Nevertheless, devoutly grateful though he was, it would take him time properly to fathom the full radical and disorienting character of his new patron. Initially, he viewed the Christian god as merely a variant upon a theme. The claim that there existed a single, all-powerful deity was hardly original to Jews or Christians, after all. Philosophers had been teaching it since at least the time of Xenophanes. That the Supreme Being ruled the universe much as an emperor ruled the world, delegating authority to functionaries, was an assumption that many in the Roman world had come to take for granted. Caracalla, arriving in Alexandria, had essentially been auditioning Serapis for the role. Others had awarded it to Jupiter or to Apollo. The ambition, as it had been for a century, was to define for all Roman citizens a single, universally accepted due of *religiones*— and thereby to provide for the empire, amid all the many crises racking it, the favour of the heavens. Constantine, by acknowledging the primacy of Christ, aspired to see Christians join with their fellow

citizens in the pursuit of this urgent goal. In 313, issuing a proclamation that for the first time gave a legal standing to Christianity, he
coyly refused to name 'the divinity who sits in heaven'.[54] The vague-
ness was deliberate. Christ or Apollo, Constantine wished to leave
the choice of whom his subjects identified as 'the supreme divinity'[55]
to them. Where there were divisions, he aimed to blur.

But then, sailing from Carthage, came Donatus. A man less committed to compromise it would have been hard to imagine. Even
before his election as bishop, he and his followers had taken the
momentous step of complaining to Constantine about Caecilian,
and demanding his deposition. The emperor, puzzled at finding such
divisions among Christians, nevertheless permitted Donatus to make
his case before a panel of bishops in Rome—who promptly found
against him. Donatus appealed; and again had his case rejected. Still
he pestered Constantine with complaints. When, in 316, he managed to slip the guards who had been placed on him by the weary
emperor, and make it back to Africa, his escape only confirmed Constantine's dark opinion of the bishop's contumacy. Henceforward,
in the bitter clash between Donatists and Caecilianists, it was the
latter who would have the might of the Roman state on their side.
'What business has the emperor with the Church?'[56] Donatus' question, suffused with outrage and resentment though it might be, was
in truth rhetorical. Constantine, no less than any bishop, believed
himself entrusted with a heavenly mission to uphold the unity of the
Christian people. The tradition embodied by Donatus, the conviction that the Church was most pleasing to God when its members
repudiated those of their fellows who had fallen into sin, perplexed
and infuriated him. 'Such squabbles and altercations,' he fretted,
'may perhaps provoke the highest deity not only against the human
race, but against myself.'[57] By giving Caecilian his support, Constantine was assuring bishops across the empire that, provided only that
they assented to the emperor's desire for a unified Church, they too
could rely on his backing. Donatus, meanwhile, had to live with the
painful knowledge that his claim to the leadership of Christians in

Africa was accepted by few beyond the limits of the province. It was the followers of Caecilius, in the eyes of the world, who were the authentic 'Catholics'; those of Donatus were 'Donatists' still.

Yet if bishops had to scramble to adjust to the new circumstances heralded by Constantine's victory at the Milvian Bridge, so too did the emperor himself. Fully committed as he was to understanding what it meant to be a servant of Christ, he found himself embarked on a steep learning curve. His altercations with Donatus had brought home to him just what he faced in the Church: an organisation over which, despite his rule of the world, he had no formal control whatsoever. Unlike the priests who traditionally had mediated between Rome and the heavens, bishops did not bother themselves with rites in which he, as the heir of Augustus, could take the lead. Instead, to Constantine's intense frustration, they insisted in squabbling over issues that seemed better suited to philosophers. In 324, alerted to the inveterate taste of theologians in Alexandria for debating the nature of Christ, he did not bother to conceal his impatience. 'When all this subtle wrangling of yours is over questions of little or no significance, why worry about harmonising your views? Why not instead consign your differences to the secret custody of your own minds and thoughts?'[58] Yet it was dawning on Constantine that these questions might be naïve. The issues of who Christ had truly been, in what way he could have been both human and divine, and how the Trinity was best defined, were hardly idle ones, after all. How could God properly be worshipped, and his approval for Rome's rule of the world thereby be assured, if his very nature was in dispute? Constantine's predecessors, with their attempts to appease the heavens by offering them their ancient dues of sacrifices and honours, had grievously misunderstood what was required of an emperor. 'It matters not how you worship, but what you worship.'[59] True *religio*, Constantine was coming to understand, was a matter less of ritual, less of splashing altars with blood or fumigating them with incense, than of correct belief.

A decisive moment. In 325, only a year after he had been advising rival theologians to resolve their differences, Constantine summoned bishops from across the empire, and even beyond, to a council. Its ambition was fittingly imperious: to settle on a statement of belief, a creed, that churches everywhere could then uphold. Canons, measures to prescribe the behaviour of the faithful, were to be defined as well. The venue for this great project, the city of Nicaea in the north-west of Asia Minor, was pointedly not a Christian powerbase. Constantine himself, 'clothed in raiment which blazed as though with rays of light',[60] welcomed his guests with a display that mingled graciousness with just the faintest hint of menace. When at length, after an entire month of debate, a creed was finally settled upon, and twenty canons drawn up, those few delegates who refused to accept them were formally banished. The fusion of theology with Roman bureaucracy at its most controlling resulted in an innovation never before attempted: a declaration of belief that proclaimed itself universal. The sheer number of delegates, drawn from locations ranging from Mesopotamia to Britain, gave to their deliberations a weight that no single bishop or theologian could hope to rival. For the first time, orthodoxy possessed what even the genius of Origen had struggled to provide: a definition of the Christian god that could be used to measure heresy with precision. In time, weighed in the balance against the Nicaean Creed, Origen's own formulations on the nature of the Trinity would themselves be condemned as heretical. A new formulation, written, as Origen's had been, in the language of philosophy, declared the Father and the Son to be *homoousios*: 'of one substance'. Christ, so the Nicaean Creed proclaimed, was 'the only Son of God, eternally begotten of the Father, God from God, Light from Light, true God from true God, begotten not made'. Never before had a committee authored phrases so far-reaching in their impact. The long struggle of Christians to articulate the paradox that lay at the heart of their faith, to define how a man tortured to death on a cross could also have been divine, had at last attained an enduring resolution. A creed that still, many centuries after it was written, would continue to join otherwise divided churches, and give substance to the ideal of a single Christian people, had more than met Constantine's hopes for his council. Only a seasoned imperial administrator could possibly have pulled it off. A century after Caracalla's grant of citizenship to the entire Roman world, Constantine had hit upon a momentous discovery: that the surest way to join a people as one was to unite them not in common rituals, but in a common belief.

Yet faith, as he had already discovered, could divide as well as unify. His triumph at Nicaea was only a partial one. Bishops and theologians continued to quarrel. Even Constantine himself, in the final years of his life, found his loyalty to the provisions of the Nicaean Creed starting to fray. On his death in 337, he was succeeded to the rule of the eastern half of the empire by a son, Constantius, who actively rejected them, and promoted instead an understanding of Christ as subordinate to God the Father. Disputes that previously had been of concern only to obscure sectarians were now the very stuff of imperial politics. Approval or repudiation of the Nicaean Creed added to the endless swirl of dynastic ambitions an entirely new dimension of rivalry. At issue, though, was not merely personal ambition. The entire future of humanity, so Constantine and his heirs believed, was at stake. The duty of an emperor to secure the stability of the world by practising the correct *religio* meant, increasingly, that theologians were as likely to feature in his concerns as generals or bureaucrats. Unless the favour of God could be secured, what value armies or taxes? Christianity was 'the true worship of the true god',[61] or it was nothing.

In Carthage, of course, they had long known that. In 325, when Caecilian returned from Nicaea, his part in the great council held there did nothing to temper the loathing felt for him by the followers of Donatus. Even when Donatus died in exile some three decades later, the schism refused to be healed. This was hardly surprising. It was not the personal ambitions of the rival bishops that had stoked the mutual hatreds of their followers—nor anything else that provincial officials, desperate to keep order in Africa, could read-ily understand. When Donatists stripped a Catholic bishop naked, hauled him to the top of a tower and flung him into a pile of excre-ment, or tied a necklace of dead dogs around the neck of another, or pulled out the tongue of a third, and cut off his right hand, they were behaving in a manner that might have appeared calculated to baffle the average Roman bureaucrat. That differences of doctrine might divide the Christian people was a realisation that Constantine had fast had to come to terms with; but it was not doctrine that divided them in Africa. The hatred ran much deeper than that. Donatists who seized a church from Catholics would make sure to paint its walls white, scrub its floors with salt and wash its furnishings. Only in this manner, they believed, could the building be cleansed of con-tamination: the contamination of opponents who had compromised with the world.

What was the surest way to plant anew the Garden of Eden on earth? Was it, as the Donatists argued, to raise a wall against the clutching of briars and nettles, and to tend only those narrow flower beds that were manifestly clear of weeds? Or was it, as their oppo-nents insisted, to attempt the planting of the whole world with seeds? 'Grant to God that His garden be spread far and wide.' So one Cath-olic bishop, responding to the Donatist charge that he had made common cause with the world as it was, rather than as it should be, urged his opponents. 'Why do you deny to God the Christian peoples of East and North, let alone those of the provinces of the West, and of all the innumerable islands with whom you share no fellowship of communion, and against whom you—rebels that you are, and few in number—range yourselves?'[62] The hatreds roused by this bitter disagreement—perplexing though they might seem to anyone not raised in the traditions of the African church—proved impossible to resolve. Constantine himself, after his brief foray into the Donatist controversy, had ended up distracted by more pressing issues. The terrorism practised by Catholics and Donatists, endemic though it fast became, was not of an order to disturb the transport of grain from the province to Rome—and so, by and large, they were left alone. Decades on from the deaths of both Caecilian and Donatus, the killings continued, the divisions widened, and the sense of moral certitude on both sides grew ever more entrenched.

For the first time, two fundamental dimensions of Christian behaviour had been brought into direct conflict on the public stage of an imperial province. Whether God's people were best understood as an elect of the godly or as a flock of sinners was a question without a conclusive answer. For all the ultimate success of the Catholic leadership in isolating their rivals from the mainstream of the Church, the appeal of the cause represented by the Donatists could not entirely be suppressed. A signpost was pointing to a new and radical future. Throughout Christian history, the yearning to reject a corrupt and contaminated world, to refuse any compromise with it, to aspire to a condition of untainted purity, would repeatedly manifest itself. The implications of this tendency would, in time, be felt far beyond the Church itself. A pattern had been set that, over the course of millennia, would come to shape the very contours of politics. Constantine, by accepting Christ as his Lord, had imported directly into the heart of his empire a new, unpredictable and fissile source of power.

5

CHARITY

AD 362: Pessinus

The new emperor, heading across Galatia, found signs of decay in every temple he visited. Paint flaked from statues, and altars stood unsplashed by blood. The strut of the ancient gods had, in recent decades, become a cringe. Nowhere, perhaps, was this more evident than in Pessinus. Here, since primordial times, Cybele had her seat. Once her castrated priests had ruled the entire city. It was from Pessinus, in 204 BC, that the first statue of the goddess to arrive in Rome had been sent. Half a millennium on, pilgrims still took the road there to pay honour to the Divine Mother. Fewer and fewer, though. Even in Pessinus itself, Cybele's hold was slipping. The great bulk of her temple, which for centuries had dominated the city, increasingly stood as a monument not to her potency, but to her fading.

The shock of this cut Flavius Claudius Julianus to the quick. The nephew of Constantine, he had been raised a Christian, with eunuchs set over him to keep him constant in his faith. As a young man, though, he had repudiated Christianity—and then, after becoming emperor in 361, had committed himself to claiming back from it those who had 'abandoned the ever-living gods for the corpse of the Jew'.[1] A brilliant scholar, a dashing general, Julian was also a man as devout in his beliefs as any of those he dismissively termed

'Galileans'. Cybele was a particular object of his devotions. It was she, he believed, who had rescued him from the darkness of his childhood beliefs. Unsurprisingly, then, heading eastwards to prepare for war with Persia, he had paused in his journey to make a diversion to Pessinus. What he found there appalled him. Even after he had made sacrifice, and honoured those who had stayed constant in their worship of the city's gods, he could not help but dwell in mingled anger and despondency on the neglect shown Cybele. Clearly, the people of Pessinus were unworthy of her patronage. Leaving the Galatians behind, he did as Paul had done three centuries before: he wrote them a letter.

Or rather, he wrote to their high priest. Julian, in his struggle to explain why the worship of Cybele had fallen into such desuetude, did not content himself with blaming the ignorant and weakminded. The true blame, he charged, lay with the priests themselves. Far from devoting themselves to the poor, they lived lives of wild abandon. This had to end. In a world rife with suffering, why were priests getting drunk in taverns? Their time would be better spent, so Julian sternly informed them, in providing succour for the needy. To that end, subsidies of food and drink would be provided out of his own funds, and sent annually to Galatia. 'My orders are that a fifth be given to the poor who serve the priests, and that the remainder be distributed to travellers and to beggars.'[2] Julian, in committing himself to this programme of welfare, took for granted that Cybele would approve. Caring for the weak and unfortunate, so the emperor insisted, had always been a prime concern of the gods. If only the Galatians could be brought to appreciate this, then they might be brought as well to renew their ancient habits of worship. 'Teach them that doing good works was our practice of old.'[3]

An assertion that would no doubt have come as news to the celebrants of Cybele themselves. Behind the selfless ascetics of Julian's fantasies there lurked an altogether less sober reality: priests whose enthusiasms had run not to charity, but to dancing, and cross-dressing, and self-castration. The gods cared nothing for the poor. To think otherwise was 'airhead talk'.[4] When Julian, writing to the high priest of Galatia, quoted Homer on the laws of hospitality, and how even beggars might appeal to them, he was merely drawing attention to the scale of his delusion. The heroes of the *Iliad*, favourites of the gods, golden and predatory, had scorned the weak and downtrodden. So too, for all the honour that Julian paid them, had philosophers. The starving deserved no sympathy. Beggars were best rounded up and deported. Pity risked undermining a wise man's self-control. Only fellow citizens of good character who, through no fault of their own, had fallen on evil days might conceivably merit assistance. Certainly, there was little in the character of the gods whom Julian so adored, nor in the teachings of the philosophers whom he so admired, to justify any assumption that the poor, just by virtue of their poverty, had a right to aid. The young emperor, sincere though he was in his hatred of 'Galilean' teachings, and in regretting their impact upon all that he held most dear, was blind to the irony of his plan for combating them: that it was itself irredeemably Christian.

'How apparent to everyone it is, and how shameful, that our own people lack support from us, when no Jew ever has to beg, and the impious Galileans support not only their own poor, but ours as well.'[5] Julian could not but be painfully aware of this. The roots of Christian charity ran deep. The apostles, obedient to Jewish tradition as well as to the teachings of their master, had laid it as a solemn charge upon new churches always 'to remember the poor'.[6] Generation after generation, Christians had held true to this injunction. Every week, in churches across the Roman world, collections for orphans and widows, for the imprisoned, and the shipwrecked, and the sick had been raised. Over time, as congregations swelled, and ever more of the wealthy were brought to baptism, the funds available for poor relief had grown as well. Entire systems of social security had begun to emerge. Elaborate and well-organised, these had progressively embedded themselves within the great cities of the Mediterranean. Constantine, by recruiting bishops to his purposes, had also recruited the networks of charity of which they served as the principal patrons. Julian, clear-sighted in his loathing of the Galileans, understood this very well. Trains of clients, in the Roman world, had always been an index of power—and bishops, by that measure, were grown very powerful indeed. The wealthy, men who in previous generations might have boosted their status by endowing their cities with theatres, or temples, or bath-houses, had begun to find in the Church a new vent for their ambitions. This was why Julian, in a quixotic attempt to endow the worship of the ancient gods with a similar appeal, had installed a high priest over Galatia and urged his subordinates to practise poor relief. Christians did not merely inspire in Julian a profound contempt; they filled him with envy as well.

His adversaries named him the Apostate, a turncoat from his faith; but Julian likewise felt betrayed. Leaving Galatia, he continued eastwards into Cappadocia, a rugged landscape famed for the quality of its horses and its lettuces, and which the emperor knew well. As a boy, he had been kept there under effective detention by a suspicious Constantius, and so was perfectly familiar with the character of the local notables. One, in particular, might almost have been a mirror image of himself. Basil, like Julian, was a man deeply versed in Greek literature and philosophy, a one-time student in Athens, and renowned for his powers of oratory. He was, in short, precisely the kind of man the emperor hoped to recruit to his side— except that Basil had embarked on the opposite path to Julian. Far from repudiating his upbringing as a Christian, it was instead his initial career as a lawyer that he had abandoned. Committing both his energies and his fortune to Christ, he and his younger brother, a brilliantly original theologian named Gregory, had fast developed international reputations. Even though Basil did not meet with Julian during the emperor's progress through Cappadocia, such was his celebrity that many, feeling that the two most famous men of the age really should have confronted one another, took the matter into their own hands.* When, a year after leaving Asia Minor, Julian perished in Mesopotamia fighting the Persians, a soldier in his train wrote an account of how Basil had, in a vision, seen Christ personally send a saint to dispatch him with a spear. While there was no one, in the wake of the emperor's death, to continue his counterrevolution, both Basil and Gregory went from strength to strength. In 370, the elder brother was elected bishop of Caesarea, the capital of Cappadocia; two years later, the younger was appointed to a new bishopric on the main road to Galatia, at Nyssa. Both were renowned for their labours on behalf of the poor; both, as a consequence, came to wield an influence that extended far beyond the borders of their native land. Julian's insight was confirmed: charity might indeed breed power.

Yet that did not mean that his own strategy had been any the less doomed. A concern for the downtrodden could not merely be summoned into existence out of nothing. The logic that inspired two wealthy and educated men such as Basil and Gregory to devote their lives to the poor derived from the very fundamentals of their faith. 'Do not despise these people in their abjection; do not think they merit no respect.' So Gregory urged. 'Reflect on who they are, and you will understand their dignity; they have taken upon them the person of our Saviour. For he, the compassionate, has given them his own person.'[7] Gregory, more clearly than anyone before him, traced the implications of Christ's choice to live and die as one of the poor to its logical conclusion. Dignity, which no philosopher had ever taught might be possessed by the stinking, toiling masses, was for all. There was no human existence so wretched, none so despised or vulnerable, that it did not bear witness to the image of God. Divine love for the outcast and derelict demanded that mortals love them too.

---

* A letter from Julian to Basil would subsequently be forged, in which the emperor expressed his admiration for the recipient.

This was the conviction that in 369, on the outskirts of a Caesarea ravaged by famine, prompted Basil to embark on a radical new
building project. Other Christian leaders before him had built *pto-
cheia*, or 'poor houses'—but none on such an ambitious scale. The
Basileias, as it came to be known, was described by one awe-struck
admirer as a veritable city, and incorporated, as well as shelter for
the poor, what was in effect the first hospital. Basil, who had studied medicine while in Athens, did not himself scorn to tend the sick.
Even lepers, whose deformities and suppurations rendered them
objects of particular revulsion, might be welcomed by the bishop
with a kiss, and given both refuge and care. The more broken men
and women were, the readier was Basil to glimpse Christ in them.
The spectacle in a slave market of a boy sold by his starving parents,
the one child sacrificed that his siblings might have some few scraps
of food, provoked the bishop to a particularly scorching excoriation
of the rich. 'The bread in your board belongs to the hungry; the cloak
in your wardrobe to the naked; the shoes you let rot to the barefoot;
the money in your vaults to the destitute.'[8] The days when a wealthy
man had only to sponsor a self-aggrandising piece of architecture to
be hailed a public benefactor were well and truly gone.

Basil's brother went even further. Gregory was moved by the existence of slavery not just to condemn the extremes of wealth and poverty, but to define the institution itself as an unpardonable offence
against God. Human nature, so he preached, had been constituted
by its Creator as something free. As such, it was literally priceless.
'Not all the universe would constitute an adequate payment for the
soul of a mortal.'[9] This, for his congregation, was altogether too radical, too seditious a perspective to take seriously: for how, as Basil
himself put it, were those of inferior intelligence and capabilities to
survive, if not as slaves? Unsurprisingly, then, Gregory's abolitionism met with little support. The existence of slavery as damnable but
necessary continued to be taken for granted by most Christians—
Basil included. Only when heaven was joined with earth would it
cease to exist. Gregory's impassioned insistence that to own slaves

was 'to set one's own power above God's',[10] and to trample on a dignity that was properly the right of every man and woman, fell like seed among thorns.

But there was seed as well that fell on good ground. Lepers and slaves were not the most defenceless of God's children. Across the Roman world, wailing at the sides of roads or on rubbish tips, babies abandoned by their parents were a common sight. Others might be dropped down drains, there to perish in the hundreds. The odd eccentric philosopher aside, few had ever queried this practice. Indeed, there were cities who by ancient law had made a positive virtue of it: condemning to death deformed infants for the good of the state. Sparta, one of the most celebrated cities in Greece, had been the epitome of this policy, and Aristotle himself had lent it the full weight of his prestige. Girls in particular were liable to be winnowed ruthlessly. Those who were rescued from the wayside would invariably be raised as slaves. Brothels were full of women who, as infants, had been abandoned by their parents—so much so that it had long provided novelists with a staple of their fiction. Only a few peoples—the odd German tribe and, inevitably, the Jews—had stood aloof from the exposure of unwanted children. Pretty much everyone else had always taken it for granted. Until, that was, the emergence of a Christian people.

What the implications might be for infants tossed out with the trash was best demonstrated not by Basil, nor by Gregory, but by their sister. Macrina, the eldest of nine siblings, was in many ways the most influential of them all. She it was who had persuaded her brother to abandon the law and devote himself to Christ; similarly, she could be hailed by Gregory as the most brilliant of his instructors. Erudite, charismatic and formidably ascetic, she devoted herself to a renunciation of the world's pleasures so absolute as to fill her contemporaries with awe; and yet she did not abandon the world altogether. When famine held Cappadocia in its grip, and 'flesh clung to the bones of the poor like cobwebs',[11] then Macrina would make a tour of the refuse tips. Those infant girls she rescued she would take home and raise as her own. Whether it was Macrina who had taught Gregory, or Gregory Macrina, both believed that within even the most defenceless newborn child there might be glimpsed a touch of the divine. Perhaps it was no coincidence that Cappadocia and its neighbouring regions, where—even by the standards of other lands—the abandonment of infants was a particular custom, should also have been where the first visions of Christ's mother had lately begun to be reported. Mary, the virgin *Theotokos*, 'the bearer of God', had herself known what it was to have a baby when poor, and homeless, and afraid. So it was recorded in the gospels of Matthew and Luke. Obliged by a Roman tax-demand to travel from her native Galilee to Bethlehem, Mary had given birth to Christ in a stable, and laid him down on straw. Macrina, taking up the slight form of a starving baby in her arms, could know for sure that she was doing God's work.

Yet Gregory, when he came to write in praise of his sister after her death, did not compare her to Mary. Of good family though she was, born to wealth, she had always slept at night on planks, as though on a cross; and so it was, on her deathbed, that she prayed to God to receive her into his kingdom, 'because I have been crucified with you'.[12] It was not his brother, the celebrated bishop, the founder of the *Basileias*, whom Gregory thought to compare to Christ, but his sister. Here, in a world where lepers could be treated with dignity, and the abolition of slavery be urged on the rich, was yet another subversion of the traditional way of ordering things. Solid as these hierarchies were, very ancient, and with foundations deeply laid, they were not to be toppled as readily as Gregory might have hoped; and yet, for all that, in his homilies there was an intimation of reverberations that lay far distant in the future. Much was imma-nent, in the new faith clasped to its bosom by the Roman ruling classes that they could barely comprehend. 'Give to the hungry what you deny your own appetite.'[13] Gregory's urging, which to previous generations would have appeared madness, was one with which the wealthy increasingly found themselves bound to wrestle.

Sharing and Caring

In 397, in a village beside the Loire, two rival gangs gathered outside a bare stone chamber where an old man lay dying. It was late afternoon by the time he finally breathed his last; and at once a violent argument broke out as to where his body should be taken. The two groups, one from Poitiers, the other from Tours, both pressed the case for their respective towns. The shadows lengthened, the sun set, and still the dispute raged. The men from Poitiers, agreeing amongst themselves that they would spirit away the corpse at first light, settled down to sit in vigil over it; but gradually all fell asleep. The men from Tours, seizing their chance, crept into the cell. Lifting up the body from the cinders in which it had been lying, they smuggled it out through a window and sped away upriver. Arriving in Tours, they were greeted by exultant crowds. The old man's burial in a tomb outside the city walls set the seal on a triumphant expedition.

Stories like these, told by people proud of the might of the dead in their midst, had a venerable pedigree.* In Greece, the bones of heroes—readily distinguishable by their colossal size—had long been prized as trophies. It was not unknown for entire skeletons to be chiselled out of rock and abducted. Tombs as well, great mounds of earth raised over the ashes of fallen heroes, had for a millennium been sites of pilgrimage. Julian, even before becoming emperor, and making public his devotion to the ancient gods, had made a point of visiting Troy. There, he had been shown the tombs of Homer's heroes, and the temples raised to them, by none other than the local bishop. Seeing Julian's raised eyebrow, the bishop had only shrugged. 'Is it not natural that people should worship a brave man who was their fellow citizen?'[14] Pride in ancestral warriors ran very deep.

---

* The reliability of this particular story, which was written two centuries after the events it describes, is hard to gauge. For what it is worth, a contemporaneous account makes no mention of the contest between the men of Poitiers and Tours.

The old man claimed for burial by the party from Tours had once been a soldier. Indeed, he had served in the cavalry under Julian. It was not, however, for any feats on the battlefield that Martin was admired by his followers. Nor was it for his lineage, nor for beauty, nor for splendour, nor for any other of the qualities that traditionally had ranked as those of a hero. Among the notoriously haughty noblemen of Gaul, Martin had inspired many an appalled curling of the lip. 'His looks were those of a peasant, his clothes shoddy, his hair a disgrace.'[15] Yet such had been his charisma, such his mystique, that various aristocrats, far from despising him, had been inspired by his example to leave their estates and come to live as he did. Three miles downriver from Tours, on a grassy plain named Marmoutier, an entire community of them was to be found, camped out in wooden shacks, or else in the caves that honeycombed a facing cliff. It was a venture that brought a flavour of distant Egypt to the banks of the Loire. There, out in the desert, amid the haunts of bandits and wild beasts, men and women had been living for many years. Their ambition it was to reject the delusions of civilisation, to commit to a lifetime of chastity and self-abnegation, to live as *monachoi*: 'those who live alone'. True, the Loire Valley was no desert. The *monachoi*—the 'monks'—who had settled there did not think to sacrifice everything. They kept their land. Peasants still worked fields for them. As they might have done in their leisure time back in their villas, they passed their time reading, talking, fishing. And yet for all that, to live as they did, after having been bred to greatness, and luxury, and worldly expectations, was undoubtedly a sacrifice. Seen in a certain light, it might almost be heroic.

And if so, then Martin—judged by the venerable standards of the aristocracy in Gaul—represented a new and disconcerting breed of hero: a Christian one. Such was the very essence of his magnetism. He was admired by his followers not despite but because of his rejection of worldly norms. Rather than accept a donative from Julian, he had publicly demanded release from the army altogether. 'Until now it is you I have served; from this moment on I am a servant of Christ.'[16] Whether indeed Martin had truly said this, his followers found it easy to believe that he had. That he had breathed his last on a bare floor, his head resting on a stone, was the measure of how he had lived his life. Not even the most exacting standards of military discipline could have compared with the austerities to which he had consistently subjected himself. In an age when the rich, arrayed in gold and silk, shimmered like peacocks, Martin's followers, camped out with him in their cells, dressed in nothing but the coarsest robes, looked on him as raw recruits might, gazing admiringly at a battle-hardened captain. By choosing to live as a beggar, he had won a fame greater than that of any other Christian in Gaul. In 371, it had even seen him elected as bishop of Tours. The shock, both to the status-conscious elite of the city, and to Martin himself, had been intense. Ambushed by those who had come with news of his elevation, he had run away and concealed himself in a barn, until his hiding place had been betrayed by geese. Or so the story went. It was evidence of Martin's celebrity that many such tales were told of him. The first monk in Gaul ever to become a bishop, he was a figure of rare authority: elevated to the heights precisely because he had not wanted to be.

Here, for anyone bred to the snobbery that had always been a characteristic of Roman society, was shock enough. Yet it was not only the spectacle of a smelly and shabbily dressed former soldier presiding as the most powerful man in Tours that had provoked a sense of a world turned upside down, of the last becoming first. Martin's disdain for the appurtenances of power—a palace, servants, fine clothes—was more than just a slap in the face of those who measured status by the possession of such things. It had charged him with a potency that, in the opinion of his admirers, owed nothing to human agency. Fabulous stories were told of its reach: of how fire would turn back at his command; of how water fowl, if they offended him by gorging too greedily on fish, would be ordered to migrate, and do so. None of his followers doubted the source of this authority. Martin, so they believed, was touched by Christ himself.

'If you want to be perfect, go, sell your possessions and give to the poor, and you will have treasure in heaven.'[17] So Jesus, asked by a wealthy young man how he might obtain eternal life, had replied. The rich man, greatly saddened, had beaten a retreat; but Martin had not. Even as bishop, he had lived his Saviour's advice to the full, shunning the palace that was his by right of office, and living instead in a shack out at Marmoutier. That he had indeed stored treasure in heaven for himself was evident from the sound, heard as he lay dying, of psalms being sung in the sky; but also from the miraculous services that he had been able, while alive, to do the sick and wretched. Reports of his feats were lovingly treasured: of how the paralysed had been made to walk by his touch; of how lepers had been healed by his kiss; even of how a suicide, found hanging from a ceiling, had been brought back from the dead. Here, in these tales, was a challenge to the wealthy that grew more pointed with every retelling. Anecdotes no less than homilies could serve to instruct the faithful. Martin was not, as Gregory of Nyssa had been, a great scholar. It was his deeds rather than his words that his disciples tended most to admire. Unlike Gregory, whose vision of God as 'the helper of the lowliest, the protector of the weak, the shelter of the hopeless, the saviour of the rejected'[18] was powerfully informed by Origen, Martin's genius was for the memorable gesture. Such was his truest and most influential legacy: the stories told about him.

And one in particular. The setting was the dead of winter, back in the days of Martin's youth, before his resignation from the army. The cold that year was exceptionally bitter. A beggar in rags stood shivering by the gateway of Amiens, a city in northern Gaul. The townsmen, wrapped up warm as they crunched through the snow, gave him nothing. Then came Martin. Dressed for duty, he had no money, only his arms. As a soldier, though, he did have his heavy military cloak; and so, taking out his sword, he cut it in two, and gave one half to the beggar. No other story about Martin would be more cherished; no other story more repeated. This was hardly surprising. The echo was of a parable told by Jesus himself. The setting, as recorded in

Luke's gospel, was the road leading eastwards from Jerusalem. Two travellers, a priest and a Temple attendant, passed a fellow Jew who had been attacked by thieves and left for dead. Then came a Samaritan; and he tended to the injured man, taking him to an inn, and paying the landlord to care for him. Shocking to the sensibilities of Jesus' original listeners, who would have taken for granted the thorough contemptibility of Samaritans, it was shocking as well to those of distant Gaul. To the tribalism that had always run deep there, Roman urbanism had added its own assumptions: that the wealthy, if they felt a responsibility to the unfortunate at all, owed it only to those of their own city. Martin, though, was not from Amiens. Born beside the eastern foothills of the Alps, and raised in Italy, he was not even a Gaul. More than any legal prescription could have done, then, more than any sermon, the compassion he had shown to a shivering stranger in the Gallic snow made vivid the principles to which he had devoted his life: that those with possessions owed a due of charity to those who had none; and that no bounds, no limits, existed on that due. The night after his encounter with the beggar, so it is said, Martin had dreamed; and in his dream he had seen Christ dressed in the very portion of the cloak that he had given away that day. 'And the Lord said to him, as he had done on earth, "Whatever you did for one of the least of these brothers of mine, you did for me."'[19]

There could be no doubting, then, the sheer potency of Martin's reputation; nor the prize that those who had abducted his corpse from his deathbed had won for Tours. The miracles which he was reported to have performed in life did not cease now that he was dead. In dreams, he would appear to the sick and the disadvantaged, straightening twisted limbs, giving voice to the mute. Yet if this inspired devotion, then so also—among the leading families of Tours—did it provoke unease. At Marmoutier, the monks put up signs indicating where he had prayed, and sat, and slept; but in Tours he tended to be remembered with less fondness. His successor as bishop, although he built a small shrine over Martin's tomb, did not promote its fame. In the upper reaches of a church dominated by the urban elite, Martin was an embarrassment. His shabbiness; his lack of breeding; his demand that the gap between rich and poor be closed: none of it had been welcome. This, so Martin's admirers charged, was because he had put other bishops to shame, by serving as a living reproach; but the bishops themselves, unsurprisingly, disagreed. They had a more elevated sense of their role: as the defenders of the natural order of things. How, if they were to give all their possessions to the poor, could they possibly be expected to maintain their authority? Why would God wish to see the very fabric of society fall apart? What, without the rich, would be the source of charity?

Here, in a world where the wealthy were becoming ever more Christian, were questions that would not go away.

Treasure in Heaven

Far beyond the horizons of a provincial town like Tours, in villas sweet-smelling with expensive perfumes, adorned with marble of every colour, and brilliant with gold and silver furnishings, there shimmered the dimension of the super-rich. The very wealthiest of families owned estates that reached back centuries, and spanned the Roman world. By virtue of their pedigree and their income, the men who headed them were enrolled in the empire's most exclusive club. The Senate, an assembly that could trace its origins back to the very beginnings of Rome, constituted the apex of a rigidly stratified society. Its members—albeit in private—might even sneer at emperors as parvenus. There was no snob quite like a senatorial snob.

How, though, for Christian plutocrats, was all this to be squared with one of their Saviour's most haunting warnings: that it was easier for a camel to go through the eye of a needle than for a rich man to enter the kingdom of God? In 394, an answer to this question was proposed so radical that it sent shock waves through the empire's elite, thrilling some, appalling many others. Meropius Pontius Paulinus was the epitome of privilege. Fabulously well-connected, and the owner of a vast array of properties in Italy, Gaul and Spain, he had enjoyed every advantage that breeding could bring. He had talent as well. Both in the Curia, the venerable building in the heart of Rome where the Senate met, and as an administrator, Paulinus had won himself a brilliant reputation while still only young. Nevertheless, he was tormented by self-doubt. A keen admirer of Martin, who had miraculously healed him of an eye complaint, Paulinus had come to believe that the surest blindness was that caused by worldly goods. Encouraged by his wife, Therasia, he began to contemplate a spectacular gesture of renunciation. When, after many years of trying, the couple had a son, only to lose him eight days later, their minds were made up. Their plan was 'to purchase heaven and Christ for the price of brittle riches'.[20] All their property and possessions, Paulinus announced, would be sold, and the proceeds given to the poor. Just for good measure, he renounced his rank as a senator and sexual relations with his wife. When together they left Therasia's native Spain, and headed for Italy, it was as a couple pledged to poverty. 'The deadly chains of flesh and blood were broken.'[21]

For the rest of his life, Paulinus would live in a simple hut inland from the bay of Naples, in the city of Nola. Here, where as a young man he had served a term as governor, he devoted himself to prayer, to vigils, and to giving alms. Gold that would once have been lavished on silks or spices was now spent on clothes and bread for the poor. When wealthy travellers came to gawp, 'their swaying coaches gleaming, their horses richly caparisoned, the carriages of the women gilded',[22] Paulinus would present himself as a visual reproach to their extravagance. Pale from his sparse diet of beans, and with his hair roughly cropped like a slave's, his appearance was calculated to shock. His body odour too. In an age when there existed no surer marker of wealth than to be freshly bathed and scented, Paulinus hailed the stench of the unwashed as 'the smell of Christ'.[23]

And yet to stink was, for a billionaire, as much of a fashion choice as it was to be expensively fragrant. Decades after his declaration that he would dispose of all his property, and despite his undoubted commitment to doing so, the precise details of Paulinus' affairs remained opaque. One thing, though, was evident: he never lacked for cash to spend on his chosen projects. The poor were not the only focus of his ambitions. In the showiest tradition of the Roman super-rich, he had a fondness for *grands projets*. That he sponsored churches rather than temples did nothing to diminish the spectacular extravagance of their fittings. Despite his pointed refusal of the dues that had been his as a senator, Paulinus remained, at heart, a recognisably patrician figure: a grandee dispensing largesse. Perhaps this was why, despite his renown as a camel who had passed through the eye of a needle, he himself rarely made allusion to the famous saying. Instead, he far preferred another passage from the gospels. The story had been told by Jesus of a rich man, *Dives*, who refused to feed a beggar at his gates named Lazarus. The two men died. Dives found himself in fire, while Lazarus stood far above him, by Abraham's side. 'Have pity on me,' Dives called up to Abraham, 'and send Lazarus to dip the tip of his finger in water and cool my tongue, because I am in agony in this fire.' But Abraham refused. 'Son, remember that in your lifetime you received your good things, while Lazarus received bad things, but now he is comforted here and you are in agony.'[24] Such was the fate that haunted Paulinus—and that he was resolved at all costs to avoid. Every act of charity, every scattering of gold coin, promised a drop of cooling water on his tongue. Wealth, if diverted to the needy, might serve to extinguish the flames of the afterlife. Here was the comfort to which Paulinus clung. 'It is not riches in themselves that are either offensive or acceptable to God, but only the uses to which they are put by men.'[25]

This, as a means for resolving the anxieties of wealthy Christians, was a proposition that seemed to offer something for everyone. The poor profited from the generosity of the rich; the rich stored up treasure for themselves in heaven by displaying charity to the poor. The more a man had to give, the greater would be his ultimate reward. In this way—unsettling reflections on camels and the eyes of needles notwithstanding—traditional proprieties could be preserved. Rank, even among Christians as literal in their interpretation of the gospels as Paulinus, might still count for something. Yet not all were so sure. The fixed order of things was tottering. Ancient certainties were literally under siege. In 410, a decade and a half after Paulinus had renounced his wealth, a far greater spectacle of abasement shocked the world. Rome herself, the ancient mistress of empire, was starved into submission by a barbarian people, the Goths, and stripped of her gold. Senators were bled white to pay their city's ransom. The shock was felt across the entire Mediterranean. Yet there were some Christians, rather than sharing in the outrage, who saw in the sack of Rome merely the latest expression of a primordial lust for riches. 'Pirates on the ocean waves, bandits on the roads, thieves in towns and villages, plunderers everywhere: all are motivated by greed.'[26] True of the Gothic king, it was no less true of senators. Rare was the fortune that had not been raised on the backs of widows and orphans. The very existence of wealth was a conspiracy against the poor. Alms-giving, no matter what Christian plutocrats might hope, could not possibly serve to sanctify it. The fires were waiting. The rich would never make it to Abraham's side.

This reading of God's purposes, grim though it might seem to Paulinus, was no less derived from an attentive reading of the gospels than his own had been. Those who proclaimed it made sure to cite their Saviour. 'Christ did not say, "Woe to you who are the evil rich", but simply, "Woe to you who are rich."'[27] Yet radicals, in the troubled decade that witnessed the sack of Rome, did not confine themselves to quoting scripture. In their ambition to fathom what Christ's teachings on wealth and poverty might mean for a society dominated by billionaires, and how the differences between the rich and the poor might be erased, they turned for inspiration to the most fashionable ascetic of the age. Pelagius, a burly and intellectually brilliant Briton, had made such a name for himself after settling in Rome that he had become the toast of high society. His teachings, though, had an appeal that extended far beyond exclusive salons. Man, Pelagius believed, had been created free. Whether he lived in obedience to God's instructions or not, the decision was his own. Sin was merely a habit—which meant that perfection might be achieved. 'There is no reason why we should not do good, other than that we have become accustomed to doing wrong from our childhood.'[28] Pelagius, in formulating this maxim, had in mind the life of the individual Christian; but there were some among his followers who applied it to the entire sweep of history. Expelled from Eden, they argued, humanity had fallen into the fatal habit of greed. The strong, stealing from the weak, had monopolised the sources of wealth. Land, livestock and gold had become the property of the few, not the many. The possibility that riches might ever have been a blessing bestowed by God, untainted by exploitation, was a grotesque self-deception. There was no coin dropped into a beggar's shrivelled palm that had not ultimately been won by criminal means: lead-tipped whips, and cudgels, and branding irons. Yet if, as Pelagius argued, individual sinners could cleanse themselves of their sin and win perfection by obedience to God's commands, then so too could all of humanity. Evidence for what this might mean in practical terms was to be found in the Acts of the Apostles, the book written by Luke in which he had described Paul's vision on the road to Damascus, and which had come to be incorporated into the New Testament. There, preserved for the edification of all, it was recorded that the first generation of Christ's followers had held everything in common. 'Selling their possessions and goods, they gave to anyone as he had need.'[29] A just and equal society was, then, an ambition for which there existed the direct sanction of scripture itself. Only achieve it, and there would be no need for charity. Grandstanding philanthropists like Paulinus would become one with the beggars who thronged his churches. 'Get rid of the rich, and where will the poor be then?'[30]

In practice, of course, as a manifesto, this was barely less implausible than Gregory of Nyssa's urging that slavery be abolished. Indeed, in the years that followed the sack of Rome, the western half of the empire became ever more a playground for the strong. The sinews that had long held it together were starting to snap. The mighty bulk of it was falling apart. A century on from Paulinus' great gesture of renunciation, and the complex infrastructure that had sustained the existence of the super-rich was gone for good. In place of a single Roman order extending from the Sahara to northern Britain, there was instead a patchwork of rival kingdoms, spear-won by an array of barbarous peoples: Visigoths, Vandals, Franks. In this new world, those among the Christian nobility who had managed to avoid utter impoverishment were rarely inclined to feel guilty about it. The poverty embraced by Martin and Paulinus was more liable to appear to them now as a fate to be avoided at all costs than an example to be followed. What they wanted from bishops and holy men was not admonishment on the inherent evil of riches, but something very different: an assurance that wealth might indeed be a gift from God. And this, sure enough, in the various barbarian kingdoms of the West, was precisely what churchmen had come to provide.

Behind them lay the massive authority of a man who, back when Paulinus had still been the talk of the empire, and Pelagius the toast of Rome, was serving as the bishop of an isolated port on the African coast—and yet whose influence had far outshone them both. To Augustine of Hippo, it was precisely the diversity of the Christian people, the joining together of every social class, that constituted its chief glory. 'All are astonished to see the entire human race converging on the Crucified One, from emperors down to beggars in their rags.'[31] Augustine himself had known what it was to be brought to Christ. His conversion had come when he was already in his thirties. Had he not turned to a passage in Paul, after hearing, as though in a hallucination, a child chant 'Pick it up and read' in a neighbouring garden, perhaps he would never have become a Christian at all. Certainly, Augustine had led a restless life. Prior to his baptism, he had clawed his way up from provincial obscurity to the margins of the imperial court; he had moved from city to city, from Carthage to Rome to Milan; he had dabbled in a whole range of cults and philosophies; he had picked up women in churches. Such a man knew perfectly well just how various humanity was. Nevertheless, returning from Italy to his native Africa, and in due course to election as the bishop of Hippo, he had dared to dream of a Christianity that was properly catholic—universal—in practice as well as name. 'It is high time for all and sundry to be inside the Church.'[32] Yet this conviction had not—as it had the more radical followers of Pelagius—encouraged Augustine to claim that divisions of class and wealth might be erased, and all goods be held in common. Quite the contrary. The bishop of Hippo was far too sombre, far too pessimistic, in his view of human nature to imagine that charity could ever not be needed. 'The poor you will always have with you.'[33] So Christ himself had warned. The wealthy and the wretched: both were destined to exist for as long as the world endured.

Augustine's mistrust of where social upheaval might lead had been bred in part of personal experience. In Hippo, as in the rest of Africa, the schism in the church had remained something violent and raw. Ambushes on the roads beyond the city were a constant danger; acid attacks a particular risk. Augustine, as a Catholic bishop, had always known himself a potential target. Donatist radicals, he had charged, were rebels not just against his own authority, but against everything that made for order. Attacking villas, they would seize the owners, 'well-educated men of superior birth', and chain them to gristmills, 'forcing them by the whip to turn it in a circle as if they were the lowest kind of draught animal'.[34] Not for Augustine the conviction that the poor were purer in heart than the rich. All were equally fallen. Divisions of class were as nothing compared to the condition of sinfulness that all of humanity shared in common. This meant that a billionaire who, like Paulinus, gave away his entire fortune could be no more certain of salvation than the destitute widow who, according to the gospels, had been watched by Jesus donating to the Temple treasury all that she had: two tiny copper coins. It meant as well that any dream of establishing an earthly society in which the extremes of wealth and poverty were banished, and all rendered equal, was just that: a dream.

Indeed, to Augustine, the teaching of Pelagius that Christians might live without sin was not merely fantasy, but a pernicious heresy. It risked damnation for all who believed it. Men and women could not possibly, in a fallen world, attain perfection. The doctrine formulated centuries earlier by Jesus Ben Sirah, that Eve's disobedience in Eden had doomed all her descendants to share in her original sin, had largely been forgotten by Jewish scholars; but not by Augustine. Every day was a day that demanded penance: not just prayers for forgiveness, but the giving of alms. Here, for everyone who could afford it, from the poorest widow to the wealthiest senator, was the surest way to expiate the fatal taint of original sin. Position and wealth, so long as those entrusted with them put them to good purposes, were not inherent evils. The wild demands of the more radical among the Pelagians, that all possessions be held in common, could be dismissed as a folly and a delusion. 'Get rid of pride, and riches will do no harm.'[35] Augustine's message, in the centuries that followed the collapse of Roman rule in the West, was one that found many listeners. Amid the rubble of the toppled imperial order, it offered both to local aristocrats and to barbarian warlords a glimpse of how their authority might be set upon novel and secure foundations. If the old days of marble-clad villas were gone for ever, then there was now another index of greatness that might more readily win God's blessing: the ability to defend dependants, and to grant them not just alms, but armed protection. Power, if employed to defend the powerless, might secure the favour of heaven.

The surest evidence of all for this, perhaps, was to be found at Tours. There, a century and more after Martin's death, it was no longer his cell at Marmoutier that provided the focus of pilgrims' devotions, but his tomb. All the reservations about his memory had long since been swept away. A succession of ambitious bishops had adorned the site of his burial with a great complex of churches, courtyards and towers. Over the tomb itself there glittered a gilded dome.* Here, dominating the approaches to Tours itself, was a monument that proclaimed an awesome degree of authority. Martin, who in life had shunned the trappings of worldly power, in death had become the very model of a mighty lord. As he had ever done,

---

* Assuming, that is, that the dome which in the tenth century was reported to have 'glittered in the sun like a mountain of gold' had already been gilded by the sixth century.

he continued to care for the sick, and the suffering, and the poor with manifold acts of charity; chroniclers of his miracles lovingly recorded how he had healed children and provided for impoverished widows. Martin, though, like any lord in the troubled years that had followed the collapse of Roman order, knew how to look after his own. Even the most grasping kings, in dread of his potency, made sure to treat Tours with a certain grudging respect. Clovis, the Frankish warlord who in the last years of the fifth century had succeeded in establishing his rule over much of Gaul, ostentatiously prayed to Martin for his backing in battle—and then, after receiving it, sent him appropriately splendid gifts. Clovis' heirs, the rulers of a kingdom that would come to be called Francia, tended to avoid Tours altogether—as well they might have done. Sensitive to the parvenu quality of their own dynasty, they knew better than to compete with the blaze of its patron's charisma. When, in due course, one of them obtained the *capella*, the very cloak that Martin had divided for the beggar at Amiens, it fast came to serve as the badge of Frankish greatness. Guarded by a special class of priest, the *capellani* or 'chaplains', and carried in the royal train in times of war, it bore intimidating witness to the degree to which holiness had become a source of power. Martin's death, far from diminishing his authority, had only enhanced it. No longer, as they had been back in Paul's day, were 'Saints' held to be the living faithful. Now the title was applied to those who, like Martin, had died and gone to join their Saviour. More than any Caesar had been, they were loved, petitioned, feared. Amid the shadows of a violent and an impoverished age, their glory offered succour both to the king and to the slave, to the ambitious and to the humble, to the warrior and to the leper.

There was no reach of the fallen world so dark, it seemed, that it could not be illumined by the light of heaven.

6

HEAVEN

492: Mount Gargano

The story brought from the mountain seemed scarcely believable. That a bull, wandering from its herd, had discovered the mouth of a cave. That its owner, indignant that the animal had gone rogue, had shot it with a poisoned arrow. That the arrow, its trajectory reversed by the blast of a sudden wind, had 'struck the one who loosed it'. All this, reported by the peasants who had witnessed the miraculous event, left the local bishop intrigued. Anxious to make sense of what had happened, he embarked on a fast. After three days, a figure of radiant beauty armoured in light appeared to him. 'Know that what happened,' the figure told the bishop, 'was a sign. I am the guardian of this place. I stand watch over it.'[1]

Gargano, a rocky promontory jutting out from south-eastern Italy into the Adriatic Sea, had long been a haunted spot. In ancient times, pilgrims to the mountain would climb its summit, and there make sacrifice of a black ram, before sleeping overnight in its hide. Glimpses of the future were granted in dreams. A soothsayer lay buried nearby who, according to Homer, had interpreted the will of Apollo to the Greeks, and instructed them, at a time when the archer god had been felling them with his plague-tipped arrows, how to appease his anger. Times, though, had changed. In 391, sacrifices had been banned on the orders of a Christian Caesar. Apollo's golden presence had been scoured from Italy. Paulinus, in his poetry, had repeatedly celebrated the god's banishment. Apollo's temples had been closed, his statues smashed, his altars destroyed. By 492, he no longer visited the dreams of those who slept on the slopes of Gargano.

His fading, though, reached back long before the conversion of Constantine. The same convulsions that, over the course of the third century, had inspired various emperors to attempt the eradication of Christianity had proven devastating to the cults of the ancient gods. Amid war and financial chaos, temples had begun literally to crumble. Some had collapsed altogether; others had been converted into barracks or military storehouses. The decay witnessed by Julian at Pessinus had owed less to any crisis of faith than to the erosion of traditional patterns of civic patronage. Naturally, though, given the opportunity, some bishops had not hesitated to press for the *coup de grâce*. The hunger of the gods for sacrifice, for the perfume of blood on blackened altars, had never ceased to horrify Christians. Before their righteous and militant indignation, even the most venerable of cults had proven powerless. In 391, the endemic aptitude of the Alexandrian mob for rioting had turned on the Serapeum and levelled it; four decades later, the worship of Athena had been prohibited in the Parthenon. Time would see it converted to a church. Nevertheless, despite loud Christian crowing, these celebrated monuments were the exceptions that proved the rule. No matter how much the biographers of saints might claim for their heroes the triumphant annihilation of a great swathe of temples, or their conversion to the worship of Christ, the reality was very different. Most shrines, deprived of the sponsorship on which they had always depended for their upkeep and rituals, had simply been abandoned. Blocks of masonry were not readily toppled, after all. Easier by far to leave them to weeds, and wild animals, and bird-droppings.*

---

* 'As a result of recent work, it can be stated with confidence that temples were neither widely converted into churches nor widely demolished in Late Antiquity.' (Lavan and Mulryan, p. xxiv).

By the end of the fifth century, it was only out in the wildest reaches of the countryside, where candles might still be lit besides springs or crossroads, and offerings to time-worn idols made, that there remained men and women who clung to 'the depraved customs of the past'.[2] Bishops in their cities called such deplorables *pagani*: not merely 'country people', but 'bumpkins'. The name of 'pagan', though, had soon come to have a broader application. Increasingly, from the time of Julian onwards, it had been used to refer to all those—senators as well as serfs—who were neither Christians nor Jews. It was a word that reduced the vast mass of those who did not worship the One God of Israel, from atheist philosophers to peasants fingering grubby charms, to one vast and undifferentiated mass. The concept of 'paganism', much like that of 'Judaism', was an invention of Christian scholars: one that enabled them to hold up a mirror to the Church itself.

And to much more besides. Reflected in the idols and cults of pagans, Christians beheld a darkness that imperilled the very reaches of time and space. Just as Origen, amid the smoking altars of Alexandria, had dreaded the vampiric appetites of beings that demanded blood, so Augustine, even with sacrifices banned, had still warned against the ancient gods, and 'the hellish yoke of those polluted powers'.[3] The danger was particularly acute in a landscape such as Gargano. Here, where the gods had long been in the habit of haunting dreams, was precisely the kind of wilderness in which they might be expected to have taken refuge. Certainly no Christian could imagine that it was enough merely to have closed down their temples. The forces of darkness were both cunning and resolute in their evil. That they lurked in predatory manner, waiting for Christians to fail in their duty to God, sniffing out every opportunity to seduce them into sin, was manifest from the teachings of Christ himself. His mission, so he had declared, was to 'drive out demons'.[4] Such a conflict was not bounded merely by the dimensions of the mortal. The challenge of defeating demons spanned heaven as well as earth.

Which was why Gargano's bishop, visited by the figure arrayed in blazing light, could feel so relieved that it was not Apollo who had appeared to him, but rather the celestial general of the armies of God. Angels had been serving as messengers since the time of Abraham. That, in Greek, was what the word meant. Most, even the angel who had appeared to Abraham as he was raising his cleaver to kill Isaac, even the angel who had brought death on the eve of the Exodus to the first-born of Egypt, had been nameless. They were defined by their service to God. Repeatedly, in the Old Testament, visions were described of the celestial court: of the Seraphim, six-winged angels who sang the praises of the Lord Almighty from above his throne, and of the numberless hosts of heaven assembled to his left and right. For Christians, when they sought to imagine what angels might look like, it was as natural to envisage them as bureaucrats in the service of Caesar, in medallions and crimson tunics, as it had been for the author of the Book of Job to model God's court on that of the Persian king. Yet not all angels were anonymous. Two in the New Testament were named. One of them, Gabriel, had brought the news to Mary that she was to give birth to Christ. The other, Michael, was defined simply as 'the archangel':[5] greatest of all the servants of God. Charismatic as only a lord of the heavens could be, he exerted a cross-cultural appeal. Jews hailed him as 'the great prince',[6] the watcher over the dead, the guardian of Israel; pagans carved his name on amulets, and conjured him in spells. At Pessinus he had even shared a shrine with Cybele. Christians, warned by Paul on no account to worship angels, had traditionally shrunk from offering Michael open honour; but increasingly, across what remained of the Roman Empire, in the eastern Mediterranean, his fame had spread. He was said to have appeared in Galatia; then near Constantinople, the great capital founded back in 330 to serve as a second Rome, in a church built by Constantine himself. Never, though, had Michael been seen in the west—until, that was, he alighted on Gargano, and proclaimed himself its guardian.

Further wonders soon followed. Overnight, inside the cave discovered by the errant bull, an entire church appeared, and then the
mysterious imprint in marble of the archangel's feet. The people of
Gargano were fortunate in their heavenly guardian. The century
that followed Michael's appearance on the mountain saw the very
fabric of civilisation in Italy start to shrivel and fall apart. War, then
plague, swept the peninsula. Bands of rival militias ravaged landscapes that were being lost to marshes and weeds. Entire villages
vanished; entire towns. Even on the slopes of Gargano, where black
mists would veil the mountain against the depredations of freeboo-
ters, and which the plague never reached, people knew that Michael's
patronage had its limits. They had only to look to the skies, and 'the
flashes of fire there that foretold the blood that was to be shed',[7] to
recognise that there could be no escaping the cosmic clash of good
and evil. For all Michael's potency, he and the hosts of heaven were
faced by adversaries who did not readily yield. Demons too had their
captain. He and Michael were well matched. Foul-smelling though
the chief of the demons had become, with 'the bloody horns of an
ox',[8] and skin as black as night, he had not always dwelt in darkness.
Once, in the beginning, when the Lord God had laid the earth's
foundation, and the morning stars had sung together, and all the
angels had shouted for joy, he, like Michael, had been a prince of
light.

Many centuries had passed since the writing of the Book of
Job. Inevitably, in the wake of Alexander's conquests, memories of
the Great King of Persia and his secret agents had begun to dim.
The word *satan* had come to serve many Jews, not as the title of
an official in God's court, but as a proper noun. Nevertheless, not
every Persian influence had dimmed. The conviction of Darius that
the cosmos was a battleground between good and evil, between
light and darkness, between truth and falsehood, was one that
many Jews had come to share. Satan—the 'Adversary' or *Diabo-
los*, as he was called in Greek—had grown to stalk the imaginings

of various Jewish sects. The first generation of Christians, when they sought to fathom why their Saviour had become man, and what precisely might have been achieved by his suffering on the cross, had identified as the likeliest answer the need to put Satan in his place. Christ had taken on flesh and blood, so one of them explained, 'that by his death he might destroy him who holds the power of death—that is, the Devil'.[9] Unsurprisingly, then, in the centuries that followed, Christian scholars had parsed scripture with great care for clues as to Satan's story. It was Origen who had pieced together the definitive account: how originally the Devil had been Lucifer, the morning star, the son of the dawn, but had aspired to sit in God's throne, and been cast down like lightning from heaven, 'to the depths of the pit'.[10] More vividly than Persian or Jewish scholars had ever done, Christians gave evil an individual face. Never before had it been portrayed to such dramatic and lurid effect; never before endowed with such potency and charisma.

'Two companies of angels are meant by the terms "Light" and "Darkness".'[11] Augustine, when he wrote this, had known the heresy that he was skirting: the Persian conviction that good and evil were principles equally matched. As a young man, he had subscribed to it himself. Then, following his conversion, he had robustly set this doctrine aside. To be a Christian was, of course, to believe in a single, omnipotent god. Evil, so Augustine had argued, possessed no independent existence, but was merely the corruption of goodness. Indeed, there was nothing mortal that was not the merest, faintest glimmering of the heavenly. 'That City, in which it has been promised that we shall reign, differs from this earthly city as widely as the sky from the earth, life eternal from temporal joy, substantial glory from empty praises, the society of angels from the society of men, the light of the Maker of the sun and moon from the light of the sun and moon.'[12] Demons, when they tempted mortals with the swagger of greatness, all the trumpets and battle-standards so beloved of kings and emperors, were offering nothing but delusions made out of smoke. What were angels of darkness themselves, after all, if not the shadows of angels of light?

Yet still, in the imaginings of many Christians, there seemed more to Satan than merely the absence of good. The more vividly he was evoked, the more autonomous he came to seem. His great empire of sin seemed hard to square with the sovereignty of an all-powerful and beneficent God. Why, if Christ had defeated death, was Satan's reach still so long? How, when the very armies of heaven remained in the field against him, armed and ready for war, could mortals in a fallen world hope to stand proof against his powers? What were the prospects, if any, of overcoming the Devil for good?

Answers to these questions existed; but they had not come easily. This, of course, was no surprise. Christians knew that they were not mere spectators in the great drama of Satan's claim on the world, but participants—and that the stakes were cosmically high. The shadows cast by this conviction were deep ones—and destined to extend far into the future.

War in Heaven

In November 589, the Tiber burst its banks. Granaries were flooded, several churches swept away on the currents, and a great school of water-snakes—the largest 'a massive dragon the size of a tree-trunk'[13]—washed up on the shore. Two months later, plague returned to Rome. Among the first to die was the pope. His death sent a chill through the city. Although nominally the city was ruled by the emperor in far-off Constantinople, responsibility for Rome's protection had effectively devolved upon its bishop. Its citizens, ravaged by plague as they were, and menaced by predatory barbarians, did not delay in electing a replacement. Their choice was unanimous. Amid the evils of a debased age, they craved a touch of class. In the spring of 590, in the great basilica that Constantine had raised over the site of Saint Peter's tomb, a man from the very heart of the Roman establishment was consecrated as pope.

Gregory's ancestors, so it was reported in awed tones by his admirers in Francia, had been senators. The claim, although an exaggeration, was understandable. The new pope did indeed have something of the vanished age of Roman greatness about him. He had inherited a palace on the Caelian hill, in the heart of the city, and various estates in Sicily; served as urban prefect, an office that reached back to the time of Romulus; lived for six years among the imperial elite in Constantinople. Gregory, though, had no illusions as to the scale of Rome's decline. A city that at its peak had boasted over a million inhabitants now held barely twenty thousand. Weeds clutched at columns erected by Augustus; silt buried pediments built to honour Constantine. The vast expanse of palaces, and triumphal arches, and race-tracks, and amphitheatres, constructed over the centuries to serve as the centre of the world, now stretched abandoned, a wilderness of ruins. Even the Senate was no more. When Gregory, emerging from his consecration into the plague-ravaged streets, raised his eyes to the sky, he claimed to see arrows raining down, fired from an invisible bow. Time would see him dread that all traces of life might be expunged from the city. 'For since the Senate failed, the people perish, and the sufferings and the groans of the few survivors are multiplied day on day. Rome, now empty, burns!'[14]

Yet Gregory did not despair. He never doubted that redemption from the plague was possible. 'God is full of mercy and compassion, and it is his will that we should win his pardon through our prayers.'[15] The crowds, listening to the new pope deliver this message of hope, were primed to listen. The attachment of the Roman people to their ancient *religiones*, to the rites and rituals that for so long had governed their city's calendar, had been decisively broken. Only a century before, in February 495, a predecessor of Gregory's had been scandalised by the spectacle of young men in skimpy loincloths haring through Rome, lashing the breasts of women with goat-skin thongs, just as young men had been doing every February since the time of Romulus; half a century before that, another pope had been no less shocked to see some among his flock greet the dawn by bowing to the sun. Those days, though, were past. The rhythms of the city—its days, its weeks, its years—had been rendered Christian. The very word *religio* had altered its meaning: for it had come to signify the life of a monk or a nun. Gregory, when he summoned his congregation to repentance, did so as a man who had converted his palace on the Caelian into a monastery, who had lived there as a monk himself, pledged to poverty and chastity, a living, breathing embodiment of *religio*. The Roman people, hearing their new pope urge them to repentance, did not hesitate to obey him. Day after day, they walked the streets, raising prayers and chanting psalms. Eighty dropped dead of the plague as they went in procession. Then, on the third day, an answer at last from the heavens. The plague-arrows stopped falling. The dying abated. The Roman people were spared obliteration.

Pagans, brought up on Homer, had been perfectly capable of attributing pestilence to the murderousness of an indignant and vengeful Apollo. Christians, though, knew better. Gregory never doubted that the sufferings of the times in which he lived were bred in part of human sinfulness. God, whose presence was to be felt in every breath of every breeze, in the passage of every cloud, was always close, nor was there anyone who could escape his judgement. Gregory had only to count his own faults to recognise this. 'Every day I transgress.'[16] This did not mean, though, that salvation lay beyond the reach of sinful humanity. Christ had not died in vain. Hope still remained. Gregory, when he sought to make sense of the calamities being visited on Italy, turned above all to the Book of Job. Its hero, given through no fault of his own into the hands of Satan, and plunged into abject wretchedness, had endured his sufferings with steadfast fortitude. Here, so Gregory argued, was the key to understanding the shocks of his own age. Satan was abroad again. Just as Job had been cast into the dust, so now were the blameless suffering disaster alongside sinners. 'Cities are sacked, strongholds razed to the ground, churches destroyed, fields emptied of farmers. Swords rage incessantly against those few of us who—for now, at any rate—remain, and blows rain down on us from above.' Gregory, after listing these tribulations, did not hesitate to declare what he believed they portended. 'Evils long foretold. The destruction of the world.'[17]

That the earthly order was destined to come to an end, and the dimension of the mortal to be joined for all eternity with the divine, had long been kept from the mass of humanity. Time, so most people assumed, went in cycles. Even the Stoics, who taught that the universe was destined to be consumed by fire, never doubted that a new universe would emerge from the conflagration, as it had done before, and as it would do again. Philosophers, though, had never had any particular cause to hope for anything different. First under Alexander and his successors, and then under Rome, they had been prized, sponsored, fêted. Men to whom the status quo had been kind could view with some equanimity the prospect of its perpetual renewal. Yet not everyone had been content to view time as a ceaseless cycle. The Persians, in the wake of their conquest by Alexander, had come to believe that it was destined to have an end, and that Ahura Mazda, in a final reckoning, would triumph over the Lie once and for all. In AD 66, the yearning for a very similar consummation had fuelled the Jews in their doomed revolt against Rome. Jesus himself, only a few decades earlier, had proclaimed the Kingdom of God to be at hand. Christians, right from the beginning, had dreamed of their Saviour's return, when the dead would be raised from their graves and all humanity be judged, and a kingdom of the just be established forever, on earth as it was in heaven. That dream, over the course of six centuries, had never faded. When Gregory, contemplating the miseries of the world, foretold its imminent destruction, he spoke in hope as much as dread.

'This is how it will be at the end of the age. The angels will come and separate the wicked from the righteous and throw them into the

fiery furnace, where there will be weeping and gnashing of teeth.'[18]
So Christ himself had warned. Similar prophecies—of how, on the
day of judgement, both the living and the dead would be sorted into
two groups, like good fruit and bad, like wheat and weeds, like
sheep and goats—appeared throughout the gospels. So too, no less
chilling, did lists of the signs that would herald the fateful moment.
These were the portents that Gregory, when he looked about him
at the agonies of the age, could recognise: wars, and earthquakes,
and famines; plagues, and terrors, and wonders in the sky. Beyond
that, however, detail in the gospels was lacking. Instead, for those
Christians who longed to stare fully into the face of the end times,
it was a very different work of scripture that provided them with an
apocalypsis—a 'lifting of the veil'. The Revelation of Saint John—
whom Irenaeus, for one, had confidently identified with the disciple
beloved of Jesus—offered the ultimate account of the judgement that
was to come. Like a troubled dream, it provided no clear narrative,
but rather a succession of haunting and hallucinatory visions. Of
war in heaven, between Michael and his angels and 'that ancient serpent called the devil, or Satan, who leads the whole world astray'.[19]
Of how Satan would be cast down and bound for a thousand years.
Of how martyrs, raised from the dead and given thrones, were to
reign with Christ for the length of the millennium. Of a whore drunk
with the blood of the saints, who sat on a scarlet beast, and whose
name was Babylon. Of how a great battle would be fought at the
place 'that in Hebrew is called Armageddon'.[20] Of how Satan, after
the thousand years had passed, was to be released, and would deceive
the four corners of the earth, before being thrown forever into a lake
of burning sulphur. Of how the dead, great and small, would stand
before the throne of Christ, and be judged according to what they
had done. Of how some would be written in the book of life, and
some—those who did not appear in its pages—would be cast into the
lake of fire. Of how there would be a new heaven and a new earth. Of
how the Holy City, the new Jerusalem, would descend out of heaven
from God. Of how heaven and earth would become one.

Here, in this apocalypse, was a vision of the future more over-whelming in its impact than that of any pagan oracle. No riddling pronouncement of Apollo had ever served to reconfigure the very concept of time. Yet this, across the Roman world, was what the Old and New Testaments had combined to achieve. Those who lacked the Christian understanding of history, so Augustine had written, were doomed to 'wander in a circuitous maze finding nei-ther entrance nor exit'.[21] The course of time, as sure and direct as the flight of an arrow, proceeded in a straight line: from Genesis to Revelation; from Creation to the Day of Judgement. Gregory was certainly not alone in measuring the events of the world against his knowledge of where time was destined to end. In Galatia, one bishop—a noted ascetic named Theodore, who insisted on wearing a fifty-pound metal corset and only ever eating lettuce—predicted the imminent materialisation of the Beast; in Tours, another, who shared with the pope the name of Gregory, anticipated 'the moment foretold by our Lord as the beginning of our sorrows.'[22] From east to west, the same anxiety, the same hope was expressed. The end days were drawing near. Time was running out.

And yet there was, for all that, a certain pulling of punches. Bish-ops, charged though they might be with shepherding the Christian people towards the time of judgement, flinched from calculating the exact hour. Pointedly, they refused to draw a precise correspondence between the events described in Revelation and the convulsions of their own age. The chance to identify who the Beast might be, or the Whore of Babylon, was spurned. Leaders of the Church had long dreaded the speculations that St John's vision of the Apocalypse might foster among those given to wild and violent imaginings. Ori-gen, ever the philosopher, had dismissed the idea that the thousand-year reign of the saints was to be taken literally. Augustine had agreed: 'The thousand years symbolise the course of the world's his-tory.'[23] In the Greek East, councils were held which denied Revela-tion a place in the New Testament at all. Few in the Latin West went that far: John's vision of the Apocalypse was too firmly inscribed in their canon for that. Equally, though, the leaders of the Western Church could not help but dread how the ignorant and excitable might interpret its prophecies. The veil had been lifted; but it was perilous to look too closely at what lay beneath. Christ, as Gregory put it, 'wants the final hour unknown to us'.[24]

Which did not mean that Christians should be unprepared for it. Quite the opposite. The vision of the end days was a vision as well of what awaited everyone after death. As such, it was bound to unsettle. 'Many are called, but few are chosen.'[25] So Christ himself had warned. The new Jerusalem and the lake of fire were sides of the same coin. For the earliest Christians, a tiny minority in a world seething with hostile pagans, this reflection had tended to provide reassurance. The dead, summoned from their graves, where for years, centuries, millennia they might have been mouldering, would face only two options. The resurrection of their physical bodies would ensure an eternity either of bliss or torment. The justice that in life they might either have been denied or evaded would, at the end of days, be delivered them by Christ. Only the martyrs, those who had died in their Saviour's name, would have been spared this period of waiting. They alone, at the moment of death, were brought by golden-winged angels in a great blaze of glory directly to the palace of God. All others, saints and sinners alike, were sentenced to wait until the hour of judgement came.

This, though, was not the vision of the afterlife that had come to prevail in the West. There, far more than in the Greek world, the awful majesty of the end of days, of the bodily resurrection and the final judgement, had come to be diluted. That this was so reflected in large part the influence—ironically enough—of an Athenian philosopher. 'When death comes to a man, the mortal part of him perishes, or so it would seem. The part which is immortal, though, retires at death's approach, and escapes unharmed and indestructible.'[26] So had written Plato, a contemporary of Aristophanes and the teacher of Aristotle. No other philosopher, in the formative years of the Western Church, had exerted a profounder influence over its greatest thinkers. Augustine, who in his youth had classed himself as a Platonist, had still, long after his conversion to Christianity, hailed his former master as the pagan 'who comes nearest to us'.[27] That the soul was immortal; that it was incorporeal; that it was immaterial: all these were propositions that Augustine had derived not from scripture, but from Athens' greatest philosopher. Plato's influence on the Western Church had, in the long run, proven decisive. The insistence of Augustine's opponents that only God was truly immaterial, and that even angels were created out of delicate and ethereal fire, had ended up dead and buried. So, as time went by, had the primordial teaching of the Church that only martyrs could be welcomed directly into heaven. The conviction that the souls of even the holiest saints were destined to join Abraham, just as Lazarus had done, and there await the hour of judgement, had faded. They too, so Augustine had taught, went straight to heaven. Yet even saints, before they could be received by Michael among the angels, still had to be judged. Gregory, the bishop of Tours, when he wrote in praise of his patron saint, described how Martin, as he died, had been visited by the Devil and obliged to render account for his life. Naturally, it had not taken long. Martin had soon been on his way to join his fellow saints in paradise. The episode had redounded entirely to his glory. Nevertheless, in describing it, Gregory of Tours could not refrain from a certain nervous gulp. After all, if even Martin could be subjected to interrogation by Satan when he died, then what of sinners? Simply by asking this question, Gregory was speaking for a new age: one in which all mortals, not just martyrs, not just saints, could expect to meet with judgement at the moment of their death.

Here, then, as Christians in the West began to go their own way, was a deep paradox: that the more distinctive a vision of the afterlife they came to have, the more it bore witness to its origins in the East. Jewish scripture and Greek philosophy, once again, had blended to potent effect. Indeed, across what had once been Roman provinces, in lands pockmarked by abandoned villas and crumbling basilicas, few aspects of life were as coloured by the distant past as the dread of death. What awaited the soul after it had slipped its mortal shell? If not angels, and the road to heaven, then demons black as the Persians had always imagined the agents of the Lie to be; Satan armoured with an account book, just as tax officials of the vanished empire might have borne; a pit of fire, in which the torments of the damned echoed those described, not by the authors of Holy Scripture, but by the poets of pagan Athens and Rome. It was a vision woven out of many ancient elements; but not a vision that Christians of an earlier age would have recognised. Revolutionary in its implications for the dead, it was to prove revolutionary as well in its implications for the living.

Powerhouses of Prayer

There were places wilder than Gargano where those with a sufficient love of God could hope, perhaps, to glimpse angels. Yet it was dangerous. At the limits of the world, where the grey and heaving ocean stretched as far as the eye could see, monks served as Christ's vanguard, and by their prayers kept sentry against the Devil and his legions. Tales would be told of those who sailed beyond the horizon, and found there both mountains of eternal fire, where burning flakes of snow fell on the damned, and the fields of Paradise, rich with fruit and precious stones. True or not, it was certain that some monks, taking to the treacherous waters of the Atlantic, had made landfall on a jagged spike of rock—or *sceillec*, as it was called in the local language—and there lived in bare cells. Cold and hunger, which kings built great feasting-halls to keep at bay, were valued by those who settled on Skellig as pathways to the radiant presence of God. Monks who knelt for hours in sheeting rain, or laboured on empty stomachs at tasks properly suited to slaves, did so in the hope of transcending the limitations of the fallen world. The veil that separated the heavenly from the earthly seemed, to their admirers, almost parted by their efforts. 'Mortal men, so people believed, were living the lives of angels.'[28] Nowhere else in the Christian West were saints quite as tough, quite as manifestly holy, as they were in Ireland.

That the island had been won for Christ was a miracle in itself. Roman rule had never reached its shores. Instead, sometime in the mid-fifth century, Christianity had been preached there by an escaped slave. Patrick, a young Briton kidnapped by pirates and sold across the Irish Sea, was revered by Irish Christians not just for having brought them to Christ, but for the template of holiness with which he had provided them. Whether working as a shepherd, or fleeing his master by ship, or returning to Ireland to spread the word of God, angels had spoken to him, and guided him in all he did; nor had he hesitated, when justifying his mission, to invoke the imminence of the end of the world. A century on from Patrick's death, the monks and nuns of Ireland still bore his stamp. They owed no duty save to God, and to their 'father'—their 'abbot'. Monasteries, like the ringforts that dotted the country, were proudly independent. An iron discipline served to maintain them. Only a rule that was 'strict, holy and constant, exalted, just and admirable'[29] could bring men and women to the dimension of the heavenly. Monks were expected to be as proficient in the strange and book-learned language of Latin as at felling trees; as familiar with the few, ferociously cherished classics of Christian literature that had reached Ireland as toiling in a field. Like Patrick, they believed themselves to stand in the shadow of the end days; like Patrick, they saw exile from their families and their native land as the surest way to an utter dependence upon God. Not all headed for the gale-lashed isolation of a rock in the Atlantic. Some crossed the sea to Britain, and there preached the gospel to the kings of barbarous peoples who still set up idols and wallowed in paganism: the Picts, the Saxons, the Angles. Others, heading southwards, took ship for the land of the Franks.

Columbanus—'the Little Dove'—arrived in Francia in 590: the same year that Gregory was elected pope. The Irish monk, unlike the Roman aristocrat, came from the ends of the earth, without status, without pedigree; and yet, by sheer force of charisma, he would set the Latin West upon a new and momentous course. Schooled in the ferociously exacting monasticism of his native land, Columbanus appeared to the Franks a figure of awesome and even terrifying holiness. Unlike their own monks, he consciously sought out wilderness in which to live. His first place of retreat was an old Roman fort in the Vosges, in eastern Francia, long since lost to trees and brush; his second, the ruins of a city burned a century and a half before by invading barbarians. Luxeuil, the monastery he founded there, was built as a portal to heaven. Columbanus and his tiny band of followers, clearing away brambles, draining marshes, building an enclosure out of the shattered masonry, seemed to the Franks men of supernatural fortitude. When hungry, they would gnaw on bark; when weary after a long day of physical labour, they would devote themselves to study, and prayer, and penance. This routine, far from scaring away potential recruits, was soon attracting them in droves. To enter the monastery enclosure, and to submit to Columbanus' rule, was to know oneself in the company of angels. The discipline imposed on novices was designed not merely to break their pride, to annihilate their self-conceit, but to offer them, sinners though they were, the hope of paradise. Columbanus had brought with him from Ireland a novel doctrine: that sins, if they were regularly confessed, were manageable. Penances, calibrated in exacting detail, could enable sinners, once they had performed them, to regain the favour of God. Punitive though Columbanus' regime was, it was also medicinal. To those who lived in dread of the hour of judgement, and of the Devil's accounting book, it promised a precious reassurance: that human weakness might be forgiven.

'Let us, since we are travellers and pilgrims in this world, keep the end of our road always in our minds—for the road is our life, and its end is our home.'[30] Not to journey, not to live in exile from the world, was to spurn heavenly rewards for earthly ones. Columbanus, when he preached this message, did so as a man who had literally turned his back on his family and his native land. As a result, he was able to serve his Frankish admirers as a living embodiment of the potency of *religio*: of a life utterly committed to God. A shimmer-hint of the supernatural attached itself to almost everything he did. Miraculous stories were told of him: of how bears would obey his commands not to steal fruit, and squirrels sit on his shoulders; of how the simple touch of his saliva could heal even the most painful workplace accident; of how his prayers had the power to cure the sick and to keep the dying alive. Favoured by kings, who knew authority when they saw it, Columbanus nevertheless disdained to play by the rules. In 610, asked to give his blessing to four princes who had been fathered by the local king on various concubines, he refused. Instead, he pronounced doom on them; and as he did so, a great clap of thunder sounded from the heavens. Even confronted by soldiers, Columbanus did not back down. Escorted to the coast, and put on a ship bound for Ireland, his prayers saw violent winds three times blow the ship back onto the mud-flats. Freed by his guards, who had come to fear his potency far more than that of their king, he crossed the Alps and descended into Italy. News came to him that, just as he had prophesied, the four princes had met with miserable deaths. Columbanus, though, did not turn back. Instead, as he travelled, he continuously sought out the wildest places that he could, remote spots haunted by wolves and pagans, far from the temptations of the world; and wherever he paused, there he would plant a monastery. The last of his foundations, built in a river-scored defile named Bobbio some fifty miles south of Milan, was where, in 615, the aged exile finally died.

Life itself, though—for the sinner adrift from heaven—was an exile. For all that Columbanus' departure from his homeland struck Franks and Italians as a peculiarly drastic gesture of penance, and a distinctively Irish one at that, the resonances that it stirred in them reached back deep into the past of the Latin West. Augustine, looking about him at the great cities of the world, at Rome, and Carthage, and Milan, had imagined the City of God as a pilgrim, unshackled by worldly cares. 'There, instead of victory, is truth; instead of high rank, holiness; instead of peace, felicity; instead of life, eternity.'[31] This, when supplicants ventured through the woods that surrounded Luxeuil and approached the settlement founded by Columbanus, was what they hoped to find. The very wall that enclosed the monastery, raised by the saint's own hand, proclaimed the triumph of the City of God over that of man. The shattered fragments of bath-houses and temples had been built into its fabric: pillars, pediments, broken statuary. These, converted to the uses of *religio*, were the bric-à-brac of what Augustine, two centuries previously, had identified as the order of the *saeculum*. The word had various shades of meaning. Originally, it had signified the span of a human life, whether defined as a generation, or as the maximum number of years that any one individual could hope to live: a hundred years. Increasingly, though, it had come to denote the limits of living recollection. Throughout Rome's history, from its earliest days to the time of Constantine, games to mark the passing of a *saeculum* had repeatedly been held: 'a spectacle such as no one had ever witnessed, nor ever would again'.[32] This was why Augustine, looking for a word to counterpoint the unchanging eternity of the City of God, had seized upon it. Things caught up in the flux of mortals' existence, bounded by their memories, forever changing upon the passage of the generations: all these, so Augustine declared, were *saecularia*—'secular things'.[33]

The potency of Columbanus' mission lay in the vivid way that he gave physical expression to the conception of these twin dimensions: of *religio* and of the *saeculum*. Even after his death, stories told of the men and women who submitted to his rule left admirers in no doubt that it could indeed open the gates to heaven. In Columbanus' own lifetime, a dying brother had told him of seeing an angel waiting by his sickbed, and begged him to cease his prayers, which were only serving to keep the angel at bay; in a nunnery founded by one of his disciples, a sister on the point of death had ordered the candle in her cell snuffed out. 'For do you not see what splendour approaches? Do you not hear the choirs singing?'[34] Stories like these, told wherever Columbanus or one of his followers had established a foundation, gave to their monasteries and convents a charge, and a sense of potency, that not even the greatest basilicas could rival. Those who dwelt in them were living embodiments of *religio*: *religiones*. To pass their walls, to cross the ditches and palisades that marked out their limits, was to leave the earthly behind and approach the heavenly.

No surprise, then, that in time the wings of the most powerful angel of them all should have been heard beating golden over Columbanus' native land. Almost certainly, it was Irish monks studying in Bobbio who brought home with them the cult of Saint Michael. From Italy to Ireland, the charisma of the warrior archangel came to radiate across the entire West. In time, even the furthermost spike of rock, as far out into the ocean as it was possible for monks to go and not vanish beyond the horizon, would end up under his protection. Skellig became Skellig Michael. There was nowhere so remote, it seemed, nowhere so far removed from the centres of earthly power, that the presence of an angel—and perhaps even his voice—might not be experienced there.

The summons to be born anew, to repent and be absolved of sin, was one that would prove to have many takers.

7

EXODUS

632: Carthage

In the spring of 632, a ship bearing a letter from Caesar glided into the great harbour at Carthage. So ships had been doing since the time of Augustus. Generations after the disintegration of Roman rule in the West, the shadows of the ancient past still lay deep over Africa. Carthage, like Rome, stood on the periphery of a great agglomeration of provinces that still spanned the eastern Mediterranean and had as their capital Constantinople, the second Rome. Lost for decades, as Rome had been, to barbarian conquerors, Carthage had been recaptured for the Empire—again, just as Rome had been—almost a century previously. Unlike Italy, though, where imperial rule was moth-eaten and embattled, the province of Africa lay securely under Roman control. The emperor himself, a battle-hardened Cappadocian named Heraclius, had seized the throne after launching a coup from there. By 632, he had been in power for twenty-two years. The commands of such of a man were not lightly set aside. The prefect of Africa, opening the imperial missive, certainly had no hesitation in scrabbling to obey them. On 31 May, Heraclius' command was put into effect. All the Jews in Africa—'visitors as well as residents, their wives, their children, their slaves'[1]—were forcibly baptised.

Here was a brutal solution to what had always been a source of frustration. Ever since the time of Paul, Christians had been fretting over the obdurate refusal of God's original chosen people to accept his Son as the Messiah. Their perplexity was compounded by the fact that the Jews, according to the unimpeachable evidence of the gospels, had willingly accepted responsibility for the death of Christ. 'Let his blood be on us and on our children!'[2] Why, then, confronted by this transparent act of deicide, had the Almighty not exacted a terrible vengeance? The response of theologians was to insist that he had. The Temple was no more, after all, and the Jews' ancient homeland—its name long since changed by the Romans from Judaea to Palestine—reconsecrated as a Christian 'Holy Land'. Meanwhile, the Jews themselves lived as exiles, 'witnesses to their own iniquity, and to the truth'.[3] Clear and awful were the proofs of divine disapproval; and so the imperial authorities, eager to serve the will of the Almighty, had naturally made sure to add some refinements of their own. The site of the Temple had been converted into a rubbish tip, a dumping-ground for dead pigs and shit; Jews themselves—except for one day a year, when a delegation was permitted to climb Mount Moria, there to lament and weep—were banned from Jerusalem; legal restrictions on their civic status grew ever more oppressive. It was forbidden them to serve in the army; to own Christian slaves; to build new synagogues. In exchange, Jews were granted the right to live according to their own traditions—but only so that they might then better serve the Christian people as a spectacle and a warning. Now, with his abrupt new shift of policy, Heraclius had denied them even that.

Many Christians, it is true, were appalled: some because they feared the damage that reluctant converts might do to the Church, and others because they believed, as Gregory had put it, that 'humility and kindness, teaching and persuasion, are the means by which to gather in the foes of the Christian faith'.[4] Yet even before Heraclius' decree, many had come to dread that it was too late for such an approach. The same consciousness of living in the end days that so haunted Gregory had already prompted a few bishops in Francia to force baptism on the local Jews. In Spain, in 612, the king of the Visigoths had followed suit. Heraclius, too, for the entire length of his reign, had lived with a consciousness that the world was coming apart. 'The Empire will fall.'[5] So Theodore, the lettuce-munching ascetic from Galatia, had prophesied in the year of Heraclius' accession—and so it had almost proved. War had ravaged the Roman Empire. The tides of a great Persian invasion had lapped at the very walls of Constantinople. Syria, Palestine, Egypt: all had fallen. Jerusalem had been stormed. Only a spectacular series of campaigns led by Heraclius himself had succeeded in hauling his empire back from the brink. Reclaiming the provinces lost to the Persians, riding through Syria, entering Jerusalem, he had repeatedly been told stories of Jewish treachery—and even of the occasional Christian, despairing of Christ, who had submitted to circumcision. Not merely accursed of God, then, the Jews were a plain and active menace. Heraclius, weary after his long struggle to save the Christian people from ruin, was in no mood to show them clemency. Now that the Persians were defeated, he aimed as well to eliminate the enemy within. His ambition: to fashion an exclusively, an impregnably Christian realm.

So it was, in Carthage, that the emperor's policy was punctiliously applied. Any Jew who landed in the city risked arrest and forcible baptism. All he had to do was cry out in Hebrew when twisting an ankle, or perhaps expose himself at the baths, to risk denunciation. Most Jews, in their hearts, remained resolutely unbaptised; but there were some, persuaded by argument, or on occasion a vision, who did truly come to feel themselves brought to Christ.[6] It was in consternation, then, in the summer of 634, that such converts listened to startling news brought from Palestine. There, it was reported, the Jews were cheering a fresh insult to Heraclius. The province had been invaded by 'Saracens': Arabs. They had killed an eminent official. They were led by a 'prophet'. Some Jews, it was true, doubted his right to this title, 'for prophets do not come with a sword and a war-chariot'.[7] Many more were afire with excitement. They, no less than Christians, could recognise in the convulsions of the age the seeming imminence of the end days. Perhaps, they dared to wonder, the advent of a Saracen prophet portended God's liberation at last of his Chosen People, the rebuilding of the Temple, and the coming of the Messiah?

What it certainly portended was an upheaval in the affairs of the Near East on a scale not witnessed since the time of Alexander. Palestine, although the initial target of the invaders, was not the last. Provinces of the battle-wearied Roman and Persian empires, like over-cooked meat slipping off the bone, melted into the grasp of Arab warbands. From Mesopotamia to central Asia, the lands ruled by the King of Kings were swallowed whole by the conquerors; those ruled by Caesar reduced to a bloody trunk. Heraclius, so lately triumphant, had barely been able to hold the line in the mountains of his native Cappadocia. The fate of Gaul and Spain—rule by barbarian overlords—was now visited on Syria and Egypt.

Yet the Arabs, despite the hearty contempt for them felt by the peoples of more settled lands, were hardly ignorant of civilisation. The influence of Rome and Persia had reached deep into Arabia. Even those tribes not employed as mercenaries on the borders of the rival empires had come to feel the seductive appeal of the superpowers' gold—and of their gods. The Arabs had particular reason to feel flattered by Jewish and Christian scripture. Alone among the barbarian peoples who lurked beyond the borders of the Roman Empire, they featured in it. Isaac, so it was recorded in Genesis, had not been Abraham's only son. The patriarch had also fathered a second, Ishmael, on an Egyptian slave. This meant that the Arabs—whom commentators had long since identified with the descendants of Ishmael—could claim a lineal descent from the first man to reject idolatry. Not only that, they were cousins of the Jews. Christian scholars were not long in waking up to the unsettling implications of this. Paul, warning the Galatians against circumcision, had declared that peoples everywhere—provided only that they accepted Christ as Lord—were the heirs of Abraham. But now, as though in direct repudiation of this, a circumcised people had seized the rule of the world—and done so, what was more, as claimants to an inheritance 'promised by God to their ancestor'. So, at any rate, it was reported by a Christian writing in Armenia some three decades after the conquest of Palestine by the Saracens. Their mysterious 'prophet'—left unnamed in the report sent to the Jews of Carthage—was now identified as a man named Muhammad. 'No one will be able to resist you in battle,' he was supposed to have told his followers. 'For God is with you.'[8]

Here, of course, was nothing that Christians had not heard before. Constantine had offered an identical assurance; so too, in the course of his campaigns against the Persians, had Heraclius. Even in the furthest reaches of the world, in the rain-lashed monasteries and monks' cells of Ireland, many of the claims made by the Saracens for their prophet would not have seemed strange. That an angel had appeared to him. That he, unlike the Jews, had acknowledged Jesus as the Messiah, and displayed a particular devotion to Mary. That he had revealed to them visions of both heaven and hell, and that the Day of Judgement was terrifyingly near. No less than Columbanus, Muhammad had preached the importance of pilgrimage, and prayer, and charity. 'What will explain to you what the steep path is? It is to free a slave, to feed at a time of hunger an orphaned relative or a poor person in distress, and to be one of those who believe and urge one another to steadfastness and compassion.'[9] Here were teachings with which Gregory of Nyssa would readily have concurred.

Yet Muhammad had not been a Christian. In 689, on Mount Moria, work began on a building that broadcast this in the most public manner possible. The Dome of the Rock, as it would come to be known, occupied the very spot where the Holy of Holies was supposed to have stood, and was a deliberate rubbing of Jewish noses in the failure, yet again, of all their hopes: of their messiah to appear; of the Temple to be rebuilt. Even more forthright, though, was the lesson taught to Christians: that they clung to a corrupted and superseded faith. Running along both sides of the building's arcade, a series of verses disparaged the doctrine of the Trinity. 'The Messiah, Jesus, son of Mary, was only a messenger of God.'[10] This was not merely to reopen theological debates that Christians had thought settled centuries before, but to condemn the entire New Testament, Gospels and all, as a fabrication. Squabbles among those who had written it, so the Dome of the Rock sternly declared, had polluted the original teachings of Jesus. These, like the revelations granted prophets before him, Abraham, and Moses, and David, had originally been identical to those proclaimed by Muhammad. There was only the one true *deen*, the one true expression of allegiance to God, and that was submission to him: in Arabic, *islam*.[11]

Here was a doctrine with which 'Muslims'—those who practised *islam*—were already well familiar. It was not only to be found emblazoned on buildings. Most of the verses on the Dome of the Rock derived from a series of revelations that Muhammad's followers believed had been given to him by none other than the angel Gabriel. These, assembled after his death to form a single 'recitation', or *qur'an*, constituted for his followers what Jesus represented to Christians: an intrusion into the mortal world, into the sublunar, into the diurnal, of the divine. Muhammad had not written this miraculous text. He had merely served as its mouthpiece. Instead, every word, every last letter of the Qur'an derived from a single author: God. This gave to its pronouncements on Christians, as on everything else, an awful and irrevocable force. Unlike pagans, but like Jews, they were owed the respect due a people who had their own scriptures, as a 'People of the Book'. Self-evidently, though, the errors in these same scriptures ensured that God had no choice but to ordain their perpetual subjugation. The very deal that the Roman authorities had prescribed for the Jews was now, to Christians' dismay, imposed on them as well. Tolerance, so it was written in the Qur'an, should be granted both Peoples of the Book; but only in exchange for the payment of a tax, the *jizya*, and humble acknowledgement of their own inferiority. Stubbornness could not be allowed to go unpunished. Why, for instance, when it had been revealed conclusively in the Qur'an that Jesus, rather than suffering execution, had only appeared to be crucified, did Christians persist in glorifying the cross? Paul, and the writers of the canonical Gospels, and Irenaeus, and Origen, and the drafters of the Nicaean Creed, and Augustine had all been wrong; Basilides had been right. 'Those who disagree on this know nothing, but merely follow conjecture.'[12]

Even more threatening to Christian assumptions than the Qur'an's flat denial that Jesus had been crucified, however, was the imperious, not to say terrifying, tone of authority with which it did so. Very little in either the Old or the New Testament could compare. For all the reverence with which Christians regarded their scripture, and for all that they believed it illumined by the flame of the Holy Spirit, they perfectly accepted that most of it, including the Gospels themselves, had been authored by mortals. Only the covenant on the tablets of stone, given to Moses amid fire and smoke on the summit of Sinai, 'and written with the finger of God',[13] owed nothing to human mediation. Perhaps it was no surprise, then, that Moses, of all the figures in the Old and New Testaments, should have featured most prominently in the Qur'an. He was mentioned 137 times in all. Many of the words attributed to him had served as a direct inspiration to Muhammad's own followers. 'My people! Enter the Holy Land which God has prescribed for you!'[14] The Arab conquerors, in the first decades of their empire, had pointedly referred to themselves as *muhajirun*: 'those who have undertaken an exodus'. A hundred years on from Muhammad's death, when the first attempts were made by Muslim scholars to write his biography, the model that they instinctively reached for was that of Moses. The age at which the Prophet had received his first revelation from God; the flight of his followers from a land of idols; the way in which—directly contradicting the news brought to Carthage in 634—he was said to have died before entering the Holy Land: all these elements echoed the life of the Jews' most God-favoured prophet.[15] So brilliantly, indeed, did

Muslim biographers paint from the palette of traditions told about Moses that the fading outlines of the historical Muhammad were quite lost beneath their brushstrokes. Last and most blessed of the prophets sent by God to set humanity on the straight path, there was only the one predecessor to whom he could properly be compared. 'There has come to him the greatest Law that came to Moses; surely he is the prophet of this people.'[16]

Heraclius, two years before the Arab invasion of Palestine, had commanded that Jews be forcibly baptised out of dread for the security of the Christian empire. Not even in his darkest nightmares could he have anticipated the calamities that had then rapidly followed and left Constantinople shorn of her richest provinces. Yet the threat presented by the Saracens to Christian rule was not merely a military one. The challenge was much greater than that. It was the same, in its essentials, as had prompted Paul, centuries previously, to write in desperate terms to the Galatians. The principle that Paul had fought for, and which had come to render Christianity irrevocably distinctive from Judaism, was clearer, perhaps, to Jewish converts than to Christians—most of whom had never met with, still less talked to, a Jew. To accept Christ was to accept that God could write his commandments on the heart. Again and again, among those Jews in Carthage whose compulsory baptism had been followed by an authentic conversion, this was the reflection, this the change in assumptions, that they had found the most overwhelming. 'It is not by means of the Law of Moses that creation has been saved, but because a new and different Law has risen up.'[17] The death of Christ upon the cross had offered humanity a universal salvation. There was no longer any need for Jews—or for anyone else—to submit to circumcision, or to avoid pork, or to follow detailed rules of sacrifice. The only laws that mattered were those inscribed by God on the conscience of a Christian. 'Love, and do as you want.'[18]

So Augustine had declared. Nowhere in the Latin West had the implications of Christian teaching been more brilliantly elucidated than in Africa—or to such influential effect. That there were Jews in Carthage who had been brought to accept them was, perhaps, due reflection of the distinctive quality of the city's Christianity: austere and passionate, autocratic and turbulent. Its self-confidence was that of a Church assured that it had indeed fathomed the laws of God.

But now a new understanding of the laws of God had emerged— and those who proclaimed it enjoyed, unlike the Jews, the muscle of a mighty and expanding empire. In 670, terrified reports reached Carthage of a raid on Africa that had carried away thousands of Christians into slavery. Over the succeeding decades, ever more incursions were recorded. Fortresses, towns, entire swathes of the province: all fell to permanent occupation. Finally, in the autumn of 695, sentries on the walls of Carthage spotted a smudge of dust on the horizon— and that it was growing larger. Then the glint of weapons catching the sun. Then, emerging from the dust, men, horses, siege-engines.

The Saracens had arrived.

The Full English

In the event, two sieges were required to wrest Carthage from Christian rule. After the city had been captured the second time, and its inhabitants slaughtered or enslaved, its conqueror razed its buildings to the ground. The masonry was then loaded into wagons and carted along the bay. There, on a hill, stood the small town of Tunis. Long in the shadow of Carthage, its time had now come. The building of a new capital from the rubble of the old proclaimed the triumph of Islam in one of the strongholds of the Christian West: the home of Cyprian, of Donatus, of Augustine. Such a thing was not meant to happen. For many centuries, the Christians of Africa had tended the flame of their faith. Just as the Israelites had followed Moses through the desert, so had they, members of the pilgrim Church, been guided through the centuries by the Holy Spirit. But now a new people, warriors who themselves claimed to be on an exodus, had seized the rule of Africa; and the Africans, for the first time in four hundred years, found themselves under the rule of masters who scorned the name of Christian. As in Jerusalem, so in Tunis, the conquerors did not hesitate to proclaim that a new revelation, God-given and uncorrupted, had superseded the old. It was not churches that were built out of the demolished walls and columns of Carthage, but places of worship called by the Arabs *masajid*: 'mosques'.

Yet even as the ancient heartlands of Christianity were brought to submit to Saracen rule, new frontiers lay open. Refugees from the *muhajirun* who settled in Rome did not necessarily stay there. Some three decades before the fall of Carthage, a Greek from Paul's home town of Tarsus, a celebrated scholar who had studied in both Syria and Constantinople, took ship for Marseille. Theodore brought with him a sense of ancient horizons. He could reminisce about camels laden with watermelons in Mesopotamia, the tableware used by Persians, the cities visited by Paul. The further north he went, travelling under royal permit through Francia, so the more evocative of scripture his memories were liable to seem. Yet Theodore, sent by the Pope to take up a distant and arduous posting, was never merely a foreigner. The bonds of the universal Church held true. In Paris, over the winter, Theodore was hosted by the city's bishop. Then, with the coming of spring, he headed on northwards. Late in his sixties though he was, and feeling the strain of travel, he embarked for his ultimate destination: 'an island of the ocean far outside the world'.[19] Theodore was heading for Britain.

And specifically for the kingdom of Kent. Canterbury, a complex of Roman ruins and thatched halls in the far south-east of the island, might not have seemed the obvious seat for a bishop who claimed a primacy over the whole of Britain. It was, however, conveniently located for Rome; and it was from Rome, back in 597, that a band of monks sent by Pope Gregory had arrived in Kent. Britain, the home of Pelagius and Patrick, boasted ancient Christian roots; but many of these, in the centuries following the collapse of Roman rule, had either withered or been pulled up and trampled underfoot. Germanic-speaking warlords, carving out kingdoms for themselves, had seized control of the richest third of the island. Calling themselves variously Angles, or Saxons, or Jutes, they had been proudly and swaggeringly pagan. Rather than accept the Christianity of the conquered natives, as the Franks had done, they had scorned it. All the same, they had kept a careful eye on the world beyond their shores. They had been alert to the potency of Frankish kingship, and to the allure of Rome. When the Pope's emissary arrived in Britain, he had been given a cautious welcome. The king of Kent, after contemplating the mysteries revealed to him by Augustine, and weighing up the various opportunities that acceptance of them promised, had submitted to baptism. Over the following decades, a succession of other warlords across eastern Britain had done the same. Naturally, it had not been plain sailing. The tide had ebbed as well as flowed: the occasional bishop, caught out by an abrupt reversal of royal policy, had been forced to flee; the occasional king, cut down by a pagan rival, had been ritually dismembered. Nevertheless, by the time of Theodore's arrival in Canterbury, a majority of the Saxon and Anglian elites had tested the Christian god to their satisfaction. Like a sparrow flying swiftly through a hall and out again, into the storms of winter, so the brief life of man had seemed to these lords. 'For of what went before it or of what comes after, we know nothing. Therefore, if these new teachings can inform us more fully, it seems only right that we should follow them.'[20]

The dimensions opened up by this decision were not exclusively those of the afterlife, however. The enthronement as archbishop of Canterbury of a scholar who had studied in Syria provided converts in Britain with the glimpse of a thrillingly exotic world. Travelling with Theodore from Rome had come a second refugee, an African named Hadrian; and together they set up a school at Canterbury that taught both Latin and Greek. 'Eagerly, people sought the new-found joys of the kingdom of heaven; and all who wished to learn how to read scripture found teachers ready at hand.'[21] Such was the tribute that Bede, a young Anglian monk, felt moved to pay them in the wake of their death. Bede himself, a man of prodigious learning, offered living testimony to the sense of possibility that the two exiles had between them done so much to foster. Wistfully, in his commentaries on scripture, he would mourn that Arabia or India, Judaea or Egypt were places that he would never live to see; but then, in the same breath, rejoice that he could read about them instead. Time as well, from its beginning to its end, was his to measure and calibrate. Faced by a confusing multitude of dating systems, Bede saw, more clearly than any Christian scholar before him, that there was only the one fixed point amid the great sweep of the aeons, only the single pivot. Drawing on calendrical tables compiled some two centuries earlier by a monk from the Black Sea, he fixed on the Incarnation, the entry of the divine into the womb of the Virgin Mary, as the moment on which all of history turned. Years, for the first time, were measured according to whether they were before Christ or *anno Domini*: in the year of the Lord. The feat was as momentous as it was to prove enduring: a rendering of time itself as properly Christian.

No less than the Muslim general who had ransacked Carthage to build the mosques of Tunis, Bede believed himself to be living in an age of divinely ordained transformation. Jarrow, the monastery in which he spent most of his life, stood at what had once been the northernmost limits of Roman power, and had been built by Frankish architects out of the remains of ancient fortifications. Bede could not help but live with an awed sense of the sheer improbability of all that had been achieved. A mere generation had passed since Jarrow's founding. Now, beside the mud and sand of a great estuary, the chanting of psalms could be heard above the keening of seabirds; now, in a land only lately brought to Christ, a library was to be found as large as any in Rome. The wonder of it never ceased to move Bede. Kings had been known to break up silver dishes and share the fragments out among the poor; noblemen to lavish plunder on touring the great centres of Christian learning. Jarrow's founder, an Anglian lord named Biscop Baducing, had himself travelled six times to Rome, and brought back 'a boundless store of books',[22] as well as embroidered silks, the relics of saints, and an Italian singing-master. When Theodore and Hadrian travelled to Canterbury, Biscop had been by their side. The request that he serve the new archbishop as his guide had come from the very top: the Pope himself. Even Biscop's name had been latinised, to Benedict. No one in Britain had been quite so Roman for a very long time indeed.

Bede and his monastery, though, had been doubly washed by the floodtide of Christ. Not all of the blessings that watered Jarrow had flowed from the ancient heartlands of Christianity. They had flowed as well from Ireland. The conversion of Northumbria, the great Anglian kingdom in which Jarrow stood, owed at least as much to Irish monks as to bishops from the Mediterranean. The same indomitable spirit of self-abnegation that had so impressed the Franks had moved and awed the Northumbrians as well. Bede, for all that he had devoted his life to scholarship, recorded with love and honour the doings of those monks who, inspired by the Irish example, had lived a sterner life: standing vigil in the icy waters of the sea; braving plague to comfort and heal the sick; communing in the wild with ravens, and eagles, and sea-otters. Although, in the ordering of its calendar and its festivals, the Northumbrian Church had been persuaded to adopt Roman over Irish practice, Bede never doubted that it had been nourished by the traditions of both. The spirit of Columbanus was owed nothing but respect. Theodore, meeting with a bishop who insisted always on travelling humbly on foot, had ordered him to ride whenever he had to make a long journey; but then, giving him a horse, had helped him like a servant up into his saddle. 'For the archbishop,' Bede explained, 'had perfectly recognised his holiness.'[23]

What, though, might this confluence, this blending of the Roman and Irish, imply about God's plans for Bede's own people? This, in the final years of his life, was the question to which the great scholar sought to provide an answer. After a lifetime of studying scripture, he knew exactly where to look. Just as Arab scholars had looked to the life of Moses to help them compose the biography of their prophet, so had Bede, when he sought to make sense of his own people's history, turned to the Old Testament. Like the Pentateuch, his great work was divided into five books. It cast Britain, an island rich in precious metals, good pasturage and whelks, as a promised land. It told of how the Britons, judged by God and found wanting, had been deprived of their inheritance. It related how the Angles, the Saxons and the Jutes, landing in Britain after an exodus across the sea, had served as the rod of divine anger, and thereby come into their own. It described again and again how Northumbrian kings, redeemed from idolatry, had dealt with their pagan enemies much as Moses had dealt with Pharaoh, not merely by inflicting slaughter on them, but by consigning them to a watery grave. 'More were drowned while trying to escape than perished by the sword.'[24] So Bede noted with satisfaction of one particularly decisive Christian victory. If baptism had brought the Angles into membership of the universal Church, then so also, in Bede's history, had it brought them something else: the hint of a possibility that they might be a chosen people.

Bede could not, of course, as Arab scholars had done, claim a bloodline from Abraham. In Northumbria, there was nothing like the variety of traditions, Jewish, and Samaritan, and Christian, that for so long had been bubbling away together in the great cauldron of the Near East. Bede used, though, what he could. Why had Gregory sent a mission to be the salvation of his people? Because, so Bede reported, he had seen blond-haired boys for sale in Rome's market and, struck by their beauty, asked from where they came; then, on being told that the slaves were Angles, made a fateful pun. 'It is fitting,' he said, 'for their faces are those of angels—and so they should properly share with the angels an inheritance in heaven.'[25] This wordplay, not surprisingly, was much cherished by Northumbrians. When Judgement Day came, they claimed, it was Gregory who would stand by Christ's side and make plea for them. Bede, though, went further. In his history, he cast the glamour of the angelic over all the kingdoms founded in Britain by those who had made their exodus across the northern sea: Saxon and Jutish as well as Anglian. Not merely a new Israel, they were lit by something of the blaze of the heavenly. Such, at any rate, was Bede's hope. To many, it would have seemed a vain one. The Angles, let alone the Saxons and the Jutes, did not think of themselves as a single people. Their lands remained, in the wake of their baptism, what they had always been: a patchwork of rival kingdoms, governed by ambitious warlords. Yet the allure of Bede's vision would prove too bright to be snuffed out. In time, the Saxons and the Jutes would indeed come to think of themselves as sharing a single identity with the Angles—and even to accept their name. Their kingdoms, following their union, would be known as *Anglia* and, in their own language, *Englalonde*. Just as the inheritance of scripture had inspired a momentous new configuration of identities in the Near East, so also in Britain. The elements of Exodus, so evident in the stories that Muslims told of their origins, were shaping, at the far end of the world, the cocoon of myth in which another people were being formed: the English.

A Clash of Civilisations

Bede knew nothing of Islam. Its empire was too far distant. Even the Byzantines, as the inhabitants of Constantinople called themselves, cared little for the details of what their Muslim enemies actually believed. Islam, so they assumed, was merely another head sprung from the hydra of heresy. As such, it merited nothing from Christians but disdain and contempt. Bede, though, in his monastery beside the remote northern sea, could not even be certain of that. Vaguely, from his study of scripture and from the reports of pilgrims to the Holy Land, he had a sense of the Saracens as a pagan people, worshippers of the Morning Star; but it was their prowess as conquerors that most concerned him. Their destruction of Carthage, Bede knew, had been only a waypoint. In 725, in the final entry of a chronicle that had begun with the Creation, he recorded further details of their onslaughts. That they had launched an attack on

Constantinople itself, and only been foiled after a three-year siege; that Saracen pirates had come to infest the western Mediterranean; that the body of Augustine had been transported to Italy in a desperate attempt to keep it safe from their depredations. Then, four years later, the appearance in the sky of two comets, trailing fire as though to set the whole north alight, seemed to Bede a portent of even worse: that the Saracens were drawing closer. And so it proved.

In 731, the great monastery founded by Columbanus at Luxeuil was raided by Arab horsemen. Those monks who could not escape were put to the sword. A mere two decades had passed since the first landing on Spanish soil of a Muslim warband. In that short space of time, the kingdom of the Visigoths had been brought crashing down. Christian lords across the Iberian peninsula had submitted to Muslim rule. Only in the mountainous wilds of the north had a few maintained their defiance. Meanwhile, beyond the Pyrenees, the wealth of Francia had tempted the Arabs into ever more far-ranging razzias. The daughter of the Duke of Aquitaine had been captured and sent to Syria as a trophy of war. Then, in 732, the Duke himself was defeated in pitched battle. Bordeaux was put to the torch. But the Arabs were not done yet. On the Loire, tantalisingly close, stood the richest prize in Francia. The temptation proved too strong to resist. That October, despite the lateness of the campaigning season, the Arabs took the road northwards. Their target: the shrine of Saint Martin at Tours.

They never made it. Martin was not a saint lightly threatened. The prospect that sacrilegious hands might tear at Martin's shrine was one fit to appal any Frank. Sure enough, north of Poitiers, the Arabs were confronted by a force of warriors. Motionless the phalanx stood, 'like a glacier of the frozen north'.[26] The Arabs, rather than withdraw and cede victory to a Christian saint, sought to shatter it. They failed. Broken on the Franks' swords, and with their general among the slain, the survivors fled under cover of night. Burning and looting still as they went, they retreated to al-Andalus, as they called Spain. The great tide of their westwards expansion had reached its fullest flood. Never again would Arab horsemen threaten the resting-place of Saint Martin. Even though their raids across the Pyrenees would continue for decades to come, any hopes they might have nurtured of conquering the Frankish kingdom as they had won al-Andalus were decisively ended. Instead, it was the Franks who went on the attack. The victor at Poitiers had a talent for ravaging the lands of his enemies. Although Charles 'Martel'— 'the Hammer'—was not of royal stock, he had forged for himself a dominion that left the heirs of Clovis as mere hapless ciphers. North of the Loire, he was the master of a realm that fused two previously distinct Frankish kingdoms, one centred on Paris, the other on the Rhine; now, in the wake of Poitiers, he moved to bring Provence and Aquitaine securely under his rule as well. Arab garrisons were scoured from the great fortresses of Arles and Avignon. An amphibious relief-force sent from al-Andalus was annihilated near Narbonne. The fugitives, desperately trying to swim back to their ships, were pursued by the victorious Franks and speared in the shallows of lagoons. By 741, when Charles Martel died, Frankish armies had the range of lands stretching from the Pyrenees to the Danube.

It was the victory at Poitiers, though, that would most enduringly gild the Hammer's fame. He was not, it was true, universally popular in Francia. Some, suspicious of his lust for power, claimed that his corpse had been snatched from its tomb by a dragon, and hauled away to the underworld. This, however, was a minority view. Most Franks saw in the sheer scale of Charles' achievements evidence for that favourite conceit of the age: that God had anointed them as a chosen people. In 751, when Charles' son Pepin deposed the line of Clovis for good, his coup drew its sustenance from the prowess of his father. 'The name of your people has been raised up above all the other nations.'[27] So the Pope himself reassured the king. That Charles Martel had been a second Joshua, conquering a promised land, was a staple of Frankish self-congratulation. The Saracens had been as stubble to his sword. Ever more startling estimates of how many had fallen at Poitiers came to be bruited. Within only a few decades of the battle, the total was already nudging four hundred thousand.

There was much, then, that the Franks had in common with their most formidable adversaries. Both believed themselves possessed of a license from God to subdue other peoples, and both drew on the inheritance of Jewish scripture to substantiate this militant calling. Certainly, a pagan traveller from beyond the eastern frontiers of the Frankish empire, a Saxon or a Dane, would have found it hard to distinguish between the rival combatants on the battlefield of Poitiers. Christians and Muslims alike worshipped a single, omnipotent deity; claimed to fight beneath the watchful protection of angels; believed that they stood in a line of inheritance from Abraham.

Yet the very similarities between them served only to sharpen the differences. More had hung in the balance at Poitiers than the Franks could possibly have realised. Far distant from their kingdom, in the great cities of the Near East, Muslim scholars were in the process of shaping a momentous new legitimacy for Islam, and its claim to a global rule. The Arabs, after their conquest of what for millennia had been the world's greatest concentration of imperial and legal traditions, had been faced with an inevitable challenge. How were they to forge a functioning state? Not every answer to the running of a great empire was to be found in the Qur'an. Similarly absent was guidance on some of the most basic aspects of daily life: whether it was acceptable for the faithful to urinate behind a bush, for instance, or to wear silk, or to keep a dog, or for men to shave, or for women to dye their hair black, or how best to brush one's teeth. For the Arabs simply to have adopted the laws and customs of the peoples they had subdued would have risked the exclusive character of their rule. Worse, it would have seen their claim to a divinely sanctioned authority fatally compromised. Accordingly, when they adopted legislation from the peoples they had conquered, they did not acknowledge their borrowing, as the Franks or the Visigoths had readily done, but derived it instead from that most respected, that most authentically Muslim of sources: the Prophet himself. Even as Poitiers was being fought, collections of sayings attributed to Muhammad were being compiled that, in due course, would come to constitute an entire corpus of law: *Sunna*. Any detail of Roman or Persian legislation, any fragment of Syrian or Mesopotamian custom, might be incorporated within it. The only requirement was convincingly to represent it as having been spoken by the Prophet— for anything spoken by Muhammad could be assumed to have the stamp of divine approval.

Here, then, for Christians was a fateful challenge. Their time-honoured conviction that the true law of God was to be found written on the heart could not have been more decisively repudiated. No longer was it the prerogative of Jews alone to believe in a great corpus of divine legislation that touched upon every facet of human existence, and prescribed in exacting detail how God desired men and women to live. The Talmud, an immense body of law compiled by Jewish scholars—*rabbis*—in the centuries prior to the Arab conquest of the Near East, had never threatened the inheritance of Paul's teachings as the Sunna did. Muslims were not a beleaguered minority, prey to the bullying of Christian emperors and kings. They had conquered a vast and wealthy empire, and aspired to conquer yet more. Had Francia gone the way of Africa, and been lost for good to Christian rule, then the Franks too would doubtless have eventually been brought to the Muslim understanding of God and his law. The fundamental assumptions that governed Latin Christendom would thereby have been radically and momentously transformed. Few, if any, who fought at Poitiers would have realised it, but at stake in the battle had been nothing less than the legacy of Saint Paul.

'For you are a chosen people, a royal priesthood, a holy nation, a people belonging to God.'[28] The Pope, when he quoted this line of scripture in a letter to Pepin, was not merely flattering the Franks, but acknowledging a brute reality. Increasingly, it was the empire ruled by the heirs of Charles Martel—the Carolingians—that defined for the papacy the very character of Christian rule. Paul I, unlike his predecessors, had failed to notify the emperor in Constantinople of his election. Instead, he had written to Pepin. The Byzantines, struggling for survival as they were against relentless Muslim onslaughts, appeared to Christians in Rome—let alone in Francia or Northumbria—an ever more alien and distant people. Even more spectral were the lands that for centuries had constituted the great wellsprings of the Christian faith: Syria and Palestine, Egypt and Africa. The days when a man like Theodore might freely travel from Tarsus to Canterbury were over. The Mediterranean was now a Saracen sea. Its waters were perilous for Christians to sail. The world was cut in half. An age was at an end.

Part II

———— ❖ ————

CHRISTENDOM

8

CONVERSION

754: Frisia

As dawn broke, the camp on the banks of the river Boorne was already stirring. Boniface, its leader, was almost eighty, but as tireless as he had ever been. Forty years after his first journey to Frisia, he had returned there, in the hope of reaping from its lonely mudflats and marshes a great harvest of souls. Missionary work had long been his life. Born in Devon, in the Saxon kingdom of Wessex, he viewed the pagans across the northern sea as his kinsmen. In letters home he had regularly solicited prayers for their conversion. 'Take pity upon them; for they themselves are saying: "We are of one blood and bone with you."'[1] Now, after weeks of touring the scattered homesteads of Frisia, Boniface had summoned all those won for Christ to be confirmed in their baptismal vows. It promised him a day of joy.

The first boats arrived as sunlight was starting to pierce the early morning cloud. A mass of men, after clambering onto dry land, walked up from the river and approached the camp. Then, abruptly, the glint of swords. A charge. Screams. Boniface came out of his tent. Already it was too late. The pirates were in the camp. Desperately, Boniface's attendants fought back. Not the old man himself, though. Christ, when he was arrested, had ordered Peter to put up his sword; and now Boniface, following his Lord's example, commanded his followers to lay down their weapons. A tall man, he gathered his fellow priests around him, and urged them to be thankful for the hour of their release. Felled by a pirate's sword, he was cut to pieces. So violently did the blows rain down that twice a book he had in his hands was hacked through. Found long afterwards at the scene of his murder, it would be treasured ever after as a witness to his martyrdom.

'Therefore, go and make disciples of all nations.'[2] So Christ himself had commanded. Augustine, insisting that the Church was for all humanity, had drawn on Genesis to emphasise his point. There, the story was told of how God had sent a flood that covered the entire world; but also of how a righteous man named Noah, forewarned of what was to happen, had built a great ark, in which two of every living creature had found a refuge. The mission of Christians was to build an ark that could shelter all the world. 'The Heavenly City calls out to citizens from every nation, and thereby collects a society of aliens, speaking every language.'[3] Yet Augustine, true to the missionary spirit of Paul though he was, had been the exception that proved the rule. Most of his contemporaries, schooled in a deep contempt for barbarians, had regarded Christianity as far too precious to be shared with the savages who lurked beyond the limits of Roman power. Those few missions that did venture past the frontier had been sent not to convert the natives, but to minister to Christian captives. In 340, for instance, the priest Ulfilas—the descendant of Cappadocians enslaved a century previously by Gothic raiders—had been appointed 'bishop of the Christians who live among the Goths'. Despite ministering beyond the Danube for seven years, he had not hesitated, when faced with a sudden bout of persecution, to lead his flock to Roman soil. That, after all, was where Christians properly belonged. Even centuries on, long after the collapse of the empire in the West, such attitudes died hard. The division between kingdoms that had once been Roman and the world beyond was one that even the most outward-looking bishops still tended to take for granted. Gregory, when he sent his mission to Kent, had been motivated in part by his awareness that Britain had once been an imperial province. The paganism of its new rulers had offended him not merely as a Christian, but as a Roman.

To Angles and Saxons, however, such considerations meant nothing. Grateful though they were to Gregory for his role in bringing them to Christ, their loyalty to the papacy implied no devotion to any long-vanished Roman imperial order. For Anglo-Saxon monks, the pagan darkness that loured over the eastern reaches of Germany, from the North Sea coast to the great forests of the interior, spoke not of an invincible savagery, not of a barbarism best left alone, but of a pressing need for light. All the world was theirs to illumine with the blaze of Christ. It was not the inheritance of Roman imperialism that inspired them, but the example of Patrick and Columbanus. To experience hardship was the very point. Fearsome stories were told of what missionaries might face. Woden, king of the demons worshipped by the Germans as gods, was darkly rumoured to demand a tithe of human lives. In the Low Countries, prisoners were drowned beneath rising tides; in Saxony, hung from trees, and run through with spears. Runes were dyed in Christian blood. Or so it was reported. Such rumours, far from intimidating Anglo-Saxon monks, only confirmed them in their sense of purpose: to banish the rule of demons from lands that properly belonged to Christ.

As vividly as anyone, they understood what it was to be born again. 'The old has gone, the new has come!'[4] The tone of revolution in Paul's cry, the sense that an entire order had been judged and found wanting, still retained a freshness for men like Boniface in a way that it did not in more venerable reaches of the Christian world. So august a presence was the Church in Rome or Constantinople that people there might struggle to imagine that it had ever been something insurgent. Yet still, fissile within its scriptures and rituals, the portrayal of change as a force for good, as a process to be embraced, as a road capable of leading humanity to a brighter future, continued to radiate. Boniface, as a West Saxon, a man whose people had only lately been brought to Christ, stood in awe of it. He suffered no anxiety in contemplating the world turned upside down. Quite the opposite. Taking to the roads, he felt himself called to serve just as Paul had once served: as an agent of disruption.

To banish the past, to overturn custom: here was a fearsome project, barely comprehensible to the peoples of other places, other times. The vast mass of humanity had always taken for granted that novelty was to be mistrusted. Boniface's own countrymen had been no different. Many among the Angles and the Saxons had been afraid to let go of the past: kings who prided themselves on their descent from Woden; peasants who resented monks for 'abolishing the old ways of worship'.⁵ Now, though, time itself was being transfigured. Barely a decade after Boniface's arrival in the Low Countries, missionaries had begun to calculate dates in the manner of Bede: *anno Domini*, in the year of their Lord. The old order, which to pagans had seemed eternal, could now more firmly be put where it properly belonged: in the distant reaches of a Christian calendar. While the figure of Woden bestowed far too much prestige on kings ever to be erased altogether from their lineages, monks did not hesitate to demote him from his divine status and confine him to the remote beginnings of things. The rhythms of life and death, and of the cycle of the year, proved no less adaptable to the purposes of the Anglo-Saxon Church. So it was that *hel*, the pagan underworld, where all the dead were believed to dwell, became, in the writings of monks, the abode of the damned; and so it was too that Eostre, the festival of the spring, which Bede had speculated might derive from a goddess, gave its name to the holiest Christian feast-day of all. Hell and Easter: the garbing of the Church's teachings in Anglo-Saxon robes did not signal a surrender to the pagan past, but rather its rout. Only because the gods had been toppled from their thrones, melted utterly by the light of Christ, or else banished to where monsters stalked, in fens or on lonely hills, could their allure safely be put to Christian ends. The victory of the new was adorned with the trophies of the old.

It was Boniface who had demonstrated this most ringingly. In 722, he had been consecrated a bishop by the pope in Rome, and given a formal commission to convert the pagans east of the Rhine. Arriving in central Germany, he had headed for the furthermost limits of the Christian world. At Geisner, where Thuringia joined with the lands of the pagan Saxons, there stood a great oak, sacred to Thunor, a particularly mighty and fearsome god, whose hammer-blows could split mountains, and whose goat-drawn chariot made the whole earth shake. Boniface chopped it down. Then, with its timbers, he built a church. The woodman's axe had long served to humble demons. In Utrecht, a fortress on the north bank of the Rhine that had provided Anglo-Saxon monks with the base for their mission to the Frisians, an axe made of polished stone was confidently identi-fied as having once belonged to Martin. Stories were told of how, to demonstrate the power of Christ's name, the saint had stood in the path of a falling tree, and lived to tell the tale. Boniface, by chopping down Thunor's oak, had shown courage of a similar order. That he had not been struck by lightning, nor slain for his temerity by out-raged locals, was widely noted. The bare stump of the oak served as a proof of what the missionary had been claiming. Christ had tri-umphed over Thunor. Pilgrims still travelled to Geisner; but now, when they did so, it was to worship in an oratory made from freshly sawn oaken planks.

Boniface had not been so naïve as to think that his mission was thereby done. The task of winning people for Christ could not be achieved merely by cutting down a tree. Converts, even after bap-tism, continued to practise any number of pestiferous customs: offering sacrifice to springs, inspecting entrails, claiming to read the future. Such backsliding was not the worst. Travelling through the lands east of the Rhine that lay under the rule of the Franks—Hesse, and Thuringia, and Swabia—Boniface had been horrified by what he found. Churches that in many cases reached back cen-turies seemed rotten with pagan practices. Merchants who sold slaves to the Saxons for sacrifice; noblemen who hid their worship of idols 'under the cloak of Christianity';[6] priests who made sacrifice of goats and bulls; bishops who fornicated, and inherited their sees from their fathers, and indulged in spectacular blood-feuds: these were not the kinds of Christian that Boniface was content to leave to their own devices. Rather than venture further into the forests of Saxony, as he had long dreamed of doing, he had embarked instead on a great labour of reform. Flinty, prickly and exacting, he had not stinted in his efforts to set the churches of eastern Francia on what he saw as a proper footing. The loathing of the local bishops for his finger-wagging he had met with a matching contempt. Not merely a man of unyielding principle, he had displayed a rare talent for securing powerful patrons. As well as the Pope, he had won the backing of Charles Martel. The Frankish warlord, no less keen to break the eastern marches to his own purposes than the Anglo-Saxon bishop, had found in Boniface a man after his own heart. Tortured though Boniface was by the need to curry favour at court, and by his frustrated yearning to save the souls of pagans, he had succeeded, by the end of his life, in shaping the churches east of the Rhine to something like his own image. Returning, in the last year of his life, to the mission that had always been closest to his heart, he had done so as the dominant figure in the Frankish church.

To convert was to educate. This, the great lesson taught by Boniface, was one that the Franks would not forget. Touched as it was by the aura of sanctity that clung to him as a martyr, it would bequeath to kings as well as to priests a stern and implacable sense of their duty to God. Yet even as Boniface was being cut down amid the reeds and mud of Frisia, the lead given by missionaries in the spread of Christianity eastwards was passing. A new and altogether more militant approach to paganism was being prepared. The willingness of Boniface to meet death rather than permit his attendants to draw their swords was not one that the Frankish authorities tended to share. Three days after his murder, a squad of Christian warriors tracked down the killers, cornered them and wiped them out. Their women and children were taken as slaves. Their plunder was plundered. The news, spreading through the pagan redoubts of Frisia, achieved what Boniface himself had failed to do. 'Struck with terror at the visitation of God's vengeance, the pagans embraced after the martyr's death the teaching which they had rejected while he still lived.'[7]

It was a model of conversion that the Carolingian monarchy, for one, would not forget.

Sword and Pen

In the summer of 772, fifty years after Boniface's felling of Thunor's oak, another tree—the greatest of all the Saxons' totems—was brought crashing down. Fearsome, phallic, and famed across Saxony, the Irminsul was believed by devotees of the ancient gods to uphold the heavens. But it did not. The skies remained in their place, even once the sanctuary had been demolished. Yet to the Saxons themselves, it might well have seemed as though the pillars of the world were crumbling. Devastation on a scale never before visited on their lands was drawing near. The desecrator of the Irminsul was no missionary, but a king at the head of the most menacing war-machine in Europe. Charles, the younger son of Pepin, had ascended to the sole rule of the Franks only the previous December. Not since the vanished age of the Caesars had anyone in the West commanded such resources. Prodigious both in his energies and in his ambitions, he exerted a sway that was Roman in its scope. In 800, the pope set an official seal on the comparison in Rome itself: for there, on Christmas Day, he crowned the Frankish warlord, and hailed him as 'Augustus'. Then, having done so, he fell before Charles' feet. Such obeisance had for centuries been the due of only one man: the emperor in Constantinople. Now, though, the West had its own emperor once again. Charles, despite his reluctance to admit that he might owe anything to an Italian bishop, and his insistence that, had he only known what the pope was planning, he would never

have permitted it, did not reject the title. King of the Franks and
'Christian Emperor',[8] he would be remembered by later generations
as Charles the Great: Charlemagne.

Many were his conquests. During the four decades and more of his
rule, he succeeded in annexing northern Italy, capturing Barcelona
from the Arabs, and pushing deep into the Carpathian Basin. Yet
of all Charlemagne's many wars, the bloodiest and most exhaust-
ing was the one he launched against the Saxons. For years it raged.
Charlemagne, despite his overwhelming military strength, found
it impossible to bring his adversaries to submit. Treaties were no
sooner agreed than they were broken. The whole of Saxony seemed
a bog. Charlemagne, faced with the choice of retreating or draining
it for good, opted for the unyielding, the protracted, the merciless
course. Every autumn, his men would burn the harvests and leave
the local peasants to starve. Settlement after settlement was wiped
out. Entire populations were deported. These were atrocities on a
Roman scale—but Augustus, whose own efforts to pacify the lands
east of the Rhine had ended in bloody failure, was not the only model
to hand. Charlemagne's lordship had been sanctified as that of the
kings of Israel had been: by the pouring of holy oil upon his head.
He ruled as the new David; as the anointed one of God. The record
of Israelite warfare was a formidable one. Centuries before, translating the scriptures into Gothic, Ulfilas had deliberately censored it,
on the principle that barbarian peoples needed no encouragement
to fight; but the Franks, as the new Israel, had long ceased to rank
as barbarians. In 782, when Charlemagne ordered the beheading of
4500 prisoners on a single day, it was the example of David, who
had similarly made a great reaping of captives, that lay before him.
'Every two lengths of them were put to death, and the third length
was allowed to live.'[9]

There was more to the bloody rhythms of Frankish campaigning, however, than the goal merely of securing for the new Israel a
troubled flank. Charlemagne aimed as well at something altogether
more novel: the winning of the Saxons for Christ. This ambition

was one that he had only arrived at gradually. Like any king in the post-Roman world, he had been raised to view pagans primarily as a nuisance. The point of attacking barbarians was to keep them in order and plunder plenty of loot. Charlemagne, unlike Boniface, could not convert pagans on the cheap. Toppling the Irminsul, he had been as anxious to strip it of the gold and silver that adorned it as to humble the pride of Thunor. The longer it took him to subdue the Saxons, however, and the more blood and treasure it cost him, so the more he came to realise that his adversaries would have to be born again. Rare was the uprising that did not begin with a burning of churches, a massacre of priests. The taint of the demonic lay heavy on the Saxons. Only by washing away all that they had been, and erasing entirely their former existence, could they be brought to a proper submission. In 776, Charlemagne imposed a treaty on the Saxons that obliged them to accept baptism. Countless men, women and children were led into a river, there to become Christian. Nine years later, after the crushing of yet another rebellion, Charlemagne pronounced that 'scorning to come to baptism'[10] would henceforward merit death. So too, he declared, would offering sacrifice to demons, or cremating a corpse, or eating meat during the forty days before Easter. Ruthlessly, determinedly, the very fabric of Saxon life was being torn apart. There would be no stitching it back together. Instead, dyed in gore, its ragged tatters were to lie for ever in the mud. As a programme for bringing an entire pagan people to Christ, it was savage as none had ever been before. A bloody and imperious precedent had been set.

But was it Christian? Forcing pagans to convert at sword-point was hardly the cause for which Boniface had died, after all. Perhaps it was telling, then, that the most pointed criticism of the policy should have come from a compatriot of the sainted martyr. 'Faith arises from the will, not from compulsion.'[11] So wrote Alcuin, a brilliant scholar from Northumbria who in 781 had met Charlemagne while returning from a visit to Rome, and been recruited to his court. Pagans, he urged the king, should be persuaded, not forced to convert. 'Let peoples newly brought to Christ be nourished in a mild manner, as infants are given milk—for instruct them brutally, and the risk then, their minds being weak, is that they will vomit everything up.'[12] Charlemagne, far from objecting to this advice, appears to have taken it in good spirit. In 796, the policy of forcible baptism was eased; a year later, the laws that governed the conquered Saxons reissued in a milder form. The king, who enjoyed nothing more than discussing theology with Alcuin while soaking with him in a hot bath, had full confidence in his advisor. He knew that the Northumbrian's commitment to the creation of a properly Christian people was absolute. Alcuin's conviction that there was no improvement so radical that it might not be achieved by education was precisely why Charlemagne had employed him. 'For without knowledge no one can do good.'[13] Alcuin, schooled in the sternest traditions of Northumbrian scholarship, wished everyone in his patron's empire to share in the fruits of Christian learning. Monasteries, in his opinion, had a greater role to play in the pacification of Saxony than fortresses. It was not only Saxons, though, who caused Alcuin anxiety. Christians in lands from which paganism had been scoured many centuries before still laboured in darkness. How, when they were illiterate, and their priests semi-lettered, could they possibly profit from the great inheritance of writings from the ancient past: the Old and New Testaments, the canons of Nicaea and other councils, the teachings of the fathers of the Church? How, without these timeless texts, could they be brought to a proper knowledge of God's purposes and desires? How could they even know what Christianity was? It was not enough to take the light of Christ into the forests of Saxony. It had to be taken into the manors, and farms, and smallholdings of Francia. An entire society needed reform.

Charlemagne did not duck the challenge. He knew that greatness brought with it grave responsibilities. A king who permitted his people to stray, who indulged their mistakes, who failed to guide them, would be sure to answer for it before the throne of God. Charlemagne, declaring in 789 his ambition to see his subjects 'apply themselves to a good life', cited as his model a king from the Old Testament: Josiah, who had discovered in the Temple a copy of the law given to Moses. 'For we read how the saintly Josiah, by visitation, correction and admonition, strove to recall the kingdom which God had given him to the worship of the true God.'[14] But Charlemagne could not, as Josiah had done, cite a written covenant. His subjects were not, as Josiah's had been, governed by the law given to Moses. Different peoples across his empire had different legal systems—nor, provided only that these codes did not subvert Frankish supremacy, did Charlemagne object. The one law that he wished his subjects to obey, the one law that existed to guide all the Christian people, could not be contained in a single book. Only on their hearts could it be written. Yet this imposed on Charlemagne a ferocious obligation: for how could God's law possibly be written on the hearts of the Christian people if they were not properly Christian? Without education, they were doomed; without education, they could not be brought to Christ. *Correctio*, Charlemagne termed his mission: the schooling of his subjects in the authentic knowledge of God.

'May those who copy the pronouncements of the holy law and the hallowed sayings of the fathers sit here.'[15] Such was the prayer that Alcuin, following his appointment as abbot of Tours in 797, ordered to be inscribed over the room where monks would toil daily at their great task of writing. Under his leadership, the monastery became a powerhouse of penmanship. Its particular focus was the production of single-volume collections of scripture. Edited by Alcuin himself, these were written to be as user-friendly as possible. No longer did words run into one another. Capital letters were deployed to signal the start of new sentences. For the first time, a single stroke like a lightning-flash was introduced to indicate doubt: the question mark. Each compendium of scripture, so one monk declared, was 'a library beyond compare'.[16] In ancient Alexandria, it had been called *ta biblia ta hagia*, 'the holy books'—and in time, so as to emphasise the unique holiness of what they were producing, monks in Francia would transliterate the Greek word *biblia* into Latin. The Old and

New Testaments would come to be known simply as *Biblia*—'the Books'. The sheer number of editions produced at Tours was prodigious. Large-format, easy to read, and distributed widely across Charlemagne's empire, they gave to the various peoples across the Latin West something new: a shared sense of God's word as a source of revelation that might be framed within one single set of covers.

Yet Alcuin and his colleagues were not content that scripture and the great inheritance of Christian learning be made available merely to the literate. Familiar as they were with the shrunken settlements that huddled within even the most imposing Roman city walls, they knew that there could be no true *correctio* without reaching deep into the countryside. The entire span of the Latin West, from its ancient heartlands to its newest, rawest marches, needed to function as a great honeycomb of dioceses. Even the meanest peasant scratching a living beside the dankest wood had to be provided with ready access to Christian instruction. This was why, every time Saxon rebels burned down a church, the Frankish authorities would hurry to rebuild it. It was why as well, under the stern and tutelary gaze of Charlemagne, the project of *correctio* had as a particular focus the education of the priesthood. This was a topic on which Boniface, only a generation previously, had expressed robust views. Frankish priests, he had charged, 'spend their lives in debauchery, adultery, and every kind of filth'.[17] Some were barely distinguishable from serfs: ordained at the behest of their lords, they were more practised in holding the leashes of hunting dogs or the reins of a lady's horse than in teaching the word of God. That, as ever more instructions flowed from Charlemagne's court, was now starting to change. Everyone in the empire, so the king ordained, was to know the Creed. So too were they all to learn the words which Christ himself, asked by his disciples how they should pray, had taught: the Lord's Prayer. Small books written specifically to serve the needs of rural priests began to appear in ever increasing numbers. Battered, scruffy and well-thumbed, these guides were the index of an innovative experiment in mass education. Charlemagne's death in 814 did nothing to slow it. Four decades on, the archbishop of Reims could urge the priests under his charge to know all forty of Gregory the Great's homilies, and expect to be obeyed. One was jailed for having forgotten 'everything that he had learned'.[18] Ignorance had literally become a crime.

Increasingly, in the depths of the Frankish countryside, there was no aspect of existence that Christian teaching did not touch. Whether drawing up a charter, or tending a sick cow, or advising on where best to dig a well, rare was the priest who did not serve his flock as the ultimate fount of knowledge. The rhythms of the Lord's Prayer and the Creed, repeated daily across the Frankish empire and beyond, in the kingdoms of Britain, and Ireland, and Spain, spoke of a Christian people becoming ever more Christian. The turning of the year, the tilling, the sowing, the reaping, and the passage of human life, from birth to death—all now lay in the charge of Christ. As generation succeeded generation, so the teachings of priests to labourers in the fields, and to expectant mothers, and to old men and women on their deathbeds, and to children mouthing their first prayers, came to seem ever more set on foundations that transcended time. Christian order could proclaim itself eternal, and be believed.

Earthly order, meanwhile, was like a rainbow, 'which adorns the vault of heaven with dazzling colours, and then quickly disappears'. So wrote Sedulius Scottus, an Irish teacher who, some time in the 840s, arrived at the Frankish court. The age was darkening. Charlemagne's empire, divided among his heirs, had become a thing of shreds and patches. Meanwhile, the borders of the Latin world were everywhere being made to bleed. Saracen pirates, who had long been pillaging the Italian coastline of its riches and seizing human livestock for the slave-markets of Africa, in 846 sailed up the Tiber and sacked St Peter's itself. In Britain and Ireland, entire kingdoms were overthrown by armies of robbers, *wicingas*, from across the northern sea: Vikings. In the skies, phantom armies were to be seen clashing amid the clouds, their ranks formed of plumes of fire. 'Now the earthly kingdom, because it is transitory and fleeting, never reveals the truth, but only some slight semblance of the truth and of the eternal kingdom.' Sedulius Scottus, writing to Charlemagne's great-grandson, did not mince his words. 'Only that kingdom is real which endures forever.'[19]

Time, then, would be the decisive test of just how firmly the foundations of Christian order had been laid.

Turning Back the Tide

The crisis had long been building. Year after year warbands of pagans had been coming, crossing from the steppes of the Carpathian Basin into Swabia and Bavaria, horsemen possessed of terrifying speed, and the nightmarish ability to fire arrows from the saddle. 'Of disgusting aspect, with deep-set eyes and short stature,'[20] they were darkly rumoured to feed on human blood. They certainly had a talent for battening onto the possessions of Christians. Wherever they went, they left behind them a trail of smoking churches and blackened fields. Various policies had been attempted to stem their onslaughts: carrots, in the form of financial subsidies, and sticks, in the form of strengthened border controls. Nothing seemed to work. Now, for the authorities in eastern Francia, the moment of truth was drawing near. The choice they faced was a stark one: either to secure a definitive solution to the crisis, or else to lose control of their borders altogether.

The storm finally broke in the summer of 955. 'A multitude of Hungarians, such as no living person can remember having seen in any one region before, invaded the realm of the Bavarians which they devastated and occupied simultaneously from the Danube to the dark forest on the rim of the mountains.'[21] It was not only the scale of the invasion force that chilled Christian onlookers, but the evident scope of its preparations. Previously, when the Hungarians had come sweeping out of their steppe-lands, they had done so exclusively on horseback, setting a premium on speed, the better to strip a landscape bare, and then to retreat back to the Danube before the more heavily armoured German cavalry could corner them. Plunder, not territorial acquisitions, had been their goal. Now, though, it seemed that they had a different strategy. Crossing into Bavarian territory, their horsemen rode at a measured pace. Alongside them marched huge columns of infantry. Siege engines creaked and rumbled in their train. This time, the Hungarians had come to conquer.

Early in August, they arrived before the walls of Augsburg. The city, rich and strategically vital though it was, stood perilously exposed. In the hour of its darkest peril, it was Ulrich, the city's aged and formidably learned bishop, who took command of its defence. While men laboured to shore up the walls, and women walked in procession, raising fearful prayers, the old scholar toured the battlements, inspiring the garrison to trust in Christ. Yet so overwhelming were the forces besieging the city, and so menacing their preparations, that it seemed to many that Augsburg was bound to fall. On 8 August, as the siege engines crawled towards the fortifications, and infantry were driven forwards under the lash, a gateway above the river Lech was breached. Ulrich, 'wearing only his vestments, protected by neither shield, nor chain mail, nor helmet',[22] rode out to block the Hungarians' path. Miraculously, despite the hissing of arrows all around him, and the thudding of stones, he succeeded in holding the attackers at bay. The open gate was secured. The Hungarians did not enter the city.

And already, relief was on its way. Otto, a king crowned in the very throne-room of Charlemagne, famed for his piety, his martial valour and the quite spectacular hairiness of his chest, had been brought the news of the invasion in the marches of Saxony. Furiously he rode southwards to confront it. With him he brought three thousand heavily armoured horsemen and the single most precious treasure in his entire realm: the very spear that had pierced the side of Christ. These advantages, in the terrible battle that followed, would gain the relief force a stunning victory against the odds. A great surging cavalry charge crushed the Hungarians; the Christian cavalry, pursuing their foes across the floodplain of the Lech, then hacked and speared them down; of the mighty force that had laid siege to Augsburg almost nothing was left. The Hungarians would later claim that only seven had escaped the slaughter. Such was the glory of it that the exultant victors, standing on the battlefield amid the tangle of corpses and banners, could hail their triumphant king as 'emperor'. Sure enough, within seven years, Otto was being crowned by the Pope in Rome.

A portentous moment. Long before, a bare couple of decades after Charlemagne's death in 814, a Saxon poet, writing in praise of the god brought by the Franks to his people, had contrasted 'the bright, infinitely beautiful light' of Christ with the waxing and waning of mortals. 'Here in this world, in Middle Earth, they come and go, the old dying and the young succeeding, until they too grow old, and are borne away by fate.'[23] The coronation of Otto in the ancient capital of the world bore potent witness to just how unpredictable were the affairs of men. The throne of empire had stood vacant for over half a century. The last descendant of Charlemagne to occupy it had been deposed, blinded and imprisoned back in 905. The *Regnum Francorum*, the 'Kingdom of the Franks', had fractured into a number of realms. Of these, the two largest were on the western and eastern flanks of the one-time Frankish empire: kingdoms that in time would come to be known as France and Germany. The dynasty to which Otto belonged, and which had been elected to the rule of eastern Francia in 919, had no link to Charlemagne's. Indeed, it was not even Frankish. Otto the Great, the heir of Constantine, the shield of the West, the wielder of the Holy Spear, was sprung from the very people who, less than two centuries before, had been so obdurate in their defiance of Christian arms: the Saxons.

'I am a soldier of Christ—it is not lawful for me to fight.'[24] So Martin, the future bishop of Tours, had informed the emperor Julian when resigning his military commission. It was hardly surprising that Otto, the descendant of men and women brought to baptism at sword-point, should not have felt any great calling from his Saviour to rule as a pacifist. Even had he done so, the times would not have permitted it. For a century, the frontiers of the Latin West had repeatedly been slashed, and uprooted, and burned. To attempt their repair, and to defend the Christian people, was to fight 'the demons who permanently assail God's Church'.[25] The defeat of such adversaries, risen up from hell as it was assumed they were, had naturally required an unrelenting effort of courage and fortitude. Otto's great victory beside the Lech was not the only sign that the tide might be turning at last. Four decades previously, on the banks of another river, the Garigliano, less than a hundred miles south of Rome, a great lair of Saracen pirates had been smoked out. The Pope himself, riding in the train of the victorious army, had twice in his excitement charged the enemy. That heaven had forgiven him his offence was demonstrated by the startling but widely reported appearance of Saints Peter and Paul in the battle-line.

Meanwhile, in the northern seas, the forces of Christian order were recovering from near implosion. In 937, a great Viking invasion of Britain was defeated by the king of Wessex, a formidable warrior by the name of Athelstan. The triumph, though, was not Athelstan's alone. For three generations, under his father and grandfather, the West Saxons had been locked in a desperate struggle for survival. They alone, of all the Anglo-Saxon peoples, had managed to preserve their kingdom from Viking conquest—and even then, only just. For a spell, the very future of Christianity in the lands cast by Bede as a new Israel had seemed to hang by a thread. God, though, had saved it from being cut. Not only had the Vikings been brought to submit to Christ, but an entire new Christian kingdom had been built out of the ruins of the old. Athelstan had emerged from a lifetime of relentless campaigning as the first king of a realm that, by the time of his death, stretched from Northumbria to the Channel. 'Through God's grace he ruled alone what previously many had held among themselves.'[26] Redeemed from the brink of disaster, Bede's vision of the Angles and the Saxons as a single people had been fulfilled.

Great conquerors such as Otto and Athelstan stood in no barbarian's shadow. After a long century of reverses and defeats, Christian kingship had recaptured its swagger, its mystique. What god could possibly rival the power of the celestial emperor who had brought the Saxons from sinister obscurity to such greatness, or the House of Wessex to feed so many of their foes to the wolves and the ravens? It was only natural for a pagan warlord defeated by Christian arms to ponder this question long and hard. Battle was the ultimate testing-ground of a god's authority. Not only that, but the rewards of suing for terms from Christ were evident. To accept baptism was to win entry into a commonwealth of realms defined by their antiquity, their sophistication and their wealth. From Scandinavia to central Europe, pagan warlords began to contemplate the same possibility: that the surest path to profiting from the Christian world might not be to tear it to pieces, but rather to be woven into its fabric. Sure enough, two decades after the great slaughter of his people beside the Lech, Géza, the king of the Hungarians, became a Christian. Reproached by a monk for continuing to offer sacrifice 'to various false gods', he cheerily acknowledged that hedging his bets 'had brought him both wealth and great power'.[27] Only a generation on, the commitment to Christ of his son, Waik, was altogether more full-blooded. The new king took the name Stephen; he built churches across the Hungarian countryside; he ordered that the head be shaved of anyone who dared to mock the rites performed within them; he had a rebellious pagan lord quartered, and the dismembered body parts nailed up in various prominent places. Great rewards were quick to flow from these godly measures. Stephen, the grandson of a pagan chieftain, was given as his queen the grand-niece of none other than Otto the Great. Otto's own grandson, the reigning emperor, bestowed on him a replica of the Holy Spear. The pope sent him a crown. In time, after a long and prosperous reign, he would end up proclaimed a saint.

By 1038, the year of Stephen's death, the leaders of the Latin Church could view the world with an intoxicating sense of possibility. It was not just the Hungarians who had been brought to Christ. So too had the Bohemians and the Poles, the Danes and the Norwegians. Ambitious chieftains, once they had been welcomed into the order of Christian royalty, were rarely tempted to renew the worship of their ancestral gods. No pagan ritual could rival the anointing of a baptised king. The ruler who felt the stickiness of holy oil upon his skin, penetrating his pores, seeping deep into his soul, knew himself joined by the experience to David and Solomon, to Charlemagne and Otto. Who was Christ himself, if not the very greatest of kings? Over the course of the centuries, he 'had gained many realms and had triumphed over the mightiest rulers and had crushed through his power the necks of the proud and the sublime'.[28] It was no shame for even the most peerless of kings, even the emperor himself, to acknowledge this. From east to west, from deepest forest to wildest ocean, from the banks of the Volga to the glaciers of Greenland, Christ had come to rule them all.

Yet there was a paradox. Even as kings bowed the knee to him, the hideousness of what he had undergone for humanity's sake, the pain and helplessness that he had endured at Golgotha, the agony of it all, was coming to obsess Christians as never before. The replica of the Holy Spear sent to Stephen served as a sombre reminder of Christ's suffering. Christ himself—unlike Otto—had never borne it into battle. It was holy because a Roman soldier, standing guard over his crucifixion, had jabbed it into his side. Blood and water had flowed out. Christ had hung from his gibbet, dead. Ever since, Christians had shrunk from representing their Saviour as a corpse. But now, a thousand years on, artists had begun to break that taboo. In Cologne, above the grave of the archbishop who had commissioned it, a great sculpture was erected, one that portrayed Christ slumped on the cross, his eyes closed, the life gone from his body. Others beheld a similar scene in their visions. A monk in Limoges, rising in the dead of night, saw 'the image of the Crucified One, the colour of fire and deep blood for half a full night hour',[29] high against the southern sky, as if planted in the heavens. The closer that 1033, the millennial anniversary of Christ's death, drew near, so the more did vast crowds, in an ecstasy of mingled yearning, and hope, and fear, begin to assemble. Never before had a movement of such a magnitude been witnessed in the lands of the West. Many gathered in fields outside towns across France, 'stretching their palms to God, and shouting with one voice, "Peace! Peace! Peace!", as a sign of the perpetual covenant which they had vowed between themselves and God'.[30] Others, taking advantage of the land-route that the conversion of the Hungarians had opened up, followed the road to Constantinople, and thence to Jerusalem. The largest number of all set out in 1033, 'an innumerable multitude of people from the whole world, greater than any man before could have hoped to see'.[31] Their journey's end: the site of Christ's execution, and the tomb that had witnessed his resurrection.

What were they hoping for? If they declared it, they did so under their breath. Christians were not oblivious to Augustine's prohibition. They knew the orthodoxy: that the thousand-year reign of the saints mentioned in Revelation was not to be taken literally. In the event, the millennium of Christ's death came and went, and he did not descend from the heavens. His kingdom was not established on earth. The fallen world continued much as before. Nevertheless, the longing for reform, for renewal, for redemption did not fade. On one level, this was nothing new. Christ, after all, had called on his followers to be born again. The longing to see the entire Christian people purged of their sins had deep roots. It was what, some two and a half centuries previously, had inspired Charlemagne in his great project of *correctio*. Yet though his heirs still claimed the right to serve as the shepherds of their people, to rule—as Charlemagne had done—as priest as well as king, the ambition to set the Christian world on new foundations was no longer the preserve of courts. It had become a fever that filled meadows with swaying, moaning crowds, and inspired armies of pilgrims to tramp dusty roads. To cross Hungary in the reign of King Stephen was to know just how remarkably the world might change. It had become a place of miracles. In 1028, a monk from Bavaria named Arnold travelled there, and was startled to see a dragon swooping over the Hungarian plains, 'its plumed head the height of a mountain, its body covered with scales like shields of iron'.[32] What marvel was this, though, compared to the true wonder: a land that was once the home of blood-drinking demons brought to Christ, its king serving as the guardian to thousands of pilgrims bound for Jerusalem, its towns filled with cathedrals and churches sounding to the praises of God? Arnold could recognise the shock of the new when he saw it. Far from unsettling him, the prospect of even further change filled him with a giddy excitement. In a world animated as never before by the fire-rush of the Holy Spirit, why should anything stand still? 'Such is the dispensation of the Almighty—that many things which once existed be cast aside by those who come in their wake.'[33]

Arnold was right to foretell upheaval. Much that had been taken for granted was on the verge of titanic disruption. Revolution of a new and irreversible order was brewing in the Latin West.

9

REVOLUTION

1076: Cambrai

The feverish spirit of the times was dangerous. Gerard, the bishop of Cambrai, had no doubt as to that. Christians who believed themselves endowed by revelation with insights into God's purposes were a menace to the Church, and to the great fabric of its order, constructed with such care and effort over the thousand years since Christ. In the shadow of the millennium, the great serpent of heresy, which for centuries had seemed scotched for good, had begun to shake its coils again. Various clerics in Orléans, one of them high in royal favour, were said to have claimed 'there was no such thing as the Church';[1] the inhabitants of a castle near Milan, swearing themselves to chastity, had laid claim to a purity that put married priests to shame; a peasant, only a hundred miles from Cambrai, had dreamed that a swarm of bees entered his anus, and revealed to him the iniquities of the clergy. This madness, it seemed, was capable of infecting every level of society. The charge, though, was customarily the same: that unworthy priests were disqualified from practising the rites and rituals of the Church; that they were polluted, tarnished, corrupted; that they were not truly Christian. The echo of the Donatists, reverberating down the centuries, was palpable.

Gerard, nervous of where such ravings might lead, was on his guard. Brought news that a man named Ramihrd was 'preaching

222

many things outside the faith, and had won a large number of disciples of both sexes',[2] the bishop was quick to act. Ramihrd was summoned to Cambrai. There, he was questioned by a panel of abbots and learned scholars. His answers, however, proved impeccably orthodox. He was then invited to celebrate with Gerard the ritual of the eucharist: the transformation, by means of a sublime mystery, of bread and wine into the very body and blood of Christ. Only a priest could perform this miracle—but Ramihrd, accusing the bishop of being filthy with sin, denied him the title of priest. The resulting uproar exploded into violence. Gerard's servants, seizing the man who had so insulted their master, bundled him into a wooden hut. A crowd set it on fire. Ramihrd, kneeling in prayer, was burned alive.

This lynching—although obviously an embarrassment to Gerard—was not without salutary effect. There was precedent for putting heretics to death. Half a century earlier, the clerics of Orléans charged with scoffing at the existence of the Church had been publicly burned: the first people to be executed for heresy in the entire history of the Latin West.* Ugly moods demanded ugly measures. The rush of Ramihrd's followers to scoop up his ashes and consecrate him as a martyr spoke of an enthusiasm for his teachings that had become a kind of madness. The demand—a wild, an impractical one!—was for a Church that could shine amid the darkness of the fallen world as radiantly as the most discipline-hallowed monastery. Priests, unlike monks, had never been obliged to pledge themselves to celibacy—and yet this, in recent years, had become a subject of violent agitation. In Milan, where the clergy had long lived openly with their wives, riots had been convulsing the city for two decades. Married priests had found themselves boycotted, abused, assaulted. Their touch was publicly scorned as 'dog shit'.[3] Paramilitaries had barricaded the archbishop inside his own cathedral, and then, when he died, tried to foist their own candidate on the city.

---

* Priscillian, a Spanish bishop executed in 385, is sometimes cited as the earliest—but he was convicted on a charge of sorcery, not heresy.

Gerard, who had only been invested as a bishop a few months previously, had no wish to see such turmoil rock Cambrai. This was
why, rather than punish the murderers of Ramihrd, he was content
to regard them as the agents of a higher purpose. Heresy, after all,
had to be rooted out. Ramihrd's admirers were weavers, peasants,
labourers—nothing more. What were the complaints of such people
to a bishop?

But Ramihrd, it turned out, also had admirers further afield. Early
in 1077, a letter arrived in Paris, addressed to the city's archbishop. It
reported in shocked tones the news of Ramihrd's fate. 'We view it as
something monstrous.'[4] Ramihrd, so the letter declared, had been no
criminal. The criminals were those who had murdered him. Here, to
Gerard, was not merely a reprimand but a body-blow. The letter had
been written by a bishop—and not just by any bishop. The burning
of Ramihrd stood condemned by the Pope himself.

Hildebrand had always been a radical. Born—some said—the
son of a Tuscan carpenter, the blaze of his future greatness had been
presaged by miraculous sparks of fire on his swaddling clothes, and
a flame seen issuing from his head. Defying his humble origins, he
had never doubted himself entrusted by God with a fateful mission.
When, as a young man, he was granted a vision of St Paul shovel-
ling cow dung out of a Roman monastery, it had confirmed him in
the ambition that he would hold to all his life: to sluice the Church
clean of every spot of filth. This, elsewhere, might have been sufficient to condemn him as a heretic; but Rome, during Hildebrand's
youth, was a city in the throes of an intoxicating sense of renewal.
For too long the papacy had been an institution pawed at and squab-
bled over by local dynasts. Pope after pope had served as a byword
for scandal. The shame of it had finally prompted intervention by
the emperor himself. Henry III, a man possessed of formidable piety
and the self-confidence that came naturally to an anointed king, had
briskly deposed and appointed a number of popes, before finally, in
1048, installing a distant cousin. A high-handed policy, certainly—
but one that had fast served to raise the papacy from the gutter.

A succession of popes as astute as they were devout had laboured to set it on a new course. *Reformatio*, they had termed this great project: 'reformation'. Its ambition was not merely the redemption of the papacy from the canker of worldliness and parochialism, but the whole world. Papal agents—'legates'—had been dispatched in increasing numbers north of the Alps. Meanwhile, talented clerics were recruited to the papacy's service from across the Latin West. Increasingly, these had given to Rome a feel that the city had not possessed for many centuries: that of a capital at the heart of the world's affairs.

Hildebrand, rising through the ranks of the Roman Church, had certainly not hesitated to view its sway as universal in its scope. Earnest, austere and implacable of purpose, he was a man perfectly suited to its ever more soaring spirit of ambition. By 1073, he had emerged as the most formidable agent of a papacy primed to claim a supreme authority over the entire Christian people. There had been no thought that year, when the throne of Saint Peter became vacant, of waiting for Henry III's son, the young and headstrong Henry IV, to appoint a new pope. 'Hildebrand for bishop!'[5] the crowds had roared. Swept up onto their shoulders, the people's choice had been carried to his enthronement in the Lateran, an ancient palace donated to the bishop of Rome centuries previously by Constantine. As a signal of his ambition, Hildebrand took the name of the Roman aristocrat who had famously devoted his life to preparing the Church for the end of days—the seventh pope to bear it. 'He was a man on whom the spirit of the first Gregory truly rested.'[6]

In truth, though, Gregory VII's ambitions for the papacy were of a momentously original order. For all that his predecessors had consistently laid claim to a position of leadership among the Christian people, none had ever proclaimed it so baldly or forcefully. Among the great accretion of documents stored in musty papal libraries—the canons of church councils, the proclamations of successive popes— there were numerous precedents suited to Gregory's needs; and so he duly made sure to harvest them. Where necessary, though, he was more than ready to introduce innovations of his own. That the Pope alone had a license to be called 'Universal'; to place inferiors in judgement over their superiors; to release those who had sworn obedience to a lord from their oaths: here were prerogatives to set the whole world on its head. Even before becoming Pope, Gregory had been eager to put them into practice. Far from condemning the militants in Milan, he had given them his personal blessing. It was no sin, Gregory believed, to amplify moral exhortation by threatening those who ignored it with violence. The heir of Saint Peter should not hesitate to draw on the support of the militant faithful. The very future of the Christian people was at stake. The proofs of this were manifest. An angel, so one of Gregory's supporters reported, had appeared before the full view of a church as a priest was celebrating the eucharist, and begun scrubbing him down. The water had turned black. Finally, the angel had tipped the filthy contents of the bucket over the priest's head. The priest, a man of hitherto spotless reputation, had broken down in tears, and confessed to the congregation that only the previous night he had slept with a servant girl. Gregory, no less than the angel, felt himself called to a mighty labour of cleaning. The clergy were leprous. Only he, the heir of Saint Peter, could bring them to purity. Priests had to be virginal, like monks. 'To pluck up and to break down, to destroy and to overthrow, to build and to plant':[7] such was Gregory's mission.

Never before had a pope made the foundations of the Christian world tremor so palpably. The excitement of Gregory's followers was outweighed by the alarm of his opponents. Gerard was far from alone in feeling disoriented. Heresy seemed to have captured the commanding heights of the Church. The hierarchies on which bishops had always depended for their authority appeared under attack from the very man who stood at their head. Priests who polluted themselves by surrendering to their lusts were not the only objects of Gregory's reforming zeal. Ramihrd, refusing to celebrate the eucharist with Gerard, had done so on a very particular basis. The bishop of Cambrai, following his election to the post in June 1076, had travelled to the German court. There, in obedience to venerable custom, he had sworn an oath of loyalty to Henry IV. The King, in return, had presented him with a shepherd's crook, and a ring: the symbol of marriage. That bishops in lands ruled by the emperor might owe their investiture to him had long been taken for granted. Not by Gregory, though. When Ramihrd refused to acknowledge Gerard as a priest, he had done so in direct obedience to a decree of the Roman Church. Issued only the year before, it had formally prohibited 'the King's right to confer bishoprics'.[8] A momentous step: for this—prohibiting kings from poking their noses into the business of the Church—had struck at the very heart of how the world was ordered.

Which was, of course, precisely why Gregory had sponsored it. Defilement came in many forms. A bishop who owed his investiture to a king was no less leprous than a priest who slept with a servant girl. To whore after baubles, and estates, and offices was to betray the King of Heaven. The scale of the change that Gregory was forcing on the Latin West could be measured by the fact that even reformers like him, only three decades previously, had depended on Henry III to secure them the papacy. That emperors had been hailed as *sanctissimus*, 'most holy', and that imperial bishops had long been administering royal fiefdoms: none of this mattered to him. For too long the rival dimensions of earthly appetites and commitment to Christ, of corruption and purity, of *saecularia* and *religio*, had been intermixed. Such pollution could not be permitted to continue. Bishops were servants of God alone, or they were nothing. Church had to be freed from state.

'The Pope is permitted to depose emperors.' This proposition, one of a number of theses on papal authority drawn up for Gregory's private use in March 1075, had shown him more than braced for the inevitable blow-back. No pope before had ever claimed such a licence; but neither, of course, had any pope dared to challenge imperial authority with such unapologetic directness. Gregory, by laying claim to the sole leadership of the Christian people, and trampling down long-standing royal prerogatives, was offending Henry IV grievously. Heir to a long line of emperors who had never hesitated to depose troublesome popes, the young king acted with the self-assurance of a man supremely confident that both right and tradition were on his side. Early in 1076, when he summoned a conference of imperial bishops to the German city of Worms, the assembled clerics knew exactly what was expected of them. The election of Hildebrand, so they ruled, had been invalid. No sooner had this decision been reached than Henry's scribes were reaching for their quills. 'Let another sit upon Saint Peter's throne.' The message to Gregory in Rome could not have been blunter. 'Step down, step down!'[9]

But Gregory also had a talent for bluntness. Brought the command to abdicate, he not only refused, but promptly raised the stakes. Speaking from the Lateran, he declared that Henry was 'bound with the chain of anathema'[10] and excommunicated from the Church. His subjects were absolved of all their oaths of loyalty to him. Henry himself, as a tyrant and an enemy of God, was deposed. The impact of this pronouncement proved devastating. Henry's authority went into meltdown. Numerous of his princely vassals, hungry for the opportunity that his excommunication had given them, set to dismembering his kingdom. By the end of the year, Henry found himself cornered. To such straits was his authority reduced that he settled on a desperate gambit. Crossing the Alps in the dead of winter, he headed for Canossa, a castle in the northern Apennines where he knew that Gregory was staying. For three days, 'barefoot, and clad in wool',[11] the heir of Constantine and Charlemagne stood shivering before the gates of the castle's innermost wall. Finally, ordering the gates unbarred, and summoning Henry into his presence, Gregory absolved the penitent with a kiss. 'The King of Rome, rather than being honoured as a universal monarch, had been treated instead as merely a human being—a creature moulded out of clay.'[12]

The shock was seismic. That Henry had soon reneged on his promises, capturing Rome in 1084 and forcing his great enemy to flee the city, had done nothing to lessen the impact of Gregory's papacy on the mass of the Christian people. For the first time, public affairs in the Latin West had an audience that spanned every region, and every social class. 'What else is talked about even in the women's spinning-rooms and the artisans' work-shops?'[13] Here, so Gregory's opponents charged, was yet another black mark against his name. To encourage woolworkers and cobblers to sit in judgement on their betters was to play with fire. The sheer violence of the propaganda levelled against Henry—that he was a pervert, an arsonist, a violator of nuns—threatened the very fabric of society. So too, of course, did Gregory's readiness to stir up mobs against priests who had opposed his programme of *reformatio*. Only start howling down the clergy, and who knew where it might all end?

The travails of the bishop of Cambrai suggested one particularly alarming answer: the eruption of entire cities into rebellion. In 1077, desperate not to be deposed for accepting a ring from Henry IV, Gerard had travelled the long road to Rome, there to plead his case. Gregory, though, had refused to see him. Only after he had headed back north and begged for mercy from a papal legate in Burgundy had Gerard's election finally been approved. Meanwhile, during the bishop's absence, workers and peasants had seized control of Cambrai. Declaring a commune, they swore never to have him back. Gerard, faced with open insurrection, found himself with no choice but to beg the assistance of a neighbouring count. A humiliating recourse—and even once the rebels had been routed, and their leaders put to death, the sense of a world turned on its head would not go away. 'Knights are armed against their lords, and children rise against their parents. Subjects are stirred up against kings, right and wrong are confounded, and the sanctity of oaths is violated.'[14]

Yet Gerard, following the pacification of Cambrai, did not repudiate the pledge of loyalty that he had made to Gregory. No sooner had the rebellion been crushed than he set to imposing on his clergy the very measures which, only a year previously, had caused Ramihrd to be lynched. Not even the death of Gregory himself, shortly after his flight from Rome, shook Gerard's new-found commitment to *reformatio*. His eyes, like those of other bishops across the empire, had been opened. The humiliation of Henry IV had made visible a great and awesome prize. The dream of Gregory and his fellow reformers—of a Church rendered decisively distinct from the dimension of the earthly, from top to bottom, from palace to meanest village—no longer appeared a fantasy, but eminently realisable. A celibate clergy, once disentangled from the snares and meshes of the fallen world, would then be better fitted to serve the Christian people as a model of purity, and bring them to God. No longer would it be monasteries and nunneries alone that stood separate from the flux of the *saeculum*, but the entire Church. Bishops who pledged themselves to the radicalism of this vision could reassure themselves that it was in reality nothing new, nothing out of tune with the teachings of their Saviour. In the Gospels, after all, it was recorded that Jesus, approached by questioners looking to trip him up, had been asked whether it was permitted to pay taxes to pagan Rome. Telling them to show him a coin, he had asked them whose image was stamped on it. 'Casear's,' they had replied. 'Then give to Caesar what is Caesar's,' Jesus had answered, 'and to God what is God's.'[15]

Nevertheless, deep though the roots of Gregory's *reformatio* lay in the soil of Christian teaching, the flower was indeed something new. The concept of the 'secular', first planted by Augustine, and tended by Columbanus, had attained a spectacular bloom. Gregory and his fellow reformers did not invent the distinction between *religio* and the *saeculum*, between the sacred and the profane; but they did render it something fundamental to the future of the West, 'for the first time and permanently'.[16] A decisive moment. Lands that had long existed in the shadow both of the vanished order of Rome, and of the vastly wealthier, more sophisticated empires on their eastern flank, had been set at last upon a distinctive course of their own. Nor was it merely the division of European society into twin dimensions of church and state that was destined to prove enduring. So too was the demonstration of just how convulsive and transformative in its effects Christianity might be. It was no longer enough for Gregory and his fellow reformers that individual sinners, or even great monasteries, be consecrated to the dimension of *religio*. The entire sweep of the Christian world required an identical consecration. That sins should be washed away; the mighty put down from their seats; the entire world reordered in obedience to a conception of purity as militant as it was demanding: here was a manifesto that had resulted in a Caesar humbling himself before a pope. 'Any custom, no matter how venerable, no matter how commonplace, must yield utterly to truth—and, if it is contrary to truth, be abolished.'[17] So Gregory had written. *Nova consilia*, he had called his teachings—'new counsels'.

A model of *reformatio* had triumphed that, reverberating down the centuries, would come to shake many a monarchy, and prompt many a visionary to dream that society might be born anew. The earthquake would reach very far, and the aftershocks be many. The Latin West had been given its primal taste of revolution.

Laying Down the Law

The most intoxicating of all the reformers' slogans was *libertas*—'freedom'. One place more than any other served as its emblem: a monastery charged with a sense of holiness so strong that Gregory had taken it as his model for the entire Church. First established back in 910, amid wooded Burgundian hills, Cluny had been placed by its founder under the protection of the distant papacy. The local bishop, to all intents and purposes, had been frozen out. Cluny's independence had fast become the mainstay of its greatness. A succession of formidably able abbots, defying the violence and rapacity for which the local warlords were notorious, had succeeded in establishing their monastery as an impregnable outpost of the City of God. So unspotted that they would wash the shoes as well as the feet of visitors, so angelic that they were known to levitate while singing psalms, the monks of Cluny appeared to their admirers as close to celestial as fallen mortals could approach. Almost two centuries on

from its foundation, the monastery had not only endured, but flourished mightily. As though from a chrysalis, an immense new church,
on a scale never before witnessed, was emerging from the shell of the
old. The ribs of its half-completed vault seemed to swell and reach
for the skies. To visit it was to see proclaimed in stone just what freedom could truly mean.

By 1095, the east end of the church had been sufficiently completed
to permit the dedication of its two great altars. Cluny being Cluny,
the man invited to do the honours was a pope. Urban II had once
been a prior in the abbey but had then left for Italy, where he had
served Gregory as a notably shrewd and committed advisor, before
himself being raised to the papacy in 1087. Travelling to Cluny, the
new pope was doing honour not only to the monastery itself, but
to the great ideal of a Church independent and free. Arriving on 18
September, and dedicating the two altars a week later, he hailed it
as a reflection of the heavenly Jerusalem. The praise was heartfelt;
but Urban had his attention fixed as well on a more distant horizon.
Travelling on from Burgundy, he headed for central France, and the
town of Clermont. There, as at Cluny, his talk was all of freedom. At
a great council of bishops and abbots, priests were formally forbidden to do homage to earthly lords. Then, on 27 November, the Pope
travelled outside the town walls, and addressed an eager crowd in a
muddy field. No less than Gregory, Urban understood the value of
harnessing popular fervour. The great cause of *reformatio* could not
merely be the stuff of councils. If it failed to liberate the Christian
people across the entire globe, to light heaven and earth, to prepare
the fallen world for the return of Christ and the day of judgement,
then it was nothing. The Church, so the bishops and abbots gathered
in Clermont had proclaimed, should be 'chaste from all contagion of
evil'.[18] A fine ambition—but how could it be achieved while Jerusalem itself lay under Saracen rule? Not all the radiant purity of Cluny
could make up for the horror of it. Urban, who gloried in the convulsions that *reformatio* had brought to Christian kingdoms, dared to
dream of a greater convulsion still. Daringly, he offered his listeners

an electrifying new formula for salvation. Listed as an official decree of the council held at Clermont, it promised warriors a means by which their trade of arms, rather than offending Christ and requiring penance to be forgiven, might itself serve to cleanse them of their sin. 'For, if any man sets out from devotion, not for reputation or monetary gain, to liberate the Church of God at Jerusalem, his journey shall be reckoned in place of all penance.'[19]

In the Book of Revelation it was foretold that, at the end of days, an angel would gather grapes from the earth's vine, and trample them in the winepress of God's wrath, and that blood would flow out of the press, and rise as high as a horse's bridle. The passage was one that Gregory's followers knew well. One bishop who had travelled in Urban's train to Clermont openly wondered whether it was the enemies of *reformatio* who were destined to be crushed in the final harvest. In the event, though, it was not in the battlegrounds of the papacy's great conflict with Henry IV that blood would be made to flow through streets, but in Jerusalem. Urban's speech had reverberated to miraculous effect. A great host of warriors drawn from across the Latin West had taken a familiar road. As pilgrims had been doing since the time of the millennium, they had journeyed across Hungary to Constantinople; and then from Constantinople to the Holy Land. Every attempt by the Saracens to halt them had been defeated. Finally, in the summer of 1099, the great army of warrior pilgrims had arrived before Jerusalem. On 15 July, they stormed its walls. The city was theirs. Then, once the slaughter was done, and they had dried their dripping swords, they headed for the tomb of Christ. There, in joy and disbelief, they offered up praises to God. Jerusalem—after centuries of Saracen rule—was Christian once again.

So extraordinary was the feat as to be barely believable—and the news redounded gloriously to the credit of the papacy. Urban himself died a fortnight after the city's capture, too soon for news of the great victory that he had inspired to reach him; but the programme of reform to which he had devoted his life was much burnished by the winning of the Holy City. Emperors since the time of Charlemagne had fought wars of conquest beneath the banner of Christ; but none had ever sent an entire army on pilgrimage. Warriors present at the capture of Jerusalem reported having seen 'a beautiful person sitting atop a white horse'[20]—and there were some prepared to wonder if it might not have been Christ himself. Whatever the truth of the mysterious horseman's identity, one thing was clear: the Holy City had been won, not in the name of any king or emperor, but in that of a much more universal cause.

But what name to give this cause? Back in the Latin West, the word starting to be used was one that, until the capture of Jerusalem, had barely been heard. The warrior pilgrims, so it came to be said, had fought under the banner of *Christianitas*: Christendom. Such a categorisation—divorced as it was from the dynasties of earthly kings and the holdings of feudal lords—was one well suited to the ambitions of the papacy. Who better to stand at the head of Christendom than the heir of Saint Peter? Less than a century after Henry III had deposed three popes in a single year, the Roman Church had carved out a role of leadership for itself so powerful that Henry's grandson, the son of Henry IV, was brought in 1122 to sue for peace. In that year, in Worms, where his father had once commanded Gregory VII to abdicate, Henry V agreed to a momentous concordat. By its terms, the fifty-year-old quarrel over the investiture of imperial bishops was finally brought to an end. Although ostensibly a compromise, time would demonstrate that victory was decisively the papacy's. Decisive too was the increasing acceptance of another key demand of the reformers: that the clergy distinguish themselves from the great mass of the Christian people—the *laicus*, or 'laity'—by embracing celibacy. By 1148, when yet another papal decree banning priests from having wives or concubines was promulgated, the response of many was to roll their eyes. 'Futile and ludicrous—for who does not know already that it is unlawful?'[21]

Increasingly, then, the separation of church from state was an upheaval manifest across the whole of Christendom. Wherever a priest was called upon to minister to the laity, even in the humblest, the most isolated village, there the impact of *reformatio* could be felt. The establishment of the Roman Church as something more than merely a first among equals, as 'the general forum of all clergy and all churches',[22] gave clerics across the Latin West a common identity that they had not previously possessed. In the various kingdoms, fiefdoms and cities that constituted the great patchwork of Christendom, something unprecedented had come into being: an entire class that owed its loyalty, not to local lords, but to a hierarchy that exulted in being 'universal, and spread throughout the world'.[23]

Emperors and kings, although they might try to take a stand against it, would repeatedly find themselves left bruised by the attempt. Not since the age of Constantine and his heirs had any one man exercised an authority over so wide a sweep of Europe as did the bishop of the ancient capital of the world. His open claim was to the 'rights of heavenly and earthly empire';[24] his legates travelled to barbarous lands and expected to be heard; his court, in an echo of the building where the Roman Senate had once met, was known as the 'Curia'. Yet the pope was no Caesar. His assertion of supremacy was not founded on force of arms, nor the rank of his ministers on their lineage or their wealth. The Church that had emerged from the Gregorian *reformatio* was instead an institution of a kind never before witnessed: one that had not merely come to think of itself as sovereign, but had willed itself into becoming so. 'The Pope,' Gregory VII had affirmed, 'may be judged by no one.'[25] All Christian people, even kings, even emperors, were subject to his rulings. The Curia provided Christendom with its final court of appeal. A supreme paradox: that the Church, by rending itself free of the secular, had itself become a state.

And a very novel kind of state, what was more. The pope's writ was above all a legal one. His supremacy over the clergy; his regulation of the borders between church and court; his provision of justice to those who sought restitution from what, a century on from Canossa, was coming to be called the 'secular arm': all were dependent on armies of lawyers. It was clerks with pens, not knights with lances, who were the papacy's shock-troops. 'Who but God has written the law of nature in the hearts of men?'[26] So Augustine had once asked. Here, in a conviction that reached ultimately back to Saint Paul, lay the surest basis for the papacy's claim to a universal authority. The order defined by the Roman Church was one that consciously set itself against primordial customs rooted in the sump of paganism, or ephemeral codes drawn up on the whims of kings, or mildewed charters. Only one law could maintain for the entirety of Christendom the ties of justice and charity that bound together a properly Christian society: 'the eternal law, that creates and rules the universe'.[27] This was not an order that could be administered by priests alone.

Yet lawyers, back in the first flush of *reformatio*, had counted for little. Their entrance onto the great stage of Christendom—certainly compared to that of the warrior pilgrims who, inspired by Urban II, had marched on Jerusalem—was little celebrated in chronicle or song; but would prove, in the long run, incalculably more decisive. In 1088, the same year that Urban became pope, one of his most eminent supporters had helped to establish a new nerve-centre for the transfiguration of Christian society: a law school in the Italian city of Bologna. The Countess Matilda, heiress to a great swathe of lands in Tuscany, and a woman as indomitable as she was pious, had consistently stood in the eye of the Gregorian storm. It was she, in 1077, who had been Gregory's host at Canossa; and it was she, in the decade that followed his death, who had inflicted such military damage on Henry IV that he had eventually withdrawn from Italy for good. Perhaps the most enduring contribution made by Matilda to the cause of *reformatio*, though, would prove to be her sponsorship of Irnerius, a Bolognese jurist. His commentaries on a vast corpus of Roman legal rulings, discovered only a few years previously mouldering in an ancient library, had made accessible to the Christian West what the Islamic world had long taken for granted: an entire system of law with ambitions to cover every aspect of human existence. That the texts studied by Irnerius were of human rather than divine origin did not prevent him from assuming that they possessed a timeless significance: that they were as applicable in the present as they had been back in the days of the Caesars. The enthusiasm for his researches, and for the great field of study that they opened up, proved immense. Enterprising young men began flocking to Bologna. Anxious to set themselves on a secure legal footing, those from Italy and those from north of the Alps formed themselves into twin guilds: *universitates*. Within decades, Bologna had become the prototype of something never seen before: a university town. Even though Irnerius himself was no enthusiast for *reformatio*, there could no doubting whose cause this most benefited. Certainly, it did not take long for the path from university to Curia to become a thoroughly well-trodden one.

Bologna, though, was not merely a finishing school for papal clerks. There were scholars in the city with broader horizons. Partisans of *reformatio*, perusing the rediscovered corpus of Roman law, could not help but note a glaring absence. For centuries, ever since the great assembly of bishops convened by Constantine at Nicaea, councils of the Church had been meeting and issuing canons. No one, however, had ever thought to collate them. Various efforts had been made to rectify this in the decades that followed the millennium; but only in the wake of Irnerius' labours was it definitively achieved. The *Decretum*—ascribed by tradition to a single monk named Gratian, and completed around 1150—was a labour of decades.[28] Indisputably, the effort required was prodigious. Canon law did not consist merely of canons. There were papal rulings to be tracked down as well, and decrees passed by other bishops, and compilations of penances. Not merely scattered, these were often downright contradictory. The challenge faced by Gratian in making sense of them was freely acknowledged by the alternative title given to the *Decretum*: the *Concordance of Discordant Canons*.

How to iron out the inconsistencies? Gratian and his colleagues had two recourses. There was the guidance provided by scripture, of course, and by the Church Fathers—men such as Irenaeus, and Origen, and Augustine. Yet even these authorities did not provide Gratian with what Muslim lawyers had long taken for granted: a comprehensive body of written rulings supposedly deriving from God himself. No Christians had ever had such a resource. God, so they believed, wrote his rulings on the human heart. Paul's authority on this score was definitive. 'The entire law is summed up in a single command: "Love your neighbour as yourself."' Here, for Gratian, was the foundation-stone of justice. So important to him was the command that he opened the *Decretum* by citing it. Echoing the Stoics much as Paul had done, he opted to define it as natural law—and the key to fashioning a properly Christian legal system. All souls were equal in the eyes of God. Only if it were founded on this assumption could justice truly be done. Anything obstructing it had to go. 'Enactments, whether ecclesiastical or secular, if they are proved to be contrary to natural law, must be totally excluded.'[29]

Much flowed from this formulation that earlier ages would have struggled to comprehend. Age-old presumptions were being decisively overturned: that custom was the ultimate authority; that the great were owed a different justice from the humble; that inequality was something natural, to be taken for granted. Clerks trained in Bologna were agents of revolution as well as of order. Legally constituted, university-trained, they constituted a new breed of professional. Gratian, by providing them with both a criterion and a sanction for weeding out objectionable customs, had transfigured the very understanding of law. No longer did it exist to uphold the differences in status that Roman jurists and Frankish kings alike had always taken for granted. Instead, its purpose was to provide equal justice to every individual, regardless of rank, or wealth, or lineage—for every individual was equally a child of God.

Gratian, by inscribing this conviction into the *Decretum*, had served to set the study of law upon a new and radical course. The task of a canon lawyer, like that of a gardener, was never done. The weeds were always sprouting, always menacing the flowers. Unlike the great corpus of Roman law, which scholars in Bologna regarded as complete, and therefore immutable, canon law was oriented to the future as well as to the past. Commentators on the *Decretum* worked on the assumption that it could always be improved. To cite an ancient authority might also require reflection on how best to provide it with legal sanction in the here and now. How, for instance, were the Christian people to square the rampant inequality between rich and poor with the insistence of numerous Church Fathers that 'the use of all things should be common to all'?[30] The problem was one that, for decades, demanded the attention of the most distinguished scholars in Bologna. By 1200, half a century after the completion of the *Decretum*, a solution had finally been arrived at—and it was one fertile with implications for the future. A starving pauper who stole from a rich man did so, according to a growing number of legal scholars, *iure naturali*—'in accordance with natural law'. As such, they argued, he could not be reckoned guilty of a crime. Instead, he was merely taking what was properly owed him. It was the wealthy miser, not the starving thief, who was the object of divine disapproval. Any bishop confronted by such a case, so canon lawyers concluded, had a duty to ensure that the wealthy pay their due of alms. Charity, no longer voluntary, was being rendered a legal obligation.

That the rich had a duty to give to the poor was, of course, a principle as old as Christianity itself. What no one had thought to argue before, though, was a matching principle: that the poor had an entitlement to the necessities of life. It was—in a formulation increasingly deployed by canon lawyers—a human 'right'.

Law, in the Latin West, had become an essential tool of its ongoing revolution.

Standing on the Shoulders of Giants

In 1140, half a century after Urban II's visit to Cluny, the most famous man in Christendom arrived in the abbey. Peter Abelard's celebrity was founded, not on feats of arms, but on the vocation of learning which, as a young man, he had exuberantly embraced in preference to knighthood. Renowned for his 'inestimable cleverness, unsurpassed memory and superhuman capacity',[31] Abelard had made his name on the great stage of the most glamorous city in the Latin world: Paris. Home to the court of the French king, it was also a powerhouse of scholarship. Nowhere else, not even Bologna, could rival the sheer brilliance, self-conceit and daring of its intellectuals. Abelard's star had shone with a particular intensity. Thousands, it was said, had flocked to his lectures. Necks would crane when he walked down the street. Girls would swoon. No one had contributed more to the lustre of the schools in Paris, and to their international reputation, than the master who, with typical modesty, liked to think of himself as 'the only philosopher in the world'.[32]

Abelard's fame, though, had long since shaded into notoriety. Combative as well as vain, his ability to bounce back from crises was rivalled only by his genius for precipitating them in the first place. His status as the leading light of the Paris schools had been secured on the back of repeated quarrels with his own teachers. Then, in 1115, he had embarked on the most scandalous of all his adventures: a secret affair with a brilliantly precocious student, 'supreme in the abundance of her learning, and not at all bad-looking',[33] named Héloïse. Shortly after a clandestine marriage, Abelard had been cornered by thugs hired by his new wife's uncle, pinned down in his bed and castrated. The humiliated victim had retired to a monastery; Héloïse, on his insistence, to a convent. Yet even as a monk, Abelard had found it impossible to stay out of trouble. It was a measure of his prestige that Saint-Denis, the monastery six miles north of Paris where he had been offered sanctuary, was the mother house of the very kingdom of France; and yet Abelard, investigating its early history, had delighted in demonstrating that the traditional account of its origins was almost certainly bogus. Naturally, this had not gone down well with his fellow monks; and so Abelard, defying the rule that required *religiones* never to leave a monastery without express permission, had returned to the road. Variously, he had lived as a hermit, as an abbot on the wild Atlantic coast, and as a teacher once again in Paris. His charisma, despite the passing of the years, remained undimmed. So too his capacity for attracting mingled hostility and adulation. Finally, in his seventh decade, there came the gravest crisis of all: his formal condemnation as a heretic. The terms of his punishment were expressed in two letters sent from Rome in the summer of 1140. Christendom's most brilliant scholar was sentenced to have his books burned 'wherever they may be found';[34] its most brilliant orator to submit to perpetual silence.

Abelard had skirted such a fate once before. Back in 1121, he had been convicted of heretical teachings on the Trinity, and ordered to burn one of his own books: a sentence that had caused him more agony, he subsequently declared, than the loss of his testicles. His judge then, as in 1140, had been a papal legate. The papacy, in its determination to provide justice for the whole of Christendom, was determined as well to patrol the acceptable frontiers of belief. This was hardly surprising. Without the sanction provided by the great framework of Christian teaching, the right of the Roman Church to sit in judgement over king and peasant alike would be as nothing. A scholar such as Abelard, whose entire career had been a restless buffeting against the claims to authority of bishops and abbots, was bound to cause them alarm. By 1140, when he was brought to his second trial, the capacity of papal lawyers to define the bounds of orthodoxy was set on firmer foundations than it had been even two decades previously. The king of France himself attended Abelard's second summons to court. Abelard, rather than answer his accusers, appealed directly to the pope. When news of his sentence arrived, he promptly headed for Rome, on the grounds that—in the long run—its justice 'never failed anyone'. His trial, as public a topic of gossip as any ever administered by papal lawyers, appeared decisively to have affirmed their grip on what Christians might and might not believe.

And yet there was, for all that, no consensus that Abelard deserved to be silenced. The charges of heresy were furiously disputed—not

least by Abelard himself. Even though it had taken him over a decade
to recover from his first conviction and return to teaching in Paris, he
had never once doubted that it was his critics who were in the wrong.
Abelard's devotion to God was as unstinting as his conceit. When
Héloïse, writing to him from her convent, confessed that she dreamed
of him even while participating in the eucharist, and that she would
rather renounce heaven than her passion for him, his reply was only
seemingly severe. By urging her to devote herself, not to memories of
their love, but to her duties as a nun, his hope was to set his wife back
on the road to salvation. Abelard himself had embarked in a very similar spirit on a great study of the Church Fathers. Discovering in their
writings repeated contradictions, repeated challenges to the tenets of
Christian belief, he had compiled entire lists of them, carefully catalogued and ordered—but not out of any ambition to challenge the
Church's teachings. Quite the contrary. Abelard no more aimed at
rending the great fabric of Christian orthodoxy than did the compilers of canon law. His goal, like that of Gratian, was to bring harmony
where there was discord. He too believed in progress. 'By doubting
we come to inquiry, and by inquiry we perceive the truth.'[35] Here was
the maxim that defined Abelard's entire theology—and enabled him
to promise his students an understanding more profound than that
of the Church Fathers themselves. By applying the standards of reason to their writings, so he taught, a scholar could aspire to behold
Christian truth in its proper perspective: clear, and whole, and logi-
cally ordered. Not even Abelard was so immodest as to claim a stature equivalent to that of Origen or Augustine; but he did aspire, by
standing on their shoulders, to see further than they had done. This,
to his accusers, was the expression of a monstrous arrogance, one
that, 'by assuming the entire nature of God to lie within the grasp of
human reason, threatens the good name of the Christian faith'.[36] But
to his admirers, it was thrilling. And there were, among these admirers, some who stood very high in the Church indeed.

This was why, in the summer of 1140, when Abelard stopped at
Cluny on his way to Rome, he was treated as an honoured guest. No

one could provide a surer sanctuary than its abbot. Peter the Venerable was, as his sobriquet implied, a man of unimpeachable sanctity, and the greatness of his monastery bestowed upon him a standing that was, perhaps, second only to that of the pope himself. Although Peter could not redeem Abelard's heresies from condemnation, he was able, by virtue of his office and his connections, to secure a personal absolution for the embattled fugitive. When, two years after his arrival at Cluny, Abelard finally succumbed to exhaustion and old age, the respect shown his memory was startling. Not only did Peter, against all convention, send the body to Héloïse for burial, he escorted the coffin himself. In an epitaph intended to be widely read, the abbot described the dead philosopher as 'the Aristotle of our age'. The attempt by Abelard's enemies to damn his reputation, and to cast as heretical his insistence that the mysteries of the divine word might be deciphered by means of logic, was denied a decisive victory. His mystique survived his death. When, some two decades after burying her husband, Héloïse followed him into the grave, he is said to have reached out to hold her as she was laid beside him. Generations of students likewise folded themselves into Abelard's posthumous embrace. By 1200, Paris could boast a university as vibrant as Bologna's. The conviction Abelard had devoted his life to promoting—that God's order was rational and governed by rules that mortals could aspire to comprehend—had become, less than a century after his death, an orthodoxy upheld by papal legates. Those who taught it, far from being seen as a menace, were now allies to be defended. In 1215, a statute was promulgated in the name of the pope, legally affirming the independence of Paris' university from the bishop. A year earlier, a similar measure had established the legal status of the colleges that, over the preceding decades, had begun to appear in the English town of Oxford. Universities were soon mushrooming across Christendom. Not merely tolerated, the methods of enquiry pioneered by Abelard had been institutionalised.

'It is by God's laws that the whole scheme of things is governed.'[37] So Augustine, contemplating the immensity of the cosmos, had declared. Although theology, unsurprisingly, reigned in Paris and Oxford as the queen of sciences, there was no lack of other fields of study in which God's laws were also to be distinguished. The workings of nature—of the sun, and the moon, and the stars, and of the elements, and of the distribution of matter, and of wild animals, and of the human body—all bore witness to their existence. It was no offence against God, then, to argue, as Abelard did, 'that the constitution or development of everything that originates without miracles can be adequately accounted for'.[38] Quite the contrary. To identify the laws that governed the universe was to honour the Lord God who had formulated them. This conviction, far from perturbing the gatekeepers of the new universities, was precisely what animated them. Philosophy, which to many of Abelard's opponents had been a dirty word, came to lie at the heart of the curriculum. Investigation into the workings of nature provided its particular foundation. The study of animals and plants, of astronomy, even of mathematics: all came to be categorised as natural philosophy. The truest miracle was not the miraculous, but the opposite: the ordered running of heaven and earth.

To believe this was not to doubt God's absolute power. Anything was possible to him, and his will was unfathomable. On this, the record of scripture was clear. He had divided seas, and halted the passage of the sun across the sky, and might readily do so again. Yet scripture was clear as well that even the Almighty God might submit himself to a legal obligation. So it was, after flooding the world, that he had set a rainbow in the clouds, as the sign of a compact, that never again would he send waters 'to destroy all life';[39] so it was, in conversation with Abraham, that he had sworn a covenant, and with Moses decreed its terms. Yet the profoundest submission, the most shocking, was neither of these. 'He freed us from our sins, and from his own wrath, and from hell, and from the power of the Devil, whom he came to vanquish for us, because we were unable to do it, and he purchased for us the kingdom of heaven; and by doing all these things, he manifested the greatness of his love for us.'[40] Thus

Anselm, writing as Abelard was coming of age, had described the crucifixion. Humanity, lost to sin, had been redeemed by Christ. But how? The question was one that had haunted Abelard and his generation. Various answers had been attempted. Some had cast Christ's death as a ransom paid to Satan; others as the resolution of a lawsuit between heaven and hell. Abelard, following in Anselm's wake, had been more subtle. Christ had submitted to torture on the Cross, not to satisfy the demands of the Devil, but to awaken humanity to love. 'This it is to free us from slavery to sin, to gain for us the true liberty of the sons of God.'[41] The demands of justice had been met; and by meeting them, Christ had affirmed to all humanity that heaven and earth were indeed structured by laws. Yet he had done more as well. Abelard, writing to Héloïse, had urged her to contemplate Christ's sufferings, and to learn from them the true nature of love. To press this argument on his anguished and abandoned wife was not to torment her, nor to abandon his lifelong commitment to reason. Abelard had seen no contradiction between his career as a logician and his passionate commitment to the tortured Christ. The road to wisdom led from the Cross.

Mystery and reason: Christianity embraced them both. God, who had summoned light and darkness into being by the power of his voice, and separated the seas from the land, had ordained as well that the whole of his creation be a monument to harmony. 'It is upon distinctions of number that the underlying principles of everything depend.'[42] So Abelard had written. A century on from his death, monuments to the cosmic order created by God, to its fusion of the miraculous and the geometric, were starting to rise above towns across Christendom. To enter Saint-Denis, where Abelard had first lived as a monk, was to behold an abbey utterly transformed. The rays of the sun, filtered through windows patterned with exquisitely coloured glass, illumined the interior with an unprecedented light, radiant as, at the end of days, the descent of the New Jerusalem from heaven would be radiant, with a brilliance 'like that of a very precious jewel, like a jasper, clear as silver'.[43] Yet if Saint-Denis, in the play of coloured rays across its interior, offered its visitors a glimpse of revelation, so also, in the soaring of its flying buttresses, in the elongation of its vaulted arches, did it proclaim its architect's mastery of proportion and geometry. Dedicated in 1144, in the presence of the French king himself, the abbey had provided a model for a spectacular new style of cathedral. 'The dull mind rises to the truth through material things.'[44] So it was written on the doors of Saint-Denis. The cathedrals built in the abbey's wake provided a physical expression, on a scale never before attempted, of the distinctive order that had emerged in the Latin West. *Modernitas*, its enthusiasts called it: the final age of time. They were spokesmen for revolution: a revolution that had triumphed.

10

PERSECUTION

1229: Marburg

Count Paviam was shocked by the gruelling nature of the work in the hospital. Every day, dressed in coarse grey tunics, women would attend the sick: bathing them, changing their linen, cleaning their sores. One, anxious for a paralysed boy who suffered from dysentery, went so far as to put him in her own bed, and carry him outside whenever his stomach began to cramp. Since this would happen upwards of six times each night, her sleep was repeatedly disturbed; but the demands on her time were far too relentless for her to have any hope of catching up with it by day. When she was not working in the hospital, she was obliged to toil in the kitchen, preparing vegetables, washing dishes, being barked at by a deaf and exacting housekeeper. If there was no work to be done in the scullery, then she would sit at a wheel and spin wool: her only source of income. Even when ill herself and confined to bed, she would still wind thread with her bare hands. The Count, entering her quarters, could only bless himself in admiration. 'Never before,' he exclaimed, 'has the daughter of a king been seen spinning wool.'[1]

The Lady Elizabeth had been born to greatness. Descended from a cousin of Stephen, Hungary's first truly Christian king, she had been sent as a child to the court of Thuringia, in central Germany, and groomed there for marriage. At the age of fourteen, she had

joined Louis, its twenty-year-old ruler, on the throne. The couple
had been very happy. Elizabeth had borne her husband three children; Louis had gloried in his wife's demonstrable closeness to God.
Even when he was woken in the night by a maid tugging on his foot,
he had borne it patiently, knowing that the servant had mistaken
him for his wife, whose custom it was to get up in the early hours to
pray. Elizabeth's insistence on giving away her jewellery to the poor;
her mopping up of mucus and saliva from the faces of the sick; her
making of shrouds for paupers out of her finest linen veils: here were
gestures that had prefigured her far more spectacular self-abasement
in the wake of her husband's death. Her only regret was that it did
not go far enough. 'If there were a life that was more despised, I
would choose it.'[2] When Count Paviam urged Elizabeth to abandon
the rigours and humiliations of her existence in Marburg, and return
with him to her father's court, she refused point blank.

She stood heir, of course, to a long tradition: to that of Basil,
and Macrina, and Paulinus. Thuringia too provided her with a role
model, and a royal one at that: Radegund, a queen who, back in the
age of Clovis, had cleaned toilets and picked out nits from the hair
of beggars. Elizabeth, though, had a much more immediate source
of inspiration to hand. She lived in a world that had been set on its
head by reformers who, for a century and more, had laboured to
wash Christendom clean of its filth, to swab and tend to its leprous
sores. The supreme exemplar that Elizabeth had before her was not
a saint but an institution: the Church itself. Like her, it had escaped
the embrace of princes. Like her, it had pledged itself to a perpetual chastity. Like her, it had enshrined poverty as an ideal. 'The
only men fit to preach are those who lack earthly riches, because—
possessing nothing of their own—they hold everything in common.'[3]
Such was the battle-cry that, back in the age of Gregory VII, had
helped to trigger the great convulsion of *reformatio*. It was the same
battle-cry that Elizabeth, giving away all her wealth, becoming one
with porters and kitchen-maids, had raised herself.

Yet she had to tread carefully. All those who followed the path to voluntary poverty did. The scorching lava-flow of *reformatio*, which for decades had swept away everything before it, had begun to cool, to harden. Its supreme achievement—the establishment across Christendom of a single, sovereign hierarchy—was no longer best served by the zeal of revolution. Its leaders had won too greatly to welcome the prospect of further upheaval. Their need now was for stability. Clerks in the service of the papal bureaucracy and scholars learned in canon law had long been toiling to strengthen the foundations of the Church's authority. They understood the awful responsibility that weighed upon their shoulders. Their task was to bring the Christian people to God. 'There is one Catholic Church of the faithful, and outside of it there is absolutely no salvation.'[4] So it had been formally declared during Elizabeth's childhood, in 1215, at the fourth of a series of councils convened at the Lateran. To defy this canon, to reject the structures of authority that served to uphold it, to disobey the clergy whose solemn prerogative it was to shepherd souls, was to follow the path to hell.

Yet that this needed stating, and by an assembled mass of bishops and abbots too, 'from every nation which is under heaven',[5] only served to highlight an awkward truth: that the Church's authority was not universally acknowledged. There were many, over the course of the century that followed Gregory VII's papacy, who felt that the potential of *reformatio* was still to be met. The passions of revolution were not easily calmed. The more reformers who had risen to power in the Church sought to stabilise the condition of Christendom, so the more did those on the extreme fringes of *reformatio* accuse them of betrayal. A momentous pattern was being set. Revolution had bred an elite—and this elite had bred demands for revolution.

Most of the agitators, preachers who clung to the ideal of living as the apostles had done, of holding all their possessions in common, and of disdaining anything that smacked of the world, railed against the new model of the Church much as Gregory had railed against the old. Roaming the countryside barefoot, carrying crosses of bare and unadorned iron, they lambasted the clergy for failing to practise what they preached: for being leprous with lechery, and pride, and greed. The most radical campaigners went even further. Rather than holding out for further reform, they had come to despair of the very edifice of the Church. Built by popes and bishops out of blood, it lay beyond saving. Corruption was its entire fabric. There was no alternative but to pull it down. Prelates, dreading the spread of these teachings, naturally condemned them as heresy. By the time of Elizabeth's birth, the panic in papal circles was at full flood. Heretics seemed everywhere. In 1215, at the Fourth Lateran Council, a programme for combating their spread was laid out in a detailed canon. 'Every heresy that rises against the holy, orthodox and Catholic faith we excommunicate and anathematise. All heretics we condemn under whatever names they may be known.'[6]

Yet the boundary between heresy and sainthood could be a narrow one. The Lady Elizabeth, while still at court, had shared fantasies with her maids of becoming a beggar. With their help, in her private quarters, she had even dressed up in rags. But this was their secret. Elizabeth had not wished to embarrass her husband. It was not only his courtiers that she had risked scandalising. Out on the roads beyond the great castle of the Wartburg, where Louis had established his court, bands of preachers roamed, summoning the wealthy to do as they had done, and give away all their riches to the poor. Even though some of these preachers were women, Elizabeth had known better than to join them. To become a Waldensian was to risk damnation. Named after Waldes, a wealthy Lyons merchant who in 1173 had been inspired by Christ's teachings to sell all his possessions, they had repeatedly been refused permission to proclaim their teachings. Appealing to the pope himself, they had been laughed out of court. Clerics had not put themselves through a gruelling course of university education merely to license laymen—*idiotae*—to pontificate on the scriptures. 'Shall pearls of wisdom be

cast before swine?'[7] The Waldensians, rather than submitting obedi-
ently to this verdict, had responded by turning on the men who had
thought to sit in judgement on them. Denouncing the pride and corruption of the clergy with a vitriol that would have done the Donatists credit, they were soon proclaiming their contempt for the very
concept of a priesthood. Christ alone was their bishop. This heresy,
rank and gross as it was, offered Elizabeth a chilling demonstration of just how far disobedience to the Church might go. That the
Waldensians led precisely the kind of lifestyle to which she aspired,
holding everything in common, subsisting on alms, only rendered
them all the more salutary a warning.

Waldes, though, was not the only merchant to have embraced
poverty in the name of Christ. In 1206, a one-time playboy by the
name of Francis, a native of the Italian city of Assisi, had spectacularly renounced his patrimony. Taking off his clothes, he had handed
them over to his father. 'Moreover he did not even keep his drawers, but stripped himself naked before all the bystanders.'[8] The local
bishop, impressed rather than appalled by this display, had tenderly
covered him with his own cloak, and sent him on his way with a
blessing. Here, with this episode, had been set the pattern of Francis' career. His genius for taking Christ's teachings literally, for dra-
matising their paradoxes and complexities, for combining simplicity
and profundity in a single memorable gesture, would never leave
him. He served lepers; preached to birds; rescued lambs from butch-
ers. Rare were those immune to his charisma. Admiration for his
mission reached to the very summit of the Church. Innocent III, the
pope who in 1215 had convened the Fourth Lateran Council, was not
a man easily impressed. Imperious, daring and brilliant, he gave way
to no one, overthrowing emperors, excommunicating kings. Unsurprisingly, then, when Francis, at the head of twelve ragged 'brothers',
or 'friars', first arrived in Rome, Innocent had refused to see him.
The whiff of heresy, not to mention blasphemy, had seemed altogether too rank. Francis, though, unlike Waldes, never stinted in his
respect for the Church, in his obedience to its authority. Innocent's

doubts were eased. Imaginative as well as domineering, he had come to see in Francis and his followers not a danger, but an opportunity. Rather than treating them as his predecessors had treated the Waldensians, he ordained them a legally constituted order of the Church. 'Go, and the Lord be with you, brethren, and as He shall deign to inspire you, preach repentance to all.'[9]

By 1217, less than a decade after this proclamation, a Franciscan mission had reached Germany. Elizabeth would grow up profoundly inspired by its example. By dressing in secret as a beggar, she had been paying tribute to Francis. Other demonstrations of her enthusiasm for his teachings were more public. In 1225, she provided the Franciscans with a base at the foot of the Wartburg, in the town of Eisenach. Three years later, following the death of her husband, she made her way there and formally renounced her ties to the world. Yet no matter how desperately she longed to do so, she did not then go begging from door to door. Elizabeth had properly absorbed the lessons of Francis' example. She understood that to embrace poverty without obedience was to risk the fate of Waldes. No mortification, no gesture of abasement, could possibly be undertaken unless at the command of a superior. Here, for a princess, the mistress of many servants, was a realisation that was itself a form of submission. So Elizabeth, even as she sat enthroned by her husband's side, had employed a *magister disciplinae spiritualis*: a 'master of spiritual discipline'. Not just any master, either. 'I could have sworn obedience to a bishop or an abbot who had possessions, but I thought it better to swear obedience to one who has nothing and relies totally on begging. And so I submitted to Master Conrad.'[10]

Personal austerity was not, however, the quality for which Master Conrad was principally famed. Across Germany, and even in distant Rome, he was celebrated above all as 'a most bitter critic of vice'.[11] Of humble background and formidable eloquence, he was tireless in his defence of the Church and its authority. Talent-spotters in the papal establishment had taken note. In 1213, armed with a personal mandate from Innocent, Conrad had taken to the roads of Germany, riding a tiny mule, preaching from village to village. 'Innumerable crowds of people of both sexes and from various provinces followed him, enticed by the words of his teaching.'[12] By 1225, when Elizabeth recruited him as her master, he had years of experience in schooling heretics. Now, with a princess to discipline, he did not hesitate to wield the rod. Even before Louis' death, he had punished her for missing one of his sermons with a beating so violent that the stripes were still visible three weeks later. It was on her master's orders that Elizabeth, following her renunciation of the world, had travelled to Marburg, his native town, in the easternmost reaches of Thuringia, there to found a hospital. Deprived first of her children, and then of her much-loved personal servants, she patiently endured his every attempt to break her. Even when punished for offences she had not committed, she rejoiced in her submission. 'Willingly she sustained repeated lashes and blows from Master Conrad—being mindful of the beatings endured by the Lord.'[13]

To suffer was to gain redemption. In 1231, when Elizabeth died of her austerities at the tender age of twenty-four, Conrad did not hesitate to hail her as a saint. As gold is purified by fire, so had she been purged of sin. The same strictness that had brought her to an early grave had brought her to heaven. Proof of this was manifest in the numerous miracles reported at her tomb. A woman who had stuck a pea in her ear when she was a young girl regained her hearing; numerous hunchbacks were healed. Most telling of all, perhaps, from Conrad's own point of view, was the story told of a Waldensian widow, whose hideously disfigured nose had been beautified upon an appeal to the Lady Elizabeth. The lesson taught by this edifying report was one fit to reassure Conrad that all his sternness, all his flintiness, was justified. Sixteen years previously, at the Fourth Lateran Council, it had been prescribed for the first time that all Christians should make annual and individual confession of their sins. The venerable reassurance of Columbanus that any fault might be forgiven, had received the official seal of the Church's approval. God's mercy was for everyone. All that it required was a genuine repentance. Even the most obdurate heretics might ultimately be brought to heaven.

It was with a renewed sense of urgency, then, that Conrad, in the wake of Elizabeth's death, embarked upon a fresh campaign to win them back for Christ. He did so armed with an innovative array of powers. For decades, a succession of popes had been labouring to enhance the legal resources available in the fight against heresy. Impatient with a tradition that had always tended to emphasise charity over persecution, they had introduced an escalating battery of punitive measures. In 1184, bishops who previously might have been content to let sleeping heretics lie had been instructed actively to sniff them out. Then, in 1215, at the great Lateran Council presided over by Innocent III, sanctions explicitly targeting heresy had provided the Church with an entire machinery of persecution. Now, in 1231, there came a fresh refinement. A new pope, Gregory IX, authorised Conrad not merely to preach against heresy, but to devote himself to the search for it—the *inquisitio*. No longer was it the responsibility of a bishop to bring heretics to trial, and sit in judgement on them, but rather that of a cleric especially appointed to the task. Even though, as a priest, Conrad could not himself 'decree or pronounce a sentence involving the shedding of blood',[14] he was licensed by Gregory to compel the secular authorities to impose it. Never before had power of this order been given to a campaigner against heresy. Now, when Conrad rode on his mule from village to village, summoning the locals to answer his interrogation of their beliefs, he did so not merely as a preacher, but as a whole new breed of official: an *inquisitor*.

'In all things he broke her will, to ensure that the merit of her obedience to him would increase.'[15] So Conrad had justified his handling of Elizabeth. Now, with all of Germany his to discipline, he could not afford to soften. The truest kindness was cruelty; the truest mercy harshness. The swarm of heretics that confronted Conrad were not readily to be redeemed from damnation. Only fire could smoke them out. Pyres needed to be stoked as they had never been stoked before. The burning of heretics—hitherto a rare and sporadic expedient, only ever reluctantly licensed, if at all—was the very mark of Conrad's inquisition. In towns and villages along the Rhine, the stench of blackened flesh hung in the air. 'So many heretics were burned throughout Germany that their number could not be comprehended.'[16] Conrad's critics, unsurprisingly, accused him of a killing spree. They charged him with believing every accusation that was brought before him; of rushing the process of law; of sentencing the innocent to the flames. No one, though, was innocent. All were fallen. Better to suffer as Christ had suffered, tortured in a place of public execution for a crime that he had not committed, than to suffer eternal damnation. Better to suffer for a few fleeting moments than to burn for all eternity.

With Master Conrad, the yearning to cleanse the world of sin, to heal it of its leprosy, had turned murderous. That made it no less revolutionary. The suspicion of the worldly order that had brought Gregory VII to humble an anointed king before the gates of Canossa was one that Conrad more than shared. As Elizabeth's master, he had forbidden her to eat food 'about which she did not have a clear conscience'. Anything on her husband's table that might have derived from exploitation of the poor, that might have been extracted from peasants as a tribute or a tax, she had dutifully spurned. 'As a result, she often suffered great penury, eating nothing but rolls spread with honey.'[17] The Lady Elizabeth had been a saint. Her peers were not. In the summer of 1233, Conrad dared to accuse one of them, the Count of Sayn, of heresy. A frantically convened synod of bishops, in the presence of the German king himself, threw out the case. Conrad, nothing daunted, began to prepare charges against further noblemen. Then, on 30 July, as he was returning from the Rhine to Marburg, he was ambushed by a group of knights and cut down. The news of his death was greeted with rejoicing throughout Germany. In the Lateran, though, there was indignation. As Conrad was laid to rest in Marburg, by the side of the Lady Elizabeth, Gregory mourned him in sombre terms. The murderers, so the Pope warned, were harbingers of a rising darkness. All of heaven and earth had shuddered at their crime. Their patron was literally hellish: none other than the Devil himself.

A Great and Holy War

When clerics pondered the mysterious upsurge of heresy, they tended to glimpse in its shadowy outline something all the more disturbing for appearing not altogether unfamiliar to them. Conrad, when he interrogated Waldensians, refused to accept that he faced some minuscule and upstart sect. Instead, he distinguished something altogether more menacing. They belonged, so he believed, to an institution that was almost the mirror image of the Church: hierarchical in its organisation, universal in its claims. Writing to Gregory IX, Conrad warned that the true loyalty of heretics belonged to the Devil, 'who they claim was the creator of the celestial bodies, and will ultimately return to glory when the Lord has fallen from power'.[18] Sinister rituals parodied those of the Church. Initiates into the ranks of Satan's followers were obliged to suck on the tongue of a giant toad. Faith in Christ was banished upon the kiss of a cadaverous man, whose lips were as cold as ice. At a ritual meal, devotees would lick the anus of a black cat the size of dog. The entire congregation would then hail Satan as Lord.

Gregory IX, on reading this sensational report, took an unprecedented step: he gave it his full imprimatur. Similar stories had long been current—but never before had they received confirmation from a pope. Christian scholars had traditionally condemned talk of devil-worship as superstitious folly. No one with any sense or education took it seriously. It smacked too much of paganism. Only gullible peasants and novices afraid of their own shadow feared that demons stalked the earth, recruiting adherents, hosting covens. Belief in such nonsense was itself the work of the Devil. Such was the solemn verdict of Gratian and other canon lawyers. 'Who is there that is not led out of himself in dreams and nocturnal visions, and sees much when sleeping which he had never seen waking?'[19]

Yet this bracing scepticism did not preclude the learned from dreading the existence of an infernally inspired conspiracy. The Waldensians were not the only heretics in the Rhineland who, in the decades before Conrad's ministry, were identified as belonging to a distinctive and pernicious sect. In 1163, six men and two women were burned in Cologne for belonging to an obscure group called *Cathari*—'the pure ones'. More executions of Cathars followed, here and there, although never in any great numbers. The precise nature of their beliefs remained obscure. Some, in the manner of Conrad, identified them with Devil-worshippers, and suggested that they derived their name from the cat that devotees of Satan were reputed to kiss on its anus. Some confused them with Waldensians. Some conflated them with other, equally enigmatic groups of heretics: 'those whom some call Patarenes, others Publicans, and others by different names'.[20] Only scholars well-versed in the history of the Church knew who the Cathars had actually been: schismatics who, back in the time of Constantine, had been singled out for a dismissive mention in a canon of the Council of Nicaea. That now, almost a thousand years on, they were suddenly popping up in the Rhineland only emphasised just how dangerous, just how undead heresy could be. Always there in the shadows, a constant danger, it endured across space and time.

Except that most of the Christians identified by nervous Church officials as 'Cathars' did not remotely think of themselves as heretics—nor indeed, come to that, as Cathars. Just as the dread of devil-worship drew on the fantasies of the uneducated, so was the fear of a revenant heresy, stirred up from its grave, nourished by scholarship. The clerics who staffed the Curia and provided the immense apparatus of the Catholic Church with its bureaucrats, and lawyers, and teachers, had too easily forgotten that they themselves were the innovators. Radicals who criticised them for betraying the cause of *reformatio* were counterbalanced by large numbers of Christians who lived still ignorant—or resentful—of its claims. Remote from the cathedrals and the universities, old habits of worship died hard. This was especially so in those regions of Christendom where a central authority barely existed, where the writ of kings was weak, and that of bishops too. Clerics schooled in the classrooms of Paris or Bologna, venturing off the beaten track, might well find themselves among entire populations who cared nothing for *reformatio*, and felt only contempt for those it had brought to power. To label these deplorables 'Cathars' was pointedly to ignore what they actually were: Christians left behind by the new orthodoxies of the age.

Nowhere were the resulting tensions more evident than in southern France. Here, where local loyalties were as intense as they were splintered, Paris seemed a long way away indeed. In 1179, a council convened by the pope specified 'the lands around Albi and Toulouse'[21] as an especially noxious breeding ground of heresy. Papal legates who visited the region found there a fractious, disputatious people, resentful of many of the founding ideals of *reformatio*: the claim to authority of the Church's international hierarchy; its demands for obedience, and deference, and tithes; the insistence that an insuperable divide distinguished the clergy from those to whom they ministered. Sacral authority, among those dismissively termed 'Albigensians' by papal agents, was not viewed as a prerogative of priests. Anyone might lay claim to it. Out in the fields that surrounded Albi and Toulouse, a peasant might well be more honoured than a bishop. A widower who won a name for himself as a model of courtesy and self-restraint; a matron who secluded herself from the world: these were honoured as *boni homines*, 'good men', 'good women'. The very holiest were believed to approach the perfection of Christ himself: to become 'friends of God'. There was no gesture they could make so humble, no gesture so everyday, that it might not be suffused with a sense of the divine. Deeply rooted in the local soil, the Christianity of the good men was one that cast *reformatio* as the heresy, a thing of 'ravening wolves, hypocrites and seducers'.[22]

In 1165, ten miles south of Albi, the bishop had engaged with his opponents in a village square, before a great audience of noblemen and prelates. Much that the good men had revealed about their beliefs that day was deeply shocking to the assembled clergy. In forthright terms, they had dismissed the Old Testament as worthless; declared that 'any good man, cleric or layman', might preside over the eucharist; insisted that they owed priests 'no obedience, for they were wicked, not good teachers, but hired servants'.[23] Nevertheless, much that they believed was perfectly orthodox. 'We believe in one God, living and true, three in one and one in three, the Father, the Son, and the Holy Spirit.'[24] Christ had become flesh; he had suffered, died and been buried; he had risen on the third day and ascended into heaven. Such was the creed to which the bishops also subscribed. But this did not reassure them. Instead, it only confirmed them in their darkest fear: that heresy was a plague, rotting away those who might not even realise that they were infected. And plague unchecked was bound to spread.

'Wounds that do not respond to the treatment of a poultice should be cut away with a knife.'[25] By November 1207, when this sombre medical ruling was pronounced by Innocent III, dread that heresy might come to poison all the Christian people had reached a fever pitch. Innocent himself, thanks to a combination of ability and good fortune, wielded an authority of which Gregory VII could only have dreamed. More plausibly than any pope before him, he aspired to sway the fate of the world. Yet the very scope of his power seemed only to mock him. Gazing as he did from east to west, and painfully conscious of the awesome mandate that had been entrusted to him by God, he feared that everywhere Christian fortunes were in retreat. In the Holy Land, Jerusalem had been lost to the Saracens. A campaign led by the kings of France and England to recapture it had failed. A second expedition, launched in 1202 in obedience to Innocent's own summons, had been diverted to Constantinople. In 1204 it had stormed and sacked the city. A stronghold that for long centuries had withstood the envy of pagan warlords had fallen at last—to a Christian army. Its captors justified their storming of the city by charging that its inhabitants were rebels against the papacy: for the churches of Rome and Constantinople, ever since the age of Gregory VII, had been divided by an ever-widening schism. Innocent, however, appalled by the despoliation of Christendom's bulwark, lamented the fall of Constantinople as a work of hell. Meanwhile, in Spain, where Christian arms had for many centuries been determinedly pushing back the frontier of al-Andalus, the advance had lately been brought to a juddering halt. In 1195, a particularly disastrous defeat—which had seen an entire field army wiped out and three bishops killed—had inspired the Muslim general to boast that he would stable his horses in Rome. To Innocent, the reason for God's anger was glaring. There could be no prospect of reclaiming Jerusalem while heresy festered. Evil as the Saracens were, they were not so evil as heretics. In January 1208, the murder of a papal legate on the banks of the Rhône decided Innocent once and for all. His duty was clear. He could not risk the contamination of the entire Christian people by the Albigensians. There was no alternative but to destroy their heresy at the point of a sword.

Back in 1095, when Urban II had summoned the warriors of Christendom to set out for the Holy Land, he had instructed them, as a symbol of their vow, to wear the sign of the cross. Now, in July 1209, when an immense army of knights unmatched since the time of Urban assembled at Lyon, they too were *crucesignati*: 'signed with the cross'. It marked them as pilgrims who, like their Saviour, were so aflame with love of mankind that they were ready to be killed in the cause of redeeming them from hell. 'The cross that is fixed to your coats with a soft thread,' a preacher reminded them, 'was fixed to His flesh with iron nails.'[26] Even those in the path of the great force as it lumbered down the Rhine and then along the coast towards the town of Béziers could recognise in the invaders a formidable sense of identification with the sufferings of Christ. A *crozada*, they called the campaign: a 'crusade'. Yet although the word would in time be applied retrospectively to the great expedition that had been launched by Urban, the crusade against the Albigensians was war of a kind that Christians had never fought before. It was not, as Charlemagne's campaigns against the Saxons had been, an exercise in territorial expansion; nor was it, in the manner of the crusades that aimed at the liberation of Jerusalem, an armed pilgrimage to a destination of transcendent holiness. Rather, it had as its goal the extirpation of dangerous beliefs. Only blood could wash Christendom clean of the pollution presented to the Christian people by heresy.

Storming Béziers, there were some who worried how the faithful were to be distinguished from heretics. 'Lord,' they asked the papal legate, 'what shall we do?' 'Kill them all,' came the blunt reply. 'God knows his own.'[27] So, at any rate, it was later reported. The story spoke powerfully of the peculiar horror that shadowed the crusaders' minds. That a heretic might seem at first glance a dutiful Christian, that the diseased might be mistaken for the healthy, that infection might often prove impossible to diagnose, was precisely what gave steel to their resolve. The risk was a chilling one: that they themselves, if they did not scour the pestilence thoroughly from the lands where it had taken a grip, might fall victim to it. The slaughter in Béziers, merciless and total, set the precedent. Even those sheltering in churches fell to the swords of the crusaders; blood darkened the river; fire, incinerating the survivors and bringing the cathedral crashing down in molten ruin, completed the holocaust. 'Divine vengeance,' Innocent's legate reported back to Rome, 'raged marvellously.'[28]

Béziers was reduced to corpse-strewn wreckage in a single afternoon. The cycles of slaughter and ruin that it heralded would last two decades. Only in 1229, by which time Innocent had died and Gregory IX was pope, did a treaty signed in Paris finally bring the killing to a close. The war had long outrun the ability of the papacy to control it. Terror had become the order of the day. Garrisons were blinded; prisoners mutilated; women thrown down wells. Innocent, without whose iron-clad sense of mission the crusade would never have been launched, had havered between exultation at the victories won for Christ and agony at the cost. The crusaders had shown fewer qualms. Although, throughout the campaign, the ambition had always been to win back heretics to the Church, its leaders had never regretted their obligation to punish obdurate defiance with death. In 1211, after the capture of the castle of Cassés, bishops had preached to the good men there, and urged them to turn from error. But to no effect. The effort of the bishops had ended in failure. 'And since they could not convert so much as one heretic, the pilgrims seized them all. And then they burned them. And they did it with the utmost joy.'[29]

When Gregory gave his mandate to Conrad of Marburg and other inquisitors, he could do so in the full confidence that persecution worked. Innocent's surgery on the diseased body of Christendom had manifestly been a success. The enemies of Christ were everywhere in retreat. In Spain, below the Sierra Morena, the great mountain range that stretches across the south of the Iberian peninsula, God's favour had granted Christian arms a decisive victory. The Saracens' defeat at Las Navas de Tolosa in the summer of 1212 had left them fatally exposed. Two decades on, their greatest cities—Cordoba, Seville—stood on the brink of capture by the king of Castile. Meanwhile, in the heartlands of the Albigensians, those among the good men who had survived the exterminating zeal of the crusaders were fugitives, skulking in forests and cattle-sheds, their days of haranguing bishops in village squares gone for good. To Gregory, and to many others, it seemed evident that a great conspiracy had been defeated. Before their defeat at Las Navas de Tolosa, the Saracens were reported to have been plotting to march to the rescue of the Albigensians. The Albigensians themselves—now that the good men were broken, and the reality of what they had been distorted for good—were increasingly seen as the agents of an entire heretical church. This church was said to have existed since ancient times; to have derived from Bulgaria; to span the world. Scholars knowledgeable in the heresies of antiquity traced its ultimate origins to a prophet in Persia. 'They follow him in believing that there are two sources of life: one a good god and the other an evil god—in other words, the Devil.'[30]

Such was the measure of the crusaders' victory: that ghosts summoned from the unimaginably distant age of Darius would come to have a more vivid presence in the imaginings of the Christian people than those of the good men and good women themselves. The fantasy that the Albigensians had belonged to an ancient church consecrated to a belief in rival principles of good and evil—a church that in time would be given the name of 'Cathar'—would prove a particularly vivid one; but it was no less of a fantasy for that. The readiness of Gregory IX to sanction a belief in satanic conspiracies was nurtured by the blood of those who had perished in the Albigensian crusade. The slaughter had demonstrated that a diseased limb might indeed be amputated from the body of Christendom—but it had shown as well just how hard it could be to distinguish rottenness from solidity, dark from light, heretic from Christian.

The dread of this realisation—and of what it might mean for those entrusted by God with the defence of his people—would not rapidly go away.

The Eternal Jew

Shortly before the great victory of Las Navas de Tolosa, another Christian army, preparing for battle against the Saracens on the Portuguese coast, had seen riding in their vanguard a force of angelic horsemen. 'Clad in white, they had worn red crosses upon their surcoats.'[31] The sense of Spain as a great battlefield between good and evil, between the heavenly and the infernal, had a long heritage in Christendom. The reconquest of lands lost to the Saracens had been tracked by the leaders of *reformatio* with an obsessive interest. It had literally helped to build Cluny. The abbey's church, the largest in the world, had been paid for with the loot of al-Andalus. In 1142, its great abbot, Peter the Venerable, had crossed the Pyrenees, the better to understand what the Saracens actually believed. Meeting with scholars fluent in Arabic, he had employed them on a momentous project: the first translation of the Qur'an into Latin. Better persuasion than compulsion—such had always been Peter's motto. Sure enough, the translation delivered, he had addressed the Saracens directly, 'not as our men often do, with arms, but with words, not with violence but reason, not with hate but love'.[32] Yet these emollient sentiments had not prevented Peter from feeling thoroughly appalled by the Qur'an. No more monstrous a compound of heresies, confected as it was 'from both Jewish fables and heretical teachers',[33] could possibly have been imagined. Even its vision of heaven blended gourmandising with sex. Cluny it was not. Far from building bridges, Peter's translation of the Qur'an had only confirmed Christians in their darkest suspicions of its contents. Islam was the sump of all heresies, and Muhammad 'the foulest of men'.[34]

The Qur'an, though, was not the only book to have been plundered from Saracen libraries. In 1085, Toledo, the ancient capital of the Visigothic monarchy and a celebrated centre of learning, had fallen to the king of Castile, the greatest of the various Spanish realms. Within only a few decades, a vast team of translators had been assembled by the city's archbishop: Muslims, Jews, monks from Cluny. They had much to keep them busy. As well as texts by Muslim and Jewish scholars, Toledo had a treasure trove of Greek classics, works by ancient mathematicians, doctors, philosophers. These, although long available in Arabic translation, had been lost to the Latin West for many centuries. One author in particular was the focus of Christian obsession. 'Only two books by Aristotle are still known to the use of the Latins.'[35] So Abelard, shortly before 1120, had lamented. Within a decade, his complaint was out of date. Iacopo, a Venetian cleric long resident in Constantinople, had embarked on an astonishing labour that would see, by the time of his death in 1147, various works by Aristotle translated directly from Greek.* To this stream of translation the efforts of the school in Toledo had soon added a flood. By 1200, almost all of Aristotle's known works were available in Latin. University teachers committed to the proposition that God's creation was governed by rules, and that reason might enable mortals to comprehend them, fell on the writings of antiquity's most renowned philosopher with a mixture of avidity and relief. That an authority such as Aristotle had been given voice again promised to set their own investigations into the functioning of the universe on a more rigorous footing than ever before. Paris in particular had fast become a hotbed of Aristotelian study. The sense of excitement generated by its schools had attracted students from across Christendom. Among them had been two future popes: Innocent III and Gregory IX.

Yet the resurrection of a sage who had lived long before Christ, nor had any familiarity with scripture, presented challenges as well as opportunities. If numerous aspects of his teaching—the fixity of species, or the unchanging motion of sun, and moon, and stars as they revolved around the earth—could readily be integrated into the fabric of Christian teaching, then others were more problematic. The very notion of a rationally ordered cosmos, so appealing to natural philosophers, continued to unsettle many in the Church. Aristotle's insistence that there had been no creation, that the universe had always existed and always would, was a particularly glaring contradiction of Christian scripture. How, then, when crusaders were struggling to cleanse southern France of heresy, could students in the kingdom's capital possibly be permitted to study such a noxious doctrine? Anxieties in Paris were heightened by the discovery in 1210 of various heretics whose reading of Aristotle had led them to believe that there was no life after death. The reaction of the city's bishop was swift. Ten of the heretics were burned at the stake. Various commentaries on Aristotle were burned as well. Aristotle's own

---

* It is equally possible that he was a Greek resident in Venice. His self-description—*Iacobus Veneticus Graecus*—is ambiguous.

books on natural philosophy were formally proscribed. 'They are not to be read at Paris either publicly or in private.'[36]

But the ban failed to hold. In 1231, Gregory IX issued a decree that guaranteed the university effective independence from the interference of bishops, and by 1255 all of Aristotle's texts were back on the curriculum. The people best qualified to learn from them, it turned out, were not heretics, but inquisitors. The days of annihilating entire towns on the grounds that God would know his own were over. The responsibility for rooting out heresy had now been entrusted to friars. Taking the lead was an order that had been established by papal decree back in 1216, to provide the Church with a shock force of intellectuals. Its founder, a Spaniard by the name of Dominic, had toured where the good men were to be found, matching them in all their austerities, and harrying them in debate. In 1207, two years before the annihilation of Béziers, he had met with a good man just north of the city, and argued publicly with him for over a week. To friars schooled in this tradition of militant preaching, Aristotle had come as a godsend. The obligation of the Dominicans was to question, to investigate, to evaluate evidence. Who better to serve as a model for this approach than history's most famous philosopher? Aristotle, far from lending succour to the enemies of the Church, was successfully summoned to its defence. Institutionalised by the universities, and licensed by the papacy, the study of his philosophy was made ever safer for Christian scholars. If the standard of investigation into heresy benefited from this trend, then so too did investigation into the workings of the universe. To fathom these workings was to fathom the very ordinances of God.

The labour of reconciling Aristotle's philosophy with Christian doctrine did not come easily. Many contributed to it; but none more so than a Dominican called Thomas, a native of Aquino, a small town just south of Rome. The book he worked on between 1265 and his death in 1274, a great compendium of 'things pertaining to Christianity',[37] was the most comprehensive attempt ever undertaken to synthesise faith with philosophy. Thomas Aquinas himself died thinking that he had failed in his efforts, and that, before the radiant unknowability of God, everything he had written was the merest chaff; in Paris, two years after his death, various of his propositions were condemned by the city's bishop. It did not take long, though, for the sheer scale of his achievement to be recognised and gratefully acknowledged. In 1323, the seal was set on his reputation when the pope proclaimed him a saint. The result was to enshrine as a bedrock of Catholic theology the conviction that revelation might indeed co-exist with reason. A century after the banning in Paris of Aristotle's books on natural philosophy, no one had to worry that the study of them might risk heresy. The dimensions that they had opened up—of time, and of space, and of the unchanging order of the stars—were rendered as Christian as scripture itself.

To those who read him in the decades that followed his death, Aquinas seemed like a voice from the radiance of heaven. To Christians long fearful of heresy he offered a double reassurance: that the teachings of the Church were true; and that the light of that truth was manifest even in dimensions that might seem to threaten it. Aristotle was not the only philosopher cited by Aquinas in his great work. There were other pagans too; there were even Saracens and Jews. His readiness to acknowledge them as authorities was a sign, not of any cultural cringe, but of the opposite: an absolute confidence that wisdom was Christian, no matter where it might be found. Reason was a gift from God. Everybody possessed it. The Ten Commandments served not as prescriptions, but as reminders to humanity of what it already knew. They were manifest in the very fabric of the universe. The love of God for his creation was the centre of a circle, to which all parts of the circumference stand in an equal relation. 'So orderly has everything been fashioned which wheels through mind and space that to contemplate its harmony is to taste of Him.'[38]

Yet this very sublimity had its shadow. If all of eternity were Christian, then it rendered those who persisted in the ways of heresy, obdurate in their folly, only the more damnable. The slaughter of the Albigensians had set a precedent that was not readily forgotten.

Dominicans, for all the care they brought to their work as inquisitors, the painstaking manner in which they applied the methods of Aristotle to the task of identifying heretics, were not immune to fantasies of mass extermination. In 1274, the same year that Aquinas became convinced that his life's labours had been in vain, a former head of his order, Humbert de Romans, urged crusaders at a council held in Lyon to take their inspiration from Charles Martel, 'who killed 370,000 of those who came against him with very little loss of his own men'.[39] Saracens, heretics, pagans: all, if they threatened Christendom, were to be viewed as legitimate targets for eradication.

Yet against the most determined of all Christ's foes, there could be no campaign of slaughter. The Jews, Humbert de Romans reminded the council of Lyon, were not to be eliminated. At the end of days, so it had been foretold, they would be brought to baptism; but their fate it was, until then, to serve the Christian people as living witnesses to the workings of divine justice. 'Although,' as Innocent III had put it, 'the Jewish perfidy is in every way worthy of condemnation, nevertheless, because through them the truth of our faith is proved, they are not to be severely oppressed by the faithful.'[40] A pallid and mocking display of mercy. Founded as it was on the conviction that the Jews, unlike the Saracens, presented no threat to Christendom, it took for granted their superannuated quality: that they and all their laws, their customs and their learning had been superseded, and now lay withered in the dust. Yet the backwardness of the Jews was not quite as manifest as the Church authorities liked to pretend. Unlike the Waldensians, they had a degree of erudition that put most Christians to shame. Aquinas was not alone in admiring the achievements of their scholarship. Even the pope's own household had long been managed by Jewish administrators. As a pupil of Abelard had freely acknowledged, 'A Jew, however poor, if he had ten sons would put them all to letters, not for gain, as the Christians do, but for the understanding of God's law—and not only his sons, but his daughters.'[41]

Perhaps it was hardly surprising, then, that the course of *reformatio*, impatient as it was of rivals, should have brought much suffering to Jews. The ideals that it proclaimed—of a Christendom cleansed of corruption, of a Church robed in light—had provoked among many Christians, in towns and villages across Europe, an escalating hostility to their Jewish neighbours. Long before Conrad of Marburg's letter to Gregory IX, warning the pope that heretics were consorting with demons, Jews had been fingered as willing agents of the Devil. They were sorcerers; they were blasphemers; they were enemies of the Church, who, whenever they had the chance, would pollute the sacred vessels used in the eucharist with their spit, their sperm, their shit. Darkest of all, they were murderers. In 1144, the discovery of a young boy's corpse in a wood outside the English city of Norwich had prompted a priest eager for a local martyr to concoct a host of sensational accusations: that the boy had been kidnapped by the local Jews; that he had been tortured as Christ had been tortured; that he had been offered up as a sacrifice. The story, although widely discounted, had not entirely been discredited; and so, like a plague, it had began to spread. In time, as similar tales were reported, a further hellish refinement had been added: that the Jews, in a grotesque parody of the eucharist, were in the habit of mixing children's blood into their ritual bread. That this claim was condemned as a libel first by an imperial commission, and then, in 1253, by the papacy itself, did nothing to stop its spread. Two years later—again in England—another mortal blow to the good name of the Jews was struck. The discovery in Lincoln of the body of a small boy named Hugh at the bottom of a well saw ninety Jews arrested for the murder on the orders of the king himself. Eighteen were hanged. The dead boy, entombed in Lincoln cathedral, was hailed by locals as a martyr. That the papacy pointedly refused to confirm this canonisation did little to check the growth of the cult of Little Saint Hugh.

'We are confined and oppressed,' Abelard had imagined a Jew as lamenting, 'as if the whole world had conspired against us alone. It is a wonder we are allowed to live.' A century on, there were few Christians ready to follow Abelard's example and think themselves into Jewish shoes. As never before, the ambition of the Church to provide a salvation to peoples of every race and background had become a weapon to be turned against all who spurned its offer. The Jews, whose claim to the great inheritance of scripture was no less passionate than its own, and whose devotion to learning had long served Christians as a standing reproach, presented an adversary infinitely more formidable than the good men. Yet the Church, confronted by such a threat, had no need of crusaders to do its work. Clerics in the age of Aquinas could feel more confident of putting Jews in their place than ever before. With theology enthroned as the queen of sciences in universities across Europe, and with friars specifically licensed by the pope to defend and promote the faith, they were able to view Jewish pretensions with mounting contempt. It was a measure of this, perhaps, that increasingly, when referring to the scriptures that were the common inheritance of both themselves and the Jews, they no longer used the word *biblia* as a plural, but rather as a singular: *the* Bible. In other ways too, any hint of a common fellowship that Jews might once have shared with Christians was being systematically razed. No longer, it had been ordained at the Fourth Lateran Council, were they to dress as those they lived among dressed, but were instead 'at all times to be marked off in the eyes of the public from other peoples through the character of their clothing'.[42] Christian artists, for the first time, began to represent Jewish men as physically distinctive: thick-lipped, hook-nosed, stooped. In 1267, sexual relations between Jews and Christians was banned by formal decree of a church council; in 1275, a Franciscan in Germany drew up a law code that made it a capital offence. In 1290, the king of England, pushing the logic of this baneful trend to its ultimate conclusion, ordered all the Jews in his kingdom to leave for good. In 1306, the king of France followed suit.*

A Church that proclaimed itself universal had, it seemed, no response to those who rejected it, save persecution.

---

* Recalled on and off throughout the fourteenth century, the Jews were finally expelled for good from France in 1394.

11

FLESH

1300: Milan

When the Dominicans and their agents arrived at the abbey of Chiaravalle, they headed straight for the final resting place of Guglielma. Almost twenty years had passed since her death, and in that time there had been a steady stream of pilgrims to her tomb. Although she was not a native of Milan—and indeed had only come to Italy in 1260, when she was fifty—the aura of mystery that clung to her had done much to enhance her fame. She was said to have had royal blood; to have been the daughter of the king of Bohemia; to have spent time in England married to a prince. True or not, it was certain that in Milan Guglielma had lived a life of spotless poverty. And so it was, after her death, that people had come to leave candles and offerings before her tomb. Twice a year, the monks of Chiaravalle would publicly celebrate her memory. Crowds would flock to pay their respects. Like Elizabeth of Hungary, a woman of similar miracle-working power, and quite possibly her cousin, Guglielma was hailed as a saint.

The inquisitors knew better. They had not come to light candles. Instead, taking crowbars to Guglielma's tomb, they levered it open, and scooped out the mouldering corpse. A great fire was lit. The bones were burned to ashes, and scattered on the winds. Guglielma's tomb was smashed to pieces. Her images were crushed underfoot.

Brutal though these measures might have seemed, they were urgently required. Shocking revelations had come to light. All that summer, inquisitors had been catching on their nostrils the stench of a truly monstrous heresy. Following where it led, they had tracked it to the very summit of Milanese society. The ringleader, a nun named Maifreda da Pirovano, was the cousin of Mateo Visconti, the effective lord of the city. But once the truth was out no one—not even her cousin—had been able to save her. She was burned at the stake. Fitting punishment for a woman whose ambition could not possibly have been more subversive, more arrogant, more grotesque. In any heretic it would have been shocking—but in a woman especially so. Maifreda had taught her followers that she was destined to rule all Christendom: that she would be elected pope.

Incubating in Milan had been a cult of rare and awful daring. Guglielma, so it was reported a year after Maifreda's execution, had come to the city 'saying that she was the Holy Spirit made flesh for the redemption of women; and she baptised women in the name of the Father, and of the Son, and of herself'.[1] This conviction, that Christendom stood on the brink of a radical new beginning, was not original to her. Back in the time of Innocent III, a monk named Joachim, brooding over the Bible in the abbey of Fiore, deep in the wilds of southern Italy, had fathomed in its pages a prophetic message. The ages of the world, so he had taught, were threefold. First, spanning the aeons that separated the Creation from the coming of Christ, had been the Age of the Father; then had come the Age of the Son. Now that too was drawing to a close. In its place was dawning the Age of the Spirit. Such a prospect was one that many found thrillingly seductive. Large numbers of Franciscans assumed that it referred to them. No one, though, had given it quite so distinctive a gloss as Guglielma: 1260, the year of her arrival in Milan, was the very date foretold by Joachim as the beginning of the new age. Whether sanctioned by Guglielma herself or not, her followers had come to believe that she was 'the Holy Spirit and the true God'.[2] Her death had done nothing to dampen this conviction. Her disciples, under the charismatic leadership of Maifreda, claimed to have seen her risen again. The Church, in the new age of the Spirit, would be scoured of its corruption. Boniface VIII, the reigning pope, and a man notorious for his cruelty, greed and corruption, would be deposed and replaced by Maifreda. The cardinals—senior officials in the Church who, from 1179 onwards, had been granted exclusive voting rights in papal elections—would all be women as well. The Age of the Spirit was to be a feminine one.

Here was a heresy that was bound to seem, to any inquisitor, almost a personal affront. Talk of female priests, let alone a female pope, was laughable. God, expelling Eve from Eden, had sentenced her not just to suffer the pains of childbirth, but to be ruled over by her husband. It was a judgement that numerous Church Fathers had upheld: 'Do you not know that you are each an Eve?'³ Augustine especially, by embedding in his works the doctrine of original sin, had bequeathed a sombre sense of the muscle and blood of every womb as infected by the ineradicable taint of disobedience to God. Formidably though women had served as patrons of the Church—as queens, as regents, as abbesses—they had rarely thought to aspire to the priesthood. The great convulsion of *reformatio*, by enshrining chastity as the supreme proof of a man's closeness to God, had only confirmed priests in their dread of women as temptresses. The monk freed from his lusts after dreaming that a man 'ran at him with a terrible swiftness, and cruelly mutilated him with a knife',⁴ was typical in his yearning to be spared any sense of dependence on women. Friars, who did not immure themselves in monasteries, but instead walked streets crowded with the opposite sex, observing their hair, their breasts, their hips, had to be even more sternly on their guard. Woman, so one Dominican thundered, was 'the confusion of man, an insatiable beast, a continuous anxiety, an incessant warfare, a daily ruin, a house of tempest, a hindrance to devotion'.⁵ What were priests to do, confronted by such a menace, but maintain the opposite sex in its divinely sanctioned state of subordination?

This, of course, was to flatter prejudices that had always come naturally to men. Theologians who justified the masculinity of the priesthood by pointing out that neither Jesus nor any of his apostles had been women could cite an authority even older than the gospels. 'The female,' Aristotle had written, 'is, as it were, an inadequate male.'[6] Just as the great philosopher had provided inquisitors with a model of how to conduct an interrogation, so had his writings on biology swung the immense weight of his prestige behind a perspective on female inferiority that many clerics were all too ready to embrace. Steeled as they were to see in their own virginity the proof of an almost angelic fortitude, they found in the model of physiology taught by the ancients confirmation of all their darkest, their most festering fears. Women oozed; they bled; like bogs at their most treacherous, they were wet, and soft, and swallowed up men entire. Increasingly, wherever Aristotle was taught, Eve's daughters were being measured by standards that were less biblical than Greek.

Women, physically the weaker sex and formed by nature for pregnancies, could never be reckoned the equals of men. If Guglielma's was the most radical protest against this assumption, then it was not the only one. Scholars who cited Aristotle as justification for viewing women as biologically inferior had to reckon with profound ambivalences within the Bible itself. The sanction given husbands to rule over their wives was not the only perspective provided by scripture on relations between the two sexes. Thomas Aquinas—great admirer of Aristotle though he was—had struggled to square the assumption that a woman was merely a defective version of a man with the insistence in Genesis that both had been divinely crafted for precise and specific purposes. Eve's body, 'ordained as it was by nature for the purposes of generation', was no less the creation of God, 'who is the universal author of nature', than Adam's had been.[7] The implications of this for the understanding of the divine were too glaring to be ignored. 'But you, Jesus, good lord, are you not also a mother?' Anselm had asked. 'Are you not that mother who, like a hen, collects her chickens under wings? Truly, master, you are a mother.'[8] Abbots, even as they lived their lives in chastity, might not hesitate to compare themselves to a nursing woman, breasts filled with 'the milk of doctrine'.[9] It was no shame for a priest to talk of himself in such a manner—for the feminine as well as the masculine was a reflection of the divine. God the Father was also a mother.

But what did such teaching mean for women themselves? Paul, writing to the Galatians, had insisted that there was no longer either male or female, for all were one in Christ Jesus. Yet even he, on occasion, had felt unsettled by the sheer subversiveness of this message. The equality of men and women before God was a concept that he had often flinched from putting into practice. Hence his prevarications over the vexed issue of whether women should be permitted to lead prayers and to prophesy, one moment insisting that they should not, and another that they might—but only if veiled. Letters written in his name after his death, and incorporated into the canon of scripture, had provided an altogether more emphatic resolution. 'I do not permit a woman to teach or to have authority over a man; she must be silent.'[10] Here, in this single verse, was all the justification that the inquisitors had needed to suppress Guglielma's cult: to haul her corpse from out of its tomb, and to consign Maifreda to the flames.

Yet the Dominicans, great scholars that they were, and thoroughly steeped in Paul's teachings, were not blind to the value that the apostle had placed on the role of women in his churches. Dominic himself, only two years after the establishment of his order, had founded a convent in Madrid. His successor as Master General, a Saxon nobleman by the name of Jordan, had been a great sponsor of Dominican nuns. Writing regularly to one of these, the prioress of a convent in Bologna, he had done so not merely as her spiritual director, but as an admirer of her often imperious charisma. The pattern set by this relationship was one that many Dominicans had followed. Priests though they were, they readily stood in awe of the closeness their female correspondents seemed to have to God. They knew that their Lord, risen from the dead, had first revealed himself, not to his disciples, but to a woman. In John's gospel, it was told how Mary Magdalene, a follower of Jesus cured by him of possession by demons, had initially mistaken the risen Christ for the gardener—but then had recognised him. 'I have seen the Lord!'[11] The Dominicans, while they never doubted their own authority as clerics, knew that authority had its limits. Power—even that of a man over a woman—was of necessity an ambivalent and treacherous thing. It was those without it who were most surely the favourites of God.

'My soul glorifies the Lord, and my spirit rejoices in God my Saviour, for he has been mindful of the humble state of his servant.'[12] So the Virgin Mary, after learning that she was to bear the Son of God, had sung. No human being had been so honoured; no human being raised so high. Even as the bones of Guglielma were being reduced to ashes, even as the legal and political status of women across Christendom was steadily deteriorating, even as the female body was being excoriated in ever more abusive terms by preachers and moralists as a vessel of corruption, so the radiance of the Queen of Heaven, full of grace, blessed among women, blazed with the brightness of the brightest star. 'O womb, O flesh, in whom and from whom the creator was created, and God was made incarnate.'[13] The virgin mother who had redeemed the fault of Eve, the mortal who had conceived within her uterus the timeless infinitude of the divine, Mary could embody for even the humblest and most unlettered peasant all the numerous paradoxes that lay at the heart of the Christian faith. It needed no years of study in a university, no familiarity with the works of Aristotle, to comprehend the devotion that a mother might feel to her son. Perhaps this was why, the more that scholars laboured to elucidate in vast and intimidating works of theology the subtleties of God's purpose, fusing revelation and logic in profound and learned ways, so the more, in works of art, were Mary and her son portrayed as joined in simple joy. So too, in scenes of Christ's death, was the Virgin increasingly represented as the equal in suffering and dignity of her son. No longer was the gaze of the Queen of Heaven as serene as once it had been. Emotions common to all were being rendered that much more Christian. Enshrined at the very heart of the great mysteries elucidated by Christianity, of birth and death, of happiness and suffering, of communion and loss, was the love of a woman for her child.

Here, to Christians fearful of where the world might be heading, was a precious reassurance: one that did not depend upon any policing of heresy, any demands for *reformatio*. Maifreda, teaching her followers that she was destined to be pope, had stood in the line of a thoroughly familiar tradition: one that aimed at setting all of Christendom on the correct foundations, and scouring it clean of corruption. Confident that the papacy remained the surest vehicle of reform, she had dreamed of doing as Gregory VII had done, and seizing the commanding heights of the Roman Church. Her ambition had always been a vain one, of course; but even popes themselves, amid all the gathering challenges and upheavals of the age, were discovering the limits of their authority. Two years after Maifreda's execution, Boniface VIII was prompted by the open defiance of Philip IV, the king of France, to issue the most ringing statement of papal supremacy ever made: 'We declare, state and define that it is absolutely necessary for salvation that every human creature be subject to the Roman Pontiff.' What, though, from the lips of Innocent III might have sounded intimidating, from the lips of Boniface was merely shrill. In September 1303, Philip's agents seized the pope at his summer retreat outside Rome. Even though he was freed after three days of captivity, the shock of it all proved too much for him, and within a month he was dead. The new pope, a Frenchman, was altogether more securely under Philip's thumb. In 1309, he settled in Avignon. Decades passed, popes came and went, but none returned to Rome. An immense palace, complete with banqueting halls, gardens and a private steam-room for the pope, came to sprawl above the Rhône. Moralists appalled by its display of luxury and wealth began to speak of a Babylonian captivity. Hopes for the dawning of an age of the Holy Spirit seemed bitterly disappointed.

Still worse shocks were to come—and Christians, amid the struggle to cope with them, would be obliged to negotiate in new and momentous ways the relationship between spirit and flesh.

Brides of Christ

When workmen digging the foundations of a new house uncovered the statue, experts from across Siena flocked to admire the find. It did not take them long to identify the nude woman as Venus, the goddess of love. Buried and forgotten for centuries, she constituted a rare trophy for the city: an authentic masterpiece of ancient sculpture. Few people were better qualified to appreciate it than the Sienese. Renowned across Italy and far beyond for the brilliance of their artists, they knew beauty when they saw it. Everyone agreed that it would be a scandal for such a prize to be hidden away. Instead, the statue was taken to the Campo, the city's great central piazza, and placed on top of a fountain. 'And she was paid great honour.'[14]

At once, everything began to go wrong. A financial crash was followed by a rout of the Sienese army. Then, some five years after the discovery of the Venus, horror almost beyond comprehension brought devastation to the city. A plague, arriving from the east, and spreading with such lethal virulence across the whole of Christendom that it came to be known simply as the Great Dying, reached Siena in May 1348. For months it raged. 'The infected perished almost immediately, swelling beneath the armpits and in the groin, and dropping down while talking.'[15] Pits were filled to overflowing with the dead. Work on the city's cathedral was abandoned forever. By the time the plague finally eased, over half of Siena's population had been wiped out. But still disasters kept coming. An army of mercenaries extorted a massive bribe from the government. There was a coup. A humiliating military defeat was inflicted on the city by its nearest and bitterest rival, Florence. Leaders in the new governing council, looking from the Palazzo Pubblico to the statue in the Campo outside, knew what to blame. 'From the moment we found the statue, evils have been ceaseless.'[16] This paranoia was hardly surprising. Admiration for ancient sculpture could not outweigh the devastating evidence for divine anger. Almost eight hundred years before, during the pontificate of Gregory the Great, it was cries of repentance that had halted the plague. It was told how Saint Michael, standing above the Tiber, had held aloft a blazing sword—and then, accepting the Romans' prayers, had sheathed it, and at once the plague had stopped. Now, overwhelmed by calamity, the Sienese scrabbled to show repentance. On 7 November 1357, workmen pulled down the statue of Venus. Hauling it away from the piazza, they smashed it into pieces. Chunks of it were buried just beyond the border with Florence.

The insult offered by the honouring of Venus had been very great. Siena was the city of the Virgin. Her tutelary presence was everywhere. In the Palazzo Pubblico, an immense fresco of her dominated the room where the governing council did its business; in the Campo, the fan-shaped design of the piazza evoked the folds of her protective cloak. Those who had demanded the destruction of the Venus were right to see in its delectable and unapologetic nudity a challenge to everything that Mary represented. A thousand years had passed since the original toppling of the statue. In that time, the understanding of the erotic had been transfigured to a degree that would have been unimaginable to those who, in cities across the Roman world, had offered sacrifice to the goddess of love. Convulsive though the experience of *reformatio* had certainly been, it was merely the aftershock of a far more seismic event: the coming of Christianity itself. Nowhere, perhaps, was this more evident than in the dimensions of desire. It was not just Venus who had been banished. So too had gods fêted for their rapes. A sexual order rooted in the assumption that any man in a position of power had the right to exploit his inferiors, to use the orifices of a slave or a prostitute to relieve his needs much as he might use a urinal, had been ended. Paul's insistence that the body of every human being was a holy vessel had triumphed. Instincts taken for granted by the Romans had been recast as sin. Generations of monks and bishops, of emperors and kings, looking to tame the violent currents of human desire, had laboured to erect great dams and dykes, to redirect their floodtide, to channel their flow. Never before had an attempt to recalibrate sexual morality been attempted on such a scale. Never before had one enjoyed such total success.

'We say with the dear apostle Paul: "Through Christ crucified, who is within me and strengthens me, I can do anything." When we do this, the Devil is left defeated.'[17] Three decades after the coming of the plague to Siena, a young woman from the city by the name of Catherine wrote to a monk much troubled by how chill and inscrutable the workings of the universe appeared. Nothing, she reassured him—not disease, not despair—could snuff out a gift that was given in love to every mortal by God: free will. The phrase was one with an ancient pedigree. First coined by Justin, the great apologist of the generation before Irenaeus, it had offered to Christians a transformative reassurance: that they were not the slaves of the stars, nor of fate, nor of demons, but were instead their own masters. No surer way existed to demonstrate this, to stand free and autonomous in defiance of all the manifold evils of the fallen world, than to exercise continence. Catherine herself, by 1377, had become Christendom's most celebrated exemplar of this. From childhood, she had made a sacrifice of her appetites. She fasted for days at a time; her diet, on those rare occasions when she did eat, would consist exclusively of raw herbs and the eucharist; she wore a chain tightly bound around her waist. Naturally, it was with sexual yearnings that the Devil most tempted her. 'He brought vile pictures of men and women behaving loosely before her mind, and foul figures before her eyes, and obscene words to her ears, shameless crowds dancing around her, howling and sniggering and inviting her to join them.'[18] But join them she never did.

Yet virginity, to Catherine, was not an end in itself. Rather, it was an active and heroic state. Proof against the touches of a man, her body was a vessel of the Holy Spirit, radiant with power. Catherine, the illiterate daughter of a dyer, was acknowledged by all as a *donna*, a 'free woman': 'the owner and mistress of herself'. On 'the tempestuous sea that is this life of shadows',[19] her virgin body was her vessel. Navigating the tides and currents of a cruelly troubled age, she came to offer to great multitudes of Christians a precious reassurance: that holiness might indeed be manifest on earth. Even the greatest were not immune to her charisma. In June 1376, she arrived in Avignon, where she set to urging the pope, Gregory XI, that he should signal his commitment to God's purpose by returning to Rome. Three months later, he was on his way. The venture, to Catherine's bitter disappointment, proved a disaster. Barely a year after arriving in Rome, Gregory XI was dead. Two rival popes, one an Italian and one an aristocrat from Geneva, were elected in his place. At stake was the issue of where the papacy should be based: the Lateran or Avignon. Catherine, loyally rallying to the Italian pope, Urban VI, hurried to his side. Her presence in Rome proved a key factor in shoring up his base. At one point, Urban even summoned his cardinals to one of the city's churches, there to hear Catherine lecture them on the rights and wrongs of the schism. 'This weak woman,' he declared admiringly, 'puts us all to shame.'[20]

Her death in the spring of 1380 did nothing to shake this conviction. Catherine's emaciated body, witness as it was to her spectacular feats of fasting, served as a salutary reminder to the pope and his court of what the Church itself should properly be. Not merely a virgin, she had been a bride. As a young girl pledging herself to Christ, she had defied her parents' plans to marry her by hacking off all her hair. She was, so she had told them, already betrothed. Their fury and consternation could not make her change her mind. Sure enough, in 1367, when she was twenty years old, and Siena was celebrating the end of carnival, her reward had arrived. In the small room in her parents' house where she would fast, and meditate, and pray, Christ had come to her. The Virgin and various saints, Paul and Dominic included, had served as witnesses. King David had played his harp. The wedding ring was Christ's own foreskin, removed when he had been circumcised as a child, and still wet with his holy blood.* Invisible though it was to others, Catherine had worn it from that moment

---

* According to her confessor, the ring was a gold band; but Catherine herself in her letters, states otherwise.

on. Intimacy of this order with the divine was beyond the reach of any man. True, there were some who mocked Catherine's claims. In Avignon, when she went into one of her states of ecstasy, a cardinal's mistress had pricked her foot with a pin to see if she was faking. Gregory XI and Urban VI, though, had both known better than to doubt. They understood the mystery revealed to them by Catherine. The Church, too, was a bride of Christ. 'Wives, submit to your husbands as to the Lord.' So a letter attributed to Paul, and included in the canon of scripture, had instructed. 'For the husband is the head of the wife as Christ is the head of the church, his body, of which he is the Saviour.'[21] In Catherine's devotion to her Lord—a devotion that she had not hesitated to define in burning and exultant tones as desire—was both a reproach and an inspiration to all the Church.

Here, in this sacral understanding of marriage, was another marker of the revolution that Christianity had brought to the erotic. The insistence of scripture that a man and a woman, whenever they took to the marital bed, were joined as Christ and his Church were joined, becoming one flesh, gave to both a rare dignity. If the wife was instructed to submit to her husband, then so equally was the husband instructed to be faithful to his wife. Here, by the standards of the age into which Christianity had been born, was an obligation that demanded an almost heroic degree of self-denial. That Roman law—unlike the Talmud, and unlike the customs of most other ancient peoples—defined marriage as a monogamous institution had not for a moment meant that it required men to display life-long fidelity. Husbands had enjoyed a legal right to divorce—and, of course, to forcing themselves on their inferiors—pretty much as they pleased. This was why, in its long and arduous struggle to trammel the sexual appetites of Christians, the Church had made marriage the particular focus of its attentions. The double standards that for so had long been a feature of marital ethics had come to be sternly patrolled. Joined together under the watchful eye of Christ, men were commanded to be as faithful to their wives as their wives were to them. Divorce—except in the very rarest of circumstances—was prohibited. To cast off a wife was to 'render her an adulteress'.[22] So Jesus himself had declared. The bonds of a Christian marriage, mutual and indissoluble as they were, served to join man and woman together as they had never been joined before.

Christ, placing his ring on Catherine's finger, had defined salvation as an 'everlasting wedding-feast in heaven'.[23] That marriage was a sacrament, a visible symbol of God's grace, was a doctrine that it had taken the Church many centuries to bring Christians to accept. The assumption that marriage existed to cement alliances between two families—an assumption as universal as it was primordial—had not easily been undermined. Only once the great apparatus of canon law was in place had the Church at last been in a position to bring the institution firmly under its control. Catherine, refusing her parents' demands that she marry their choice of husband, insisting that she was pledged to another man, had been entirely within her rights as a Christian. No couple could be forced into a betrothal, nor into wedlock, nor into a physical coupling. Priests were authorised to join couples without the knowledge of their parents—or even their permission. It was consent, not coercion, that constituted the only proper foundation of a marriage. The Church, by pledging itself to this conviction, and putting it into law, was treading on the toes of patriarchs everywhere. Here was a development pregnant with implications for the future. Opening up before the Christian people was the path to a radical new conception of marriage: one founded on mutual attraction, on love. Inexorably, the rights of the individual were coming to trump those of family. God's authority was being identified, not with the venerable authority of a father to impose his will on his children, but with an altogether more subversive principle: freedom of choice.

So strange was the Christian conception of marriage that it had always raised eyebrows in the lands beyond Christendom. From the very earliest days of Islamic scholarship, Muslims—whose license to enjoy a variety of wives and slaves was sanctioned directly by the Qur'an itself—had viewed the Church's insistence on monogamy with amused bewilderment. Yet Christians, far from feeling nonplussed by such contempt, had only been confirmed in their determination to bring proper order to pagan appetites. Saint Boniface, acknowledging the appeal of polygamy to fallen man, had shuddered in revulsion at the bestiality it represented: 'a base defilement of everything, as though it were whinnying horses or braying asses mixing it up with their adulterous lusts'.[24] His disgust, at the entanglement of limbs that should never have been permitted to intertwine, at the joining of flesh that should forever have been kept apart, had run very deep. Most repellent of all, a constant menace among those ignorant of Christ's love and of his laws, was the proclivity for incest. Again and again, writing to Rome, Boniface had demanded reassurance on a particularly pressing point: the degree of relationship within which a couple might legitimately be permitted to marry. The pope, in his replies, had made a great show of liberality. 'Since moderation is better than strictness of discipline, especially toward so uncivilised a people, they may contract marriage after the fourth degree.'[25] Almost half a millennium on, and the canons of the great council summoned by Innocent III to the Lateran had ordained the same. This as well had been advertised as a liberalising measure. After all, as a canon of the council served notice, the degrees within which marriages were forbidden had for a long while been seven.

Of all the measures taken by the Church to shape and mould the Christian people, few were to prove more enduring in their consequences. Back in ancient times, when the statue of Venus retrieved from a building site in Siena had been worshipped as a portrait of a living goddess, the word *familia* had signified a vast and sprawling household. Clans, dependents, slaves: all were family. But that had changed. The Church, in its determination to place married couples, and not ambitious patriarchs, at the heart of a properly Christian society had tamed the instinct of grasping dynasts to pair off cousins with cousins. Only relationships sanctioned by canons were classed as legitimate. No families were permitted to be joined in marriage except for those licensed by the Church: 'in-laws'. The hold of clans, as a result, had begun to slip. Ties between kin had progressively weakened. Households had shrunk. The fabric of Christendom had come to possess a thoroughly distinctive weave.

Husbands, wives, children: it was these, in the heartlands of the Latin West, that were increasingly coming to count as family.

Casting the First Stone

On one occasion, when Christ appeared to Catherine of Siena, he did so accompanied by Mary Magdalene. Catherine, weeping with an excess of love, remembered how Mary, kneeling before the feet of her Lord, had once wet his feet with her own tears, and then wiped them with her hair, and kissed them, and anointed them with perfume. 'Sweetest daughter,' Christ told her, 'for your comfort I give you Mary Magdalene for your mother.' Gratefully, Catherine accepted the offer. 'And from that moment on,' so her confessor reported, 'she felt entirely at one with the Magdalene.'[26]

To be paired with the woman who had first beheld the risen Christ was, of course, a rare mark of divine favour. From childhood, Catherine had taken the Magdalene as a particular role model. Far from betraying complacency, though, this had borne witness to the opposite: Catherine's own gnawing sense of sin. As reported by Luke, the woman who wept before Jesus, and anointed his feet, had 'lived a sinful life'.[27] Although she was never named, the identification of her with the Magdalene was one that had enjoyed wide currency ever since Gregory the Great, back in 591, had first made it in a sermon. Over time—and despite the lack of any actual evidence for it in the gospels—the precise character of her 'sinful life' had become part of the fabric of common knowledge. Kneeling before Jesus, seeking his forgiveness, she had done so as a penitent whore. Catherine, by accepting the Magdalene as her mother, was embracing the full startling radicalism of a warning given by Christ: that prostitutes would enter the kingdom of God before priests.

Here, for a Church that demanded celibacy of its priesthood and preached the sanctity of marriage, was an unsettling reminder that its Saviour had been quite as ready to forgive sins of the flesh as to condemn them. The lesson was one that many moralists understandably struggled to take on board. Women who made their living by tempting men into transgression seemed the ultimate manifestation of everything that the Church Fathers had condemned in Eve. The more attractive a whore, so one of Abelard's students had argued, the less onerous should be the penance for buying her services. The quickening pulse of *reformatio* had only intensified this characterisation of a prostitute's embraces as a cess-pit into which men might not help but fall. Keeping pace with the escalating campaign against heresy, a series of initiatives had aimed at draining the swamp. In Paris, for instance, as the great cathedral of Notre Dame was being built, the offer from a collective of prostitutes to pay for one of its windows, and dedicate it to the Virgin, had been rejected by a committee of the university's leading theologians. Two decades later, in 1213, one of the same scholars, following his appointment as papal legate, had ordered that all woman convicted of prostitution be expelled from the city—just as though they were lepers. Then, in 1254, a notably pious king had sought to banish them from the whole of France. The predictable failure of this measure had only confirmed the Church authorities in their anxiety to have sex-work quarantined. Just like Jews, prostitutes were commanded to advertise their own infamy. It was forbidden them to wear a veil; on their dresses, falling from their shoulders, they were obliged to sport a knotted cord. So dreaded was their touch that, in cities as far afield as London and Avignon, they were banned altogether from handling goods on market stalls.

Yet always, lurking at the back of even the sternest preacher's mind, was the example of Christ himself. In John's gospel, it was recorded that a woman taken in adultery had been brought before him by the Pharisees. Looking to trap him, they had asked if, in accordance with the Law of Moses, she should be stoned. Jesus had responded by bending down and writing in the dust with his finger; but then, when the Pharisees persisted in questioning him, he had straightened up again. 'If any of you is without sin, let him be the first to throw a stone at her.' The crowd, shamed by these words, had hesitated—and then melted away. Finally, only the woman had been left. 'Has no one condemned you?' Jesus had asked. 'No one, Sir,' she had answered. 'Then neither do I condemn you. Go now and leave your life of sin.'

Contempt, then, was not the only response that women who had succumbed to sexual temptation might provoke among dutiful Christians. There was sympathy for them too, and compassion. Innocent III, that most formidable of heresy's foes, never forgot that his Saviour had kept company with the lowest of the low: tax-collectors and whores. Endowing a hospital in Rome, he specified that it offer a refuge to sex-workers from walking the streets. To marry one, he preached, was a work of the sublimest piety. Friars—although prevented by their vows from going quite as far as that—felt themselves charged with a particular mission to do as Christ had done, and welcome fallen women into the kingdom of God. The French nickname for Dominicans—*jacobins*—had soon become a nickname for prostitutes too. Prostitutes themselves, perfectly aware of the example offered them by the Magdalene, veered between tearful displays of repentance and the conviction that God loved them just as much as any other sinner. Catherine, certainly, whenever she met with a sex-worker, would never fail to assure her of Christ's mercy. 'Turn to the Virgin. She will lead you straight into the presence of her son.'[28]

Yet there were some sins that could not be forgiven. In the decades that followed Catherine's death, the Christian people continued to look with dread to the heavens, and shudder before the divine anger that was so plainly brewing. Plague; war; the papal schism: evils of such an order could only be God's judgement on Christendom.

Moralists versed in the Old Testament knew all too well what might follow. In Genesis, the annihilation was recorded of two cities: Sodom and Gomorrah. Because they had become rotten through with sin, God had condemned them to a terrible collective punishment. Burning sulphur had rained down from the heavens; smoke like that from a furnace had risen up from the plain on which the two cities stood; everything living, even the very weeds, had been destroyed. Only melted rock had been left to mark the spot. From that moment on, the memory of Sodom and Gomorrah had served God's people as a terrible warning of what might happen to them, were their own society to become similarly cancerous with evil. Old Testament prophets, arraigning their countrymen of sin, were forever prophesying their ruin. 'They are all like Sodom to me.'[29]

But what precisely had been the sin of Sodom? The key to understanding that lay not in Genesis, but in Paul's letters. Writing to the Christians of Rome, the apostle had identified as the surest and most terrifying measure of humanity's alienation from God's love the sexual depravity of gentile society. One aspect of it more than any other had disgusted him. 'Men committed indecent acts with other men.'[30] Here, in Paul's formulation, was a perspective on sexual relations that Roman men would barely have recognised. The key to their erotic sense of themselves was not the gender of the people they slept with, but whether, in the course of having sex, they took the active or the passive role. Deviancy, to the Romans, was preeminently a male allowing himself to be used as though he were a female. Paul, by condemning the master who casually spent himself inside a slaveboy no less than the man who offered himself up to oral or anal penetration, had imposed on the patterns of Roman sexuality a thoroughly alien paradigm: one derived, in large part, from his upbringing as a Jew. Paul had been steeped in Torah. Twice the Law of Moses prohibited the lying of men with other men 'as one lies with a woman'.[31] Paul, though, in his letter to the Romans, had given this prohibition a novel twist. Among the gentiles, he warned, it was not only men who committed indecent acts with others of their own sex. 'Even their women exchanged natural relations for unnatural ones.'[32] A momentous denunciation. By mapping women who slept with women onto men who slept with men, Paul had effectively created an entire new category of sexual behaviour. The consequence was yet another ramping-up of the revolution brought by Christianity to the dimension of the erotic. Just as the concept of paganism would never have come into existence without the furious condemnation of it by the Church, so the notion that men and women who slept with people of their own sex were sharing in the same sin, one that obscenely parodied the natural order of things, was a purely Christian one.

The originality of Paul's conception was manifest, in the early centuries of the Church, by the struggle to find a word for it. Nothing existed in either Greek or Latin, nor in the Hebrew of the Old Testament. Conveniently to hand, though, was the story of Sodom. Christian scholars, noting the city's fate, could not help but wonder what its inhabitants might have been up to, that God had felt called to obliterate them. 'That we should understand sulphur as signifying the stench of the flesh,' opined Gregory the Great, 'the history of the holy Scriptures itself testifies, when it narrates that God rained down fire and sulphur upon Sodom.'[33] Nevertheless, it was only amid the convulsions of that revolutionary period, the age of Gregory VII, that the word 'sodomy' itself gained widespread currency[34]—and even then its definition remained imprecise. Same-sex intercourse, although its primary meaning, was not its only one. Moralists regularly used the word to describe a broad range of sinister deviancies. Inevitably, perhaps, it was left to Thomas Aquinas to offer clarity. 'Copulation with a member of the same sex, male with male, or female with female, as stated by the Apostle—this is called the vice of sodomy.'

The effect of this clarification, among those charged with the moral stewardship of the Christian people, was to give a new and sharper definition to their anxieties about angering God. In Italy especially, where cities were both wealthier and more numerous than in the rest of Christendom, the shadow of the doom that had claimed Sodom and Gomorrah lay particularly dark. By 1400, amid recurrent bouts of plague, dread that the failure to cleanse a city of sodomy might risk the annihilation of its entire population was general across the peninsula. In Venice, a succession of spectacular sex scandals saw the establishment in 1418 of the *Collegium Sodomitarum*: a magistracy specifically charged with the eradication of 'a crime which threatens the city with ruin'.[35] Whether in dancing schools or in fencing classes, its agents sought to sniff out sodomites wherever they might consort. Six years later, in Florence, the greatest preacher of his day was invited to mark the approach of Easter by giving three consecutive sermons on sodomy—a commission which he accepted with alacrity. Bernardino, a Franciscan from Siena, was a master in the art of working a crowd, 'now sweet and gentle, now sad and grave, with a voice so flexible that he could do with it whatever he wished'[36]—and the evils of sodomy were a theme on which he waxed particularly hot.

Walking the streets of his native city, he would sometimes hear the spectral calling-out of unborn infants against the sodomites who were denying them existence. One night, waking with a start, he listened to them make the whole of Siena—the courtyards, the streets, the towers—echo to their cries: 'To the fire, to the fire, to the fire!'[37] Now, preaching in Florence, Bernardino had come to a city so notorious for its depravities that the German word for sodomite was, quite simply, *Florenzer*. The friar, making play with his listeners' emotions as only he could, roused them to repeated climaxes of shame, disgust and fear. When he warned his congregation that the fate of Sodom and Gomorrah threatened to be theirs, they swayed, and moaned, and sobbed. When he urged them to show what they thought of sodomites by spitting on the floor, the din of expectorations was like that of a thunderstorm. When, in the great square outside the church, he set fire to a massive pile of the fripperies and fashions to which sodomites were notoriously partial, the crowds stood reverently, feeling the heat of the flames against their cheeks, gazing in awe at the bonfire of the vanities.

Seventy years previously, in 1348, as Florence was reeling before the first devastating impact of the plague, and its streets were choked by piles of the dead, a man named Agostino di Ercole had been consigned, like Bernardino's vanities, to fire. A 'dedicated sodomite',[38] he had been wallowing in sin for years. Nevertheless, at a time when the most terrifying proof of God's anger imaginable was devastating Florence, he had refused to show repentance. Indeed, he had barely acknowledged his guilt. It was quite impossible, so Agostino had insisted, for him to extinguish the furnace of his desires. He had been unable to help himself. Naturally, this excuse had cut no ice with his judges. No one committed sin except by choice. The possibility that a man might sleep with other men, not out of any perverse inclination to evil, but simply because it was his nature, was too much of a paradox for any decent Christian to sanction. Even Bernardino, despite his obsession with rooting out sodomy, struggled to keep Aquinas' definition of it clearly before him. At various times, he might use the word to describe bestiality, or masturbation, or anal sex between a man and his wife. Aquinas and Agostino, the saint and the sinner, the celibate and the sodomite, were both of them ahead of their times. Almost fifteen hundred years after Paul, the notion that men or women might be defined sexually by their attraction to people of the same gender remained too novel, too incomprehensible for most to grasp.

In matters of the flesh—as in so much else—the Christian revolution still had a long way to run.

12

APOCALYPSE

1420: Tabor

There had never been anywhere quite like it. The castle, perched on a rock above the Lužnice river, had been abandoned decades before, and the blackened ruins of the settlement that had once surrounded it were choked by weeds. It was not an obvious place to seek shelter. The site had to be cleared, and a new town built from scratch. There was an urgent need of fortifications. The nights were bitterly cold. Yet still the refugees came. All March they had been making the trek, drawn from every class of society, from every corner of Bohemia. By the end of the month, camped out in tents within the half-built perimeter walls, there were contingents of men who had been blooded in battle while making their journey there, and women with their children, in flight from burning villages; tavern-keepers from Prague and peasants armed with flails; knights, and clerics, and labourers, and vagrants. 'Selling their possessions and goods, they gave to anyone as he had need.'[1] As it had been in the Acts of the Apostles, so it was now. All shared in the common danger—and all shared a common status. Every man was called brother, and every woman sister. There were no hierarchies, no wages, no taxes. Private property was illegal. All debts were forgiven. The poor, it seemed, had inherited the earth.

The town was called by those who had moved to it Tabor. The name was one that broadcast a defiant message to its gathering enemies. In the Bible, it was recorded that Jesus had climbed a mountain to pray. 'And as he was praying, the appearance of his face changed, and his clothes became as bright as a flash of lightning.'[2] The site of this miracle had long been identified by Christian scholars as a mountain in Galilee: Tabor. The radiance of the divine had suffused its summit, and heaven been joined with earth. Now it was happening again. The Bohemians who flocked to the lonely crag above the Lužnice were following in the footsteps of those crowds who once, beneath open skies, had gathered to hear the preaching of their Lord. 'Woe to you who are rich, for you have already received your comfort. Woe to you who are well fed now, for you will go hungry.'[3] These were words that the radicals among the followers of Pelagius had seized on, and which had been troubling the wealthy since the time of Paulinus; but no one—not Martin, not Francis, not Waldes— had ever thought to do as the Taborites were now doing, and attempt to build an entire new society upon them. As lords laboured alongside peasants, toiling day and night to provide Tabor with an impregnable screen of fortifications, they were not merely constructing a stronghold, but aiming to rebuild the entire world.

In this ambition, at any rate, they were following in well-worn footsteps. The immense edifice of the Catholic Church, raised in defiance of earthly monarchs, and fashioned with such boldness and effort to serve the needs of all the Christian people, stood as the ultimate monument to what a revolution might achieve. The lava of its radicalism, though, had long since set. By an irony that was not yet familiar, the papal order had become the status quo. Increasingly, three centuries and more after the heroic age of Gregory VII, there were many Christians who, when they contemplated the claims to a universal rule of the papacy, could no longer recognise in it an agent of *reformatio*. Instead, so they dreaded, it had become an impediment to the change that was so clearly and desperately needed. The shadow of divine disapproval was unmistakable. A third of Christendom, it was estimated, had perished of the plague. Wars were ravaging its most prosperous kingdoms. On its eastern flank, the Byzantine Empire—which, following the expulsion of the crusaders from its capital in 1261, had been struggling to recover from the terrible blow inflicted on it back in the pontificate of Innocent III—was imperilled by a yet more formidable enemy. A new Muslim power, the empire of the Ottoman Turks, had expanded across the Hellespont, directly threatening Constantinople. Its armies had even begun to probe the defences of Hungary. Yet nothing was ultimately more debilitating to the claims of the Roman Church to be the bride of Christ than the enduring abomination of the papal schism. Attempts to resolve it had only made the crisis worse. In 1409, a council of bishops and university masters, meeting in Pisa, had declared both rival popes deposed, and crowned a new candidate of its own—but this, far from delivering Christendom a single pope, had merely left it stuck with three. Small wonder, then, confronted by such a scandal, that a few bold souls, pushing at the very limits of what it was acceptable to think, had begun to contemplate a nightmarish possibility: that the papacy, far from holding the keys to the gates of heaven, might in truth be an agent of hell.

And that in particular it might be Antichrist. At the end of days, Saint John had foretold, a beast with ten horns and seven heads was destined to emerge from the sea; this same beast, according to venerable tradition, would be a false prophet, a blasphemy against the church, and destined to rule the world. Rival popes, recognising an obvious way to rally their supporters when they saw it, had not hesitated to hurl the name of Antichrist at one another; but there were some Christians, marking the propaganda war with contempt, who had scorned to back either side. Their dissidence, communicated via the very network of universities that provided the Church with its clerical elite, had reverberated across Christendom. It was in Oxford that the theologian John Wycliffe had openly dared to denounce both factions in the schism as demonic, and the papacy itself as lacking all divine foundation; but it was in Prague that these sparks of subversion had ignited the most explosive reaction. Already, by the time of Wycliffe's death in 1384, the city was a tinder box. The Bohemian nobility, subject as they were to emperors who stood in a line of inheritance from Otto the Great, chafed under German dominance. Czech-speaking scholars at the university, similarly disadvantaged, nurtured their own grievance. Meanwhile, out in the slums, the resentment was of the rich. The most popular preachers were those who condemned the wealth of monasteries adorned with gold and sumptuous tapestries, and demanded a return to the stern simplicity of the early days of the Church. The Christian people, they warned, had taken a desperately wrong turn. The reforms of Gregory VII, far from serving to redeem the Church, had set it instead upon a path to corruption. The papacy, seduced by the temptations of earthly glory, had forgotten that the Gospels spoke most loudly to the poor, to the humble, to the suffering. 'The cross of Jesus Christ and the name of the crucified Jesus are now brought into disrepute and made as it were alien and void among Christians.'[4] Only Antichrist could have wrought such a fateful, such a hellish abomination. And so it was, in the streets of Prague, that it had become a common thing to paint the pope as the beast foretold by Saint John, and to show him wearing the papal crown, but with the feet of a monstrous bird.

To imagine that an entire order might be overturned had rarely come naturally to people. In Babylon, the ideal of kingship honoured by its inhabitants had reached back millennia, to the very beginnings of civilisation; in Greece, philosophers had cast society as the expression of a divinely ordered pattern; in Rome, anything that smacked of *res novae*, 'new things', had invariably been regarded as a catastrophe at all costs to be avoided. Not the least revolutionary aspect of Christianity had been the sanction that it provided for the very notion of revolution. Yet the papacy, which in the age of Gregory VII had weaponised it as no other institution had ever thought to do, had now become the embodiment of the status quo. The *moderni*, those reformers who back in the twelfth century had proclaimed the world to be standing on the threshold of eternity, had turned out to be mistaken. *Modernitas*—the new age that, with its dawning, would herald the end of time—had failed to arrive. This did not mean, though, that it never would. The prognosis provided by the Book of Revelation was clear. To read in the cracking of the world the events foretold by Saint John was inevitably to feel a certain shiver of dread; but also, perhaps, to dream that upheaval and transformation might be for the best.

One man more than any other had come to serve as a lightning rod for the gathering storm. In 1414, when church leaders from across Christendom met in the imperial city of Constance, on the edge of the Swiss Alps, their agenda had been an especially demanding one. As well as the running sore of the papal schism, there had been a second challenge: the defiant heresy of Prague's most celebrated preacher. Jan Hus, a man of immense charisma, intellectual brilliance and personal integrity, had emerged from the scholarly confines of the city's university to become the toast of Bohemia. Denouncing both the church hierarchy in Prague and the German-speaking elites who had long been profiting from imperial favour, he had helped to bring an already febrile mood to boiling point. The more rapturously his teachings were greeted, the more radical they had become. Inspired by Wycliffe, Hus had openly derided the claim of the papacy to a primacy sanctioned by God. That he had refrained from going the whole hog and denouncing it as Antichrist had not prevented his excommunication; nor, in turn, had excommunication served to rein in his defiance. Quite the contrary. Enjoying as he did adulatory support both in the slums of Prague and in the castles of Czech noblemen, Hus had stood firm. Increasingly, it seemed that the very structures of authority in Bohemia were collapsing. If this was a cause of panic in papal circles, then it was no less so for the imperial high command. Particularly alarmed was Sigismund, a ginger-haired veteran of the Turkish front and prince of the royal blood, who in 1410 had been proclaimed emperor-elect. Desperate to secure a compromise that all the various factions in Bohemia could accept, he had invited Hus to travel to Constance and negotiate directly with the delegates. Hus had accepted. Leaving the castle in Bohemia where he had been sheltering from papal agents, he had done so under a safe conduct personally guaranteed by Sigismund. On 3 November, he had arrived in Constance. Three weeks later, he had been arrested. Put on trial, he had refused to recant. Sentenced to death as a heretic, he had been burnt at the stake. His ashes had been dumped in the Rhine.

'The time of greatest suffering, prophesied by Christ in his scriptures, the apostles in their letters, the prophets, and Saint John in the Apocalypse, is now at hand; it has begun; it stands at the gates!'[5] Five years on from the death of Hus, the Taborites had gathered in their rocky stronghold confident that they would soon be seeing him again—him and all the risen saints. Far from extinguishing the flames of Hussite subversion, the Council of Constance had served only to stoke them further. Not even its success in finally ending the schism and installing again a single pope upon the throne of Saint Peter had been enough to redeem its reputation in Bohemia. In the wake of Hus' execution, denunciations of the papacy as Antichrist had begun to be made openly across Prague. Of Sigismund as well—for it was presumed that it was by his treachery that Hus had been delivered up to the flames. Then, in 1419, an attempted crackdown by conservatives had precipitated open revolt. Hussites had stormed the city hall; flung their opponents out of its windows; seized control of churches across Prague. It was out in the mountains, though, that the true revolution was coming to a head. There, when the faithful assembled in flight from their homes, it was in the conviction that Prague was Babylon. The past and the future, manifest as they had always been in the books of the Bible, were now being mapped onto the contours of Bohemia. Nowhere was this more evident than behind the rising walls of Tabor. Radiant with light as the clothes of Christ had been, the emerging stronghold blazed as well with every kind of precious stone, as it had been foretold that the New Jerusalem would blaze. Or so it seemed to the Taborites. Labouring in the mud, mixing mortar, hauling stone, they knew what was approaching. Christ was destined to return within months. All sinners would perish. The reign of the saints would begin. 'Only God's elect were to remain on earth—those who had fled to the mountains.'[6]

The Taborites were hardly the first Christians to believe themselves living in the shadow of Apocalypse. The novelty lay rather in the scale of the crisis that had prompted their imaginings: one in which all the traditional underpinnings of society, all the established frameworks of authority, appeared fatally compromised. Confronted by a church that was the swollen body of Antichrist, and an emperor guilty of the most blatant treachery, the Taborites had pledged themselves to revolution. But it was not enough merely to return to the ideals of the early church: to live equally as brothers and sisters; to share everything in common. The filth of the world beyond Tabor, where those who had not fled to the mountains still wallowed in corruption, had to be swept away too. Its entire order was rotten. 'All kings, princes and prelates of the church will cease to be.' This manifesto, against the backdrop of Sigismund's determination to break the Hussites, and the papacy's declaration of a crusade against them, was one calculated to steel the Taborites for the looming struggle. Yet it was not only emperors and popes whom they aspired to eliminate. All those who had rejected the summons to Tabor, to redeem themselves from the fallen world, were sinners. 'Each of the faithful ought to wash his hands in the blood of Christ's foes.'[7]

Many Hussites, confronted by this unsparing refusal to turn the other cheek, were appalled. 'Heresy and tyrannical cruelty,' one of them termed it. Others muttered darkly about a rebirth of Donatism. The summer of 1420, though, was no time for the moderates to be standing on their principles. The peril was too great. In May, at the head of a great army of crusaders summoned from across Christendom, Sigismund advanced on Prague. Ruin of the kind visited on Béziers two centuries earlier now directly threatened the city.

Moderates and radicals alike accepted that they had no choice but to make common cause. The Taborites, leaving behind only a skeleton garrison, duly marched to the relief of Babylon. At their head rode a general of genius. Jan Žižka, one-eyed and sixty years old, was to prove the military saviour that the Albigensians had never found. That July, looking to break the besiegers' attempt to starve Prague into submission, he launched a surprise attack so devastating that Sigismund was left with no choice but to withdraw. Further victories quickly followed. Žižka proved irresistible. Not even the loss late in 1421 of his remaining eye to an arrow served to handicap him. Crusaders, imperial garrisons, rival Hussite factions: he routed them all. Innovative and brutal in equal measure, Žižka was the living embodiment of the Taborite revolution. Noblemen on their chargers he met with rings of armoured wagons, hauled from muddy farmyards and manned by peasants equipped with muskets; monks he would order burnt at the stake, or else personally club to death. Never once did the grim old man meet with defeat. By 1424, when he finally fell sick and died, all of Bohemia had been brought under Taborite rule.

On his deathbed, so his enemies reported, Žižka had ordered the Taborites to flay his corpse, feed his flesh to carrion beasts, and use his skin to make a drum. 'Then, with this drum in the lead, they should go to war. Their enemies would turn to flight as soon as they heard its voice.'[8] The anecdote was tribute both to Žižka's fearsome reputation and to the continuing success of his followers on the battlefield after his death. In truth, the Taborite drum had begun to sound a muffled beat even while Žižka was alive. In the summer of 1420, in the wake of the great victory over Sigismund, it had still been possible for the Taborites to believe that Christ's return was imminent. Readying Prague for their Lord's arrival, they had systematically targeted symbols of privilege. Monasteries were levelled; the bushy moustaches much favoured by the Bohemian elite forcibly shaved off wherever they were spotted; the skull of a recently deceased king dug up and crowned with straw. As the months and then the years passed, however, and still Christ failed to appear, so the radicalism of the Taborites had begun to fade. They had elected a bishop; negotiated to secure a king; charged the most extreme in their ranks with heresy and expelled them from Tabor. Žižka, displaying a brusque lack of concern for legal process that no inquisitor would ever have contemplated emulating, had rounded up fifty of them and burnt the lot.* Well before the abrupt and crushing defeat of the Taborites by a force of more moderate Hussites in 1434, the flame of their movement had been guttering. Christ had not returned. The world had not been purged of kings. Tabor had not, after all, been crowned the New Jerusalem. In 1436, when Hussite ambassadors—achieving a startling first for a supposedly heretical sect—succeeded in negotiating a concordat directly with the papacy, the Taborites had little choice but to accept it. There would be time enough, at the end of days, to defy the order of the world. But until it came, until Christ returned in glory, what option was there except to compromise?

A New Earth

Pulling back the veil from the prophecies in the Bible was a dangerous thing to attempt. The Franciscans, admirers of Joachim of Fiore though they might be, had learned to tread carefully. Any friar tempted to do as the Taborites had done and draw on scripture to speculate about the end days, was carefully monitored. In 1485, when a German Franciscan named Johann Hilten finished a detailed study of the prophetic passages in the Bible, his superiors were less than amused. The papacy, Hilten foretold, was in its last days. Its 'disturbance and destruction'[9] was sure. When placed under house-arrest in Eisenach, in the friary that had been donated to the order by Saint Elizabeth, Hilten doubled down. It was not only the papacy that was doomed, he warned. So too was monasticism. A man was

---

* Only one man was spared, to provide an account of his sect's beliefs.

coming, a great reformer, destined to bring about its ruin. So sure of this was Hilten that he even provided a date: 'the year 1516 after the birth of Christ'.*

It was not only the decayed condition of the Church that had been weighing on his mind. There was geopolitics too. In 1453, Constantinople had finally fallen to the Turks. The great bulwark of Christendom had become the capital of a Muslim empire. The Ottomans, prompted by their conquest of the Second Rome to recall prophecies spoken by Muhammad, foretelling the fall to Islam of Rome itself, had pressed on westwards. In 1480, they had captured Otranto, on the heel of Italy. The news of it had prompted panic in papal circles—and not even the expulsion of the Turks the following year had entirely settled nerves. Terrible reports had emerged from Otranto: of how the city's archbishop had been beheaded in his own cathedral, and some eight hundred others martyred for Christ. True or not, these stories gave a decided edge to another of Hilten's prophecies. Both Italy and Germany, he warned, were destined to be conquered by the Turks. Their streets, like Otranto's, would be washed in the blood of martyrs. Such were the horrors that would presage the coming of Antichrist. Once again, Hilten made sure to give precise dates for his prophecies. The end of the world, he specified, was due in the 1650s.

Hilten's forebodings drew on an ancient wellspring. Saint John, when he warned that Satan, at the end of days, would lead entire nations out of the four corners of the earth, and that in number they would be 'like the sand on the seashore',[10] had himself been channelling primordial fears. A dread of migrants came naturally to the peoples of settled lands. Darius, condemning barbarians as agents of the Lie, had articulated a perspective that Caesars too had come to share. Christians, though, were not merely the heirs of Roman paranoia. 'Preach the good news to all creation':[11] so the risen Jesus had instructed his disciples. Only when the gospel had been brought to

---

* Although some alternative accounts give 1514.

the ends of the earth would he finally return in glory. The dream of a world become one in Christ was as old as Paul. Hilten, prophesying the fall of Christendom to the Turks, had foretold as well their conversion. That Islam was destined to vanish upon the approach of the end days, and the Jews too be brought to Christ, had long been the devout conviction of every Christian who dared to map the contours of the future. Hilten too, for all the blood-curdling quality of his prognostications, never thought to doubt it.

Across Christendom, then, dread of what the future might hold continued to be joined with hope: of the dawning of a new age, when all of humanity would be gathered under the wings of the Spirit, that holy dove which, at Jesus' baptism, had descended upon him from heaven. The same sense of standing on the edge of time that in Bohemia had led the Taborites to espouse communism elsewhere prompted Christians to anticipate that all the world would soon be brought to Christ. In Spain, where war against Muslim potentates had been a way of life for more than seven hundred years, this optimism was particularly strong. Men spoke of *El Encubierto*, the Hidden One: the last Christian emperor of all. At the end of time, he would emerge from concealment to unify the various kingdoms of Spain, to destroy Islam for good, to conquer Jerusalem, to subdue 'brutal kings and bestial races'[12] everywhere, and to rule the world. Even as the people of Otranto were repairing the sacrilege done to their cathedral, and Johann Hilten was foretelling the conquest of Germany by the Turks, rumours that El Encubierto had come at last were sweeping Spain. Isabella, the queen of Castile, did not rule alone. By her side, her equal in everything, was her husband, the king of the neighbouring realm: Ferdinand of Aragon. Before the combined might of these two monarchs, the truncated rump of al-Andalus stood perilously exposed. Of the great Muslim empire that had once reached to the Pyrenees and beyond, only the mountainous kingdom of Granada, on the southernmost shore of Spain, survived. Its continuing independence, to monarchs as devout and ambitious as Ferdinand and Isabella, was a standing affront. In 1482, their forces duly embarked on its conquest, fortress by fortress, port by port. By 1490, only Granada itself still held out. Two years later, on 2 January 1492, its king finally surrendered. Ferdinand, handed the keys to the royal palace, could be well pleased. The conquest of Spain's final Muslim stronghold was a feat worthy of El Encubierto.

Last emperor or not, Ferdinand was certainly free now to look to broader horizons. Among the cheering crowds watching the royal entry into Granada was a Genoese seafarer by the name of Christopher Columbus. His own mood was downbeat. For years he had been trying to persuade Ferdinand and Isabella to fund an expedition across the uncharted waters of the western ocean. Confident that the world was smaller than geographers had calculated, he was notorious in courts across Christendom for his claim that there lay across the Atlantic a short and ready route to the riches of the Orient: to 'India', as Europeans termed it. Wealth, though, was not an end in itself. Shortly before the fall of Granada, Columbus, pressing his suit, had pledged the profits of his enterprise to a very particular cause: the conquest of Jerusalem. Ferdinand and Isabella, listening to this, had smiled, and said that this plan for a crusade pleased them, and that it was their wish too. Then nothing. Columbus' appeal for funding had been rejected by a panel of experts appointed by the two monarchs to investigate his proposal. Turning his back on Granada, its palace now topped by a cross, he rode despondently away. After only a day on the road, though, he was overtaken by a messenger from the royal court. There had been a change of heart, he was told. The two monarchs were ready to sponsor him.

Columbus sailed that August. In the event, despite making landfall barely two months after his departure from Spain, he did not reach India. The day after his first Christmas in the West Indies (as he would come to call the islands he had arrived among), he prayed to God that he would soon discover the gold and spices promised in his prospectus; but the wealthy entrepôts of the Orient were destined always to lie beyond his grasp.* Nevertheless, even as the realisation of this began to dawn on Columbus, he betrayed no disappointment. He understood his destiny. In 1500, writing to the Spanish court, he spoke in unabashed terms of the role that he had been called to play in the great drama of the end times. 'God made me the messenger of the new heaven and the new earth of which he spoke in the Apocalypse of Saint John after having spoken of it through the mouth of Isaiah. And he showed me the spot where to find it.'[13] Three years later, during the course of a voyage blighted by storms, hostile natives and a year spent marooned on Jamaica, Columbus' mission was confirmed for him directly by a voice from heaven. Speaking gently, it chided him for his despair, and hailed him as a new Moses. Just as the Promised Land had been granted to the Children of Israel, so had the New World been granted to Spain. Writing to Ferdinand and Isabella about this startling development, Columbus insisted reassuringly that it had all been prophesied by Joachim of Fiore. Not for nothing did his own name mean 'the dove', that emblem of the Holy Spirit. The news of Christ would be brought to the New World, and its treasure used to rebuild the Temple in Jerusalem. Then the end of days would come. Columbus could even identify the date. Just as Johann Hilten had done, he specified the 1650s.

This sense of time as a speeding arrow, its destination sure, was one that Columbus always took for granted. It gave to him—even as he might feel small before the ineluctable potency of God's plans, and the vagaries of his own career—his feelings of self-assurance, of purpose, of destiny. Yet there existed in the New World, in cities as yet unglimpsed beyond the western horizon, a very different understanding of time. In 1519, more than a decade after Columbus' death, a Spanish adventurer named Hernán Cortés disembarked with five hundred men on the shore of an immense landmass that was already coming to be called America. Informed that there lay inland the capital of a

---

* Columbus first used the phrase '*Indias Occidentales*'—'West Indies'—in late 1501 or early 1502. It was an implicit acknowledgement that they lay in a totally different hemisphere from India.

great empire, Cortés took the staggeringly bold decision to head for it. He and his men were stupefied by what they found: a fantastical vision of lakes and towering temples, radiating 'flashes of light like quetzal plumes',[14] immensely vaster than any city in Spain. Canals bustled with canoes; flowers hung over the waterways. Tenochtitlan, wealthy and beautiful, was a monument to the formidable prowess of the conquerors who had built it: the Mexica. It was also a monument to something much more: their understanding of time itself. The city, only recently built, existed in the shadow of other, earlier cities, once no less magnificent, but long since abandoned. The emperor of the Mexica, going on foot, would often make pilgrimage to one of these massive ruins. No more awesome warning could have been served him that the world was endlessly mutable, governed by cycles of greatness and collapse, than to visit the wreckage of such a city. The anxiety of the Mexica that their own power might crumble shaded readily into an even profounder dread: that the world itself might darken and turn to dust. So it was, across Tenochtitlan, that they had raised immense pyramids; on the summit of these, at times of particular peril, when the very future of the cosmos seemed to hang in the balance, priests would smash knives of flint into the chests of prisoners. Without sacrifice, so the Mexica believed, the gods would weaken, chaos descend, and the sun start to fade. Only *chalchiuatl*, the 'precious water' pumped out by a still-beating heart, could serve to feed it. Only blood, in the final reckoning, could prevent the universe from winding down.

To the Spaniards, the spectacle of dried gore on the steps of Tenochtitlan's pyramids, of skulls grinning out from racks, was literally hellish. Once Cortés, in a feat of unparalleled audacity and aggression, had succeeded in making himself the master of the great city, its temples were razed to the ground. So Charlemagne, smashing with his mailed horsemen through dripping forests, had trampled down the shrines of Woden and Thunor. The Mexica, who had neither horses nor steel, let alone cannon, found themselves as powerless as the Saxons had once been to withstand Christian arms. The true clash, though, had been not between Toledo sword and stone axe, but between rival visions of the end of the world. The Spanish were prepared for it as no Christian people had ever been before. A decade before the conquest of Granada, Ferdinand had proclaimed it his intention 'to dedicate Spain to the service of God'.[15] In 1478, he had secured permission from the pope to establish, as the one institution common to both Aragon and Castile, an inquisition directly under royal control. 1492, the year of Granada's fall and of Columbus' first voyage, had witnessed another fateful step in the preparation of Spain for its mission to bring the gospel to the world. The Jews, whose conversion was destined to presage Christ's return, had been given the choice of becoming Christian or going into exile. Many had opted to leave Spain; more, including the chief rabbi of Castile himself, had accepted baptism. It was hardly to be expected, then, three decades on, that agents of the Spanish monarchy would spare the altars of a people who knew nothing of the God of Israel. Travelling to Mexico in Cortés' wake, Franciscans were revolted by the demands of sacrifice imposed by the Mexica's gods. None doubted they were demons. There was Huitzilopochtli, the great patron of the Mexica, whose temple in Tenochtitlan, it was said, had been consecrated with the blood of eighty thousand victims; Xipe Totec, 'the Flayed One', whose devotees wore the skins of those offered to their patron, and stabbed their penises with cactus thorns; Tlaloc, the god of the rains, whose favours could be won only by the sacrifice of small children who had first been made to weep. Such cruelties cried out to the heavens. 'It was the clamour of so many souls, and so much blood shed as an affront to their Creator,' wrote one Franciscan, that had inspired God to send Cortés to the Indies—'like another Moses in Egypt.'[16]

Yet even Cortés himself had lamented the cost. The glories of Tenochtitlan had been obliterated; its canals filled with floating corpses. In the Spaniards' wake had come killers even more terrible: diseases borne from Europe, against which the Indians had no resistance. Millions upon millions would die. And then there were the Spanish themselves. The wealth of the Indians, fallen into Christian hands, was not spent on bringing the world into the fold of Christ. Instead, shipped back to Spain, it was used to fund wars against the king of France. The Indians, crushed beneath the hooves of Spanish greatness, were worked as slaves. Resistance was savagely punished. Friars who travelled to the New World, labouring to bring the natives to Christ, reported in consternation on the atrocities they had seen: men wrapped in straw and set on fire; women cut to pieces like sheep in an abattoir; newborn infants smashed against rocks, or tossed into boiling rivers.

What kind of Moses, then, had Columbus and Cortés proved?

Sheep Among Wolves

In 1516, any lingering hopes that Ferdinand might prove to be the last emperor were put to rest by his death. He had not led a great crusade to reconquer Jerusalem; Islam had not been destroyed. Nevertheless, the achievements of Ferdinand's reign had been formidable. His grandson, Charles, succeeded to the rule of the most powerful kingdom in Christendom, and to a sway more authentically globe-spanning than that of the Caesars. Spaniards felt no sense of inferiority when they compared their swelling empire to Rome's. Quite the contrary. From lands unknown to the ancients came news of feats that would have done credit to Alexander: the toppling against all the odds of mighty kingdoms; the winning of dazzling fortunes; men who had come from nowhere to live like kings.

Yet there lay over the brilliance of these achievements a pall of anxiety. No people in antiquity would ever have succeeded in winning an empire for themselves had they doubted their licence to slaughter and enslave the vanquished; but Christians could not so readily be innocent in their cruelty. When scholars in Europe sought to justify the Spanish conquest of the New World, they reached not for the Church Fathers, but for Aristotle. 'As the Philosopher says, it is clear that some men are slaves by nature and others free by nature.'[17] Even in the Indies, though, there were Spaniards who worried whether this was truly so. 'Tell me,' a Dominican demanded of his fellow settlers, eight years before Cortés took the road to Tenochtitlan, 'by what right or justice do you keep these Indians in such a cruel and horrible servitude? On what authority have you waged a detestable war against these people, who dwelt quietly and peacefully in their own land?'[18] Most of the friar's congregation, too angered to reflect on his questions, contented themselves with issuing voluble complaints to the local governor, and agitating for his removal; but there were some colonists who did find their consciences pricked. Increasingly, adventurers in the New World had to reckon with condemnation of their exploits as cruelty, oppression, greed. Some, on occasion, might even come to this realisation themselves. The most dramatic example occurred in 1514, when a colonist in the West Indies had his life upended by a sudden, heart-stopping insight: that his enslavement of Indians was a mortal sin. Like Paul on the road to Damascus, like Augustine in the garden, Bartolomé de las Casas found himself born again. Freeing his slaves, he devoted himself from that moment on to defending the Indians from tyranny. Only the cause of bringing them to God, he argued, could possibly justify Spain's rule of the New World; and only by means of persuasion might they legitimately be brought to God. 'For they are our brothers, and Christ gave his life for them.'[19]

Las Casas, whether on one side of the Atlantic, pleading his case at the royal court, or on the other, in straw-thatched colonial settlements, never doubted that his convictions derived from the mainstream of Christian teaching. Formulating his objections to Spanish imperialism, he drew on the work of Aquinas. 'Jesus Christ, the king of kings, was sent to win the world, not with armies, but with holy preachers, as sheep among wolves.'[20] Such was the judgement of Thomas Cajetan, an Italian friar whose commentary on Aquinas was the great labour of his life.* Appointed head of the Dominicans in 1508, and a cardinal in 1517, he spoke with a rare authority. News

---

* Born de Vio, he took 'Thomas' as his name in tribute to Thomas Aquinas. 'Cajetan' derives from Gaeta, the city midway between Rome and Naples where he was born.

of the sufferings inflicted on the Indians filled him with a particular anger. 'Do you doubt that your king is in hell?,'[21] he demanded of one Spanish visitor to Rome. Here, in his shock that a Christian ruler should think to justify conquest and savagery in the name of the crucified Christ, was the expression of a scholarly tradition that reached all the way back to Alcuin. Cajetan, in his efforts to provide the Indians with a legal recourse against their oppressors, never imagined that he was breaking new ground. The discovery of continents and peoples unimagined by Aquinas did not render the great Dominican any the less qualified to serve as a guide as to how they should be treated. The teachings of the Church were universal in their reach. That the kingdoms of the Indians were legitimate states; that Christianity should be imposed, not by force, but solely by means of persuasion; that neither kings, nor emperors, nor the Church itself had any right to ordain their conquest: here, in Cajetan's opinion, were the principles fit to govern a globalised age.

There was, in this innovative programme of international law, a conscious attempt to lay the foundations of something enduring. Cajetan did not think that the discovery of a New World presaged the return of Christ. The days when popes imagined themselves living in the end times were gone. The concern now of the papacy and its servants was to invest in the long term. Evidence for this in Rome itself was to be found amid a great din of hammering and chiselling. On the opposite side of the Tiber from the Lateran, in the Vatican, the ancient quarter where Saint Peter lay buried, work had begun in 1506 on an immense new church, intended to be the largest in the world. In the Lateran, at a council held in 1513, a formal prohibition had been issued against preaching the imminence of Antichrist. In the spring of 1518, when Cajetan arrived in Augsburg on his first foreign mission, his aim was pre-eminently a diplomatic one: to form a united German front against the Turks. Rather than interpreting the Ottoman onslaught on Christendom as a fulfilment of prophecies in the book of Revelation, he preferred to see it as something quite else: a military challenge best met by raising taxes.

Yet Cajetan, now that he was beyond the Alps, could not help but feel the swirl and tug of apocalyptic expectations all around him. Hilten had died at the turn of the century, confined to a cell in Eisenach, and writing at the end—so it was said—in his own blood; but prophecies of the kind that he had so forcefully articulated, of the ruin of the papacy and the coming of a great reformer, were still circulating widely. 1516, the year foretold by Hilten as the one in which the great reformer was destined to appear, had come and gone; but Cajetan could not afford to relax. Even as he pressed the German princes to invest in a crusade against the Turks, he knew that financial demands from the Church were generating widespread resentment. In 1517, a theological dispute about the methods employed by Dominicans to raise funds for the papal building programme had led to a particular stir in the Saxon fortress town of Wittenberg. There, a friar who served the recently founded university as its professor of biblical studies had issued a formal objection, in the form of ninety-five written theses. Various Dominicans, closing ranks against this display of impudence, had responded with indignant counterblasts. Academic spats like this were nothing unusual, of course, and attempts to resolve it followed a process that would have been perfectly familiar to Abelard. The papacy, sent the ninety-five theses by the local archbishop, had pondered them for eight months before finally pronouncing, in August 1518, that they were indeed heretical. The author had been summoned to Rome. Yet this, far from settling the matter, had only stoked the flames. Already, in Wittenberg, writings by the local inquisitor had been burnt in the market square. Cajetan, tracking events from his residence in Augsburg, fretted that the bush fires of controversy might spread out of control. As papal legate, it was his responsibility to stamp them out. The best and most Christian way of doing this, he decided, was to summon the troublesome author of the ninety-five theses to Augsburg and persuade him in person to recant. Austere, learned and devout, Cajetan was a man whom even those normally suspicious of inquisitors knew that they could trust. His invitation was accepted. On 7 October 1518, Martin Luther arrived in Augsburg.

Perhaps, in greeting his troublesome guest, Cajetan reflected on how, almost four centuries before, Peter the Venerable had similarly welcomed a monk summoned to Rome on a charge of heresy and afforded him peace. Like Abelard, Luther was a theologian whose capacity for daring speculation was combined with a quite exceptional talent for self-publicity. It was typical of him that, travelling to Augsburg, he should have done so on foot. Intellectually brilliant, he knew as well how to present himself as a man of the people. As quick with a joke as he was with a Latin tag, as adept at speaking the language of taverns as he was at debating with scholars, he had followed up his ninety-five theses with an escalating volume of pamphlets. Indeed, such was public enthusiasm for what Luther had to say that Wittenberg, a town so poor and remote that it barely had an economy at all, was well on its way to becoming Europe's most improbable centre of the publishing industry. In the space of barely a year, as Luther himself modestly observed, 'it has pleased heaven that I should become the talk of the people'.[22] To win such a man back from the brink of heresy would redound as gloriously to Cajetan's order as the redemption of Abelard had redounded to Cluny's. There was little, then, of the inquisitor about the Cardinal's initial welcome. Fondly he spoke to the gaunt, spare man before him like a father to a son. Far from haranguing Luther, Cajetan aimed to persuade him in a gentle tone of his errors, and thereby spare him a trial in Rome. Recognisably, the cardinal spoke as the philosopher who had condemned the use of force against the Indians.

His hopes were to be bitterly disappointed. Over the course of his first meeting with Luther, Cajetan found his voice steadily rising. By the end of it, he was shouting his opponent down. At stake, the cardinal had come to realise, were not the details of Luther's ninety-five theses, but an altogether more fundamental question: how Christians were best to pursue holiness. To Cajetan, the answer appeared self-evident. Outside of the Roman Church, there could be no salvation. Its immense structure was nothing less than the City of God. Generation upon generation of Christian had laboured to build it. The popes who had followed in a line of succession from Saint Peter himself, and the lawyers who had compiled the canons and commentaries, and the scholars who had succeeded in integrating divine revelation with pagan philosophy—all had contributed to its edifice. Yet Luther, it began to dawn on Cajetan, was content to put all of this in question. He seemed to despise every buttress of the Church's authority: Aquinas, and canon law, and even the papacy itself. Over them all, defiantly and unyieldingly, he affirmed the witness of scripture. 'For the pope is not above but under the word of God.'[23] Cajetan, stupefied that an obscure monk should think to place his personal interpretation of the Bible on such a pedestal, dismissed the argument as 'mere words'; but Luther, quoting verses with a facility that came naturally to a professor of scripture, appealed for the first time to a concept that he had discovered in Paul: 'I must believe according to the testimony of my conscience.'[24]

The result was deadlock. After three meetings, during which Luther obdurately held firm to his position, Cajetan lost patience for good. Expelling the monk from his presence, he ordered him not to return unless he was ready to recant. Luther took the cardinal at his word. Released from his monastic vows by the head of his order, who had accompanied him to Augsburg, he clambered over the city wall and beat a speedy retreat. Naturally, the moment he was back in Wittenberg, he made sure to publish a full account of all his dealings with Cajetan. Luther understood, infinitely better than his adversary, how important it was to seize control of the narrative. His very life now seemed likely to depend on it. 'I was afraid because I was alone.'[25] Yet fear was not Luther's only emotion. He felt exhilaration as well, and a sense of exultation. Now that he was no longer a monk, and his bonds to the dimension of Catholic *religio* had been cut once and for all, he was free to forge something different: a new and personal understanding of *religio*.

The need for it was pressing. Time was running out. The hour of judgement was drawing near. The signs of it were everywhere. Two months after leaving Augsburg, Luther confessed in private to a dark and growing suspicion: 'that the true Antichrist mentioned by Paul reigns in the court of Rome'.[26]

Only by means of a new *reformatio*, Luther was coming to believe, could the Christian people hope to be redeemed from its darkening shadow.

13

REFORMATION

1520: Wittenberg

The papacy had given Martin Luther sixty days to recant, or else be damned as a heretic. Now, on 10 December, the time was up. That morning, at nine o'clock, Luther walked through one of the three town gates, to where a carrion pit lay. A large crowd had gathered there. One of Luther's colleagues from the university, a theologian named Johann Agricola, lit a fire. The spot was where the clothes of those who had died in the nearby hospital were burned; but Agricola, rather than rags, used books as fuel. All that morning he and Luther had been ransacking libraries for collections of canon law. Had the two men been able to find a volume of Aquinas, they would have burnt that as well. Their kindling, though, proved sufficient. The fire began to catch. Agricola continued to feed books into the flames. Then Luther stepped out from the crowd. Trembling, he held up the papal decree that had condemned his teachings. 'Because you have confounded the truth of God,' he said in a ringing voice, 'today the Lord confounds you. Into the fire with you.'[1] He dropped the decree into the flames. The parchment blackened, and curled, and turned to smoke. As Luther turned and walked back through the city gate, ashes skittered and swirled on the winter breeze.

He had opposed the burning of heretics well before self-interest might have prompted him to do so. Among the ninety-five theses which he had posted in Wittenberg three years previously was a denunciation of the practice as contrary to the will of the Spirit. It was an ominous sign, then, that the papacy, in its decree, had specifically condemned this proposition. Luther, absconding from Augsburg, had dreaded that Cajetan was planning to have him arrested. Wittenberg, his home, was reassuringly distant from Rome. It also provided him with the protection of a formidable patron. Friedrich of Saxony was one of the seven electors who, on the death of an emperor, were charged with choosing a new one: a responsibility that brought him much influence and respect. But Friedrich wanted more. Painfully aware how backward his lands were compared to those of other electors, he had founded the university in Wittenberg to act as a beacon of sophistication amid the muddy wastes of Saxony. Luther's growing celebrity had put it spectacularly on the map. Friedrich had no wish to lose his star professor to the stake. The best course, he decided, would be for Luther's case to be heard by the emperor. That January, a great assembly of the empire's power brokers, a 'diet', was convened on the banks of the Rhine, in Worms. Presiding over it was Charles of Spain, the grandson of Ferdinand and Isabella who, just a year and a half previously, had become the fifth person of his name to be elected emperor. Friedrich, as one of the men who had chosen him, was well placed to pull strings. Sure enough, on 26 March, a summons arrived in Wittenberg, instructing Luther 'to answer with regard to your books and teachings'.[2] He was given three weeks to comply. He also received a personal assurance from Charles V of safe conduct to the diet.

Naturally, travelling to Worms, Luther could not help but feel himself in the shadow of another reformer's fate. 'We are all Hussites, and did not realise it. Even Paul and Augustine are in reality Hussites.'[3] There could be no serving God's purpose, Luther had come to understand, without seeing the past in a new and radical light. For centuries, in the garden of Christendom, flowers had been pulled up as weeds, and weeds tended as flowers. Now, and forever, that had to change. Already, even before his meetings with Cajetan,

Luther had come to believe that true *reformatio* would be impossible without consigning canons, papal decrees and Aquinas' philosophy to the flames. Then, in the wake of his meeting with the cardinal, he had come to an even more subversive conclusion. It was not enough merely to renovate the fabric of the Church: to fix its abuses, to clean up its scandals. Its very architecture was rotten through. The whole structure needed to be condemned, demolished. That Cajetan, a man of transparent holiness, had placed obedience to the pope above the witness of scripture precisely illustrated the problem. Even at its very best, the Roman Church was a perversion of what Christianity should properly be. Far from bringing the Christian people closer to God, it had seduced them into paganism and idolatry. Luther, contemplating the sheer terrifying scale of its reach, the way in which it had infected every nook and cranny of life with its rot, had no doubt who was to blame. 'Hell's brand, the mask of the devil, also called Gregory VII, is the Monster of Monsters, the very first Man of Sin and Son of Perdition.'[4] His papacy had ushered in the last and fatal age of the world. The world shaped by Hildebrand and his heirs, so Luther warned, the world of a church that for over four centuries had been motivated by nothing except a ravening appetite for power, was a literally hellish abomination: 'sheer robbery and violence'.[5]

Yet there was, in the very savagery of this abuse, the spectral hint of a compliment. Luther's condemnation of the road taken by the Church in the age of Gregory VII was an acknowledgement as well of the revolutionary character of its ambitions and achievements. Now, by setting himself openly against the papacy and its works, Luther was aiming at a *reformatio* no less seismic. His mastery of publicity, his readiness to harness riot to his own purposes, his attempt to bleed from the most awesome office in all of Christendom its authority: here were displays of boldness worthy of Hildebrand. In Wittenberg, on the day that Luther had staged his bonfire, students had built a float, festooned it with parodies of papal decrees, and finally, after driving it around the town to raucous cheers, burnt the lot. A man dressed up as the pope had then tossed his tiara into the fire. Now, travelling to the diet, Luther was greeted with matching displays of exuberance. Welcoming committees toasted him at the gates of city after city; crowds crammed into churches to hear him preach. As he entered Worms, thousands thronged the streets to catch a glimpse of the man of the hour. Late the following afternoon, brought before Charles V and asked whether he would recant, Luther was so disappointed at finding himself denied the chance to argue his case that he asked for twenty-four hours to mull things over. The crowds outside continued to cheer him. As Luther left the bishop's palace where the meeting had been held, 'he was admonished by various voices to be brave, to act manfully, and not to fear those who can kill the body but cannot kill the soul'.[6] One enthusiast even compared him to Jesus.

On what basis, Cajetan had demanded of Luther, did he think to defy the accumulated wisdom of the Church? Now, that night in Worms, the question hung even more urgently in the air. Luther's mission, no less than Hildebrand's had been, was to redeem Christendom from darkness, to purify it of corruption, to baptise it anew. He could not, though, as the earlier reformers had done, seize control of the commanding heights of the Roman Church— for that was precisely the strategy that had resulted in everything he aspired to reverse. Standing before the emperor, he did so as a counter-revolutionary: one who mourned that Gregory VII had ever succeeded in bringing Henry IV 'under his heel—for Satan was with him'.[7] That Charles V appeared immune to the appeal of this message was, to be sure, a disappointment: for Luther had come to believe that it was the duty of the emperor to check the conceit of the papacy and demolish all its claims to a universal jurisdiction. Fortunately, the responsibility was not solely that of princes. Luther's summons was to all the Christian people. For centuries, priests had been deceiving them. The founding claim of the order promoted by Gregory VII, that the clergy were an order of men radically distinct from the laity, was a swindle and a blasphemy. 'A Christian man is a perfectly free lord of all, and subject to none.'

So Luther had declared a month before his excommunication, in a pamphlet that he had pointedly sent to the pope. 'A Christian is a perfectly dutiful servant of all, subject to all.'[8] The ceremonies of the Church could not redeem men and women from hell, for it was only God who possessed that power. A priest who laid claim to it by virtue of his celibacy was playing a confidence trick on both his congregation and himself. So lost were mortals to sin that nothing they did, no displays of charity, no mortifications of the flesh, no pilgrimages to gawp at relics, could possibly save them. Only divine love could do that. Salvation was not a reward. Salvation was a gift.

As a monk, Luther had lived in dread of judgement, starving himself and praying every night, confessing his sins for long hours at a time, wearying his superiors, all in a despairing attempt to render himself deserving of heaven. Yet the more he had studied the Bible, and reflected on its mysteries, so the more had he come to see this as so much wasted effort. God did not treat sinners according to their just deserts—for, were he to do so, then none would ever be saved. If this was the sombre lesson that had been taught by Augustine, then even more so was it evident in scripture. Paul, a Pharisee upright in every way, had not been redeemed by his zealousness for the law. Only after he had been directly confronted by the risen Christ, dazzled by him, and set on a spectacularly different path, had God marked him out as one of the elect. Luther, reading Paul, had been overwhelmed by a similar consciousness of divine grace. 'I felt I was altogether born again and had entered paradise itself through open gates.'[9] Unworthy though he was, helpless and fit to be condemned, yet God still loved him. Luther, afire with the intoxicating and joyous improbability of this, loved God in turn. There was no other source of peace, no other source of comfort, to be had. It was in the certitude of this that Luther, the day after his first appearance before Charles V, returned to the bishop's palace. Asked again if he would renounce his writings, he said that he would not. As dusk thickened, and torches were lit in the crowded hall, Luther fixed his glittering black eyes on his interrogator and boldly scorned all the pretensions of popes and councils. Instead, so he declared, he was bound only by the understanding of scripture that had been revealed to him by the Spirit. 'My conscience is captive to the Word of God. I cannot and I will not retract anything, since it is neither safe nor right to go against conscience.'[10]

Two days after listening to this bravura display of defiance, Charles V wrote a reply. Obedient to the example of his forebears, he vowed, he would always be a defender of the Catholic faith, 'the sacred rituals, decrees, ordinances and holy customs'.[11] He therefore had no hesitation in confirming Luther's excommunication. Nevertheless, he was a man of his word. The promise of safe passage held. Luther was free to depart. He had three weeks to get back to Wittenberg. After that, he would be liable for 'liquidation'.[12] Luther, leaving Worms, did so as both a hero and an outlaw. The drama of it all, reported in pamphlets that flooded the empire, only compounded his celebrity. Then, halfway back to Wittenberg, another astonishing twist. Travelling in their wagon through Thuringia, Luther and his party were ambushed in a ravine. A posse of horsemen, pointing their crossbows at the travellers, abducted Luther and two of his companions. The fading hoofbeats left behind them nothing but dust. As to who might have taken Luther, and why, there was no clue. Months passed, and still no one seemed any the wiser. It was as though he had simply vanished into thin air.

All the while, though, Luther was in the Wartburg. The castle belonged to Friedrich, whose men had brought him there for safekeeping. Disguised as a knight, with two servant boys to attend him, but no one to argue with, no one to address, he was miserable. The devil nagged him with temptations. Once, when a strange dog came padding into his room, Luther—who loved dogs dearly—identified it as a demon and threw it out of his tower window. He suffered terribly from constipation. 'Now I sit in pain like a woman in childbirth, ripped up, bloody.'[13] He did not, as Saint Elizabeth had done when she lived in the castle, welcome suffering. He had come to understand that he could never be saved by good works. It was in the

Wartburg that Luther abandoned forever the disciplines of his life as a monk. Instead, he wrote. Lonely in his eyrie, he could look down at the town of Eisenach, where Hilten had prophesied the coming of a great reformer, and believe himself—despite his isolation from the mighty convulsions that he himself had set in train—to be the man foretold. At Worms, the emperor had charged him with arrogance, and demanded to know how it was that a single monk could possibly be right in an opinion 'according to which all of Christianity will be and will always have been in error both in the past thousand years and even more in the present'.[14] It was to answer that question, to share his good news of God's grace, that Luther kept to his writing desk.

Only in October, though, did he finally settle on a project that proved sufficient to ease his anguish. It was by reading scripture that he had opened his heart to the Spirit, and thereby had revealed to him the startling fact of God's love. What better could he do, then, than break down the barrier that had for so long existed between the learned and the unlearned, and give to Christians unfamiliar with Latin the chance to experience a similar joy? Already, back in 1466, the Bible had been printed in German; but in a shoddy translation. Luther's ambition was not merely to translate directly from the original Greek, but also to pay tribute to the beauties of everyday speech. Eleven weeks it took him to finish his rendering of the New Testament. The words flowed from his pen, phrases that might have been heard in a kitchen, or a field, or a marketplace, short, simple sentences, language that anyone could understand. Easily, fluently it came. By the time that Luther had finished, even his constipation had eased.

'If you picture the Bible to be a mighty tree and every word a little branch, I have shaken every one of these branches because I wanted to know what it was and what it meant.'[15] Now, with his translation, Luther had given Germans everywhere the chance to do the same. All the structures and the traditions of the Roman Church, its hierarchies, and its canons, and its philosophy, had served merely to render scripture an entrapped and feeble thing, much as lime might prevent a bird from taking wing. By liberating it, Luther had set Christians everywhere free to experience it as he had experienced it: as the means to hear God's living voice. Opening their hearts to the Spirit, they would understand the true meaning of Christianity, just as he had come to understand it. There would be no need for discipline, no need for authority. Antichrist would be routed. All the Christian people at long last would be as one.

Here I Stand

They found him hiding in an attic, in a house beside the city gate of Frankenhausen. When he insisted that he was an invalid and knew nothing about the terrible battle that had just been fought, they emptied out the contents of his bag. A letter left no doubt as to his identity: Thomas Müntzer, the notorious revolutionary who had been preaching the imminent extermination of the mighty, and the reign of the downtrodden, when all—as in the days of the Apostles—would be held in common. Dragged through the streets of the city, where piles of corpses bore witness to the full terrible scale of the slaughter inflicted on his ragtag army, he was led into the presence of his conqueror. Duke George of Saxony, the cousin of Prince Friedrich, was a man who had long dreaded where the elector's sponsorship of Luther might lead; now, in the charnel house of Frankenhausen, he seemed to have his answer. Interrogating his prisoner, all his darkest suspicions were confirmed. Müntzer insisted on calling him 'brother'; repeatedly quoted the Old Testament; justified the insurrection of the poor against the rich as the necessary sorting of the wheat from the chaff. The duke had heard enough. Müntzer was put to torture. Some said that he had been brought to recant his views; but nothing in his final message suggested that he had. 'Do not allow my death to be a stumbling block to you,' he wrote to his followers. 'It has come to pass for the benefit of the good and uncomprehending.'[16]

Luther, brought the news that Müntzer had been executed, and his head displayed on a pikestaff, was grimly delighted. For three years, ever since he had finally succeeded in slipping the Wartburg and returning to Saxony, he had been wrestling with an unsettling conundrum: the failure of the Spirit to illumine all those inspired by his teachings as he himself had been illumined. When Argula von Grumbach, a Bavarian noblewoman, publicly praised Luther's translation of the New Testament, she did so in terms that perfectly corresponded to Luther's own elevated sense of his mission. 'Ah, but how splendid it is,' she wrote, 'when the spirit of God teaches us and, more, helps us understand first this passage then that one, God be praised! revealing to me the real, authentic light shining forth.'[17] Yet the coming of enlightenment, it turned out, revealed different things to different people. Many of Luther's followers, inspired by the premium that he had put on freedom, complained that he was dragging his feet. That a man who had dared to oppose both pope and emperor should now seem to shrink from campaigning for a universal liberty, one in which the poor might be freed forever from the exactions of the rich, struck them as a sorry disappointment. Müntzer, a former priest who believed himself appointed by God to bring the oppressed to the lordship of the world, had been particularly vituperative. Making play with the one-time monk's growing bulk, he mocked Luther as a mound of soft-living flesh, and fantasised about cooking him as a dainty for the Devil.

It did not need the culinary fantasies of Müntzer to inspire in peasants and miners across the various territories of the empire a mood of insurrectionary ferment. The uprising crushed so bloodily at Frankenhausen was only one of a number of such revolts. Again and again, rebellion was justified as obedience to the Bible. In 1525, when thousands of peasants assembled in Baltringen, a village in northern Swabia, they proclaimed it their ambition 'to hear the gospel and to live accordingly'.[18] It was not they who were responsible for the war, but the lords and abbots, who oppressed them as Pharaoh had oppressed the Israelites. They wanted nothing that was not promised them by scripture. Unsurprisingly, then, the entire course of the peasants' revolt, once the imperial nobility had rallied against it to brutal effect, slaughtering some hundred thousand rebels and bringing devastation to vast swathes of the empire, was charged by Luther's critics to his account. 'There were many peasants slain in the uprising, many fanatics banished, many false prophets hanged, burned, drowned, or beheaded who perhaps would still live as good obedient Christians had he never written.'[19] The accusation was one that preyed on Luther's conscience. Anxiety that he might have been responsible for sending multitudes to hell tormented him. So desperate was he not to be held responsible for the uprising that, as it reached its bloody climax, he condemned the rebels in terms so hysterical than even his admirers were taken aback. Luther did not care. He understood what was at stake. He knew that to acknowledge the rebels as his own would be to threaten his entire life's work. Without the backing of supportive princes, there could be no possible future for his great project of *reformatio*.

'Frogs need storks.' Luther had no illusions as to the beneficence of earthly rulers. He knew how blessed he was in his patron. Few princes were as steadfast or wise as Friedrich. The majority, Luther acknowledged, were at best 'God's gaolers and hangmen'.[20] Yet this was sufficient. In a world that was fallen, there could be no prospect of arriving at a law that adequately reflected the eternal law of God—nor was it the task of the Church to make the attempt. It was one of the more grotesque enterprises of the papacy to have created an entire legal system, and then foisted it on the Christian people. This was why Luther had consigned volumes of canon law to his bonfire in Wittenberg. It was the duty of princes, not of popes, to uphold the frameworks of justice. Yet what were the proper frameworks of justice? Luther, precisely because he scorned to think of himself as a lawyer, took for granted much of what, over the course of long centuries, had been achieved by the very legal scholars whose books he had so publicly burned. Rulers who embraced Luther's programme of *reformatio* had little option but to do the same. Anxious to govern their subjects in a correctly Christian manner, they settled on a simple expedient: to appropriate large portions of canon law and make it their own.

The result was not to dissolve the great division between the realms of the profane and the sacred that had characterised Christendom since the age of Gregory VII, but to entrench it. Rulers inspired by Luther, laying claim to an exclusive authority over their subjects, were able to set about designing a model of the state that no longer ceded any sovereignty to Rome. Meanwhile, in the privacy of their souls, true Christians had lost nothing. In place of canon lawyers, they now had God. Subject though they might be to a newly muscular understanding of the secular, liberty was theirs in a parallel dimension: the one dimension that truly mattered. Only those who opened their hearts to the gift of divine grace, to a direct communion with the Almighty, could feel themselves truly free. No longer was it the *religiones*—the monks, the friars, the nuns—who had *religio*. All believers had it—even those who, lacking Latin and speaking only German, might call it 'religion'.

The world consisted of two kingdoms. One was a sheepfold, in which all who had answered the summons of Christ, the Good Shepherd, were fed and governed in peace; the other belonged to those who had been set to watch over the sheep, to keep them from dogs and robbers with clubs. 'These two kingdoms must be sharply distinguished, and both be permitted to remain; the one to produce piety, the other to bring about external peace and prevent evil deeds; neither is sufficient in the world without the other.'[21] That ambitious rulers should have been quick to sniff out the potential of such a formulation was hardly surprising. The most startling, the most outrageous move of all was made by a king who, far from ranking as an admirer of Luther, had not merely written a best-selling pamphlet against him, but been commended for it by the pope. Henry VIII—who, as king of England, lived in fuming resentment of the much greater prestige enjoyed by the emperor and the king of France—had been mightily pleased to have negotiated the title of Defender of the Faith for himself from Rome. It had not taken long, though, for relations between him and the papacy to take a spectacular turn for the worse. In 1527, depressed by a lack of sons and obsessed by a young noblewoman named Anne Boleyn, Henry convinced himself that God had cursed his marriage. As wilful as he was autocratic, he demanded an annulment. The pope refused. Not only was Henry's case one to make any respectable canon lawyer snort, but his wife, Catherine of Aragon, was the daughter of Ferdinand and Isabella—which meant in turn that she was the aunt of Charles V. Anxious though the pope might be to keep the English king on side, his prime concern was not to offend Christendom's most powerful monarch. Henry, under normal circumstances, would have had little option but to admit defeat. The circumstances, though, were hardly normal. Henry had an alternative recourse to hand. He did not have to accept Luther's views on grace or scripture to relish the reformer's hostility to the pope. Opportunistic to the point of megalomania, the king seized his chance. In 1534, papal authority was formally repudiated by act of parliament. Henry was declared 'the only supreme head on Earth of the Church of England'. Anyone who disputed his right to this title was guilty of capital treason.

Simultaneously, in the German city of Münster, another king was pushing the implications of Luther's teachings to an opposite, but no less radical, extreme. Jan Bockelson—'John of Leiden'—had no palaces, no parliaments. Instead, he was a tailor. For a year, as the forces of the expelled bishop laid siege to the town, attempting to starve it into submission, he governed Münster as a second David, the self-anointed king of the world. Confident that the thousand-year reign of the saints prophesied in Revelation was imminent, preachers in the city summoned the faithful to the slaughter of the unrighteous. 'God will be with his people; he will give them iron horns and bronze claws against their enemies.'[22] A familiar rallying cry. Müntzer had raised it only a decade earlier at Frankenhausen. Escaping the slaughter of that terrible battle, a handful of men had lived to inspire a new generation. One, a former bookseller named

Hans Hut, had taken refuge in Augsburg, where he had preached an uncompromising rejection of traditions lacking the sanction of scripture. A particular object of his ire had been the baptism of infants. Though the custom reached back to the earliest days of the Church, it lacked any mention in the Bible—and so Hut had duly denounced it as 'a cunning trick on all Christendom'.[23] In 1526, on Pentecost, the feast day that commemorated the descent of the Spirit onto the first apostles, he had received a second baptism: an *anabaptismos*. Hut's death in prison the following year had not prevented thousands of Christians from following his example. Bockelson's reign in Münster was an Anabaptist coup. A host of policies for which scriptural licence could readily be cited, but which the Church had long set its face against, were instituted: the smashing of images; communism; polygamy. Riot alternated with repression. John of Leiden personally beheaded a suspected spy. The scandal and the horror of it reverberated across Christendom. By June 1535, when Münster finally fell, Lutheran princes had joined forces with the bishop, and Anabaptist become a byword for violence and depravity.

'Here I stand. I can do no other.' So Luther, appearing before the emperor at Worms, was said to have declared. John of Leiden, equally convinced of his obedience to God's Word, had suffered for it more terribly. His flesh was tortured with red-hot pincers; his tongue pulled out with pliers; his corpse left to moulder in an iron cage. Other Anabaptists, wherever the news from Münster was reported, from England to Austria, were hunted down. They too died in the certainty of their obedience to God's Word. They too could do no other. Yet the men who condemned them, Lutheran as well as Catholic, when they imagined themselves preventing a second Münster, might often have their victims badly wrong. Many Anabaptists, when they pondered the writings that had inspired John of Leiden and his followers to exact God's vengeance on the unrighteous, understood them to mean the precise opposite: never to wield a sword. The verses of scripture were many, and the ways of interpreting them as numerous as those who read them. If some

Anabaptists found in the Bible a summons to trample God's enemies in the winepress of his wrath, then so did many others, pondering the life and the death of their Saviour, absorb a very different lesson. Hut himself, escaping the slaughter at Frankenhausen, had repented for his time as a soldier. Other Anabaptists too, committing themselves to an absolute pacifism, had sought, not to overthrow the order of the world, but to withdraw from it. Whether in the loneliness of isolated valleys or in the anonymity of crowded cities, they turned their backs on earthly power. It seemed to them the only proper, the only Christian thing to do.

'Where the Spirit of the Lord is,' Paul had written to the Corinthians, 'there is freedom.'[24] Between this assertion and the insistence that there existed only the one way to God, only the one truth, only the one life, there had always been a tension. The genius of Gregory VII and his fellow radicals had been to attempt its resolution with a programme of reform so far-reaching that the whole of Christendom had been set by it upon a new and decisive course. Yet the claim of the papacy to embody both the ideal of liberty and the principle of authority had never been universally accepted. For centuries, various groups of Christians had been defying its jurisdiction by making appeal to the Spirit. Luther had lit the match—but others before him had laid the trail of gunpowder. This was why, in the wake of his defiant appearance at Worms, he found himself impotent to control the explosions that he had done so much to set in train. Nor was he alone. Every claim by a reformer to an authority over his fellow Christians might be met by appeals to the Spirit; every appeal to the Spirit by a claim to authority. The consequence, detonating across entire reaches of Christendom, was a veritable chain reaction of protest.

Flailingly, five Lutheran princes had sought to put this process on an official footing. In 1529, summoned to an imperial diet, they had dared to object to measures passed there by the Catholic majority by issuing a formal 'Protestation'. By 1546, when Luther died, commending his spirit into the hands of the God of Truth, other princes too had come to be seen as 'Protestant'—and not only in the empire. Denmark had been Lutheran since 1537; Sweden was well on its way to becoming so. Yet elsewhere, the spectrum of what it might mean to be Protestant yawned as unbridgably as it had ever done. Luther, a man whose genius for vituperation had helped to make the whole of Christendom shake, had never been content merely to insult the pope. Those who, like him, had dared to repudiate the Roman Church but had then been guilty of what Luther condemned as a failure properly to understand the Spirit, had also been the objects of his ire. Theologians in Swiss or German cities who presumed to dispute his views on the eucharist; Anabaptists, with their wild contempt for infant baptism and secular authority; Henry VIII, who seemed to think he was God. Luther, fretting where it all might lead, had not shrunk from contemplating a nightmarish prospect: a world in which the very concept of truth might end up dissolving, and everything appear relative. 'For whoever has gone astray in the faith may thereafter believe whatever he wants.'[25]

Certainly, in the years that followed Luther's death, the task of steering the great project of *reformatio* between rocks and shoals appeared an ever more desperate one. Lutheran princes were crushed in battle by Charles V, and cities that had long echoed to the impassioned debates of rival reformers brought to submit. Many exiles, in their desperation to find sanctuary, headed for England, where— following the death of Henry VIII in 1547—his young son, Edward VI, had come to be hailed by Protestants as a new Josiah. This was no idle flattery. Edward might be a boy, but he was committed to the cause. Indeed, the only aspect of it he in any way seemed to dislike was the style of beard sported by German Protestants. Heir as he was to the title of head of the English Church, the young king provided the radicals on his council with a formidable instrument of reform. It was one they exploited to the full. 'The greater change was never wrought in so short a space in any country since the world was.'[26] Yet the thread on which all this hung was a delicate one. What a monarchy charged with the governance of the Church could give, it might also take away. In 1553, Edward died, to be succeeded by his elder sister Mary, the daughter of Catherine of Aragon. Devoutly Catholic, it did not take her long to reconcile England with Rome. Many leading reformers were burned; others fled abroad. The lesson to Protestants on the perils of placing their trust in a secular authority was a harsh one. Yet there was peril too in being a stateless exile. To refugees in flight from Mary's England, it seemed an impossible circle to square. The liberty to worship in a manner pleasing to God was nothing without the discipline required to preserve it—but how were they to be combined? Was it possible, amid the storms and tempests of the age, for a seaworthy ark to be built at all?

The most formidable, the most influential attempt to answer these questions was undertaken by a reformer who was himself an exile. Jean Calvin was a Frenchman, a scholar whose intellectual brilliance was rivalled only by his genius for the detail and grind of administration. Schooled as he was in law, he might under normal circumstances have enjoyed a profitable career at court; but instead, embracing what the French authorities condemned as a sinister and foreign heresy, he had been obliged in 1534, at the age of twenty-five, to abandon his homeland. Fortunately for the young fugitive, there had lain, just across the border, a number of cities renowned as hotbeds of reform. Calvin, restless and anxious to play his part, had made a tour of them: Zurich, Strasbourg, Bern. When he did finally put down roots, though, it was in a city that had barely registered in the consciousness of most Protestants: Geneva. Calvin had first visited it in 1536; but then, after two years of attempting to create a godly community, had ended up being run out of town. Invited back in 1541 to have a second go, he had demanded official assurance of their backing from the city magistrates. This they had provided. Geneva was a city racked by political and social tensions, and Calvin—a man of evidently formidable talents—seemed to its leaders the man likeliest to heal them. And so it proved. Calvin, recognising a rare opportunity when he saw it, had moved with what proved to be decisive speed. It took him only a couple of months to set the Genevan church on new foundations, to recalibrate its relationship with the civic authorities and to commit the entire city to an unsparing programme of moral regeneration. 'If you desire to have me as your pastor,' he had warned the council, 'then you will have to correct the disorder of your lives.'[27] He was nothing if not true to his word.

Naturally, there was opposition. Calvin brusquely, even brutally, overrode it. The means he used, though, were always within the law, never violent. He lived unarmed, unguarded. He turned the other cheek when he was spat at by his enemies in the street. His only weapon was the pulpit. Lacking any civic office, or even—until 1559—citizenship, he relied solely on his authority as a minister of the Word to bend the Genevans to his purposes. This, to the growing numbers of his admirers beyond the city, only confirmed that his achievements enjoyed divine sanction. In 1555, when a group of exiles from England arrived in Geneva, they found themselves in what appeared to their stupefied gaze the very model of a Christian commonwealth: a society in which freedom and discipline were so perfectly in balance that none of them would ever forget the experience.

To a degree exceptional among reformers, Calvin had always wrestled with the practicalities of defining a godly order. That the 'privilege of liberty'[28] was one to which all Christians were entitled he took for granted. Accordingly, in his vision of what the Church should properly be, he set a premium on every Christian's freedom both to join it and to leave. The dictates of conscience, so Calvin believed, had always, 'even when the whole world was enveloped in the thickest darkness of ignorance, held like a small ray of light which remained unextinguished';[29] but he knew, nevertheless, that it was not given to everyone to be saved. Only an elect few, reaching out to God with their faith, would be met by God with his grace. All the descendants of Adam were predestined either to heaven or to eternal death. That this decree was 'a dreadful one',[30] Calvin freely admitted; and yet he did not shrink before it. It was precisely because he knew that many would spurn the gifts of the Spirit that he laboured so hard, not just to gather together a community of the elect, but to bring it into harmony with God's plans. Four offices existed to uphold it. There were ministers to preach the word of God; teachers to instruct the young; deacons to meet the needs of the unfortunate. Then, watchdogs elected to stand guard over the morals of the laity, there were the 'elders': the *presbyters*. Meeting every Thursday, it was they and the city's ministers who provided the church with its court: the 'Consistory'. Fail to attend a service on Sunday, or transgress the Ten Commandments, or break the laws devised by Calvin to define the doctrines of the Church, and a summons was bound to come—no matter the rank of the offender. Every year, almost one in fifteen Genevans would end up making an appearance before it.[31] For those in the city who hated Calvin, who rejected his theology, who resented the endless lectures and harangues from the pulpit, it was this that constituted the worst intrusion: the dread that the eyes of the Consistory were always on them, watching, marking, judging. Conversely, for Protestants fleeing persecution, uprooted from their homes and desperate to believe that the disorder of the fallen world might yet be brought into harmony with God's plan, it was precisely Calvin's concern to rectify sinners that made Geneva seem such a model. He had created in it, as one admirer put it, 'the most perfect school of Christ that ever was in earth since the days of the apostles'.[32]

The shelter that the city could offer refugees was like streams of water to a panting deer. Charity lay at the heart of Calvin's vision. Even a Jew, if he needed assistance, might be given it. 'Remember this: Whoever sows sparingly will also reap sparingly, and whoever sows generously will also reap generously.'[33] The readiness of Geneva to offer succour to refugees was, for Calvin, a critical measure of his success. He never doubted that many Genevans profoundly resented the influx of impecunious foreigners into their city. But nor did he ever question his responsibility to educate them anew. The achievement of Geneva in hosting vast numbers of refugees was to prove a

momentous one. The example of charity that it provided; the reassurance that a godly society was indeed possible; the comfort offered
to persecuted exiles that there was a purpose to their suffering, and
that everything in life was shaped by divine intention: all were top-
ics discussed whenever refugees made it home. 'Calvinists' they
were called by their enemies, a term of abuse that was also a tribute.
Loyal to God's purposes as they understood them, those inspired by
Calvin would prove themselves ready to follow his teachings even at
the utmost cost: to abandon their past; to leave behind their homes;
to travel, if they had to, the ends of the earth.

The Clearing Mist

One night in 1581, a group of men carried the corpse of an executed
robber through the dark streets of Shrewsbury. Ahead of them, on a
hill overlooking the river Severn, rose one of the tallest spires in England. Founded back in the age of Athelstan, the church of St Mary's
was where, during the turbulent centuries that preceded the English
conquest of Wales, some ten miles to the west, a succession of papal
legates had based themselves. But those days were history. What Protestants had come to call 'popery' was banished from England. The
Catholic queen Mary had died in 1558, and her half-sister, Elizabeth,
the daughter of Anne Boleyn, now sat on the English throne. Over one
of the church doors her coat of arms had been carved, and a verse from
the Bible: 'Many daughters have done virtuously, but thou excellest
them all.'[34] Not every taint of popery, though, had yet been erased. In
the churchyard there stood a giant cross. That it was much cherished
in Shrewsbury only made the task of destroying it all the more urgent.
Working under cover of darkness, the party of bodysnatchers set to
pulling it down. Then, once the cross had been demolished, they dug
a grave where it had formerly stood, and slung in the corpse. Better an
executed criminal than a monument to popery.

'A perpetual forge of idols.'[35] So Calvin had described the human
mind. This conviction, that fallen mortals were forever susceptible

to turning their backs on God, to polluting the pure radiance of his commands, to erecting in his very sanctuary a golden calf, was the dread that had constantly shadowed all his reforms. Now, a decade and more after his death, his warnings against superstition had won a readership far beyond the limits of Geneva. In London, where more editions of his works were published than anywhere else, printers struggled to keep pace with demand. One enterprising editor had even commissioned a compilation of his greatest hits. Nor was it only in England that Calvin had become, almost overnight, a bestseller. The reverberations of his influence had reached as far afield as Scotland—a land freely acknowledged by its own nobility to lie 'almost beyond the limits of the human race'.[36] In 1559, the preaching of John Knox, an exile returned from Geneva, had inspired an eruption of godly vandalism across the kingdom. One congregation, after listening to Knox inveigh against idolatry, had promptly set to dismantling the local cathedral. Other bands of enthusiasts had incinerated abbeys, chopped down the orchards of friaries, and pulled up flowers in monastery gardens. A year later—after a short but vicious civil war, and a vote by the Scottish parliament for a reformation of the country's Church that was unmistakably Calvinist in flavour—the ambition to rout idolatry had been set on an official footing. There was now no relic of papist superstition in Britain so remote that it might not be liable for legal destruction. Whether to islands lashed by Atlantic gales, where Irish monks, back in the age of Columbanus, had raised crosses amid the heather and the rock, or to the wildest reaches of Wales, where moss-covered chapels stood guard over gushing springs, workmen armed with sledgehammers made their way, and did their work. The reach of magistrates inspired by Calvin had become a long one indeed.

Why, then, in the churchyard of St Mary's, had there been any need for the clandestine destruction of its cross? It had been done by men who feared that time was running out. Across the Channel, the forces of darkness, hell-bound and predacious, were drowning famous Christian cities in the blood of the elect. In 1572, on the feast-day of Saint Bartholomew, thousands of Protestants had been butchered on the streets of Paris. In other cities too, throughout Calvin's native France, there had been a general slaughter of his followers. New martyrs had been made in Lyon. Meanwhile, in the Low Countries, an even more murderous conflict was being fought. Its cities, brilliant and rich, had long been incubators of every shade of Protestant. As early as 1523, Charles V had hanged two monks in Antwerp on a charge of heresy and levelled their monastery. The king of Münster, John of Leiden, had been Dutch. Over the course of the succeeding decades, more Protestants had been put to death in the Low Countries than anywhere else. Yet still the ranks of the godly there had continued to grow. Insurgents against a monarchy with all the wealth of the New World at its back, many had found in Calvin's teachings a life-altering reassurance: that to be outnumbered did not mean being wrong. To take up arms against tyranny was no sin, but rather a duty. God would look after his own. If the toppling of a cross in an English market town could hardly compare as a feat with the successful defiance of the most formidable military machine in Christendom, then it was no less godly for that. The loyalty shown by the Dutch rebels to the will of the divine; their readiness to risk their fortunes and their lives; the courage and the intelligence that they brought to their fight against idolatry: here were inspirations to anyone with eyes to see.

In England no less than in the embattled Dutch Republic, the yearning was for purity. One year after the demolition of the cross in St Mary's, when a new minister arrived to lead the church, he lauded his monarch as God's faithful servant, 'who hath worthily triumphed over spiritual tyranny'.[37] But in his own congregation, and across the length and breadth of the kingdom, there were plenty who disagreed. England was not the Dutch Republic, where the exertions of Calvinists in the cause of independence had helped to secure for their church—the 'Reformed Church', as they proudly termed it—a pre-eminent and public status. Elizabeth's Protestantism was of a distinctively wilful kind. Her taste for the trappings of popery—bishops, choirs, crucifixes—appalled the godly. The more that she dismissed their calls for further reform, they more they fretted whether the Church of England over which she presided as its first Supreme Governor could be reckoned truly Protestant at all. The name first given them by a Catholic exile in 1565—'Puritans'*—seemed less an insult than a fair description. Knowing as they did that only a small number were destined to be saved, they saw in the obduracy of the queen and her ministers all the confirmation they needed of their own status as an inner core of the elect. It was not just their right to shoulder the responsibility for reform, but their duty. What were all the titles of bishops if not mere vanities 'drawn out of the Pope's shop'?[38] What were the affectations of monarchy if not tyranny? True authority lay instead with the fellowship of the godly, led by its elected pastors and presbyters. Their charge it was to continue the great labour of cleansing the world of delusion and of scraping away from the ark of Christianity all the accumulated barnacles and seaweed of human invention. Before the urgency of such a mission, all the raging of the traditional guardians of church and state, of archbishops and kings, were as nothing. The task was nothing less than to right the disorder of the cosmos. To join God with man.

Yet for all the revolutionary character of the Puritans' programme—its dismissal of custom, its contempt for superstition—it was not nearly as radical a break with the past as either their supporters or their enemies liked to insist. Godly examples of idol-toppling were hardly confined to the Bible. In 1554, while Mary was still on the throne, the papal legate sent to welcome England back into the fold had addressed members of parliament and reminded them of how it was from the papacy that they had first received the gift of Christ, which had redeemed their country from the worship of stock and stone. Meanwhile, in the Low Countries, Catholic leaders desperate to steel their flock urged veneration of Saint Boniface,

---

* It is testimony to the enduring obsession of Christians with purity, and the way in which this has repeatedly been cast as an insult, that 'Cathar' can be translated as 'Puritan'.

who had brought the light of the Gospel to their forebears, and constructed churches out of Thunor's oak. This was a line of attack with the power to make Protestants feel uneasy. Various defences were employed against it. Some insisted that the first Christian mission to England had in fact arrived, not in the papacy of Gregory the Great but long before, back in the age of the apostles, and therefore owed nothing to the Antichrist of Rome; others that the saints celebrated by Bede had never existed, but instead been fabricated to fill the gap left by the banished gods. The thesis did not catch on. To many Protestants, the record of the Anglo-Saxon Church was a model and an inspiration. Clearly, its corruption, and that of Christendom as a whole, had been the fault of Gregory VII. Puritans, then, even as they rejected the old and familiar, could not entirely deny a lurking paradox: that their rejection of tradition was itself a Christian tradition.

Back in the earliest days of English Christianity, when the first king of Northumbria to hear the gospel had consented to be baptised, and was heading down to the river with his followers, a crow had appeared, croaking in a manner that every pagan knew to be a warning. But the missionary who had been preaching to them, a Roman sent by Gregory the Great, had ordered the bird shot dead. 'If that heedless bird could not avoid death,' he had declared, 'then still less was it able to reveal the future to men who have been reborn and rebaptised into the image of God.'[39] No Puritan would have thought to disagree. Mockery of the tall stories told by papists, of the folly of their claims that the footprints of the devil were to be found imprinted on rocks, or that the bones of saints might in any way be reckoned holy, or that Christ, during the eucharist, became physically present among the congregation, did not imply any doubt that the divine was manifest in every aspect of the universe. Calvin had believed this quite as devoutly as Abelard. If reason had no role to play in fathoming the mysteries of faith, then in its proper sphere, where the stars moved on their inexorable course, and the birds sang their songs of love to their creator, and 'grass and flowers laugh out to him',[40] it existed to reveal to mortals the traces and purposes of God.

A century on from Luther, Protestants could cast themselves as the heirs of a revolution that had transformed Christendom utterly. No longer merely a staging post in a lengthy process of *reformatio*, it was commemorated instead as an episode as unique as it had been convulsive: as *the* Reformation. It had been, in the opinion of its admirers, a liberation of humanity from ignorance as well as error. Once, when the world had been lost to darkness, there had been no limit to the stories of marvels and wonders that Christians had greedily swallowed; but then, 'when the mist began to clear up, they grew to be esteemed but as old wives' fables, impostures of the clergy, illusions of spirits, and badges of Antichrist'.[41] If God was to be found in the interior experience of individual believers, then so also could he be apprehended in the immensity and complexity of the cosmos.

The truest miracles needed no popery to be rendered miraculous.

14

COSMOS

1620: Leiden

A sense of themselves as a people redeemed from the chariots and horses of Pharaoh had never left the Dutch. Forty-six years on from the relief of Leiden, memories of the terrible siege were still proudly tended in the city. Of how troops sent by Charles V's son, Philip II, the king of Spain, had almost succeeded in starving the inhabitants into submission. Of how, in desperation, the Dutch rebels had breached the dykes, to permit a relief force to sail up to the city walls. Of how a great storm had forced the besiegers to turn tail before rising floodwaters. Every year on 3 October, the anniversary of this miraculous event, a public day of atonement and thanksgiving was held. While many chose to fast, others preferred to eat meals in commemoration of how Leiden, 'through God's almighty rule, had been miraculously saved and set free'.[1] Herring and bread, the food distributed to its starving people by the relief force back in 1574, were popular choices; but so too was stewed rodent. Leiden, by 1620, had become a city 'flowing with abundance of all sorts of wealth and riches';[2] but this might be as readily a source of anxiety to its citizens as a reassurance. Every good thing, they knew, was a temptation. Just as it was the duty of a man to labour in his calling, so was it his responsibility to remember that all rewards came from the Almighty. Deeply read in the Bible as they were, the Dutch needed no reminding of what had befallen the children of Israel when they broke their covenant with God. The same divine anger that had sent the Spanish scattering before floods and winds might equally be a rod for their own backs. Once again, should they succumb to sin and profligacy, the people of Leiden might be reduced to gnawing on rat.

Calvinists in the city had good reason to worry. For all the prestige that they enjoyed as members of the Dutch Republic's established church, Leiden was no Geneva. Its consistory exercised discipline only over those who willingly submitted to it. This was, perhaps, no more than 10 per cent of the population. The consequences, it appeared to the godly, were as malign as they were self-evident. Attempts had been made by professors in the university to soften the impact of Calvin's teachings on predestination. Rival factions had clashed in the streets. So violently had tempers flared that in 1617 barricades had gone up around the city hall. Not even a purge of dissident preachers in 1619 had entirely calmed the controversy. Meanwhile, others in Leiden devoted themselves to dancing, or going to plays, or gorging themselves on enormous cheeses. Parents cuddled their children in public. Lutherans, and Anabaptists, and Jews all worshipped much as they pleased. The reluctance of magistrates to regulate these excesses had become, by 1620, a matter of voluble protest from members of the Reformed Church. The identification of the Dutch with the children of Israel was, in pulpits across Leiden, less a reassurance than a warning.

Yet even in the ambition to separate themselves from idolatry and to create a land that might be pleasing to the Almighty, at once godly and abundant, there lurked just the hint of a reproach. 'O Lord when all was ill with us You brought us up into a land wherein we were enriched through trade and commerce, and have dealt kindly with us.'[3] What, though, of those who had not been brought dry-footed through the floodwaters, but still, beyond the limits of the republic that the Dutch had established for themselves with such effort and fortitude, suffered oppression at the hands of Pharaoh?

That October, as the people of Leiden celebrated their liberation from the Spanish, and Reformed preachers pushed with ever more determination for their country to serve worthily as a new Israel, war was threatening the Protestants of the Rhineland and Bohemia. As in the days of Žižka, a Catholic emperor had mustered armies to march on Prague. His ambition: to extirpate Protestantism. The Dutch, true to their conviction that the promises made by God were promises made to the entire world, and that nothing in the whole of human existence possessed so much as a shred of authority that did not derive from his will, steeled themselves for the fight. Troops were sent across the border to buttress Protestant princes. A column of cavalry advanced up the Rhine. Outside Prague, on a mountainous ridge pockmarked by chalk pits, the army that had taken position there to defend the city from the onslaught of Antichrist included some five thousand men either funded or provided by the Dutch.

The centre did not hold. On 8 November, the Protestant forces on White Mountain were broken. Prague fell the same day. The war, though, was far from over. Quite the opposite. It was only just beginning. Like the blades of a terrible and revolving machine, the rivalries of Catholic and Protestant princes continued to scythe, mangling ever more reaches of the empire, sucking into the mulch of corpses ever more foreign armies, turning and ever turning, and only stopping at last after thirty years. Christian teachings, far from blunting hatreds, seemed a whetstone. Millions perished. Wolves prowled through the ruins of burnt towns. Atrocities of an order so terrible that, as one pastor put it, 'those who come after us will never believe what miseries we have suffered',[4] were committed on a numbing scale: men castrated; women roasted in ovens; little children led around on ropes like dogs. The Dutch, increasingly imperilled in their own fastnesses, abandoned any thought of sending armies into the slaughterhouse that lay beyond their borders. Not merely a sensible strategy, it was the godly thing to do. The prime duty of the Republic was to maintain its independence, and thereby sustain its Church, for the good of all Christendom. In Leiden, where the needs of the defence budget saw extortionate taxes levied on bread and beer, even the poorest citizens could feel that they were doing their bit. Calvinists who held firm to the fundamentals of their faith, and had the wealth to back it up, made sure to provide charity to refugees. Here, then, amid the spreading darkness of the age, was a model of Christian behaviour that might serve as an inspiration to the whole world.

This was not a perspective shared by everyone. To many in the killing fields of Germany and central Europe, it seemed that the roots of the Republic's greatness were being fed by blood. Munitions, and iron, and the bills of exchange that funded the rival armies: all were monopolised by Dutch entrepreneurs. The great dream of the godly—that by their example they might inspire anguish-torn humanity to reach out to the joy and the regeneration that only divine grace could ever provide—was shadowed by the nightmare of a Christendom being torn to pieces. How, amid the throes of such a calamity, were the elect ever to avoid the taint of compromise and hypocrisy? How were they to shutter themselves away from the evils of the age, and yet at the same time serve as the light of the world—as a city upon a hill?

Raising taxes on beer was not the only attempt to answer these questions that Leiden had fostered. On 9 November 1620, one day after the battle of the White Mountain, a ship named the *Mayflower* arrived off a thin spit of land in the northern reaches of the New World. Crammed into its holds were a hundred passengers who, in the words of one of them, had made the gruelling two-month voyage across the Atlantic because 'they knew they were pilgrims'[5]—and of these 'pilgrims', half had set out from the Dutch port of Delfshaven. These voyagers, though, were not Dutch, but English. Leiden had been only a waypoint on a longer journey: one that had begun in an England that had come to seem to the pilgrims pestiferous with sin. First, in 1607, they had left their native land; then, sailing for the New World thirteen years later, they had turned their backs on Leiden as well. Not even the godly republic of the Dutch had been able to satisfy their yearning for purity, for a sense of harmony with the divine. The Pilgrims did not doubt the scale of the challenge they faced. They perfectly appreciated that the new England which it was their ambition to found would, if they were not on their mettle, succumb no less readily to sin than the old. Yet it offered them a breathing space: a chance to consecrate themselves as a new Israel on virgin soil. Just as an individual sinner, reaching out to God, might be blessed by the gift of his grace, so might an entire people. It was in this conviction that the Pilgrims, making landfall in America, founded a settlement which they named Plymouth, to serve the whole world as a model. When, a decade later, a second settlement was established just up the coast, on Massachusetts Bay, its leaders were equally determined to demonstrate that the dream of a godly community might be more than a dream. 'Thus stands the cause between God and us,' declared one of them, a lawyer and preacher named John Winthrop, on the voyage out to the New World. 'We are entered into Covenant with him for this work.'[6] Liberty was the freedom to submit to this covenant: to be joined in a society of the godly that was hedged about by grace.

From the beginning, however, the leaders of New England found themselves negotiating a paradox. Their gaze, for all that they had settled on the margins of what seemed to them an immense and unexplored wilderness, was fixed on the entire expanse of the globe. Were they to fail in keeping their covenant, so Winthrop warned his fellow settlers, then the scandal of it would make them a story and a byword through the world. The fate of fallen humanity rested on their shoulders. They were its last, best hope. Yet for that very reason they had to be exclusive. No one could be permitted to join their community who might threaten its status as an assembly of the elect. Too much was at stake. It being the responsibility of elected magistrates to guide a colony along its path to godliness, only those who were visibly sanctified could possibly be allowed a vote. 'The covenant between you and us,' Winthrop told his electorate, 'is the oath you have taken of us, which is to this purpose, that we shall govern you and judge your causes by the rules of God's laws and our own, according to our best skill.'⁷ The charge was a formidable one: to chastise and encourage God's people much as the prophets of ancient Israel had done, in the absolute assurance that their understanding of scripture was correct. No effort was spared in staying true to this mission. Sometimes it might be expressed in the most literal manner possible. In 1638, when settlers founded a colony at New Haven, they modelled it directly on the plan of an encampment that God had provided to Moses. This it was to be a chosen people.

Except that New England was not, as the desert around Sinai had been, a wilderness. Even in the earliest days of its settlement, there had been colonists who had no wish to live as Puritans. Here, to the godly, was a nagging source of anxiety. When, during the course of their second winter, the Pilgrims found unregenerates celebrating Christmas Day by playing cricket, they promptly confiscated their bats. As the colonies grew, so too did the determination to keep in check the sinful nature of those who did not belong to the elect. Their lack of a vote did not prevent them from being expected to help support ministers, attend church and listen to sermons in which their faults would be sternly excoriated. The urge both to educate and to discipline ran deep. Both were expressions of the same deep inner sense of certitude: that the gift that God had made to the Puritans of the New World, to be a flourishing garden and a vineyard, was far too precious to be allowed to go to weed.

'Fruitful and fit for habitation,' it had seemed to the Pilgrims, 'being devoid of all civil inhabitants, where there are only savage and brutish men, which range up and down, little otherwise than the wild beasts of the same.'⁸ That the Almighty had given them a new England to settle, to light up the entire world with the perfection of their example, did not mean that they had no duty to the Indians (as the English—following the example of the Spanish—persisted in calling the natives of America). On the seal of the expedition led by John Winthrop was an Indian dressed as Adam had been in Eden, and from his mouth there came an appeal: 'Come over and help us.' The grace of God was free and capricious, and there was no reason why it might not be granted as readily to a savage as to an Englishman. The image of the Lord was in everyone, after all, and there was not a minister in New England who did not know himself commanded to love his enemies. Within decades of the first landing of the Pilgrims at Plymouth, there were Puritans applying themselves to the task of bringing the word of God to the local tribes with the same devoted sense of duty that they brought to all their tasks. Missionaries preached to the Indians in their own languages; they laboured on translations of the Bible. Yet if God had commanded Christians to bring his word to all of humanity, then so also, in defence of his chosen people, had he revealed himself a god of wrath. In 1622, an English soldier elected by the Pilgrims to serve as their captain had learned that a band of Massachusett warriors were planning to attack the colony and duly launched a pre-emptive attack of his own. Many in Plymouth expressed their qualms; but the head of the Massachusett leader was put on a pole, for all that, and exhibited in the settlement's fort. Fifteen years later, a force of colonists joined with native allies to launch another, far more devastating attack on a hostile tribe called the Pequots. Four hundred men, women and children were left dead amid the torching of their wigwams. 'It was a fearful sight to see them thus frying in the fire and the streams of blood quenching the same, and horrible was the stink and scent thereof.' Again, there were Puritans who expressed their disgust; and again, they were answered with God's licensing of slaughter in defence of Israel. 'Sometimes the Scripture declareth women and children must perish with their parents,' they were assured. 'We had sufficient light from the Word of God for our proceedings.'[9]

So Charlemagne might have answered Alcuin. Settled in a new world the Puritans may have been, in flight from the degeneracy of the old, and proudly born again; but the challenges that they faced as Christians, and the ambivalences of their solutions, had no less an ancient pedigree for that.

All Things to All Men

One morning in the summer of 1629, on the opposite side of the globe from the crude clapboard houses and timber palisades of Plymouth, the sky began to darken above the largest city on earth. Astronomers in Beijing were used to keeping track of eclipses. In the Ministry of Rites, one of a cluster of government buildings that stood south of the emperor's great complex of palaces, records were kept that reached back to the very beginnings of China. *Lifa*—the science of correctly calculating a calendar—had been assiduously sponsored by dynasty after dynasty. To neglect the movement of the stars was to risk calamity: for nothing ever happened in the heavens, so Chinese scholars believed, that was not interfused with the pattern of events on earth.

This was why, in China, the compilation and promulgation of calendars was a strict monopoly of state. Only by accurately keeping track of eclipses could an emperor hope to avert disaster. Over recent decades, however, the Ministry of Rites had made a succession of embarrassing mistakes. In 1592, its prediction of an eclipse had been off by an entire day. Reform had begun to seem essential. With an eclipse predicted for 23 June, the vice-president of the Ministry of Rites had insisted on a competition. Xu Guangqi, a distinguished scholar from Shanghai, had come to mistrust the entire methodology upon which astronomers in China had always relied. Another way of understanding the workings of the cosmos, developed in the barbarian lands of the furthermost West, had recently been introduced to Beijing. Xu Guangqi—who was not merely a patron but a friend to the foreign astronomers—had been angling for years to have them given official posts. Now he had his chance. Once the eclipse had come and gone, and daylight returned to Beijing, the forecast of the Chinese astronomers was compared to that of the barbarians; and it was the barbarians who proved to have won. Their reward was quick in coming. That September, they were commissioned by the emperor himself to reform the calendar.

Dressed in the long sweeping robes that were the uniform of Chinese scholars, they took possession of Beijing's observatory and set to work. Their triumph was a testimony to their learning: to their knowledge of the heavens, and of their ability to track the stars. It also bore witness to something more: to their understanding of the purposes of their god. It was not only the foreigners from the distant West who believed this; so too did Xu Guangqi. All of them, barbarian astronomers and Chinese minister alike, shared in the common baptism. All of them were loyal servants of the Catholic Church.

The news that Christians were to be found in the heart of an empire as remote, as mighty and as enigmatic as China, in a city that stood a whole three years' travel from Europe, was naturally a cause of great rejoicing in Rome. Of reassurance too. The times had not been easy. For a century and more, the entire fabric of Christendom had seemed at risk of rotting away. Ancient kingdoms had been lost to heresy. Others had been swallowed up by the Turks. Much of Hungary—the land of Saint Stephen, of Saint Elizabeth—had come to lie under the rule of the Ottoman sultan. Embattled on many fronts, Catholics had strained every sinew to stabilise them. The risk otherwise was of becoming—like the heretics with their swarms of sects—just one among a whole multitude of churches: less Catholic than Roman. Faced with this hellish prospect, the papacy and its servants had adopted a two-pronged strategy. Within its own heartlands, there had been a renewed insistence on discipline. In 1542, an inquisition modelled on the Spanish example had been established in Rome; in 1558, it had drawn up a lengthy index of prohibited books; a year later, ten thousand volumes had been publicly burnt in Venice. Simultaneously, beyond the seas, in the new worlds opened up by Spanish and Portuguese adventurers, great harvests of souls had been reaped by Catholic missionaries. The fall of Mexico to Christian arms had been followed by the subjugation of other fantastical lands: of Peru, of Brazil, and of islands named—in honour of Philip II—the Philippines. That God had ordained these conquests, and that Christians had not merely a right but a duty to prosecute them, remained, for many, a devout conviction. Idolatry, human sacrifice and all the other foul excrescences of paganism were still widely cited as justifications for Spain's globe-spanning empire. The venerable doctrine of Aristotle—that it was to the benefit of barbarians to be ruled by 'civilised and virtuous princes'[10]—continued to be affirmed by theologians in Christian robes.

There was, though, an alternative way of interpreting Aristotle. In 1550, in a debate held in the Spanish city of Valladolid on whether or not the Indians were entitled to self-government, the aged Bartolomé de las Casas had more than held his own. Who were the true barbarians, he had demanded: the Indians, a people 'gentle, patient and humble', or the Spanish conquerors, whose lust for gold and silver was no less ravening than their cruelty? Pagan or not, every human being had been made equally by God and endowed by him with the same spark of reason. To argue, as las Casas' opponent had done, that the Indians were as inferior to the Spaniards as monkeys were to men was a blasphemy, plain and simple. 'All the peoples of the world are humans, and there is only one definition of all humans and of each one, that is that they are rational.'[11] Every mortal—Christian or not—had rights that derived from God. *Derechos humanos*, las Casas had termed them: 'human rights'. It was difficult for any Christians who accepted such a concept to believe themselves superior to pagans simply by virtue of being Christian. The vastness of the world, not to mention the seemingly infinite nature of the peoples who inhabited it, served missionaries both as an incentive and as an admonition. If Indians could be scorned by Spanish and Portuguese adventurers as barbarians, then there were other lands in which it was Europeans who were liable to appear the barbarians. Nowhere was this more soberingly evident than in China. Even to live on its margins was to wonder at 'people who are so civilised and ingenious in the sciences, government and everything else that they are in no way inferior to our ways in Europe'.[12] To journey along the roads and rivers of the empire, to marvel at its wealth, to gawp at the sheer scale of its cities, was—for a missionary—to feel much as

Paul had done, travelling the world ruled by Rome. 'I have become all things to all men.'[13] So the apostle had defined his strategy for bringing the world to Christ. Cortés, crushing the Mexica, had felt no obligation to copy his example; but China was not to be treated as the Spanish had treated the New World. It was too ancient, too powerful, too sophisticated for that. 'It is,' as the first missionary to reach Beijing after crossing the oceans had put it, 'very different from other lands.'[14] If missionaries, obedient to their Saviour's command to preach the gospel to all creation, were to travel there, they could not afford to be defined as European. The Christian message was universal, or it was nothing.

The man appointed by Xu Guangqi to reform the calendar had consecrated his entire life to this conviction. Johann Schreck was a polymath of astonishing abilities: not just an astronomer, but a physician, a mathematician, a linguist. Above all, though, he was a priest, a member of an order that, ever since its founding in 1540, had aspired to operate on a global scale. Like friars, those who joined the Society of Jesus swore themselves to poverty, chastity and obedience; but they swore as well a vow of obedience to the pope to undertake any mission that he might give them. Some Jesuits expressed their commitment to this by devoting their lives to teaching; others by risking martyrdom to redeem England from heresy; others by sailing to the ends of the earth. Their mandate, when they travelled to lands beyond Europe, was—without ever offending against Christian teaching—to absorb as many of the customs as they could. In India they were to live as Indians, in China as Chinese. The policy had been pushed to notable extremes. So successfully had the first Jesuit to reach Beijing integrated himself into the Chinese elite that, following his death there in 1610, the emperor himself had granted a plot of land for his burial: an honour without precedent for a foreigner. Matteo Ricci, an Italian who had arrived in China in 1582 speaking not a word of the language, had transformed himself into Li Madou, a scholar so learned in the classical texts of his adopted home that he had come to be hailed by Chinese mandarins as their peer. Although Confucius, the ancient philosopher whose teachings served as the fountainhead of Chinese morality, had plainly not been a Christian, Ricci had refused to dismiss him as merely a pagan. That he had been able to do this in good faith had owed much to two particular convictions: first, that Confucius had been illumined by the same divinely bestowed gift of reason that was evident in the writings of Aristotle; and second, that his teachings had been corrupted over the centuries by his followers. Only strip the accretions away, so Ricci had believed, and Confucians might be led to Christ. Confucian philosophy, in its fundamentals, was perfectly compatible with Christianity. This was why, sending to Rome for astronomers, Ricci had made no apology for aspiring to serve the Chinese emperor by reforming his calendar. 'According to the disposition of Divine Providence, various ways have been employed at different times, and with different races, to interest people in the Christian faith.'[15] Schreck, by travelling from his native Constance to Beijing, had committed his life to this policy.

Yet there were some among his superiors who had their doubts. A couple of months before the fateful eclipse had secured for Schreck his appointment to the Bureau of Astronomy, a senior Jesuit had arrived in Beijing to inspect its mission. Although much impressed by the calibre of the various priests he found working there, André Palmeiro had raised a quizzical eyebrow at their guiding assumption. It did not seem to him at all apparent that Confucian philosophy, beneath the skin, resembled Christianity. 'If the priests believe that among the books of the Chinese there are some moral documents that serve to instill virtue, I respond by asking what sect there has ever been or is today that does not have some rules for correct living?'[16] Leaving Beijing a week before the morning turned dark over the city, Palmeiro could reflect on various aspects of Chinese behaviour that had perturbed him: the haughtiness shown by mandarins towards the poor; their inability to grasp the distinction between church and state; their obscene number of wives. Most unsettlingly of all, though, Palmeiro could detect not the slightest trace of the worship of the One Creator God of Israel. The Chinese seemed to have no concept either of creation or of a god. Rather than a universe obedient to the laws of an omnipotent deity, they believed instead in a naturally occurring order, formed by constituent elements—fire, water, earth, metal, wood—that were forever waxing and waning in succession. Everything went in cycles. Bound together by their bonds of mutual influence, cosmos and humanity oscillated eternally between rival poles: *yin* and *yang*. The duty of the emperor, one granted him by the heavens, was to negotiate these oscillations, and to maintain order as well he could. Hence his need for an accurate calendar. Without one, after all, how would he know to perform the rituals that kept heaven and earth in harmony? This was a question for which Schreck, now that he had formally entered the imperial civil service, was responsible for providing an answer.

Palmeiro, although contemptuous of Confucian philosophy, had not forbidden the Jesuits from taking up office in Beijing. He could accept that, in an immense empire like China, any chance to bring its ruler to Christ was too precious to be wasted. He could accept as well that there were grounds for hope. Xu Guangqi was a model of what might be achieved. Once, like any mandarin, he had believed that humanity was of one substance with the stars. 'Man is born from amidst heaven and earth, which means that his origin is fundamentally the same as Heaven.'[17] But then Xu had met Matteo Ricci. In 1603, he had been baptised and taken the name Paul. Ricci, noting the effects on his friend of his conversion, had observed with satisfaction the mandarin's attentiveness to converts of a lesser class. It was Xu's understanding of the cosmos, however, that had been most significantly transformed. His eagerness to recruit the Jesuits into the Bureau of Astronomy reflected his new, and very Christian, understanding of the universe: that it had had a beginning, and would have an end; that its workings were governed by divinely authored laws; that the God who had fashioned it was a geometer. Generations of mandarins, Xu lamented, had been operating in the dark. 'We have been ignorant of the Author of the world. We have interested ourselves in this and in that, thus naturally losing from view the First Source. Alas! How many losses and how many deceptions!'[18]

Even Xu, though, had failed to recognise the full scale of the threat that Christian assumptions about the universe represented to China's traditions. A loyal servant of his monarch, he never doubted the role of the emperor in maintaining a cosmic harmony. No less than his unbaptised peers, Xu believed that it would be a simple matter to melt down the Jesuits' astronomy and cast it in a Chinese mould. The only necessity for achieving this was to translate the barbarians' books and source their most up-to-date instruments for tracking the stars. This, once the emperor had granted his permission, was precisely what Xu ordered to be done. Yet the task of transforming Beijing into a centre for cutting-edge European astronomy was more challenging than he cared to imagine. Mandarins were not alone in having been shaped by a highly distinctive tradition of scholarship. Schreck's understanding of how and why the stars revolved on their course derived from one as well. Padua, the university he had attended before becoming a Jesuit, was the oldest in Italy after Bologna. Many generations of students before him had taken courses such as he had done, in medicine and mathematics, and in universities across the whole of Christendom. The autonomy of such institutions, guaranteed as early as 1215 by papal statute, had endured through war and reformation. Nothing in China, where access to learning had always been strictly regulated by the state, could compare. If to be a Jesuit was to serve in obedience to the pope, then it was also to know that God's purposes were revealed through the free and untrammelled study of natural philosophy.

'Holy Scripture,' Aquinas had written, 'naturally leads men to contemplate the celestial bodies.'[19]

To take that path was the very essence of being a Christian.

The Starry Messenger

Exploring the unknown might sometimes entail taking a risk. Schreck, a man as fascinated by the workings of the human body as of the cosmos, did not confine himself to tracking stars; and on 11 May 1630, investigating a herb that was reported to induce sweating, he tested it out on himself. A few hours later he was dead. The loss of such a brilliant astronomer, less than a year after his appointment to reform the Chinese calendar, was a grievous one; but not, as it turned out, fatal to the Jesuits' mission. Schreck had prepared well for it. Two of his younger colleagues, sent to China precisely because of their command of natural philosophy, proved equal to the challenge of replacing him. This was due in part to their own talents, and in part to the close links that Schreck had succeeded in establishing with the most brilliant figures in his field. Fabulously distant from Europe though they were, the Jesuits in Beijing were not working in isolation. Thanks to Schreck's efforts, they had the most advanced equipment in the world for observing the heavens. They also had the use of the most up-to-date star tables. The Jesuits never doubted what they were living through: a revolution in the study of the cosmos without precedent in history.

Schreck, a couple of years before his death, had sought to explain it to his Chinese readers. 'In these late years,' he wrote, 'a celebrated mathematician of the kingdoms of the West has constructed a lens which permits one to see afar.'[20] Schreck had known the 'celebrated mathematician' well. On 14 April 1611, the two men had met at a dinner party held on a hill above the Vatican. A previously obscure professor at the university of Padua, where he had been one of Schreck's teachers, Galileo Galilei had become famous overnight. His 'lens'—an improvement on an original Dutch prototype—had enabled him to make sense of the heavens as never before. He had observed that the surface of the moon was alternately cratered and mountainous; that the Milky Way consisted of an inordinate number of stars; that Jupiter had four moons. These claims, published in a jauntily self-aggrandising pamphlet, had created a sensation. The dinner party at which Schreck had joined Galileo, and at which it had been agreed by the guests that his lens should be christened a 'telescope', had been held in his honour by a prince, no less. Yet if his discoveries were widely toasted, they had also provoked alarm. The blow dealt to Aristotle's model of the universe, which for centuries had exercised a domineering authority over Christian cosmology, appeared mortal. How was the appearance of a moon pitted with craters to be reconciled with the philosopher's understanding of it as unchanging, imperishable, incorruptible?

Galileo, a man as impatient for fame as he was derisive of anyone who presumed to obstruct him from obtaining it, failed to see this as an issue. His contempt for Aristotle, whom he ranked alongside all the most miserable things in life—'plague, urinals, debt'[21]—was matched only by his impatience with the philosopher's admirers: 'the potbellied theologians who locate the limits of of human genius in his writings'.[22] Galileo, though, was no Luther. His instincts were those of a social climber, not a rebel. His craving was for the celebrity that he knew would be his if he could only persuade the leaders of the Catholic Church—the Jesuit superiors, the cardinals, the pope—to replace Aristotle as an authority on the workings of the cosmos with himself. That was why, in the spring of 1611, he had travelled to Rome and hawked around his telescope. His efforts to make a name for himself among the city's movers and shakers had reaped spectacular success. Aristotle's cosmology had effectively been toppled. Schreck was only one among crowds of fans. Other Jesuits too—among them some of the most eminent mathematicians in Christendom—had corroborated Galileo's claims. A cardinal, Maffeo Barberini, had gone so far as to praise him in verse. Other, even more decisive marks of favour had followed twelve years later, in 1623, when Barberini was elected to the throne of Saint Peter. Now, as Urban VIII, he could grant his friend honours that were only a pope's to grant: private audiences, pensions, medals. Galileo, naturally enough, basked in the attention. But still he wanted more.

Schreck, praising the great astronomer to the Chinese, had celebrated him for one discovery in particular. Galileo's telescope had enabled him to keep close track of the planet Venus. 'Sometimes it is obscure, sometimes it is completely illuminated, sometimes it is illuminated either in the superior quarter or in the inferior quarter.' Just in case the implication of this was not clear, Schreck had made sure to spell it out. 'This proves that Venus is a satellite of the sun and travels around it.'[23] Here, as the Jesuits readily accepted, was yet another body blow to the model of the cosmos that the Church had inherited from Aristotle. The possibility that planets might revolve around the sun rather than the earth was not one that the philosopher had ever countenanced. How, then, was it to be explained? The model favoured by Schreck, one that had been in existence for some forty years, placed the planets in orbit around the sun, and the sun and moon in orbit around the earth. Complex though this was, it appeared to a majority of astronomers the one that best corresponded to the available evidence. There were some, however, who preferred an altogether more radical possibility. Among them was a Czech Jesuit, Wenceslas Kirwitzer, who had met Galileo in Rome, and then sailed with Schreck to China, where he had died in 1626. Prior to his departure, he had written a short pamphlet, arguing for heliocentrism: the hypothesis that the earth, just like Venus and the other planets, revolved around the sun.[24] The thesis was not Kirwitzer's own. The first book to propose it had been published back in 1543. Its author, the Polish astronomer Nicolaus Copernicus, had in turn drawn on the work of earlier scholars at Paris and Oxford, natural philosophers who had argued variously for the possibility that the earth might rotate on its axis, that the cosmos might be governed by laws of motion, even that space might be infinite. Daring though Copernicus' hypothesis seemed, then, it stood recognisably in a line of descent from a long and venerable tradition of Christian scholarship. Kirwitzer was not the only astronomer to have been persuaded by it. So too had a number of others; and of these the most high profile, the most prolific, the most pugnacious, was Galileo.

That heliocentrism ran contrary to the teachings of Aristotle was precisely part of the appeal it held for him; but there was another, even more formidable authority that could not so easily be brushed aside. In the book of Joshua, it was reported that God had commanded the sun to stand still; in the Book of Psalms, it was said of the world that 'it cannot be moved'.[25] Galileo, in his own way a devout Christian, never thought to argue that the Bible was wrong. All of scripture was true. That did not mean, however, that every passage had to be read literally. In support of this opinion, Galileo could—and did—cite the authority of the church fathers: Origen, Basil, Augustine. 'Thus, given that in many places the Scripture is not only capable but necessarily in need of interpretations different from the apparent meaning of the words, it seems to me that in disputes about natural phenomena it should be reserved to the last place.'[26]

Galileo was saying nothing new. His argument was one that had been serving as a licence for the study of natural philosophy since the time of Abelard. Nevertheless, in circles neurotically alert to the sulphur-stench of Lutheranism, it was enough to get nostrils flaring. The inquisition, while it was perfectly content for Galileo to report what he might observe through his telescope, had no intention of permitting him to interpret scripture simply as he pleased. Nevertheless, anxious not to make fools of themselves, the Roman inquisitors had taken pains to investigate what the case for Copernicus' hypothesis might actually be—and specifically whether it appeared to be contradicted by natural philosophy as well as by scripture. Eminent astronomers had been consulted; the temperature of expert opinion on the matter scrupulously taken. On 24 February 1616, a panel of eleven theologians had delivered their considered judgement: that certain proofs for heliocentrism did not exist, and that it should therefore be condemned as 'foolish and absurd in philosophy'.[27] Then, a few days later, a second shot had been fired across Galileo's bows. Roberto Bellarmino, a cardinal battle-hardened in the fight against heresy, and the Jesuits' most distinguished theologian, had invited him for a friendly chat. Any continued promotion of heliocentrism as established fact rather than merely as a hypothesis, Bellarmino had politely explained, would be met with a signal lack of enthusiasm by the Inquisition. The astronomer, recognising the glint of steel behind his host's smile, had bowed to the inevitable. 'The same Galileo,' it was recorded by Bellarmino's secretary, 'acquiesced in this injunction and promised to obey.'[28]

A demand for empirical evidence had gone head to head with wild supposition—and the demand for empirical evidence had won. That, at any rate, was how it appeared to the Inquisition. Speculation that the earth revolved around the sun continued to be perfectly licit; nor—despite the urging of the committee established to investigate it—was heliocentrism itself condemned as heretical. Only provide proof, Bellarmino had assured Galileo, and the Church would reconsider its opinion. 'But I will not believe that there is such a demonstration, until it is shown me.'[29] This, to Galileo's frustration, was a challenge he found himself unable to meet.

As the years slipped by, so his impatience only mounted. Painfully aware that Protestant astronomers were busy making the case for heliocentrism without risk or censorship, he longed to redeem the papacy from an error that he dreaded was making it a laughing stock. The argument was one that Galileo, following the papal election of 1623, had been able to press directly on the pope himself. Urban VIII, convinced that there would be no harm in his friend revisiting the issue of heliocentrism, provided only that he made sure to label it a hypothesis, was persuaded to give him the nod. For six years Galileo worked on his masterpiece: a fictional dialogue between an Aristotelian and a Copernican. Obedient to Urban's instructions, he made sure to balance his book's transparent enthusiasm for heliocentrism by citing the pope himself, who had sternly warned what folly it would be for any natural philosopher 'to limit and restrict the Divine power and wisdom to some particular fancy of his own'.[30] This statement, though, in the *Dialogue*, was put into the mouth of the Aristotelian: a man of such transparent stupidity that Galileo had named him Simplicio. The pope, alerted to what his friend had written, was persuaded by advisors hostile to Galileo that all his generosity was being flung back in his face.[31] Conscious as only an Italian nobleman could be of his own personal dignity, Urban felt himself called upon as well to defend the authority of the Universal Church. Galileo, summoned to Rome by the Inquisition, was put on trial. On 22 June 1633, he was condemned for having defended as 'probable' the hypothesis that 'the Earth moves and is not the centre of the world'.[32] Dressed in the white robe of a penitent, and kneeling arthritically before his judges, he abjured in a shaking voice all his heresies. His book was placed on the index of books that it was forbidden Catholics to read. Galileo himself was sentenced to imprisonment at the pleasure of the Inquisition. Spared their dungeons by Urban, the most celebrated natural philosopher in the world spent the remaining nine years of his life under house arrest.

The entire debacle had been a concatenation of misunderstandings, rivalries and wounded egos—but the scandal of it, all the same, reverberated across Christendom. The stakes appeared to many ferociously high. It had never been the rival claims of scripture and natural philosophy that were at issue: for, as Cardinal Bellarmino had pointed out back in 1616, both served to confirm that definite backing for Copernicus did not exist. Nor even, in the final reckoning, was it an argument about whether the sun moved: for a much more seismic issue was at stake. Galileo had been put on trial as Catholic fortunes, amid the killing fields of Germany, appeared in desperate straits. A succession of dramatic victories won by the Lutheran king of Sweden in defence of his fellow heretics had brought him almost as far south as the Alps. Even though the Swedish king himself had been killed in battle in 1632, Catholic fortunes still hung very much in the balance. Urban, snarled in a complex web of alliances and rivalries, was in no mood to cede an inch of his authority to a supercilious and egocentric natural philosopher. This in turn ensured that Protestants—whose dread of where the course of war in Germany might lead was no less than Catholics'—would attribute to the pope the blackest motives. Rather than a desperate attempt by the papacy to shore up its authority, they saw instead in the condemnation of Galileo an illustration of everything that they most detested and feared about the Roman Church. In 1638, when John Milton, a young English Puritan, visited Italy, he made a point of visiting Florence. 'There it was that I found and visited the famous *Galileo* grown old, a prisoner to the Inquisition, for thinking in Astronomy otherwise than the Franciscan and Dominican licencers thought.'[33] This, in the years to come, was how Protestants would consistently portray their Catholic opponents: as fanatics too bigoted to permit the study of the heavens. Galileo, meanwhile, they hailed as one of their own. A martyr to superstition, he was also a titan: one who, in the noblest tradition of Luther, had dispelled with the brilliance of his discoveries the murk of popery and Aristotle.

Yet natural philosophers knew better. They knew themselves, as Christians, bonded together in a single, common endeavour. The Jesuits in Beijing, certainly, did not hesitate to consult a heretic if they thought that it might aid their cause. Schreck had depended heavily on star-tables sent to him by a Lutheran. Protestant and Catholic, communicating with each other halfway across the world, had together shared their hopes that the Chinese might be brought to Christ. There was no better way to appreciate, perhaps, just how truly distinctive the Christian understanding of natural philosophy was, just how deeply rooted in the soil of Christendom, then to be a Jesuit in China. In 1634, the presentation to the Chinese emperor of a telescope had provided Galileo with an unexpectedly global seal of approval; but in Beijing there had been no great wave of excitement, no rush by princes and scholars to stare at craters on the moon, such as there had been in Rome. 'It is better to have no good astronomy than to have Westerners in China.'[34] So Yang Guangxian, a scholar resentful of the Jesuits' stranglehold on the Bureau of Astronomy, complained in the wake of Schreck's death. Correctly, he had identified the degree to which their ability to make sense of the heavens was rooted in assumptions that were exclusive to Christians. The obsession of the Jesuits with fathoming laws that might govern the cosmos, Yang charged, had led them to neglect what Confucian scholarship had always known to be the proper object of astronomy: divination. Briefly, he succeeded in having them removed from their posts. For six months, they were kept in prison, shackled to wooden stakes. Only the fortuitous intervention of an earthquake prevented their execution. Yet within four years the Jesuits were back in office. Yang's attempts to forecast eclipses had proven an embarrassing failure. There were no other Chinese astronomers capable of improving on his efforts. The understanding of the cosmos that underpinned the Jesuits' ability to draw up accurate calendars did not, it seemed, come easily to scholars from a radically different tradition. The Christian inheritance of natural philosophy had revealed itself to be nothing if not Christian through and through.

Amid the slaughter of the age, the communication of scholars across the lines that separated Protestant and Catholic was a reminder that, despite all their mutual hatreds, they still had much in common. 1650, the date that both Columbus and Luther had believed would herald the end of days, instead saw Germany, after thirty years of war, restored to peace. The world had not come to an end. The Turk had been kept at bay; Christianity still endured. Certainly, much had been lost. The venerable ideal of a shared unity in Christ—one to which so many over the centuries had committed themselves, even at the cost of their lives—had been irreparably shattered. There could be no soldering the fragments of Christendom back together, no reversing the process of its disintegration. For all that, the dust left by its shattered masonry still hung thick in the air; and if it was in what people had begun to call Europe that it was inhaled most deeply, then there were others too, whether in lonely settlements on the North Atlantic coast, or in Mexico, or in the lands of the distant Pacific, who breathed in its particles too. Galileo, looking to the future, had imagined his successors set on a course that was impossible for him to contemplate. 'There will be opened a gateway and a road to a large and excellent science, into which minds more piercing than mine shall penetrate to recesses still deeper.' It was not only sciences, though, that waited. There were many gateways, many roads.

The only constant was that they all had their origins in Christendom.

A nail driven through the heel bone of a crucifixion victim. Discovered in a tomb in Jerusalem, and dating from the first century AD, it is one of only two pieces of physical evidence ever found for the most notorious of Roman tortures. (Peter Oxley)

Jesus on the cross. Carved in the early fifth century, it is part of a series of ivory panels that together constitute the earliest known depiction of the Passion. Buff and ripped, Jesus boasts the physique of a victorious athlete. (British Museum)

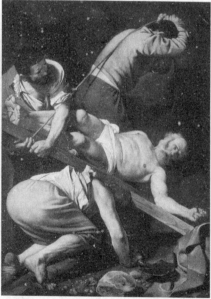

'When you are old you will stretch out your hands, and someone else will dress you and lead you where you do not want to go.' Caravaggio's painting of 1601, illustrating how Jesus' prophecy to Peter came to be fulfilled. (Heritage Image Partnership/Alamy Stock Photo)

'You, who shall be king hereafter, be firmly on your guard against the Lie. The man who shall be a follower of the Lie — punish him well.' Darius the Great, as portrayed on the side of Mount Bisitun, standing triumphant before a line of tethered liar kings. (© B. A. Tafreshi/Novapix/Bridgeman Images)

Demetrius of Phaleron: playboy, philosopher, ruler of Athens, librarian. (Peter Horree/Alamy Stock Photo)

This coin, minted in Persian-ruled Judah, is exceptional for portraying what Jews would come to believe should never be portrayed: the god they worshipped as the creator of the heavens and the earth, the Lord of Hosts, the Most High God, one, almighty, eternal. (Wikipedia)

Saint Paul, author of the most influential letters ever written, as portrayed in a fourth-century catacomb in Rome. (Courtesy of the Vatican's Pontifical Commission for Sacred Archaeology)

Saint Mark, who was believed to have founded the Church of Alexandria, with the walls and balconies of the great city rising behind him. Celebrated as a powerhouse of scholarship, Alexandria was home in the third century to Origen, a Christian as versed in Greek literature as he was in Jewish scripture. 'No one can truly do duty to God,' he declared, 'who does not think like a philosopher.' (Wikipedia)

Christ watches on approvingly as Saint Martin shares his cloak with a beggar. (Staatsbibliothek Bamberg)

Saint Michael, greatest of the angels, who at the end of days will hurl down 'that ancient called the devil, or Satan, who leads the whole world astray'. (Cameraphoto Arte Venezia/Bridgeman Images)

The book which Saint Boniface – the 'Apostle of the Germans' – reputedly held up to defend himself from the swords of the Frisian pirates who murdered him. (Hessisches Staatsarchiv Darmstadt)

Canossa, the castle where Henry IV sought absolution from Gregory VII on a freezing winter's day in 1076, has become emblematic of the conflict between empire and papacy: the cracking of an ancient order, and the onset of the first European revolution. (Tom Holland)

'The dull mind rises to the truth through material things.' The interplay of darkness and light in Saint-Denis. (Tom Holland)

Elizabeth of Hungary submits to her master of spiritual discipline. 'Willingly she sustained repeated lashes and blows from Master Conrad – being mindful of the beatings endured by the Lord.'

(Akg-images/Jean-Claude Varga)

Jesus before Caiphas, the Jewish high priest. It was in the thirteenth century, when this manuscript was produced, that Jews first began to be portrayed by Christian illustrators as physically repulsive: hook-nosed and stooped. (British Library/Bridgeman Images)

Guglielma, an enigmatic aristocrat reported by inquisitors to have claimed that 'she was the Holy Spirit made flesh for the redemption of women'. The nun kneeling before her is most likely Maifreda, an abbess from Milan who aspired to become pope, and ended up burnt at the stake. (Tom Holland)

Bernardino of Siena, the most famous preacher of his day, and a notably implacable scourge of sodomites, preaches in the central piazza of his native city. (World History Archive/Alamy Stock Photo)

The Four Horsemen of the Apocalypse, one of a series of fifteen woodcuts by Albrecht Dürer illustrating the book of Revelation. Published in 1498, they gave vivid form to an expectation widespread across Christendom that the end of days was approaching fast. (British Museum)

The bubbles on this statue represent lumpy fat deposits of flayed human skin. Xipe Totec, worshipped in central America as the Flayed One, appeared to the Christian conquerors of the Mexica not a god but a demon.

(De Agostini Picture Library/G. Dagli Orti/Bridgeman Images)

Martin Luther, who as a monk had been notably scrawny, ended up putting on so much weight that he was denounced by one adversary as a dainty for the Devil. (PRISMA ARCHIVO/Alamy Stock Photo)

John Calvin, as portrayed on the Reformation Wall, built in Geneva to commemorate the four-hundredth anniversary of his birth. 'If you desire to have me as your pastor,' he told the people of his adopted city, 'then you will have to correct the disorder of your lives.' (James Holland)

Matteo Ricci, the Christian who became a mandarin, with Xu Guangqi, the mandarin who became a Christian.

(AF Fotografie/Alamy Stock Photo)

Galileo's condemnation by the Inquisition for having defended the hypothesis that 'the Earth moves and is not the centre of the world' was not, as subsequent myth would have it, due to a reluctance on the part of the Catholic Church to pay attention to the opinion of eminent astronomers, but the precise opposite. (De Agostini Picture Library/U. Marsani/Bridgeman Images)

A stone carved in 1999 to commemorate the 350th anniversary of the occupation by the Diggers of St George's Hill. It could not be established on the actual site of the Diggers' attempt to set the earth free 'from intanglements of Lords and Landlords' because St George's Hill is now a gated community, and therefore off-limits to the general public.

(Tom Holland)

'A book forged in hell.' Spinoza's attempt to disguise his authorship of the *Theological-Political Treatise* did not fool its readers for long. (Eric Grangeon)

Benjamin Lay, the four-foot hunchback who devoted his life to an ultimately successful campaign to persuade his fellow Quakers to condemn the slave trade.

(History and Art Collection/Alamy Stock Photo)

The Declaration of the Rights of Man and of the Citizen, portrayed as though delivered on tablets of stone from Mount Sinai. (Musée de la Ville de Paris, Musée Carnavalet, Paris, France/Bridgeman Images)

The Marquis de Sade, whose conviction that some people were naturally masters and some were naturally slaves, saw him incarcerated in a succession of prisons and lunatic asylums. 'The doctrine of loving one's neighbour,' he insisted, 'is a fantasy that we owe to Christianity and not to Nature'. (Wikipedia)

A cartoon published in 1815 shows Brahmins bribing the Governor General of Bengal and the Bishop of Calcutta to allow the continuance of 'suttee': the self-immolation of widows on the pyres of their husbands. British officials, nervous of doing damage to their business interests by offending against Indian custom, were reluctant to ban suttee until it could be proven that the practise was not, after all, a universally accepted feature of the 'Hindoo religion'. (Wellcome Collection)

Cologne Cathedral, begun in 1248 and left unfinished by workmen in 1473. When Friedrich Wilhelm, the young crown prince of Prussia, first visited the building site in 1814, he was enraptured. In 1842, two years after becoming king, he ordered work to begin on it again. The cathedral was finally completed in 1880. (Wikipedia)

Richard von Krafft-Ebing, the German psychiatrist who in the second half of the nineteenth century popularised the novel concept of 'homosexuality'. A sexual practice condemned by the Church as 'sodomy' was, Krafft-Ebing argued, perfectly compatible with the ideal that he saw as Christianity's great contribution to civilisation: lifelong monogamous love. (Stefano Bianchetti/Getty)

Andrew Carnegie unveils the cast of a *Diplodocus* in London's museum of natural history: a building intended by its founder to have the ambience of a cathedral, and to 'return good for evil'. (Natural History Museum)

'After a terrible earthquake, a tremendous *reflection*, with new questions.' Otto Dix's life-size bust of Friedrich Nietzsche. (Tom Holland)

The Lord of the Rings was the best-selling book by a Christian published in the twentieth century. Its success spoke powerfully of the strong hold that Christianity continued to exert on the imagination of people in the West – but also of its fading. (The Bodleian Library, University of Oxford folio 21)

Love is all you need.

(David Magnus/REX/Shutterstock)

'You have heard that it was said, "Love your neighbour and hate your enemy." But I tell you: love your enemies and pray for those who persecute you, that you may be sons of your Father in heaven.'

(Sipa USA/REX/Shutterstock)

Protestors summon men to exercise control over their lusts — just as the Puritans had once done. (Matt Rourke/AP/REX/Shutterstock)

Part III

❖

MODERNITAS

15

SPIRIT

1649: St George's Hill

On 26 May, the day that the Lord General with his train of officers came riding to St George's Hill, there were twelve people working on the heath. They were variously digging, and planting, and spreading manure. The venture was a bold one. The land had been crown property since ancient times. The law of trespass strictly forbade any sowing on it. Times, though, were hard, and there were some locals, faced with destitution, who had come to despise the very notion of private property. Leading them was a smallholder named Gerrard Winstanley, a former cloth-merchant who had moved out of London into the Surrey countryside after going bankrupt in 1643. The entire earth, he declared, was 'a common Treasury for all, both Rich and Poor'.[1] On 1 April 1649, obedient to a direct command of the Holy Spirit, he had taken his spade and gone to the nearby St George's Hill, and there broken the ground. Various other men and women had joined him. Now, almost two months on, and despite all the hostility they had provoked among neighbouring landowners, the 'Diggers' were still busy among their corn, their carrots and their beans. 'For in this work of restoration,' so Winstanley defiantly insisted, 'there will be no beggar in Israel.'[2]

The approach of soldiers on horseback would normally have filled any trespassers on crown lands with terror. The times, though, were not normal. Four months earlier, on a bitterly cold winter day, the king of England had been beheaded outside his own palace of Whitehall. The charge had been high treason. Shortly afterwards the monarchy itself had been abolished. To royalists—of whom there remained many in England—the execution of Charles I, God's anointed, had been not just a crime, but a blasphemy. Nothing like it had ever been seen before. Yet that, for supporters of the new English commonwealth, was precisely the point. The causes that had brought the king into armed conflict with his parliament were many, and the road that had led him to the scaffold long and winding; but none of those who had sat in judgement on him ever doubted that God's finger was manifest in the redrawing of England. Winstanley agreed. Monarchy, he declared, was a usurpation of the power of God. So too was the rule of every lord. Like the followers of Pelagius who, long before, had mocked any notion that wealth might not be tyranny, Winstanley took literally the warnings of scripture, which 'threaten misery to rich men, bidding them Howl and weep'.[3] The return of Christ, which he believed imminent, would not be from the heavens, but in the flesh of men and women. All were to share equally in the treasury of the earth. The evils of Adam's fall were destined to be reversed. If Winstanley, in preparing for this happy eventuality, was perfectly content to sanction the whipping of those who refused to pull their weight, and even—in extreme cases—their enslavement, then that was due reflection of his utter confidence in his cause. To dig on St George's Hill was to regain paradise.

Quite what the Lord General might make of all this, however, was open to question. Sir Thomas Fairfax—although he commanded the army which, following its remodelling in 1645 into the most formidable fighting force in Europe, had brought the king to defeat—did not approve of regicide. Already, on 16 April, he had been alerted to the activities of the Diggers. Winstanley, summoned to Whitehall to explain himself, had on that occasion succeeded in persuading Fairfax that he and his project presented no threat to the order of the Commonwealth; but now, one month on, circumstances had changed. Mutiny had broken out. Only swift action by Fairfax and his deputy Oliver Cromwell, a general as formidable as he was devout, had succeeded in breaking it. The mutineers had been taken by surprise at night in Burford, a town west of Oxford. The next morning, three of them had been executed in a churchyard. Order had successfully been restored. Fairfax, however, as he headed back to London, had good reason to view the Diggers with renewed suspicion. Christ, who had foretold the doom of the rich, and whose return would see the poor inherit the earth, was hailed by Winstanley as 'the greatest, first, and truest Leveller that ever was spoke of in the world'.[4] The title of 'Leveller' was not in fact original to him. It was one that the mutineers had already claimed as their own. Like Winstanley, they believed that rank and wealth were evils; that all were by nature equal; that Christ's work was to be 'the Restorer and Repairer of man's loss and fall'.[5] Soldiers, though, could not be Diggers. Without rank there would be no discipline; and without discipline there would be no army. Godliness in England did not stand so secure that it could afford that. Cromwell, leaving Burford, had begun to prepare an expedition to Ireland, a notorious sump of popery, where royalists continued to plot the return of monarchy to England, and the overthrow of everything that the army had fought so long and hard to achieve. The responsibility of Fairfax, meanwhile, was to keep his lieutenant-general's rear secure. The Lord General, as he turned off the highway to London and rode with his attendants to inspect St George's Hill, had much on his mind.

Arriving before the Diggers, he gave them a short speech of admonition. Winstanley, though, was nothing daunted. Scorning to remove his hat, he scorned as well to moderate his views. Soberly though he spoke, he was not the man to bit or bridle the Spirit. More than a century before, in the first throes of the Reformation, Thomas Müntzer had proclaimed that scripture itself was a less certain witness of truth than God's direct speaking to the soul; and now, in the hothouse of the English Commonwealth, the Spirit was once again bringing enlightenment to common men and women. 'I have nothing,' Winstanley insisted, 'but what I do receive from a free discovery within.'[6] The proofs of God's purpose were more surely to be found in a ploughboy whose heart had been suffused with an awareness of the essential goodness of mankind than they ever were in churches. Just as Müntzer had done, Winstanley despised the book-wrangling of pastors. 'All places stink with the abomination of Self-seeking Teachers and Rulers.' True wisdom was the knowledge of God that all mortals could have, if only they were prepared to open themselves to the Spirit: for God, Winstanley proclaimed, was Reason. It was Reason that would lead humanity to foreswear the very concept of possessions; to join in building a heaven on earth. His foes might dismiss Winstanley as a dreamer; but he was not the only one. The occupation of St George's Hill was a declaration of hope: that others some day would join the Diggers, and the world would be as one.

Wild talk such as this had always provoked alarm. 'Anabaptist' remained a dirty word across Europe. If common men and women were to cast themselves as vessels of the Spirit, unmediated by the guidance of their betters, then who knew where it might end? Truth could not compromise with error. Pastors and presbyters—anxious to preserve from damnation the souls of those in their care—believed this no less devoutly than any inquisitor. The horrors of Münster had not been forgotten. Liberty might readily become a menace. Heresy, idolatry, schism: all had to be sternly guarded against. There might even be need—should an offender prove contumacious—to invoke the ultimate sanction. Calvin himself, in 1553, had approved the burning at the stake of a particularly notorious heretic, a propagandist for views on the Trinity so shocking as barely to be trinitarian at all. Within living memory, in 1612, a heretic had been burned in England for questioning in a similar manner the divinity of Christ and the Spirit. The vast majority of Puritans, taking up arms against the king in 1642, had fought him in the conviction that toleration was 'the whore of Babylon's back door'.[7] If the elements of popery in the Church of England were a palpable evil, then so too were the blasphemies of Protestant sectarians. When even scripture might count for nothing before the claims of tinkers and housemaids to direct revelations from God, there was a risk, it seemed to many Puritans, that God himself would end up doubted. 'A liberty of judgment is pretended, and queries are proposed, until nothing certain be left, nothing unshaken.'[8]

Victory over the king, though, had not led to a tightening of the reins of discipline. Quite the opposite. Despite the passing in 1648 of a blasphemy ordinance that punished anti-trinitarianism with death, and a host of other heresies with imprisonment, it had proved impossible to enforce. The streets of London—which had witnessed an archbishop of Canterbury as well as a king being led to the block—seethed with contempt for the very notion of authority. Practices and beliefs that previously had lurked in the shadows burst into spectacular flower. Baptists who, as the more radical of the first generation of Protestants had done, dismissed infant baptism as an offence against scripture; Quakers, who would shake and foam at the mouth with the intensity of their possession by the Spirit; Ranters, who believed that every human being was equally a part of God: all made a mockery of any notion of a single national church. Their spread, to enthusiasts for Presbyterian discipline, was like that of the plague. Christian order in England seemed at risk of utter disintegration.

Yet one believer's anarchy might just as well be another's freedom. Presbyterians who sought to make criminals of other Protestants for laying claim to the gifts of the Spirit had to tread carefully. Aflame as they were with the transformative effect of God's grace, they might easily be cast as hypocrites. Milton, whose visit to Galileo had steeled him in his loathing for censorship, warned his fellow Puritans that Calvin's example risked dazzling them. To idolise the reformers of an earlier age was to behave no better than papists. The course of true reform was never done. It was always a work in progress. Every

Christian had to be free to seek his own path to God. It was not the business of a state, still less that of a church, to trammel the workings of the Spirit. 'No man or body of men in these times can be the infallible judges or determiners in matters of religion to any other men's consciences but their own.'[9]

But what, in a Protestant country, was 'religion'? Cut from its Catholic moorings, the word had come to evolve two distinct meanings. It was, so Charles I had declared, 'the only firm foundation of all power: that cast loose, or depraved, no government can be stable'.[10] Presbyterians agreed. The conception of religion for which both sides in the civil war had been fighting was essentially the same: an understanding of what England's proper relationship to God should be. If this alone was to be viewed as true, then plainly it could not tolerate a rival. The Reformation needed to be completed; its victory had to be total. Yet that was not the whole story. Religion was also something intimate, personal. A word once used to describe the communal life in an abbey or a convent had come to take on a very different meaning: the private relationship that a Protestant might have with the workings of the Spirit. Fairfax, admonishing the Diggers, spoke both as a Presbyterian and as a man charged by his office with the maintenance of true religion in England; but Winstanley, when he spoke of his duty to God and refused point blank to abandon St George's Hill, was equally being obedient to his religion. Fairfax, aware of this, opted not to force the issue. Satisfied a second time that the Diggers presented no threat to public order, he returned to the road, and continued on his way to London. Winstanley and his companions, meanwhile, went back to their digging.

Between the demands of those who believed that there was only the one true religion, and those who believed that God wished all to practise their religion freely, there could be no easy reconciliation. That Fairfax had even attempted to steer a middle course reflected the fact that, as Lord General, he held a more pre-eminent position of authority in the Commonwealth than any civilian. The true victory in the war against the king had gone not to parliament, but to the army.

To command it was—inevitably—to be charged with attempting to square a circle. By 1650, Fairfax had had enough. A man much happier in the saddle than in the council chamber, he resigned his commission. His replacement was a man altogether more comfortable in the exercise of power, and who also, unlike Fairfax, was no Presbyterian: Oliver Cromwell. When, in late 1653, he was appointed Lord Protector of the Commonwealth, he ruled both as a military autocrat and as England's first-ever Protestant head of state to support liberty of conscience. A civil war that had been fought between two rival programmes of authoritarian rule was recast by his propagandists as a struggle for freedom. The founding constitution of the Protectorate made this explicit. 'Such as profess faith in God by Jesus Christ,' it proclaimed, 'shall not be restrained from, but shall be protected in, the profession of the faith and the exercise of their religion.'[11]

A ringing declaration—but shadowed by ambivalence. Who precisely were to be defined as those professing faith in God by Jesus Christ? Not Catholics, that was to be sure. In May 1649, on the eve of Cromwell's expedition to Ireland, leaflets had circulated among the mutineers at Burford, lamenting the slaughter that was to come. 'We have waded too far in that crimson stream (already) of innocent and Christian blood.'[12] Here was an expression of the same revulsion and despair that on the continent, the previous year, had helped at last to end thirty years of slaughter. By terms of a series of treaties signed in the German territory of Westphalia, a 'Christian, general and permanent peace'[13] had been brought to the blood-manured lands of the Empire. The princes who signed it pledged themselves not to force their own religion on their subjects. Catholics, Lutherans, Calvinists: all were granted the freedom to worship as they pleased. This formula, far from an attempt to banish religion from the workings of the state, constituted the precise opposite: a project to establish a properly Christian order. Rather than a betrayal of Christ, who had urged his followers to love their enemies, and to turn the other cheek, it expressed a conscious ambition to measure up to his teachings. Toleration of religious difference had been enshrined as a Christian virtue.

Cromwell, victorious in his own wars to a degree that no general on the continent had succeeded in matching, and confident of God's backing because of it, had felt no call to extend a matching toleration to the Catholic rebels in Ireland. His campaigning there had been obedient to the same rules of war that had brought such ruin to Germany; but Cromwell himself, far from lamenting its horrors, had exulted in his role as an instrument of divine justice. As Lord Protector, he was similarly unbending. Papists, while free to believe what they liked, could not be licensed to practise their ungodly rituals. That there were Protestants in England bold enough to condemn this as hypocrisy did not sway him. Arguments such as that made by a one-time publisher of Milton, that 'a Protestant sermon is as idolatrous to a Papist, as a Popish Mass is to a Protestant',[14] only provoked his indignation. Radicals, when they pushed at the limits of what he regarded as acceptable opinion, bewildered and aggravated him. They were, he declared, 'a despicable and contemptible generation of men'.[15]

Revolution had come to England amid the tumult of battles and executions. Nevertheless, throughout Cromwell's protectorate, it wore as well a more sober aspect: that of a trade-off. Between the yearning of Presbyterians for a purified commonwealth, and the demands of radicals for an absolute liberty of religion, the Lord Protector trod a delicate path. When an anti-trinitarian was sentenced to exile, and a Quaker who had impersonated Christ to mutilation, neither side was satisfied. Yet it was clear, from Cromwell's personal interventions to ensure that both were spared the death penalty, and his readiness to allow the blasphemy ordinance of 1648 to wither on the vine, where his convictions ultimately lay. It was not—as it had been for the diplomats who had drawn up the treaties of Westphalia—the need to patch up a peace with his enemies that prompted him to accept toleration as a Christian duty. Rather, it was his sense of himself as a vessel of the Spirit, and his attentive reading of scripture. 'You, then,' Paul had demanded of the Romans, 'why do you judge your brother? Or why do you look down on your brother? For we will all stand before God's judgement seat.'[16]

Cromwell, despite the ambition that had helped to raise him from provincial obscurity to the rule of Britain, was a man far too conscious of God's prerogatives ever to contemplate usurping them. He had rather see Islam practised in England, he declared, 'than that one of God's Children should be persecuted'.[17] Books might be burnt; but not the men who wrote them. Even Papists, despite Cromwell's loathing for their religion, were known to be guests at his table. In 1657, in a particularly startling gesture, he moved to ensure that the son of the founder of Maryland—a colony established in the New World specifically to provide a haven for English Catholics—should not be deprived of his rights to the province. Toleration, then, was a principle that even God's most faithful servants might opt to uphold in a range of ways. The illumination of the Spirit was not always easy to translate into policy. On occasion, rather than in an ecstasy of certainty, it might need to be answered with compromises. Godliness, it seemed, might sometimes be expressed through ambiguity.

No Other Teacher but the Light

When Cromwell joked about Islam, he could afford to be insouciant. There was not the remotest prospect of Muslims wishing to settle in England, of course. Nevertheless, the issue of whether a godly Commonwealth should tolerate those who did not acknowledge Christ as Lord was a topical one. In 1655, a rabbi resident in Amsterdam arrived in London. Menasseh ben Israel had come with a request. Appealing directly to Cromwell, he begged that Jews be granted a legal right of residency in England. The ban imposed in 1290 had never been rescinded. There were plenty of Protestants who thought it never should be. Christian hostility to Jews, far from being moderated by the Reformation, had in many ways been refined by it. Luther, reading Paul's letter to the Galatians, had found in it a direct inspiration for his own campaign against the papacy. The Spirit was all. Those who denied the primacy of faith as the way to God—be they papists, be they Jews—were guilty of a baneful legalism. Desiccated and sterile, they blocked the panting sinner from the revivifying waters of the truth. To Luther, the enduring insistence of the Jews that they were God's Chosen People was a personal affront. 'We foolish Gentiles, who were not God's people, are now God's people. That drives the Jews to distraction and stupidity.'[18] If anyone had been driven to distraction, though, it was Luther. By the end of his life, he had come to nurture fantasies of persecution that went far beyond anything the papacy had ever sanctioned. The Jews, he had demanded, should be rounded up, housed beneath one roof, put to hard labour. Their prayer books, their Talmuds, their synagogues: all should be burned. 'And whatever will not burn should be buried and covered with dirt, so that no man will ever again see so much as a stone or cinder of them.'[19]

Even Luther's admirers tended to regard this as a bit extreme. Widespread though resentment of the Jews might be among Protestants, there were also some who felt sympathy for them. In England, where the self-identification of Puritans as the new Israel had fostered a boom in the study of Hebrew, this might on occasion shade almost into admiration. Even before Menasseh's arrival in London, there were sectarians who claimed it a sin 'that the Jews were not allowed the open profession and exercise of their religion amongst us'.[20] Some warned that God's anger was bound to fall on England unless repentance was shown for their expulsion. Others demanded their readmission so that they might the more easily be won for Christ, and thereby expedite the end of days. Cromwell, who convened an entire conference in Whitehall to debate Menasseh's request, was sympathetic to this perspective. Nevertheless, he failed to win formal backing for it. Accordingly—in typical fashion—he opted for compromise. Written permission for the Jews to settle in England was denied; but Cromwell did give Menasseh the private nod, and a pension of a hundred pounds. The practical effect of this was noted by a diarist that same December. 'Now were the Jews admitted.'[21]

Yet in not nearly large enough numbers to satisfy some in England. Friends, as Quakers called themselves, felt charged with a mission to the Jews. 'The Lord moved his good spirit in me, and his word came unto me, (which was in me as a fire).'[22] It was this burning impulse to proclaim God's kingdom—which might inspire some Friends to preach naked, and others in sackcloth and ashes—that had frustrated all attempts by the authorities to extinguish it. Unlike the Diggers, all of whom had ended up evicted from their various communes by local landowners, the Quakers had positively flourished in the face of official hostility. Women were particularly active. One, marching into Cromwell's private quarters in Whitehall, boldly addressed the Protector as a 'dunghill', and then spent an hour urging him to repentance; another, a one-time housemaid, travelled to Constantinople, where she somehow succeeded in preaching to the sultan himself. It was the Jews, though, who were a particular object of Quaker hopes. The refusal of Cromwell to grant them a formal right of admission prompted missionaries to head for Amsterdam. The early signs were not promising. The Jews there seemed resolutely uninterested in the Quakers' message; the authorities were hostile; only one of the missionaries spoke Dutch. Nevertheless, it was not the Quaker way to despair. There was, so one of the missionaries reported, 'a spark in many of the Jews' bosoms, which in process of time may kindle to a burning flame'.[23]

Here, to any Friend, was encouragement enough. Well read though Quakers might be in scripture, they, like other radicals, did not view it as the most direct source of truth. The most excitable among them—to the embarrassment of their leaders—were known on occasion to burn Bibles in public. Only an unmediated openness to the Spirit could enable the rancorous sectarianism that bedevilled other Christians to be transcended. 'He that puts the letter for the light, when the letter says Christ is the light, is blind.'[24] Quite how this light was to be defined—whether as the conscience natural to all humans mentioned by Paul, or as the Spirit, or as Christ, or as a mingling of all three, or perhaps as something else entirely—was a question to which Quakers could never provide a consistent answer. This, though, did not greatly bother them. To feel the light was to know it. Such was the message that Margaret Fell, one of the founding members of the Friends, addressed directly to Menasseh. A second pamphlet, *A Loving Salutation, to the Seed of Abraham Among the Jews*, quickly followed. Anxious to get both tracts into Hebrew, the Quaker missionaries in Amsterdam were delighted to report back to Fell that they had successfully procured the services of a translator. This translator was not only a skilled linguist; he had also been a pupil of none other than Menasseh himself.[25]

Baruch Spinoza was no ordinary Jew. Indeed, he barely considered himself a Jew at all. In July 1656, he had been formally expelled, cursed and damned by the synagogue in Amsterdam. Such a sentence was not unheard of, and was issued in the full expectation that offenders—rather than risk being cut off permanently from their own community—would scrabble to make their peace with the synagogue's governing board. But Spinoza refused to make peace. He had alternative ports of call. Rather than the Quaker missionaries in Amsterdam approaching him, it was he who had approached the Friends. Writing to Margaret Fell, one of them explained that Spinoza had been 'Cast out (as he himself and others sayeth) because he owneth no other teacher but the light...'[26] Whether this was an accurate report or not, it was certainly the case that Spinoza, in the wake of his excommunication, did not lack for companionship and support. Rather than with the Quakers, though, it was with their nearest Dutch equivalents that he had sought refuge. Collegiants, as they were called, were recognisably bred of the same soil as their fellow radicals in England. They scorned the claims to authority of the public Church; disdained all ideals of hierarchy and priesthood; despaired of sectarian rivalries and quarrels. Spinoza's Dutch friends, like his Quaker contacts, believed that true holiness was enlightenment. 'This it is which leads man in truth, into the way to

God, which excuseth him in well-doing, giving him peace in his conscience, yea, brings him to union with God, wherein all happiness and salvation consist.'[27]

To settle among such Protestants—as Spinoza did in 1660, when he moved to Rijnsberg, a village outside Leiden that had become the centre of Collegiant life—was very consciously to take sides in what had become the major division in Dutch society. The purging of dissident preachers in 1619 had provided the Reformed Church with only a temporary victory. For decades, rival promoters of discipline and toleration had been locked in effective stalemate. Meanwhile, in England, fresh upheavals were serving to sharpen the sense of what was at stake. Two years after the death of Cromwell in 1658, the monarchy was restored—and the Church of England with it. An Act of Uniformity served to push Quakers and other religious dissenters to the margins. The warning to Protestants in the Netherlands who rejected the pretensions of institutional churches, who affirmed that personal enlightenment was the surest guide to truth, who read the word of God as something written pre-eminently on their consciences, appeared a grim one. The enemies of toleration were everywhere. Freedom could never be taken for granted—not even in the Dutch Republic. When Spinoza, in 1665, began preparing a book in defence of religious liberty, the praise he offered his homeland was touched by irony as well as gratitude. 'We are fortunate to enjoy the rare happiness of living in a republic where every person's liberty to judge for himself is respected, everyone is permitted to worship God according to his own mind, and nothing is thought dearer or sweeter than freedom.'[28]

It was Calvin himself who had proposed that true obedience to God should be grounded in liberty.[29] Spinoza, when he pushed the case for toleration, was participating in a debate that had always been fundamental to Protestantism. This did not mean, however, that he saw himself as bounded by it. Quite the opposite. Spinoza's ambition was to demonstrate that to quarrel at all over religion, let alone to fight over it, was idiocy. By profession a lens grinder, fine-tuning glasses for both telescopes and microscopes, he knew what it was to hone an instrument that could reveal wonders invisible to the naked eye. Spinoza beheld the cosmos, not as a Christian, still less as a Jew, but as a philosopher. Rather than pick at the Gordian knot of theology, he sought instead to cut directly through it. Already, by 1662, rumours of his shocking opinions had begun to swirl around Amsterdam. Spinoza, it was reported, believed every substance to be infinite, and incapable of producing another. That being so, there could exist only a single substance. God was 'nothing other than the whole universe'.[30] He did not exist beyond the laws that governed the cosmos, and which generations of natural philosophers had committed themselves to identifying: he was those laws. Abelard, declaring that 'everything that originates without miracles can be adequately accounted for', had spoken more truly than he had ever imagined. Miracles did not exist. They were an impossibility. There was only nature, and all God's decrees, all his commandments, all his providence, were in truth only nature's order. No less than Calvin, Spinoza saw the destiny of every human being as irrevocably preordained. God, though, was no divine judge. He was geometry. 'For all things follow from God's eternal decree with the same necessity as from the essence of a triangle it follows that its three angles are equal to two right angles.'[31]

This was not, of course, a God that most pastors would have recognised—which was, for Spinoza, precisely the point. His ambition in questioning the very fundamentals of Christian belief was political as well as philosophical. 'How pernicious it is,' he declared, 'both for religion and the state to allow ministers of things sacred to acquire the right to make decrees or handle the business of government.'[32] There were plenty of Protestants who agreed; but increasingly, in the Dutch Republic, the tide seemed to be turning against them. In 1668, a Reformed preacher who had come strongly under Spinoza's influence was arrested; his brother, convicted on a charge of blasphemy, died in prison a year later. Spinoza, putting the finishing touches to his book, did so in the conviction that the only way to annihilate the authority of the Reformed Church was to attack the deep foundations on which it ultimately depended. Religion itself had to be discredited. Simultaneously, Spinoza knew how dangerously he was treading. The *Theological-Political Treatise*, when it was published in Amsterdam early in 1670, did not have his name on the cover. It also declared its place of publication to be Hamburg. The guardians of Reformed orthodoxy were not fooled. By the summer of 1674, the Dutch authorities had been persuaded to issue a formal ban on Spinoza's book. The directive imposing it listed an entire litany of its most monstrous blasphemies: 'against God and his attributes, and his worshipful trinity, against the divinity of Jesus Christ and his true mission, along with the fundamental dogmas of the true Christian religion, and in effect the authority of Holy Scripture...'[33] The notoriety of Spinoza as an enemy of the Christian religion was assured.

Yet in truth, the *Theological-Political Treatise* was a book that only a man utterly saturated in Protestant assumptions could ever have written. What rendered it so unsettling to the Dutch authorities was less that it served as a repudiation of their beliefs than that it pushed them to a remorseless conclusion. Spinoza's genius was to turn strategies that Luther and Calvin had deployed against popery on Christianity itself. When he lamented just how many people were 'in thrall to pagan superstition',[34] when he dismissed the rituals of baptism or the celebration of feast days as mere idle 'ceremony',[35] and when he lamented that the original teachings of Christ had been corrupted by popes, he was arguing nothing that a stern Reformed pastor might not also have argued. Even the most scandalous of his claims—that a belief in miracles was superstitious nonsense, and that a close reading of scripture would demonstrate it to have been of human rather than divine origin—were merely Protestant arguments pushed to a radical extreme. When Spinoza sought to substantiate them, he described himself—just as he had done to the Quakers—as a pupil of 'the light'. Naturally, he did not cast his own experience of enlightenment as anything supernatural. Those who claimed to be illumined by the Spirit were, he scoffed, merely fabricating a sanction for their own fantasies. True enlightenment derived from reason. 'I do not presume that I have found the best philosophy,' Spinoza wrote to a former pupil who, to his dismay, had converted to Catholicism, 'but I know that I understand the true one.'[36] Here too he was pursuing a familiar strategy. Protestants had been insisting on the correctness of their own readings of scripture, their own understandings of God's purpose, since the time of Luther's confrontation with Cajetan. Now, in the person of Spinoza, this tradition had begun to cannibalise itself.

Spinoza himself, though, saw it as something more than merely Protestant. A Jew learned in the law of his ancestors, who had left his own community to preach a radical and unsettling new message, he did not hesitate to hint at whom he saw as his most obvious forebear. 'Paul, when he was first converted, saw God as a great light.'[37] This light, so Spinoza strongly implied, had been authentically divine. Paul, unlike Moses or the prophets, had adopted the methods of a philosopher: debating with his opponents, and submitting his teachings to the judgement of others. Spinoza's critique of Judaism, for all that it might be disguised by a tone of scholarly detachment, was recognisably Christian. He admired Paul much as Luther had done: as the apostle who had brought to all of humanity the good news that God's commandments were written on their hearts. Unlike the Old Testament—a term pointedly used throughout the *Theological-Political Treatise*—the New bore witness to a law that was for all peoples, not just the one; that constituted 'true liberty'[38] rather than a burdensome legalism; that was best comprehended by means of the light. 'Anyone therefore who abounds in the fruits of love, joy, peace, long-suffering, kindness, goodness, faithfulness, gentleness and self-control, against whom (as Paul says in his Epistle to the Galatians 5.22) there is no law, he, whether he has been taught by reason alone or by Scripture alone, has truly been taught by God, and is altogether happy.'[39]

Spinoza certainly did not approve of all the Christian virtues. Humility and repentance he dismissed as irrational; pity as 'evil and unprofitable'.[40] Nevertheless, his equation of Christ's teachings with the universal laws of nature was a manoeuvre as audacious as it was brilliant. To Christians unenthused by the prospect of worshipping a triangle, it offered what would prove a momentous reassurance: that much of Christianity, even without a belief in the creator God of Israel, might still be retained. Although Spinoza was privately disdainful of any notion that Jesus might have risen from the dead, he unhesitatingly affirmed in the *Theological-Political Treatise* that Christ—as he always made sure to call him—was a man who had indeed attained a superhuman degree of perfection. 'Therefore his voice may be called the voice of God.'[41] Even in his unpublished writings, Spinoza maintained this tone of awe. Liberty—the cause which he valued above all others, and to which he had devoted his entire career—he identified directly with 'the Spirit of Christ'.[42] Notorious as an enemy of religion though Spinoza rapidly became throughout Europe, there remained in his attitude to Jesus the sense of a profound enigma. When, in the decades that followed his death in 1677, both his enemies and his admirers hailed him as 'the chief atheist of our age',[43] the ambivalences in his attitude to Christianity, and the way in which his philosophy constituted less a beginning than a mutation, were rapidly occluded. Quakers, when they preached that it was the inner light which enabled the truth to be known, and Collegiants, when they preached that it was Christ, had both been beating a path for Spinoza. All of them, whether they trusted in the Spirit, or reason, or both, had dreamed that sectarian disputes might be resolved for good; and all of them had failed.

Spinoza, far from quieting the babel of competing doctrines, had instead only added to them yet another variant on Christian belief.

The Hunchback's Progress

To be a Christian was to be a pilgrim. This conviction, widely shared by Protestants, did not imply any nostalgia for the dark days of popery, when monks had gulled the faithful into trekking vast distances to bow and scrape before bogus relics. Rather, it meant to journey through life in the hope that at its end the pilgrim would be met by shining angels, and dressed in raiment that shone like gold, and led into heaven, a city on a hill. Such a commitment was not lightly undertaken. There were bound to be many impediments along the way: sloughs of despond, and fairs full of vanities, and times when despair seemed to loom up like a giant. Many, rather than toil along such a road, shouldering the burden that was the consciousness of their own sin, understandably chose to stay where they were. But that, for those who had come to realise that they were living in the city of Destruction, could never be an option. 'Down I fell, as a Bird that is shot from the top of a Tree, into great guilt and fearful despair.'[44] So recalled one itinerant preacher, of the darkness that had preceded the light of the coming of the Spirit. From that time on, all his life had been a tireless journeying towards holiness. Such it was to be a pilgrim. True Christianity was nothing if it were not progress.

Pilgrimage to the celestial city did not, of course, require Christians to kick up literal dust. They also served who only stood and waited. Nevertheless, something of the restlessness that had led in 1620 to the founding of Plymouth continued to inspire in numerous Protestants a yearning to leave behind the miseries and temptations of the old world and begin afresh. Some were willing to go halfway round the world to achieve this. In 1688, taking ship, 150 of the Calvinists who had recently been expelled by royal command from France—'Huguenots'—made for Cape Colony, a settlement founded by Dutch traders on the southernmost tip of Africa. Most Protestants, though, continued to head for America. In Massachusetts, where a law passed in 1661 had prescribed that Quakers be tied to a cart and flogged, Puritans continued to uphold a uniformity of worship that, back in the mother country, Cromwell's protectorate had served to doom for good. The New World, though, was not New England. South of Boston and Plymouth, there was no lack of places where dissenters might settle without fear of harassment. The most visionary of all was a colony named Philadelphia: 'Brotherly Love'. William Penn, its founder, was a man of paradox. The son of one of Cromwell's admirals, he was simultaneously a dandy with close links to the royal court, and a Quaker who had repeatedly suffered imprisonment for his beliefs. Philadelphia, the capital of a huge tranche of territory granted Penn by royal charter, was designed to serve as 'a holy experiment':[45] a city without stockades, at peace with the local Indians, in which all 'such as profess faith in Jesus Christ'[46] might be permitted to hold office. Just as the godly colonies of New England had been founded to serve the whole world as models, so too was Philadelphia—but as a haven of tolerance. By the early eighteenth century, its streets were filled with Anabaptists as well as Quakers, and with Germans as well as English. There were Jews. There were even Catholics. Increasingly, it was New England—once the vanguard of Protestant expansion overseas—that seemed out of step with the times.

To cross the Atlantic, then, was to lay claim to the liberty that Paul had proclaimed to be every Christian's. 'It is for freedom that Christ has set us free.'[47] In the autumn of 1718, when a Quaker named Benjamin Lay sailed for the Caribbean with his wife, Sarah, he could do so confident that they would literally be among Friends. Barbados, an English colony for almost a century, now belonged— following the union of England with Scotland in 1707—to a British empire. It was, in the words of one settler, 'a Babel of all Nations and Conditions of men'.[48] Yet even amid the colour and clamour of Bridgetown, the island's principal port, the Lays stood out. Both were hunchbacks; both were barely four feet tall. Lay, despite having legs 'so slender, as to appear almost unequal to the purpose of supporting him',[49] had already, by the age of forty-one, led an astonishingly active life. Of humble background, he had worked variously as a glover, a shepherd and a sailor; he had visited a well in Syria beside which Jesus was supposed to have sat; he had personally lobbied the British king. His small stature had made him only the more determined to be true to 'the counsel and direction of the Holy Spirit',[50] and oppose anything that he viewed as contrary to Christ. In an age when many Quakers were coming to set a premium on respectability, Lay was a throwback to their wilder, more confrontational beginnings. In England, this had made him plenty of enemies. Now, arriving in Barbados, he was about to make many more.

Not everyone who came to the New World did so by choice. One day, visiting a Quaker who lived some miles outside Bridgetown, Sarah Lay was shocked to find a naked African suspended outside his house. The man had just been savagely whipped. Blood, dripping from his twitching body, had formed a puddle in the dust. Flies were swarming over his wounds. Like the more than seventy thousand other Africans on Barbados, the man was a slave. The Quaker, explaining to Sarah that he was a runaway, felt no need to apologise. As in the time of Gregory of Nyssa, so in the time of the Lays: slavery was regarded by the overwhelming majority of Christians as being—much like poverty, or war, or sickness—a brutal fact of life. That there was no slave nor free in Christ Jesus did not mean that the distinction itself was abolished. Europeans, who lived on a continent where the institution had largely vanished, rarely thought for that reason to condemn it out of hand. Even Bartolomé de las Casas, whose campaign to redeem the Indians from slavery had become the focus of his entire life, never doubted that servitude might be merited as punishment for certain crimes. In the Caribbean as in Spanish America, the need for workers who could be relied upon to toil in hot and sticky climates without dying of the tropical diseases to which European labourers were prone made the purchase of Africans seem an obvious recourse. No Christian should feel guilt. Abraham had owned slaves. Laws in the Pentateuch regulated their treatment. A letter written by Paul's followers, but attributed to Paul himself, urged them to obey their owners. 'Do it, not only when their eye is on you and to win their favour, but with sincerity of heart and reverence for the Lord.'[51] The punishment of a runaway, then, might well be viewed as God's work. Even Lay, despite not owning slaves himself, had been known to reach for a whip when other people's slaves stole from him,. 'Sometimes I could catch them, and then I would give them Stripes.'[52]

Lay, when he remembered bringing down the lash on a starving slave's back, did not reach for scriptural justifications. On the contrary, he felt only a crushing sense of self-abhorrence. His guilt was that of a man who had suddenly discovered himself to be in the city of Destruction. 'Oh my Heart has been pained within me many times, to see and hear; and now, now, now, it is so.'[53] Las Casas, brought to a similar consciousness of his sin, had turned for guidance to the great inheritance of Catholic scholarship: to Cajetan, and Aquinas, and the compilers of canon law. Lay turned for guidance to the Spirit. When he and his wife, fearlessly confronting the slave-owners of Barbados, beseeched them to 'examine your own Hearts',[54] it was with an inner certitude as to the ultimate meaning of Scripture. The God that Lay could feel as enlightenment had bought his Chosen People out of slavery in Egypt; his son had washed feet, and suffered a death of humiliating agony, and redeemed all of humanity from servitude. To trade in slaves, to separate them from their children, to whip and rack and roast them, to starve them, to work them to death, to care nothing for the mixing into raw sugar of their 'Limbs, Bowels and Excrements',[55] was not to be a Christian, but to be worse than the Devil himself. The more that the Lays, opening their home and their table to starving slaves, learned about slavery, the more furiously they denounced it—and the more unpopular they became. Forced to beat a retreat from Barbados in 1720, they were never to escape the shadow of its horrors. For the rest of their lives, their campaign to abolish slavery—quixotic though it seemed—was to be their pilgrims' progress.

They were not the first abolitionists in the New World. Back in the 1670s, an Irish Quaker named William Edmundson had toured both Barbados and New England, campaigning to have Christianity taught to African slaves. Then, on 19 September 1676, writing to his fellow Friends in the Rhode Island settlement of Newport, he had been struck by a sudden thought. 'And many of you count it unlawful to make slaves of the Indians, and if so, then why the Negroes?'[56] This again was to echo las Casas. The great Spanish campaigner for human rights, in his anxiety to spare Indians enslavement, had for many decades backed the importation of Africans to do forced labour. This he had done under the impression that they were convicts, sold as punishment for their crimes. Then, late in life, he had discovered the terrible truth: that the Africans were unjustly enslaved, and no less the victims of Christian oppression than the Indians. The guilt felt by las Casas, the revulsion and dread of damnation, had been sharpened by the sustenance that he knew he had provided to the argument of Aristotle: that certain races were suited to be slaves. 'God has made of one blood all nations.'[57] When William Penn, writing in prison, cited this line of scripture, he had been making precisely the same case as las Casas: that all of humanity had been created equally in God's image; that to argue for a hierarchy of races was an offence against the very fundamentals of Christ's teaching; that no peoples were fitted by the colour of their skins to serve as either masters or slaves. Naturally—since this was an argument that so self-evidently went with the grain of Christian tradition—it was capable of provoking some anxiety among the owners of African slaves. Just as opponents of the Dominican had cited Aristotle, so opponents of Quaker abolitionists might grope after obscure verses in the Old Testament. Particularly popular was a passage that related a curse laid by Noah on his grandson, whose descendants—by means of various tortuous deductions—had come to be identified with Africans. So unconvincing was this argument, however, that no one ever took it very seriously. Slave-owners with delicate consciences, and who wished to salve them, preferred instead an altogether more solidly founded justification: that the enslavement of pagans, and their transportation to Christian lands, was done for the good of their souls. This, as Benjamin Lay had discovered in Barbados, was a licence for slavery widely accepted by Quakers. Even William Penn had been convinced. It was why the founder of

Philadelphia, that great and undoubted enthusiast for 'the Right of Liberty,'[58] had himself been an owner of slaves.

To Lay, all this was the rankest hypocrisy. In 1731, when he and his wife arrived in Philadelphia, he was appalled to discover whips, and chains, and slave-markets in the City of Brotherly Love. Rather than stay in such a Babylon, they settled instead in the nearby town of Abington. There, much as Elizabeth of Hungary had once done, they sought to boycott anything that might have been procured at the cost of another creature's suffering. The couple made their own clothes; drank nothing but water and milk; lived entirely on vegetables. Unlike Elizabeth, though, they did not attempt to keep their commitment to ethical living between themselves and God. Their ambition instead was to draw attention to their lifestyle: to make a public spectacle of it. In 1735, when Sarah Lay died, her husband mourned her by pushing his activism to a new level. By 1737, the Quaker slave-holders in Abington had grown so fed up with his endless protests that they banned him from their meeting hall. The following year, attending the annual assembly of Philadelphia Friends, Lay pulled off his most spectacular publicity stunt yet. Called to address his fellow Quakers, he rose to his feet, smoothed back his coat, and drew out a sword that he had been concealing within its folds. The enslavement of Africans, he declared in a resounding voice, was 'as justifiable in the sight of the Almighty, who beholds and respects all nations and colours of men with an equal regard, as if you should thrust a sword through their hearts as I do through this book.'[59] Then, holding up a hollowed-out Bible in which he had concealed a bladder full of blood-red pokeberry juice, he ran it through. The juice spattered everywhere. The meeting hall erupted in indignation. Lay, turning on his heel, hobbled out. He had made his point.

Summons to repentance were, of course, nothing new. The Bible was full of them. Yet Lay's campaign, for all that it drew on the example of the prophets, and for all that his admonitions against

slavery were garlanded with biblical references, did indeed constitute something different. To target it for abolition was to endow
society itself with the character of a pilgrim, bound upon a continuous journey, away from sinfulness towards the light. It was to cast
slavery as a burden, long borne by fallen humanity, but which, by the
grace of God, might one day loose from its shoulders, and fall from
off its back, and begin to tumble. It was at once a startling repudiation of an institution that most Christians had always taken utterly
for granted, and yet bred of Christianity's marrow. It bore witness,
no less than did the spirit of toleration in neighbouring Philadelphia,
no less than did those who in distant Amsterdam pondered the writings of Spinoza, to the workings of the Spirit. It was founded upon
the conviction that had for centuries, in the lands of the Christian
West, served as the great incubator of revolution: that society might
be born again. 'Flesh gives birth to flesh, but the Spirit gives birth to
spirit.'[60]

Never once did Lay despair of these words of Jesus. Twenty
years after he had gatecrashed the annual assembly of Philadelphia
Friends, as he lay mortally sick in bed, he was brought news that
a new assembly had voted to discipline any Quaker who traded in
slaves. 'I can now die in peace,'[61] he sighed in relief. His own progress through life, for all its discouragements, for all the dismal stories that had beset him round, for all the hobgoblins and foul fiends
that had sought to daunt his spirit, had never turned aside from its
object. Benjamin Lay had succeeded, by the time of his death in
1759, in making the community in which he had lived just that little
bit more like him—in making it just that little bit more progressive.

16

ENLIGHTENMENT

1762: Toulouse

On 13 October, the evening calm of the rue des Filatiers, a shop-lined street in the heart of Toulouse's commercial district, was disturbed by a terrible howl of anguish. More cries followed. The screams were coming from a shop owned by Jean Calas, a cloth-merchant in his sixties. As a crowd began to build, he and his family, who occupied the two storeys above the shop, could be seen through the window, clustered around what appeared to be a body. A surgeon's assistant arrived; then, towards midnight, a magistrate at the head of some forty soldiers. The accounts of what had happened that evening, as they emerged over the course of the next few days, were confused. First it was reported that Marc-Antoine, Jean Calas' eldest son, had been found by his family lying dead on the shop floor. The surgeon's assistant, pulling back the young man's cravat, had found on his neck the unmistakable imprint of a rope. It appeared, then, that he had been garrotted. Yet this version of events, which derived from the father's initial deposition, was soon being contradicted by Jean Calas himself. Changing his story, he declared that he had not, after all, found his son lying on the floor. Instead he had discovered Marc-Antoine hanging from a rope. He had taken down the corpse of his son. He had laid it on the floor. He had even—in the pathetic hope that his

387

son might still be alive—sought to make him comfortable by providing him with a pillow. Marc-Antoine Calas had not been murdered. He had hanged himself.

How were these contradictions to be explained? There was one obvious answer. Calas, disoriented by grief, had been desperate to spare his son the posthumous ignominy of being condemned as a suicide: for then his corpse would be dragged through the streets, and slung into the municipal tip. The investigating magistrate, however, was unconvinced. He had a different hypothesis. Marc-Antoine had indeed been murdered—by his own father. It had not taken the magistrate long to unearth what seemed a literally killer fact. Calas, in a country where it was illegal to be anything other than Catholic, was a Protestant: a Huguenot. What if Marc-Antoine, brought up in his father's heretical faith, had discovered the light? What if Calas, determined not to let his son convert to Catholicism, had killed him? What if all the talk of suicide were nothing but a cover-up? These suppositions, against a backdrop of growing hysteria in Toulouse, had soon come to take on the solidity of fact. On 8 November, amid awful and lachrymose solemnity, Marc-Antoine was commemorated in the city's cathedral as a martyr for the Catholic faith. Ten days later, his father was condemned to death. The following March, after a failed appeal, the old man was readied for execution. First, in a vain attempt to make him confess his crime, he was waterboarded. Then he was led in chains to the place St-Georges, a square in the heart of Toulouse. There he was lashed to a wheel. His limbs were broken with an iron bar. For two hours he endured the agony of his splintered bones with a grim fortitude. 'I die innocent,' he declared. 'I do not pity myself. Jesus Christ, who was innocence itself, died for me by even more cruel torments.'[1] By the time he breathed his last, even the priest who had been at his side, urging him to embrace the Catholic faith, felt moved to compare him to the martyrs of the early Church.

Jean Calas had been executed as a murderer, not a heretic. Four months later, a Catholic peasant convicted of parricide was similarly put to death in the place St-Georges—with the added refinement that his right hand was first cut off. Nevertheless, the centrality of Calas' Calvinism to the case brought against him provoked widespread alarm among Huguenots. It did not take long for the news of his miserable fate to reach Geneva; nor, from there, to reach the estate just beyond the city walls where the most famous man in Europe had one of his three homes. Voltaire, France's greatest writer, the confidant and adversary of kings, a man feared and admired in equal measure for the incomparable brilliance of his wit, immediately became obsessed by the case. Inclined at first to believe in Calas' guilt, he had soon changed his mind. When two of Calas' sons arrived in Geneva as refugees, he interviewed the younger of them—'a simple child, ingenuous, with the most gentle and interesting cast of features'[2]—at length. What the boy had to say left Voltaire convinced that a monstrous miscarriage of justice had taken place: a scandal that seemed conjured up from the blackest shadows of Toulouse's past. To Voltaire, Calas seemed as much a victim of murderous fanaticism as the Albigensians had once been. Such a wrong could not be permitted to stand. Innocent blood cried out to heaven. The great writer, summoning all his immense reserves of talent and energy, set himself to winning a posthumous pardon for the executed Huguenot.

But Voltaire—baptised into the Catholic Church and educated by the Jesuits, whom he publicly lambasted as power-hungry paedophiles, but privately saluted for their learning—did not take up the cause out of any sympathy for Protestantism. That September, as he was busy preparing his case, a letter arrived which addressed him as 'Antichrist'. The title was one appropriate to his often-sulphurous reputation. Voltaire, a gaunt, short man with a wide, mocking smile, had something of the look of a devil. His grin, though, was only the half of it. Even more shocking to devout opinion—Protestant no less than Catholic—was the dawning realisation that Europe's most celebrated writer, a man whom even his enemies could not help but admire, viewed Christianity with a hatred that bordered on fixation.

For decades he had veiled it, knowing just how far he could go, skilful like no other in deploying irony, the private joke, the knowing wink. Recently, though, he had become more forthright. With one property beyond the reach of the French authorities in Geneva, and two beyond the reach of the Genevan authorities in France, Voltaire felt secure as never before. Anonymously though he continued to publish his more shocking pasquinades, and publicly though he continued to insist on his membership of the Catholic Church, nobody was fooled. The deftness with which he mocked Christians for their god who could be eaten in a morsel of pastry, their scriptures rife with the most glaring contradictions and idiocies, their inquisitions, and scaffolds, and internecine wars, was too recognisably the work of Voltaire to be mistaken for that of anyone else. When he publicly called for *l'infâme*—'the abomination'—to be smashed, he did not need to specify his target. The fanaticism that had brought Calas to his death, far from being an aberration, was the very essence of the Christian sect. Its entire history was nothing but a sorry record of persecution. Its bigotry and intolerance had served 'to cover the earth with corpses'.[3]

Such blasphemies—while profoundly shocking to Christians—were to some a summons to battle. The letter in which Voltaire was hailed as the Antichrist had been written not by an opponent, but by an admirer: a philosopher and notorious free-thinker by the name of Denis Diderot. It was tribute that the great man received as his due. There could be no place for any modesty or self-abasement in the war against fanaticism. Fame was a weapon and self-promotion an obligation. Influence such as Voltaire had come to wield in the courts and salons of Europe would only be wasted if not exploited to the full. This was why, fusing conviction with invincible self-regard, he insisted on his status as the patriarch of an entire 'new philosophy'. Voltaire was far from alone in his contempt for Christianity. Diderot's was, if anything, even more inveterate. Ranged alongside them were a whole host of *philosophes*—metaphysicians and encyclo-paedists, historians and geologists—whose scorn for *l'infâme* was often no less than Voltaire's. Whether in Edinburgh or in Naples, in Philadelphia or in Berlin, the men most celebrated for their genius were increasingly those who equated churches with bigotry. To be a *philosophe* was to thrill to the possibility that a new age of freedom was advancing. The demons of superstition and unwarranted privilege were being cast out. People who had been walking in darkness had seen a great light. The world was being born again. Voltaire himself, in his more sombre moments, worried that the malign hold of priestcraft might never be loosened; but in general he was inclined to a cheerier take. His age was a *siècle des lumières*: 'an age of enlightenment'. For the first time since the reign of Constantine, the commanding heights of European culture had been wrested from Christian intellectuals. The shock of Calas' conviction was precisely that it had happened when *la philosophie* had been making such advances. 'It seems, then, that fanaticism, outraged by the progress of reason, is thrashing about in a spasm of outrage.'[4]

Yet in truth, there was nothing quite so Christian as a summons to bring the world from darkness into light. When Voltaire joked that he had done more for his own age than Luther and Calvin had done for theirs, it was a typically feline display of ingratitude. His complaint that the two great reformers had only scotched the papacy, not killed it, echoed any number of Protestant radicals. Voltaire, as a young man, had spent time in England. There, he had seen for himself how faith, in the transformative potency of enlightenment, from aristocratic salons to the meeting halls of Quakers, had resulted in what appeared to him an enviable degree of tolerance. 'If there were only one religion in England, there would be danger of tyranny; if there were two, they would cut each other's throats; but there are thirty, and they live happily together in peace.'[5] Voltaire, though, as he surveyed this religious landscape with an amused condescension, did not rest content with it. The impact of Calas' execution was precisely that it served to jolt him out of any complacency. Christian sects were incorrigible. They would always persecute one another, given only half a chance. The ideal, then, was a religion that could transcend their mutual hatreds. The wise man, Voltaire wrote in the midst of his campaign to exonerate Calas, knows such a religion not only to exist, but to be 'the most ancient and the most widespread' of any in the world. The man who practises it does not quibble over points of doctrine. He knows that he has received no divine revelations. He worships a just God, but one whose acts are beyond human comprehension. 'He has his brethren from Beijing to Cayenne, and he reckons all the wise his brothers.'⁶

Yet this, of course, was merely to proclaim another sect—and, what was more, one with some very familiar pretensions. The dream of a universal religion was nothing if not catholic. Ever since the time of Luther, attempts by Christians to repair the torn fabric of Christendom had served only to shred it further. The charges that Voltaire levelled against Christianity—that it was bigoted, that it was superstitious, that its scriptures were rife with contradictions—were none of them original to him. All had been honed, over the course of two centuries and more, by pious Christians. Voltaire's God, like the Quakers', like the Collegiants', like Spinoza's, was a deity whose contempt for sectarian wrangling owed everything to sectarian wrangling. 'Superstition is to religion what astrology is to astronomy, that is the very foolish daughter of a wise and intelligent mother.'⁷ Voltaire's dream of a brotherhood of man, even as it cast Christianity as something fractious, parochial, murderous, could not help but betray its Christian roots. Just as Paul had proclaimed that there was neither Jew nor Greek in Christ Jesus, so—in a future blessed with full enlightenment—was there destined to be neither Jew nor Christian nor Muslim. Their every difference would be dissolved. Humanity would be as one.

'You are all sons of God.'⁸ Paul's epochal conviction that the world stood on the brink of a new dispensation, that the knowledge of it would be written on people's hearts, that old identities and divisions would melt and vanish away, had not released its hold on the *philosophes*. Even those who pushed their quest for 'the light of reason'⁹ to overtly blasphemous extremes could not help but remain its heirs. In

1719—three years before the young Voltaire's arrival in the Dutch Republic, on his ever first trip abroad—a book had been printed there so monstrous that its 'mere title evoked fear'.[10] *The Treatise of the Three Imposters*, although darkly rumoured to have had a clandestine existence since the age of Conrad of Marburg, had in reality been compiled by a coterie of Huguenots in The Hague. As indicated by its alternative title—*The Spirit of Spinoza*—it was a book very much of its time. Nevertheless, its solution to the rival understandings of religion that had led to the Huguenots' exile from France was one to put even the *Theological-Political Treatise* in the shade. Christ, far from being 'the voice of God', as Spinoza had argued, had been a charlatan: a sly seller of false dreams. His disciples had been imbeciles, his miracles trickery. There was no need for Christians to argue over scripture. The Bible was nothing but a spider's web of lies. Yet the authors of the *Treatise*, although they certainly aspired to heal the divisions between Protestants and Catholics by demonstrating that Christianity itself was nothing but a fraud, did not rest content with that ambition. They remained sufficiently Christian that they wished to bring light to the entire world. Jews and Muslims too were dupes. Jesus ranked alongside Moses and Muhammad as one of three imposters. All religion was a hoax. Even Voltaire was shocked. No less committed than any priest to the truth of his own understanding of God, he viewed the blasphemies of the *Treatise* as blatant atheism, and quite as pernicious as superstition. Briefly taking a break from mocking Christians for their sectarian rivalries, he wrote a poem warning his readers not to trust the model of enlightenment being peddled by underground radicals. The *Treatise* itself was an imposture. Some sense of the divine was needed, or else society would fall apart. 'If God did not exist, it would be necessary to invent him.'[11]

But what kind of God? By the time that Voltaire came to pen his celebrated *aperçu*, he had achieved a stunning victory in his campaign to have Jean Calas pardoned. In 1763, the queen herself had received Madame Calas and her daughters. A year later, the royal council had declared the conviction of Calas null and void. In 1765, on the anniversary of the death sentence pronounced against him, he was conclusively exonerated. Voltaire, exhilarated by this triumph, had then embarked on further campaigns. The memory of a young nobleman mutilated and beheaded for blaspheming a religious procession was fearlessly defended; a second Huguenot cleared of murder—and this time while he was still alive. The bigotry and cruelty of l'infâme had always provoked in Voltaire a particular revulsion. Now, prompted by the success of his campaign to overturn miscarriages of justice, he dared to imagine its final rout. The exoneration of Calas, an innocent man tortured to death before a mocking and bloodthirsty crowd, had not merely been a triumph for the cause of enlightenment, but a defeat for Christianity. 'It is philosophy alone that is responsible for this victory.'[12]

Yet this was not necessarily how it appeared to Christians. There were many Catholics who saluted Voltaire's intervention. Had there not been, his campaign would never have succeeded—for there were hardly enough philosophes in France to sway the country on their own. Even in Toulouse, the city cast by Voltaire as a hellhole of superstition, there were plenty who agreed with his warnings against religious intolerance, nor saw any contradiction between them and Catholic teaching. 'Jesus Christ has given us examples for everything in his Bible,' wrote the wife of one prominent politician in Toulouse to her son. 'The one who looks for a strayed lamb does not bring it back by the whip; he carries it on his back, caresses it, and tries to attach it to himself by his benevolence.'[13] The paradox that weakness might be a source of strength, that a victim might triumph over his torturers, that suffering might constitute victory, lay at the heart of the Gospels. Voltaire, when he sketched a portrait of Calas broken on the wheel, could not help but evoke in the imaginings of his readers the image of Christ on the cross. The standards by which he judged Christianity, and condemned it for its faults, were not universal. They were not shared by philosophers across the world. They were not common from Beijing to Cayenne. They were distinctively, peculiarly Christian.

Even the most radical *philosophes* might on occasion betray an awareness of this. In 1762, during the first throes of the Calas affair, Diderot wrote admiringly of Voltaire's readiness to deploy his genius in the cause of the persecuted family. 'For what are the Calas to him? What is it that can interest him in them? What reason has he to suspend labours he loves, to occupy himself in their defence?' Atheist though he was, Diderot was too honest not to acknowledge the likeliest answer. 'If there were a Christ, I assure you that Voltaire would be saved.'[14]

The roots of Christianity stretched too deep, too thick, coiled too implacably around the foundations of everything that constituted the fabric of France, gripped too tightly its venerable and massive stonework, to be pulled up with any ease. In a realm long hailed as the eldest daughter of the Church, the ambition of setting the world on a new order, of purging it of superstition, of redeeming it from tyranny, could hardly help but be shot through with Christian assumptions. The dreams of the *philosophes* were both novel and not novel in the slightest. Many before them had laboured to redeem humanity from darkness: Luther, Gregory VII, Paul. Christians, right from the very beginning, had been counting down the hours to an upheaval in the affairs of the earth. 'The night is nearly over; the day is almost here.'

Revolution, in the lands that were once Christendom, had been known to convulse churches and kingdoms before. Who was to say, then, that it might not do so again?

Woe to You Who Are Rich

It took effort to strip bare a basilica as vast as the one that housed Saint Martin. For a millennium and more after the great victory won by Charles Martel over the Saracens, it had continued to thrive as a centre of pilgrimage. A succession of disasters—attacks by Vikings, fires—had repeatedly seen it rebuilt. So sprawling had the complex of buildings around the basilica grown that it had come to be known as Martinopolis. But revolutionaries, by their nature, relished a challenge. In the autumn of 1793, when bands of them armed with sledgehammers and pickaxes occupied the basilica, they set to work with gusto. There were statues of saints to topple, vestments to burn, tombs to smash. Lead had to be stripped from the roof, and bells removed from towers. 'A sanctuary can do without a grille, but the defence of the Fatherland cannot do without pikes.'[15] So efficiently was Martinopolis stripped of its treasures that within only a few weeks it was bare. Even so—the state of crisis being what it was—the gaunt shell of the basilica could not be permitted to go to waste. West of Tours, in the Vendée, the Revolution was in peril. Bands of traitors, massed behind images of the Virgin, had risen in revolt. Patriots recruited to the cavalry, when they arrived in Tours, needed somewhere to keep their horses. The solution was obvious. The basilica of Saint Martin was converted into a stable.

Horse shit steaming in what had once been one of the holiest shrines in Christendom gave to Voltaire's contempt for *l'infâme* a far more pungent expression than anything that might have been read in a salon. The ambition of France's new rulers was to mould an entire 'people of *philosophes*'.[16] The old order had been weighed and found wanting. The monarchy itself had been abolished. The erstwhile king of France—who at his coronation had been anointed with oil brought from heaven for the baptism of Clovis, and girded with the sword of Charlemagne—had been executed as a common criminal. His decapitation, staged before a cheering crowd, had come courtesy of the guillotine, a machine of death specifically designed by its inventor to be as enlightened as it was egalitarian. Just as the king's corpse, buried in a rough wooden coffin, had then been covered in quicklime, so had every division of rank in the country, every marker of aristocracy, been dissolved into a common citizenship. It was not enough, though, merely to set society on new foundations. The shadow of superstition reached everywhere. Time itself had to be recalibrated. That October, a new calendar was introduced. Sundays were swept away. So too was the practice of dating years from the incarnation of Christ. Henceforward, in France, it was the proclamation of the Republic that would serve to divide the sweep of time.

Even with this innovation in place, there still remained much to be done. For fifteen centuries, priests had been leaving their grubby fingerprints on the way that the past was comprehended. All that time, they had been carrying 'pride and barbarism in their feudal souls'.[17] And before that? A grim warning of what might happen should the Revolution fail was to be found in the history of Greece and Rome. The radiance that lately had begun to dawn over Europe was not the continent's first experience of enlightenment. The battle between reason and unreason, between civilisation and barbarism, between philosophy and religion, was one that had been fought in ancient times as well. 'In the pagan world, a spirit of toleration and gentleness had ruled.'[18] It was this that the sinister triumph of Christianity had blotted out. Fanaticism had prevailed. Now, though, all the dreams of the *philosophes* were coming true. *L'infâme* was being crushed. For the first time since the age of Constantine, Christianity was being targeted by a government for eradication. Its baleful reign, banished on the blaze of revolution, stood revealed as a nightmare that for too long had been permitted to separate twin ages of progress: a middle age.

This was an understanding of the past that, precisely because so flattering to sensibilities across Europe, was destined to prove infinitely more enduring than the makeshift calendar of the Revolution. Nevertheless, just like many other hallmarks of the Enlightenment, it did not derive from the *philosophes*. The understanding of Europe's history as a succession of three distinct ages had originally been popularised by the Reformation. To Protestants, it was Luther who had banished shadow from the world, and the early centuries of the Church, prior to its corruption by popery, that had constituted the primal age of light. By 1753, when the term 'Middle Ages' first appeared in English, Protestants had come to take for granted the existence of a distinct period of history: one that ran from the dying years of the Roman Empire to the Reformation. The revolutionaries, when they tore down the monastic buildings of Saint-Denis, when they expelled the monks from Cluny and left its buildings to collapse, when they reconsecrated Notre Dame as a 'Temple of Reason' and installed beneath its vaulting a singer dressed as Liberty, were paying unwitting tribute to an earlier period of upheaval. In Tours as well, the desecration visited on the basilica was not the first such vandalism that it had suffered. Back in 1562, when armed conflict between Catholics and Protestants had erupted across France, a band of Huguenots had torched the shrine of Saint Martin and tossed the relics of the saint onto the fire. Only a single bone and a fragment of his skull had survived. It was hardly unsurprising, then, in the first throes of the Revolution, that many Catholics, in their bewilderment and disorientation, should initially have suspected that it was all a Protestant plot.

In truth, though, the origins of the great earthquake that had seen the heir of Clovis consigned to a pauper's grave extended much further back than the Reformation. 'Woe to you who are rich.' Christ's words might almost have been the manifesto of those who could afford only ragged trousers, and so were categorised as men 'without knee-breeches': *sans-culottes*. They were certainly not the first to call for the poor to inherit the earth. So too had the radicals among the Pelagians, who had dreamed of a world in which every man and woman would be equal; so too had the Taborites, who had built a town on communist principles, and mockingly crowned the corpse of a king with straw; so too had the Diggers, who had denounced property as an offence against God. Nor, in the ancient city of Tours, were the *sans-culottes* who ransacked the city's basilica the first to be outraged by the wealth of the Church, and by the palaces of its bishops. In Marmoutier, where Alcuin had once promoted scripture as the inheritance of all the Christian people, a monk in the twelfth century had drawn up a lineage for Martin that cast him as the heir of kings and emperors—and yet Martin had been no aristocrat. The silken landowners of Gaul, offended by the roughness of his manners and his dress, had detested him much as their heirs detested the militants of revolutionary France. Like the radicals who had stripped bare his shrine, Martin had been a destroyer of idols, a scorner of privilege, a scourge of the mighty. Even amid all the splendours of Martinopolis, the most common depiction of the saint had shown him sharing his cloak with a beggar. Martin had been a *sans-culotte*.

There were many Catholics, in the first flush of the Revolution, who had recognised this. Just as English radicals, in the wake of Charles I's defeat, had hailed Christ as the first Leveller, so were there enthusiasts for the Revolution who saluted him as 'the first *sans-culotte*'.[19] Was not the liberty proclaimed by the Revolution the same as that proclaimed by Paul? 'You, my brothers, were called to be free.' This, in August 1789, had been the text at the funeral service for the men who, a month earlier, had perished while storming the Bastille, the great fortress in Paris that had provided the French monarchy with its most intimidating prison. Even the Jacobins, the Revolution's dominant and most radical faction, had initially been welcoming to the clergy. For a while, indeed, priests were more disproportionately represented in their ranks than any other profession. As late as November 1791, the president elected by the Paris Jacobins had been a bishop. It seemed fitting, then, that their name should have derived from the Dominicans, whose former headquarters they had made their base. Certainly, to begin with, there had been little evidence to suggest that a revolution might precipitate an assault on religion.

And much from across the Atlantic to suggest the opposite. There, thirteen years before the storming of the Bastille, Britain's colonies in North America had declared their independence. A British attempt to crush the revolution had failed. In France—where the monarchy's financial backing of the rebels had ultimately contributed to its own collapse—the debt of the American revolution to the ideals of the *philosophes* appeared clear. There were many in the upper echelons of the infant republic who agreed. In 1783, six years before becoming their first president, the general who had led the colonists to independence hailed the United States of America as a monument to enlightenment. 'The foundation of our Empire,' George Washington had declared, 'was not laid in the gloomy age of Ignorance and Superstition, but at an Epoch when the rights of mankind were better understood and more clearly defined than at any former period.'[20] This vaunt, however, had implied no contempt for Christianity. Quite the opposite. Far more than anything written by Spinoza or Voltaire, it was New England that had provided the American republic with its model of democracy, and Pennsylvania with its model of toleration. That all men had been created equal, and endowed with an inalienable right to life, liberty and the pursuit of happiness, were not remotely self-evident truths. That most Americans believed they were owed less to philosophy than to the Bible: to the assurance given equally to Christians and Jews, to Protestants and Catholics, to Calvinists and Quakers, that every human being was created in God's image. The truest and ultimate seedbed of the American republic—no matter what some of those who had composed its founding documents might have cared to think—was the book of Genesis.

The genius of the authors of the United States constitution was to garb in the robes of the Enlightenment the radical Protestantism that was the prime religious inheritance of their fledgling nation. When, in 1791, an amendment was adopted which forbade the government from preferring one Church over another, this was no more a repudiation of Christianity than Cromwell's enthusiasm for religious liberty had been. Hostility to imposing tests on Americans as a means of measuring their orthodoxy owed far more to the meeting houses of Philadelphia than to the salons of Paris. 'If Christian Preachers had continued to teach as Christ & his Apostles did, without Salaries, and as the Quakers now do, I imagine Tests would never have existed.'[21] So wrote the polymath who, as renowned for his invention of the lightning rod as he was for his tireless role in the campaign for his country's independence, had come to be hailed as the 'first

American'. Benjamin Franklin served as a living harmonisation of New England and Pennsylvania. Born in Boston, he had run away as a young man to Philadelphia; a lifelong admirer of Puritan egalitarianism, he had published Benjamin Lay; a strong believer in divine providence, he had been shamed by the example of the Quakers into freeing his slaves. If, like the *philosophes* who much admired him as an embodiment of rugged colonial virtue, he dismissed as idle dogma anything that smacked of superstition, and doubted the divinity of Christ, then he was no less the heir of his country's Protestant traditions for that. Voltaire, meeting him in Paris, and asked to bless his grandson, had pronounced in English what he declared to be the only appropriate benediction: 'God and liberty.'[22] Franklin, like the revolution for which he was such an effective spokesman, illustrated a truth pregnant with implications for the future: that the surest way to promote Christian teachings as universal was to portray them as deriving from anything other than Christianity.

In France, this was a lesson with many students. There, too, they spoke of rights. The founding document of the country's revolution, the sonorously titled 'Declaration of the Rights of Man and of the Citizen', had been issued barely a month after the fall of the Bastille. Part-written as it was by the American ambassador to France, it drew heavily on the example of the United States. The histories of the two countries, though, were very different. France was not a Protestant nation. There existed in the country a rival claimant to the language of human rights. These, so it was claimed by revolutionaries on both sides of the Atlantic, existed naturally within the fabric of things, and had always done so, transcending time and space. Yet this, of course, was quite as fantastical a belief as anything to be found in the Bible. The evolution of the concept of human rights, mediated as it had been since the Reformation by Protestant jurists and *philosophes*, had come to obscure its original authors. It derived, not from ancient Greece or Rome, but from the period of history condemned by all right-thinking revolutionaries as a lost millennium, in which any hint of enlightenment had at once been snuffed out by monkish, book-burning fanatics. It was an inheritance from the canon lawyers of the Middle Ages.

Nor had the Catholic Church—much diminished though it might be from its heyday—abandoned its claim to a universal sovereignty. This, to revolutionaries who insisted that 'the principle of any sovereignty resides essentially in the Nation',[23] could hardly help but render it a roadblock. No source of legitimacy could possibly be permitted that distracted from that of the state. Accordingly, in 1791—even as legislators in the United States were agreeing that there should be 'no law respecting an establishment of religion, or prohibiting the free exercise thereof'[24]—the Church in France had been nationalised. The legacy of Gregory VII appeared decisively revoked. Only the obduracy of Catholics who refused to pledge their loyalty to the new order had necessitated the escalation of measures against Christianity itself. Even those among the revolutionary leadership who questioned the wisdom of attempting to eradicate religion from France never doubted that the pretensions of the Catholic Church were insupportable. By 1793, priests were no longer welcome in the Jacobins. That anything of value might have sprung from the mulch of medieval superstition was a possibility too grotesque even to contemplate. Human rights owed nothing to the flux of Christian history. They were eternal and universal—and the Revolution was their guardian. 'The Declaration of Rights is the Constitution of all peoples, all other laws being variable by nature, and subordinated to this one.'[25]

So declared Maximilien Robespierre, most formidable and implacable of the Jacobin leaders. Few men were more icily contemptuous of the claims on the future of the past. Long an opponent of the death penalty, he had worked fervently for the execution of the king; shocked by the vandalising of churches, he believed that virtue without terror was impotent. There could be no mercy shown the enemies of the Revolution. They bore the taint of leprosy. Only once they had been amputated, and their evil excised from the state, would the triumph of the people be assured. Only then would France be fully born again. Yet there hung over this a familiar irony. The ambition of eliminating hereditary crimes and absurdities, of purifying humanity, of bringing them from vice to virtue, was redolent not just of Luther, but of Gregory VII. The vision of a universal sovereignty, one founded amid the humbling of kings and the marshalling of lawyers, stood recognisably in a line of descent from that of Europe's primal revolutionaries. So too their efforts to patrol dissidence. Voltaire, in his attempt to win a pardon for Calas, had compared the legal system in Toulouse to the crusade against the Albigensians. Three decades on, the mandate given to troops marching on the Vendée, issued by self-professed admirers of Voltaire, echoed the crusaders with a far more brutal precision. 'Kill them all. God knows his own.' Such was the order that the papal legate was reputed to have given before the walls of Béziers. 'Spear with your bayonets all the inhabitants you encounter along the way. I know there may be a few patriots in this region—it matters not, we must sacrifice all.'[26] So the general sent to pacify the Vendée in early 1794 instructed his troops. One-third of the population would end up dead: as many as a quarter of a million civilians. Meanwhile, back in the capital, the execution of those condemned as enemies of the people was painted by enthusiasts for revolutionary terror in recognisably scriptural colours. Good and evil locked in a climactic battle, the entire world at stake; the damned compelled to drink the wine of wrath; a new age replacing the old: here were the familiar contours of apocalypse. When, demonstrating that its justice might reach even into the grave, the revolutionary government ordered the exhumation of the royal necropolis at Saint-Denis, the dumping of royal corpses into lime pits was dubbed by those who had commissioned it the Last Judgement.

The Jacobins, though, were not Dominicans. It was precisely the Christian conviction that ultimate judgement was the prerogative of God, and that life for every sinner was a journey towards either heaven or hell, that was the object of their enlightened scorn. Even Robespierre, who believed in the eternity of the soul, did not on that count imagine that justice should be left to the chill and distant deity that he termed the Supreme Being. It was the responsibility of all who cherished virtue to work for its triumph in the here and now. The Republic had to be made pure. To imagine that a deity might ever perform this duty was the rankest superstition. In the Gospels, it was foretold that those who had oppressed the poor would only receive their due at the end of days, when Christ would return in glory, and separate 'the people one from another as a shepherd separates the sheep from the goats'.[27] But this would never happen. A people of *philosophes* could recognise it to be a fairy tale. So it was that the charge of sorting the goats from the sheep, and of delivering them to punishment, had been shouldered—selflessly, grimly, implacably—by the Jacobins.

This was why, in the Vendée, there was no attempt to do as the friars had done in the wake of the Albigensian crusade and apply to a diseased region a scalpel rather than a sword. It was why as well, in Paris, the guillotine seemed never to take a break from its work. As the spring of 1794 turned to summer, so its blade came to hiss ever more relentlessly, and the puddles of blood to spill ever more widely across the cobblestones. It was not individuals who stood condemned, but entire classes. Aristocrats, moderates, counter-revolutionaries of every stripe: all were enemies of the people. To show them mercy was a crime. Indulgence was an atrocity; clemency parricide. Even when Robespierre, succumbing to the same kind of factional battle in which he had so often triumphed, was himself sent to the guillotine, his conviction that 'the French Revolution is the first that will have been founded on the rights of humanity'[28] did not fade. There needed no celestial court, no deity sat on his throne, to deliver justice. 'Depart from me, you who are cursed, into the eternal fire prepared for the devil and his angels.'[29] So Christ, at the day of judgement, was destined to tell those who had failed to feed the hungry, to clothe the naked, to visit the sick in prison. There was no requirement, in an age of enlightenment, to take such nonsense seriously. The only heaven was the heaven fashioned by revolutionaries on earth. Human rights needed no God to define them. Virtue was its own reward.

The Misfortunes of Virtue

'The darkness of the middle ages exhibits some scenes not unworthy of our notice.'[30] Condescension of this order, an amused acknowledgement that even amid the murk of the medieval past the odd flickering of light might on occasion be observed, was not unknown among the *philosophes*. To committed revolutionaries, however, compromise with barbarism was out of the question. The Middle Ages had been a breeding ground of superstition, and that was that. Unsurprisingly, then, there was much enthusiasm among Jacobins for the customs and manners that had existed prior to the triumph of Christianity. The role played by the early Church in the imaginings of the Reformation was played in the imaginings of the French Revolution by classical Greece and Rome. Festivals designed to celebrate the dawning of the new age drew their inspiration from antique temples and statuary; the names of saints vanished from streets in Paris, to be replaced by those of Athenian philosophers; revolutionary leaders modelled themselves obsessively on Cicero. Even when the French Republic, mimicking the sombre course of Roman history, succumbed to military dictatorship, the new regime continued to plunder the dressing-up box of classical antiquity. Its armies followed eagles to victories across Europe. Its victories were commemorated in Paris on a colossal triumphal arch. Its leader, a general of luminescent genius named Napoleon, affected the laurel wreath of a Caesar. The Church meanwhile—grudgingly tolerated by an emperor who had invited the pope to his coronation, but then refused to be crowned by him—functioned effectively as a department of state. Salt was rubbed into the wound when a saint named Napoleon was manufactured in honour of the emperor, and given his own public fête. Augustus would no doubt have approved.

Nevertheless, the notion that antiquity offered the present nothing save for models of virtue, nothing save for exemplars appropriate to an enlightened and progressive age, had limitations. In 1797, a book was published in Paris that provided a very different perspective. Emphasis on the 'toleration and gentleness' of the ancients there was not. The Persians, 'the world's most ingenious race for the invention of tortures',[31] had devised the *scaphe*. The Greeks, when they captured a city, had licensed rape as a reward for valour. The Romans had stocked their households with young boys and girls, and used them as they pleased. Everyone in antiquity had taken for granted that infanticide was perfectly legitimate; that to turn the other cheek was folly; that 'Nature has given the weak to be slaves'.[32] Over many hundreds of pages, the claim that empires in the remote past had regarded as perfectly legitimate customs that under the influence of Christianity had come to be regarded as crimes was rehearsed in painstaking detail. Provocatively, it was even suggested that a relish for displays of suffering—such as in ancient Rome had been staged as public entertainments in the very heart of the city—had been a civic good. 'Rome was mistress of the world all the while she had these cruel spectacles; she sank into decline and from there into slavery as soon as Christian morals managed to persuade her that there was more wrong in watching men slaughtered than beasts.'[33]

This reflection was not altogether an original one: the thesis that Christianity had contributed to the decline and fall of the Roman Empire was popular among historically minded *philosophes*. In other ways, though, the author had indeed pushed originality to an extreme. So shocking was his book that it was published without any hint of his name. *The New Justine* was not a work of history at all, but of fiction. Its observations on the character of ancient civilisations formed merely one strand in a vast tapestry, woven to demonstrate a disorienting proposition: that 'virtue is not a world of priceless worth, it is just a way of behaving that varies according to climate and consequently has nothing real about it'.[34] To think otherwise was imbecility. The plot of the novel—which related the adventures of two sisters, one virtuous, the other libertine—demonstrated this in obscene and relentless detail. Justine, ever trusting in the essential goodness of humanity, was repeatedly raped and brutalised; Juliette, ever contemptuous of any hint of virtue, whored and murdered her way to spectacular wealth. Their respective fortunes demonstrated the way of the world. God was a sham. There was only Nature. The weak existed to be enslaved and exploited by the strong. Charity was a cold and pointless process, and talk of human brotherhood a fraud. That anyone should ever have thought otherwise was due solely to a monstrous scam. 'The religion of that wily little sneak Jesus—feeble, sickly, persecuted, singularly desirous to outmanoeuvre the tyrants of the day, to bully them into acknowledging a doctrine of brotherhood from whose acceptance he calculated to gain some respite—Christianity sanctioned these laughable fraternal ties.'[35]

The scandal of the novel was sufficient, when the identity of its author was finally uncovered by Napoleon's chief of police in 1801, to have him flung into jail. The blasphemy, though, was only incidentally against Christianity. The Marquis de Sade was a man who had been brought up in the bosom of the Enlightenment. Schooled from an early age in the writings of the *philosophes*, and with an uncle who had been a close friend of Voltaire, he had always been a freethinker. Freedom, though, had its limits. Sade's refusal to submit to convention was complicated by the often violent character of his desires. Born in 1741, he had spent his sexual prime frustrated by laws that decreed that even prostitutes and beggars had a right not to be kidnapped, or whipped, or force-fed Spanish fly. Titled though the Marquis was, his escapades in the years before the fall of the Bastille had culminated in his incarceration in France's most notorious prison. There, denied his much-cherished liberty, he had found himself with no lack of time to dwell on the contemptibility of Christian teaching. 'The doctrine of loving one's neighbour is a fantasy that we owe to Christianity and not to Nature.'[36] Yet even once Sade, set free by the Revolution, had found himself living under 'the reign of philosophy',[37] in a republic committed to casting off the clammy hold of superstition, he had found that the pusillanimous doctrines of Jesus retained their grip. Specious talk of brotherhood was as common in revolutionary committee rooms as it had been in churches. In 1793—following his improbable election as president of a local committee in Paris—Sade had issued instructions to his fellow citizens that they should all paint slogans on their houses: 'Unity, Indivisibility of the Republic, Liberty, Equality, Fraternity'.[38] Sade himself, though, was no more a Jacobin than he was a priest. The true division in society lay not between friends and enemies of the people, but between those who were naturally masters and those who were naturally slaves. Only when this was appreciated and acted upon would the taint of Christianity finally be eradicated, and humanity live as Nature prescribed. The inferior class of man, so a *philosophe* in *The New Justine* coolly observed, 'is simply the species that stands next above the chimpanzee on the ladder; and the distance separating them is, if anything, less than that between him and the individual belonging to the superior caste.'[39]

Yet if this was the kind of talk that would see Sade spend his final years consigned to a lunatic asylum, the icy pitilessness of his gaze was not insanity. More clearly than many enthusiasts for enlightenment cared to recognise, he could see that the existence of human rights was no more provable than the existence of God. In 1794, prompted by rebellion in Saint-Domingue, a French-ruled island in the West Indies, and by the necessary logic of the Declaration of Rights, the revolutionary government had proclaimed slavery abolished throughout France's colonies; eight years later, in a desperate and ultimately futile attempt to prevent the blacks of Saint-Domingue from establishing their own republic, Napoleon reinstated it. The shamelessness of this would not have surprised Sade. Those in power were hypocrites. Throughout *The New Justine*, there was not an abbot, not a bishop, not a pope who did not prove to be an atheist and a libertine. Nor, when Sade contemplated the slave trade, was he any the more convinced by the godliness of Protestants.

English plantation-owners in the Caribbean—masters of life and death over their human chattels as they were—were among the few contemporaries worthy to be compared to the ancients. 'Wolves eating lambs, lambs devoured by wolves, the strong killing the weak, the weak falling victim to the strong, such is Nature, such are her designs, such is her plan.'[40] The English, like the Spartans or the Romans, understood this. It was why, Sade wrote, they were in the habit of chopping up their slaves and boiling them in vats, or else crushing them in the sugar-cane mills—'as slow a way to die as it is dreadful'.[41] There was only the one timeless language: the language of power.

Progress, that venerable Christian ideal that Abelard had cherished and Milton hymned, was no less a fantasy for having provided revolution with its battle-cry. In 1814, eleven years after Sade's incarceration in a lunatic asylum, the monarchy was restored to France. Napoleon, whose ambitions had shaken thrones across Europe, was exiled to an island off Italy. Aristocrats returned to Paris. That September, when foreign ministers arrived in Vienna to negotiate a new balance of power in Europe, there was no wild talk of a brotherhood of man. Too many doors that should have been kept locked had been prised open. It was time to close them again, and slide the bolts across. Sade, who knew what it was to be consigned to a prison, would not have been unduly surprised at the end to which a century of enlightenment had come. That November, when his cousin visited him on his sickbed, and spoke to him of liberty, he did not reply. On 2 December he breathed his last. Meanwhile, in Vienna, amid the glittering of diamonds and the smashing of wine bottles, emperors and kings continued to draw lines on maps, and to work at making Europe secure against progress.

Yet even amid the concert of the great powers there was evidence that it lived on as an ideal. That June, on his return from preparatory negotiations in Paris, the British Foreign Secretary had been greeted by his fellow parliamentarians with a standing ovation. Among the terms of the treaty agreed by Lord Castlereagh had been one particularly startling stipulation: that Britain and France would join in a campaign to abolish the slave trade. This, to Benjamin Lay, would have been fantastical, an impossible dream. The treaty, though, in the view of some in the British parliament, did not go nearly far enough. Castlereagh, anxious not to destabilise France's recently restored monarchy, had agreed that French merchants should be permitted to continue trafficking slaves for a further five years. This, it had turned out, was a concession too far. Within days of the Foreign Secretary's seemingly triumphant return from Paris, an unprecedented campaign of protest had swept Britain. Petitions on a scale never before witnessed had deluged Parliament. A quarter of all those eligible to sign them had added their names. Never before had the mass of the British public committed themselves so manifestly to a single issue. It had become for them, the French Foreign Minister noted in mingled bemusement and disdain, 'a passion carried to fanaticism, and one which the ministry is no longer at liberty to check'.[42] Castlereagh, negotiating with his opposite numbers at Vienna, knew that his hands were tied. He had no option but to secure a treaty against the slave trade.

Barely sixty years had passed since the Philadelphia Friends had banned Quakers from dealing in slaves. In that short space of time, a cause that had rendered Benjamin Lay an object of mockery had evolved to shape the counsels of nations. Both in the United States and in Britain, dread that slavery ranked as a monstrous sin, for which not just individuals but entire nations were certain to be chastised by God, had come to grip vast swathes of the population. 'Can it be expected that He will suffer this great iniquity to go unpunished?'[43] Such a question would, of course, have bewildered earlier generations of Christians. The passages in the Bible that appeared to sanction slavery remained. Plantation owners—both in the West Indies and in the southern United States—did not hesitate to quote them. But this had failed to stem the rising swell of protest. Indeed, it had left slave owners open to a new and discomfiting charge: that they were the enemies of progress. Already, by the time of the

American Revolution, to be a Quaker was to be an abolitionist. The gifts of the Spirit, though, were not confined to Friends. They had come to be liberally dispensed wherever English-speaking Protestants were gathered. Large numbers of them, ranging from Baptists to Anglicans, had been graced with good news: *euangelion*. To be an Evangelical was to understand that the law of God was the law not only of justice, but of love. No one who had felt the chains of sin fall away could possibly doubt 'that *slavery* was ever detestable in the sight of God'.[44] There was no time to lose. And so it was, in 1807, in the midst of a deadly struggle for survival against Napoleon, that the British parliament had passed the Act for the Abolition of the Slave Trade; and so it was, in 1814, that Lord Castlereagh, faced across the negotiating table by uncomprehending foreign princes, had found himself obliged to negotiate for the eradication of a business that other nations still took for granted. Amazing Grace indeed.

To Sade, of course, it all had been folly. There was no brotherhood of man; there was no duty owed the weak by the strong. Evangelicals, like Jacobins, were the dupes of their shared inheritance: their belief in progress; their conviction in the potential of reform; their faith that humanity might be brought to light. Yet it was precisely this kinship, this synergy, that enabled Castlereagh, faced by the obduracy of his fellow foreign ministers, to craft a compromise that was, in every sense of the word, enlightened. Unable to force through an explicit outlawing of the slave trade, he settled instead for something at once more nebulous and more far-reaching. On 8 February 1815, eight powers in Europe signed up to a momentous declaration. Slavery, it stated, was 'repugnant to the principles of humanity and universal morality'.[45] The language of evangelical Protestantism was fused with that of the French Revolution. Napoleon, slipping his place of exile three weeks after the declaration had been signed, and looking to rally international support for his return, had no hesitation in proclaiming his support for the declaration. That June, in the great battle outside Brussels that terminally ended his ambitions, both sides were agreed that slavery, as an institution, was an abomination. The twin traditions of Britain and France, of Benjamin Lay and Voltaire, of enthusiasts for the Spirit and enthusiasts for reason, had joined in amity even before the first cannon was fired at Waterloo. The irony was one that neither Protestants nor atheists cared to dwell upon: that an age of enlightenment and revolution had served to establish as international law a principle that derived from the depths of the Catholic past. Increasingly, it was in the language of human rights that Europe would proclaim its values to the world.

17

RELIGION

1825: Baroda

Late in the afternoon of 29 November, a British surgeon arrived on the banks of the Vishwamitri river, there to watch a young woman be burnt alive. Richard Hartley Kennedy was no idle gawper. He had a long and distinguished record of service in India. The improbable empire there that, over the course of the previous decades, the East India Company had succeeded in carving out for itself, and which by 1825 had come to span most of the subcontinent, depended for its smooth running on doctors no less than on soldiers. For years, Kennedy had been charged with maintaining the health of the Company's employees; first in Bombay, and then, from 1819, in the city of Baroda, some three hundred miles to the north. This, on paper, was the capital of an independent kingdom. Paper, though, in British India, invariably worked to the Company's advantage. By terms of a treaty it had signed with the Maharaja of Baroda, responsibility for the kingdom's external affairs now rested with the Company. Its representative in the city—the resident, as he was known—was certainly no plenipotentiary; but nor was he merely an ambassador. British rule in Baroda, as in other princely states across India, functioned best by veiling itself. Kennedy, as a surgeon employed in the residency, perfectly understood this. Arriving that afternoon by the great bridge that spanned the Vishwamitri,

he knew that no one in the procession he could see approaching the
river would dare forbid him to watch it; but he knew as well that he
had no authority to stop what was about to happen.

Some months earlier, when her husband was still alive, Kennedy
had met Ambabai. He remembered her as a happy woman. Now,
though, with her husband dead of fever, she looked very different:
her hair dishevelled, her expression determined and severe. That
afternoon, following in the dead man's train and then watching
as the pyre was built, it was Ambabai, not her husband, who was
the centre of attention. The sun began to set. The funeral-bed was
given the look of 'the domestic couch of nightly repose'.[1] Ambabai washed herself in the shallows, poured out libations, raised her
arms and looked up at the sky. Then, stepping out of the river, she
exchanged her wet sari for clothes of a dull saffron colour. A crowd
gathered round her. She handed out bequests. Soon there was nothing left for her to give away, and the crowd fell back again. Ambabai,
after a brief pause, so momentary as barely to be observable, circled
the pyre, her eyes fixed all the time on the body of her husband. A
fire was lit in a great metal dish. Ambabai tended it, feeding it with
sandalwood. She rose to her feet. She was handed a mirror. She
looked into it; then gave it back, declaring that she had seen in it
the history of her soul, which soon enough would be returning 'into
the bosom and substance of the Creator'.[2] For now, though, her husband was calling. Climbing onto the pyre, she made herself comfortable beside his corpse, and began to sing her own funeral song.
Even as the pyre was lit, she continued to chant. Soon, the heat of
the flames had forced the spectators back. Ambabai, though, never
changed her position. Nor did she ever scream. Smoke billowed.
The sun set. Beside the dark-flowing river, the embers glowed, then
faded. By midnight, nothing was left of the pyre save a heap of grey
and powdery ashes. Ambabai had become what she had set out to
become: a 'good woman', a *sati*.

Here, in this exotic and shocking scene, was everything that
a respectable British family might care to read about over the

breakfast table. Reports of 'suttee'—as Kennedy termed Ambabai's self-immolation—filled the pages of London newspapers and periodicals. The image of a beautiful widow consigning herself to fire combined titillation with all the evidence that was needed of Christianity's invincible superiority to paganism. Looming behind Kennedy's report was a horror of idolatry that reached back unbroken through Christian history. Cortés, confronted by racks of skulls in Tenochtitlan, and Boniface, venturing deep into the forests of Saxony, and Origen, scorning the blood-caked altars of Alexandria, had all borne witness to it. The venerable conviction that idols were raised to demons, witness to 'the extent and power of Satan's empire',[3] exerted a firm grip on British evangelicals. Even Kennedy, watching Ambabai, found himself comparing her to a priestess of Apollo. The implication was clear. Whether in ancient Greece or in British India, idolatry always wore the same face. Paganism was paganism.

Except that Kennedy knew there was more to what he had seen on the banks of the Vishwamitri than that. Witnessing the courage with which Ambabai had embraced her fate, he had saluted 'the heavenly aspirations and glowing enthusiasm of her mind'.[4] He knew how far back the traditions of India reached. The very name used by the British to describe its inhabitants—'Hindoos'—derived ultimately from the court of Darius. Hard-nosed though officials of the East India Company might be, the sheer antiquity of Indian civilisation could not help but inspire in many of them a sense of awe. Unsurprisingly, then—given that their own ancestors had been savages in forests at a time when India was already fabled for its wealth and sophistication—they were reluctant to dismiss 'the Hindoo superstition'[5] merely as superstition. Indeed, so one British officer declared, there was little need of Christianity 'to render its votaries a sufficiently correct and moral people for all the useful purposes of a civilised society'.[6] While few Christians went quite that far, there was, even so, an increasing readiness to accept that Hindus could not simply be dismissed as pagans. They had scriptures as old as the Bible. They had temples that, in terms of scale and beauty, rivalled the cathedrals of Europe. They had an entire social class—'Brahmins'—who appeared to Europeans much like priests. It was Brahmins who had accompanied Ambabai to the Vishwamitri; Brahmins who had built her pyre; Brahmins who had readied her for death. It seemed reasonable enough to reckon, then, that Hindus had a religion.

Yet British observers, when they sought to view India through this prism, faced an obvious challenge. Three hundred years had passed since the onset of the Reformation, and in that time the word religion had come to take on shades of meaning that would have baffled a Christian in medieval England. How much more foreign, then, was it bound to seem to a Hindu. No word remotely approximating to it existed in any Indian language. To Protestants, the essence of religion appeared clear: it lay in the inner relationship of a believer to the divine. Faith was a personal, a private thing. As such, it existed in a sphere distinct from the rest of society: from government, or trade, or law. There was the dimension of the religious, and then there was the dimension of everything else: the 'secular'. That other societies too could be divided up in this manner might—to a people less self-confident than the British—have appeared farfetched: for it was, in truth, a most distinctive way of seeing the world. Nevertheless, to officials in India possessed of a scholarly turn of mind, intrigued by the ancient land they found themselves administering, and forever conscious of just how different it was from their own, the conviction that such a thing as a 'Hindoo religion' existed was simply too useful to abandon. In ancient Greece, the story had been told of a robber named Procrustes, who, after inviting a guest to lie down on a bed, would then rack his limbs or amputate them, as required to ensure a trim fit. It was in a very similar spirit that British scholars, confronted by all the manifold riches, complexities and ambivalences of Indian civilisation, set to shaping out of them something that might be recognisable as a religion.

Inevitably, there was much stretching and editing of definitions. The most urgent need was to decide who 'Hindoos' actually were:

people from India or people who practised the 'Hindoo religion'? Increasingly, since talk of 'Hindoo Muslims' or 'Hindoo Christians' risked obvious confusion, the British found themselves opting for the second definition. This in turn facilitated another linguistic innovation. The more that British officials identified Hindus with a religion native to India, so the more they required a convenient shorthand for it. 'Hindooism', the word that came to fill the gap, had originally been coined back in the 1780s. The first man known to have used it was an Evangelical. Charles Grant, a Scot who had served the Company both as a soldier and on its board of trade, had initially felt little sense of Christian mission. He had travelled to India with the goal of getting rich. Accordingly, he had seen no reason to disagree with the settled policy of the Company: that its only business was business. Any attempt to convert Hindus to Christianity would risk the precarious foundations of its rule. Its purpose was the making of money, not the winning of souls. But then had come the great crisis in Grant's life. Gambling debts had threatened his finances. Two of his children had died of smallpox within ten days of each other. Grant, in the depths of his agony, had found himself redeemed by grace. From that moment on, the great object of his life had been to win the Hindus for Christ. Convinced that they were lost in ignorance, he had pledged himself to saving them from all their idolatries and superstitions. These were what he had meant by 'Hindooism'.

His mission, so he believed, was one of emancipation. This was why, returning to London in 1790, he had made common cause with the Abolitionists. Slavery, after all, came in many forms. If divine providence had bestowed upon Britain the chance to end the transportation of human chattels across the Atlantic, then so also had it granted to the East India Company an incomparable opportunity to abolish the practices that kept Hindus in servitude to superstition. In 1813, while the Company was embroiled in negotiations with the British government over a renewal of its charter, Grant had seized his chance. For decades, he had been demanding that its directors be legally obliged to work for the 'religious and moral improvement'[7] of the Hindus. Now, in a decisive moment, the campaign had come to the very heart of power. Evangelicals had enthusiastically rallied to the cause; 908 petitions had been delivered to Parliament. The British government—as it would the following year, when pressed to alter its policy on the slave trade—had bowed to public opinion. The charter had been amended. Yet even with this success under his belt, Grant had persisted in his activism. One Hindu practice more than any other had loomed in his nightmares. 'If we had conquered such a kingdom as Mexico, where a number of human victims were regularly offered every year upon the altar of the sun, should we have calmly acquiesced in this horrid mode of butchery?'[8] Grant's question, addressed to the directors of the Company, was one that even after his death in 1823 continued to reverberate. As Kennedy, in distant Baroda, watched Ambabai performing the rituals required of a *sati*, so Britain was seized by one of its periodic fits of morality. Demands were becoming overwhelming for a ban on the self-immolation of widows.

All of which put the Company in a bind. Despite the change to its charter, it remained reluctant to interfere in the religious practices of its Hindu subjects. What, though, if it could be proven that suttee was not a religious practice? The question, of course, was one that would have made no sense at all before the coming of the British to India; but increasingly, after decades of rule by the Company, there were Indians who understood its implications well enough. Hindus who used words such as religion, or secular, or Hinduism were not merely displaying their fluency in English. They were also adopting a new and alien perspective on their country and turning it to their advantage. Evangelicals were not alone in opposing the immolation of widows. There were Hindus who opposed it as well. For centuries, praise of the *sati* had alternated with forthright condemnation. A thousand years and more before the self-immolation of Ambabai, a Hindu poet had denounced deaths such as hers as 'a mere freak of madness, a path of ignorance'.[9] The British conviction that there existed in India a religion named Hinduism, comparable to Christianity, complete with orthodoxies and ancient scriptures, provided Hindus fluent in English with the perfect opportunity to shape what this religion should look like. Brahmins, because of their reputation for learning, enjoyed a particular advantage. In 1817, one of them had presented the government in Calcutta with a paper which insisted that it was purely optional for widows to incinerate themselves; a year later, another had gone even further, and demonstrated that there was no evidence at all for the practice in Hinduism's oldest texts. Insisting on this to the British, Raja Rammohun Roy had known exactly what he was doing. Sufficiently intrigued by Christianity to have taught himself Hebrew and Greek, and familiar with the workings of the Company after years of working in its various departments, he understood precisely how to give its officials what they so desperately needed: a justification acceptable to Hindus for the banning of suttee.

The burning of widows on pyres, Roy assured the British, was a purely secular phenomenon. That there were Brahmins who officiated at such rituals was due solely to their ignorance of Hindu scripture. There was authentic Hinduism, and then there was a Hinduism that had been corrupted by the greed and superstition of malevolent priests. Bogus tradition was like the creepers that, left unchecked, would subsume an ancient temple, and swallow it up into the jungle. If this all sounded rather Protestant, then so indeed it was. Roy's resentment of Christians as 'persons who travel to a distant country for the purpose of overturning the opinions of its inhabitants and introducing their own'[10] had not prevented him from recognising their usefulness. Each had much to offer the other. Roy was able to reassure the British that suttee was not a religious practice, and might therefore legitimately be banned; the British were able to back Roy in his efforts to prescribe how Hinduism should properly be defined. In 1829, the Governor-General of India issued a decree, forbidding 'the practice of Suttee; or of burning or burying alive the widows of Hindoos'.[11] One year later, fearing that the British government might overturn the ban, Roy travelled to London. There, in the imperial capital, he secured a definitive victory. Brought to his grave soon afterwards by the inclemencies of the English climate, he was widely mourned. Evangelicals had been able to recognise him—Hindu though he was—as one of their own.

'Christianity spreads in two ways,' an Indian historian has written: 'through conversion and through secularisation.'[12] Missionaries who dreamed of reaping a great harvest of Indian souls were destined to be disappointed. There was to be no humbling of the Hindu gods, no triumphant toppling of their idols into the dust. British officials continued to tread a delicate and careful path. Even so much as a rumour that the Company was working for the conversion of India had the potential to cripple its rule. In 1857, indeed, these would trigger an uprising so explosive that briefly, for a few blood-soaked months, the entire future of Britain's empire in India would be left hanging by a thread. The shock of it would never be forgotten by the imperial authorities. Their determination not to risk the promotion of Christianity in India was left even more rock-solid. Nevertheless, they had no hesitation in fostering assumptions bred of Christian theology. That there existed a religion called Hinduism, and that it functioned in a dimension distinct from entire spheres of human activity—spheres called 'secular' in English—was not a conviction native to the subcontinent. Instead, it was distinctively Protestant. That, though, would not prevent it from proving perhaps the most successful of all British imports to India. In time, indeed—when, after two centuries, Britain's rule was brought at last to an end, and India emerged to independence—it would do so as a self-proclaimed secular nation. A country did not need to become Christian, it turned out, to start seeing itself through Christian eyes.

Jew-ish

In 1842, the king of Prussia visited Europe's oldest building site. Friedrich Wilhelm IV ruled a state that, over the course of the preceding century, had established itself as the most formidable in

Germany. Humiliated by Napoleon, who had occupied its capital, Berlin, and sought to neuter it for good, Prussia had ended up playing a key role in his defeat. It was a Prussian army that had forced him from his throne in 1814, and a Prussian army that had sealed his fate at Waterloo. Napoleon's empire, though, was not alone in having been ended. So too had an infinitely more venerable order. On 6 August 1806, barely noticed amid all the storm-tides of revolution and war, the line of Caesars founded by Otto the Great had been formally terminated. An empire that for almost a millennium had prided itself on being both holy and Roman was no more. Even with Napoleon's defeat, there had been no bringing it back from the dead.

This was why, at the Congress of Vienna, the representatives of the great powers had devoted most of their time, not to discussions of the slave trade, but to redrawing the map of central Europe. Prussia had played its hand well. A state that had been shorn by Napoleon of many of its provinces had emerged from the Congress much expanded. It had absorbed almost half of Saxony. Wittenberg had become a Prussian possession. So too, on the western border of what had once been the Holy Roman Empire, had a great tranche of the Rhineland. Friedrich Wilhelm had first travelled there in 1814. The highlight of the young crown prince's journey had been a visit to Cologne. The city—unlike Berlin, an upstart capital far removed from the traditional heartlands of Christendom—was an ancient one. Its foundations reached back to the time of Augustus. Its archbishop had been one of the seven electors. Its cathedral, begun in 1248 and abandoned in 1473, had for centuries been left with a crane on the massive stump of its southern tower. Friedrich Wilhelm, visiting the half-completed building, had been enraptured. He had pledged himself there and then to finishing it. Now, two years after his accession to the Prussian throne, he was ready to fulfil his vow. That summer, he ordered builders back to work. On 4 September he dedicated a new cornerstone. Then, in a spontaneous and heartfelt address to the people of Cologne, he saluted their city. The cathedral, he declared, would rise as a monument to 'the spirit of German unity'.[13]

Startling evidence of this was to be found on the executive committee set up to supervise the project. Simon Oppenheim, a banker awarded a lifelong honorary membership of the board, was fabulously wealthy, highly cultured—and a Jew. Even within living memory his presence in Cologne would have been illegal. For almost four hundred years, Jews had been banned from the devoutly Catholic city. Only in 1798, following its occupation by the French, and the abolition of its ancient privileges, had they been allowed to settle there again. Oppenheim's father had moved to Cologne in 1799, two years before its official absorption into the French Republic. Since France's revolutionary government, faithful to the Declaration of Rights, had granted full citizenship to its Jews, the Oppenheims had been able to enjoy a civic equality with their Catholic neighbours. Not even a revision of this by Napoleon, who in 1808 had brought in a law expressly designed to discriminate against Jewish business interests, had dampened their sense of identification with Cologne—nor their ability to run a highly successful bank from the city. It helped as well that Prussia, by the time it came to annex the Rhineland, had already decreed that its Jewish subjects should rank as both 'natives' and 'citizens'. That Napoleon's discriminatory legislation remained on the statute book, and that the Prussian decree had continued to ban Jews from entering state employment, did nothing to diminish Oppenheim's hopes for further progress. The cathedral was for him as a symbol not of the Christian past, but of a future in which Jews might be full and equal citizens of Germany. That was why he agreed to help fund it. Friedrich Wilhelm, rewarding him with a house call, certainly had no hesitation in saluting him as a patriot. A Jew, it seemed, might indeed be a German.

Except that the king, by visiting Oppenheim, was making a rather different point. To Friedrich Wilhelm, the status of Cologne Cathedral as an icon of the venerable Christian past was not some incidental detail, but utterly fundamental to his passion for seeing it finished. Half-convinced that the French Revolution had been a harbinger of the Apocalypse, he dreamed of restoring to monarchy the sacral quality that it had enjoyed back in the heyday of the Holy Roman Empire. That he himself was fat, balding and short-sighted in the extreme did nothing to diminish his enthusiasm for posing as a latter-day Charlemagne. 'Fatty Flounder', as he was nicknamed, had even renovated a ruined medieval castle, and inaugurated it with a torchlit procession in fancy dress. Unsurprisingly, then, confronted by the challenge of integrating Jews into his plans for a shimmeringly Christian Prussia, he had groped after a solution that might as well have been conjured up from the Middle Ages. Only Christians, Friedrich Wilhelm argued, could be classed as Prussian. Jews should be organised into corporations. They would thereby be able to maintain their distinctive identity in an otherwise Christian realm. This was not at all what Oppenheim wished to hear. Shortly before the king's arrival in Cologne, he had gone so far as to write an open protest. Others in the city rallied to the cause. The regional government pushed for full emancipation. 'The strained relationship between Christians and Jews,' thundered Cologne's leading newspaper, 'can be resolved only through unconditional equalisation of status.'[14] The result was deadlock. Frederick William—channelling the spirit of a mail-clad medieval emperor—refused to back down. Prussia, he insisted, was a state Christian through and through. Its monarchy, its laws, its values—all derived from Christianity. Accordingly, so conservatives argued, its prime responsibility was the 'protection and advancement of the Christian religion.'[15] From this it followed in turn that there could be no place for Jews in its administration. If they wished to become properly Prussian, then they had a simple recourse: conversion. This was why Frederick William, on his visit to Cologne, had been willing to pay a social call on Oppenheim. What was a Jew prepared to fund a cathedral, after all, if not one close to finding Christ?

But the king had been deluding himself. Oppenheim had no intention of finding Christ. Instead, he and his family continued with their campaign. It was not long before Cologne, previously renowned as a bastion of chauvinism, was serving as a trailblazer for Jewish emancipation. In 1845, Napoleon's discriminatory legislation was definitively abolished. Time would see a sumptuous domed synagogue, designed by the architect responsible for the cathedral, and funded—inevitably—by the Oppenheims, rise up as one of the great landmarks of the city. Well before its construction, though, it was evident that Friedrich Wilhelm's dreams of resurrecting a medieval model of Christianity were doomed. In 1847, one particularly waspish theologian portrayed the king as a modern-day Julian the Apostate, chasing after a world forever gone. Then, as though to set the seal on this portrait, revolution returned to Europe. History seemed to be repeating itself. In February 1848, a French king was deposed. By March, protests and uprisings were flaring across Germany. Slogans familiar from the time of Robespierre could be heard on the streets of Berlin. The Prussian queen briefly dreaded that only the guillotine was lacking. Although, in the event, the insurrectionary mood was pacified, and the tottering Prussian monarchy stabilised, concessions offered by Friedrich Wilhelm would prove enduring. His kingdom emerged from the great crisis of 1848 as—for the first time—a state with a written constitution. The vast majority of its male inhabitants were now entitled to vote for a parliament. Among them, enrolled at last as equal citizens, were Prussia's Jews. Friedrich Wilhelm, appalled by the threat to the divine order that he had always pledged himself to upheld, declared himself sick to the stomach. 'If I were not a Christian I would take my own life.'[16]

Nevertheless, as the king might justifiably have pointed out, it was not Judaism that had been emancipated, but only those who practised it. Supporters of the Declaration of Rights had always been explicit on that score. The shackles of superstition were forged in synagogues no less than in churches. 'We must grant everything to Jews as individuals, but refuse to them everything as a nation!' This was the slogan with which, late in 1789, proponents of Jewish emancipation in France had sought to reassure their fellow revolutionaries. 'They must form neither a political body nor an order in the state, they must be citizens individually.'[17] And so it had come to pass. When the French Republic granted citizenship to Jews, it had done so on the understanding that they abandon any sense of themselves as a people set apart. No recognition or protection had been offered to the Mosaic law. The identity of Jews as a distinct community was tolerated only to the degree that it did not interfere with 'the common good'.[18] Here—garlanded with the high-flown rhetoric of the Enlightenment though it might be—was a programme for civic self-improvement that aimed at transforming the very essence of Judaism. Heraclius, a millennium and more previously, had attempted something very similar. The dream that Jewish distinctiveness might be subsumed into an identity that the whole world could share—one in which the laws given by God to mark the Jews out from other peoples would cease to matter—reached all the way back to Paul. Artists in the early years of the French Revolution, commissioned to depict the Declaration of Rights, had not hesitated to represent it as a new covenant, chiselled onto stone tablets and delivered from a blaze of light. Jews could either sign up to this radiant vision, or else be banished into storm-swept darkness. If this seemed to some Jews a very familiar kind of ultimatum, then that was because it was. That the Declaration of Rights claimed an authority for itself more universal than that of Christianity only emphasised the degree to which, in the scale of its ambitions and the scope of its pretensions, it was profoundly Christian.

The price paid by Jews for their freedom was, then, a real one. Citizenship required them to become just that bit more Christian. This, perhaps, was more evident in Germany even than in France. Devout Lutherans—Luther's own hatred for the Jews notwithstanding—were no less capable than Jacobins of making the case for Jewish emancipation. Some, indeed, had been doing so since before the fall of the Bastille. Their case was rich in the familiar rhetoric of Luther's writings: that the Law of Moses, which was withered, and desiccated, and arid, still held all those who obeyed it in its corpse-like embrace; that the papacy, by persecuting the Jews throughout the Middle Ages, had left them so degraded in character that they had remained ever since in a backward and corrupted condition.

Only liberate them from those two favourite objects of Lutheran obloquy, and all would be well. Judaism would reform itself. Jews would become productive citizens. This programme—no matter that it was shot through with Protestant assumptions—was one with which German Jews had generally been willing to ally themselves. While naturally offended by any suggestion that the Mosaic law might have been superseded by the law of Christ, they did not hesitate to promote it as compatible with the law of Prussia. The days of an independent Jewish state were long gone. In place of Israel, Jews now had Judaism. This word—Christian invention that it was—was one that they had never thought to use until the prospect of emancipation began to glimmer before them. Pressed by Protestant theologians to accept a status for Jewish law as something merely private and ceremonial, they were being pressed to accept something more: that they belonged not to a nation, but to a religion.

Many Jews had no problem with this concept. Some, indeed, found it liberating. In 1845, a group of Jewish intellectuals in Berlin issued a formal appeal for a Judaism that, transcending the written prescriptions of Torah, might be transformed into a religion 'that corresponds with our age and the sentiments of our heart'.[19] Already, even as Friedrich Wilhelm was attempting to re-erect the barriers between Jews and Christians, rabbis across the Lutheran heartlands of Germany had begun to proclaim the primacy of faith over law. Other Jews, meanwhile, appalled by any suggestion that the covenant revealed to Moses on Sinai might not have been definitive, condemned them as heretics. Two rival traditions—'Reform' and 'Orthodox'—began to emerge. In time, the Prussian state itself would come to formalise these divisions. Jews insistent on the enduring authority of the Mosaic law would be given official licence to establish themselves as a separate community. 'Judaism,' its founder insisted, 'is not a religion'[20]—and yet, for all that, he protested too much. Beliefs, privately and passionately held, were becoming the mark of Jewish as well as of Protestant congregations. Christians, it seemed, were no longer alone in bearing witness to the Reformation.

The great claim of what, in 1846, an English newspaper editor first termed 'secularism' was to neutrality. Yet this was a conceit. Secularism was not a neutral concept. The very word came trailing incense clouds of meaning that were irrevocably and venerably Christian. That there existed twin dimensions, the secular and the religious, was an assumption that reached back centuries beyond the Reformation: to Gregory VII, and to Columbanus, and to Augustine. The concept of secularism—for all that it was promoted by the editor who invented the word as an antidote to religion—testified not to Christianity's decline, but to its seemingly infinite capacity for evolution. Manifest in English, this was manifest in other languages too. When, in 1842, the word *laïcité* first appeared in French, it signified both a similar concept to 'secularism', and a similar pedigree: the *laicus* had originally been none other than the people of God. In Europe as in India, then, the process by which peoples who were not Christian came to be identified with a religion was inevitably a Procrustean one. For Jews—so similar to Christians, so profoundly different—the task of negotiating a new identity was, perhaps, especially delicate; and nowhere more so than in Germany. There, as the doomed efforts of Friedrich Wilhelm to resurrect medieval Christendom bore witness, Christians too were increasingly uncertain of their place in a fast-changing world. What, amid the ruins of the Holy Roman Empire, did it mean to be a German? Jews, by fashioning a religion that could take its place in a secular order alongside Christianity, had won the right to help solve this puzzle. Yet whether their fellow Germans would welcome their contribution, or resent them for making the attempt, remained an open question. Emancipation was not merely a solution; it was an ongoing challenge. The problem of how a defiantly distinctive culture that reached back millennia might best be squared with a secular order shot through with Christian assumptions was one that lacked a ready solution. The search for it, though, could hardly be ducked. Jews had little option, then, but to continue negotiating the boundaries of secularism, and to hope for the best.

A Crime Against Humanity

For almost two and a half millennia, one of the inscriptions commissioned by Darius to justify his rule of the world—written in three distinct languages, and featuring a particularly imperious portrait of the king himself—had been preserved on the side of a mountain by the name of Bisitun. Carved into a cliff some two hundred feet above the road that led from the Iranian plateau to Iraq, its survival had been ensured by its sheer inaccessibility. The chance to risk life and limb in the cause of deciphering ancient scripts, however, was one that the odd adventurer might positively relish. One such was Henry Rawlinson, a British officer on secondment from India to the Persian court. He first scouted out Bisitun in 1835, scaling the cliff as best as he was able, and recording as much of the inscription as he could make out. Then, eight years later, he returned to the site properly equipped with planks and ropes. Balanced precariously on a ladder, he was able to complete his transcription. 'The interest of the occupation,' he later recalled, 'entirely did away with any sense of danger.'[21] By 1845 Rawlinson had completed a full translation of the section written in Persian, and sent it for publication to London. The Great King spoke once more.

The boasts recorded on the cliff-face of Bisitun were ones that an officer in the employ of the East Indian Company might well appreciate. Darius had combined ambition on a global scale with a mastery of all the various political arts required to satisfy it: ruthlessness, cunning, self-confidence. Rawlinson, as seasoned a spy as he was a soldier, knew perfectly well that empires did not magic themselves into being. British power, already securely established in India, depended for its maintenance on agents willing to fight dirty. Rawlinson did not devote all his time to hunting down ancient inscriptions. Whether sweet-talking the Shah of Persia, manoeuvring against the Russians, or winning medals for gallantry in Afghanistan, he was a talented player in what a fellow intelligence officer, writing to him in 1840, had termed the 'great game'.[22] Darius

too, whose depiction at Bisitun showed him crushing a rival underfoot, had been a player in the great game of imperial advancement—
a player, and a victor. Nine kings had thought to defy him; nine
kings had been brought to defeat. The sculptor at Bisitun, obedient
to his master's commission, had portrayed them as dwarfs, tethered
together by their necks and cowering before their conqueror. Here,
for an officer such as Rawlinson, was timeless testimony to the brute
realities of empire-building.

Yet Darius, when he set himself to the conquest of barbarous and
fractious peoples, had claimed to be doing so for the good of the
cosmos. His mission had been to combat the Lie. Here, in his conviction that evil needed to be opposed wherever it was found, and truth
brought to the outermost limits of the world, had lain a justification
for empire of such enduring potency that Rawlinson himself, two
and a half thousand years on, bore witness to it. The 'great game'
was not an end in itself. The duty of a Christian nation, so Rawlinson's colleague had advised him, was to work for the regeneration of
less fortunate lands: to play a 'noble part'.[23] This, of course, was to
cast his own country as the very model of civilisation, the standard
by which all others might be judged: a conceit that came so naturally to imperial peoples that the Persians too, back in the time of
Darius, had revelled in it. Yet the British, despite the certitude felt
by many of them that their empire was a blessing bestowed on the
world by heaven, could not entirely share in the swagger of the Great
King. Pride in their dominion over palm and pine was accompanied
by a certain nervousness. The sacrifice demanded by their God was
a humble and a contrite heart. To rule foreign peoples—let alone
to plunder them of their wealth, or to settle their lands, or to hook
their cities on opium—was also, for a Christian people, never quite
to forget that their Saviour had lived as the slave, not the master, of
a mighty empire. It was an official of that empire who had sentenced
him to death; it was soldiers of that empire who had nailed him to
a cross. Rome's dominion had long since passed away. The reign of
Christ had not.

Every British Foreign Secretary—no matter how hard-nosed he might be, no matter how bluff—lived with the consciousness of this. Command of the oceans would be for nothing unless it served 'the Hands of Providence'.[24] One sin more than any other weighed heavily on the conscience of the British: a sin that only recently had hung like a millstone about their necks, ready to sink them to their perdition. In 1833, when the ban on the slave trade had been followed by the emancipation of slaves throughout the British Empire, abolitionists had greeted their hour of victory in rapturously biblical terms. It was the rainbow seen by Noah over the floodwaters; it was the passage of the Israelites through the Red Sea; it was the breaking of the Risen Christ from his tomb. Britain, a country that for so long had been lost in the valley of the shadow of death, had emerged at last into light. Now, in atonement for her guilt, it was her responsibility to help all the world be born again.

Nonetheless, British abolitionists knew better than to trumpet their sense of Protestant mission too loudly. Slavery was widespread, after all, and one that had made many in Portugal, Spain and France exceedingly rich. A campaign against the practice could never hope to be truly international without the backing of Catholic powers. No matter that it was Britain's naval muscle that enabled slave-ships to be searched and their crews to be put on trial, the legal frameworks that licensed these procedures had to appear resolutely neutral. British jurists, conquering the deep suspicion of anything Spanish that was an inheritance from the age of Elizabeth I, brought themselves to praise the 'courage and noble principle'[25] of Bartolomé las Casas. The result was an entire apparatus of law—complete with treaties and international courts—that made a virtue out of merging both Protestant and Catholic traditions. In 1842, when an American diplomat defined the slave trade as a 'crime against humanity',[26] the term was one calculated to be acceptable to lawyers of all Christian denominations—and none. Slavery, which only decades previously had been taken almost universally for granted, was now redefined as evidence of savagery and backwardness. To oppose it was to side with progress. To support it was to stand condemned before the bar, not just of Christianity, but of every religion.

All of which was liable to come as news to Muslims. In 1842, when the British consul-general to Morocco sought to press the cause of abolitionism, his request that the trade in African slaves be banned was greeted with blank incomprehension. It was a matter, the sultan declared, 'on which all sects and nations have agreed from the time of Adam'.[27] As proof, he might well have pointed to the United States, a nation that had proclaimed in its founding document that all men were created equal, and yet where the House of Representatives had only two years earlier ruled that it would no longer receive anti-slavery petitions. If this was testimony, on one level, to the sheer weight of abolitionist opinion, then it also reflected the obdurate determination of slave-owners in the south of the country never to relinquish their human property. American supporters of slavery scoffed at any claim that it might be incompatible with civilisation. Abolitionism, they pointed out, was a movement that had emanated from only a single small corner of the world. Against it was ranged the authority of Aristotle, and the jurists of ancient Rome, and the Bible itself. In the United States, there were still pastors convinced by a case almost totally abandoned by Protestants elsewhere: that the laws issued by God licensing slavery held eternally good. 'He has given them his sanction, therefore, they must be in harmony with his moral character.'[28]

A sentiment with which the sultan of Morocco would certainly have concurred. Missions by British abolitionists continued to be swatted aside. In 1844, the governor of an island off the Moroccan coast flatly informed one of them that any ban on slavery would be 'against our religion'.[29] Such bluntness was hardly surprising. Wild claims that the spirit of scripture might be distinguished from its letter was liable to strike most Muslims as a foolish and sinister blasphemy. The law of God was not to be found written in the heart, but in the great inheritance of writings that derived from the lifetime of the Prophet. These, aflame with the divine as they were, brooked no contradiction. The owning of slaves was licensed by the Qur'an, by the example of Muhammad himself, and by the Sunna, that great corpus of Islamic traditions and practices. Who, then, were Christians to demand its abolition?

But the British, to the growing bafflement of Muslim rulers, refused to leave the question alone. Back in 1840, pressure on the Ottomans to eradicate the slave trade had been greeted in Constantinople, as the British ambassador in the city put it, 'with extreme astonishment and a smile at the proposition of destroying an institution closely interwoven with the frame of society'.[30] A decade later, when the sultan found himself confronted by a devastating combination of military and financial crises, British support came at a predictable price. In 1854, the Ottoman government was obliged to issue a decree prohibiting the slave trade across the Black Sea; three years later the African slave trade was banned. Also abolished was the *jizya*, the tax on Jews and Christians that reached back to the very beginnings of Islam, and was directly mandated by the Qur'an. Such measures, of course, risked considerable embarrassment to the sultan. Their effect was, after all, to reform the Sunna according to the standards of the thoroughly infidel British. To acknowledge that anything contrary to Islamic tradition had been forced on a Muslim ruler by Christians was clearly unthinkable; and so Ottoman reformers instead made sure to claim a sanction of their own. Circumstances, they argued, had changed since the time of the Prophet. Rulings in Islamic jurisprudence that appeared to condone slavery were as nothing compared to those that praised the freeing of slaves as an act most pleasing to God. The Qur'an, if it were only to be read in the correct light, would open the eyes of the believer to the true essence of Islam: an essence that now, more than twelve centuries after the death of Muhammad, stood revealed as abolitionist through and through. Yet this manoeuvre, for all that it might seem to save the sultan's face, threatened as well to infect Islam with profoundly Christian assumptions about the proper functioning of law. The spirit of the Sunna, it turned out, might after all trump its letter. Insidiously, among elite circles in the Islamic world, a novel understanding of legal proprieties was coming to be fostered: an understanding that derived ultimately not from Muhammad, nor from any Muslim jurist, but from Saint Paul.

In 1863, barely twenty years after the sultan of Morocco had declared slavery an institution approved since the dawn of time, the mayor of Tunis wrote a letter to the American consul-general, citing justifications drawn from Islamic scripture for its abolition. In the United States, escalating tensions over the rights and wrongs of the institution had helped to precipitate, in 1861, the secession of a confederacy of southern states, and a terrible war with what remained of the Union. Naturally, for as long as Americans continued to slaughter one another in battle, there could be no definitive resolution of the issue. Nevertheless, at the beginning of 1863, the United States president, Abraham Lincoln, had issued a proclamation, declaring all slaves on Confederate territory to be free. Clearly, should the Unionists only emerge victorious from the civil war, then slavery was liable to be abolished across the country. It was in support of this eventuality that the mayor of Tunis sought to offer his encouragement. Aware that the Americans were unlikely to be swayed by citations from Islamic scripture, he concluded his letter by urging them to act instead out of 'human mercy and compassion'.[31] Here, perhaps, lay the ultimate demonstration of just how effective the attempt by Protestant abolitionists to render their campaign universal had become. A cause that, only a century earlier, had been the preserve of a few crankish Quakers had come to spread far and wide like the rushing wildfire of the Spirit. It did not need missionaries to promote evangelical doctrines around the world. Lawyers and ambassadors might achieve it even more effectively: for they did it, in the main, by stealth. A crime against humanity was bound to have far more resonance beyond the limits of the Christian world than a crime against Christ. A crusade, it turned out, might be more effective for keeping the cross well out of sight.

All of which promised great advantage to the empire that had first launched it. The British had not begun their campaign to stamp out the slave trade in any mood of cynicism. At odds with their immediate interests, both geopolitical and economic, it was also extremely expensive. Nevertheless, the more the tide of global opinion turned against slavery, so the more the prestige of the nation that had first recanted it was inevitably burnished. 'England,' exclaimed a Persian prince in 1862, 'assumes to be the determined enemy of the slave trade, and has gone to an enormous expense to liberate the African races, to whom she is no way bound save by the tie of a common humanity.'[32] Yet already, even as he was expressing his wonderment at such selflessness, the British were busy capitalising on the prestige it had won them. In 1857, a treaty that committed the shah to suppressing the slave trade in the Persian Gulf had also served to consolidate Britain's influence over his country. Meanwhile, in the heart of Africa, missionaries were starting to venture where Europeans had never before thought to go. Reports they brought back, of the continuing depredations of Arab slavers, confirmed the view of many in Britain that slavery would never be wholly banished until the entire continent had been won for civilisation. That this equated to their own rule was, of course, taken for granted. 'I will search for the lost and bring back the strays.' So God had declared in the Bible. 'I will bind up the injured and strengthen the weak, but the sleek and the strong I will destroy.'[33] Here—not just for Britain, but for any power that might plausibly lay claim to it—lay a licence for conquest that, in due course, would foster a headlong scramble for colonies. It was not the slavers who would end up settling Africa, and subjugating it to foreign rule, but—by an irony familiar from Christian history—the emancipators.

18

SCIENCE

1876: The Judith River

Every night the professor would suffer from nightmares. As dry thunder rumbled over the Montana badlands, Edward Drinker Cope would toss and moan in his sleep. Sometimes, one of his companions would wake him. Understandably, the nerves of everyone on the expedition were drawn tight. The American West was a dangerous place. Cope, prospecting for fossils in regions as yet unmapped by the US Army, was crossing the hunting grounds of a particularly formidable native people: the Sioux. Only a few weeks previously, a seasoned general and veteran of the Unionist victory in the recent civil war, George Armstrong Custer, had been defeated by their warbands on the banks of the Little Bighorn River. At one point, Cope and his expedition had come within a day's ride of where—as one of them put it—'thousands of warriors, drunk with the blood of Custer and the brave men of the 7th US Cavalry',[1] were camped out. A scout and a cook, both terrified for their scalps, had fled. But it was not thoughts of the Sioux that gave Cope his nightmares. Instead, his dreams were haunted by finds that he and his companions had made in the great labyrinth of canyons and ravines that stretched all around them where they had made base. Beneath the brightness of the stars these appeared impenetrably black. The drop in many places was a thousand feet. One slip on the loose shale and a man might well plunge to his death. Yet there was a time when the now barren landscape had been teeming with life. Buried amid the gorges were the bones of monsters that once, many millions of years before, had roamed what was then a coastal plain. For most of history, no one had realised that such creatures had even existed. It was only in 1841, in distant England, that they had been given a name. Yet now, camped out in the wilds of Montana, in the heights above the Judith River, Cope knew himself to be surrounded by the remains of untold numbers of them: an immense and uncharted graveyard of dinosaurs.

The ambition of fathoming the deep past of the earth was one that had always come naturally to Christians. 'Of old,' the psalmist had written in praise of the Creator, 'You founded the earth, and the heavens—Your handiwork. They will perish and You will yet stand. They will all wear away like a garment.'[2] Here, in this vision of a world that had both a beginning and a history, linear and irreversible, lay an understanding of time in decisive contrast to that of most peoples in antiquity. To read Genesis was to know that it did not go round in endless cycles. Unsurprisingly, then, scholars of the Bible had repeatedly sought to map out a chronology that might reach back before humans. 'We must not suppose,' Luther had declared, 'that the appearance of the world is the same today as it was before sin.'[3] Increasingly, though, enthusiasts for what by the late eighteenth century had come to be termed geology were basing their investigations not on Genesis, but directly on their study of God's creation: rocks and fossils, and the very contours of the earth.

Among the clergy in Britain this had grown to become a particular obsession. In 1650, when James Ussher, the archbishop of Armagh and one of the most brilliant scholars of his day, sought to establish a global chronology, his exclusive reliance on written records—and in particular on the Bible—led him to identify the date of the Creation as 4004 BC. In 1822, when William Buckland, another clergyman, published a paper demonstrating that life on earth, let alone the deposition of rocks, was infinitely older than Noah's flood, it was his dating of the fossils he had found in a Yorkshire cave that enabled him to demonstrate his point. Two years later, he wrote the first full account of a dinosaur. In 1840, he argued that great gouges across the landscape of Scotland bore witness to an ancient—and decidedly unbiblical—Ice Age. Buckland, a noted eccentric with a taste for eating his way through every kind of animal, from bluebottles to porpoises, saw not the slightest contradiction between serving as dean of Westminster and lecturing on geology at Oxford.* Nor did most Christians. Although some, clinging to a literal interpretation of Genesis, refused to accept that the earth's history might stretch back immeasurable distances before man, the vast majority felt only awe before a Creator capable of working on such a prodigious scale. Geology, bred as it was of the biblical understanding of time, seemed less to shake than to buttress Christian faith.

Yet there were signs, even as Cope embarked on his fossil-harvesting in the wilds of the American West, that this was changing. Cope himself—so unsettled by the dinosaurs he found entombed in rock that they came to visit him in his dreams, 'tossing him into the air, kicking him, trampling upon him'[4]—was a man suffering from a crisis of faith. The descendant of a Quaker who had settled in Philadelphia after buying land there from William Penn, he had been raised by his father to believe in the literal truth of Noah's flood. A precocious fascination with ichthyosaurs, prehistoric monsters of the deep, had soon put paid to that; but not to Cope's faith. Toiling through the badlands, he would hold prayer meetings every evening, and readings from the Bible. His very obsession with animals, alive as well as extinct, marked him out as a distinctive kind of Christian. That God, filling the world with living creatures, had looked on them and seen that they were good, had long suggested to careful readers of Genesis that they bore witness to his design. 'He is the source of all that exists in nature,' Augustine

---

* Buckland's most startling feat, perhaps, was to gobble down what was reliably reported to have been the heart of King Louis XIV of France.

had long ago written, 'whatever its kind, whatsoever its value, and of the seeds of forms, and the forms of seeds, and the motions of seeds and forms.'[5] William Buckland, whose fascination with all aspects of the animal kingdom was such that he had been the first to identify the faeces of an ichthyosaur, and could distinguish bat urine by taste, had been only one of a great number of clergymen committed to the minutest examination of the natural world. In Britain and America especially, the conviction that God's workings were manifest in nature—'natural theology'—had become, by the middle of the nineteenth century, a key weapon in the armoury of Christianity's defenders. An English parson illustrating the goodness of God was as likely to cite the life cycle of a butterfly as the theology of Calvin. The teeming of insects in a hedgerow had come to seem to many Christians in the English-speaking world a more certain witness to their faith than any appeal to revelation. And yet this confidence had been shown up as something grievously misplaced. What appeared an unassailable support of the Christian religion had proved to be nothing of the kind. A position of strength had been transformed into a grievous source of weakness. Natural theology had become, almost overnight, an Achilles' heel.

Charles Darwin, who as a youth had obsessively collected beetles, and gone on field trips with a geology professor in holy orders, and had himself for a short while been destined for a career in the Church, was a product of the same milieu as William Buckland and all the other prominent defenders of natural theology in England. Yet Darwin, far from joining their ranks, had emerged instead to become their bane. In 1860, writing to Asa Gray, America's most eminent botanist, he confessed his motivation. 'I had no intention to write atheistically. But I own that I cannot see, as plainly as others do, & as I sh^d wish to do, evidence of design & beneficence on all sides of us. There seems to me too much misery in the world.'[6] Job, of course, had raised much the same complaint; and Darwin, just like Job, had suffered from boils and the death of a child. But God had not spoken to him from a whirlwind; and Darwin, when he contemplated the natural world, found in it too many examples of cruelty to believe that they might ever have been the result of conscious design. One more than any other haunted him: a species of parasitic wasp. 'I cannot persuade myself that a beneficent & omnipotent God would have designedly created the Ichneumonidæ with the express intention of their feeding within the living bodies of caterpillars.'[7]

A year earlier, Darwin had published a book in which the life cycle of the ichneumon wasp had similarly featured. The thesis elaborated in *On the Origin of Species* was liable to seem, to any supporter of natural theology, a profoundly unsettling one. 'It may not be a logical deduction,' Darwin had written, 'but to my imagination it is far more satisfactory to look at such instincts as the young cuckoo ejecting its foster-brothers, — ants making slaves, — the larvae of ichneumonidae feeding within the live bodies of caterpillars, — not as specially endowed or created instincts, but as small consequences of one general law, leading to the advancement of all organic beings, namely, multiply, vary, let the strongest live and the weakest die.'[8] Here, with this theory of evolution, he was inflicting on natural theology something of the hideous fate visited by an ichneumon on its host. The parsons who in growing numbers had come to roam the fields of England with their butterfly nets and their flower presses took certain propositions as manifest. That the immense plenitude of species bore witness to a single guiding hand; that only in relation to their environment could the full perfection of their design be understood; that the purposes manifest in nature were irreversible. Darwin, in *The Origin of Species*, was not disputing any of these assumptions. They were, though, to his theory of evolution by natural selection, what the innards of a caterpillar were to the larvae of an ichneumon. 'The Creator creates by...laws.'[9] So, decades previously, at a time when he was still a believing Christian, Darwin had recorded in a notebook. Abelard had claimed much the same. For centuries, in the Christian world, it had been the great project of natural philosophy to identify the laws that animated

God's creation, and thereby to arrive at a closer understanding of God himself. Now, with *The Origin of Species*, a law had been formulated that—even as it unified the realm of life with that of time—seemed to have no need of God at all. Not merely a theory, it was itself a startling display of evolution.

But was it right? By 1876, the most impressive evidence for Darwin's theory had been uncovered in what was fast proving to be the world's premier site for fossil beds: the American West. Cope was not the only palaeontologist to have made spectacular discoveries there. So too had Othniel Charles Marsh, a Yale professor with the beard, bulk and bombast of a middle-aged Henry VIII. Over the course of six years' work in the field, he had succeeded in excavating no less than thirty species of prehistoric horse. So complete a chain of evidence did these finds constitute that Darwin could hail them as 'the best support to the theory of evolution which has appeared in the last 20 years'.[10] Cope, whose envy and detestation of Marsh was cordially reciprocated, did not dispute this. He had long accepted that the evidence for evolution was overwhelming. Nevertheless, unlike his great rival, he refused to accept that it was driven by natural selection. He longed still to find in the natural world a place for a beneficent God. The only deity for which the theory of natural selection had room, he fretted, was one content to botch a species here, to tinker with it there. Certainly, no place was left by it for any sense of a divine design. Yet divine design, so Cope believed, was precisely what the evolution of the horse served to illustrate. Back from the Judith River, he delivered a paper that made this case in forceful terms. The fossils found by Marsh, he told an assembly of American naturalists in 1877, spoke of changes far too regular to be explained by random variation. 'The ascending development of the bodily structure in higher animals has thus been, in all probability, a concomitant of the evolution of mind.'[11] The modern horse, in other words, had willed itself into being. Far from being at the mercy of its environment, the species had always been in charge of its own destiny. The course of its evolution, long foreseen by its Creator, bore witness not to chaos and confusion, but rather to an order that suffused the whole of nature. Borne on the flow of time, every species was bound for a goal preordained by God.

But to accept this was, of course, to accept something more: that humans too were a product of evolution. Darwin, in *The Origin of Species*, had only coyly hinted at what the implication of his theory might be for humanity's understanding of itself. This, though, had not prevented others from indulging in their own speculations. Bishops demanded to know of Darwin's defenders the precise details of their descent from gorillas; satirists delighted in portraying Darwin himself as an ape; Cope declared it his belief that humanity had evolved from a lemur. Yet not all the debating society sallies, not all the cartoons of monkeys in frock coats, not all the theorising about possible lines of human descent could entirely conceal what yawned behind them: an immense abyss of anxiety and doubt. Nervousness at the idea that humanity might have evolved from another species was not bred merely of a snobbery towards monkeys. Something much more was at stake. To believe that God had become man and suffered the death of a slave was to believe that there might be strength in weakness, and victory in defeat. Darwin's theory, more radically than anything that previously had emerged from Christian civilisation, challenged that assumption. Weakness was nothing to be valued. Jesus, by commending the meek and the poor over those better suited to the great struggle for survival that was existence, had set *Homo sapiens* upon the downward path towards degeneration.

For eighteen long centuries, the Christian conviction that all human life was sacred had been underpinned by one doctrine more than any other: that man and woman were created in God's image. The divine was to be found as much in the pauper, the convict or the prostitute as it was in the gentleman with his private income and book-lined study. Darwin's house, despite its gardens, private wood and greenhouse filled with orchids, stood on the margins of an unprecedented agglomeration of brick and smoke. Beyond the fields where he would lovingly inspect the workings of worms there stretched what Rome had been in Augustus' day: the capital of the largest empire in the world. Just as Rome had once done, London sheltered disorienting extremes of privilege and squalor. The Britain of Darwin's day, though, could boast what no one in Augustus' Rome had ever thought to sponsor: campaigns to redeem the poor, the exploited, the diseased. Darwin himself, the grandson of two prominent abolitionists, knew full well the impulse from which these sprang. The great cause of social reform was Christian through and through. 'We build asylums for the imbecile, the maimed and the sick; we institute poor-laws; and our medical men exert their utmost skill to save the life of every one to the last moment.'[12] And yet the verdict delivered by Darwin on these displays of philanthropy was a fretful one. Much as the Spartans had done, when they flung sickly babies down a ravine, he dreaded the consequences for the strong of permitting the weak to propagate themselves. 'No one who has attended to the breeding of domestic animals will doubt that this must be highly injurious to the race of man.'[13]

Here, for any Quaker, was a peculiarly distressing assertion. Cope knew the traditions to which he was heir. It was Quakers who had first lit the fire which, in the recent civil war, had come to consume the institution of American slavery; it was Quakers who, in America as in Britain, had taken the lead in campaigning for prison reform. Whatever they did for the least of their Saviour's brothers and sisters, they did for Christ himself. How, then, could this conviction possibly be squared with what Cope, in mingled scorn and dread, termed 'the Darwinian law of the "survival of the fittest"'?[14] The question was one that had perturbed Darwin himself. He remained sufficiently a Christian to define any proposal to abandon the weak and the poor to their fate as 'evil'.[15] The instincts that had fostered a concern for the disadvantaged must themselves, he noted, have been the product of natural selection. Presumably, then, they had to be reckoned to serve some evolutionary purpose. Yet Darwin havered. In private conversations he would confess that, because 'in our modern civilisation natural selection had no play',[16] he feared for the future. Christian notions of charity—however much he might empathise with them personally—were misplaced. Only continue to give them free rein, and the peoples who clung to them were bound to degenerate.

And this, were it to happen, would be to the detriment of the entire human race. Here, at any rate, Cope was in perfect accord with Darwin. He had taken the railroad across the vast expanses of the Great Plains, and he had sent telegrams from forts planted in the lands of the Sioux, and he had seen their hunting grounds littered for miles around with the bleached bones of bison, felled by the very latest in repeating rifles. He knew that Custer's defeat had been only a temporary aberration. The native tribes of America were doomed. The advance of the white race was inexorable. It was their manifest destiny. This was evident around the world. In Africa, where a variety of European powers were scheming to carve up the continent; in Australia, and New Zealand, and Hawaii, where there was no resisting the influx of white colonists; in Tasmania, where an entire native people had already been driven to extinction. 'The grade of their civilisation,' as Darwin put it, 'seems to be a most important element in the success of competing nations.'[17]

How were these differences, between a white and a native American, between a European and a Tasmanian, most plausibly to be explained? The traditional response of a Christian would have been to assert that between two human beings of separate races there was no fundamental difference: both had equally been created in the image of God. To Darwin, however, his theory of natural selection suggested a rather different answer. As a young man, he had sailed the seas of the world, and he had noted how, 'wherever the European has trod, death seems to pursue the aboriginal'.[18] His feelings of compassion for native peoples, and his matching distaste for white settlers, had not prevented him from arriving at a stark conclusion: that there had come to exist over the course of human existence a natural hierarchy of races. The progress of Europeans had enabled them, generation by generation, to outstrip 'the intellectual and social faculties'[19] of more savage peoples. Cope—despite his refusal to accept Darwin's explanation for how and why this might have happened—conceded that he had a point. Clearly, in humanity as in any other species, the operations of evolution were perpetually at work. 'We all admit the existence of higher and lower races,' Cope acknowledged, 'the latter being those which we now find to present greater or less approximation to the apes.' So it was that an attempt by a devout Quaker to reconcile the workings of God with those of nature brought him to an understanding of humanity that would have appalled Benjamin Lay. Cope's conviction that a species could will itself towards perfection enabled him to believe as well that different forms of the same species could co-exist. Whites, he argued, had elevated themselves to a new degree of consciousness. Other races had not.

In 1877, a year after he had lain amid the fossil beds of Montana, oppressed by terrible dreams, Edward Drinker Cope formally resigned from the Society of Friends.

A New Reformation

Not everyone who read Darwin interpreted his theory as licensing a bleak and carnivorous vision of human society. Among the more pugnacious of his followers, the banishment of God from the realm of nature was viewed as an unalloyed blessing. 'A veritable Whitworth gun in the armoury of liberalism'[20]—so The Origin of Species was hailed by one of its earliest and most positive reviewers. Thomas Henry Huxley, an anatomist whose genius for savaging bishops led to him being described as 'Darwin's bulldog', was a self-professed enthusiast for progress. Impatient with the influence of men like Buckland over the study of geology and natural history, he yearned to see it professionalised. Not only would the rout of 'Theology & Parsondom'[21] lead to more opportunities for men like himself—self-educated, middle class, contemptuous of privilege—but it would help to spread the blessings of enlightenment. The more that the fog of superstition was banished, the more apparent would become the contours of truth. Even though the sunlit uplands of reason were beckoning, the road to them still had to be cleared. It was only by stepping over the corpses of extinguished theologians that humanity would be able to leave delusion behind. If this required Darwin's theory to be employed as a muzzle-loader, then so be it. The age demanded nothing less. Huxley, writing a few months before *The Origin of Species* was published, had recognised that a great conflict was brewing. 'Few see it, but I believe we are on the Eve of a new Reformation and if I have a wish to live thirty years, it is that I may see the foot of Science on the necks of her Enemies.'[22]

But what did Huxley mean by 'Science'? The answer was not at all obvious. Branches of knowledge ranging from grammar to music had all traditionally ranked as sciences. Theology had long reigned as their queen. At Oxford, 'science' still, even in the 1850s, meant 'attainment in Aristotle'.[23] Huxley, though, was hardly the man to rest content with that. The early decades of the nineteenth century had seen a new and altogether more cutting-edge definition of the word establish itself. When palaeontologists or chemists used 'science' to mean the sum of all the natural and physical sciences, they made it appear to their contemporaries a concept simultaneously novel and familiar—much as 'Hinduism' was to Indians. Huxley, with the assiduity of a general keen to make sure of a recently annexed province, went to great pains to secure its borders. 'In matters of the intellect,' he warned, 'do not pretend that conclusions are certain which are not demonstrated or demonstrable.'[24] Such was the principle of 'agnosticism', a word that Huxley had come up with himself, and which he cast as the essential requirement for anyone who wished to practise science. It was, he flatly declared, 'the only method by which truth could be ascertained'.[25] Everyone reading him knew his target. Truth that could be neither demonstrated nor proven, truth that was dependent for its claims on a purportedly supernatural revelation, was not truth at all. Science—as a practitioner of the fashionable new art of photography might have put it—was defined by its negative: religion.

Here, then, lay a striking paradox. Although the concept of science, as it emerged over the course of the nineteenth century, was defined by men who assumed it to be the very opposite of novel, something timeless and universal, this was conceit of a very familiar kind. Science, precisely because it was cast as religion's doppelgänger, inevitably bore the ghostly stamp of Europe's Christian past. Huxley, however, refused to recognise this. The same man whose genius as an anatomist enabled him to identify what only now has become almost universally accepted, that modern birds are descended from dinosaurs that once, millions of years ago, were scampering through Jurassic forests, had no problem in believing that 'science' had always existed. Just as colonial officials and missionaries, travelling to India, had imposed the concept of 'religion' on the societies they found there, so did agnostics colonise the past in similar manner. The ancient Egyptians, and Babylonians, and Romans: all were assumed to have had a 'religion'. Some peoples—most notably the Greeks—were also assumed to have had 'science'. It was this that had enabled their civilisation to serve as the wellspring of progress. Philosophers had been the prototypes of scientists. The library of Alexandria had been 'the birthplace of modern science'.[26] Only Christians, with their fanatical hatred of reason and their determination to eradicate pagan learning, had prevented the ancient world from being set on a path towards steam engines and cotton mills. Wilfully, monks had set themselves to writing over anything that smacked of philosophy. The triumph of the Church had been an abortion of everything that made for a humane and civilised society. Darkness had descended on Europe. For a millennium and more, popes and inquisitors had laboured to snuff out any spark of curiosity, or enquiry, or reason. The most notable martyr to this fanaticism had been Galileo. Tortured for demonstrating beyond all shadow of a doubt that the earth revolved around the sun, 'he groaned away his days,' as Voltaire had put it, 'in the dungeons of the Inquisition'.[27] Bishops who scoffed at Darwin's theory of evolution by asking sneery questions about gorillas were merely the latest combatants in a war that was as old as Christianity itself.

That nothing in this narrative was true did not prevent it from becoming a wildly popular myth. Nor was its appeal confined solely to agnostics. There was much in it for Protestants to relish as well. The portrayal of medieval Christendom as a hellhole of backwardness and bigotry reached all the way back to Luther. Huxley's sense of himself as a member of an elect had—as contemporaries were quick to note—a familiarly radical quality. 'He has the moral earnestness, the volitional energy, the absolute confidence in his own convictions, the desire and determination to impress them upon all mankind, which are the essential marks of the Puritan character.'[28] Yet in truth, the growing conviction of many agnostics that science alone possessed the ability to answer questions about life's larger purpose derived from a much older seedbed. Once upon a time, the natural sciences had been natural philosophy. The awe felt by medieval theologians before the works and the wonders of creation was not absent from *The Origin of Species*. Darwin, in its concluding lines, described his theory in sonorous terms. 'There is grandeur in this view of life,' he proclaimed. The conviction that the universe moved in obedience to laws which might be comprehended by human reason, and that the fruit of these laws was 'most beautiful and most wonderful', was one that joined him directly to the distant age of Abelard.[29] When, in Germany, Darwinists fantasised that churches might soon feature altars to astronomy and be decked out with orchids, their hankering after the venerable gravitas of Christianity was rendered explicit. The war between science and religion reflected—at least in part—the claims of both to a common inheritance.

Darwin's wife, a Christian to the end of her days, voiced the dread of many at what this seemed to portend. Writing to her son shortly after Darwin's death, she confessed that 'your father's opinion that *all* morality has grown up by evolution is painful to me'.[30] Already, it appeared that there was no reach of Christian teaching where a scientist might hesitate to intrude. Even as some trained telescopes on Mars or sought to track the passage of invisible rays, others were turning their attentions to the bedroom. Here, as the Marquis de Sade had insistently complained, a morality that derived ultimately from Paul continued to prescribe the acceptable parameters of behaviour. Darwin and his theory, though, had set the cat among the pigeons. The functioning of natural selection depended on reproduction. The mating habits of humans was no less legitimate a field of study than those of the birds or the bees. This—in countries less embarrassed by sex than Darwin's own—provided a licence for scientists to investigate the detail and variety of sexual behaviour on a scale that might have impressed even Sade himself. In 1886, when the German psychiatrist Richard von Krafft-Ebing published a survey of what he termed 'pathological fetishism', the sheer scope of his researches made his book a focus of interest far beyond the scholarly circles at which it was aimed. Six years later, an English translation of the *Psychopathia Sexualis* prompted one reviewer to lament its vast and undiscerning readership. The entire book, he complained, should have been rendered into the decent obscurity of Latin.

Nevertheless, classicists could still find much in it to pique their interest. One word in particular, a portmanteau of Greek and Latin, stuck out. *Homosexualität* had originally been coined in 1869, to provide the writer of a pamphlet on Prussian morality laws with a shorthand for sexual relations between people of the same gender. This, of course, was precisely the category of behaviour that Paul, in his letter to the Romans, had so roundly excoriated, and which Aquinas had defined as sodomy. Nevertheless, in the age of Enlightenment as in that of Bernadino, the word remained a slippery one. In 1772, for instance, when Sade was found guilty of having anal sex with women, it was as a sodomite that he had been legally convicted. Now, with the precision of a skilled anatomist, Krafft-Ebing had succeeded in identifying with a single word the category of sexual behaviour condemned by Paul. Only a medical man, perhaps, could have done it. Krafft-Ebing's interest in same-sex relations was as a scientist, not a moralist. Why—in seeming defiance of Darwin's theory—did men or women chose to sleep with people of their own sex? The traditional explanation, that such people were lustful predators whose failure to control their appetites had led them to weary of what God had ordained as natural, was starting to seem inadequate to psychiatrists. Much likelier, Krafft-Ebing believed, 'homosexuals' were the victims of an underlying morbid condition. Whether this was to be viewed as something hereditary, an ailment passed down the generations, or as the result of an accident suffered in the uterus, it was clear to him that homosexuality should be regarded not as a sin, but as something very different: an immutable condition. Homosexuals, he argued, were the creatures of their proclivities. As such—Christian concern for the unfortunate being what it was—they deserved to be treated with generosity and compassion.

Most Christians were unpersuaded. The challenge that Krafft-Ebing's researches presented to their understanding of sexual morality was twofold. Even as *Psychopathia Sexualis* demonstrated that there were people who could not help having a taste for sexual activities condemned by scripture as immoral, so also—just as disturbingly—did it propose that many in the Church's history might themselves have been in the grip of deviant sexual needs. When Krafft-Ebing invented the word 'sadism' to describe those who took erotic pleasure in inflicting pain, he was implicitly associating the Marquis with inquisitors such as Conrad of Marburg. Even more shocking to devout sensibilities, however, was his analysis of what he termed—after Leopold von Sacher-Masoch, an Austrian nobleman with a taste for being whipped by aristocratic ladies dressed in furs—'masochism'. 'Masochists subject themselves to all kinds of maltreatment and suffering in which there can be no question of reflex excitation of lust.' In consequence, Krafft-Ebing declared, he had no hesitation in identifying 'the self-torture of religious enthusiasts', and even martyrs, as a form of masochism.[31] Seven hundred years after Elizabeth of Hungary had surrendered herself to the strict ministrations of her confessor, the unsentimental gaze of psychiatry presumed to stare at her as she had never been stared at before. A masochist, Krafft-Ebing ruled, was the perfect counterpart of a sadist. 'The parallelism is perfect.'[32]

Yet even as psychiatry served to challenge Christian assumptions, so also did it fortify them. Krafft-Ebing's conclusions were not nearly as clinical as either his critics or his admirers cared to think. Raised a Catholic, he took for granted the primacy of the Christian model of marriage. The great labour of the Church in fashioning and upholding monogamy as a lifelong institution was one that he deeply valued. 'Christianity raised the union of the sexes to a sublime position by making woman socially the equal of man and by elevating the bond of love to a moral and religious institution.'[33] It was not despite believing this, but because of it, that Krafft-Ebing, by the end of his career, had come to believe that sodomy should be decriminalised. Homosexuals, he declared, might be no less familiar with 'the noblest inspirations of the heart' than any married couple.[34] Huge numbers of them, inspired by his researches, wrote to him, sharing their most intimate yearnings and secrets. It was on the basis of this correspondence that Krafft-Ebing was able to arrive at a paradoxical conclusion. The sexual practice condemned by the Church as sodomy was perfectly compatible with the ideal that he saw as Christianity's great contribution to civilisation: lifelong monogamy. Homosexuality, as defined by the first scientist ever to attempt a detailed categorisation of it, constituted the seamless union of Christian sin with Christian love.

In cool and dispassionate language, Krafft-Ebing put the seal on a revolution in the dimensions of the erotic that was without parallel in history. Paul, by twinning men who slept with men and women who slept with women, had set in train a recalibration of the sexual order that now, in an age of science, attained its apotheosis. 'Homosexuality' was not the only medical-sounding compound of Greek and Latin to which *Psychopathia Sexualis* introduced the world. There was a second: 'heterosexuality'. All the other categories of sexual behaviour that Krafft-Ebing had identified—sadism, masochism, fetishistic obsessions—were mere variations of the one great and fundamental divide: that which existed between heterosexual and homosexual desire. Categories that had taken almost two millennia to evolve were now impregnably defined. Soon enough, the peoples of Europe and America would forget that they had ever not been there. Exported by missionaries and embedded within colonial legal systems across the world, a way of conceptualising desire that had originated with an itinerant Jew back in the reign of Nero would come to enjoy a global sway. In the sexual order as in so much else, the roots of modernity reached deep into Christian soil.

Visiting Diplodocus

Meanwhile, in America, the Wild West was being tamed. Palaeontologists as well as cowboys found themselves obliged to adjust to the closing of the frontier. The old freebooting ways practised by Cope and Marsh with such gusto were proving hard to sustain. Both men ended up ruined. In 1890, scandalous details of what journalists called the 'Bone Wars' were published in the press: how America's two most eminent palaeontologists had been employing rival gangs of workmen to smash up each other's finds, and writing scholarly papers to destroy each other's reputations. Fossil-prospecting no longer came as cheaply as it had once done, and both Cope and Marsh found themselves increasingly short of funds. A new age was dawning—one in which the search for dinosaurs was to be dominated by plutocrats. Andrew Carnegie, an industrialist with the largest liquid fortune in the world, could bring resources to bear on the quest for prehistoric remains beyond the wildest dreams of scientists. Cope and Marsh were priced out of the market. Carnegie had no interest in roaming badlands panning for fragments of Mesozoic tooth. He wanted fossils on a scale appropriate to his gargantuan wealth. When his workmen excavated the skeleton of an eighty-foot dinosaur, he made sure to trumpet his ownership of the find by having it named *Diplodocus carnegii*. It was, his publicists screamed, the 'most colossal animal ever on earth'.[35]

To bag trophies was the way of man. Carnegie passionately believed this. An immigrant from Scotland who had gone from labouring in a cotton mill to monopolising the production of American steel, his entire career had been what the ancient Greeks might have called an *agon*. Rivals were there to be crushed, unions to be broken, the resources of capital to be concentrated in his own grasping and restless hands. Farmers, artisans, shopkeepers: all had to be broken to what his critics termed wage-slavery. Carnegie, who had once been poor himself, had no time for any idea that woe might be due the rich. Impatient with clergymen who offered lectures from the pulpit on their iniquities, he held a sterner view of the miseries suffered by the poor, for he 'had found the truth of evolution'.[36] The only alternative to the survival of the fittest was the survival of the unfittest. Indiscriminate charity served no purpose save to subsidise the lazy and the drunk. Contemptuous of any notion of the supernatural, Carnegie was contemptuous as well of what America's most distinguished social scientist had termed 'the old ecclesiastical prejudice in favor of the poor and against the rich'. William Graham Sumner, a professor at Yale, had once felt a calling to the ministry; but the experience of serving as a clergyman had led him to reject the Church's teachings on poverty. 'In days when men acted by ecclesiastical rules these prejudices produced waste of capital, and helped mightily to replunge Europe into barbarism.'[37] If only Columbanus, rather than skulking profitlessly in woods, had set up a business. If only Boniface, rather than haranguing pagans, had brought them the good news of free trade. Here was teaching of which Carnegie was proud to consider himself a disciple.

And yet he could not help, for all that, but remain the child of his Presbyterian upbringing. When Carnegie's family had travelled to America from Scotland they had brought with them, just as the Pilgrim Fathers had once done, the knowledge that regeneration did not come easily to fallen humanity. A man had to live in obedience to his calling. Only if he laboured as though everything were dependent on his own exertions would reward then come from God. Carnegie, even if he doubted the existence of a deity, never doubted that his efforts to enrich himself brought with them a stern responsibility. John Winthrop, sailing to the New World, had warned what calamity might follow were he and his fellow settlers 'to embrace this present world and prosecute our carnal intentions, seeking great things for our selves and our posterity'.[38] Carnegie, two centuries on and more, was shadowed by the same anxiety. A thoughtful man, he declared, would as soon leave his son a curse as a dollar. The article in which he wrote this had a pointed title: 'The Gospel of Wealth'. Charity was only pointless if it failed to help the poor to help themselves. 'The best means of benefiting the community is to place within its reach the ladders upon which the aspiring can rise.'[39] It was in obedience to this maxim that Carnegie, having spent his career making fabulous amounts of money, devoted his retirement to spending it. For all that he believed in helping the poor to become rich, rather than—in 'imitation of the life of Christ'[40]—living in poverty himself, he was recognisably an heir of Paulinus. Parks, libraries, schools, endowments to promote the cause of world peace: Carnegie funded them all. Self-aggrandising though these gestures might be, they were not primarily self-interested. The concern they showed to improve the lives of others was one of which John Winthrop would surely have approved. It was not enough for Carnegie to put his *Diplodocus* on display in a lavishly appointed museum in his home town of Pittsburgh. The wonder of it had to be shared far and wide. Casts of it were made and dispatched to capitals across the world.

On 12 May 1905, Carnegie was in London, where the 292 bones of the first *Diplodocus* cast ever to be assembled into a single skeleton were ready to be unveiled to an aristocratic array of dignitaries. Naturally, he gave a speech. His dinosaur, vast and stupefying like his own business empire, was the perfect emblem of what might be achieved by giving free rein to the survival of the fittest. It was his unfettered accumulation of capital, after all, that had enabled him to fund his gift, and thereby to help forge between the British and American peoples 'an alliance for peace'.[41] The setting for this message could hardly have been more appropriate: London's museum of natural history, an immense pile complete with soaring pillars and gargoyles, had the decided ambience of a cathedral. This was no accident. Its founder, Richard Owen—the naturalist who had coined the word 'dinosaur'—had consciously intended it. Science, he had once claimed, existed to 'return good for evil'.[42]

Carnegie, then, proudly surveying his *Diplodocus*, could feel that its bones had been provided with a fitting reliquary. He was not, though, the only foreign visitor to London that May who believed that a proper understanding of science would enable humanity to attain world peace. One day before the unveiling of the *Diplodocus*, a Russian named Vladimir Ilyich Ulyanov—Lenin, as he called himself—had also visited the city's museum of natural history. No less than Carnegie, he was a proponent of putting the lessons taught by evolution to practical effect. Unlike Carnegie, however, he did not believe that human happiness was best served by giving free rein to capital. Capitalism, in Lenin's opinion, was doomed to collapse. The workers of the world—the 'proletariat'—were destined to inherit the earth. The abyss that yawned between 'the handful of arrogant millionaires who wallow in filth and luxury, and the millions of working people who constantly live on the verge of pauperism'[43] made the triumph of communism certain. For two weeks, Lenin and thirty-seven others had been in London to debate how this coming revolution in the affairs of the world might best be expedited—but that the laws of evolution made it inevitable none of them doubted. This was why, as though to a shrine, Lenin had led his fellow delegates to the museum. It was only a single stop, however. London had a second, an even holier shrine. The surest guide to the functioning of human society, and to the parabola of its future, had been provided not by Darwin, but by a second bearded thinker who, Job-like, had suffered from bereavement and boils. Every time Lenin came to London he would visit the great man's grave; 1905 was no exception. The moment the congress was over, Lenin had taken the delegates up to the cemetery in the north of the city where, twenty-two years earlier, their teacher, the man who—more than any other—had inspired them to attempt the transformation of the world, lay buried. Standing before the grave, the thirty-eight disciples paid their respects to Karl Marx.

There had been only a dozen people at his funeral in 1883. None, though, had ever had any doubts as to his epochal significance. One of the mourners, speaking over the open grave, had made sure to spell it out. 'Just as Darwin discovered the law of evolution as it applies to organic matter, so Marx discovered the law of evolution as it applies to human history.'[44] Communists could be certain of their cause, not because it was moral, or just, or written—as Marx himself had mockingly put it—'in vaporous clouds in the heavens',[45] but because it was scientifically proven. For years he had sat in the Reading Room of the British Museum, crunching the numbers and analysing the data that had enabled him to identify, at last, the inexorable and unconscious forces that shape human history. Once, in the beginning, man and woman had lived in a condition of primitive equality; but then there had been a fall. Different classes had emerged. Exploitation had become the norm. The struggle between the rich and the poor had been relentless: an unforgiving tale of greed and acquisition. Now, under the blood-stained reign of capital, in the era of plutocrats like Carnegie, it had become pitiless as never before. Workers were reduced to machines. Marx, sixty years previously, had foretold it all: what the clamouring, hammering genius of capitalism had revealed. 'All that is solid melts into air, all that is holy is profaned, and man is at last compelled to face with sober senses his real conditions of life, and his relations with his kind.'[46] In the great, the climactic convulsion of the class struggle that, since the very dawn of civilisation, had determined history's course, there could be only one possible outcome. Capitalists like Andrew Carnegie were the grave-diggers of their own class. It was capitalism itself that would give birth to the classless society.

Naturally, now that Marx had succeeded in providing a scientific basis for the processes of history, there was no need for God. To believe in a deity was, for any human being, to exist in a condition of humiliating dependence. Religion, like opium, lulled its addicts into a condition of soporific passivity, numbing them with fantasies of providence and an afterlife. It was, as it had always been, merely a cipher of the exploitative classes. Marx, the grandson of a rabbi and the son of a Lutheran convert, dismissed both Judaism and Christianity as 'stages in the development of the human mind—different snake skins cast off by history, and man as the snake who cast them off'.[47] An exile from the Rhineland, expelled from a succession of European capitals for mocking the religiosity of Friedrich Wilhelm IV, he had arrived in London with personal experience of the uses to which religion might be put by autocrats. Far from amplifying the voices of the suffering, it was a tool of oppression, employed to stifle and muzzle protest. The ambitions of Christianity to change the world, its claims to have done so, were delusions. 'Epiphenomena', Marx termed them: mere bubbles thrown up on the heaving surface of things by the immense currents of production and exchange. The ideals, the teachings, the visions of Christianity: none had independence from the material forces that had generated them. To imagine that they might in any way have influenced the processes of history was to slumber indeed in an opium den. Now that Marx had issued his wake-up call, there could be no possible excuse for remaining addicted to such a baneful narcotic. The questions of morality and justice that for so long had obsessed Christians were superseded. Science had rendered them superfluous. Marx had pondered the workings of capitalism as a man unclouded by moral prejudices. Not so much as an incense-hint of the epiphenomenal clung to his writings. All his evaluations, all his predictions, derived from observable laws.

'From each according to his ability, to each according to his needs.'[48]
Here was a slogan with the clarity of a scientific formula.

Except, of course, that it was no such thing. Its line of descent was
evident to anyone familiar with the Acts of the Apostles. 'Selling
their possessions and goods, they gave to everyone as he had need.'
Repeatedly throughout Christian history, the communism practised
by the earliest Church had served radicals as their inspiration. Marx,
when he dismissed questions of morality and justice as epiphenomena, was concealing the true germ of his revolt against capitalism
behind jargon. A beard, he had once joked, was something 'without
which no prophet can succeed'.[49] Famously hirsute himself, he had
spoken more truly, perhaps, than he knew. Dispassion was a tone
that—despite his efforts—he found impossible to maintain. The
revulsion that he so patently felt at the miseries of artisans evicted
by their landlords to starve on the streets, of children aged before
their years by toiling night and day in factories, of labourers worked
to death in distant colonies so that the bourgeoisie might have sugar
in their tea, made a mockery of his claims to have outgrown moral
judgements. Marx's interpretation of the world appeared fuelled by
certainties that had no obvious source in his model of economics.
They rose instead from profounder depths. Again and again, the
magma flow of his indignation would force itself through the crust
of his scientific-sounding prose. For a self-professed materialist, he
was oddly prone to seeing the world as the Church Fathers had once
done: as a battleground between cosmic forces of good and evil.
Communism was a 'spectre': a thing of awful and potent spirit. Just
as demons had once haunted Origen, so the workings of capitalism
haunted Marx. 'Capital is dead labour which, vampire-like, lives
only by sucking living labour, and lives the more, the more labour it
sucks.'[50] This was hardly the language of a man emancipated from epiphenomena. The very words used by Marx to construct his model of
class struggle—'exploitation', 'enslavement', 'avarice'—owed less to
the chill formulations of economists than to something far older: the

claims to divine inspiration of the biblical prophets. If, as he insisted, he offered his followers a liberation from Christianity, then it was one that seemed eerily like a recalibration of it.

Lenin and his fellow delegates, meeting in London that spring of 1905, would have been contemptuous of any such notion, of course. Religion—opium of the people that it was—would need, if the victory of the proletariat were properly to be secured, to be eradicated utterly. Oppression in all its forms had to be eliminated. The ends justified the means. Lenin's commitment to this principle was absolute. Already, the single-mindedness with which he insisted on it had precipitated schism in the ranks of Marx's followers. The congress held in London had been exclusively for those of them who defined themselves as *Bolsheviks*: the 'Majority'. Communists who insisted, in opposition to Lenin, on working alongside liberals, on confessing qualms about violence, on worrying that Lenin's ambitions for a tightly organised, strictly disciplined party threatened dictatorship, were not truly communists at all—just a sect. Sternly, like the Donatists, the Bolsheviks dismissed any suggestion of compromising with the world as it was. Eagerly, like the Taborites, they yearned to see the apocalypse arrive, to see paradise established on earth. Fiercely, like the Diggers, they dreamed of an order in which land once held by aristocrats and kings would become the property of the people, a common treasury. Lenin, who was reported to admire both the Anabaptists of Münster and Oliver Cromwell, was not entirely contemptuous of the past. Proofs of what was to come were plentiful there. History, like an arrow, was proceeding on its implacable course. Capitalism was destined to collapse, and the paradise lost by humanity at the beginning of time to be restored. Those who doubted it had only to read the teachings and prophecies of their great teacher to be reassured.

The hour of salvation lay at hand.

19

SHADOW

1916: The Somme

It was not the front, but the journey to the front that was the worst. 'There was some shit in people's pants, I tell you.'[1] Two years into the war, Otto Dix had seen it all. In 1914, he had unhesitatingly signed up to the field artillery. Back then, people had assumed that victory would be swift in coming. Germany was the greatest military power in Europe. In the decades following the reign of Friedrich Wilhelm IV, Prussia had emerged to become the core of an immense German Empire. Its king now ruled as Otto the Great had once done—as a Caesar, a *Kaiser*. Naturally, such greatness had prompted envy. Russia, on the empire's eastern border, and France, brooding to the west, had sought to crush Germany in a vice. The British, fearful for their rule of the waves, had joined with the French. For a few heady weeks, as the German army had swept first through neutral Belgium and then into northern France, it had seemed that Paris was bound to fall. But the French had rallied. The capital had remained tantalisingly out of reach. A great gash of trenches had come to score the Western Front. Neither side could force a decisive breakthrough. Now, though, on the slopes above the river Somme, the British and the French armies were making a concentrated effort to smash a hole through the labyrinth of German defences. All summer the battle had been raging. Dix, approaching the Somme, had been deafened by artillery fire of a volume he had never imagined possible, and seen the western horizon lit as though by lightning. Everywhere was ruin: mud, and blasted trees, and rubble. In his dreams Dix was always crawling through shattered houses and doorways that barely permitted him to pass. Once he had arrived at his post, though, his fear left him. Stationed with a heavy machine-gun battery, he felt mingled excitement and calm. He even found time to paint.

Back in Dresden, the famously beautiful city in Saxony where he had been an art student, Dix had experimented with a range of styles. Only twenty-three when war broke out, and from an impoverished background, the sense of urgency he felt as a painter was that of a man determined to make a name for himself. Amid the mud and the slaughter of the Somme, he was witness to scenes that no previous generation of artists could possibly have imagined. By night, as Dix huddled beside a carbide lamp with his oils or his pens, flares over no man's land would light up corpses grotesquely twisted on barbed wire. Then, every morning, dawn would illumine a cratered landscape of death. On 1 July, the opening day of the battle, almost twenty thousand British soldiers had been mown down as they sought in vain to take the enemy trenches, and another forty thousand left wounded. A fortnight later, every yard of the German lines had been battered by 660 pounds of shell. New ways of killing were forever being developed. On 15 September, monstrous machines called 'tanks' by their British inventors grumbled and ground their way across the battlefield for the first time. By the end of the month, flying machines were regularly dropping bombs on the trenches below. Only in late November did the fighting finally grind to a halt. Casualties numbered a million. To Dix, hunkered behind his machine gun, it seemed that the whole world was transformed. 'Humanity,' he wrote, 'changes in demonic fashion.'[2]

There were plenty, though, who thought themselves on the side of the angels. Back in Saxony, a year before the outbreak of war, a great monument had been dedicated to commemorate the centenary of a particularly bloody victory over Napoleon. Centrepiece of the memorial was a colossal statue of Saint Michael, winged and armed with a fiery sword. That Germany's struggle against her foes mirrored the cosmic war of angel against demon was a conviction that reached all the way to the top. The Kaiser, as the war dragged on and on, and a naval blockade of Germany began to bite, grew ever more convinced that the British were in league with the Devil. Patriotic Britons, for their part, had been saying much the same about Germany since the start of the war. Bishops joined with newspaper editors in hammering the message home. The Germans had succumbed to 'a brutal and ruthless military paganism',[3] of the kind from which, more than a millennium earlier, Boniface had laboured to redeem them. They had returned to the worship of Woden. In Germany—so *The Times* announced—'Christianity is beginning to be regarded as a worn-out creed'.[4]

Yet it was easier, perhaps, for armchair warriors to believe this than for soldiers on the front. Behind the British lines at the Somme, in the small town of Albert, there stood a basilica topped by a golden statue of the Virgin and Child. A year previously, the spire had been hit by a shell. The statue had been left hanging precariously, as though by a miracle. Rumours began to spread in both the German and the British trenches that whichever side brought it down was destined to lose the war. Yet many, when they looked up at the Virgin, were inspired to dwell not on the calculus of victory and defeat, but on the suffering of both sides. 'The figure once stood triumphant on the cathedral tower,' wrote one British soldier; 'now it is bowed as by the last extremity of grief.'[5] The Virgin, after all, had known what it was to mourn a son. Unsurprisingly, amid the misery and the suffering that had become the common experience across the whole of Europe, the image of Christ tortured to death on a cross took on for many a new potency. Both sides, predictably, sought to turn this to their own advantage. In Germany, pastors compared the blockade enforced by the Royal Navy to the nails with which Christ had been fixed to the cross; in Britain, stories of German soldiers crucifying a

Canadian prisoner had long been a staple of propaganda. Even so, in the trenches themselves, where soldiers—if they did not find themselves trapped on barbed wire, or riddled by machine-gun fire, or disembowelled by an exploding shell—would live day after day in the valley of the shadow of death, the crucifixion had a more haunting resonance. Christ was their fellow-sufferer. On the battlefield of the Somme, soldiers would note in wonder the survival amid all the devastation of wayside crucifixes, chipped and riddled with bullets though they were. Even Protestants, even atheists were capable of being moved. Christ was imagined sharing in a jest passed along the trenches, standing beside soldiers in their pain and weakness. 'We have no doubts, we know that You are here.'[6]

Otto Dix, in his dug-out, had Christ's sufferings much on his mind. Raised a Lutheran, he had brought a Bible with him to France. In the course of his service on the front, he had seen enough artillery attacks to recognise in their aftermath a kind of Golgotha. With his artist's eye, he could glimpse in the spectacle of a soldier impaled on a shard of metal something of the crucifixion. Yet Dix, to a degree that would have confirmed British propagandists in all their darkest suspicions of the German character, refused to see Christ's suffering as having served any purpose. To imagine that it might have done so was to cling to the values of a slave. 'To be crucified, to experience the deepest abyss of life': this was its own reward. Dix, volunteering in 1914, had done so out of a desire to know the ultimate extremes of life and death: to feel what it was to stick a bayonet in an enemy's guts and to twist it around; to have a comrade suddenly fall, a bullet square between his eyes; 'the hunger, the fleas, the mud'.[7] Only in the intoxication of such experiences could a man be more than a man: an *Übermensch*. To be free was to be great; and to be great was to be terrible. It was not the Bible that had brought Dix to this conviction. In his determination to spurn the mindset of a slave, to revel in all the qualities that made for a master, there was a conscious repudiation of Christian morality, with its concern for the weak, and the poor, and the oppressed. A trench in the midst of the most terrible battle-scape in history seemed to Dix a fitting vantage point from which to observe what was, so he had come to believe, the collapse of a 1900-year-old order. Alongside his Bible, he had a second book. So stirred was he by its philosophy that in 1912, while still an art student in Dresden, he had made a life-size plaster bust of its author. Not just his first sculpture, it had also been his first work to be bought by a gallery. Discerning critics, inspecting the bust's drooping mous-tache, its thrusting neck, its stare shadowed by bristling eyebrows, had proclaimed it the very image of Friedrich Nietzsche.

'Do we not hear the noise of the grave-diggers who are bury-ing God? Do we not smell the divine putrefaction?—for even gods putrefy! God is dead. God remains dead. And we have killed him.'[8] To read these words beside the Somme, amid a landscape turned to mud and ash, and littered with the mangled bodies of men, was to shiver before the possibility that there might not be, after all, any redemption in sacrifice. Nietzsche had written them back in 1882: the parable of a madman who one bright morning lit a lantern and ran to the marketplace, where no one among his listeners would believe his news that God had bled to death beneath their knives. Little in Nietzsche's upbringing seemed to have prefigured such blasphemy. The son of a Lutheran pastor, and named after Friedrich Wilhelm IV, his background had been one of pious provincialism. Precocious and brilliant, he had obtained a professorship when he was only twenty-four; but then, only a decade later, had resigned it to become a shabbily genteel bum. Finally, seeming to confirm the sense of a squandered career, he had suffered a terrible mental breakdown. For the last eleven years of his life, he had been confined to a succes-sion of clinics. Few, when he finally died in 1900, had read the books that, in an escalating frenzy of production, he had written before his collapse into madness. Posthumously, though, his fame had grown with startling rapidity. By 1914, when Dix marched to war with his writings in his knapsack, Nietzsche's name had emerged to become one of the most controversial in Europe. Condemned by many as the most dangerous thinker who had ever lived, others hailed him as a prophet. There were many who considered him both.

Nietzsche was not the first to have become a byword for atheism, of course. No one, though—not Spinoza, not Darwin, not Marx— had ever before dared to gaze quite so unblinkingly at what the murder of its god might mean for a civilisation. 'When one gives up the Christian faith, one pulls the right to Christian morality out from under one's feet.'[9] Nietzsche's loathing for those who imagined otherwise was intense. Philosophers he scorned as secret priests. Socialists, communists, democrats: all were equally deluded. 'Naiveté: as if morality could survive when the *God* who sanctions it is missing!'[10] Enthusiasts for the Enlightenment, self-proclaimed rationalists who imagined that men and women possessed inherent rights, Nietzsche regarded with contempt. It was not from reason that their doctrine of human dignity derived, but rather from the very faith that they believed themselves—in their conceit—to have banished. Proclamations of rights were nothing but flotsam and jetsam left behind by the retreating tide of Christianity: bleached and stranded relics. God was dead—but in the great cave that once had been Christendom his shadow still fell, an immense and frightful shadow. For centuries, perhaps, it would linger. Christianity had reigned for two millennia. It could not easily be banished. Its myths would long endure. They were certainly no less mythical for casting themselves as secular. 'Such phantoms as the dignity of man, the dignity of labour':[11] these were Christian through and through.

Nietzsche did not mean this as a compliment. It was not just as frauds that he despised those who clung to Christian morality, even as their knives were dripping with the blood of God; he loathed them as well for believing in it. Concern for the lowly and the suffering, far from serving the cause of justice, was a form of poison. Nietzsche, more radically than many a theologian, had penetrated to the heart of everything that was most shocking about the Christian faith. 'To devise something which could even approach the seductive, intoxicating, anaesthetising, and corrupting power of that symbol of the "holy cross", that horrific paradox of the "crucified God", that mystery of an inconceivably ultimate, most extreme cruelty and self-crucifixion undertaken *for the salvation of mankind*?'[12] Like Paul, Nietzsche knew it to be a scandal. Unlike Paul, he found it repellent. The spectacle of Christ being tortured to death had been bait for the powerful. It had persuaded them—the strong and the healthy, the beautiful and the brave, the powerful and the self-assured—that it was their natural inferiors, the hungry and the humble, who deserved to inherit the earth. 'Helping and caring for others, being of use to others, constantly excites a sense of power.'[13] Charity, in Christendom, had become a means to dominate. Yet Christianity, by taking the side of everything ill-constituted, and weak, and feeble, had made all of humanity sick. Its ideals of compassion and equality before God were bred not of love, but of hatred: a hatred of the deepest and most sublime order, one that had transformed the very character of morality, a hatred the like of which had never before been seen on earth. This was the revolution that Paul— 'that hate-obsessed false-coiner'[14]—had set in motion. The weak had conquered the strong; the slaves had vanquished their masters.

'Ruined by cunning, secret, invisible, anaemic vampires! Not conquered—only sucked dry! ... Covert revengefulness, petty envy become *master*!'[15] Nietzsche, when he mourned antiquity's beasts of prey, did so with the passion of a scholar who had devoted his life to the study of their civilisation. He admired the Greeks not despite but because of their cruelty. So dismissive was he of any notion of ancient Greece as a land of sunny rationalism that large numbers of students, by the end of his tenure as a professor, had been shocked into abandoning his classes. Much as Sade had done, Nietzsche valued the ancients for the pleasure they had taken in inflicting suffering; for knowing that punishment might be festive; for demonstrating that, 'in the days before mankind grew ashamed of its cruelty, before pessimists existed, life on earth was more cheerful than it is now'.[16] That Nietzsche himself was a short-sighted invalid prone to violent migraines had done nothing to inhibit his admiration for the aristocracies of antiquity, and their heedlessness towards the sick and the weak. A society focused on the feeble was a society enfeebled itself. This it was that had rendered Christians such malevolent blood-suckers. If it was the taming of the Romans that Nietzsche chiefly rued, then he regretted as well how they had battened onto other nations. Nietzsche himself, whose contempt for the Germans was exceeded only by his disdain for the English, had so little time for nationalism that he had renounced his Prussian citizenship when he was only twenty-four, and died stateless; and yet, for all that, he had always lamented the fate of his forebears. Once, before the coming of Boniface, the forests had sheltered Saxons who, in their ferocity and their hunger for everything that was richest and most intense in life, had been predators no less glorious than lions: 'blond beasts'. But then the missionaries had arrived. The blond beast had been tempted into a monastery. 'There he now lay, sick, wretched, malevolent toward himself; filled with hatred of the vital drives, filled with suspicion towards all that was still strong and happy. In short, a "Christian".'[17] Dix, enduring the extremes of the Western Front, did not have to be a worshipper of Woden to feel that he was free at last.

'Even war,' he recorded in his notebook, 'must be regarded as a natural occurrence.'[18] That it was an abyss, across which, like a rope, a man might be suspended, fastened between beast and *Übermensch*: here was a philosophy that Dix felt no cause to abandon at the Somme. Yet it could seem a bleak one, for all that. Soldiers in the trenches rarely cared to imagine with Nietzsche that there might be no truth, no value, no meaning in itself—and that only by acknowledging this would a man cease to be a slave. The unprecedented scale of the violence that had bled Europe white did not shock most of its peoples into atheism. On the contrary: it served to confirm them in their faith. How otherwise to make sense of all the horror? As so often before, when Christians had found themselves enmired in misery and slaughter, the veil that lay between earth and heaven could appear to many hauntingly thin. As the war ground on, and 1916 turned to 1917, so the end times seemed to be drawing near. In Portugal, in the village of Fatima, the Virgin made repeated appearances, until at last, before huge crowds, the sun danced, as though in fulfilment of the prophecy recorded in Revelation that a great and wondrous sign would appear in heaven: 'a woman clothed with the sun'.[19] In Palestine, the British won a crushing victory at Armageddon and took Jerusalem from the Turks. In London, the Foreign Secretary issued a declaration supporting the establishment in the Holy Land of a Jewish homeland—a development that many Christians believed was bound to herald the return of Christ.

Yet he did not come back. Nor did the world end. In 1918, when the German high command launched a massive attempt to smash their opponents once and for all, the operation they had code-named Michael, in honour of the archangel, peaked, and broke, and ebbed. Eight months later, the war was over. Germany sued for terms. The Kaiser abdicated. A squalid peace was brought to a shattered continent. Otto Dix returned from the front. In Dresden, he painted maimed officers, and malnourished infants, and haggard prostitutes. He saw beggars everywhere. On street corners there were gangs of agitators. Some were communists. Some were nationalists. Some wandered barefoot, prophesying the end of the world and calling for man to be born again. Dix ignored them all. Asked to join a political party, he would answer that he would rather go to a brothel. He continued to read Nietzsche. 'After a terrible earthquake, a tremendous *reflection*, with new questions.'[20]

Meanwhile, in basements stale with beer and sweat, men with strident voices were talking about Jews.

The Triumph of the Will

Difficult lodgers were the bane of any landlady's life. Times in Berlin were hard, and Elisabeth Salm, as a widow, needed to make money somehow—but there were limits. The young man had always been trouble. First he had begun sharing his room with his girlfriend, a former prostitute called Erna Jaenichen—not the kind of woman that any respectable widow would want in her flat. Then groups of men had begun arriving, banging on Frau Salm's door, pushing past her, and loudly talking politics all night. Finally, on 14 January 1930, her patience snapped. She ordered Jaenichen out of her flat. Jaenichen refused to leave. Frau Salm went to the police. They told her to sort the matter out herself. By now desperate, she headed to a local pub, where she knew the friends of her late husband would be. Sure enough, there they all were, cloistered in a back room. They heard her out, but refused to help. Why should they? There was bad blood between them. Frau Salm's husband had been a man of deeply held beliefs, but his widow, rather than give him the funeral that he would have wanted, and which his friends had offered to provide, had turned instead to the local pastor for help. Now, standing in the Baer Tavern, she was surrounded by reminders of the sacrilege she had committed. Emblems stitched into flags the colour of blood. Well-thumbed sacred texts. Icons on the walls. The shrine in the corner, complete with flowers and a picture of Lenin.

The Bolsheviks had come a long way since their visit to the museum of natural history in London. The party that back in 1905 had seen fewer than forty delegates attend its congress now ruled a vast and ancient empire. So huge was Russia that it accounted for almost a quarter of the world's Christians. Scorning the pretensions of Rome, its monarchy had claimed a line of descent from Byzantium, and the title of 'Orthodox' for its church. Revolution, though, had come to the self-proclaimed Third Rome. In 1917, the Russian monarchy had been overthrown. The Bolsheviks, under the leadership of Lenin, had seized power. Marx's chosen people, the industrial proletariat, had been brought to the promised land: a communist Russia. Those unworthy to live in such a paradise— be they members of the royal family or peasants with a couple of cows—had been slated for elimination. So too had the Church. Even though Lenin himself had havered, fretting that it might prove counterproductive to offend believers, the demands of revolutionary logic had proven remorseless. 'In practice, no less than in theory, communism is incompatible with religious faith.'[21] The clergy had to go. In 1918, their churches had been nationalised. Bishops had been variously shot, crucified upside down, or imprisoned. Then, in 1926, the conversion of a particularly venerable monastery into a labour camp had enabled two birds to be killed with one stone. Still the process of weaning the masses off their opium had appeared to many communists to be grinding far too slow. Accordingly, in 1929, responsibility for religious affairs had been given to an organisation that did precisely what it said on the tin: the League of Militant Atheists. Their stated goal it was to eliminate religion once and for all. Five years, they trusted, would prove sufficient for the task. Organising themselves into missions, they set to work. Entire trains were commandeered. In the remote reaches of Siberia, where Christianity had only patchily spread, shamans were thrown out of planes and told to fly. There was no redoubt of superstition so distant that its shrines could not be demolished, its leaders liquidated, its darkness banished upon the light of reason. Religion—that farrago of unsubstantiated assertions, farfetched prophecies and nonsensical wishful thinking—was destined to disappear. That, as Marx had demonstrated, was scientific fact.

Many beyond the borders of the Soviet Union—as the Russian empire had come to be known—agreed. It was why, that January afternoon in Berlin, Frau Salm found her husband's comrades deaf to her appeals. Yet their very indignation pointed to an irony that Nietzsche had noted decades before. To insist that a church funeral might be a kind of blasphemy was less a repudiation of Christianity than an inadvertent acknowledgement of kinship with it. Increasingly, by 1930, there were Christians willing to contemplate a disorienting possibility: that the Bolsheviks, adherents of a cause as universal in its claims as it was uncompromising in its principles, might in fact be the shock troops of an 'anti-church'.[22] Like Gregory VII, they had trampled the pretensions of an emperor into winter snow; like Innocent III, they had combated the forces of reaction with fire and inquisition; like Luther, they had jeered at the excrescences of priestly superstition; like Winstanley, they had proclaimed the earth a common treasury and prescribed ferocious penalties for any objectors. For a thousand years, it had been the distinct ambition of Latin Christendom to see the entire world born anew: to baptise it in the waters of *reformatio*. Repeatedly, this ambition had brought revolution to Europe; and repeatedly, to lands shaped by very different habits of thought, it had brought ruin. Lenin, armed with the teachings of a German economist, had been no less the bane of Russian Orthodoxy than Cortés had been of the Aztec gods. That the once-Christian tradition of missionary zeal might now be sending the advance of Christianity itself into reverse was a possibility too cruel for most Christians to contemplate—and yet the shrewdest of them understood it very well. The godlessness of the Soviet Union was less a repudiation of the Church than a dark and deadly parody of it. 'Bolshevik atheism is the expression of a new religious faith'.[23]

The dream of a new order planted on the ruins of the old; of a reign of the saints that would last for a thousand years; of a day of judgement, when the unjust would be sorted from the just, and condemned to a lake of fire: this, from the earliest days of the Church, had always haunted the imaginings of the faithful. Christian authorities, nervous of where such yearnings might lead, had consistently sought to police them; but still, blurring and bonding with one another, the constituent elements of the longed-for apocalypse had never ceased to take on fresh lineaments. But now, across Germany, they were metastasising. Not all the paramilitaries in Berlin were communist. Street rivalries were ferocious. Frau Salm, making one last desperate appeal, had only to mention her lodger's name for everyone in the back room of the pub abruptly to sit up. At once, the mood was transformed. Some of the men rose to their feet. Heading out of the pub, they went with Frau Salm back to her apartment. A few days previously, a communist daily had printed an unapologetic slogan. That night, standing in the kitchen of Frau Salm's flat, waiting for her to ring the cowbell with which she habitually announced visitors, three paramilitaries readied themselves to answer the paper's battle-cry: 'Wherever you find them, beat up the Fascists!'[24]

The name derived from the palmy days of ancient Rome. The *fasces*, a bundle of scourging rods, had served the guards appointed to elected magistrates as emblems of their authority. Not every magistrate in Roman history, though, had necessarily been elected. Times of crisis had demanded exceptional measures. Julius Caesar, following his defeat of Pompey, had been appointed *dictator*: an office that had permitted him to take sole control of the state. Each of his guards had carried on their shoulders, bundled up with the scourging rods, an axe. Nietzsche, predicting that a great convulsion was approaching, a repudiation of the pusillanimous Christian doctrines of equality and compassion, had foretold as well that those who led the revolution would 'become devisers of emblems and phantoms in their enmity'.[25] Time had proven him right. The *fasces* had become the badge of a brilliantly successful movement. By 1930, Italy was ruled—as it had been two millennia previously—by a dictator. Benito Mussolini, an erstwhile socialist whose reading of Nietzsche had led him, by the end of the Great War, to dream of forming a new breed of man, an elite worthy of a fascist state, cast himself both as Caesar and as the face of a gleaming future. From the fusion of ancient and modern, melded by the white-hot genius of his leadership, there was to emerge a new Italy. Whether greeting the massed ranks of his followers with a Roman salute or piloting an aircraft, Mussolini posed in ways that consciously sought to erase the entire span of Christian history. Although, in a country as profoundly Catholic as Italy, he had little choice but to cede a measure of autonomy to the Church, his ultimate aim was to subordinate it utterly, to render it the handmaid of the fascist state. Mussolini's more strident followers exulted nakedly in this goal. 'Yes indeed, we are totalitarians! We want to be from morning to evening, without distracting thoughts.'[26]

In Berlin too there were such men. The storm troopers of a movement that believed simultaneously in racism and in the subordination of all personal interests to a common good, they called themselves *Nationalsozialisten*: 'National Socialists'. Their opponents, in mockery of their pretensions, called them Nazis. But this only betrayed fear. The National Socialists courted the hatred of their foes. An enemy's loathing was something to be welcomed. It was the anvil on which a new Germany was to be be forged. 'It is not compassion but courage and toughness that save life, because war is life's eternal disposition.'[27] As in Italy, so in Germany, fascism worked to combine the glamour and the violence of antiquity with that of the modern world. There was no place in this vision of the future for the mewling feebleness of Christianity. The blond beast was to be liberated from his monastery. A new age had dawned. Adolf Hitler, the leader of the Nazis, was not, as Mussolini could claim to be, an intellectual; but he did not need to be. Over the course of a life that had embraced living in a dosshouse, injury at the Somme, and imprisonment for an attempted putsch, he had come to feel himself summoned by a mysterious providence to transform the world. Patchily read in philosophy and science he might be, but of one thing he was viscerally certain: destiny was written in a people's blood. There was no universal morality. A Russian was not a German. Every nation was different, and a people that refused to listen to the dictates of its soul was a people doomed to extinction. 'All who are not of good race in this world,' Hitler warned, 'are chaff.'[28]

Once, in the happy days of their infancy, the German people had been at one with the forests in which they lived. They had existed as a tree might: not just as the sum of its branches, its twigs and its leaves, but as a living, organic whole. But then the soil from which the Nordic race were sprung had been polluted. Their sap had been poisoned. Their limbs had been cut back. Only surgery could save them now. Hitler's policies, although rooted in a sense of race as something primordially ancient, were rooted as well in the clinical formulations of evolutionary theory. The measures that would restore purity to the German people were prescribed equally by ancient chronicles and by Darwinist textbooks. To eliminate those who stood in the way of fulfilling such a programme was not a crime, but a responsibility. 'Apes massacre all fringe elements as alien to their community.' Hitler did not hesitate to draw the logical conclusion. 'What is valid for monkeys must be all the more valid for humans.'[29] Man was as subject to the struggle for life, and to the need to preserve the purity of his race, as any other species. To put this into practice was not cruelty. It was simply the way of the world.

Horst Wessel, the young man who for three months had been living with Frau Salm as her lodger, had not merely been convinced by this manifesto—he had been electrified by it. The son of a pastor, he had become at an early age 'an enthusiastic disciple of Adolf Hitler'.[30] Energies that he might otherwise have devoted to the Church he had consecrated to National Socialism. In 1929 alone, he had preached at almost sixty meetings. Much as his father might once have done, taking hymns to the streets, he had assembled a company of musicians and paraded with them through communist strongholds. One of the songs he had written for the band, his most famous, imagined martyred comrades marching by the side of the living. No wonder, then, that Frau Salm's mention of his name should have made her listeners sit up straight. Wessel was a man that any self-respecting band of communists might be interested in cornering. This was why, on the evening of 14 January, three of them were standing outside his door, waiting for Frau Salm to ring her cowbell. Their intentions would later be a matter of some contention. Perhaps, as they claimed, they had only ever planned to give him a beating. Perhaps the gunshot to his face had been an accident. Whatever the truth, Wessel was left critically injured. Taken to hospital, he died five weeks later. Complicating the matter yet further was the identity of the murderer: a man who had once been Erna Jaenichen's pimp. The more the police investigated the case, the more confused the details became. Only one thing about the whole squalid business was certain: Wessel's funeral was that of a street-fighter killed in a brawl.

Except that this was not at all how Wessel's superior in Berlin saw it. Joseph Goebbels, like Hitler, had been raised a Catholic. Contemptuous though he might be of Christianity, he was alert not only to the hold that it still had over the imaginations of many Germans, but also to how this might be turned to the advantage of his own movement. A propagandist of genius, Goebbels knew a martyr when he saw one. Speaking at Wessel's funeral, he proclaimed—with a stagey catch in his throat—that the dead man would come again. A shudder ran through the crowd. 'As if God,' one of the mourners later recalled, 'had made a decision and sent His holy breath upon the open grave and the flags, blessing the dead man and all who belong to him.'[31] One month later, Goebbels explicitly compared Wessel to Christ. Over the years that followed, as the National Socialists progressed from fighting in the streets to bringing the entire country under their rule, the murdered *Sturmführer* continued to serve them as the embodiment of a saint: the leader of the martyred dead. Most Church leaders—conscious that to condemn Nazis for blasphemous kitsch might prove risky—opted to bite their tongues. Some, though, actively lent it their imprimatur. In 1933, the year that Hitler was appointed chancellor, Protestant churches across Germany marked the annual celebration of the Reformation by singing Wessel's battle hymn. In Berlin Cathedral, a pastor shamelessly aped Goebbels. Wessel, he preached, had died just as Jesus had died. Then, just for good measure, he added that Hitler was 'a man sent by God'.[32]

Yet Christians, if they thought this would curry favour with the Nazi leadership, let alone influence it, were deluding themselves. To parody Christianity was not to show it respect, but to cannibalise it. Out in the woods, eager young National Socialists would burn copies of the Bible on great fires, and then—'to prove how we despise all the cults of the world except the ideology of Hitler'[33]—sing the Horst Wessel Lied. On the Rhine, in the amphitheatres of what had once been Roman cities, girls might gather by night to celebrate Wessel's birthday with dances and prayers to his spirit, 'to make them good bearers of children'.[34] Not just a saint, the son of a pastor had become a god.

Boniface, travelling across the Rhine twelve hundred years before, had witnessed very similar things. Dismay at the spectacle of pagan practices in a supposedly Christian land had led him to devote much of his life to combating them. Now, though, his heirs faced an even more grievous threat. Missionaries to Germany in the eighth century had been able to count on the support of the Frankish monarchy in their labours. No such backing was forthcoming from the Nazis. Hitler, who in 1928 had loudly proclaimed his movement to be Christian, had come to regard Christianity with active hostility. Its morality, its concern for the weak, he had always viewed as cowardly and shameful. Now that he was in power, he recognised in the claim of the Church to a sphere distinct from the state—that venerable inheritance from the Gregorian revolution—a direct challenge to the totalitarian mission of National Socialism. Although, like Mussolini, Hitler was willing to tread carefully at first—and even, in 1933, to sign a concordat with the papacy—he had no intention of holding to it for long. Christian morality had resulted in any number of grotesque excrescences: alcoholics breeding promiscuously while upstanding national comrades struggled to put food on the table for their families; mental patients enjoying clean sheets while healthy children were obliged to sleep three or four to a bed; cripples having money and attention lavished on them that should properly be devoted to the fit. Idiocies such as these were precisely what National Socialism existed to terminate. The churches had had their day. The new order, if it were to endure for a millennium, would require a new order of man. It would require *Übermenschen*.

By 1937, then, Hitler had begun to envisage the elimination of Christianity once and for all. The objections of church leaders to the state's ongoing sterilisation of idiots and cripples infuriated him. His own preference—one that he fully intended to act upon in the event of war—was for euthanasia to be applied in a comprehensive manner. This, a policy that was sanctioned both by ancient example and by the most advanced scientific thinking, was something that the German people needed urgently to be brought to accept.

Clearly, there was no prospect of them fulfilling their racial destiny while they were still cancerous with compassion. Among the *Schutz-staffel*, the elite paramilitary organisation that served as the most efficient instrument of Hitler's will, the destruction of Christianity came to be regarded as a particular vocation. Heinrich Himmler, the commander of the SS, plotted a fifty-year programme that he trusted would see the religion utterly erased. Otherwise, Christianity might once again prove the bane of the blond beast. For the Germans to continue in their opposition to policies so transparently vital for their own racial health was insanity. 'Harping on and on that God died on the cross out of pity for the weak, the sick, and the sinners, they then demand that the genetically diseased be kept alive in the name of a doctrine of pity that goes against nature, and of a misconceived notion of humanity.'[35] The strong, as science had conclusively demonstrated, had both a duty and an obligation to eliminate the weak.

Yet if Christianity—as Hitler had come to believe—was 'the heaviest blow that ever struck humanity',[36] then it was not enough merely to eradicate it. A religion so pernicious that it had succeeded both in destroying the Roman Empire and in spawning Bolshevism could hardly have emerged from nowhere. What source of infection could possibly have bred such a plague? Clearly, there was no more pressing question for a National Socialist to answer. Whatever the bacillus, it needed to be identified fast, and—if the future of the German people were to be set on stable foundations, enduring enough to last for a thousand years—destroyed.

As Goebbels, in reflective mood, would put it: 'One must not be sentimental in such matters.'[37]

In the Darkness Bind Them

For over four years, Britain had been at war with Nazi Germany. In all that time, Oxford had barely been touched by bombers. Even so, there could be no relaxing. This was why, on the evening of 17

January 1944, the Rawlinson and Bosworth Professor of Anglo-Saxon reported to the Area Headquarters in the north of the city. John Ronald Reuel Tolkien had been serving as an air-raid warden since 1941. His duties were not particularly onerous. That night, he sat up late chatting with a fellow warden. Cecil Roth, like Tolkien, was a don at the university, a Jewish historian who had written—among many other books—a biography of Menasseh ben Israel. The two men got on well, and only after midnight did they finally retire to their quarters. Roth, knowing that Tolkien was a devout Catholic and observing that he had no watch, insisted on lending him his own, so that his companion would not miss early-morning mass. Then, just before seven, he knocked on Tolkien's door, to check that he was up. Tolkien, already awake, had been lying in bed, wondering whether he had time to get to church. 'But the incursion of this gentle Jew, and his sombre glance at my rosary by my bed, settled it.' As a light in a dark place, when all other lights had gone out, Roth's kindness struck Tolkien. So moved was he that he discerned in it something of Eden. 'It seemed,' he wrote that same day, 'like a fleeting glimpse of an unfallen world.'[38]

Tolkien did not mean this as a figure of speech. Every story, he believed, was ultimately about the fall. No less than Augustine had done, he interpreted all of history as the record of human iniquity. The world, which in the Anglo-Saxon writings he so loved had been named 'Middle-earth', was still what it had ever been: the great battlefield between good and evil. In 1937, two years before the outbreak of war, Tolkien had embarked on a work of fiction which sought to hold up a mirror to this abiding Christian theme. *The Lord of the Rings* was deeply embedded in the culture to which he had devoted an entire lifetime of scholarship: that of early medieval Christendom. To be sure, the Middle-earth of his imaginings was not one that Bede or Boniface would have recognised. The familiar contours of history and geography were missing; so too was Christianity; so too was God. There were men; but there were other races too. Elves and dwarves, wizards and walking trees: all filled the pages of Tolkien's novel. There were also halflings named hobbits, and if these—with their large hairy feet and their comical names—seemed sprung from some nursery tale, then that was indeed how they had originated. Tolkien, though, could not rest content with writing a children's book. His ambitions were too epic in scale. 'The City will be hemmed in,' Augustine had written, 'hard pressed, shut up, in the straits of tribulation, yet it will not abandon its warfare.'[39] This vision, of the struggle to defy evil, and of the costs that it imposed, was one that kings and saints had held to, back in the early years of Christendom; and Tolkien was much moved by it. Marshalling their languages, drawing on their literatures, merging episodes from their histories so that, together, they came to take on something of the contours of a dream, he aimed to write a fantasy that would also— in a sense acceptable to God—be true. His hope for *The Lord of the Rings* was that others, when they came to read it, would find truth in it too.

Naturally, as a Catholic, Tolkien believed that the whole of history bore witness to Christ. He felt no call to apologise, then, for cloaking such self-knowledge as he had, and such criticisms of life as he knew them, 'under mythical and legendary dress'.[40] His fiction, nevertheless, was not shaped exclusively by ancient song. Tolkien knew what it was to stare into the heart of his own century's darkness. As a young man, he had faced Otto Dix and Adolf Hitler across the mud of the Somme. In 1944, memories of the carnage still haunted him. 'Wrenching his hands out of the bog, he sprang back with a cry. "There are dead things, dead faces in the water," he said with horror. "Dead faces!"'[41] This terrifying vision, of corpses drowned in the mire of a battlefield, and left to float for all eternity, fused the terrors of a mechanised age with medieval visions of the damned. Tolkien, when he wrote of demons riding great featherless birds, or marshalling lethal engines of war, did so as a man who had witnessed dog-fights in the skies above the trenches and tanks churning across no man's land. Sauron, the Dark Lord whose ambitions threatened all Middle-earth with darkness, ruled in the land of Mordor: at once both a vision of hell such as Gregory the Great might have recognised, and an immense military-industrial complex, black with furnaces, munition factories and slag-heaps. Unfailingly, throughout *The Lord of the Rings*, it was the blasted desecration of tree and flower that had run like a scar across France and Belgium during the Great War that featured as the marker of his rule.

Now, as Tolkien pressed on with his novel, there were fresh miseries, fresh horrors that had put the world in their shadow. That history bore witness to a war between light and darkness, aeons old, and demanding from those on the side of good an unstinting watchfulness against evil, was a conviction that Tolkien shared with the Nazis. Admittedly, when articulating the mission of National Socialism, its leaders tended not to frame it in such terms. They preferred the language of Darwinism. 'A cool doctrine of reality based on the most incisive scientific knowledge and its theoretical elucidation.'[42] So Hitler had defined National Socialism, a year before invading Poland and engulfing Europe in a second terrible civil war. The victories won by his war-machine, even as they demonstrated the fitness of his people to rank as a master race, had provided him with something even more precious: the opportunity to preserve them from a uniquely besetting peril. Scientists, when they defined racial hierarchies for National Socialism, hesitated to define the Jews as a race at all. They were a 'counter-race': a virus, a bacillus. It was no more a crime to eradicate them than it was for doctors to combat an epidemic of typhus. On 9 November 1938, when the great synagogue in Cologne that had been funded by the Oppenheims was destroyed, it was only one of an immense number of Jewish properties similarly put to the torch across Germany. It was not enough, though, merely to burn the lairs of vermin. Vermin themselves had to be destroyed. That they might wear the form of men, women and children did not render their elimination any the less pressing a duty. Only people infected by the baneful humanism of Christianity—a cult, it went without saying, 'invented by Jews and disseminated by

Jews'[43]—could possibly think otherwise. Yet Hitler, even as he cast his campaign against them as a matter of public health, would often assimilate it to another narrative: a profoundly Christian one. To be saved, the world had to be cleansed. A people threatened by perdition required redemption. Those on the side of the angels needed to be preserved from the pestiferous agents of hell. 'Two worlds face one another—the men of God and the men of Satan! The Jew is the anti-man, the creature of another god.'[44]

Conquest had enabled the tendrils of Hitler's hatred to reach far beyond the limits of Germany. Even before the war they had snaked and slithered their way into Tolkien's book-lined study. In 1938, a German editor wishing to publish him had written to ask if he were of Jewish origin. 'I regret,' Tolkien had replied, 'that I appear to have *no* ancestors of that gifted people.'[45] That the Nazis' racism lacked any scientific basis he took for granted; but his truest objection to it was as a Christian. Of course, steeped in the literature of the Middle Ages as he was, he knew full well the role played by his own Church in the stereotyping and persecution of the Jews. In his imaginings, however, he saw them not as the hook-nosed vampires of medieval calumny, but rather as 'a holy race of valiant men, the people of Israel the lawful children of God'.[46] These lines, from an Anglo-Saxon poem on the crossing of the Red Sea, were precious to Tolkien, for he had translated them himself. There was in them the same sense of identification with Exodus as had inspired Bede. Moses, in the poem, was represented as a mighty king, 'a prince of men with a marching company'.[47] Tolkien, writing *The Lord of the Rings* even as the Nazis were expanding their empire from the Atlantic to Russia, draw freely on such poetry for his own epic. Central to the plot was the return of a king: an heir to a long-abandoned throne named Aragorn. If the armies of Mordor were satanic like those of Pharaoh, then Aragorn—emerging from exile to deliver his people from slavery—had more than a touch of Moses. As in Bede's monastery, so in Tolkien's study: a hero might be imagined as simultaneously Christian and Jewish.

This was no isolated, donnish eccentricity. Across Europe, the readiness of Christians to identify themselves with the Jews had become the measure of their response to the greatest catastrophe in Jewish history. Tolkien—ever the devout Catholic—was doing nothing that popes had not also done. In September 1938, the ailing Pius XI had declared himself spiritually a Jew. One year later, with Poland defeated and subjected by German forces to an unspeakably brutal occupation, his successor had issued his first public letter to the faithful. Pius XII, lamenting the ploughing of blood-drenched furrows with swords, pointedly cited Paul: 'There is neither Jew nor Greek.' Always, from the earliest days of the Church, this was a phrase that had particularly served to distinguish *Christianismos* from *Ioudaismos*: Christianity from Judaism. Between Christians, who celebrated the Church as the mother of all nations, and Jews, appalled at any prospect of having their distinctiveness melt away into the great mass of humanity, the dividing line had long been stark. But that was not how it seemed to the Nazis. When Pius XII quoted Genesis to rebuke those who would forget that humanity had a common origin, and that all the peoples of the world had a duty of charity to one another, the response from Nazi theorists was vituperative. To them, it appeared self-evident that universal morality was a fraud perpetrated by Jews. 'Can we still tolerate our children being obliged to learn that Jews and Negroes, just like Germans or Romans, are descended from Adam and Eve, simply because a Jewish myth says so?' Not merely pernicious, the doctrine that all were one in Christ ranked as an outrage against the fundamentals of science. For centuries, the Nordic race had been infected by it. The consequence was a mutilation of what should properly have been left whole: a circumcision of the mind. 'It is the Jew Paul who must be considered as the father of all this, as he, in a very significant way, established the principles of the destruction of a worldview based on blood.'

Christians, confronted by a regime committed to the repudiation of the most fundamental tenets of their faith—the oneness of the human race, the obligation of care for the weak and the suffering—had a choice to make. Did the Church, as a pastor named Dietrich Bonhoeffer had put it as early as 1933, have 'an unconditional obligation towards the victims of any social order, even where those victims do not belong to the Christian community'[48]—or did it not? Bonhoeffer's own answer to that question would see him conspire against Hitler's life, and end up being hanged in a concentration camp. There were many other Christians too who passed the test. Some spoke out publicly. Others, more clandestinely, did what they could to shelter their Jewish neighbours, in cellars and attics, in the full awareness that to do so was to risk their own lives. Church leaders, torn between speaking with the voice of prophecy against crimes almost beyond their comprehension and a dread that to do so might risk the very future of Christianity, walked an impossible tightrope. 'They deplore the fact that the Pope does not speak,' Pius had lamented privately in December 1942. 'But the pope cannot speak. If he spoke, things would be worse.'[49] Perhaps, as his critics would later charge, he should have spoken anyway. But Pius understood the limits of his power. By pushing things too far he might risk such measures as he was able to take. Jews themselves understood this well enough. In the pope's summer residence, five hundred were given shelter. In Hungary, priests frantically issued baptismal certificates, knowing that they might be shot for doing so. In Romania, papal diplomats pressed the government not to deport their country's Jews—and the trains were duly halted by 'bad weather'. Among the SS, the pope was derided as a rabbi.

Yet there were many Christians too, seduced by evil, who entered into the realm of shadow. The Nazis, when they portrayed Jews as a pestilence, simultaneously backward and over-educated, verminous and smoothly plausible, were not, of course, weaving their propaganda out of nothing. The myths that they drew upon were Christian myths. Biologists who deployed the rational formulations of science to identify Jews as a virus were drawing as well upon stereotypes that reached back ultimately to the Gospels. 'Let his blood be on us and on our children!'[50] That the Jews had willingly accepted responsibility for the death of Christ was a doctrine that repeatedly, over the course of Christian history, had seen them condemned as agents of the Devil. Eight hundred years after a pope had first condemned as a libel the claim that they were in the habit of mixing the blood of Christian children into their ritual bread, there were still bishops in Poland who hesitated to dismiss it. In Slovakia, where Jews were first expelled from the capital, and then deported from the country altogether, the puppet regime established by the Germans was headed by a priest. Elsewhere too, from France to the Balkans, and in the very Vatican itself, Catholics were often induced by their hatred of communism to view the Nazis as the lesser of two evils. Even a bishop might on occasion be brought to speak about the campaign of eradication against the Jews with a worm tongue. In Croatia, when the archbishop of Zagreb wrote to the Interior Minister to protest against their deportation, he freely acknowledged the existence of a 'Jewish question,' and that the Jews themselves were indeed—albeit in some unspecified manner—guilty of 'crimes'.[51] More than thirty thousand would end up murdered: three-quarters of Croatia's entire Jewish population.

Yet nowhere was shadow more menacingly enthroned than in Germany. It was there—unsurprisingly—that churches lay most ruinously under the thraldom of an adversary pledged to their utter corruption. It was not only medieval Christendom that provided grist to the mill of the Nazi campaign against the Jews. So too did the Reformation. Luther's contempt for Judaism as a creed defined by hypocrisy and legalism had many heirs still. These, dazzled by the swagger of National Socialism, might well find their own faith pallid by comparison. The parade grounds, ablaze with flags and eagles, seemed to offer a sense of communion with the numinous that their own dusty pews could no longer provide. Perhaps, as Hitler himself believed, Jesus had not been a Jew at all, but of Nordic stock, blond and blue-eyed. This thesis had opened up for many Protestants in Germany a tantalising prospect: that it might be possible to forge a new and National Socialist form of Christianity. In 1939, in the Wartburg, where Luther had completed his great translation of the New Testament, distinguished scholars had met to revive the heresy of Marcion. The keynote speaker had pledged them to a second Reformation. Protestants had been urged to cleanse Christianity of every last taint of the Jew. Back then, with the world on the brink of war, it had seemed clear which way the wind was blowing. The victory of National Socialism was at hand. The rewards would be rich for those that aided it. Christians could bide their time, keeping their thoughts in their hearts, deploring maybe evils done by the way, but approving the high and ultimate purpose. Such, at any rate, was the thinking. A church of blood—racist and wraith-like—would be one that Hitler would indeed have cause to spare from destruction. A Christianity fallen under the mastery of National Socialism would provide him with a servant both potent and terrible. Those who belonged to it would be able to draw up plans for the liquidation of millions, and attend to the scheduling of cattle trucks, and toast the success of their efforts even as the smell of burning corpses drifted in through the windows, and know that they were serving the purposes of Christ.

'He who fights with monsters should look to it that he himself does not become a monster. And when you gaze long into an abyss the abyss also gazes into you.'[52] Nietzsche, a man who had renounced his citizenship, despised nationalism, and praised the Jews as the most remarkable people in history, had warned what confusions were bound to follow from the death of God. Good and evil would become merely relative. Moral codes would drift unanchored. Deeds of massive and terrible violence would be perpetrated. Even committed Nietzscheans might flinch before their discovery of what this meant in practice. Otto Dix, far from admiring the Nazis for turning the world on its head, was revolted by them. They in turn dismissed him as a degenerate. Sacked from his teaching post in Dresden, forbidden to exhibit his paintings, he had turned to the Bible as his surest source of inspiration. In 1939, he had painted the destruction of

Sodom. Fire was shown consuming a city that was unmistakably Dresden. The image had proven prophetic. As the tide of war turned against Germany, so British and American planes had begun to visit ruin on the country's cities. In July 1943, in an operation code-named Gomorrah, a great sea of fire had engulfed much of Hamburg. Back in Britain, a bishop named George Bell—a close friend of Bonhoeffer's—spoke out in public protest. 'If it is permissible to drive inhabitants to desire peace by making them suffer, why not admit pillage, burning, torture, murder, violation?'[53] The objection was brushed aside. There was no place, the bishop was sternly informed, in a war against an enemy as terrible as Hitler, for humanitarian or sentimental scruples. In February 1945, it was the turn of Dresden to burn. The most beautiful city in Germany was reduced to ashes. So too was much else. By the time the country was at last brought to unconditional surrender in May 1945, most of it lay in ruins. The liberation of the Nazis' death camps, and the dawning realisation of just how genocidal Hitler's ambitions had been, ensured that few in Britain felt many qualms. Good had triumphed over evil. The end had justified the means.

Yet to some, the victory felt almost like a defeat. In 1948, three years after the death of Hitler, Tolkien finally completed *The Lord of the Rings*. Its climax told of the overthrow of Sauron. Over the course of the novel, he and his servants had been searching for a terrible weapon, a ring of deadly power, that would have enabled him, had he only been able to find it, to rule all of Middle-earth. Naturally, Sauron's dread had been that his enemies—whom he knew had found it—would turn it against him. But they did not. Instead, they destroyed the ring. True strength manifested itself not in the exercise of power, but in the willingness to give it up. So Tolkien, as a Christian, believed. It was why, in the last year of the war against Hitler, he had lamented it as an ultimately evil job. 'For we are attempting to conquer Sauron with the Ring. And we shall (it seems) succeed. But the penalty is, as you will know, to breed new Saurons.'[54] Tolkien, although he gruffly dismissed any notion that he might have modelled *The Lord of the Rings* on the events of his own century, certainly viewed them through the prism of his own creation. The world of the concentration camp and the atom bomb was etched with the patterns of a more distant age: one when the wings of angels had beaten close over battlefields, and miracles been manifest on Middle-earth. There were few moments in the novel when its profoundly Christian character were rendered overt; but when they came, they were made to count. The fall of Mordor, so Tolkien specified, occurred on 25 March: the very date on which, since at least the third century, Christ was believed to have become incarnate in the womb of Mary, and then to have been crucified.

The first instalment of *The Lord of the Rings* was published, after a lengthy edit, in 1954. Most reviews, when not bewildered, were contemptuous. The book's roots in a distant past; its insistence that good and evil actually existed; its relish for the supernatural: all were liable to strike sophisticated intellectuals as infantile. 'This is not a work,' one of them sniffed, 'which many adults will read through more than once.'[55] But he was wrong. The popularity of the book grew and grew. Within only a few years, it had established itself as a publishing phenomenon. No other novel written over the course of the war remotely began to compare with its sales. Such success was very sweet to Tolkien. His purpose in writing *The Lord of the Rings* had not been a merely pecuniary one. His ambition had been one that Irenaeus, and Origen, and Bede had shared: to communicate to those who might not appreciate them the beauties of the Christian religion, and its truth. The popularity of his novel suggested to him that he had succeeded. *The Lord of the Rings* would end up the most widely read work of fiction of the twentieth century, and Tolkien its most widely read Christian author.

Yet this, while it might testify to Christianity's abiding hold on the imagination, testified to something else as well. *The Lord of the Rings*—as many of its critics complained—was a story with a happy ending. Sauron was vanquished, the powers of Mordor overthrown. But the victory of good did not come without cost. Loss accompanied it, and diminishment, and the passing of what had once been beautiful and strong. The kingdoms of men endured—but not those of the other races of Middle-earth. 'Together through the ages of the world we have fought the long defeat.'[56] This sentiment, expressed by an Elvish queen, was one that Tolkien felt shadowed by himself. 'I am a Christian, and indeed a Roman Catholic, so that I do not expect "history" to be anything but a "long defeat"—though it contains (and in a legend may contain more clearly and movingly) some samples or glimpse of final victory.'[57] The success of *The Lord of the Rings*—while it bore witness, Tolkien hoped, to the 'final victory' of Christianity—bore witness as well to its fading. The novel offered Tolkien's religion to its readers obliquely; and, had it not done so, it would never have enjoyed such unprecedented success. The world was changing. A belief in evil as Tolkien believed in it, and as Christians for so long had done, as a literal, satanic force, was weakening. Few doubted, in the wake of the first half of the twentieth century, that hell existed—but it had become difficult to imagine it as anything other than a muddy cesspool, surrounded by barbed wire, and with crematoria silhouetted against a wintry sky, built by men from the very heartlands of what had once been Christendom.

20

LOVE

1967: Abbey Road

Sunday, 25 June. In St John's Wood, one of London's most afflu-
ent neighbourhoods, churchgoers were heading to evensong.
Not the world's most famous band, though. The Beatles were
booked to play their largest-ever gig. For the first time, a programme
featuring live sequences from different countries was to be broadcast
simultaneously around the world—and the British Broadcasting Cor-
poration, for its segment, had put up John Lennon, Paul McCartney,
George Harrison and Ringo Starr. The studios on Abbey Road were
where, for the past five years, the Beatles had been recording the songs
that had transformed popular music, and made them the most idolised
young men on the planet. Now, before an audience of 350 million, they
were recording their latest single. The song, with a chorus that anyone
could sing, was joyously, catchily anthemic. Its message, written on
cardboard placards in an assortment of languages, was intended to be
readily accessible to a global village. Flowers, streamers and balloons
all added to the sense of a party. John Lennon, alternately singing and
chewing heavily on a wad of gum, offered the watching world a prescription with which neither Aquinas, nor Augustine, nor Saint Paul
would have disagreed: 'all you need is love'.

God, after all, was love. This was what it said in the Bible. For
two thousand years, men and women had been pondering this

revelation. Love, and do as you will. Many were the Christians who, over the course of the centuries, had sought to put this precept of Augustine's into practice.[1] For then, as a Hussite preacher had put it, 'Paradise will open to us, benevolence will be multiplied, and perfect love will abound.'[2] But what if there were wolves? What then were the lambs to do? The Beatles themselves had grown up in a world scarred by war. Great stretches of Liverpool, their native city, had been levelled by German bombs. Their apprenticeship as a band had been in Hamburg, served in clubs manned by limbless ex-Nazis. Now, even as they sang their message of peace, the world again lay in the shadow of conflict. Only three weeks before the broadcast from Abbey Road, war had broken out in the Holy Land. The blackened carcasses of Egyptian and Syrian planes littered landscapes once trodden by biblical patriarchs. Israel, the Jewish homeland promised by the British in 1917, and which had finally been founded in 1948, had won in only six days a stunning victory over neighbours pledged to its annihilation. Jerusalem, the city of David, was—for the first time since the age of the Caesars—under Jewish rule. Yet this offered no resolution to the despair and misery of those displaced from what had previously been Palestine. Just the opposite. Across the world, like napalm in a Vietnamese jungle, hatreds seemed to be burning out of control. Most terrifying of all were the tensions between the world's two superpowers, the Soviet Union and the United States. Victory over Hitler had brought Russian troops into the heart of Europe. Communist governments had been installed in ancient Christian capitals: Warsaw, Budapest, Prague. An iron curtain now ran across the continent. Armed as both sides were with nuclear missiles, weapons so lethal that they had the potential to wipe out all of life on earth, the stakes were grown apocalyptic. Humanity had arrogated to itself what had always previously been viewed as a divine prerogative: the power to end the world.

How, then, could love possibly be enough? The Beatles—although roundly mocked for their message—were not alone in believing that it might be. A decade earlier, in the depths of the American South, a

Baptist pastor named Martin Luther King had pondered what Christ had meant by urging his followers to love their enemies. 'Far from being the pious injunction of a utopian dreamer, this command is an absolute necessity for the survival of our civilisation. Yes, it is love that will save our world and our civilization, love even for enemies.'[3] King had not claimed, as the Beatles would in 'All You Need Is Love', that it was easy. He spoke as a black man, to a black congregation, living in a society blighted by institutionalised oppression. The civil war, although it had ended slavery, had not ended racism and segregation. Lawmen had combined with lynch mobs to ensure that. Thousands were signed up to the Ku Klux Klan, a paramilitary organisation that sang hymns, burned giant crosses, and rode down black Americans. White pastors—when they were not actively serving as leaders in the Klan—stood silently by. It was these clergymen and their congregations that King sought to rouse from their moral slumbers. An orator of genius, with an unrivalled mastery of the Bible and its cadences, he also possessed a rare talent for organising peaceful demonstrations. Strikes, boycotts, marches: again and again, King deployed them to force the repeal of discriminatory legislation. Yet these successes, while they made him a national figure, also made him hated. His house was firebombed; he was repeatedly thrown into prison. But King never hated in return. He knew that it cost a man to bear witness to the word of God. In the spring of 1963, writing from jail, he had reflected on how Saint Paul had carried the gospel of freedom to where it was most needed, heedless of the risks. Summoning the white clergy to break their silence and to speak out against the injustices suffered by blacks, King had invoked the authority of Aquinas and of his own namesake, Martin Luther. Above all, though—answering the charge of extremism—he had appealed to the example of his Saviour. Laws that sanctioned the hatred and persecution of one race by another, he declared, were laws that Christ himself would have broken. 'Was not Jesus an extremist for love?'[4]

The campaign for civil rights gave to Christianity an overt centrality in American politics that it had not had since the decades before the Civil War. King, by stirring the slumbering conscience of white Christians, succeeded in setting his country on a transformative new path. To talk of love as Paul had talked of it, as a thing greater than prophecy, or knowledge, or faith, had once again become a revolutionary act. King's dream, that the glory of the Lord would be revealed, and all flesh see it together, helped to animate a great yearning across America—in West Coast coffee shops as in Alabama churches, on verdant campuses as on picket lines, among attorneys as among refuse-workers—for justice to roll on like a river, and righteousness like a never-failing stream. This was the same vision of progress that, in the eighteenth century, had inspired Quakers and Evangelicals to campaign for the abolition of slavery; but now, in the 1960s, the spark that had set it to flame with a renewed brilliance was the faith of African Americans. The sound of protest was the sound of the black churches. Evident in King's soaring preacher's baritone, it was evident too in the music that could be heard on transistors and stereos across the country. In the 1950s, on picket lines and marches, black protestors had sung songs from the dark days of bondage: about Moses redeeming his people from slavery; about Joshua bringing down the walls of Jericho. In the 1960s, it began to seem that voices honed in gospel choirs might transform the world: that a change was gonna come. When James Brown, the most innovative and daring of all black superstars, emerged from poverty to blaze a trail for funk, he drew for his style on a youthful apprenticeship spent in a notably flamboyant evangelical church. Brown, a mercurial man who veered between singing the praises of capitalism and saying it loud that he was black and proud, never forgot the debt he owed the United House of Prayer for All People of the Church on the Rock of the Apostolic Faith. 'Sanctified people got more fire.'[5]

Like the perfume of a joss stick, however, the ideals and slogans of the civil rights movement might be inhaled by people who had never seen the inside of a black church. That the Beatles agreed with King on the importance of love and had refused as a matter of principle to play for segregated audiences, did not mean that they were—as James Brown might have put it—'holy'. Even though Lennon had first met McCartney at a church fête, all four had long since abandoned their childhood Christianity. It was, in the words of McCartney, a 'goody-goody thing':[6] fine, perhaps, for a lonely woman wearing a face that she kept in a jar by the door, but not for a band that had conquered the world. Churches were stuffy, old-fashioned, boring—everything that the Beatles were not. In England, even the odd bishop had begun to suggest that the traditional Christian understanding of God was outmoded, and that the only rule was love. In 1966, when Lennon claimed in a newspaper interview that the Beatles were 'more popular than Jesus',[7] eyebrows were barely raised in his home country. Only four months later, after his comment had been reprinted in an American magazine, did the backlash hit. Pastors across the United States had long been suspicious of the Beatles. This was especially so in the South—the Bible Belt. Preachers there—unwittingly backing Lennon's point—fretted that Beatlemania had become a form of idolatry; some even worried that it was all a communist plot. To many white evangelicals— shamed by the summons to repentance issued them by King, baffled by the sense of a moral fervour that had originated outside their own churches, and horrified by the spectacle of their daughters screaming and wetting themselves at the sight of four peculiar-looking Englishmen—the chance to trash Beatles records came as a blessed relief. Simultaneously, to racists unpersuaded by the justice of the civil rights movement, it provided an opportunity to rally the troops. The Ku Klux Klan leapt at the chance to cast themselves as the defender of Protestant values. Not content with burning records, they set to burning Beatles wigs. The band's distinctive hairstyle— a shaggy moptop—seemed to clean-cut Klansmen a blasphemy in itself. 'It's hard for me to tell through the mopheads,' one of them snarled, 'whether they're even white or black.'[8]

None of which did much to alter Lennon's views on Christianity. The Beatles did not—as Martin Luther King had done—derive their understanding of love as the force that animated the universe from a close reading of scripture. Instead, they took it for granted. Cut loose from its theological moorings, the distinctively Christian understanding of love that had done so much to animate the civil rights movement began to float free over an ever more psychedelic landscape. The Beatles were not alone, that summer of 1967, in 'turning funny'.⁹ Beads and bongs were everywhere. Evangelicals were appalled. To them, the emergence of long-haired freaks with flowers in their hair seemed sure confirmation of the satanic turn that the world was taking. Blissed-out talk of peace and love was pernicious sloganeering: just a cover for drugs and sex. Two thousand years of attempts to rein in the violence of the passions appeared to be going into reverse. That this was true enough did not, of course, make Christians seem any less square. Preachers, seen through the marijuana haze of a squat in San Francisco, had the look of bigots. Where was the love in short-haired men jabbing their fingers and going puce? Tense and thrumming, the sense of an unbridgeable divide, of opposites locked in an irreconcilable culture war, was always there in the Summer of Love.

Then, the following April, Martin Luther King was shot dead. An entire era seemed to have been gunned down with him: one in which liberals and conservatives, black progressives and white evangelicals, had felt able—however inadequately—to feel joined by a shared sense of purpose. As news of King's assassination flashed across America, cities began to burn: Chicago, Washington, Baltimore. Black militants, impatient even before King's murder with his pacifism and talk of love, pushed for violent confrontation with the white establishment. Many openly derided Christianity as a slave religion. Other activists, following where King's campaign against racism had led, demanded the righting of what they saw as no less grievous sins. If it were wrong for blacks to be discriminated against, then why not women, or homosexuals? But to ask this was not—as King had done—to prick the consciences of Evangelicals, and to remind them of values which they already held. Instead, it was to attack the very fundamentals of their faith. That a woman's place was the home and homosexuality an abomination were orthodoxies, so pastors thundered, that had the timeless sanction of the Bible itself. Increasingly, to Americans disoriented by the moral whirligig of the age, Evangelicals promised solid ground. A place of refuge, though, might just as well be a place under siege. To many Evangelicals, feminism and the gay rights movement were an assault on Christianity itself. Equally, to many feminists and gay activists, Christianity appeared synonymous with everything that they were struggling against: injustice, and bigotry, and persecution. God, they were told, hates fags.

But did he? Conservatives, when they charged their opponents with breaking biblical commandments, had the heft of two thousand years of Christian tradition behind them; but so too, when they pressed for gender equality or gay rights, did liberals. Their immediate model and inspiration was, after all, a Baptist preacher. 'There is no graded scale of essential worth,' King had written a year before his assassination. 'Every human being has etched in his personality the indelible stamp of the Creator. Every man must be respected because God loves him.'[10] Every woman too, a feminist might have added. Yet King's words, while certainly bearing witness to an instinctive strain of patriarchy within Christianity, bore witness as well to why, across the Western world, this was coming to seem a problem. That every human being possessed an equal dignity was not remotely self-evident a truth. A Roman would have laughed at it. To campaign against discrimination on the grounds of gender or sexuality, however, was to depend on large numbers of people sharing in a common assumption: that everyone possessed an inherent worth. The origins of this principle—as Nietzsche had so contemptuously pointed out—lay not in the French Revolution, nor in the Declaration of Independence, nor in the Enlightenment, but in the Bible. Ambivalences that came to roil Western society in the 1970s had always been perfectly manifest in the letters of Paul.

Writing to the Corinthians, the apostle had pronounced that man was the head of woman; writing to the Galatians, he had exulted that there was no man or woman in Christ. Balancing his stern condemnation of same-sex relationships had been his rapturous praise of love. Raised a Pharisee, learned in the Law of Moses, he had come to proclaim the primacy of conscience. The knowledge of what constituted a just society was written not with ink but with the Spirit of the living God, not on tablets of stone but on human hearts. Love, and do as you will. It was—as the entire course of Christian history so vividly demonstrated—a formula for revolution.

'The wind blows wherever it pleases.'[11] That the times they were a-changin' was a message Christ himself had taught. Again and again, Christians had found themselves touched by God's spirit; again and again, they had found themselves brought by it into the light. Now, though, the Spirit had taken on a new form. No longer Christian, it had become a vibe. Not to get down with it was to be stranded on the wrong side of history. The concept of progress, unyoked from the theology that had given it birth, had begun to leave Christianity trailing in its wake. The choice that faced churches—an agonisingly difficult one—was whether to sit in the dust, shaking their fists at it in impotent rage, or whether to run and scramble in a desperate attempt to catch up with it. Should women be allowed to become priests? Should homosexuality be condemned as sodomy or praised as love? Should the age-old Christian project of trammelling sexual appetites be maintained or eased? None of these questions were easily answered. To those who took them seriously, they ensured endless and pained debate. To those who did not, they provided yet further evidence—if evidence were needed—that Christianity was on its way out. John Lennon had been right. 'It will vanish and shrink. I needn't argue about that; I know I'm right and I will be proved right.'[12]

Yet atheists faced challenges of their own. Christians were not alone in struggling to square the rival demands of tradition and progress. Lennon, after walking out on his song-writing partnership with McCartney, celebrated his liberation with a song that listed Jesus alongside the Beatles as idols in which he no longer believed. Then, in October 1971, he released a new single: 'Imagine'. The song offered Lennon's prescription for global peace. Imagine there's no heaven, he sang, no hell below us. Yet the lyrics were religious through and through. Dreaming of a better world, a brotherhood of man, was a venerable tradition in Lennon's neck of the woods. St George's Hill, his home throughout the heyday of the Beatles, was where the Diggers had laboured three hundred years previously. Rather than emulate Winstanley, however, Lennon had holed up inside a gated community, complete with a Rolls-Royce and swimming pool. 'One wonders what they do with all their dough.'[13] So a pastor had mused back in 1966. The video of 'Imagine', in which Lennon was seen gliding around his recently purchased seventy-two-acre Berkshire estate, provided the answer. In its hypocrisy no less than in its dreams of a universal peace, Lennon's atheism was recognisably bred of Christian marrow. A good preacher, however, was always able to take his flock with him. The spectacle of Lennon imagining a world without possessions while sitting in a huge mansion did nothing to put off his admirers. As Nietzsche spun furiously in his grave, 'Imagine' became the anthem of atheism. A decade later, when Lennon was shot dead by a crazed fan, he was mourned not just as one half of the greatest song-writing partnership of the twentieth century, but as a martyr.

Not everyone was convinced. 'Now, since his death, he's become Martin Luther Lennon.'[14] Paul McCartney had known Lennon too well ever to mistake him for a saint. His joke, though, was also a tribute to King: a man who had flown into the light of the dark black night. 'Life's most persistent and urgent question is, "What are you doing for others?"'[15] McCartney, for all his dismissal of 'goody goody stuff', was not oblivious to the tug of an appeal like this. In 1985, asked to help relieve a devastating famine in Ethiopia by taking part in the world's largest-ever concert, he readily agreed. Live

Aid, staged simultaneously in London and Philadelphia, the city of brotherly love, was broadcast to billions. Musicians who had spent their careers variously bedding groupies and snorting coke off trays balanced on the heads of dwarves played sets in aid of the starving. As night fell over London, and the concert in Wembley stadium reached its climax, lights picked out McCartney at a piano. The number he sang, 'Let It Be', had been the last single to be released by the Beatles while they were still together. 'When I find myself in times of trouble, Mother Mary comes to me.' Who was Mary? Perhaps, as McCartney himself claimed, his mother; but perhaps, as Lennon had darkly suspected, and many Catholics had come to believe, the Virgin. Whatever the truth, no one that night could hear him. His microphone had cut out.

It was a performance perfectly appropriate to the paradoxes of the age.

Long Walk to Freedom

Seven months before Live Aid, its organisers had recruited many of the biggest acts in Britain and Ireland to a super-group: Band Aid. 'Do They Know It's Christmas?', a one-off charity record, succeeded in raising so much money for famine relief that it would end up the best-selling single in the history of the UK charts.* For all the peroxide, all the cross-dressing, all the bags of cocaine smuggled into the recording studio, the project was one born of the Christian past. Reporting on the sheer scale of the suffering in Ethiopia, a BBC correspondent had described the scenes he was witnessing as 'biblical'; stirred into action, the organisers of Band Aid had embarked on a course of action that reached for its ultimate inspiration to the examples of Paul and Basil. That charity should be offered to the needy, and that a stranger in a foreign land was no less a brother

---

* Until displaced in 1997, by 'Candle in the Wind', Elton John's tribute to Diana, Princess of Wales.

or sister than was a next-door neighbour, were principles that had always been fundamental to the Christian message. Concern for the victims of distant disasters—famines, earthquakes, floods—was disproportionately strong in what had once been Christendom. The overwhelming concentration of international aid agencies there was no coincidence. Band Aid were hardly the first to ask whether Africans knew that it was Christmastime. In the nineteenth century, the same anxiety had weighed heavily on Evangelicals. Missionaries had duly hacked their way through uncharted jungles, campaigned against the slave trade, and laboured with all their might to bring the Dark Continent into the light of Christ. 'A diffusive philanthropy is Christianity itself. It requires perpetual propagation to attest its genuineness.'[16] Such was the mission statement of the era's most famous explorer, David Livingstone. Band Aid—in their ambition to do good, if not in their use of hair dye—were recognisably his heirs.

This was not, though, how their single was marketed. Anything that smacked of white people telling Africans what to do had become, by the 1980s, an embarrassment. Admiration even for a missionary such as Livingstone, whose crusade against the Arab slave trade had been unstintingly heroic, had come to pall. His efforts to map the continent—far from serving the interests of Africans, as he had trusted they would—had instead only opened up its interior to conquest and exploitation. A decade after his death from malaria in 1873, British adventurers had begun to expand deep into the heart of Africa. Other European powers had embarked on a similar scramble. France had annexed much of north Africa, Belgium the Congo, Germany Namibia. By the outbreak of the First World War, almost the entire continent was under foreign rule. Only the Ethiopians had succeeded in maintaining their independence. Missionaries, struggling to continue with their great labour of conversion, had found themselves stymied by the brute nature of European power. How were Africans to believe talk of a god who cared for the oppressed and the poor when the whites, the very people who worshipped him, had seized their lands and plundered them for diamonds, and ivory, and rubber? A colonial hierarchy in which blacks were deemed inferior had seemed a peculiar and bitter mockery of the missionaries' insistence that Christ had died for all of humanity. By the 1950s, when the tide of imperialism in Africa had begun to ebb as fast it had originally flowed, it might have seemed that Christianity was doomed to retreat as well, with churches crumbling before the hunger of termites, and Bibles melting into mildewed pulp. But that—in the event—was not what had happened at all!

Did Africans, as Band Aid stormed its way to the top of the UK charts, know that it was Christmas? Not all of them, perhaps. Many were pagan; many more were Muslim. In 1984, though, some 250 million of them were Christian. In 1900, the total had been a bare ten million. The rate of growth, far from going into decline with the end of colonial rule, had exploded. Nothing quite like it had been seen since the expansion of Christendom in the early Middle Ages. As then, so now, the worship of Christ had spectacularly slipped the bonds of a vanished imperial order. Even in the early years of the twentieth century, when the European empires had seemed invincible, Africans had found in the Bible the promise of redemption from foreign rule. Just as Irish hermits and Anglo-Saxon missionaries had once claimed an authority that, deriving as it did from heaven, instilled in them the courage to upbraid kings, so in Africa, native preachers had repeatedly confronted colonial officials. There were some who had led armed uprisings, and been put to death for it; some, obedient to the commands of angels, who had only had to enter a village for idols to go up in flames; some who had cured the sick, and raised the dead, and ended up clapped in irons for it by twitchy chiefs of police. To many white missionaries, these prophets, with their wild talk of the Spirit and of the powers of darkness, had appeared the very essence of savagery: hysterics who risked polluting the pure waters of Christianity with their primitive superstitions. This, though, had been the nervousness of Europeans who could not imagine their faith arrayed in any garb other than their own. African Christians, far from compromising with the paganism of their ancestors, tended to dread it far more than any foreign missionary might do: for they could recognise in it, just as Boniface had once done, the worship of demons. Decades after the end of colonial rule, there were clergymen across Africa who continued to despair of the condescension shown them by Europe. 'We thank her for what she has done to us, and we appreciate her worries and anxieties about us.' So Emmanuel Milingo, the Catholic archbishop of Lusaka, had declared in 1977. 'But we believe that she, as a grandmother to us, should now worry much more about her problems of old age, than about us.'[17]

Milingo's belief in the reality of evil spirits, and his conviction that—with God's blessing—they might be cast out from those they afflicted, had seen him, throughout the 1970s, perform spectacular feats of exorcism across Zambia. Summoned to Rome in 1982 by a suspicious Vatican, he had promptly established a no less successful healing ministry in Italy. That church leaders in Europe seemed to have stopped believing in the reality of the demonic was their problem, not his. To rid the sick of demons was no sin, after all. Rather than apologise for performing what Christ himself had repeatedly performed, Milingo preferred instead to charge European bishops with a faith grown too desiccated to accept the reality of the miracles and terrors revealed in the Bible. To be African was no impediment to fathoming the Christian message. Rather, it was a positive advantage. 'If God made a mistake by creating me an African, it is not yet evident.'[18] Implicit in such defiance was a conviction that Africa, far from owing the revelation of Christ's light to white missionaries, had always been touched by its fire. Any notion that Ethiopians might never have heard of Christmas was worse than mistaken—it was grotesque. The Psalms themselves had foretold that Ethiopia would submit to God—and so it had proved.[19] Christianity had been the country's state religion since the age of Constantine. For 1700 years it had endured as a Christian realm. What European kingdom could claim as much?

Of course, then, Ethiopians knew what Christmas was. The example of their Christianity had long been an inspiration across the whole of Africa. Nowhere, indeed, had it been more fruitfully treasured than at the far end of the continent: in South Africa. In 1892, a black clergyman resentful of the paternalism with which white Christians were treating him and his fellow Africans had founded what he named *Ibandla laseTiyopiya*: the Ethiopian Church. Ninety years on, and the sense of South Africa as a land aflame with holiness was widespread. It was not just to Ethiopia that churches now compared themselves. New Jerusalems were to be found dotted across the country. A second Mount Moria stood in the northern reaches of the Transvaal. The breath of the Spirit was felt from Cape Town to Zululand. Even in the Churches brought to South Africa by Europeans, black Christians could rejoice in the distinctive relationship that Africans were believed always to have enjoyed with the divine. 'It has helped to give the lie to the supercilious but tacit assumption that religion and history in Africa date from the advent in that continent of the white man.'[20]

Yet Desmond Tutu, even as he made this point, never doubted that he was part of a global communion. As an Anglican bishop, he belonged to a Church that traced its origins back to the reign of a sixteenth-century English king. A natural showman, he delighted in blending the traditions of Canterbury with those of Soweto. In 1986, when he became the first black man to be elected to the archbishopric of Cape Town, he was able to offer himself as a living symbol of how, in Christ Jesus, there was neither black nor white. Yet this was not simply to make a theological statement. Questions about the purposes of God had become, in South Africa, tumultuously, explosively political. Blacks were not alone in seeing the country as a new Israel. So too did many whites. The Dutch Calvinists who in the seventeenth century had settled the Cape—Afrikaners, as they would come to be known—had viewed themselves not as colonists, but as a chosen people brought into a promised land. Just as the Israelites had wrested Canaan from the native heathen, so had the Afrikaners defied the fury of 'the stark naked black hordes'[21] to carve out a homeland of their own. Absorption into the British Empire had done nothing to diminish their sense of themselves as a people bound by a covenant with God. In 1948, when a government dominated by Afrikaner conservatives had come to power, it had set to solidifying this conviction into an entire political programme. A policy of *apartheid*—'separateness'— had been formalised. Racial segregation had become the animating principle of the entire state. Whether it was buying a house or falling in love, getting an education or choosing which bench to sit on in a park, there was almost no aspect of life in South Africa that the government had not aimed to regulate. White rule was enshrined as the expression of God's purpose. Afrikaner churchmen, incorrectly attributing to Calvin a doctrine that certain peoples were more likely to be saved than others, had enabled supporters of apartheid to view it as Christian through and through. To its supporters, it was an expression not of racism, but of love: a commitment to providing the different races of South Africa with the 'separate development' that was needed for them all to come to God. It was not prisons that ultimately served to maintain apartheid, nor guns, nor helicopters, nor police dogs. Apartheid was maintained by theology.

'Totally un-Christian, evil and a heresy.'[22] This condemnation of apartheid, proposed by Tutu, and passed by the Anglican Church, could easily be dismissed by the government's supporters as hand-wringing waffle. Yet it was in truth something altogether more ominous: a trumpet-blast, of the kind that had brought down the walls of Jericho. If it was as a theological construct that apartheid had been built, then it was as a theological construct that it would need to be dismantled. An unjust regime stood condemned before the throne of God. 'It is not a legitimate sovereignty, but a usurpation.'[23] So Calvin himself had written. When clergymen both black and white, quoting the theologian most admired by Afrikaners, were able to demonstrate in scrupulous and forensic detail that no possible backing for racial segregation was to be found in his writings, but only the opposite, condemnation stern and uncompromising, a hammer-blow was dealt to the apartheid regime as decisive as anything delivered by armed insurgents.

This was a lesson well understood by Nelson Mandela, most celebrated and formidable of all South Africa's revolutionaries, and a man who, ever since his conviction in 1964 on charges of sabotage, had been kept firmly under lock and key. In prison, he had slept on damp concrete and been put to hard labour, and had his eyesight permanently damaged by the glare of the quarry in which he had been made to toil; but he had come to recognise, during those long decades of incarceration, that forgiveness might be the most constructive, the most effective, the most devastating tactic of all. Mandela, a Methodist of discreet but committed faith, had time enough in his cell to read the Bible, and to ponder the teachings of Christ. 'You have heard that it was said, "Love your neighbour and hate your enemy." But I tell you: Love your enemies and pray for those who persecute you, that you may be sons of your Father in heaven.'[24] By 1989, with Afrikaner confidence in apartheid as an expression of God's plan crumbling, and a new president, F. W. de Klerk, desperate to make sense of the divine purpose, Mandela was ready to act on his long years of reflection. Freed at last on 11 February 1990, he returned into the world resolved to be free as well of all his bitterness and hatred. Meeting with those who had kept him a prisoner for twenty-seven years and oppressed his people for many years longer, he did so with a belief in the redemptive power of forgiveness.

The ending of apartheid and the election in 1994 of Mandela as South Africa's first black president was one of the great dramas of Christian history: a drama woven through with deliberate echoes of the Gospels. Without protagonists long familiar with the script they had been given to speak, it could not possibly have succeeded. 'When confession is made, then those of us who have been wronged must say "We forgive you."'[25] Had de Klerk not known that Tutu was bound to say this, then perhaps he would never have dared trust his people's fate to the readiness of black South Africans to pardon them their sins. The same faith that had inspired Afrikaners to imagine themselves a chosen people was also, in the long run, what had doomed their supremacy. The pattern was a familiar one.

Repeatedly, whether crashing along the canals of Tenochtitlan, or settling the estuaries of Massachusetts, or trekking deep into the Transvaal, the confidence that had enabled Europeans to believe themselves superior to those they were displacing was derived from Christianity. Repeatedly, though, in the struggle to hold this arrogance to account, it was Christianity that had provided the colonised and the enslaved with their surest voice. The paradox was profound. No other conquerors, carving out empires for themselves, had done so as the servants of a man tortured to death on the orders of a colonial official. No other conquerors, dismissing with contempt the gods of other peoples, had installed in their place an emblem of power so deeply ambivalent as to render problematic the very notion of power. No other conquerors, exporting an understanding of the divine peculiar to themselves, had so successfully persuaded peoples around the globe that it possessed a universal import. When, a month before his inauguration as president, Mandela travelled to the Transvaal, there to celebrate Easter in the holy city of Moria, it was as a Saviour who had died for the whole world that he saluted Christ. 'Easter is a festival of human solidarity, because it celebrates the fulfilment of the Good News! The Good News borne by our risen Messiah who chose not one race, who chose not one country, who chose not one language, who chose not one tribe, who chose all of humankind!'[26]

Ironically, however, even as Mandela was hailing Easter as a festival for all the world, elites in the old strongholds of Christendom were growing ever more nervous of using such language. This was not because they had ceased to believe in the universality of their values. Quite the opposite. The collapse of apartheid had been merely the aftershock of a far more convulsive earthquake. In 1989, even as de Klerk was resolving to set Mandela free, the Soviet empire had imploded. Poland, Czechoslovakia, Hungary: all had cast off the chains of foreign rule. East Germany, a rump hived off by the Soviets in the wake of the Second World War, had been absorbed into a reunified—and thoroughly capitalist—Germany. The Soviet Union itself had ceased to exist. Communism, weighed in the scales of history, had been found wanting. To de Klerk, pious Calvinist that he was, all this had manifestly appeared the writing of God's finger on the affairs of the world. This was not, however, how it tended to be seen by policymakers in America and Europe. They drew a different lesson. That the paradise on earth foretold by Marx had turned out instead to be closer to a hell only emphasised the degree to which the true fulfilment of progress was to be found elsewhere. With the rout of communism, it appeared to many in the victorious West that it was their own political and social order that constituted the ultimate, the unimprovable form of government. Secularism; liberal democracy; the concept of human rights: these were fit for the whole world to embrace. The inheritance of the Enlightenment was for everyone: a possession for all of mankind. It was promoted by the West, not because it was Western, but because it was universal. The entire world could enjoy its fruits. It was no more Christian than it was Hindu, or Confucian, or Muslim. There was neither Asian nor European. Humanity was embarked as one upon a common road.

The end of history had arrived.

The Management of Savagery

'Why do they hate us?'

The president of the United States, in his address to a joint session of Congress, knew that he was speaking for Americans across the country when he asked this question. Nine days earlier, on 11 September, an Islamic group named al-Qaeda had launched a series of devastating attacks against targets in New York and Washington. Planes had been hijacked and then crashed into the World Trade Center and the Pentagon. Thousands had died. George W. Bush, answering his own question, had no doubt as to the motives of the terrorists. They hated America's freedoms. Her freedom of religion, her freedom of speech. Yet these were not exclusively

American. Rather, they were universal rights. They were as much the patrimony of Muslims as of Christians, of Afghans as of Americans. This was why the hatred felt for Bush and his country across much of the Islamic world was based on misunderstanding. 'Like most Americans, I just can't believe it because I know how good we are.'[27] If American values were universal, shared by humans across the planet, regardless of creed or culture, then it stood to reason that Muslims shared them too. Bush, sitting in judgement on the terrorists who had attacked his country, condemned them not just for hijacking planes, but for hijacking Islam itself. 'We respect the faith. We honor its traditions. Our enemy does not.'[28] It was in this spirit that the President, even as he ordered the American war machine to inflict a terrible vengeance on al-Qaeda, aimed to bring to the Muslim world freedoms that he believed in all devoutness to be no less Islamic than they were Western. First in Afghanistan, and then in Iraq, murderous tyrannies were overthrown. Arriving in Baghdad in April 2003, US forces pulled down statues of the deposed dictator. As they waited to be given sweets and flowers by a grateful people, they waited as well to deliver to Iraq the dues of freedom that Bush, a year earlier, had described as applying fully to the entire Islamic world. 'When it comes to the common rights and needs of men and women, there is no clash of civilizations.'[29]

Except that sweets and flowers were notable by their absence on the streets of Iraq. Instead, the Americans were greeted with mortar attacks, and car bombs, and improvised explosive devices. The country began to dissolve into anarchy. In Europe, where opposition to the invasion of Iraq had been loud and vocal, the insurgency was viewed with often ill-disguised satisfaction. Even before 9/11, there were many who had felt that 'the United States had it coming'.[30] By 2003, with US troops occupying two Muslim countries, the accusation that Afghanistan and Iraq were the victims of naked imperialism was becoming ever more insistent. What was all the President's fine talk of freedom if not a smokescreen? As to what it might be hiding, the possibilities were multiple: oil, geopolitics, the interests of Israel. Yet Bush, although a hard-boiled businessman, was not just about the bottom line. He had never thought to hide his truest inspiration. Asked while still a candidate for the presidency to name his favourite thinker, he had answered unhesitatingly: 'Christ, because he changed my heart.'[31] Here, unmistakably, was an Evangelical. Bush, in his assumption that the concept of human rights was a universal one, was perfectly sincere. Just as the Evangelicals who fought to abolish the slave trade had done, he took for granted that his own values—confirmed to him in his heart by the Spirit— were values fit for all the world. He no more intended to bring Iraq to Christianity than British Foreign Secretaries, back in the heyday of the Royal Navy's campaign against slavery, had aimed to convert the Ottoman Empire. His ambition instead was to awaken Muslims to the values within their own religion that would enable them to see everything they had in common with America. 'Islam, as practised by the vast majority of people, is a peaceful religion, a religion that respects others.'[32] Bush, asked to describe his own faith, might well have couched it in similar terms. What bigger compliment, then, could he possibly have paid to Muslims?

But Iraqis did not have their hearts opened to the similarity of Islam to American values. Their country continued to burn. To Bush's critics, his talk of a war against evil appeared grotesquely misapplied. If anyone had done evil, then it was surely the leader of the world's greatest military power, a man who had used all the stupefying resources at his command to visit death and mayhem on the powerless. In 2004 alone, US forces in Iraq variously bombed a wedding party, flattened an entire city, and were photographed torturing prisoners. To many, it seemed that violence had always been the essence of the West. 'Europe's well-being and progress were built with the sweat and corpses of blacks, Arabs, Indians, and Asians.'[33] So had written Frantz Fanon, a psychiatrist from the French Caribbean, who in 1954 had joined the Algerian revolution against France, and devoted his life to rousing the colonised against their colonisers. To insurgents impatient with talk of peace and reconciliation, Fanon's insistence that true redemption from their bondage could only be achieved through armed insurrection had provided a bracing antidote to the pacifism of a Martin Luther King. It was not just among the colonised, however, that his message had cut through. Fanon had come to seem a prophet to many in the West who viewed themselves as the vanguard of the progressive. 'It is naked violence, and only gives in when confronted with greater violence.'[34] Fanon's analysis of imperialism was, to Bush's more radical critics, as clear-sighted as it was prescient. The occupation of Iraq was yet another blood-stained chapter in the history of the West's criminality. To target the forces of occupation with car-bombs or kidnappings was to fight for freedom. Without armed resistance, how were the shackles of imperialism ever to be cast off, and the wretched of the earth set free? To recognise this was to recognise—as the Stop the War Coalition, a British campaign group, put it in the autumn of 2004—'the legitimacy of the struggle of Iraqis, by whatever means they find necessary, to secure such ends'.[35]

Putting this rhetoric in its shadow, however, was a familiar irony. On what basis was it assumed that empires were evil? In Iraq, of all countries, evidence for the timelessness of imperialism lay everywhere. Persians, Romans, Arabs, Turks: all had taken for granted their entitlement to rule. The readiness of anti-war activists to condemn the West for its colonialist adventuring derived from the heritage not of the colonised countries, but of the colonisers. This was evident enough in the career of Fanon himself. Although he had been born and bred on Martinique, his education was impeccably French. His vision of terror as a means of purifying the world, of banishing oppression, of raising up the poor and casting down the rich, would have been perfectly familiar to Robespierre. Yet Fanon, a man of rare intellectual honesty, had recognised as well the ultimate source of this revolutionary tradition. Although contemptuous of religion as only a man who had spent his schooldays in a library emblazoned with the name of Voltaire could be, he had been raised a Catholic. He had read the Bible. Explaining what was meant by 'decolonisation', he had turned to the words of Jesus. 'Its definition can, if we want to describe it accurately, be summed up in the well-known words: "The last shall be first."'[36]

To imagine, then, that the insurgency in Iraq was a campaign of decolonisation such as Fanon would have understood it was to view the Muslim world through spectacles barely less Christian than those worn by Bush himself. Insurgents fighting the Americans tended not to object to empires per se—only to empires that were not legitimately Islamic. Muslims, like Christians, had their dreams of apocalypse; but these, amid the killing fields of Iraq, tended to foster fantasies of global conquest rather than of social revolution. As the world had once been, so it would be again. The fighting against the Americans was a mirror held up to the fighting, back in the early centuries of Islam, against the Romans and the crusaders—and foreshadowed what was yet to come. 'The spark has been lit here in Iraq, and its heat will continue to intensify—by Allah's permission—until it burns the crusader armies in Dabiq.'[37] This vaunting prophecy, delivered by an insurgent named Abu Musab al-Zarqawi two weeks before Stop the War gave him and his fellow paramilitaries their backing, articulated a venerable yearning: for the whole world to be brought to submit to Islam. Dabiq was a small town in Syria, where—according to a saying attributed to Muhammad—the armies of Christianity were destined to be annihilated in a final, climactic defeat. Islam's empire would then span the world. The end days would arrive; God's plans would be fulfilled at last.

Al-Zarqawi claimed that in a dream he had seen a sword descend to him from the heavens. The reality was more sordid. A thug and a rapist, he had a taste for atrocities so gruesome that even al-Qaeda would eventually denounce him. There was method, though, to his bombings and beheadings. Although barely literate, he had received a formidable education from one of the most influential of all Muslim radicals. In 1994, arrested for planning terrorist offences in Jordan, al-Zarqawi had stood trial alongside a Palestinian scholar named Abu Muhammad al-Maqdisi. For five years, while serving his prison term, he had been tutored by al-Maqdisi in the crisis that was facing Islam. Muslims, despite God's gift to them of a perfect and eternal law, had been seduced into obeying laws authored by men. They had become, al-Maqdisi warned, like Christians: infidels who took legislators as their lords 'instead of God'.[38] Governments across the Muslim world had adopted constitutions that directly contradicted the Sunna. Worse, they had signed up to international bodies that, despite their claims to neutrality, served to foist on Muslims alien law codes. Most menacing of all was the United Nations. Established in the aftermath of the Second World War, its delegates had proclaimed a Universal Declaration of Human Rights. To be a Muslim, though, was to know that humans did not have rights. There was no natural law in Islam. There were only laws authored by God. Muslim countries, by joining the United Nations, had signed up to a host of commitments that derived, not from the Qur'an or the Sunna, but from law codes devised in Christian countries: that there should be equality between men and women; equality between Muslims and non-Muslims; a ban on slavery; a ban on offensive warfare. Such doctrines, al-Maqdisi sternly ruled, had no place in Islam. To accept them was to become an apostate. Al-Zarqawi, released from prison in 1999, did not forget al-Maqdisi's warnings. In 2003, launching his campaign in Iraq, he went for a soft and telling target. On 19 August, a car bomb blew up the United Nations headquarters in the country. The UN's special representative was crushed to death in his office. Twenty-two others were also killed. Over a hundred were left maimed and wounded. Shortly afterwards, the United Nations withdrew from Iraq.

'Ours is a war not against a religion, not against the Muslim faith.'[39] President Bush's reassurance, offered before the invasion of Iraq, was not one that al-Zarqawi was remotely prepared to accept. What most people in the West meant by Islam and what scholars like al-Maqdisi meant by it were not at all the same thing. What to Bush appeared the markers of its compatibility with Western values appeared to al-Maqdisi a fast-metastasising cancer. For a century and a half, ever since the first Muslim rulers had been persuaded to abolish slavery, Islam had been on an ever more Protestant course. That the spirit trumped the letter of the law had come to be widely accepted by Muslims across the globe. It was what had enabled reformers to argue that any number of practices deeply embedded in Islamic jurisprudence, but offensive to the United Nations, might in fact not be Islamic at all. To al-Maqdisi, the spectacle of Muslim governments legislating to uphold equality between men and women, or between Islam and other religions, was a monstrous blasphemy. The whole future of the world was at stake. God's final revelation, the last chance that humanity had of redeeming itself from damnation, was directly threatened. The only recourse was to return to scripture: to rid Islam of all the nettles and brambles that, over the centuries, had come to choke the pure revelation that the first Muslims—the 'Ancestors', or *Salaf*—had known. What it needed was a *reformatio*.

Salafists, then, even as they sought to cleanse Islam of foreign influences, could not help but bear witness to them. 'Modern Islam,' as the scholar Kecia Ali has put it, 'is a profoundly Protestant tradition.'[40] For a millennium, Muslims had taken for granted that the teachings of their *deen* were determined by the scholarly consensus on the meaning of the Qur'an and the Sunna. As a result, over the course of the centuries, it had accrued an immense corpus of commentary and interpretation. Salafists, in their ambition to restore a pristine form of Islam, were resolved to pull this cladding down. Al-Zarqawi, armed with the bombs and the knives that led him to be known by Iraqis as the Sheikh of the Slaughterers, was certainly exceptional for the savagery with which he set to achieving this. Nevertheless, widely reviled though he was across the Muslim world, there were some who admired his example. His incineration by a US jet strike in 2006 did not serve to kill the hydra. Below the surface of an Iraq that, by 2011, appeared largely pacified, it lurked, and coiled, and bided its time.

Opportunity came that same year, as the hold of the dictatorship that had long ruled Syria began to slip, and the country to implode. Al-Zarqawi's acolytes seized their chance. By 2014, they had come to preside over an empire that spanned much of Syria and large swathes of northern Iraq. With a bloody punctiliousness, they sought to transform it into a state from which every trace of foreign influence, every hint of alien legislation, had been scoured: an Islamic State. All that counted was the example of the *Salaf*. When al-Zarqawi's disciples smashed the statues of pagan gods, they were following the example of Muhammad; when they proclaimed themselves the shock troops of a would-be global empire, they were following the example of the warriors who had humbled Heraclius; when they beheaded enemy combatants, and reintroduced the *jizya*, and took the women of defeated opponents as slaves, they were doing nothing that the first Muslims had not gloried in. The only road to an uncontaminated future was the road that led back to an unspoilt past. Nothing of the Evangelicals, who had erupted into the Muslim world with their gunboats and their talk of crimes against humanity, was to remain. Only scripture was to count. Yet the very literalness with which the Islamic State sought to resuscitate the vanished glories of the Arab empire was precisely what rendered it so inauthentic. Of the beauties, of the subtleties, of the sophistication that had always been the hallmarks of Islamic civilisation there was not a trace. The god they worshipped was not the god of Muslim philosophers and poets, all-merciful and all-compassionate, but a butcher. The licence they drew upon for their savagery derived not from the incomparable inheritance of Islamic scholarship, but from a bastardised tradition of fundamentalism that was, in its essentials, Protestant. Islamic the Islamic State may have been; but it also stood in a line of descent from Anabaptist Münster. It was, perhaps, the most gruesome irony in the whole history of Protestantism.

Like Nietzsche, the Islamic State saw in the pieties of Western civilisation—its concern for the suffering, its prating about human rights—a source of terrible and sickly power. Like Sade, they understood that the surest blow they could strike against it was a display of exultant and unapologetic cruelty. The cross had to be redeemed from Christianity. In the Qur'an it served as it had served under the Caesars: as an emblem of righteously sanctioned punishment. 'The penalty for those who wage war against God and His messenger, and who strive in fomenting corruption on the earth, is that they be killed or crucified...'[41] Wherever the Islamic State brought their justice, up would go rough-hewn crosses. Criminals and pagans would be lashed to them. Birds would gather on the cross-beams. Corpses would rot in the sun. Some prisoners, though, endured an even more public punishment. On 19 August 2014, a video appeared on the internet. It showed an American journalist, James Foley, kneeling in front of a masked man dressed all in black, wielding a knife. The man, speaking with an English accent, arraigned America for its crimes, and then—off-camera—hacked off Foley's head. More killings, similarly uploaded to the internet, followed over the succeeding weeks. The executioner—revealed the following year to have been a Londoner named Muhammed Emwazi—was known to the unfortunates in his custody as 'John'. His three fellow guards—all of them, like Emwazi, masked and speaking with English accents—were nicknamed 'Paul', 'George' and 'Ringo'. Collectively, they were, of course, 'the Beatles'.

Within days of Foley's murder, the as yet anonymous Emwazi was featuring in headlines around the world as 'Jihadi John'. It was a telling soubriquet. In reports of Foley's death, little was made of the Catholicism in which he had been raised, and of how, during a previous spell as a hostage, his prayers had enabled him to feel that he was communicating with his mother 'through some cosmic reach of the universe'.[42] *Mother Mary comes to me.* To the outside world, the blasphemy of Foley's fate was not against the Lord whom, Christians believed, had been humiliatingly and publicly put to death, but rather against something more vague: a conviction that love was all anybody needed, and that peace should be given a chance. 'It's bullshit. What they are doing out there is against everything the Beatles stood for.'[43] So protested an indignant Ringo Starr. His namesake agreed. Interviewed after his capture, 'Ringo' was asked for his response to being nicknamed after a Beatle. 'I don't listen to music,' he replied in a dull monotone, 'so I'd rather not speak about a rock band.' But then, after a long silence, he abruptly arched his eyebrows, and darted a quick, sparrow-like glance at the microphone. 'John Lennon won't like it much.'[44]

But that, of course, had been precisely the point.

21

WOKE

2015: Rostock

Politics is sometimes hard.' Angela Merkel, speaking to an audience of teenagers in the gymnasium of their school, knew what she was talking about. Brought up under communist rule, she had risen to become chancellor of a united Germany, Europe's largest and most important economy. Ten years in office had taught her that decisions rarely came without cost. Now, live on television, she found herself face to face with what one of her policies might mean for a fourteen-year-old girl. Reem Sahwil, a Palestinian born in a refugee camp, had travelled to Germany to be treated for cerebral palsy. Fluent in German and top of her class, she had proven a model immigrant. Why, then, did she and her family face deportation? Merkel, visibly uncomfortable, sought to explain. 'You know that in the Palestinian refugee camps in Lebanon there are thousands and thousands, and if we were to say you can all come, and you from Africa, you can all come here—we just couldn't manage.' Turning to the moderator, she sought to elaborate—but then, mid-sentence, paused. Sahwil had begun to cry. Merkel, going over to her, touched her awkwardly, then stroked her hair. 'I know it's difficult for you.' Sahwil, blinking back tears, tried to smile. Merkel, her hand resting on the girl's shoulder, consoled her as best she could. 'You have explained very well a situation that many others find themselves in.'[1]

The key to staying at the top in politics, the Chancellor understood, was to take the path of least resistance. Hostility to migrants was a timeless emotion. Rulers had been putting up walls since the beginnings of civilisation. Violence against people who looked and sounded different had been a constant throughout history. A couple of decades previously, Rostock itself had been convulsed by two days of rioting against refugees. Back then, in 1992, the sight of people from distant continents on the city's streets had been unusual. Europeans belonged to a civilisation that had long been exceptional for its degree of cultural homogeneity. For centuries, pretty much everyone—with the exception of the occasional community of Jews—had been Christian. Otto the Great's victory over the Hungarians had marked a decisive turning point in the ability of outsiders to penetrate the heartlands of Christendom. Nowhere else in Eurasia had stood so secure against the mounted archers who tended otherwise to dominate the medieval battlefield. Only with the expansion of Ottoman power, which twice brought Muslim armies to the very gates of Vienna, had Christian Europe faced a serious threat from adversaries who did not subscribe to its own faith. Even that had ended in retreat. Increasingly, as their fleets swept distant oceans, their flags fluttered over distant colonies, and their emigrants settled across the world, Europeans had been able to take for granted the impregnability of their own continent. Mass migration was something that they brought to the lands of non-Europeans—not the other way round.

Since the end of the Second World War, however, that had changed. Attracted by higher living standards, large numbers of immigrants from non-European countries had come to settle in Western Europe. For decades, the pace and scale of immigration into Germany had been carefully regulated; but now it seemed that control was at risk of breaking down. Merkel, explaining the facts to a sobbing teenager, knew full well the crisis that, even as she spoke, was building beyond Germany's frontiers. All that summer, thousands upon thousands of migrants and refugees from Muslim countries had been moving through the Balkans. The spectacle stirred deeply atavistic fears. In Hungary, there was talk of a new Ottoman invasion. Even in Western Europe, in lands that had never been conquered by Muslim armies, there were many who felt a sense of unease. Dread that all the East might be on the move reached back a long way. 'The plain was dark with their marching companies, and as far as eyes could strain in the mirk there sprouted, like a foul fungus growth, all about the beleaguered city great camps of tents, black or sombre red.'[2] So Tolkien, writing in 1946, had described the siege of Minas Tirith, bulwark of the free lands of the West, by the armies of Sauron. The climax of *The Lord of the Rings* palpably echoed the momentous events of 955: the attack on Augsburg and the battle of the Lech. A wise and battle-seasoned scholar, consecrated in his mission by a supernatural power, standing in the gateway of a breached city and blocking the enemy's advance. An army of mail-clad horsemen arriving to contend the battlefield just as the invaders seemed to have victory in their grasp. A king armed with a sacred weapon, laying claim to an empty imperial throne. In 2003, a film of *The Lord of the Rings* had brought Aragorn's victory over the snarling hordes of Mordor to millions who had never heard of the battle of the Lech. Burnished and repackaged for the twenty-first century, Otto's defence of Christendom still possessed a spectral glamour.

Its legacy, though, that summer of 2014, was shaded by multiple ironies. Otto's mantle was taken up not by the chancellor of Germany, but by the prime minister of Hungary. Victor Orbán had until recently been a self-avowed atheist; but this did not prevent him from doubting—much as Otto might have done—whether unbaptised migrants could ever truly be integrated. 'This is an important question, because Europe and European culture have Christian roots.' That September, ordering police to remove refugees from trains and put up fences along Hungary's southern border, he warned that Europe's soul was at stake. Merkel, as she tracked the migrant crisis, had come to an identical conclusion. Her response, however, was the opposite of Orbán's. Although pressed by ministers in her own ruling coalition to close Germany's borders, she refused. Huge crowds of Syrians, Afghans and Iraqis began crossing into Bavaria. Soon, upwards of ten thousand a day were pouring in. Crowds gathered at railway stations to cheer them; football fans raised banners at matches to proclaim them welcome. The scenes, the chancellor declared, 'painted a picture of Germany which can make us proud of our country'.[3]

Merkel, no less than Orbán, stood in the shadow of her people's history. She knew where a dread of being swamped by aliens might lead. Earlier generations had been more innocent. Tolkien, when he drew on episodes from early medieval history for the plot of *The Lord of the Rings*, had never meant to equate the Hungarians or the Saracens with the monstrous evil embodied by Mordor. The age of migrations was sufficiently remote, he had assumed, that there was little prospect of his readers believing that. He had never had any intention of demonising entire peoples—ancient or modern. 'I'm very anti that kind of thing.'[4] Sauron's armies, although they might come from the east, symbolised the capacity for murderousness that Tolkien had seen for himself on the Western Front. Hell's shadow knew no national boundaries. Its reach was universal. Already, though—even as Tolkien was writing his account of the siege of Minas Tirith—the long reign of the Devil as its embodiment was drawing to a close. Evil had come to wear a new face. In 1946 the trial had opened in Nuremberg of the most prominent surviving members of the Nazi leadership. A year on from the liberation of Auschwitz, reports of the proceedings had made clear to the world the full scale of Nazism's crimes. Like dry rot spreading back through time, the horror of it had served to contaminate the entire fabric of German history. Himmler, a man whose loathing for Christianity had not prevented him from admiring the martial feats of Christian emperors, had hallowed Otto's father as the supreme model of Germanic heroism. It was darkly rumoured that he claimed to be the Saxon king's reincarnation. Hitler, although privately contemptuous of Himmler's more mystical leanings, had himself been obsessed by the Holy Lance. A relic of the crucifixion had been transmogrified into an emblem of Nazism. Seventy years on from Hitler's suicide, in a country still committed to doing penance for his crimes, there had never been any prospect of Angela Merkel riding to fight a new battle of the Lech. The truly, the only Christian thing to do, faced by the floodtide of misery lapping at Europe's borders, was to abandon any lingering sense of the continent as Christendom and open it up to the wretched of the earth.

Always, from the very beginnings of the Church, there had been tension between Christ's commandment to his followers that they should go into the world and preach the good news to all creation, and his parable of the Good Samaritan. Merkel was familiar with both. Her father had been a pastor, her mother no less devout. Her childhood home had been a hostel for people with disabilities—people much like Reem Sahwil. 'The daily message was: Love your neighbour as yourself. Not just German people. God loves everybody.'[5] For two millennia, Christians had been doing their best to put these teachings into practice. Merkel, by providing refuge to the victims of war in the Middle East, was doing nothing that Gregory of Nyssa, sixteen centuries previously, had not similarly done. Offer charity, he had urged his congregants, for the spectacle of refugees living like animals was a reproach to every Christian. 'Their roof is the sky. For shelter they use porticos, alleys, and the deserted corners of the town. They hide in the cracks of walls like owls.'[6] Yet Merkel, when she sought to justify the opening of her country's borders—a volte-face all the more dramatic for seeming so out of character—pointedly refused to frame it as a gesture of Christian charity. Six weeks after telling a sobbing girl that Germany could never play Good Samaritan to the entire world, her new take was to insist that she was merely doing what anyone in her position would do. Her own faith was irrelevant. A morality existed that trumped all differences of culture—and differences of religion too. It was with this argument that Merkel sought to parry the objection of Orbán that a Muslim influx into Europe risked irrevocably transforming the Christian character of the continent. Islam, in its essentials, was little different from Christianity. Both might equally be framed within the bounds of a liberal, secular state. Islam, the chancellor insisted—slapping down any members of her own party who dared suggest otherwise—belonged in Germany.

Yet this position was not quite the polar opposite of Orbán's that it appeared to be. Implicit within the anxieties of the Hungarian prime minister about 'a new mixed, Islamised Europe'[7] was the assumption that Muslims, if they were only willing to accept baptism, might then take their place within the continent's Christian order. This, after all, was the lesson taught by his own people's history. A couple of generations on from the Lech, and the king of Hungary had been sent a replica of the Holy Lance by the pope. Residency visas had rarely come so sanctified. Not for Merkel, though, anything that smacked of Holy Lances. As the leader of a country that within living memory had wiped out six million Jews, she was understandably anxious not to appear prescriptive about what might constitute European identity. Nevertheless, there was no bucking history. Germany remained, in its assumptions about how a society should best be structured, profoundly and distinctively Christian. As in the nineteenth century, when Jews had won citizenship of Prussia, Muslims who wished to integrate into German society had no choice but to become practitioners of that decidedly Christian concept: a 'religion'. *Islam*—which traditionally had signified to those who practised it merely the activity of submission—had to be moulded, and twisted, and transmuted into something very different. This was not, of course, a process that had begun in 2015. For a century and a half, ever since the heyday of European colonialism, it had been picking up speed. Its progress could be measured by the number of Muslims across the world brought to accept that laws authored by humans might trump those authored by God; that Muhammad's mission had been religious rather than political; that the relationship of worshippers to their faith was, in its essentials, something private and personal. Merkel, when she insisted that Islam belonged in Germany just as much as Christianity, was only appearing to be even-handed. To hail a religion for its compatibility with a secular society was decidedly not a neutral gesture. Secularism was no less bred of the sweep of Christian history than were Orbán's barbed-wire fences.

Naturally, for it to function as its exponents wished it to function, this could never be admitted. The West, over the duration of its global hegemony, had become skilled in the art of repackaging Christian concepts for non-Christian audiences. A doctrine such as that of human rights was far likelier to be signed up to if its origins among the canon lawyers of medieval Europe could be kept concealed. The insistence of United Nations agencies on 'the antiquity and broad acceptance of the conception of the rights of man'[8] was a necessary precondition for their claim to a global, rather than a merely Western, jurisdiction. Secularism, in an identical manner, depended on the care with which it covered its tracks. If it were to be embraced by Jews, or Muslims, or Hindus as a neutral holder of the ring between them and people of other faiths, then it could not afford to be seen as what it was: a concept that had little meaning outside of a Christian context. In Europe, the secular had for so long been secularised that it was easy to forget its ultimate origins. To sign up to its premises was unavoidably to become just that bit more Christian. Merkel, welcoming Muslims to Germany, was inviting them to take their place in a continent that was not remotely neutral in its understanding of religion: a continent in which the division of church and state was absolutely assumed to apply to Islam.

To secularists battle-hardened in their long fight against the myths of Christianity—what *Charlie Hebdo*, a French satirical magazine, summed up as 'the myth of a God as architect of the universe, the myth of Mary's virginity, the myth of Christ's resurrection'[9]—it was easy to forget that secularism too was founded on a myth. In France—more, perhaps, than anywhere else in Europe—the story told of its origins stood at variance with its history. *Laïcité*, among its more fiery partisans, was valued less as a separation of church from state than as a quarantining of religion from those who might otherwise be infected by its nonsense. *Charlie Hebdo* defined itself proudly as '*laïc*, joyful and atheist'.[10] With its scabrous satirising of popes and priests, it laid claim to what, for two hundred years and more, had been a peculiarly French brand of anti-clericalism. Its roots, though, reached back much further than the Revolution. The cartoonists of *Charlie Hebdo*, when they mocked Christ, or the Virgin, or the saints, tended to an obscenity that owed little to Voltaire. Their true line of inheritance could be traced back instead to a far more rambunctious generation of iconoclasts. Back in the first flush of the Reformation, revellers had exulted in their desecration of idols: ducking a statue of the Virgin in a river as a witch, pinning asses' ears to an image of St Francis, parading a crucifix through brothels, and bath-houses, and taverns. To trample on superstition was to lay claim to the light. To be enlightened was, in turn, to lay claim to a status as the people of God—the *laicus*. The journalists of *Charlie Hebdo*, then, were doubly *laïc*. The tradition in which they stood—of satire, of blasphemy, of desecration—was not a repudiation of Christian history, but its very essence. For five hundred years, Catholics had repeatedly been obliged to test their faith against it. Now it was the turn of Muslims. In 2011, a cartoon of Muhammad appeared on the cover of *Charlie Hebdo*. The following year he was depicted crouching on all fours, his genitals bared. The mockery would not cease, so *Charlie Hebdo*'s editor vowed, until 'Islam has been rendered as banal as Catholicism'.[11] This it was, in a secular society, for Muslims to be treated as equals.

Except that they were not being treated as equals. Only those who believed in the foundation myths of secularism—that it had emerged as though from a virgin birth, that it owed nothing to Christianity, that it was neutral between all religions—could possibly have believed that they were. In January 2015, after two gunmen had forced their way into the *Charlie Hebdo* offices and shot dead twelve of the staff, Muslim sensitivities were repeatedly weighed in the balance by a bewildered and frightened public, and found wanting. Why the murderous over-reaction to a few cartoons? Why, when Catholics had again and again demonstrated themselves capable of swallowing blasphemies directed against their faith, could Muslims not do the same? Was it not time for Islam to grow up and enter the modern world, just as Christianity had done? Yet to ask these questions was, of course, to buy into the core conceit of secularism: that all religions were essentially the same. It was to assume that they were bound, much like butterflies, to replicate an identical life cycle: reformation, enlightenment, decline. Above all, it was to ignore the degree to which the tradition of secularism upheld by *Charlie Hebdo*, far from an emancipation from Christianity, was indelibly a product of it. Three days after the shootings, as world leaders marched alongside millions of demonstrators through the heart of Paris, placards declared solidarity with the murdered journalists: *'Je suis Charlie'*. As a spectacle, it was a powerful demonstration of what had become the West's guiding orthodoxy: one that had been millennia in the evolving. Back in the age of Otto, there had been no settling in Christendom for pagan chieftains without baptism. Now, in the age of *Charlie Hebdo*, Europe had new expectations, new identities, new ideals. None, though, was neutral; none was anything other than the fruit of Christian history. To imagine otherwise, to imagine that the values of secularism might indeed be timeless, was—ironically enough—the surest evidence of just how deeply Christian they were.

Blessed Be the Fruit

To visit the Peninsula Beverly Hills was to visit a hotel where guests were treated like gods. Set discreetly behind vine-covered walls, within striking distance of the luxury shopping on Rodeo Drive, and replete with spas, swimming pools and award-winning restaurants, it played host to a clientele as exclusive as any in the world. There were singers recording albums; film stars recovering from plastic surgery; titans of the movie industry cutting deals. Harvey Weinstein, for decades one of the most successful independent producers in the world, never stayed anywhere else when visiting Los Angeles. Checking in to the hotel, he would hold court in a particularly opulent suite on the fourth floor. Actresses invited upstairs to discuss forthcoming projects might find themselves surrounded by ice buckets of champagne and plates piled high with lobster. No effort was spared by the hotel to accommodate Weinstein's tastes. Great care was taken to provide him with the correct size of bathrobe. The bathroom was furnished with his preferred brand of toilet paper. His assistants were given personalised stationery. Nothing was too much trouble for a man of Harvey Weinstein's importance.

Everything at the Peninsula had to be perfect. Naturally, this required an army of staff. Receptionists, pedicurists, waiters. Early every morning, changing into their uniforms, packing their cleaning carts, housekeepers would ready themselves for a long day of making beds and scrubbing toilets. The average hourly wage paid a chambermaid in the United States was $9.51. A suite in the Peninsula might easily cost over two thousand dollars a night. Between a movie tycoon in his personalised bathrobe and the woman tidying up his wet towels there was an almost vertiginous imbalance of power. Perhaps it was only to be expected, then, that the occasional guest, accustomed to having his every whim catered to, should have been tempted to view the staff themselves as commodities. 'They treat workers like their property,'[12] complained one housekeeper in 2016, after she had twice been offered money in exchange for a massage. Another that same year was cornered by a guest and violently molested. Another was assaulted by a fellow worker. Even incidents such as these—the ones that were reported—were only the tip of the iceberg. Across the country, so a 2016 survey reported, one in four women was liable to experience sexual harassment in her workplace. In hotels, the figures were considerably higher. For any woman, but especially for a woman in a precarious, low-wage job, often not speaking English, and perhaps without the proper papers, there was risk in jobs that might require her to be alone with an unknown man. To work as a housekeeper, a government commission concluded, was to be 'particularly vulnerable to sexual harassment and assault'.[13]

So it had always been. Back in the Middle Ages, Bernard of Clairvaux—a contemporary of Abelard's, and an abbot of such formidable sanctity that he had ended up both a saint and a Doctor of the Church—had lamented the sheer tempestuousness of male sexual need. 'To be always with a woman and not to have sexual relations with her is more difficult than to raise the dead.'[14] The entire point of the chastity to which monks like Bernard had pledged themselves was that it was not easy. It obliged them to fit their desires with bit and rein, and serve as models of self-control. Not every man, of course, had the fortitude to live as a monk; but even those who could not live without sex had been expected to marry, and commit themselves to a life-long fidelity. The Reformation—for all the scorn with which its partisans had dismissed the ideal of chastity as monkish superstition—had served, if anything, to place an even greater premium on the sacral quality of marriage. As the Church was to Christ, so a woman was to her husband. The man who treated his wife brutally, forcing himself on her, paying no attention to her pleasure, treating her as he might a prostitute, dishonoured God. Mutual respect was all. Sex between a married couple should be 'an holy kind of rejoicing and solacing themselves'.[15]

Beverly Hills, though, rarely played host to puritans. Hollywood was Babylon. It did not make its money by selling prudery. It made it by selling cool. Back in 1994, Weinstein had enjoyed his breakout hit as a producer with *Pulp Fiction*, a movie set in the criminal underworld of Los Angeles. Electrifyingly amoral, it had alchemised sex and violence into box-office millions. Such echoes as there were in its script of the values upheld by Saint Bernard or the Pilgrim Fathers existed—like the cocaine periodically snorted in the film by Mia Wallace, wife of a local crime boss—to liven things up. Getting medieval in *Pulp Fiction* was something that gangsters did on people's asses; the Old Testament was there to be misquoted as heavies filled their victims full of lead. Even when one hitman, convinced that God has personally intervened to spare him death, has a spiritual awakening, everyone else in the movie regards him with blank incomprehension. 'You read the Bible, Ringo?' the hitman asks an English robber, his gun pointed at the his head.* The reply might just as easily have been given by the vast majority of those who occupied the commanding heights of America's entertainment industry: 'Not regularly, no.'

Drugs, violence, money: *Pulp Fiction* fashioned adrenalin-fuelled entertainment out of the human appetite for all of them. The only limit on pleasure was the threat of violence. No other impetus to self-restraint existed. That, for the movie's audience, was precisely the thrill. The sheen of coolness that clung to *Pulp Fiction* was the sheen, in large part, of the taboo. America was a country shaped by a tradition that, for two thousand years, had sought to regulate desire. Sexual appetite, in particular, had always been regarded by Christians with mingled suspicion and anxiety. This was why, beginning with Paul, such a supreme effort had been made to keep its currents flowing along a single course. Increasingly, however, the dams and dykes erected to channel it had begun to spring leaks. Whole sections had eroded. Others appeared to have vanished altogether beneath the floodwaters. Self-restraint had come to be cast as repression; summons to sexual continence as hypocrisy. It did not help that Church leaders themselves, brought under the spotlight of an ever less deferential media, had repeatedly been exposed as committing the very sins that they warned their flocks against. For decades, the moral authority of the Catholic Church in America had been corroded by accusations of child abuse brought against thousands of its priests, and of cover-ups by its hierarchy. Meanwhile, among Protestants, it seemed that a televangelist had only to fulminate against

---

* The use of a Beatle's name as shorthand for an Englishman extends from Syria to California.

sexual impropriety to be caught having an affair or arrested in a public convenience. Yet there was, of course, in the failure of priests and pastors to live up to their own teaching, nothing new. 'We are all naturally prone to hypocrisy.'[16] So Calvin had acknowledged. The flesh was weak. The change—and it was one that had occurred with a startling rapidity—was the readiness of people to accept that the exacting ideals of Christian sexual morality might not be ideals at all.

That erotic desires were natural, and therefore good, and that the coming of Christianity had been like a blast of grey breath on the world, had long been a conviction popular with the more aristocratic class of freethinker. 'Our religions, our manners and customs may easily and indeed must perforce deceive us,' as the Marquis de Sade had put it, 'whilst we shall certainly never be misled by the voice of Nature.'[17] This, over the course of the 1960s, had become a manifesto shared by millions. The Summer of Love had been a celebration of body as well as of spirit. 'Make love, not war,' the hippies urged. To many, it had seemed that two thousand years of neurosis and self-hatred were being banished upon the weaving of flowers in the hair. Desires natural to men and women, long kept in check, had at last been restored to freedom. Once again, the moving of the phallus in the bright womb of the world was praised as something precious: as 'the victory of yes and love'.[18] One music journalist, writing in San Francisco as 1967 turned to fall, had cast America as a stagnant swamp suddenly brought to life by the shimmering through its waters of a god. Ralph Gleason, the founder of *Rolling Stone*, most successful of all the many magazines inspired by the counterculture of the 1960s, had identified its spirit of sexual freedom with that of classical Greece. Society, he had declared, was being 'deeply stirred by Dionysiac currents'.[19] The ancient gods were back.

Except that the freedom to fuck when and as one liked had tended to be, in antiquity, the perk of a very exclusive subsection of society: powerful men. Zeus, Apollo, Dionysus: all had been habitual rapists. So too, in the Rome to which Paul had travelled with his unsettling message of sexual continence, had been many a head of household. Only the titanic efforts of Christian moralists, the labour of a millennium and more, had managed to recalibrate this. Their insistence on marriage as the only legitimate way to obtain erotic fulfilment had prevailed. 'Do you not know,' Paul had demanded of the Corinthians, 'that your body is a temple of the Holy Spirit, who is in you, whom you have received from God?'[20] This was the message, two thousand years later, that continued to be thundered forth from pulpits across America: the warning that sexual desire, implicated as it was in the cosmic battle between good and evil, was far too predatory, far too rapacious, ever to be left to its own devices. But it was also a message that, in the offices of men who had their fingers on the pulse of popular entertainment, who knew what sold a movie, tended to be regarded with, if not contempt, then incomprehension. Sexual repression was boring—and to be boring was box-office death.

How much leeway did this give a movie mogul to behave like an Olympian god? On 5 October 2017, allegations about what Harvey Weinstein had been getting up to in his fourth-floor suite at the Peninsula broke in the *New York Times*. An actress meeting him there for what she had thought was a business breakfast had found the producer wearing nothing but his bespoke bathrobe. Perhaps, he had suggested, she could give him a massage? Or how about watching him shower? Two assistants who had met with Weinstein in his suite reported similar encounters. Over the weeks and months that followed, further allegations were levelled against him: harassment, assault, rape. Among the more than eighty women going public with accusations was Uma Thurman, the actor who had played Mia Wallace in *Pulp Fiction* and become the movie's pin-up. Meanwhile, where celebrity forged a path, many other women followed. A campaign that urged women to report incidents of harassment or assault under the hashtag #MeToo actively sought to give a voice to the most marginalised and vulnerable of all: janitors, fruit-pickers, hotel housekeepers. Already that year, the summons to a great moral awakening, a call for men everywhere to reflect on their sins, and repent them, had been much in the air. On 21 January, a million women had marched through Washington, DC. Other, similar demonstrations had been held around the world. The previous day, a new president, Donald J. Trump, had been inaugurated in the American capital. He was, to the organisers of the women's marches, the very embodiment of toxic masculinity: a swaggering tycoon who had repeatedly been accused of sexual assault, who had bragged of grabbing 'pussy', and who, during the recently concluded presidential campaign, had paid hush money to a porn star. Rather than make the marches about Trump, however, the organisers had sought a loftier message: to sound a clarion call against injustice, and discrimination, and oppression wherever it might be found. 'Yes, it's about feminism. But it's about more than that. It's about basic equality for all people.'[21]

The echo, of course, was of Martin Luther King. Repeatedly, in the protests against misogyny that swept America during the first year of Trump's presidency, the name and example of the great Baptist preacher were invoked. Yet Christianity, which for King had been the fount of everything he ever campaigned for, appeared to many who marched in 2017 part of the problem. Evangelicals had voted in large numbers for Trump. Roiled by issues that seemed to them not just unbiblical, but directly antithetical to God's purposes—abortion, gay marriage, transgender rights—they had held their noses and backed a man who, pussy-grabbing and porn stars notwithstanding, had unblushingly cast himself as the standard-bearer for Christian values. Unsurprisingly, then, hypocrisy had been added to bigotry on the charge sheet levelled against them by progressives. America, it seemed to many feminists, risked becoming a misogynist theocracy. Three months after the Women's March, a television series made gripping drama out of this dread. *The Handmaid's Tale* was set in a country returned to a particularly nightmarish vision of seventeenth century New England. Adapted from a dystopian novel by the Canadian writer Margaret Atwood, it provided female protestors against Trump with a striking new visual language of protest. White bonnets and red cloaks were the uniform worn by 'handmaids': women whose ability to reproduce had rendered them, in a world crippled by widespread infertility, the objects of legalised rape. Licence for the practice was provided by an episode in the Bible. The parody of evangelicals was as dark as it was savage. *The Handmaid's Tale*—as all great dystopian fiction tends to be—was less prophecy than satire. The TV series cast Trump's America as a society rent in two: between conservatives and liberals; between reactionaries and progressives; between dark-souled televangelists and noble-hearted foes of patriarchy.

Yet the divisions satirised by *The Handmaid's Tale* were in truth very ancient. They derived ultimately, not from the specifics of American politics in the twenty-first century, but from the very womb of Christianity. Blessed be the fruit. There had always existed, in the hearts of the Christian people, a tension between the demands of tradition and the claims of progress, between the prerogatives of authority and the longing for reformation, between the letter and the spirit of the law. The twenty-first century marked, in that sense, no radical break with what had gone before. That the great battles in America's culture war were being fought between Christians and those who had emancipated themselves from Christianity was a conceit that both sides had an interest in promoting. It was no less of a myth for that. In reality, Evangelicals and progressives were both recognisably bred of the same matrix. If opponents of abortion were the heirs of Macrina, who had toured the rubbish tips of Cappadocia looking for abandoned infants to rescue, then those who argued against them were likewise drawing on a deeply rooted Christian supposition: that every woman's body was her own, and to be respected as such by every man. Supporters of gay marriage were quite as influenced by the Church's enthusiasm for monogamous fidelity as those against it were by biblical condemnations of men who slept with men. To install transgender toilets might indeed seem an affront to the Lord God, who had created male and female; but to refuse kindness to the persecuted was to offend against the most fundamental teachings of Christ. In a country as saturated in Christian assumptions as the United States, there could be no escaping their influence—even for those who imagined that they had. America's culture wars were less a war against Christianity than a civil war between Christian factions.

In 1963, when Martin Luther King addressed hundreds of thousands of civil rights protestors assembled in Washington, he had aimed his speech at the country beyond the capital as well—at an America that was still an unapologetically Christian nation. By 2017, things were different. Among the four co-chairs of the Women's March was a Muslim. Marching through Washington were Sikhs, Buddhists, Jews. Huge numbers had no faith at all. Even the Christians among the organisers flinched from attempting to echo the prophetic voice of a Martin Luther King. Nevertheless, their manifesto was no less based in theological presumptions than that of the civil rights movement had been. Implicit in #MeToo was the same call to sexual continence that had reverberated throughout the Church's history. Protestors who marched in the red cloaks of handmaids were summoning men to exercise control over their lusts just as the Puritans had done. Appetites that had been hailed by enthusiasts for sexual liberation as Dionysiac stood condemned once again as predatory and violent. The human body was not an object, not a commodity to be used by the rich and powerful as and when they pleased. Two thousand years of Christian sexual morality had resulted in men as well as women widely taking this for granted. Had it not, then #MeToo would have had no force.

The tracks of Christian theology, Nietzsche had complained, wound everywhere. In the early twenty-first century, they led—as they had done in earlier ages—in various and criss-crossing directions. They led towards TV stations on which televangelists preached the headship of men over women; and they led as well towards gender

studies departments, in which Christianity was condemned for het-
eronormative marginalisation of LGBTQIA+. Nietzsche had foretold
it all. God might be dead, but his shadow, immense and dreadful,
continued to flicker even as his corpse lay cold. Feminist academics
were no less in thrall to it, no less its acolytes, than were the most fire-
breathing preachers. God could not be eluded simply by refusing to
believe in his existence. Any condemnation of Christianity as patriar-
chal and repressive derived from a framework of values that was itself
utterly Christian. 'The measure of a man's compassion for the lowly
and the suffering comes to be the *measure* of the *loftiness of his soul*.'[22]
It was this, the epochal lesson taught by Jesus' death on the cross, that
Nietzsche had always most despised about Christianity. Two thousand years on, and the discovery made by Christ's earliest followers—
that to be a victim might be a source of power—could bring out
millions onto the streets. Wealth and rank, in Trump's America, were
not the only indices of status. So too were their opposites. Against the
priapic thrust of towers fitted with gold-plated lifts, the organisers of
the Women's March sought to invoke the authority of those who lay
at the bottom of the pile. The last were to be first, and the first were
to be last. Yet how to measure who ranked as the last and the first? As
they had ever done, all the multiple intersections of power, all the various dimensions of stratification in society, served to marginalise some
more than others. Woman marching to demand equality with men
always had to remember—if they were wealthy, if they were educated,
if they were white—that there were many among them whose oppression was greater by far than their own: 'Black women, indigenous
women, poor women, immigrant women, disabled women, Muslim
women, lesbian, queer and trans women.'[23] The disadvantaged too
might boast their own hierarchy.

That it was the fate of rulers to be brought down from their
thrones, and the humble to be lifted up, was a reflection that had
always prompted anxious Christians to check their privilege. It had
inspired Paulinus to give away his wealth, and Francis to strip himself naked before the Bishop of Assisi, and Elizabeth of Hungary to

toil in a hospital as a scullery maid. Similarly, a dread of damnation, a yearning to be gathered into the ranks of the elect, a desperation to be cleansed of original sin, had provided, from the very moment the Pilgrim Fathers set sail, the surest and most fertile seedbed for the ideals of the American people. Repeatedly, over the course of their history, preachers had sought to awaken them to a sense of their guilt, and to offer them salvation. Now, in the twenty-first century, there were summons to a similar awakening. When, in October 2017, the leaders of the Women's March organised a convention in Detroit, one panel in particular found itself having to turn away delegates. 'Confronting White Womanhood' offered white feminists the chance to acknowledge their own entitlement, to confess their sins and to be granted absolution. The opportunity was for the rich and the educated to have their eyes opened; to stare the reality of injustice in the face; truly to be awakened. Only through repentance was salvation to be obtained. The conveners, though, were not merely addressing the delegates in the conference hall. Their gaze, as the gaze of preachers in America had always been, was fixed on the world beyond. Their summons was to sinners everywhere. Their ambition was to serve as a city on a hill.

Christianity, it seemed, had no need of actual Christians for its assumptions still to flourish. Whether this was an illusion, or whether the power held by victims over their victimisers would survive the myth that had given it birth, only time would tell. As it was, the retreat of Christian belief did not seem to imply any necessary retreat of Christian values. Quite the contrary. Even in Europe— a continent with churches far emptier than those in the United States—the trace elements of Christianity continued to infuse people's morals and presumptions so utterly that many failed even to detect their presence. Like dust particles so fine as to be invisible to the naked eye, they were breathed in equally by everyone: believers, atheists, and those who never paused so much as to think about religion.

Had it been otherwise, then no one would ever have got woke.

The Weak Things of the World

Writing this book, I have often found myself thinking about my godmother. Deborah Gillingham died in 2009, but because I loved her very much, and because she was a constant presence during my childhood, my memories of her have never faded. This may seem, in a book that has spanned millennia, a self-indulgent note on which to end; but the story it tells, the story of how Christianity transformed the world, would never have happened without people like my Aunty Deb. A committed and faithful member of the Church of England, she took her duties as my godmother with the utmost seriousness. Having vowed at my baptism to see that I was brought up in the Christian faith and life, she did her best to keep her word. She never allowed me to forget that Easter was about much more than the chocolate eggs that she annually lavished on me. She bought me my first children's Bible, lovingly selected because it featured vibrant illustrations of pharaohs and centurions, and she knew me well enough to understand that this was the best way to ensure that I would read it. Above all, through her unfailing kindness, she provided me with a model of what, to a committed Christian, the daily practise of her faith could actually mean. At the time, of course, I did not think of her in these terms. She was just Aunty Deb. But over the years, as I read more and more about the great sweep of Christian history, about crusades, and inquisitions, and religious wars, about popes with fat, jewelled fingers and Puritans with stern, beetling frowns, and about all the great shocks and convulsions that Christianity had brought to the world, I found myself thinking of her more and more as a part of this same story. Which in turn means that I am a part of it as well.

I have sought, in writing this book, to be as objective as possible. Yet this, when dealing with a theme such as Christianity, is not to be neutral. To claim, as I most certainly do, that I have sought to evaluate fairly both the achievements and the crimes of

Christian civilisation is not to stand outside its moral frameworks, but rather—as Nietzsche would have been quick to point out—to stand within them. The people who, in his famous fable, continue to venerate the shadow of God are not just church-goers. All those in thrall to Christian morality—even those who may be proud to array themselves among God's murderers—are included among their number. Inevitably, to attempt the tracing of Christianity's impact on the world is to cover the rise and fall of empires, the actions of bishops and kings, the arguments of theologians, the course of revolutions, the planting of crosses around the world. It is, in particular, to focus on the doings of men. Yet that hardly tells the whole story. I have written much in this book about churches, and monasteries, and universities; but these were never where the mass of the Christian people were most influentially shaped. It was always in the home that children were likeliest to absorb the revolutionary teachings that, over the course of two thousand years, have come to be so taken for granted as almost to seem human nature. The Christian revolution was wrought above all at the knees of women.

The success, then, of the most influential framework for making sense of human existence that has ever existed always depended on people like my godmother: people who saw in the succession of one generation by another something more than merely the way of all the earth. Although she had no children of her own, she was a teacher, the headmistress of a much-garlanded school, and publicly honoured for it: the conviction that she had a duty to those who would outlive her provided her entire career with its cornerstone. As a Christian, though, she also believed something much more. A *saeculum*, to the Romans, had been the limit of living recollection: a brief, fleeting span of time. A baby, perhaps, can be dandled by its great-grandparent; but ashes must ultimately return to ashes, and dust to dust. Without a dimension of the celestial, all things are transitory. So my godmother knew. But she did not believe that all things are transitory. She had the hope of eternal life. It was a faith that she had received from her mother, who had received it in turn from her parents, who had received it in turn from their parents. Down the generations, down the centuries, down the millennia it had been passed. Only Jews could lay claim to anything comparable: a living tradition that could be traced back along an unbroken line to the long-vanished civilisation of the Roman Empire. And this was the tradition that my godmother passed to me.

But that was not all she passed to me. As a young child, I only had one true obsession—and it was not Bible stories. My godmother, because she was a kind and loving woman, with a teacher's long experience of small boys and their obsessions, was not remotely disappointed that all I really cared about was prehistoric animals. Her house, on the outskirts of a small town in southern England, was conveniently located for exploring the cliffs where, in 1811, the first complete skull of an ichthyosaur had been found. Sitting in the back of the car as my mother drove me there, I would gaze out at the countryside, and dream of the Mesozoic. I was not the first to do so. On the wall of a local fossil shop, hung above the ammonites and crinoids and ichthyosaur teeth, there was a reproduction of the first ever illustration of a prehistoric landscape. Painted in 1830, it showed what the neighbourhood might have looked like in the Jurassic. Palm trees sprouted from otherwise bare lumps of rock. Strange creatures, half-dragon, half-bat, soared over a teeming sea. A long-necked monster, attacked by an ichthyosaur, voided its bowels. It was all very sinister. It was all very thrilling.

God, speaking to Job from the whirlwind, had told him of drawing Leviathan with a hook, and with a cord pressing down his tongue. But I found it hard to square this with what I knew of ichthyosaurs. Slowly, like a dimmer switch being turned down, I found my belief in God fading. The reaches of time seemed too icily immense for the life and death of a single human being two thousand years ago possibly to have had the cosmic significance claimed for it by Christianity. Why should *Homo sapiens* be granted a status denied ammonites? Why, if God existed, had he allowed so many species to evolve, to flourish, and then utterly to disappear? Why, if he were merciful and good, had he permitted an asteroid to smash into the side of the planet, making the flesh on the bones of dinosaurs burst into flame, the Mesozoic seas to boil, and darkness to cover the face of the earth? I did not spend my whole time worrying about these questions; but sometimes, in the dead of night, I would. The hope offered by the Christian story, that there was an order and a purpose to humanity's existence, felt like something that had forever slipped my grasp. 'The more the universe seems comprehensible,' as the physicist Steven Weinberg famously put it, 'the more it also seems pointless.'[24]

When, in the spring of 2009, I was told that my godmother had been taken to hospital, I went to visit her. She was clearly dying. Because of a stroke, she did not speak as fluently as she had once done; but she managed to assure me of her certainty that all would be well, and all would be well, and all manner of thing would be well. When I rose and left her, I paused in the doorway and looked back. She had turned to face the wall. She lay hunched like an injured animal. I did not think I would see her again. Nor did I think, as she hoped, that we would meet in heaven. Only the atoms and the energy that had constituted her living self, and which had originated with the universe itself, would endure. Every wave of every particle that was my beloved godmother would remain, as those of every other organism that had ever existed—humans, dinosaurs, microbes—would remain; and perhaps in this there was a source of comfort. But not really. It seemed to me, driving away from the hospital, just a palliative. A story told by a species that, as I knew from my own personal experience, cannot bear very much reality.

'There is nothing particular about man. He is but a part of this world.'[25] Today, in the West, there are many who would agree with Himmler that, for humanity to claim a special status for itself, to imagine itself as somehow superior to the rest of creation, is an unwarrantable conceit. *Homo sapiens* is just another species. To insist otherwise is to cling to the shattered fragments of religious belief. Yet the implications of this view—which the Nazis, of course, claimed as their sanction for genocide—remain unsettling for many. Just as Nietzsche had foretold, freethinkers who mock the very idea of a god as a dead thing, a sky fairy, an imaginary friend, still piously hold to taboos and morals that derive from Christianity. In 2002, in Amsterdam, the World Humanist Congress affirmed 'the worth, dignity and autonomy of the individual and the right of every human being to the greatest possible freedom compatible with the rights of others'.[26] Yet this—despite humanists' stated ambition to provide 'an alternative to dogmatic religion'[27]—was nothing if not itself a statement of belief. Himmler, at any rate, had understood what licence was opened up by the abandonment of Christianity. The humanist assumption that atheism and liberalism go together was just that: an assumption. Without the biblical story that God had created humanity in his own image to draw upon, the reverence of humanists for their own species risked seeming mawkish and shallow. What basis—other than mere sentimentality—was there to argue for it? Perhaps, as the humanist manifesto declared, through 'the application of the methods of science'.[28] Yet this was barely any less of a myth than Genesis. As in the days of Darwin and Huxley, so in the twenty-first century, the ambition of agnostics to translate values 'into facts that can be scientifically understood'[29] was a fantasy. It derived not from the viability of such a project, but from medieval theology. It was not truth that science offered moralists, but a mirror. Racists identified it with racist values; liberals with liberal values. The primary dogma of humanism—'that morality is an intrinsic part of human nature based on understanding and a concern for others'[30]—found no more corroboration in science than did the dogma of the Nazis that anyone not fit for life should be exterminated. The wellspring of humanist values lay not in reason, not in evidence-based thinking, but in history.

It was always my profoundest regret, as a child, that dinosaurs no longer existed. I only had to look at a cow to wish it were a Triceratops. Yet now, in middle age, I discover that dinosaurs do still exist.

Huxley's thesis, that birds had originated from something akin to small, carnivorous dinosaurs, has been spectacularly substantiated. Today, after a century and more of being scorned by palaeontologists, proof for it has been coming thick and fast. It is now clear that feathers may be at least as old as dinosaurs themselves. Tyrannosaurs had wishbones; laid eggs; had filamentous coats of fuzz. When, in an astonishing breakthrough, collagen was extracted recently from the remains of one tyrannosaur fossil, its amino acid sequences turned out to bear an unmistakable resemblance to those of a chicken. The more the evidence is studied, the hazier the dividing line between birds and dinosaurs has become. The same, *mutatis mutandis*, might be said of the dividing line between agnostics and Christians. On 16 July 2018, one of the world's best-known scientists, a man as celebrated for his polemics against religion as for his writings on evolutionary biology, sat listening to the bells of an English cathedral. 'So much nicer than the aggressive-sounding "Allahu Akhbar",' Richard Dawkins tweeted. 'Or is that just my cultural upbringing?'[31] The question was a perfectly appropriate one for an admirer of Darwin to ponder. It is no surprise, since humans, just like any other biological organism, are products of evolution, that its workings should be evident in their assumptions, beliefs and cultures. A preference for church bells over the sound of Muslims praising God does not just emerge by magic. Dawkins—agnostic, secularist and humanist that he is—absolutely has the instincts of someone brought up in a Christian civilisation.

Today, as the flood tide of Western power and influence ebbs, the illusions of European and American liberals risk being left stranded. Much that they have sought to cast as universal stands exposed as never having been anything of the kind. Agnosticism—as Huxley, the man who coined the word, readily acknowledged—ranks as 'that conviction of the supremacy of private judgment (indeed, of the impossibility of escaping it) which is the foundation of the Protestant Reformation'.[32] Secularism owes its existence to the medieval papacy. Humanism derives ultimately from claims made in the Bible:

that humans are made in God's image; that his Son died equally for everyone; that there is neither Jew nor Greek, slave nor free, male nor female. Repeatedly, like a great earthquake, Christianity has sent reverberations across the world. First there was the primal revolution: the revolution preached by Saint Paul. Then there came the aftershocks: the revolution in the eleventh century that set Latin Christendom upon its momentous course; the revolution commemorated as the Reformation; the revolution that killed God. All bore an identical stamp: the aspiration to enfold within its embrace every other possible way of seeing the world; the claim to a universalism that was culturally highly specific. That human beings have rights; that they are born equal; that they are owed sustenance, and shelter, and refuge from persecution: these were never self-evident truths.

The Nazis, certainly, knew as much—which is why, in today's demonology, they retain their starring role. Communist dictators may have been no less murderous than fascist ones; but they—because communism was the expression of a concern for the oppressed masses—rarely seem as diabolical to people today. The measure of how Christian we as a society remain is that mass murder precipitated by racism tends to be seen as vastly more abhorrent than mass murder precipitated by an ambition to usher in a classless paradise. Liberals may not believe in hell; but they still believe in evil. The fear of it puts them in its shade no less than it ever did Gregory the Great. Just as he lived in dread of Satan, so do we of Hitler's ghost. Behind the readiness to use 'fascist' as an insult there lurks a numbing fear: of what might happen should it cease to be taken as an insult. If secular humanism derives not from reason or from science, but from the distinctive course of Christianity's evolution—a course that, in the opinion of growing numbers in Europe and America, has left God dead—then how are its values anything more than the shadow of a corpse? What are the foundations of its morality, if not a myth?

A myth, though, is not a lie. At its most profound—as Tolkien, that devout Catholic, always argued—a myth can be true. To be a

Christian is to believe that God became man and suffered a death as terrible as any mortal has ever suffered. This is why the cross, that ancient implement of torture, remains what it has always been: the fitting symbol of the Christian revolution. It is the audacity of it— the audacity of finding in a twisted and defeated corpse the glory of the creator of the universe—that serves to explain, more surely than anything else, the sheer strangeness of Christianity, and of the civilisation to which it gave birth. Today, the power of this strangeness remains as alive as it has ever been. It is manifest in the great surge of conversions that has swept Africa and Asia over the past century; in the conviction of millions upon millions that the breath of the Spirit, like a living fire, still blows upon the world; and, in Europe and North America, in the assumptions of many more millions who would never think to describe themselves as Christian. All are heirs to the same revolution: a revolution that has, at its molten heart, the image of a god dead on a cross.

No doubt I should have appreciated this earlier. As it was, only during the early stages of writing this book, when I travelled to Iraq to make a film, did it properly dawn on me. Sinjar was a town that, when I visited it, stood directly on the frontier with the Islamic State. It had been seized from their fighters just a few weeks before. Back in 2014, when they captured and occupied Sinjar, it had been home to large numbers of Yazidis, a religious minority condemned by the Islamic State as devil-worshippers. Their fate had been grim precisely as the fate of those who resisted the Romans had been grim. Men had been crucified; women had been enslaved. To stand amid the ruins of Sinjar, knowing that two miles away, across flat and open ground, were ranged the very people who had committed such atrocities, was to appreciate how, in antiquity, the stench of heat and corpses would have served a conqueror as the marker of his possession. Crucifixion was not merely a punishment. It was a means to achieving dominance: a dominance felt as a dread in the guts of the subdued. Terror of power was the index of power. That was how it had always been, and always would be. It was the way of the world.

For two thousand years, though, Christians have disputed this. Many of them, over the course of this time, have themselves become agents of terror. They have put the weak in their shadow; they have brought suffering, and persecution, and slavery in their wake. Yet the standards by which they stand condemned for this are themselves Christian; nor, even if churches across the West continue to empty, does it seem likely that these standards will quickly change. 'God chose the weak things of the world to shame the strong.'[33] This is the myth that we in the West still persist in clinging to. Christendom, in that sense, remains Christendom still.

ACKNOWLEDGEMENTS

I owe a huge debt of gratitude to many people for their help and encouragement with the writing of this book. To my wonderful editors, Richard Beswick, Lara Heimert and Zoe Gullen. To Susan de Soissons, for all her advice and patience. To Patrick Walsh, best of agents. To all the many people who read sections or the entirety of the book while it was still a draft on a computer screen, or helped with questions: Richard Beard, Nigel Biggar, Piers Brendon, Fergus Butler-Gallie, Paul Cartledge, Thony Christie, Caroline Dodds-Pennock, Charles Fernyhough, Dimitra Fimi, John Fitzpatrick, Peter Frankopan, Judith Gardiner, Michael Goldfarb, James Hannam, Damian Howard, Larry Hurtado, Christopher Insole, Julia Jordan, Frank McDonough, Anthony McGowan, Sean Oliver-Dee, Gabriel Said Reynolds, Alec Ryrie, Michael Snape, Guy Walters, Keith Ward, Tim Whitmarsh and Tom Wright. To Bob Moore, for writing the books which first helped to stimulate my interest in the themes explored in this book, for his immense generosity and for his readiness to read the chapters as they were written. To Jamie Muir, for being—as he has ever been—the first to read the manuscript when it was completed, and the most stalwart of friends. To Kevin Sim, for indulging me, and never wearying of hearing me out. To Charlie Campbell and Nicholas Hogg, for their great feat of resurrection, without which the years I have spent writing this book would not have been half as enjoyable. To Sadie, my beloved wife, and Katy and Eliza, my equally beloved daughters. Their price is far above rubies.

NOTES

PREFACE

1. Horace. *Satires* 1.8.8.
2. Ibid. *Epodes* 5.100.
3. Tacitus. *Annals* 15.60.
4. Seneca. *On Anger* 1.2.2.
5. Tacitus. *Annals* 14.44.
6. Seneca. *On Consolation, to Marcia.*
7. See Cicero. *Against Verres* 2.5.168 and 169.
8. Varro. Fragment 265.
9. Mark. 15.22.
10. Vermes. *Jesus,* p. 181.
11. Josephus. *Jewish War* 7.202.
12. Philippians. 2.9–10.
13. Pindar. *Nemean Odes* 3.22.
14. Varro. Fragment 20.
15. Justin Martyr. *Dialogue with Trypho* 131.
16. Anselm. 'Prayer to Christ' lines 79–84.
17. Eadmer. *Life of Saint Anselm* 23.
18. Fulton. p. 144.
19. Eadmer. *Life of Saint Anselm* 22.
20. Matthew. 20.16.
21. Ibid. 16.19.
22. Boyarin. *A Radical Jew,* p. 9.
23. Psalms. 9.5. Quoted by Rana Mitter in *Forgotten Ally: China's World War II, 1937–1945* (London, 2013), p. 362.
24. http://www.abc.net.au/radionational/programs/religionreport/the-god-delusion-and-alister-e-mcgrath/3213912.
25. Gibbon. *The Decline and Fall of the Roman Empire* 3, ch. 28.
26. Swinburne. 'Hymn to Proserpine'.
27. Acts of Thomas 31.

1 ATHENS
479 BC: *The Hellespont*

1. Herodotus. 9.120.
2. Darius. Bisitun, 32. The following paragraph records the same punishment being inflicted on a second rebel.
3. Plutarch. *Life of Artaxerxes* 16.
4. Darius. Bisitun, 5.
5. Ibid: 8.
6. Hammurabi. Prologue.
7. Ashurbanipal. 1221 r.12.
8. Cyrus Cylinder 20.
9. Darius. Bisitun, 49.
10. Ibid. 72. The people so condemned were from a land named Elam.
11. Ibid. 75.
12. Ibid. 76.
13. Thucydides. 2.41.
14. Xenophon. *Cyropaedia* 8.2.12.
15. Ibid.
16. An alternative explanation of Pseudartabas' name, that it means 'false measure', seems implausible.
17. Homer. *Iliad* 24.617.
18. Hesiod. *Works and Days* 158.
19. Homer. *Odyssey* 20.201.
20. Plato. *Ion* 530b.
21. Homer. *Iliad* 6.610.
22. Ibid. 5.778.
23. Ibid. 4.51–3.
24. Theognis. 381–2.
25. Aristotle. *Eudemian Ethics* 1249b.
26. Demosthenes. *Against Timocrates* 5.
27. Sophocles. *Oedipus the King* 866–9.
28. Sophocles. *Antigone* 456–7.
29. Ibid. 453–5.
30. Ibid. 1348–50.
31. Hesiod. *Theogony* 925.
32. Xenophanes. Quoted by Sextus Empiricus. *Against the Professors* 1.289.
33. Heraclitus. Quoted by Stobaeus, 3.1.179.
34. Aristotle. *Metaphysics* 12 1072a.
35. Ibid. 12 1072b.
36. Aristotle. *History of Animals* 1.2.
37. Aristotle. *Politics* 3.1287a.
38. Diogenes. Laertius 1.33.

39. Aristotle. *Politics* 1.1254a.
40. Ibid. 7.1327a.
41. Thucydides. 5.89.
42. 'Hymn to Demetrius' 15–20.
43. Theophrastus, quoting Chaeremon. *Tragicorum Graecorum Fragmenta*. Fragment 2 (p. 782).
44. Polybius. 29.21.5.
45. Ibid. 1.3.4.
46. Cicero. *On Laws* 1.6.18.
47. Alexander. *On Mixture* 225.1–2.
48. Cleanthes. *Hymn to Zeus* 1.537.
49. Cicero. *On Divination* 1.127.
50. Strabo. 11.16.

2 JERUSALEM

63 BC: Jerusalem

1. Josephus. *Antiquities of the Jews* 14.4.4.
2. Varro, as cited by Augustine. *On the Harmony of the Gospels* 1.22.30.
3. Tacitus. *Histories* 5.9.
4. Diodorus Siculus. 34.2.
5. Cicero. *Tusculan Disputations* 2.61.
6. Psalms of Solomon 2.1–2.
7. Dio Cassius. 37.6.1.
8. Genesis. 22.2.
9. Ibid. 22.18.
10. Eupolemus, a Greek-speaking Jew who lived a century before Pompey's capture of Jerusalem. Quoted by Isaac Kalimi: 'The Land of Moriah, Mount Moriah and the Site of Solomon's Temple in Biblical Historiography' (*Harvard Theological Review* 83, 1990), p. 352.
11. Isaiah. 2.2.
12. Deuteronomy. 11.26–28.
13. 2 Kings. 25.9.
14. Haggai. 2.3.
15. *Psalms of Solomon* 2.3–4.
16. Habakkuk. 2.8.
17. Ibid. 1.8.
18. Qumran pesher on Habakkuk. 9.6–7. The Romans are referred to in the text as the 'Kittim'.
19. Letter of Aristeas. 31.
20. Deuteronomy. 4.7.
21. *Enuma Elish*. Tablet 5.76.
22. Ibid. Tablet 6.7–8.
23. Genesis. 1.31.

24. Ibid. 2.9. Although God subsequently expresses anxiety that Adam and Eve will eat the fruit of a second tree, 'the tree of life', He does not explicitly ban them from picking it.
25. Ben Sirah. 25.24.
26. Judges. 5.8.
27. Deuteronomy. 30.3.
28. Psalms. 68.5.
29. Isaiah. 44.6.
30. Ibid. 41.24.
31. Ibid. 45.6.
32. Exodus. 15.11.
33. Judges. 5.4.
34. Psalms. 89.6.
35. Psalms. 82.1.
36. Ibid. 82.6–7.
37. Malachi. 1.11.
38. Job. 1.7.
39. Ibid. 1.8.
40. Ibid. 1.11.
41. Ibid. 2.8.
42. Ibid. 82.6–7.
43. Ibid. 42.7.
44. Genesis. 1.21.
45. Job. 40.25.
46. Ibid. 42.2.
47. Isaiah. 45.7.
48. Ibid. 41.17.
49. *Psalms of Solomon* 2.25.
50. Ibid. 2.29.
51. Exodus. 1.13.
52. Ibid. 12.29.
53. Ibid. 14.28.
54. Ibid. 33.17.
55. Exodus. 20.3.
56. Ibid. 20.5.
57. Deuteronomy. 34.6.
58. Assman. *Moses the Egyptian*, p. 2.
59. Exodus. 20.2.
60. Deuteronomy. 7.19.
61. 2 Kings. 22.8.
62. Ibid. 23.2.
63. Judges. 8.24.
64. Deuteronomy. 4.6.
65. Isaiah. 11.6.

66. Ibid. 11.4.
67. *Psalms of Solomon* 17.30.
68. Virgil. *Eclogues* 4.6–9.
69. Josephus. *Jewish War* 2.117.
70. Josephus. *Against Apion* 2.175.
71. Tacitus. *Histories* 5.4.
72. Strabo. 16.2.35.
73. Psalms. 47.2.
74. Isaiah. 56.6.
75. Strabo. 16.2.37.
76. Tacitus. *Histories* 5.5.
77. Philo. *Embassy to Gaius* 319.
78. Ibid. *Life of Moses* 2.20.

3 MISSION
AD 19: *Galatia*

1. Livy. 38.17.4.
2. No record of these decrees has survived, but the fact that Augustus' self-glorification was reproduced in at least three Galatian cities, and nowhere else—so far as we know—in the entire Roman empire, strongly suggests that they were issued by the *Koinon Galaton*. For the dating, see Hardin. *Galatians and the Imperial Cult*, p. 67.
3. Nicolaus of Damascus. *Fr Gr H* 90 F 125.1.
4. Seneca. Quoted by Augustine in *The City of God*, 6.10.
5. Virgil. *Aeneid* 6.792–3.
6. Galatians. 4.8. There is a hint here, perhaps, that Paul's malady was an eye infection.
7. Ibid. 4.14.
8. Ibid. 4.15.
9. Ibid. 1.14.
10. 1 Corinthians. 9.1.
11. Ibid. 15.9.
12. Romans. 8.6.
13. Galatians. 5.11.
14. 1 Corinthians. 1.23.
15. Galatians. 6.17.
16. Deuteronomy. 14.1.
17. Galatians. 5.6.
18. Plutarch. *Alexander* 18.1.
19. Philippians. 3.8.
20. Galatians. 3.28–9.
21. Ibid. 2.20.
22. 1 Corinthians. 4.13.
23. The estimate is from Hock. *Social Context*, p. 27.
24. Galatians. 3.1.

25. Ibid. 2.4.
26. Ibid. 5.12.
27. Ibid. 7.19.
28. Ibid. 5.13.
29. Ibid. 5.14.
30. 2 Corinthians. 12.4.
31. Ibid. 3.6.
32. Ibid. 3.17.
33. Horace. *Epistles* 1.17.36.
34. 1 Corinthians. 1.28.
35. Ibid. 7.22.
36. Ibid. 10.23.
37. Ibid. 9.21.
38. Ibid. 13.1.
39. Ibid. 9.22.
40. Galatians. 3.28.
41. 1 Corinthians. 11.3.
42. 2 Corinthians. 3.3.
43. Jeremiah. 31.33. Paul echoes the phrase in Romans. 2.15.
44. Romans. 2.14.
45. Ibid. 13.12.
46. 1 Thessalonians. 5.23.
47. Seneca. *Apocolocyntosis* 4.
48. Dio. 62.15.5.
49. Romans. 1.7.
50. Ibid. 8.16.
51. Musonius Rufus. Fr. 12.
52. 1 Corinthians. 6.15.
53. Ibid. 6.19.
54. Romans. 8.11.
55. Ibid. 2.11.
56. 2 Corinthians. 11.24.
57. Romans. 13.1.
58. 1 Thessalonians. 5.2.
59. Tacitus. *Annals* 15.44.
60. 1 Clement. 5.5–6.
61. Josephus. *Jewish War* 6.442.
62. 1 Corinthians. 1.22–23.
63. Matthew. 23.10.
64. Romans. 1.4.
65. Isaiah. 49.6.
66. John. 1.5.
67. Ibid. 21.17.

4 BELIEF
AD 177: Lyon

1. Irenaeus. *Against Heresies* 3.3.4.
2. Irenaeus, quoted by Eusebius. *History of the Church* 5.20.
3. Irenaeus. *Against Heresies* 3.3.2.
4. Colossians. 3.22.
5. 1 Peter. 2.17.
6. Irenaeus. *Against Heresies* 4.30.3.
7. Minucius Felix. *Octavius* 8.9.
8. *Martyrdom of Polycarp* 9.
9. 1 Corinthians. 4.9.
10. Eusebius. *History of the Church* 5.1.17.
11. Ibid. 5.1.11.
12. Ibid. 5.1.42.
13. Ibid. 5.1.41.
14. Irenaeus. *Against Heresies* 3.16.1.
15. Ibid. 1.24.4.
16. Ibid.
17. Ibid. 3.18.5.
18. Ibid. 1.13.1.
19. Ibid. 1.10.1.
20. Ignatius. 'Letter to the Smyrnaeans' 8.2.
21. Irenaeus. *Against Heresies* 2.2.1.
22. For the probability that Marcion was the first to coin the phrase 'New Testament', see Wolfram Kinzig: '*Kaine diatheke*: The Title of the New Testament in the Second and Third Centuries' (*Journal of Theological Studies* 45, 1994).
23. Irenaeus. *Against Heresies* 4.26.1.
24. Ibid. 1.8.1.
25. Eusebius. *History of the Church* 5.1.20.
26. 'Letter to Diognetus' 5.
27. Celsus, quoted by Origen. *Against Celsus* 5.59.
28. Recorded on a papyrus fragment (*P. Giss.* 40).
29. Minucius Felix. *Octavius* 6.2.
30. Herodian. 4.8.8.
31. Eusebius. *History of the Church* 6.3.6.
32. Origen. *Homilies on Joshua* 9.1.
33. Ibid. *Commentary on John* 10.35.
34. In three of his letters: to the Magnesians, the Philadelphians and the Romans.
35. Quoted Hans Urs von Balthasar: *Origen: Spirit and Fire: A Thematic Anthology of His Writings*, tr. Robert J. Daly (Washington DC, 1984), p. 244.
36. 1 Thessalonians. 4.12.
37. Celsus, quoted by Origen. *Against Celsus* 7.66.

38. Origen. *Against Celsus* 7.5.
39. The two comparisons are made in Origen's exegesis of The Song of Songs, verses 8.8 and 1.13 respectively.
40. Origen. Quoted by Trigg. *Origen*, p. 70.
41. Justin Martyr. *Second Apology* 13.4.
42. Gregory Thaumaturgus. *Oration and Panegyric Addressed to Origen* 6.
43. Ibid. 12.
44. Celsus, quoted by Origen. *Against Celsus* 3.44.
45. Irenaeus. *Against Heresies* 3.2.2.
46. Origen. *Commentary on John* 10.237.
47. Ibid. *Against Celsus* 7.38.
48. *Wisdom of Solomon* 7.26.
49. Origen. *On First Principles* 2.6.2.
50. Ibid. *Against Celsus* 8.70.
51. Tertullian. *Apology* 50.
52. Silius Italicus. 1.211–12.
53. Eusebius. *History of the Church* 10.6.4.
54. Lactantius. *On the Deaths of the Persecutors* 48.2.
55. Ibid. 48.3.
56. Optatus. 3.3.22.
57. Ibid. Appendix 3.
58. Eusebius. *Life of Constantine* 2.71.
59. Lactantius. *Divine Institutes* 4.28.
60. Eusebius. *Life of Constantine* 3.10.
61. Tertullian. *Apology* 24.
62. Optatus of Milevis. *Against the Donatists* 2.11.

5 CHARITY

AD 362: Pessinus

1. Julian. *Against the Galileans* 194d.
2. Julian. *Letter* 22.
3. Ibid.
4. Porphyry, quoted (and translated) by Brown (2016), p. 3.
5. Ibid.
6. Galatians. 2.10.
7. Gregory of Nyssa. *On the Love of the Poor*, 1. (Rhee. *Wealth and Poverty*, p. 73.)
8. Basil of Caesarea. *Homily 6: 'I Will Pull Down My Barns'*. (Rhee. *Wealth and Poverty*, p. 60.)
9. Gregory of Nyssa. *On Ecclesiastes* 4.1.
10. Gregory of Nyssa. *Homily 4 on Ecclesiastes*. (Hall. *Gregory of Nyssa*, p. 74.)
11. Basil of Caesarea. *Homily 8: In Time of Famine and Drought*. (Rhee. *Wealth and Poverty*, p. 65.)
12. Gregory of Nyssa. *Life of Macrina* 24.

13. Gregory of Nyssa. *On the Love of the Poor* 1. (Rhee. *Wealth and Poverty*, p. 72.)
14. Julian. Letter 19.
15. Sulpitius Severus. *Life of St Martin* 9.
16. Ibid. 4.
17. Matthew. 19.21.
18. Origen. *Commentary on John* 28.166.
19. Sulpitius Severus. *Life of St Martin* 3.
20. Paulinus. *Letters* 1.1.
21. Ibid. 5.5.
22. Ibid. 29.12.
23. Ibid. 22.2.
24. Luke. 16.24–25.
25. Paulinus. *Letters* 13.20.
26. *On Riches* 17.3. Tr. B. R. Rees in *The Letters of Pelagius and his Followers* (Woodbridge, 1998).
27. Ibid. 16.1, quoting Luke. 6.24.
28. Pelagius. *Letter to Demetrias* 8.3.
29. Acts of the Apostles. 2.45.
30. *On Riches* 12.1.
31. Augustine. *Dolbeau Sermon* 25.25.510. Quoted by Brown. *Augustine of Hippo*, p. 460.
32. Ibid.
33. Matthew. 26.11.
34. Augustine. *Letters* 185.4.15.
35. Ibid. *Sermon* 37.4.

6 HEAVEN
492: Mount Gargano

1. *Book of the Appearance of Saint Michael* 2.
2. Gregory I. *Letters* 5.38.
3. Augustine. *City of God* 2.28.
4. Luke. 14.32.
5. Jude. 9.
6. Daniel. 12.1.
7. Gregory I. *Homilies on the Gospels* 1.1.
8. Sulpitius Severus. *Life of St Martin* 21.
9. Hebrews. 2.14.
10. Isaiah. 14.15.
11. Augustine. *City of God* 11.33.
12. Ibid. 5.17.
13. Gregory of Tours. *History of the Franks* 10.1.
14. Gregory I. *Homilies on Ezekiel* 2.6.22.
15. Gregory of Tours. *History of the Franks* 10.1.
16. Gregory I. *Letters* 5.36.

17. Ibid. 3.29.
18. Matthew. 13.49–50.
19. Revelation. 12.9.
20. Ibid. 16.16.
21. Augustine. *City of God* 12.15.
22. Gregory of Tours. *History of the Franks* 5. Introduction.
23. Augustine. *City of God* 20.7.
24. Gregory I. *Homilies on the Gospels* 1.13.6.
25. Matthew. 24.14.
26. Plato. *Phaedo* 106e.
27. Augustine. *City of God* 8.5.
28. Jonas of Bobbio. *Life of Columbanus* 1.11.
29. *The Bangor Antiphonary*.
30. Columbanus. *Sermons* 8.2.
31. Augustine. *City of God* 2.29.
32. Zosimus. 2.
33. Augustine. *City of God* 16.26.
34. Jonas of Bobbio. *Life of Columbanus* 2.19.

7 EXODUS

632: Carthage

1. 'Letter of Saint Maximus', quoted by Gilbert Dagron and Vincent Déroche in *Juifs et Chrétiens en Orient Byzantin* (Paris, 2010), p. 31.
2. Matthew. 27.25.
3. Augustine. *Narrations on the Psalms* 59.1.19.
4. Gregory I. *Letters* 1.14.
5. *The Life of St Theodore of Sykeon* 134.
6. Such, at any rate, is the evidence of *The Teaching of Jacob*, which most scholars believe to have been written by a converted Jew. See Olster. *Roman Defeat*, pp. 158–75.
7. *Teaching of Jacob* 5.16.
8. Sebeos. 30.
9. Qur'an. 90.12–17.
10. Ibid. 4.171.
11. Ibid. 3.19.
12. Ibid. 4.157.
13. Deuteronomy. 9.10.
14. Qur'an. 5.21.
15. For the way in which the chronology of Muhammad's life echoes that of Moses', see Uri Rubin. *Eye of the Beholder*. For the tradition that Muhammad led the invasion of Palestine, see Shoemaker. *Death of a Prophet*.
16. Ibn Ishaq. *The Life of Muhammad*, tr. by Alfred Guillaume (Oxford, 1955), p. 107.
17. *Teaching of Jacob* 1.11.
18. Augustine. *Homily on the Letter of John to the Parthians* 7.8.

19. Bede. *On the Song of Songs*, Preface.
20. Bede. *Ecclesiastical History* 2.13.
21. Ibid. 4.2.
22. Bede. *Lives of the Abbots of Wearmouth and Jarrow*.
23. Bede. *Ecclesiastical History* 4.3.
24. Ibid. 3.24. I am grateful to Tom Williams for pointing this out to me.
25. Ibid. 2.1.
26. *Mozarabic Chronicle of 754*, quoted by Bernard S. Bachrach in *Early Carolingian Warfare: Prelude to Empire* (Philadelphia, 2001), p. 170.
27. Paul I to Pepin. Quoted by Alessandro Barbero in *Charlemagne: Father of a Continent*, tr. Allan Cameron (Berkeley & Los Angeles, 2004), p. 16.
28. Ibid. The quotation is from 1 Peter. 2.9.

8 CONVERSION
754: Frisia

1. Boniface. *Letters* 46.
2. Matthew. 28.19.
3. Augustine. *City of God* 19.17.
4. 2 Corinthians. 5.17.
5. Bede. *Life of Cuthbert* 3.
6. Willibald. *Life of Boniface* 6.
7. Ibid. 8.
8. Einhard. 31.
9. 2 Samuel. 8.2.
10. 1st Saxon Capitulary. 8.
11. Alcuin. *Letters* 113.
12. Ibid. 110.
13. From '*De Littoris Colendis*', a letter written in Charlemagne's name, almost certainly by Alcuin.
14. *Admonitio Generalis*. Preface.
15. Alcuin: cited in *Poetry of the Carolingian Renaissance*, ed. Peter Godman (London, 1985), p. 139.
16. *Gesta abbatum Fontanellensium*, in *MGH SRG* 28 (Hanover, 1886), p. 54.
17. Boniface. *Letters* 50.
18. Flodoard. *Historia Remensis Ecclesiae*, III, 28, p. 355.
19. Sedulius Scottus. *On Christian Rulers*, tr. E. G. Doyle (Binghamton, 1983), p. 56.
20. Otto of Freising. *The Two Cities*, tr. C. C. Mierow (New York, 1928), p. 66.
21. Gerhard, *Vita Sancti Uodalrici Episcopi Augustani*: cap. 12, tr. Charles R. Bowlus, in *The Battle of Lechfeld and Its Aftermath, August 955: The End of the Age of Migrations in the Latin West* (Aldershot: Ashgate, 2006), p. 176.
22. Ibid. p. 177.
23. *Heliand*, tr. G. Ronald Murphy (Oxford, 1992), p. 118.
24. Sulpitius Severus. *Life of St Martin* 4.

25. Haymo of Auxerre. *Commentarium in Pauli epistolas (Patrologia Latina)* 117, 732d.

26. From an 11th century list of relics kept in Exeter. Quoted by Patrick Connor in *Anglo-Saxon Exeter* (Woodbridge, 1993), p. 176.

27. Thietmar of Merseburg. *Chronicle* 8.4.

28. Radbod of Utrecht. Quoted by Julia M. H. Smith in *Europe After Rome: A New Cultural History 500–1000* (Oxford, 2005), p. 222.

29. Adémar of Chabannes. *Chronicles* 3.46.

30. Rudolf Glaber. *Histories* 4.16.

31. Ibid. 4.18.

32. Arnold of Regensburg. *Vita S. Emmerami*, in *MGH SS* 4 (Hanover, 1841), p. 563.

33. Ibid, p. 547.

9 REVOLUTION
1076: Cambrai

1. Andrew of Fleury. *Miraculi Sancti Benedicti*, ed. Eugene de Certain (Paris, 1858), p. 248.

2. *Chronicon s. Andreae (MGH SS 7)*, p. 540.

3. Arnulf of Milan. 3.15.

4. Gregory VII. *Letters* 5.17.

5. Bonizo of Sutri. *To a Friend*, in *The Papal Reform of the Eleventh Century*, tr. I. S. Robinson (Manchester, 2004), p. 220.

6. Paul of Bernried. *The Life of Pope Gregory VII*.

7. Jeremiah. 1.10.

8. Arnulf of Milan. 4.7.

9. *Die Briefe Heinrichs IV, in Monumenta Germaniae Historica, Deutsches Mittelalter* 1 (Leipzig, 1937), p. 12.

10. Gregory VII. *Register* 3.10a.

11. Ibid. 4.12.

12. Otto of Freising. *The Two Cities* 6.36.

13. Sigebert of Gembloux. Quoted by Moore. *Origins of European Dissent*, p. 53.

14. Wido of Ferrara. *De Scismate Hildebrandi* 1.7.

15. Luke. 20.25.

16. Moore. *First European Revolution*, p. 12.

17. Gregory VII. *Letters* 67.

18. Quoted by Morris. *Papal Monarchy*, p. 125.

19. Quoted by Cowdrey, H. E. J. 'Pope Urban II's Preaching of the First Crusade' (*History* 55. 1970), p. 188.

20. Quoted by Rubenstein. *Armies of Heaven*, p. 288.

21. John of Salisbury. *Historia Pontificalis* 3.8.

22. Huguccio. Quoted by Morris. *Papal Monarchy*, p. 208.

23. Bernard of Clairvaux. *De Consideratione* 2.8.

24. Gratian. *Decretum: Distinction* 22 c. 1.

25. Gregory VII. *Dictatus Papae*.

26. Augustine. *On the Sermon on the Mount* 2.9.32.

27. St Bernard. *Letter* 120.

28. Almost certainly, 'Gratian' is shorthand for the work of two compilers.

29. Quoted by Berman. *Law and Revolution*, p. 147.

30. Specifically, Saint Clement. Quoted by Tierney. *Idea of Natural Rights*, p. 71.

31. From an obituary quoted by Clanchy. *Abelard*, p. 29.

32. *The Letter Collection of Peter Abelard and Héloïse* 1.14.

33. Ibid. 1.16.

34. Innocent II. Cited in 'Les Lettres de Guillaume de Saint-Thierry à Saint Bernard' by J. Leclercq in *Revue Bénédictine* 79 (1969), p. 379.

35. *Sic et Non*, ed. B. B. Boyer and R. McKeon (Chicago, 1976), p. 103.

36. Bernard of Clairvaux. *Letters* 191.

37. Augustine. *City of God* 5.11.

38. Quoted by Huff. *Intellectual Curiosity*, p. 106.

39. Genesis. 9.15.

40. Anselm. *Why Was God a Man?* 1.6.

41. Abelard. *Commentary on the Epistle to the Romans*, tr. Steven R. Cartwright (Washington DC, 2011), p. 168 (adapted).

42. Abelard. *Theologia 'Scholarium'*, ed. E. M. Buytaert and C. J. Mews, in *Petri Abaelardi opera theologica III* (Turnhout, 1987), p. 374.

43. Revelation. 21.11.

44. Abbot Suger. *On What Was Done in His Administration* 27.

10 PERSECUTION
1229: Marburg

1. *Reports of Four Attendants*, in Wolf. *Life and Afterlife*, 40.

2. Ibid. 45.

3. Peter Damian. *Against Clerical Property* 6.

4. 1st canon of the Fourth Lateran Council.

5. A German observer at the Fourth Lateran Council. Quoted by Morris. *Papal Monarchy*, p. 417.

6. 3rd canon of the Fourth Lateran Council.

7. Walter Map. *Of the Trifles of Courtiers* 1.31.

8. Thomas of Celano. *The Life of Blessed Francis* 1.6.

9. Ibid. 1.33.

10. Elizabeth of Hungary. *Sayings* 45.

11. Caesarius of Heisterbach. *Life of Saint Elizabeth the Landgravine*, 4.

12. Ibid.

13. *Reports of Fours Attendants*, 31.

14. 18th canon of the Fourth Lateran Council.

15. Caesarius of Heisterbach. *Life of Saint Elizabeth the Landgravine*, 5.

16. Alberic of Trois-Fontaines. Quoted by Sullivan. *Inner Lives*, p. 76.

17. *Reports of Fours Attendants*, 15.

18. Gregory IX. *A Voice in Rama*. We do not have Conrad's letter to Gregory, but it is evident that the Pope is citing it.

19. Gratian. Quoted by Peters. *Magician, the Witch*, p. 73.

20. 27th canon of the Third Lateran Council.

21. Ibid.

22. *Acts of the Council of Lombers* in *Heresies of the High Middle Ages: Selected Sources Translated and Annotated*, by Walter L. Wakefield and Austin P. Evans (New York, 1969), p. 191.

23. Ibid. p. 192.

24. Ibid. p. 193.

25. Innocent III. *Register* 10.149.

26. Jacques de Vitry. Quoted by Pegg. *Most Holy War*, p. 67.

27. Caesarius of Heisterbach. *Dialogue of Miracles* 5.21.

28. Arnau Amalric. Quoted by Pegg. *Most Holy War*, p. 77.

29. Peter of Les-Vaux-de-Cernay. *Hystoria Alibigensis* (2 volumes. Ed. by Pascal Guébin and Ernest Lyon. Paris, 1926), vol. 1, p. 159.

30. Caesarius of Heisterbach. *Dialogue of Miracles* 5.21.

31. Ibid. 8.66.

32. Peter the Venerable. *Writings Against the Saracens* (tr. Irven M. Resnick), p. 75.

33. Ibid. p. 40.

34. Ibid. p. 31.

35. Abelard. *Dialogues*. Quoted by Clanchy. *Abelard*, p. 98.

36. Quoted by van Steenberghen. *Aristotle in the West*, p. 67.

37. Aquinas. *Summa Theologica*, Preface, Part 1.

38. Dante. *Paradise* 10.4–6.

39. Humber of Romans. Quoted by William J. Parkis in *Writing the Early Crusades: Text, Transmission and Memory*, ed. Marcus Graham Bull and Damien Kempf (Woodbridge, 2014), p. 153.

40. Innocent III. *Register* 2.276.

41. Quoted by Smalley. *Study of the Bible*, p. 55.

42. 68th canon of the Fourth Lateran Council.

11 FLESH
1300: Milan

1. *The Annals of Colmar* (1301). Quoted by Newman, "The Heretic Saint", p. 10.

2. Witness statement from the trial record. Quoted by Newman, "The Heretic Saint", p. 12.

3. Tertullian. *On the Apparel of Women* 1.1.

4. Caesarius of Heisterbach. *Dialogue of Miracles* 4.97.

5. A thirteenth-century translation into English of Vincent de Beauvais' *Speculum*. Quoted by G. Owst. *Literature and Pulpit in Medieval England* (Cambridge, 1933), p. 378.

6. Aristotle. *On the Generation of Animals* 2.3.737a. Medieval scholars variously translated *peperomenon*, the adjective used by Aristotle to describe the female, with words that suggested the sense of something lacking.

7. Aquinas. *Summa Theologica* 1.92.1.

8. Quoted by Bynum. *Jesus as Mother*, p. 114. Anselm is echoing the words of Jesus himself (Matthew. 23.37).

9. Bernard of Clairvaux. Ibid. p. 118.

10. 1 Timothy. 2.12.

11. John. 20.18.

12. Luke. 1.46–8.

13. Odo of Tournai. Quoted by Miri Rubin. *Mother of God*, p. 163.

14. Lorenzo Ghiberti. *I Commentari*, ed. O. Morisani (Naples, 1947), p. 56.

15. Agnolo di Tura. Quoted in John Aberth. *The Black Death: The Great Mortality of 1348–1350*, p. 81.

16. Ghiberti, p. 56.

17. Catherine of Siena. *Letter* T335. In *The Letters of St. Catherine of Siena*, tr. Suzanne Noffke (2 volumes) (Binghamton NY, 1988).

18. Raymond of Capua. *The Life of St Catherine of Siena*, tr. George Lamb (London, 1960), p. 92.

19. Catherine of Siena. *Letter* T35.

20. Quoted by Brophy. *Catherine of Siena*, p. 199.

21. Ephesians. 5.22–3.

22. Matthew. 5.32.

23. Raymond of Capua, p. 100.

24. Boniface. *Letters* 26.

25. Ibid.

26. Raymond of Capua, p. 168.

27. Luke. 7.37.

28. Catherine of Siena. *Letter* T276.

29. Jeremiah. 23.14.

30. Romans. 1.27.

31. Leviticus. 18.22.

32. Romans. 1.26.

33. Gregory I. *Morals in the Book of Job* 14.19.23.

34. It was popularised by Peter Damian, a close associate of Hildebrand's before he became pope. See Jordan. *Invention of Sodomy*, pp. 29–44. The phrase *scelus sodomiae*, "the sin of sodomy" was first used in the ninth century.

35. Venetian State Archives. Quoted by Elisabeth Pavan. 'Police des moeurs, société et politique à Venise à la fin du Moyen Age' (*Revue Historique* 264, no. 536, 1980), p. 275.

36. The praise of a contemporary, cited by Origo. *World of San Bernardino*, p. 26.

37. Quoted by Rocke. *Forbidden Friendships*, p. 37.

38. Ibid. p. 25.

12 APOCALYPSE
1420: Tabor

1. Acts of the Apostles. 2.45.
2. Luke. 9. 29.
3. Ibid. 6.22–25.
4. Matthew of Janov. Quoted by Kaminsky. *History of the Hussite*, p. 20.
5. Anonymous letter, 1420. Quoted by Kaminsky. *History of the Hussite*, p. 312.
6. John of Přibram. *The Stories of the Priests of Tabor*, quoted by McGinn. *Visions of the End*, p. 265.
7. Lawrence of Březova. *Chronicle*, quoted by McGinn. *Visions of the End*, p. 268.
8. Aeneas Sylvius Piccolomini, *Historia Bohemia*: quoted by Fudge, Thomas A. 'Žižka's Drum: The Political Uses of Popular Religion' (*Central European History* 36, 2004), p. 546.
9. Cited by Peder Palladius, a Danish Protestant, in 1555, in his introduction to a Lutheran polemic. Quoted by Cunningham and Grell. *Four Horsemen*, p. 45.
10. Revelation. 20.8.
11. Mark. 16.15.
12. Pere Azamar, *Repetición del derecho miltar e armas*. Quoted by Bryan Givens, p. 59: '"All things to all men": Political messianism in late medieval and early modern Spain', in *Authority and Spectacle in Medieval and Early Modern Europe: Essays in Honor of Teofilo F. Ruiz*, ed. Yuen-Gen Liang and Jarbel Rodriguez (London, 2017).
13. From a letter written to Juan de la Torres. Quoted by Watts. 'Prophecy and Discovery', p. 73.
14. A Nahuatal poem on Tenochtitlan, quoted by Manuel Aguilar-Moreno in *Handbook to Life in the Aztec World* (Oxford, 2006), p. 403.
15. Quoted by Felipe Fernández-Armesto in *Ferdinand and Isabella* (London, 1974), p. 95.
16. Gerónimo de Mendieta. Quoted by Phelan. *Millennial Kingdom*, p. 29.
17. John Mair. Quoted by Tierney. *Idea of Natural Rights*, p. 254.
18. Antonio de Montesinos. Quoted by Hanke. *Spanish Struggle*, p. 17.
19. Quoted by Tierney. *Idea of Natural Rights*, p. 273.
20. 'Commentaria Cardinalis Caietani ST II-II Q.66 a.8' in *Sancti Thomae Aquinatis: Opera Omnia, Iussu Impensaque Leonis XIII, P.M. Edita*, vol. 9 (Rome, 1882), p. 94.
21. Quoted by by Isacio Pérez Fernández in 'La doctrina de Santo Tomás en la mente ye en la acción del Padre Las Casas' (*Stadium* 27, 1987), p. 274.
22. 'The Proceedings of Friar Martin Luther, Augustinian, with the Lord Apostolic Legate at Augsburg', in *Luther's Works* (Minneapolis, 1957–1986), vol. 1, p. 129.
23. Ibid. p. 137.
24. Ibid. p. 147.
25. Quoted by Roper. *Martin Luther*, p. 119.
26. Quoted by David M. Whitford in 'The Papal Antichrist: Martin Luther and the Underappreciated Influence of Lorenzo Valla' (*Renaissance Quarterly* 61, 2008), p. 38.

13 REFORMATION
1520: Wittenberg

1. Quoted by Brecht. *Martin Luther*, p. 424.
2. Quoted by Harline. *World Ablaze*, p. 211.
3. Quoted by Whitford, p. 38.
4. Luther. *A Global Chronology of the Years*: entry for papacy of Gregory VII.
5. *To the Christian Nobility of the German Nation Concerning the Reform of the Christian Estate*, in *Luther's Works*, vol. 44, p. 164.
6. 'The Account and Actions of Doctor Martin Luther the Augustinian at the Diet of Worms' in *Luther's Works*, 32, p. 108.
7. Luther. 'Appeal for Prayer Against the Turks,' in *Luther's Works*, 43, p. 237.
8. Luther. 'On the Freedom of a Christian', in *Luther's Works*, 31, p. 344.
9. Luther. *Luther's Works*, 34, p. 337.
10. 'The Account and Actions of Doctor Martin Luther the Augustinian at the Diet of Worms' in *Luther's Works*, 32, p. 112.
11. Ibid. p. 114, n. 9.
12. Ibid. p. 115.
13. Quoted by Roper. *Martin Luther*, p. 186.
14. 'The Account and Actions of Doctor Martin Luther the Augustinian at the Diet of Worms' in *Luther's Works*, 32, p. 114, n. 9.
15. Luther. *Table Talk*, 1877.
16. *The Collected Works of Thomas Müntzer*, tr. Peter Matheson (Edinburgh, 1994), p. 161.
17. Argula von Grumbach. 'Letter to the rector and council of the University of Ingolstadt', in *Reformation Thought: An Anthology of Sources*, ed. Margaret L. King (Indianapolis, 2016), p. 74.
18. From the preamble to the 12 Articles, in Blickle. *The Revolution of 1525*, p. 195.
19. Johann Cochlaeus. Quoted by Mark Edwards in *Printing, Propaganda, and Martin Luther* (Berkeley & Los Angeles, 1994), p. 149.
20. Luther. 'Secular Authority: To What Extent It Should Be Obeyed'.
21. Ibid.
22. Bernhard Rothmann. Quoted by Buc. *Holy War*, p. 256.
23. Quoted by Gregory. *Unintended Reformation*, p. 90.
24. 2 Corinthians. 3.17.
25. Luther. 'The Sacrament of the Body and Blood of Christ—Against the Fanatics' in *Luther's Works* 36, p. 336.
26. Sir Richard Morrison, quoted by Diarmaid MacCulloch in *Tudor Church Militant: Edward VI and the Protestant Reformation* (London, 1999).
27. Quoted by Ozment. *Age of Reform*, p. 366.
28. Calvin. *Institutes of the Christian Religion* 3.19.14.
29. Ibid. 4.10.5.

30. Ibid. 3.23.7.
31. The figure—'somewhere in the range of 7 per cent of the population each year'—is quoted by Gordon. *Calvin*, p. 295.
32. John Knox. *Works*, ed. David Laing (Edinburgh, 1846–64). vol. 4, p. 240.
33. 2 Corinthians. 9.6.
34. Proverbs. 31.30. The inscription is quoted by Hugh Owen in *A History of Shrewsbury* II, (London, 1825) p. 320.
35. Calvin. *Institutes of the Christian Religion* 1.11.8.
36. Quoted by Philip Benedict in *Christ's Churches Purely Reformed: A Social History of Calvinism* (New Haven, Conn., 2002), p. 153.
37. John Tomkys. Quoted by Owen, p. 320.
38. *An Admonition to the Parliament* (1572). Quoted by Marshall. *Heretics and Believers*, p. 505.
39. *Earliest Life of Gregory the Great*, 15.
40. Calvin. 'Preface to the New Testament'.
41. Francis Bacon. *The Advancement of Learning* 1.4.9.

14 COSMOS
1620: Leiden

1. From a Leiden newspaper (1686), quoted in *Privacy and Privateering in the Golden Age of the Netherlands* by Virginia W. Lunsford (Basingstoke, 2005), p. 91.
2. William Bradford. *Bradford's History 'Of Plimouth Plantation'* (Boston, 1898), p. 22.
3. Adriaen Valerius. *Nederlandtsche Gedenck-Clanck*. Quoted by Schama. *Embarrassment of Riches*, p. 98.
4. Quoted by Parker. *Global Crisis*, p. 247.
5. William Bradford. *Bradford's History 'Of Plimouth Plantation'* (Boston, 1898), p. 47.
6. John Winthrop. 'A Model of Christian Charity,' in *Founding Documents of America: Documents Decoded*, ed. John R. Vile (Santa Barbara, 2015), p. 20.
7. John Winthrop. In *The Puritans: A Sourcebook of their Writings*, ed. Perry Miller and Thomas H. Johnson (Mineola, 2001), p. 206.
8. Bradford. p. 33.
9. Ibid. p. 339.
10. Juan Ginés de Sepúlveda. Quoted in J. H. Parry. *The Spanish Seaborne Empire* (Berkeley and Los Angeles, 1990), p. 147.
11. Bartolomé de las Casas. Quoted by Tierney. *Idea of Natural Rights*, p. 273.
12. João Rodrigues. Quoted by Brockey. *The Visitor*, p. 191.
13. 1 Corinthians. 9.22.
14. Matteo Ricci. Quoted by Fontana. *Matteo Ricci*, p. 177.
15. *China in the Sixteenth Century: The Journals of Matthew Ricci*, tr. Louis J. Gallagher (New York, 1953), p. 166.
16. Quoted by Brockey. *The Visitor*, p. 309.

17. Xu Guangqi. Quoted by Nicolas Standaert, 'Xu Guangqi's Conversion', in Jami et al. *Stagecraft and Intellectual*, p. 178.

18. Xu Guangqi. Quoted by Gregory Blue, 'Xu Guangqi in the West', in Jami et al. *Stagecraft and Intellectual*, p. 47.

19. Aquinas. *On the Power of God* 3.17.30.

20. Quoted by D'Elia. *Galileo in China*, p. 40.

21. Quoted by Heilbron. *Galileo*, p. 61.

22. Ibid. p. 287.

23. Quoted by D'Elia. *Galileo in China*, p. 40.

24. The pamphlet has not survived. See D'Elia. *Galileo in China*, p. 27 and Lattis. *Between Copernicus*, p. 205.

25. Psalms. 93.1.

26. Quoted in *The Galileo Affair: A Documentary History*, ed. and tr. Maurice A. Finocchiaro (Berkeley & Los Angeles), p. 50.

27. Ibid. p. 146.

28. Ibid. p. 147.

29. Ibid. p. 68.

30. Galileo. *Dialogue Concerning the Two Chief World Systems*, tr. Stillman Drake (Berkeley & Los Angeles, 1967), p. 464.

31. Though Finnochiaro, pointing out the late origins of the story and the lack of contemporary evidence for it, cautions against taking it for granted.

32. Finocchiaro. *Galileo Affair*, p. 291.

33. Milton. 'Areopagitica' in *Complete Prose Works, Volume II: 1643–1648*, ed. Ernest Sirluck (New Haven, 1959), p. 538

34. Yang Guangxian, quoted by George Wong, 'China's Opposition to Western Science during Late Ming and Early Ching' (*Isis* 54, 1963), p. 35.

15 SPIRIT

1649: St George's Hill

1. *The Complete Works of Gerrard Winstanley* (2 vols), ed. Thomas N. Corns, Ann Hughes and David Loewenstein (Oxford, 2009), 2, p. 19.

2. Ibid. p. 16.

3. *The Complete Works of Gerrard Winstanley* 1, p. 504.

4. Ibid. 2, p. 144.

5. John Lilburne. 'Londons Liberty in Chains' (1646). Quoted by Foxley. *The Levellers*, p. 26.

6. *The Complete Works of Gerrard Winstanley*. 1, p. 98.

7. Christopher Fowler (1655). Quoted by Worden. *God's Instruments*, p. 64.

8. John Owen. *Vindiciae Evangelicae; Or, The Mystery of the Gospel Vindicated and Socinianism Examined* (Fredonia, 2009) p. 62.

9. Milton. 'A Treatise of Civil Power' in *The Prose Works of John Milton*, ed. J. A. St John (London, 1984), 2, p. 523.

10. Lucy Aikin. *Memoirs of the Court of King Charles the First* (2 vols), (Philadelphia, 1833), 2, p. 317.

11. *Constitutional Documents of the Puritan Revolution*, ed. S. R. Gardiner (Oxford, 1958), p. 416.

12. 'The Soulders Demand', quoted by Norah Carlin in 'The Levellers and the Conquest of Ireland in 1649' (*Historical Journal* 30, 1987), p. 280.

13. From the first article of the two treaties that brought the Thirty Years War to an end. Quoted by Peter H. Wilson in *Europe's Tragedy: A History of the Thirty Years War* (London, 2009), p. 753.

14. Henry Robinson. Quoted by Carlin, p. 286.

15. Quoted by Andrew Bradstock in *Radical Religion in Cromwell's England: A Concise History from the English Civil War to the End of the Commonwealth* (London, 2011), p. 48.

16. Romans. 14.9.

17. Quoted by John Coffey, 'The toleration controversy during the English Revolution', in Durston and Maltby. *Religion in Revolutionary*, p. 51.

18. Luther. 'On the Jews and their Lies' in *Luther's Works* 47, p. 219.

19. Ibid. p. 268.

20. Thomas Edwards. Quoted by Glaser. *Judaism Without Jews*, p. 95.

21. John Evelyn. Diary entry for 14 December 1655.

22. Robert Turner. Quoted by Moore. *Light in Their Consciences*, p. 124.

23. William Caton. Quoted by Claus Bernet. 'Quaker Missionaries in Holland and North Germany in the Late Seventeenth Century: Ames, Caton, and Furly' (*Quaker History* 95, 2006), p. 4.

24. George Fox. Quoted by Moore. *Light in Their Consciences*, p. 54.

25. Almost certainly. See Nadler (1999), pp. 99–100.

26. William Ames. Quoted by Richard H. Popkin. 'Spinoza's Relations with the Quakers in Amsterdam' (*Quaker History* 73, 1984), p. 15. Although Ames nowhere refers to Spinoza by name, the likelihood that he was indeed 'the Jew' commissioned to translate Fell's pamphlets is overwhelming.

27. Pieter Balling. Quoted by Hunter. *Radical Protestantism*, p. 43.

28. Spinoza. *Theological-Political Treatise*: Prologue, 8.

29. See his Commentary on 1 Peter. 2.16.

30. The report of a Danish savant, Olaus Borch, on Spinoza's philosophy. Quoted by Jonathan Israel in *Radical Enlightenment: Philosophy and the Making of Modernity* (Oxford, 2001), p. 170.

31. Spinoza. *Ethics* 1. 17.

32. *Theological-Political Treatise* 18.6.1.

33. Quoted by Nadler. *Book Forged in Hell*, p. 230.

34. *Theological-Political Treatise* Preface, 8.

35. Ibid. 5.13.

36. Spinoza. *Letters* 76.

37. *Theological-Political Treatise* 1.29.

38. Ibid. 2.15.

39. Ibid. 5.20.

40. *Ethics* 4.50.

41. *Theological-Political Treatise* Prologue 19.

42. *Ethics* 4.68.

43. Johann Franz Buddeus. Quoted by Israel (2001), p. 161.

44. John Bunyan. *Grace Abounding to the Chief of Sinners*, 141.

45. *William Penn and the Founding of Pennsylvania, 1680–1684: A Documentary History* (Philadelphia, 1983), p. 77.

46. Ibid. p. 132.

47. Galatians. 5.1.

48. Thomas Walduck. Quoted by Rediker, p. 33.

49. Vaux. *Memoirs of the Lives*, p. 20.

50. Benjamin Lay. *All Slave-Keepers that Keep the Innocent in Bondage* (Philadelphia, 1737), p. 8.

51. Colossians. 3.22.

52. Lay, pp. 39–40.

53. Ibid. p. 40.

54. Ibid. p. 91.

55. Ibid. p. 34.

56. Quoted by Drake. *Quakers and Slavery*, p. 10.

57. Acts. 17.26, quoted by William Penn in *The Political Writings of William* Penn, ed. Andrew R. Murphy (Indianapolis, 2002), p. 30.

58. *Political Writings*, p. 30.

59. Vaux. *Memoirs of the Lives*, p. 27.

60. John. 3.6.

61. Vaux. *Memoirs of the Lives*, p. 51.

16 ENLIGHTENMENT

1762: Toulouse

1. Quoted by Nixon. *Voltaire*, p. 108.

2. Ibid. p. 133.

3. Voltaire. *Treatise on Tolerance*. Chapter 4.

4. Voltaire. *Treatise on Tolerance*. Chapter 1.

5. Voltaire. *Letters on England*. Letter 6.

6. Voltaire. *Philosophical Dictionary*. 'Theist'.

7. Voltaire. *Treatise on Tolerance*. Chapter 20.

8. Galatians. 3.26.

9. From the English version of *The Treatise of the Three Imposters*, quoted by Israel (2001), p. 697.

10. Bernard de La Monnoye, a French scholar writing in 1712 to deny that 'the so-called Book of the Three Imposters' existed. Quoted by Minois. *Atheist's Bible*, p. 138.

11. Voltaire. 'Epistle to the Author of the Book, The Three Imposters', line 22.

12. Voltaire. *Correspondance*. [To the d'Argentals: March 1765].

13. Mme. Du Bourg. Quoted by Bien. *Calas Affair*, p. 171.

14. Quoted by Gay. *Enlightenment*, Volume 2, p. 436.

15. A revolutionary slogan quoted by McManners. *French Revolution*, p. 93.

16. Jacques-Alexis Thuriot. Quoted in Michaël Culoma. *La Religion Civile de Rousseau à Robespierre* (Paris, 2010), p. 181.

17. Pierre Vergniaud. Quoted by Schama. *Citizens*, p. 594.

18. Montesquieu. 'Essay on the Roman Politics of Religion', in *Oeuvres Complètes* (Paris, 1876), vol. 2, p. 369.

19. Léonard Bourdon. Quoted by Kennedy. *Cultural History*, p. 336.

20. Quoted by John R. Vile in *The Constitutional Convention of 1787: A Comprehensive Encyclopedia of America's Founding* (Santa Barbara & Denver, 2005), vol. 1, p. xliv.

21. Benjamin Franklin. Letter to Richard Price, 9 October 1780.

22. Quoted by Gay. *Enlightenment*, vol. 2, p. 557.

23. Article III of the Declaration of Rights.

24. First Amendment to the United States Constitution.

25. Robespierre. Quoted by Edelstein. *Terror of Natural*, p. 190.

26. Quoted by Burleigh. *Earthly Powers*, p. 100.

27. Matthew. 25.32.

28. Quoted by Schama. *Citizens*, p. 841.

29. Matthew. 25.41.

30. Gibbon. *The Decline and Fall of the Roman Empire*, chapter LXIX.

31. Sade. *Juliette*, tr. Austryn Wainhouse (New York, 1968), p. 793.

32. Ibid. p. 177.

33. Ibid. p. 784.

34. Sade. *Justine*, tr. John Phillips (Oxford, 2012), p. 84.

35. *Juliette*, p. 178.

36. *Justine*, p. 142.

37. Quoted by Schaeffer. *Marquis de Sade*, p. 436.

38. Ibid. p. 431.

39. *Juliette*, pp. 322–3.

40. Ibid. p. 143.

41. Ibid. p. 796.

42. Talleyrand. Quoted in Jerome Reich. 'The Slave Trade at the Congress of Vienna' (*The Journal of Negro History* 53, 1968).

43. *The Case for the Oppressed Africans*. Quoted by Turley. *Culture of English*, p. 22.

44. Granville Sharp. Quoted by Anstey. *Atlantic Slave Trade*, p. 185.

45. Declaration relative to the Universal Abolition of the Slave Trade.

17 RELIGION
1825: Baroda

1. Kennedy. 'The Suttee: The Narrative of an Eye-Witness,' in *Bentley's Miscellany* 13 (1843), p. 247.
2. Ibid. p. 252.
3. Charles Goodrich. *Religious Ceremonies and Customs* (London, 1835), p. 16.
4. Kennedy. p. 244.
5. Ibid. p. 241.
6. Colonel 'Hindoo' Stewart. Quoted by David Kopf in *British Orientalism and the Bengal Renaissance: The Dynamics of Indian Modernization, 1773–1835* (Berkeley & Los Angeles, 1969), p. 140.
7. *Journals of the House of Commons* 48 (14 May 1793), p. 778.
8. Grant. Quoted by Weinberger-Thomas. *Ashes of Immortality*, p. 110.
9. The Sanskrit poet Bana, c. AD 625. Quoted by Vida Dehejia in Hawley. *Sati*, p. 53.
10. Quoted by Ghazi. *Raja Rammohun Roy*, p. 51.
11. Quoted by Hawley. *Sati*, p. 12.
12. S. N. Balagangadhara, in Bloch, et al. *Rethinking Religion*, p. 14.
13. Quoted by Barclay. *Frederick William IV*, p. 49.
14. *Kölnische Zeitung*, 4 August 1844. Quoted by Magnus. *Jewish Emancipation*, p. 103.
15. Stahl. 'The Christian State and its Relationship to Deism and Judaism', quoted in 'Protestant Anti-Judaism in the German Emancipation Era', by David Charles Smith (*Jewish Social Studies* 36, 1974), p. 215.
16. Quoted by Barclay. *Frederick William IV*, p. 183.
17. The Comte de Clermont-Tonnerre. Quoted by Graetz. *Jews in Nineteenth-Century France*, p. 177.
18. Article 1 of the Declaration of the Rights of Man and of the Citizen.
19. 'Appeal to our German Coreligionists'. Quoted by Koltun-Fromm. *Abraham Geiger's Liberal Juddism*, p. 91.
20. Samons Raphael Hirsch. Quoted by Batnitzky. *How Judaism*, p. 41.
21. Henry Rawlinson. 'Notes on some paper casts of cuneiform inscriptions upon the sculptured rock at Behistun exhibited to the Society of Antiquaries' (*Archaeologia* 34, 1852), p. 74.
22. Arthur Conolly. Quoted by Malcolm Yapp in 'The Legend of the Great Game' (*Proceedings of the British Academy* 111, 2000), p. 181.
23. Ibid.
24. Lord Palmerston, in *A Collection of Documents on the Slave Trade of Eastern Africa*, ed. R. W. Beachey (New York, 1976), p. 19.
25. Sir Travers Twiss, writing in 1856. Quoted by Koskenniemi. *Gentle Civilizer*, p. 78.
26. Henry Wheaton. Quoted by Martinez. *Slave Trade*, p. 116.
27. Quoted by Drescher, p. 3.
28. Thornton Stringfellow, a Baptist minister. Quoted by Noll. *America's God*, p. 389.

29. Quoted by Drescher. *Abolition*, p. 3.

30. Lord Ponsonby. Quoted by Christophe de Bellaigue in *The Islamic Enlightenment: The Modern Struggle Between Faith and Reason* (London, 2017), p. 190.

31. Husayn Pasha. Quoted by Toledano. *Ottoman Slave Trade*, p. 277.

32. Edward Eastwick, *Journal of a Diplomat's Three Years' Residence in Persia* (London, 1864), p. 254.

33. Ezekiel. 34.16.

18 SCIENCE
1876: The Judith River

1. Quoted by Charles H. Sternberg in *The Life of a Fossil Hunter* (New York, 1909), p. 82.

2. Psalms. 102.25–6.

3. *Lectures of Genesis 1–5*, in *Luther's Works*, vol. 1, p. 99.

4. Sternberg, p. 75.

5. *City of God*, 5.11.

6. Charles Darwin. *The Correspondence of Charles Darwin*, vol. 8 (Cambridge, 1993), p. 224.

7. Ibid.

8. Charles Darwin. *On the Origin of Species* (London, 1859), pp. 243–4.

9. Quoted by Desmond and Moore. *Darwin*, p. 218.

10. Quoted by Richard Gawne in 'Fossil Evidence in the *Origin of Species*' (*BioScience* 65, 2015), p. 1082.

11. Speech to the American Association for the Advancement of Science. Quoted by Wallace. *Beasts of Eden*, p. 57.

12. Charles Darwin. *The Descent of Man* (London, 1871), part 1, pp. 133–4.

13. Ibid. p. 134.

14. Edward D. Cope. *The Origin of the Fittest: Essays on Evolution* (New York, 1887), p. 390.

15. *The Descent of Man*, part 1, p. 134.

16. Quoted by Diane B. Paul in 'Darwin, social Darwinism and eugenics', in Hodge and Radick, p. 225.

17. *The Descent of Man* (London, 1874), Part 1, p. 183.

18. Charles Darwin. *Journal of Researches into the Geology and Natural History of the Various Countries Visited by H.M.S. Beagle* (London, 1839), p. 520.

19. *The Descent of Man*, p. 180.

20. Quoted by Desmond. *Huxley*, p. 262.

21. Ibid. p. 253.

22. Ibid.

23. Mark Pattison, rector of Lincoln College. Quoted by Harrison. *Territories of Science*, p. 148.

24. Thomas Henry Huxley. *Collected Essays. Volume 5: Science and the Christian Tradition* (London, 1894), p. 246.

25. *The Mechanics' Magazine* (1871). Quoted by Harrison. *Territories of Science*, p. 170.

26. John William Draper, *History of the Conflict Between Religion and Science* (London, 1887), p. 33.

27. Voltaire. Quoted by Finocchiaro. *Retrying Galileo*, p. 116.

28. T. S. Baynes. Quoted by Desmond. *Huxley*, p. 624.

29. *On the Origin of Species*, p. 490.

30. *The Autobiography of Charles Darwin, 1809–1882*, ed. Nora Barlow (London, 1958), p. 93.

31. Krafft-Ebing. *Psychopathia Sexualis*, tr. F. J. Redman (London, 1899), p. 210.

32. Ibid. p. 213.

33. Ibid. pp. 3–4.

34. Quoted by Robert Beachy in 'The German Invention of Homosexuality' (*Journal of Modern History* 82, 2010), p. 819.

35. Quoted by W. J. T. Mitchell in *The Last Dinosaur Book* (Chicago, 1998).

36. Andrew Carnegie. *Autobiography of Andrew Carnegie* (London, 1920), p. 339.

37. William Graham Sumner. *What Social Classes Owe To Each Other* (New York, 1833), pp. 44–5.

38. John Winthrop. 'A Model of Christian Charity,' p. 20.

39. Andrew Carnegie. *The Gospel of Wealth, And Other Timely Essays* (New York, 1901), p. 18.

40. Ibid. pp. 14–15.

41. Quoted by Rea. *Bone Wars*, p. 5.

42. Richard Owen. Quoted by Nicolaas Rupke in *Richard Owen: Biology Without Darwin* (Chicago, 2009), p. 252.

43. Lenin. 'Letter to American Workers'. https://www.marxists.org/archive/lenin/works/1918/aug/20.htm.

44. Engels. *Marx-Engels Collected Works* (Moscow, 1989), vol. 24, p. 467.

45. Marx. *MECW* (1975), vol. 4, p. 150.

46. Marx and Engels. *Manifesto of the Communist Party* (London, 1888), p. 16.

47. Marx. 'On the Jewish Question.' *Early Writings*, tr. T. B. Bottomore (London, 1963), p. 5.

48. Ibid. *Critique of the Gotha Program* (London, 1891), p. 23.

49. Ibid. *The Cologne Communist Trial*, tr. R. Livingstone (London, 1971), p. 166.

50. Ibid. *Capital* (London, 1976), vol. 1, p. 342.

19 SHADOW

1916: The Somme

1. Otto Dix. Quoted by Karcher. *Otto Dix*, p. 38.

2. Ibid. p. 18.

3. The Bishop of Hereford. Quoted by Jenkins. *Great and Holy War*, p. 99.

4. Quoted by Nicholas Martin in 'Fighting a Philosophy': The Figure of Nietzsche in British Propaganda of the First World War' (*The Modern Language Review* 98, 2003), p. 374.

5. Max Plowman. Quoted by Paul Fussell in *The Great War and Modern Memory* (Oxford, 1975), p. 133.

6. Lucy Whitmell. 'Christ in Flanders'.

7. Otto Dix. Quoted by Hartley. *Otto Dix*, p. 73.

8. Friedrich Nietzsche. *The Gay Science*, 125.

9. Ibid. *Twilight of the Idols*, 9.38.

10. Ibid. *Will to Power*, 253.

11. Ibid. 'Preface to an Unwritten Book' in *Early Greek Philosophy and Other Essays*, tr. M. Mügge (London, 1911), p. 4.

12. Ibid. *On the Genealogy of Morals*, 1.8.

13. Ibid. *Will to Power*, 176.

14. Ibid. *The Antichrist*, 42.

15. Ibid. 58.

16. Ibid. *On the Genealogy of Morals*, 2.7.

17. Ibid. *Twilight of the Idols*, 7.2.

18. Otto Dix. Quoted by Hartley. *Otto Dix*, p. 16.

19. Revelation. 12.1.

20. Nietzsche. *Will to Power*, 133.

21. N. Bukharin and E. Preobrazhensky. *The ABC of Communism* (London, 2007), p. 235.

22. Waldemar Gurian. *Bolshevism: Theory and Practice*, tr. E. I. Watkin (London, 1932), p. 259.

23. Ibid. p. 226.

24. Quoted by Siemens. *Making of a Nazi*, p. 8.

25. Nietzsche. *Thus Spoke Zarathustra*, 'Of the Tarantulas'.

26. Roberto Davanzati. Quoted by Burleigh. *Sacred Causes*, p. 61.

27. 'It's Him or Me', an article in the *SS-Leitheft*. Quoted by Chapoutot, p. 157.

28. Hitler. *My Struggle*, Chapter 11.

29. Hitler. Quoted by Chapoutot, p. 156.

30. Erwin Reitmann. Quoted by Siemens. *Making of a Nazi*, p. 57.

31. Wilfred Bade. Quoted by Siemens. *Making of a Nazi*, p. 17.

32. Joachim Hossenfelder. Quoted by Siemens. *Making of a Nazi*, p. 129.

33. Quoted by Gregor Ziemer. *Education for Death: The Making of the Nazi* (London, 1942), p. 180.

34. Ibid. p. 133.

35. From an SS magazine (1939), quoted by Chapoutot, p. 190.

36. *Hitler's Table Talk 1941–1944: His Private Conversations*, ed. Hugh Trevor-Roper (London, 1953), p. 7.

37. Joseph Goebbels. Diary entry for 27 March 1942.

38. *The Letters of J. R. R. Tolkien*, ed. Humphrey Carpenter (London, 1981), p. 67.

39. Augustine. *The City of God* 20.11.

40. J. R. R. Tolkien. *Letters*, p. 211.

41. J. R. R. Tolkien. *The Lord of the Rings* (London, 2004), p. 820.

42. Adolf Hitler. Quoted by Stone. *Histories of the Holocaust*, p. 160.

43. Werner Graul. Quoted by Chapoutot, p. 100.

44. Adolf Hitler. Quoted by Stone. *The Holocaust*, p. 49.

45. J. R. R. Tolkien. *Letters*, p. 37.

46. *The Old English Exodus: Text, Translation, and Commentary by J. R. R. Tolkien*, ed. Joan Turville-Petre (Oxford, 1981), p. 27.

47. Ibid. p. 23.

48. Quoted by Bethge. *Dietrich Bonhoeffer*, p. 208.

49. Quoted by Burleigh. *Sacred Causes*, p. 252.

50. Matthew. 27.25.

51. Alojzije Stepinac. Quoted by Stella Alexander in *The Triple Myth: A Life of Archbishop Alojzije Stepinac* (New York, 1987), p. 85.

52. Nietzsche. *Beyond Good and Evil*, Aphorism 146.

53. https://api.parliament.uk/historic-hansard/lords/1944/feb/09/bombing-policy.

54. J. R. R. Tolkien. *Letters*, p. 78.

55. Alfred Duggan. Quoted by Shippey. *J. R. R. Tolkien*, p. 306.

56. *The Lord of the Rings*, p. 464.

57. J. R. R. Tolkien. *Letters*, p. 255.

20 LOVE
1967: Abbey Road

1. Augustine. *7th Homily on the First epistle of John*, 7.

2. Martin Huska. Quoted by Kaminsky, p. 406.

3. Martin Luther King. 'Loving Your Enemies'. (Sermon delivered 17 November 1957).

4. Martin Luther King. 'Letter from Birmingham Jail'.

5. James Brown. Quoted by Stephens. *Devil's Music*, p. 45.

6. Paul McCartney. Quoted by Craig Cross in *Beatles-discography.com* (New York, 2004), p. 98.

7. Quoted by Norman. *John Lennon*, p. 446.

8. Robert Shelton. Quoted by Stephens. *Devil's Music*, p. 104.

9. An observation about the Beatles reputedly made by the Queen to Sir Joseph Lockwood, chairman of their record company, EMI.

10. Martin Luther King. *Where Do We Go from Here: Chaos or Community?* (New York, 1967), p. 97.

11. John. 3.8.

12. Quoted by Norman. *John Lennon*, p. 446.

13. Norman Vincent Peale. Quoted by Stephens. *Devil's Music*, p. 137.

14. McCartney made this comment in a 1981 interview. It was published four years later in *Woman* magazine.

15. Martin Luther King. *Strength to Love* (New York, 1963), p. 72.

16. David Livingstone. *The Last Journals of David Livingstone, Volume II*, ed. Horace Waller (Frankfurt, 2018), p. 189.

17. Emmanuel Milingo. Quoted by ter Haar. *How God Became*, p. 26.

18. Ibid. p. 28.

19. Psalms. 68.31.

20. Desmond Tutu. Quoted by Jonathan Fasholé-Luke in *Christianity in Independent Africa* (London, 1978), p. 369.

21. J. D. du Toit. Quoted by Ryrie, p. 335.

22. Declaration of the Church of the Province of South Africa, November 1982.

23. Quoted by Allan Boesak in an open letter he wrote in 1979.

24. Matthew. 5.43–4.

25. Desmond Tutu, speaking at a conference of South Africa's churches in December 1989. Quoted by Ryrie, p. 357.

26. Nelson Mandela. Address to the Zionist Christian Church Easter Conference, 3 April 1994.

27. George W. Bush. Press conference, 11 October 2001.

28. Ibid. Comments made on US humanitarian aid to Afghanistan, 11 October 2002.

29. Ibid. Address at West Point, 1 June 2002.

30. Mary Beard. *London Review of Books* 23.19 (4 October 2001), p. 21.

31. Quoted by David Aikman in *A Man of Faith: The Spiritual Journey of George W. Bush* (Nashville, 2004), p. 3.

32. George W. Bush. Press conference, 13 November 2002.

33. Frantz Fanon, in *The Wretched of the Earth*, tr. Richard Philcox (New York, 1963), p. 53.

34. Ibid. p. 23.

35. Printed in the *Morning Star* on 11 October 2004.

36. Fanon, p. 2.

37. al-Zarqawi. Quoted by Weiss and Hassan. *ISIS*, p. 40.

38. Qur'an. 9.31. The verse is one that al-Maqdisi repeatedly returns to.

39. George W. Bush. Press conference, 20 November 2002.

40. Ali. *Lives of Muhammad*, p. 238.

41. Qur'an. 5.33.

42. https://medium.com/@alyssacccc/phone-call-home-a-letter-from-james-foley-arts-96-to-marquette-4a9dd1553d83?subaction=showfull&id=1318951203&archive.

43. Interview in the *Evening Standard*, 4 September 2014.

44. https://twitter.com/jenanmoussa/status/982935563694215168.

21 WOKE

2015: Rostock

1. Transcript from *Gut leben in Deutschland*, 15 July 2015.

2. J. R. R. Tolkien: *The Return of the King* (London: Allen & Unwin, 1955; repr. 2005), p. 1075.

3. http://www.bbc.co.uk/news/world-europe-34173720.

4. Quoted by John Garth in *Tolkien and the Great War: The Threshold of Middle-earth* (London: Harper Collins, 2003), p. 219.

5. http://www.spiegel.de/international/germany/why-has-angela-merkel-staked -her-legacy-on-the-refugees-a-1073705.html.

6. Gregory of Nyssa. *On the Love of the Poor 1: 'On Good Works'*, tr. Holman, p. 194.

7. Victor Orbán. Speech at the 28th Bálványos Summer Open University and Student Camp, 22 July 2017.

8. From the UNESCO symposium *Human Rights: Comments and Interpretations* (1949). Quoted by Tierney. *Idea of Natural Rights*, p. 2.

9. *Charlie Hebdo*. Editorial, 14 December 2016.

10. Ibid. 13 January 2016.

11. Stéphane Charbonnier. http://arretsurinfo.ch/quand-la-liberte-dexpression-sert-a -propager-la-haine-raciste/.

12. https://www.nytimes.com/2017/12/17/us/harvey-weinstein-hotel-sexual -harassment.html.

13. https://www.eeoc.gov/eeoc/task_force/harassment/report.cfm.

14. Bernard of Clairvaux. Quoted by Bynum (1987), p. 16.

15. William Perkins. *Christian Oeconomie or, a Short Survey of the right Manner of Erecting and Ordering a Familie, According to the Scriptures* (London, 1609), p. 122.

16. Calvin. *Institutes of the Christian Religion* 1.1.2.

17. Sade. *Juliette*, p. 172.

18. Milton Himmelfarb. His reflection was prompted by a viewing of the Beatles' film, *Yellow Submarine*. Quoted by John Carlevale in 'Dionysus Now: Dionysian Myth-History in the Sixties' (*Arion* 13, 2005), p. 95.

19. Ralph Gleason. Quoted by Ibid. p. 89.

20. 1 Corinthians. 6.19.

21. Vanessa Wruble. https://www.vogue.com/article/meet-the-women-of-the-womens -march-on-washington.

22. Nietzsche. *The Will to Power*, 27.

23. https://staging.womensmarchglobal.org/about/unity-principles/.

24. Steven Weinberg. *The First Three Minutes* (New York, 1977), p. 154.

25. Heinrich Himmler. Quoted by Chapoutot, p. 27.

26. Amsterdam Declaration, 2002.

27. Ibid.

28. Ibid.

29. Sam Harris. *The Moral Landscape: How Science Can Determine Human Values* (New York, 2010), p. 2.

30. Amsterdam Declaration, 2002.

31. https://twitter.com/RichardDawkins/status/1018933359978909696.

32. Thomas Henry Huxley. *Collected Essays. Volume 5: Science and the Christian Tradition* (London, 1894), p. 320.

33. 1 Corinthians. 1.27.

BIBLIOGRAPHY

All Bible quotations are from the *New English Version*.

GENERAL

Almond, Philip C: *Afterlife: A History of Life after Death* (London, 2016)

Barton, John: *A History of the Bible: The Story of the World's Most Influential Book* (London, 2019)

Brague, Rémi: *The Law of God: The Philosophical History of an Idea*, tr. Lydia G. Cochrane (Chicago, 2006)

Brooke, John Hedley: *Science and Religion: Some Historical Perspectives* (Cambridge, 1991)

Buc, Philippe: *Holy War, Martyrdom, and Terror: Christianity, Violence, and the West* (Philadelphia, 2015)

Cambridge History of Christianity, 9 volumes (Cambridge, 2006)

Chidester, David: *Christianity: A Global History* (New York, 2000)

Funkenstein, Amos: *Theology and the Scientific Imagination: From the Middle Ages to the Seventeenth Century* (Princeton, 1986)

Gillespie, Michael Allen: *The Theological Origins of Modernity* (Chicago, 2008)

Gray, John: *Straw Dogs: Thoughts on Humans and Other Animals* (London, 2003)

———*Heresies: Against Progress and Other Illusions* (London, 2004)

———*Black Mass: Apocalyptic Religion and the Death of Utopia* (London, 2007)

Gregory, Brad S: *The Unintended Reformation: How a Religious Revolution Secularized Society* (Cambridge, Mass., 2012)

Harrison, Peter: *The Bible, Protestantism, and the Rise of Natural Science* (Cambridge, 1998)

———(ed) *The Cambridge Companion to Science and Religion* (Cambridge, 2010)

——— *The Territories of Science and Religion* (Chicago, 2015)

Hart, David Bentley: *Atheist Delusions: The Christian Revolution and Its Fashionable Enemies* (New Haven, Conn., 2009)

——— *The Story of Christianity: A History of 2,000 Years of the Christian Faith* (London, 2009)

Jacobs, Alan: *Original Sin: A Cultural History* (New York, 2008)

MacCulloch, Diarmaid: *A History of Christianity: The First Three Thousand Years* (London, 2009)

Nirenberg, David: *Anti-Judaism: The History of a Way of Thinking* (New York, 2013)

Nongbri, Brent: *Before Religion: A History of a Modern Concept* (New Haven, Conn., 2013)

Rubin, Miri: *Mother of God: A History of the Virgin Mary* (London, 2009)

Schimmelpfennig, Bernhard: *The Papacy*, tr. James Sievert (New York, 1992)

Shagan, Ethan H: *The Birth of Modern Belief: Faith and Judgment from the Middle Ages to the Enlightenment* (Princeton, N. J., 2019)

Shah, Timothy Samuel and Allen D. Hertzke: *Christianity and Freedom: Historical Perspectives* (Cambridge, 2016)

Siedentop, Larry: *Inventing the Individual: The Origins of Western Liberalism* (London, 2014)

Smith, William Cantwell: *The Meaning and End of Religion* (Minneapolis, Minn., 1962)

Taylor, Charles: *A Secular Age* (Cambridge, Mass., 2007)

Watkins, Basil: *The Book of Saints: A Comprehensive Biographical Dictionary* (London, 2002)

ANTIQUITY

Allison, Dale C: *Constructing Jesus: Memory, Imagination and History* (Grand Rapids, Mich., 2010)

Ando, Clifford: *The Matter of the Gods: Religion and the Roman Empire* (Berkeley, 2008)

Arnold, Clinton E: *The Footprints of Michael the Archangel: The Formation and Diffusion of a Saintly Cult, c. 300–c.800* (New York, 2013)

Assman, Jan: *Moses the Egyptian: The Memory of Egypt in Western Monotheism* (Cambridge, Mass., 1997)

Atkinson, Kenneth: *I Cried to the Lord: A Study of the Psalms of Solomon's Historical Background and Social Setting* (Leiden, 2004)

Barton, John: *Ethics in Ancient Israel* (Oxford, 2014)

Bauckham, Richard: *Jesus and the Eyewitnesses: The Gospels as Eyewitness Testimony* (Grand Rapids, Mich., 2006)

Behr, John: *Irenaeus of Lyons: Identifying Christianity* (Oxford, 2013)

Boyarin, Daniel: *A Radical Jew: Paul and the Politics of Identity* (Berkeley and Los Angeles, 1994)

———"Justin Martyr Invents Judaism" (*Church History* 70, 2001)

——— *Border Lines: The Partition of Judaeo-Christianity* (Philadelphia, 2007)

Brent, Allen: *The Imperial Cult and the Development of Church Order: Concepts and Images of Authority in Paganism and Early Christianity Before the Age of Cyprian* (Boston, 1999)

Briant, Pierre: *From Cyrus to Alexander: A History of the Persian Empire*, tr. Peter T. Daniels (Winona Lake, Ind., 2002)

Brown, Peter: *The Cult of the Saints: Its Rise and Function in Latin Christianity* (Chicago, 1981)

——— *The Body and Society: Men, Women and Sexual Renunciation in Early Christianity* (London, 1989)

——— *The Rise of Western Christendom: Triumph and Diversity, A.D. 200–1000* (Oxford, 1996)

——— *Augustine of Hippo* (London, 2000)

——— *Through the Eye of a Needle: Wealth, the Fall of Rome, and the Making of Christinaity in the West, 350–550 AD* (Princeton, 2012)

——— *The Ransom of the Soul: Afterlife and Wealth in Early Western Christianity* (Cambridge, Mass., 2015)

Burkert, Walter: *Greek Religion*, tr. John Raffan (Oxford, 1985)

Castelli, Elizabeth A: *Martyrdom and Memory: Early Christian Culture Making* (New York, 2004)

Chapman, David W: *Ancient Jewish and Christian Perceptions of Crucifixion* (Tübingen, 2008)

Cohen, Shaye J. D: *The Beginning of Jewishness: Boundaries, Varieties, Uncertainties* (Berkeley & Los Angeles, 1999)

Crislip, Andrew: *From Monastery to Hospital: Christian Monasticism and the Transformation of Health Care in Late Antiquity* (Ann Arbor, Mich., 2005)

Crouzel, Henry: *Origen*, tr. A. S. Worrall (San Francisco, 1989)

Darby, Peter and Faith Wallis (eds): *Bede and the Future* (Farnham, 2014)

Demacopoulos, George E: *Gregory the Great: Ascetic, Pastor, and First Man of Rome* (Notre Dame, Ind., 2015)

Drake, H. A.: *Constantine and the Bishops* (Baltimore, 2002)

Dunn, J. D. G: *Christology in the Making: A New Testament Inquiry into the Origins of the Doctrine of the Incarnation* (Grand Rapids, Mich., 1989)

——— *The Theology of Paul the Apostle* (Grand Rapids, Mich., 1998)

——— *Jesus, Paul, and the Gospels* (Grand Rapids, Mich., 2011)

Ehrman, Bart D: *Lost Christianities: The Battles for Scripture and the Faiths We Never Knew* (Oxford, 2003)

——— *The Triumph of Christianity: How a Forbidden Religion Swept the World* (London, 2018)

Eichrodt, Walther: *Man in the Old Testament* (London, 1951)

Elliott, Neil: *The Arrogance of Nations: Reading Romans in the Shadow of Empire* (Minneapolis, Minn., 2008)

Elliott, Susan: *Cutting Too Close for Comfort: Paul's Letter to the Galatians in its Anatolian Cultic Context* (London, 2003)

Elm, Susanna: *Sons of Hellenism, Fathers of the Church: Emperor Julian, Gregory of Nazianzus, and the Vision of Rome* (Berkeley & Los Angeles, 2012)

Engberg-Pedersen, Troels: *Paul and the Stoics* (Edinburgh, 2000)

Ferngren, Gary B: *Medicine & Health Care in Early Christianity* (Baltimore, 2009)

Finn, Richard: *Almsgiving in the Later Roman Empire: Christian Promotion and Practice (313–450)* (Oxford, 2006)

BIBLIOGRAPHY

Fortenbaugh, William W. and Eckart Schütrumpf (ed): *Demetrius of Phalerum: Text, Translation and Discussion* (New Brunswick, 2000)

Frend, W. H. C: *The Donatist Church: A Movement of Protest in Roman North Africa* (Oxford, 1952)

Gager, John G: *The Origins of Anti-Semitism: Attitudes Toward Judaism in Pagan and Christian Antiquity* (Oxford, 1983)

Green, Peter: *From Alexander to Actium: The Historical Evolution of the Hellenistic Age* (Berkeley & Los Angeles, 1990)

Greenhalgh, Peter: *Pompey: The Roman Alexander* (London, 1980)

Hall, Stuart George (ed.): *Gregory of Nyssa: Homilies on Ecclesiastes* (Berlin & New York, 1993)

Hardin, Justin K: *Galatians and the Imperial Cult: A Critical Analysis of the First-Century Social Context of Paul's Letter* (Tübingen, 2008)

Harding, Mark and Alanna Nobbs: *All Things to All Cultures: Paul Among Jews, Greeks, and Romans* (Grand Rapids, 2013)

Harper, Kyle: *From Shame to Sin: The Christian Transformation of Sexual Morality in Late Antiquity* (Cambridge, Mass., 2013)

Harrill, J. Albert: *Paul the Apostle: His Life and Legacy in Their Roman Context* (Cambridge, 2012)

Harvey, Susan Ashbrook and David G. Hunter: *The Oxford Handbook of Early Christian Studies* (Oxford, 2008)

Hayward, C. T. R: *The Jewish Temple: A Non-Biblical Sourcebook* (London, 1996)

Heine, Ronald E: *Scholarship in the Service of the Church* (Oxford, 2010)

Hengel, Martin: *Crucifixion in the Ancient World and the Folly of the Message of the Cross*, tr. John Bowden (Philadelphia, 1977)

Higham, N. J: *(Re-)Reading Bede: The Ecclesiastical History in Context* (Abingdon, 2006)

Hock, Ronald F.: *The Social Context of Paul's Ministry: Tentmaking and Apostleship* (Philadelphia, 1980)

Holman, Susan R: *The Hungry Are Dying: Beggars and Bishops in Roman Cappadocia* (Oxford, 2001)

Horrell, David G.: 'The Label χριστιανος: 1 Peter 4:16 and the Formation of Christian Identity' (*Journal of Biblical Literature* 126, 2007)

Horsley, Richard A (ed): *Paul and Empire: Religion and Power in Roman Imperial Society* (Harrisburg, Pa., 1997)

Hurtado, Larry W: *Lord Jesus Christ: Devotion to Jesus in Earliest Christianity* (Grand Rapids, 2003)

——*Destroyer of the Gods: Early Christian Distinctiveness in the Roman World* (Waco, Tex., 2016)

Johnson, Richard F: *Saint Michael the Archangel in Medieval English Legend* (Woodbridge, 2005)

Judge, E.A: *The Social Pattern of Early Christian Groups in the First Century* (London, 1960)

Kim, Seyoon: *The Origins of Paul's Gospel* (Tübingen, 1981)

———— *Christ and Caesar: The Gospel and the Roman Empire in the Writings of Paul and Luke* (Grand Rapids, Mich., 2008)

Koskenniemi, Erkki: *The Exposure of Infants Among Jews and Christians in Antiquity* (Sheffield, 2009)

Kyrtatas, Dimitris J: *The Social Structure of the Early Christian Communities* (New Yok, 1987)

Lane Fox, Robin: *Pagans and Christians* (London, 1986)

Lavan, Luke and Michael Mulryan (eds): *The Archaeology of Late Antique 'Paganism'* (Leiden, 2011)

Ledegant, F: *Mysterium Ecclesiae: Images of the Church and Its Members in Origen* (Leuven, 2001)

Lemche, Niels Peter: *Ancient Israel: A New History of Israel* (London, 2015)

Lincoln, Bruce: *Religion, Empire & Torture* (Chicago, 2007)

Longenecker, Bruce W: *Remember the Poor: Paul, Poverty, and the Greco-Roman World* (Grand Rapids, Mich., 2010)

Ludlow, Morwenna: *Gregory of Nyssa: Ancient and [Post]Modern* (Oxford, 2007)

Marietta, Don E: "Conscience in Greek Stoicism" (*Numen* 17, 1970)

Markus, R. A: *Saeculum: History and Society in the Theology of St Augustine* (Cambridge, 1970)

———— *Christianity in the Roman World* (New York, 1974)

———— *From Augustine to Gregory the Great: History and Christianity in Late Antiquity* (London, 1983)

———— *Gregory the Great and His World* (Cambridge, 1997)

Meeks, Wayne A: *The First Urban Christians: The Social World of the Apostle Paul* (New Haven, Conn., 1983)

Miles, Richard (ed): *The Donatist Schism: Controversy and Contexts* (Liverpool, 2016)

Miller, Timothy S: *The Orphans of Byzantium: Child Welfare in the Christian Empire* (Washington D.C., 2003)

Mitchell, Stephen: *Anatolia: The Celts in Anatolia and the Impact of Roman Rule* (Oxford, 1993)

Neusner, Jacob, William S. Green & Ernest Frerichs: *Judaisms and their Messiahs at the Turn of the Christian Era* (Cambridge, 1987)

Oakes, Peter: *Reading Romans in Pompeii: Paul's Letter at Ground Level* (Minneapolis, Minn., 2009)

———— *Galatians* (Grand Rapids, Minn., 2015)

Olson, S. D. (ed.): *Aristophanes: Acharnians* (Oxford, 2002)

Olster, David M: *Roman Defeat, Christian Response, and the Literary Construction of the Jew* (Philadelphia, 1994)

Osborn, Eric: *The Emergence of Christian Theology* (Cambridge, 1993)

———— *Irenaeus of Lyons* (Cambridge, 2001)

Ostwald, Martin: *Nomos and the Beginnings of the Athenian Democracy* (Oxford, 1969)

BIBLIOGRAPHY

Palmer, James: *The Apocalypse in the Early Middle Ages* (Cambridge, 2014)

Paxton, Frederick S: *Christianizing Death: The Creation of a Ritual Process in Early Medieval Europe* (Ithaca, 1990)

Peppard, Michael: *The Son of God in the Roman World: Divine Sonship in Its Social and Political Context* (Oxford, 2011)

Porter, Stanley E (ed): *Paul: Jew, Greek, and Roman* (Leiden, 2008)

Price, S. R. F: *Rituals and Power: The Roman Imperial Cult in Asia Minor* (Cambridge, 1984)

Rhee, Helen: *Wealth and Poverty in Early Christianity* (Minneapolis, 2017)

Römer, Thomas: *The Invention of God*, tr. Raymond Geuss (Cambridge, Mass., 2015)

Rubin, Uri: *The Eye of the Beholder: The Life of Muhammad as Viewed by the Early Muslims* (Princeton, N. J., 1995)

———*Between Bible and Qur'an: The Children of Israel and the Islamic Self-image* (Princeton, N. J., 1999)

Samuelsson, Gunnar: *Crucifixion in Antiquity: An Inquiry into the Background and Significance of the New Testament Terminology of Crucifixion* (Tübingen, 2013)

Sanders, E. P: *Paul: The Apostle's Life, Letters, and Thought* (Minneapolis, 2016)

Sandmel, Samuel: *Judaism and Christian Beginnings* (New York, 1978)

Satlow, Michael L: *How the Bible Became Holy* (New Haven, Conn., 2014)

Schultz, Joseph P. & Louis Spatz: *Sinai & Olympus: A Comparative Study* (Lanham, Md., 1995)

Shoemaker, Stephen J: *The Death of a Prophet: The End of Muhammad's Life and the Beginnings of Islam* (Philadelphia, 2012)

———*Mary in Early Christian Faith and Devotion* (New Haven, Conn., 2016)

Smith, Mark S: *The Early History of God: Yahweh and the Other Deities in Ancient Israel* (Grand Rapids, Mich., 1990)

———*The Origins of Biblical Monotheism: Israel's Polytheistic Background and the Ugaritic Texts* (Oxford, 2001)

Smith, Rowland: *Julian's Gods: Religion and Philosophy in the Thought and Action of Julian the Apostate* (London, 1995)

Stark, Rodney: *The Rise of Christianity: A Sociologist Reconsiders History* (Princeton, N. J., 1996)

———*Cities of God: The Real Story of How Christianity Became an Urban Movement and Conquered Rome* (New York, 2006)

Theissen, Gerd: *The Social Setting of Pauline Christianity: Essays on Corinth*, tr. John H. Schütz (Edinburgh, 1982)

Trigg, Joseph W: *Origen* (Abingdon, 1998)

Trout, Dennis E: *Paulinus of Nola: Life, Letters, and Poems* (Berkeley & Los Angeles, 1999)

Van Dam, Raymond: *Leadership and Community in Late Antique Gaul* (Berkeley & Los Angeles, 1985)

———*Saints and Their Miracles in Late Antique Gaul* (Princeton, N. J., 1993)

————Kingdom of Snow: Roman Rule and Greek Culture in Cappadocia (Philadelphia, 2002)

————Families and Friends in Late Roman Cappadocia (Philadelphia, 2003)

————Becoming Christian: The Conversion of Roman Cappadocia (Philadelphia, 2003)

Vermes, Geza: Jesus: Nativity, Passion, Resurrection (London, 2010)

Wengst, K: Pax Romana and the People of Christ (London, 1987)

Whitmarsh, Tim: Battling the Gods: Atheism in the Ancient World (London, 2016)

Winter, Bruce W: Philo and Paul Among the Sophists: Alexandrian and Corinthian Responses to a Julio-Claudian Movement (Grand Rapids, Mich., 2002)

Wright, N. T: Paul and the Faithfulness of God (London, 2013)

————Paul and His Recent Interpreters (London, 2015)

————Paul: A Biography (London, 2018)

CHRISTENDOM

Barstow, Anne Llewellyn: Married Priests and the Reforming Papacy (New York, 1982)

Bartlett, Robert: The Making of Europe: Conquest, Colonization and Cultural Change, 950–1350 (London, 1993)

————Why Can the Dead Do Such Great Things? Saints and Worshippers from the Martyrs to the Reformation (Princeton, N. J., 2013)

Berman, Constance Hoffman (ed): Medieval Religion: New Approaches (New York, 2005)

Berman, Harold J: Law and Revolution: The Formation of the Western Legal Tradition (Cambridge, Mass., 1983)

Blickle, Peter: The Revolution of 1525: The German Peasants' War from a New Perspective, tr. Thomas A. Brady and H. C. Erik Midelfort (Baltimore, 1981)

————Communal Reformation, tr. Thomas Dunlap (Atlantic Highlands, 1992)

————From the Communal Reformation to the Revolution of the Common Man, tr. Beat Kümin (Leiden, 1998)

Blumenthal, Uta-Renate: The Investiture Controversy: Church and Monarchy from the Ninth to the Twelfth Century (Philadelphia, 1995)

Bossy, John: Christianity in the West 1400–1700 (Oxford, 1985)

Brecht, Martin: Martin Luther: His Road to Reformation, 1483–1521, translated James L. Schaaf (Minneapolis, 1985)

Brockey, Liam Matthew: The Visitor: André Palmeiro and the Jesuits in Asia (Cambridge, Mass., 2014)

Brophy, Don: Catherine of Siena: A Passionate Life (London, 2011)

Bynum, Caroline Walker: Jesus as Mother: Studies in the Spirituality of the High Middle Ages (Berkeley & Los Angeles, 1982)

————Holy Feast and Holy Fast: The Religious Significance of Food to Medieval Women (Berkeley & Los Angeles, 1987)

Cameron, Euan: *Waldenses: Rejections of Holy Church in Medieval Europe* (Oxford, 2000)

Clanchy, M. T: *Abelard: A Medieval Life* (Oxford, 1997)

Coffey, John: *Persecution and Toleration in Protestant England 1558–1689* (Harlow, 2000)

Cohen, Jeremy (ed): *From Witness to Witchcraft: Jews and Judaism in Medieval Christian Thought* (Wiesbaden, 1996)

Cowdrey, H. E. J: *The Cluniacs and the Gregorian Reform* (Oxford, 1970)

——— *Popes, Monks and Crusaders* (London, 1984)

——— *Pope Gregory VII 1073–1085* (Oxford, 1998)

——— *Popes and Church Reform in the 11th Century* (Aldershot, 2000)

Cunningham, Andrew and Ole Peter Grell: *The Four Horsemen of the Apocalpyse: Religion, War, Famine and Death in Reformation Europe* (Cambridge, 2000)

Cushing, Kathleen G: *Reform and Papacy in the Eleventh Century: Spirituality and Social Change* (Manchester, 2005)

Daniel, Norman: *The Arabs and Medieval Europe* (London, 1975)

D'Elia, Pasquale M: *Galileo in China*, tr. Rufus Suter and Matthew Sciascia (Cambridge, Mass., 1960)

Dunne, John: *Generation of Giants: The Story of the Jesuits in China in the Last Decades of the Ming Dynasty* (Notre Dame, Ind., 1962)

Elliott, Dyan: *Fallen Bodies: Pollution, Sexuality, and Demonology in the Middle Ages* (Philadelphia, 1999)

Emmerson, Richard K. and Bernard McGinn: *The Apocalypse in the Middle Ages* (Ithaca, N. Y., 1992)

Finnocchiaro, Maurice A: *Retrying Galileo, 1633–1992* (Berkeley & Los Angeles, 2005)

Fletcher, Richard: *The Conversion of Europe: From Paganism to Christianity, 371–1386 AD* (London, 1997)

Fontana, Michela: *Matteo Ricci: A Jesuit in the Ming Court* (Lanham, 2011)

Frassetto, Michael (ed): *Medieval Purity and Piety: Essays on Medieval Clerical Celibacy and Religious Reform* (New York, 1998)

Fudge, Thomas A: *Jan Hus: Religious Reform and Social Revolution in Bohemia* (London, 2010)

Fulton, Rachel: *From Judgment to Passion: Devotion to Christ and the Virgin Mary, 800–1200* (New York, 2002)

Gilbert, Creighton E: "Ghiberti on the Destruction of Art" (*I Tatti Studies in the Italian Renaissance* 6, 1995)

Goody, Jack: *The Development of the Family and Marriage in Europe* (Cambridge, 1983)

Gordon, Bruce: *The Swiss Reformation* (Manchester, 2008)

——— *Calvin* (New Haven, Conn., 2009)

Grell, Ole Peter and Bob Scribner: *Tolerance and Intolerance in the European Reformation* (Cambridge, 1996)

Grundmann, Herbert: *Religious Movements in the Middle Ages*, tr. Steven Rowan (Notre Dame, Ind., 1995)

Hamilton, Bernard: *Monastic Reform, Catharism and the Crusades, 900–1300* (London, 1979)

Hancock, Ralph C: *Calvin and the Foundations of Modern Politics* (Ithaca, N. Y., 1989)

Hanke, Lewis: *The Spanish Struggle for Justice in the Conquest of America* (Dallas, Tx., 2002)

Hannam, James: *God's Philosophers: How the Medieval World Laid the Foundations of Modern Science* (London, 2009)

Harline, Craig: *A World Ablaze: The Rise of Martin Luther and the Birth of the Reformation* (Oxford, 2017)

Hashimoto, Keizo: *Hsü Kuang-Ch'i and Astronomical Reform: The Process of the Chinese Acceptance of Western Astronomy, 1629–1635* (Kansas, 1988)

Headley, John M: *Luther's View of Church History* (New Haven, Conn., 1963)

Heilbron, J. L: *Galileo* (Oxford, 2010)

Hendrix, Scott: "Rerooting the Faith: The Reformation as Re-Christianization" (*Church History* 69, 2000)

Hsia, R. Po-chia (ed): *The German People and the Reformation* (Ithaca, N. Y., 1988)

Huff, Toby E: *Intellectual Curiosity and the Scientific Revolution: A Global Perspective* (Cambridge, 2011)

———(3rd edtn) *The Rise of Early Modern Science: Islam, China, and the West* (Cambridge, 2017)

Izbicki, Thomas M: "Cajetan on the Acquisition of Stolen Goods in the Old and New Worlds" (*Revista di storia del Cristianesimo* 4, 2007)

Jami, Catherine, Peter Engelfriet and Gregory Blue: *Statecraft and Intellectual Renewal in Late Ming China: The Cross-Cultural Synthesis of Xu Guangqi (1562–1633)* (Leiden, 2001)

Jones, Andrew Willard: *Before Church and State: A Study of Social Order in the Sacramental Kingdom of St. Louis IX* (Steubenville, 2017)

Jordan, Mark D: *The Invention of Sodomy in Christian Theology* (Chicago, 1997)

Kadir, Djelal: *Columbus and the Ends of the Earth: Europe's Prophetic Rhetoric as Conquering Ideology* (Berkeley & Los Angeles, 1992)

Kaminsky, Howard: *A History of the Hussite Revolution* (Berkeley and Los Angeles, 1967)

Karras, Ruth Mazo: *Sexuality in Medieval Europe* (New York, 2005)

Kedar, Benjamin Z: *Crusade and Mission: European Attitudes Toward the Muslims* (Princeton, N. J., 1984)

Kieckhefer, Richard: *Repression of Heresy in Medieval Germany* (Liverpool, 1979)

Klaniczay, Gábor: *Holy Rulers and Blessed Princesses: Dynastic Cults in Medieval Central Europe*, tr. Éva Pálmai (Cambridge, 2000)

Lattis, James M: *Between Copernicus and Galileo: Christoph Clavius and the Collapse of Ptolemaic Cosmology* (Chicago, 1994)

MacCulloch, Diarmaid: *Reformation: Europe's House Divided, 1490–1700* (London, 2003)

Madigan, Kevin: *Medieval Christianity: A New History* (New Haven, Conn., 2015)

Marshall, Peter: *The Reformation* (Oxford, 2009)

——*Heretics and Believers: A History of the English Reformation* (New Haven, Conn., 2017)

McGinn, Bernard: *Visions of the End: Apocalyptic Traditions in the Middle Ages* (New York, 1979)

Milis, Ludo J. R: *Angelic Monks and Earthly Men* (Woodbridge, 1992)

Miller, Perry: *The New England Mind: From Colony to Province* (Cambridge, Mass., 1953)

——*The New England Mind: The Seventeenth Century* (Cambridge, Mass., 1954)

——*Errand into the Wilderness* (Cambridge, Mass., 1956)

Moore, John C: *Pope Innocent III (1160/61–1216): To Root Up and to Plant* (Leiden, 2003)

Moore, R. I: *The Birth of Popular Heresy* (London, 1975)

——*The Origins of European Dissent* (London, 1977)

——*The Formation of a Persecuting Society: Power and Deviance in Western Europe, 950–1250* (Oxford, 1990)

——*The First European Revolution, c. 970–1215* (Oxford, 2000)

Mormando, Franco: *Bernardino of Siena and the Social Underworld of Early Renaissance Italy* (Chicago, 1999)

Morris, Colin: *The Papal Monarchy: The Western Church from 1050 to 1250* (Oxford, 1989)

Newman, Barbara: *From Virile Woman to WomanChrist: Studies in Medieval Religion and Literature* (Philadelphia, 1995)

——"The Heretic Saint: Guglielma of Bohemia, Milan, and Brunate" (*Church History* 74, 2005)

Oberman, Heiko: *The Impact of the Reformation* (Grand Rapids, Mich., 1994)

Origo, Iris: *The World of San Bernardino* (London, 1963)

Ozment, Steven: *The Age of Reform, 1250–1550: An Intellectual and Religious History of Late Medieval and Reformation Europe* (New Haven, Conn., 1980)

Patzold, Steffen and Carmine van Rhijn: *Men in the Middle: Local Priests in Early Medieval Europe* (Berlin, 2016)

Pegg, Mark Gregory: *The Corruption of Angels: The Great Inquisition of 1245–1246* (Princeton, N. J., 2001)

——*A Most Holy War: The Albigensian Crusade and the Battle for Christendom* (Oxford, 2008)

Peters, Edward: *The Magician, the Witch, and the Law* (Philadelphia, 1978)

——*Inquisition* (Berkeley & Los Angeles, 1989)

Phelan, John Leddy: *The Millennial Kingdom of the Franciscans in the New World: A Study of the Writings of Gerónimo de Mendieta (1525–1604)* (Berkeley & Los Angeles, 1956)

Polecritti, Cynthia L: *Preaching Peace in Renaissance Italy: Bernardino of Siena & His Audience* (Washington, D.C., 2000)

Reuter, Timothy (ed): *The Greatest Englishman: Essays on St Boniface and the Church at Crediton* (Exeter, 1980)

Riley-Smith, Jonathan: *The First Crusade and the Idea of Crusading* (London, 1986)
———— *The First Crusaders, 1095–1131* (Cambridge, 1997)

Rocke, Michael: *Forbidden Friendships: Homosexuality and Male Culture in Renaissance Florence* (Oxford, 1996)

Roper, Lyndal: *Martin Luther: Renegade and Prophet* (London, 2016)

Rosenstock-Huessy, Eugen: *Driving Power of Western Civilization: The Christian Revolution of the Middle Ages* (Boston, 1949)

Ross, Andrew C: *A Vision Betrayed: The Jesuits in Japan and China 1542–1742* (Edinburgh, 1994)

Rubenstein, Jay: *Armies of Heaven: The First Crusade and the Quest for Apocalypse* (New York, 2011)

Schama, Simon: *The Embarrassment of Riches: An Interpretation of Dutch Culture in the Golden Age* (London, 1987)

Scott, Tom: *Thomas Müntzer: Theology and Revolution in the German Reformation* (Basingstoke, 1989)

Scott-Dixon, C: *Contesting the Reformation* (Oxford, 2012)

Scribner, R. W: *Popular Culture and Popular Movements in Reformation Germany* (London, 1987)

Smalley, Beryl: *The Study of the Bible in the Middle Ages* (Oxford, 1941)

Southern, R. W: *The Making of the Middle Ages* (London, 1953)
———— *Western Society and the Church in the Middle Ages* (London, 1970)
———— *Saint Anselm: A Portrait in a Landscape* (Cambridge, 1990)

Steenberghen, Fernand van: *Aristotle in the West: The Origins of Latin Aristotelianism*, tr. Leonard Johnston (Louvain, 1955)

Sullivan, Karen: *The Inner Lives of Medieval Inquisitors* (Chicago, 2011)

Sweet, Leonard I: "Christopher Columbus and the Millennial Vision of the New World" (*The Catholic Historical Review* 72, 1986)

Talbot, CH (ed): *The Anglo-Saxon Missionaries in Germany* (London, 1954)

Tellenbach, Gerd: *Church, State and Christian Society at the Time of the Investiture Contest*, tr. R. F. Bennett (Oxford, 1940)
———— *The Church in Western Europe from the Tenth to the Early Twelfth Century*, tr. Timothy Reuter (Cambridge, 1993)

Tylus, Jane: *Reclaiming Catherine of Siena: Literacy, Literature, and the Signs of Others* (Chicago, 2009)

Ullman, Walter: *The Growth of Papal Government in the Middle Ages: A Study in the Ideological Relation of Clerical to Lay Power* (London, 1955)

Walsham, Alexandra: *The Reformation of the Landscape: Religion, Identity, & Memory in Early Modern Britain & Ireland* (Oxford, 2011)

Watts, Pauline Moffitt: "Prophecy and Discovery: On the Spiritual Origins of Christopher Columbus's 'Enterprise of the Indies'" (*American Historical Review* 90, 1985)

Wessley, Stephen E: "The Thirteenth-Century Gugliemites: Salvation Through Women", in *Medieval Women*, ed. Derek Baker (Oxford, 1978)

Williams, George Huntston: *The Radical Reformation* (Kirksville, 1992)

Witte, John: *The Reformation of Rights: Law, Religion, and Human Rights in Early Modern Calvinism* (Cambridge, 2007)

Wolf, Kenneth Baxter: *The Poverty of Riches: St. Francis of Assisi Reconsidered* (Oxford, 2003)

———*The Life and Afterlife of St. Elizabeth of Hungary: Testimony from Her Canonization Hearings* (Oxford, 2011)

MODERNITAS

Ali, Kecia: *The Lives of Muhammad* (Cambridge, Mass., 2014)

Anderson, Allan: *Zion and Pentecost: The Spirituality and Experience of Pentecostal and Zionist/Apostolic Churches in South Africa* (Pretoria, 2000)

———*African Reformation: African Initiated Christianity in the 20th Century* (Trenton, N. J., 2001)

Anstey, Roger: *The Atlantic Slave Trade and British Abolition 1760–1810* (London, 1975)

Aston, Nigel: *Christianity and Revolutionary Europe, 1750–1830* (Cambridge, 2002)

Balagangadhara, S. N: *"The Heathen in His Blindness..." Asia, the West and the Dynamic of Religion* (Manohar, 2005)

Barclay, David E: *Frederick William IV and the Prussian Monarchy 1840–1861* (Oxford, 1995)

Batnitzky, Leora: *How Judaism Became a Religion: An Introduction to Modern Jewish Thought* (Princeton, N. J., 2011)

Beachy, Robert: *Gay Berlin: Birthplace of a Modern Identity* (New York, 2014)

Becker, Carl L: *The Heavenly City of the Eighteenth-Century Philosophers* (New Haven, 1932)

Bethge, Eberhard: *Dietrich Bonhoeffer: A Biography* (London, 1970)

Bien, David D: *The Calas Affair: Persecution, Tolerance, and Heresy in Eighteenth-Century Toulouse* (Princeton, N. J., 1960)

Bloch, Esther; Marianne Keppens and Rajaram Hegde (ed): *Rethinking Religion in India: The Colonial Construction of Hinduism* (London, 2010)

Bruckner, Pascal: *The Tyranny of Guilty: An Essay on Western Masochism*, tr. Steven Rendall (Princeton, N. J., 2010)

Burleigh, Michael: *Earthly Powers: Religion and Politics in Europe from the Enlightenment to the Great War* (London, 2005)

Sacred Causes: Religion and Politics from the European Dictators to Al Qaeda (London, 2006)

Callahan, Allen Dwight: *The Talking Book: African Americans and the Bible* (New Haven, Conn., 2006)

Carson, Penelope: *The East India Company and Religion, 1698–1858* (Woodbridge, 2012)

Chartier, Lydia G: *The Cultural Origins of the French Revolution*, tr. Lydia G. Cochrane (Durham, N. C., 1991)

Coffey, John: *Exodus and Liberation: Deliverance Politics from John Calvin to Martin Luther King Jr.* (Oxford, 2014)

Conway, John S: *The Nazi Persecution of the Churches* (London, 1968)

Cuddihy, John: *No Offense: Civil Religion and Protestant Taste* (New York, 1978)

Curry, Thomas J: *The First Freedoms: Church and State in America to the Passage of the First Amendment* (Oxford, 1986)

Davidson, Jane Pierce: *The Life of Edward Drinker Cope* (Philadelphia, 1997)

Davie, Grace: *Religion in Modern Europe: A Memory Mutates* (Oxford, 2000)

Davie, Grace, Paul Heelas and Linda Woodhead (eds): *Preaching Religion: Christian, Secular and Alternative Futures* (Aldershot, 2003)

Davies, Owen: *A Supernatural War: Magic, Divination, and Faith During the First World War* (Oxford, 2018)

Davis, David Brion: *The Problem of Slavery in Western Culture* (Ithaca, N. Y., 1966)
——*Slavery and Human Progress* (Oxford, 1984)

Desmond, Adrian: *Huxley: From Devil's Disciple to Evolution's High Priest* (Reading, 1997)

Desmond, Adrian and James Moore: *Darwin* (London, 1991)

Drake, Thomas E: *Quakers and Slavery in America* (New Haven, 1950)

Drescher, Seymour: *Abolition: A History of Slavery and Antislavery* (Cambridge, 2009)

Durston, Christopher and Judith Maltby: *Religion in Revolutionary England* (Manchester, 2006)

Edelstein, Dan: *The Terror of Natural Right: Republicanism, the Cult of Nature, and the French Revolution* (Chicago, 2009)

Elphick, Richard and Rodney Davenport (ed): *Christianity in South Africa: A Political, Social & Cultural History* (Cape Town, 1997)

Fix, Andrew C: *Prophecy and Reason: The Dutch Collegiants in the Early Enlightenment* (Princeton, N. J., 1991)

Foxley, Rachel: *The Levellers: Radical Political Thought in the English Revolution* (Manchester, 2013)

Fromm, Erich: *Marx's Concept of Man* (New York, 1961)

Gay, Peter: *The Enlightenment: An Interpretation* (2 vol) (New York, 1966–69)

Ghazi, Abidullah Al-Ansari: *Raja Rammohun Roy: An Encounter with Islam and Christianity and the Articulation of Hindu Self-Consciousness* (Iqra, 2010)

Glaser, Eliane: *Judaism Without Jews: Philosemitism and Christian Polemic in Early Modern England* (Basingstoke, 2007)

Glasson, Travis: *Mastering Christianity: Missionary Anglicanism and Slavery in the Atlantic World* (Oxford, 2012)

Golomb, Jacob and Robert S. Wistrich (ed): *Nietzsche, Godfather of Fascism? On the Uses and Abuses of a Philosophy* (Princeton, N. J., 2002)

Graetz, Michael: *The Jews in Nineteenth-Century France: From the French Revolution to the Alliance Israélite Universelle*, tr. Jane Marie Todd (Stanford, C. A. 1996)

Greenberg, David F: *The Construction of Homosexuality* (Chicago, 1988)

Gurney, John: *Gerrard Winstanley: The Digger's Life and Legacy* (London, 2013)

Haar, Gerrie ter: *How God Became African: African Spirituality and Western Secular Thought* (Philadelphia, 2009)

Hartley, Keith: *Otto Dix, 1891–1969* (London, 1992)

Harvey, David: *The Song of Middle-Earth: J. R. R. Tolkien's Themes, Symbols and Myths* (London, 1985)

Hawley, John Stratton: *Sati, the Blessing and the Curse: The Burning of Wives in India* (Oxford, 1994)

Hess, Jonathan M: *Germans, Jews and the Claims of Modernity* (New Haven, Conn., 2002)

Higonnet, Patrice: *Goodness Beyond Virtue: Jacobins During the French Revolution* (Cambridge, Mass., 1998)

Hopper, Andrew: *'Black Tom': Sir Thomas Fairfax and the English Revolution* (Manchester, 2007)

Hughes, Gordon and Philipp Blom: *Nothing but the Clouds Unchanged: Artists in World War 1* (Los Angeles, 2014)

Hunter, Graeme: *Radical Protestantism in Spinoza's Thought* (Aldershot, 2005)

Jacob, Margaret C: *The Radical Enlightenment: Pantheists, Freemasons and Republicans* (London, 1981)

Jenkins, Philip: *The Next Christendom: The Coming of Global Christianity* (Oxford, 2002)

——— *The Great and Holy War: How World War I Became a Religious Crusade* (New York, 2014)

Karcher, Eva: *Otto Dix (1891–1969): His Life and Works* (Cologne, 1988)

Katz, D. S: *Philosemitism and the Readmission of the Jews to England, 1603–1655* (Oxford, 1982)

Keith, Miller: *The Language of Martin Luther King, Jr. and Its Sources* (New York, 1992)

Kennedy, Emmet: *A Cultural History of the French Revolution* (New Haven, Conn., 1989)

Kerry, Paul E (ed): *The Ring and the Cross: Christianity and The Lord of the Rings* (Lanham, Md., 2011)

Koltun-Fromm, Ken: *Abraham Geiger's Liberal Judaism: Personal Meaning and Religious Authority* (Bloomington & Indianapolis, 2006)

Koonz, Claudia: *The Nazi Conscience* (Cambridge, Mass., 2003)

Kors, Alan: *Atheism in France, 1650–1729* (Princeton, N. J., 1990)

Koskenniemi, Martti, *The Gentle Civilizer of Nations: The Rise and Fall of International Law 1870–1960* (Cambridge, 2001)

——— "Empire and International Law: The Real Spanish Contribution" (*The University of Toronto Law Journal* 61, 2011)

Koskenniemi, Martti, Mónica García-Salmones Rovira and Paolo Amorosa: *International Law and Religion: Historical and Contemporary Perspectives* (Oxford, 2017)

Lewisohn, Mark: *The Beatles: All These Years, Volume One—Tune In* (London, 2013)

Lynskey, Dorian: *33 Revolutions Per Minute: A History of Protest Songs* (London, 2010)

Magnus, Shulamit S: *Jewish Emancipation in a German City: Cologne, 1798–1871* (Stanford, C. A. 1997)

Marshall, P. J: *The British Discovery of Hinduism in the Eighteenth Century* (Cambridge, 1970)

Martinez, Jenny S: *The Slave Trade and the Origins of International Human Rights Law* (Oxford, 2012)

Marwick, Arthur: *The Sixties: Cultural Revolution in Britain, France, Italy, and the United States, c.1958–c.1974* (Oxford, 1998)

Mason, Richard: *The God of Spinoza: A Philosophical Study* (Cambridge, 1997)

Masuzawa, Tomoko: *The Invention of World Religions: Or, How European Universalism Was Preserved in the Language of Pluralism* (Chicago, 2005)

May, Simon (ed): *Nietzsche's* On the Genealogy of Morality: *A Critical Guide* (Cambridge, 2011)

McManners, John: *The French Revolution and the Church* (London, 1969)

Meyer, Michael: *Response to Modernity: A History of the Reform Movement in Judaism* (Oxford, 1988)

Middlebrook, Martin & Mary: *The Somme Battlefields* (London, 1991)

Miller, Nicholas P: *The Religious Roots of the First Amendment: Dissenting Protestants and the Separation of Church and State* (Oxford, 2012)

Minois, Georges: *The Atheist's Bible: The Most Dangerous Book that Never Existed*, tr. Lys Ann Weiss (Chicago, 2012)

Moore, Rosemary: *The Light in their Consciences: Early Quakers in Britain 1646–1666* (University Park, 2000)

Morris, Henry: *The Life of Charles Grant: Sometime Member of Parliament and Director of the East India Company* (London, 1904)

Muravyova, L. and I. Sivolap-Kaftanova: *Lenin in London*, tr. Jane Sayer (Moscow, 1981)

Nadler, Steven: *A Book Forged in Hell: Spinoza's Scandalous Treatise and the Birth of the Secular Age* (Princeton, N. J., 2011)

———*Spinoza: A Life* (Cambridge, 1999)

Nasaw, David: *Andrew Carnegie* (New York, 2006)

Nixon, Edna: *Voltaire and the Calas Case* (London, 1961)

Noll, Mark A: *America's God: From Jonathan Edwards to Abraham Lincoln* (Oxford, 2002)

———*God and Race in American Politics* (Princeton, N. J., 2008)

Norman, Philip: *John Lennon: The Life* (London, 2008)

Numbers, Ronald L (ed): *Galileo Goes to Jail and Other Myths About Science and Religion* (Cambridge, Mass., 2009)

O'Connor, Ralph: *The Earth on Show: Fossils and the Poetics of Popular Science, 1802–1856* (Chicago, 2007)

Oddie, Geoffrey A: *Imagined Hinduism: British Protestant Missionary Construc-
tions of Hinduism, 1793–1900* (New Delhi, 2006)

Oldfield, J. R: *Popular Politics and British Anti-Slavery: The Mobilisation of Public
Opinion Against the Slave Trade, 1787–1807* (Manchester, 1995)

Oosterhuis, Harry: *Stepchildren of Nature: Krafft-Ebing, Psychiatry, and the Making of Sexual Identity* (Chicago, 2000)

Osborn, Henry Fairfield: *Cope: Master Naturalist* (Princeton, N. J., 1931)

Parker, Geoffrey: *Global Crisis: War, Climate Change and Catastrophe in the Seventeenth Century* (New Haven, Conn., 2013)

Pestana, Carla: *Protestant Empire: Religion and the Making of the British Atlantic
World* (Philadelphia, 2010)

Porterfield, Amanda: *The Transformation of American Religion: The Story of a
Late-Twentieth Century Awakening* (Oxford, 2001)

Rea, Tom: *Bone Wars: The Excavation and Celebrity of Andrew Carnegie's Dinosaur* (Pittsburgh, 2001)

Roberts, J. Deotis: *Bonhoeffer & King: Speaking Truth to Power* (Louisville, 2005)

Rowntree, C. Brightwen: "Benjamin Lay (1681–1759)" (*The Journal of the Friends'
Historical Society* 33, 1936)

Rudwick, Martin J. S: *Earth's Deep History: How It Was Discovered and Why It
Matters* (Chicago, 2014)

Schaeffer, Neil: *The Marquis de Sade: A Life* (London, 1999)

Schama, Simon: *Citizens: A Chronicle of the French Revolution* (London, 1989)

Schmidt, Alfred: *The Concept of Nature in Marx*, tr. Ben Fowkes (London, 1971)

Sheehan, Jonathan: *The Enlightenment Bible* (Princeton, N. J., 2005)

Shippey, Tom: *J. R. R. Tolkien: Author of the Century* (London, 2000)

Shulman, George M: *Radicalism and Reverence: The Political Thought of Gerrard
Winstanley* (Berkeley & Los Angeles, 1989)

Siemens, Daniel: *The Making of a Nazi Hero: The Murder and Myth of Horst Wessel*,
tr. David Burnett (London, 2013)

Soderlund, Jean R: *Quakers & Slavery: A Divided Spirit* (Princeton, N. J., 1985)

Stanley, Brian: *Christianity in the Twentieth Century: A World History* (Princeton,
N.J., 2018)

Steignmann-Gall, Richard: *The Holy Reich: Nazi Conceptions of Christianity* (Cambridge, 2003)

Stephens, Randall J.: *The Devil's Music: How Christians Inspired, Condemned, and
Embraced Rock 'n' Roll* (Cambridge, Mass., 2018)

Stone, Dan: *Histories of the Holocaust* (Oxford, 2010)

———*The Holocaust, Fascism and Memory: Essays in the History of Ideas* (London,
2013)

Tierney, Brian: *The Idea of Natural Rights* (Grand Rapids, Mich., 2001)

Toledano, Ehud R: *The Ottoman Slave Trade and Its Suppression: 1840–1890* (Princeton, N. J., 1982)

Turley, David: *The Culture of English Antislavery, 1780–1860* (London, 1991)

BIBLIOGRAPHY

Van Kley, Dale K: *The Religious Origins of the French Revolution: From Calvin to the Civil Constitution, 1560–1791* (New Haven, Conn., 1996)

Vattimo, Gianni: *After Christianity*, tr. Luca d'Isanto (New York, 2002)

Vaux, Roberts: *Memoirs of the Lives of Benjamin Lay and Ralph Sandiford: Two of the Earliest Public Advocates for the Emancipation of the Enslaved Africans* (Philadelphia, 1815)

Wallace, David Rains: *Beasts of Eden: Walking Whales, Dawn Horses, and Other Enigmas of Mammal Evolution* (Berkeley & Los Angeles, 2004)

Weinberger-Thomas, Catherine: *Ashes of Immortality: Widow-Burning in India*, tr. Jeffrey Mehlman and David Gordon-White (Chicago, 1999)

Weiss, Michael and Hassan Hassan: *ISIS: Inside the Army of Terror* (New York, 2015)

Worden, Blair: *God's Instruments: Political Conduct in the England of Oliver Cromwell* (Oxford, 2012)

INDEX

INDEX

Christian doctrine
  garnering support for apartheid, 502
  loving your enemies, 489–490
  Marx's rejection of, 456
  modeling for children, 534–536
  1960s protests challenging fundamentals, 493–494
  persistence without Christians, 533
  reconciling Aristotle's writings with, 265–267
  repackaging for non-Christian audiences, 521
Christian values, Trump's hypocrisy over, 529–530
Christianismos (Christianity), 120
Christmas, 497–499
Chronicles, the Book of, 63(fn)
Church of England, 335, 367, 375, 501, 502
church-state separation
  Charlie Hebdo's religious satire and anti-clericalism, 522
  fusing Roman bureaucracy with theology, 133–134
  Gregorian *reformatio* establishing papal supremacy, 234–236
  Gregory's prohibition against kings' involvement in the running of the Church, 227–228
  Gregory's religious reforms, 230–231
  jihadists Muslims defying governmental authority, 509–510
Cicero, 46
circumcision, 48, 52, 78, 86–87, 89–90, 96, 181–183, 186, 281–282
civil rights movement, American, 490–494
class struggles, 457–458
Clermont, 232–233
Cluny monastery, 231–232, 239–240, 242–243, 264
Collegiants, 374–375
Collegium Sodomitarum, 290
Cologne, 219–220, 421–423
Cologne Cathedral, 422–423
colonialism, 307–308, 371, 498–500, 507–509
colonies, American, 341–344
Columbanus (saint), 174–178, 194, 203, 253, 427
Columbus, Christopher, 303–304

communism, 455, 457, 468–469, 489, 504–505
compassion, 287, 464–466, 532
Confronting White Womanhood, 533
Confucius, 349
Congress of Vienna, 409–412, 421
Conrad of Marburg, 252–257, 262, 269
conscience, 34, 95–96
  Syneidesis, 34, 95
Constantine (Roman emperor), 183
  banning crucifixion, 6–7
  Carthaginian schism, 135–136
  charitable programs, 140
  conquest of Rome and acceptance of the primacy of Christ, 129–131, 132, 133
  journey through Cappadocia, 141
Constantinople, 166, 179–180, 186, 193–194, 259–260, 294, 301, 373, 432
Constantius II (Roman emperor), 134, 140
conversion, religious, 523
  of African slaves in the New World, 383–384
  Augustine of Hippo, 155–156
  Augustine's refusal to convert the savages, 202
  Boniface's conversion of Germans and Franks, 201–207
  of Britain's Angles, Saxons and Jutes, 189–191
  British presence in India, 417–418, 420
  Charlemagne's forced conversion of the Saxons, 209–210
  Christian-Muslim frame for German immigration policy, 520
  Constantine's acceptance of the primacy of Christ, 130–131, 136
  forced baptism of Africa's Jews under Heraclius, 179–182, 186–187
  of foreigners to Judaism during Roman occupation, 77–79
  Friedrich Wilhelm's attempts to convert the Jews of Cologne, 423–424
  integrating unbaptised migrants, 517–518
  Jesuits in China, 348–351
  of Mandarin Chinese, 350–351
  of New England natives, 344
  of pagan warlords defeated by Christians, 217–220
  Paul's preaching, 84–87, 90–94

love (*continued*)
   the contradiction of love, war and
      destruction, 488–490
   Mandela's commitment to love his
      enemies and persecutors, 503
   Martin Luther King and black protest,
      490–492
   Paul's preaching on the primacy of,
      93–94
Luke (saint), 84, 101, 101(fn), 115–116, 144,
   148–149
Luther, Martin, 490
   Anabaptists, 326–327
   antipathy to Mosaic law, 425–426
   defiance of the Church, 314–317
   diet of Worms, 315–319, 320
   divine grace and, 318–319
   excommunication, 311–312
   increasing Christian hostility towards
      Jews, 371–372
   Müntzer's execution, 322–323
   the peasants' revolt, 322–323
   pre-human chronology and history, 436
   rising protests of the Lutheran princes,
      327–328
   rulers appropriating canon law, 323–324
Luxeuil monastery, 175, 177, 194
Lužnice, 292–293
Lyon, martyrs of, 107–109, 111, 113

Macedon, 41–43
Macrina (saint), 143–144, 530
Maifreda da Pirovano, 272, 273, 277
Majorinus, 127
Mandela, Nelson, 503–504
al-Maqdisi, Abu Muhammad, 509–511
Marcion, 114–115, 121, 484
Marcus Aurelius Antoninus, 117
Marduke (Babylonian god), 58–59, 62
Marmoutier, 146, 149–150
marriage
   brides of Christ, 281–285
   Christian insistence on continence
      outside of, 527–528
   denial of Henry VIII's annulment, 325
   Elizabeth of Hungary, 248
   Indian funeral pyre, 414–416
   Krafft-Ebing's support of homosexual
      monogamy, 450
   married clergy, 223–224

   monogamy, 283–284, 450
   religious-secular influences over gay
      marriage, 530–531
   sacred quality of, 525
Marsh, Othniel Charles, 440, 451
Martel, Charles "the Hammer," 195–198,
   206, 268, 395–396
Martin (saint), 205
   Arab invasion of Francia, 194–195
   celebrity and humility, 147–150,
      398–399
   devotion of his followers, 145–147
   final judgement, 172
   monument to, 157–158
   pacifism, 216–217
   vandalism of the basilica, 395–398
martyrdom
   apocalypse and end times, 171
   Boniface's murder by pagans, 206–207
   of Calvinists, 334
   Christians of Lyon and Vienne, 116
   creating the schism in Carthaginian
      Christianity, 128–129
   execution of heretics in Cambrai,
      223–224
   of John Lennon, 496
   masochism as, 449–450
   Paul's execution by Nero, 102
   redefining suffering as triumph, 110–113
Marx, Karl, 455–458
Mary, mother of Jesus, 144, 276–277, 279,
   285–287, 461–462
Mary Magdalene, 275–276, 285–287
masochism, 449–450
Matthew, the Gospel according to,
   115–116, 144
McCartney, Paul, 496–497
Menasseh ben Israel, 371–373, 374
Merkel, Angela, 515–521
Mesopotamia, 24–26, 51–53
Messiah, 75–76, 103, 183–184
#MeToo movement, 528, 531
Mexico, 305, 346
Michael (archangel), 162–163, 169, 172,
   178, 279
Middle Ages, 11, 397–398, 401–402, 525
Milingo, Emmanuel, 500
Milton, John, 358, 367
missionaries
   Africa and, 498–500